British English
for American Readers

British English for American Readers

A Dictionary of the Language, Customs, and Places of British Life and Literature

David Grote

Greenwood Press ———————— WESTPORT, CONNECTICUT · LONDON

Library of Congress Cataloging-in-Publication Data

Grote, David.
    British English for American readers : a dictionary of the
language, customs, and places of British life and literature / David
Grote.
        p.   cm.
    Includes bibliographical references.
    ISBN 0–313–27851–2 (alk. paper)
    1. English language—Great Britain—Dictionaries.   2. Great
Britain—Civilization—Dictionaries.   3. English literature—
Dictionaries.   I. Title.
PE1704.G76   1992
423—dc20   91–45575

British Library Cataloguing in Publication Data is available.

Library of Congress Catalog Card Number: 91–45575
ISBN: 0–313–27851–2

First published in 1992

Greenwood Press, 88 Post Road West, Westport, CT 06881
An imprint of Greenwood Publishing Group, Inc.

Printed in the United States of America

The paper used in this book complies with the
Permanent Paper Standard issued by the National
Information Standards Organization (Z39.48–1984).

10 9 8 7 6 5 4 3 2 1

The English have everything in common with the Americans—except language.

Oscar Wilde

Contents

Introduction

This is hardly the first reference book about British literature to be published, and hardly the first book about the differences between British and American English usage. But it is perhaps the first to focus on the kinds of questions actually asked by readers or by viewers of the many British television programs and films that have become so widely available on PBS (Public Broadcasting System) and cable channels in recent years.

This is, in its way, a book about the obvious. It is an attempt to define the kind of things that British authors thought needed no explanation, because "everybody knows that." The problem for Americans is that if we ever did know it, we certainly no longer do. This became suddenly obvious to me one day when an actor with whom I was working asked, "What exactly is a vicar?" "Well," I thought, "everybody knows what a vicar is: a minister of a church." But then my mind raced on and asked: How is that different from a rector? a priest? a parson? a chaplain? a curate? a canon? a padre? a dean? a warden? Was Canon Chasuble, for example, a vicar? And suddenly it dawned on me that, after thirty-five or so years of reading British literature, for school and for pleasure, and of going to the theatre to laugh at farces about vicars by writers from Pinero to Ben Travers to Philip King to Alan Bennett, in fact I didn't know what a vicar was.

Nor did I know for certain what was in spotted dick or in a pudding, how a hussar differed from a dragoon, whether a marquis was a lord, why one character was called Sir while another who seemed more noble was not, whether Superintendent Dalgliesh outranked Chief Inspector Japp, where the Home Counties were or whether the West Country and the West Ridings were the same place, and any number of similar facts that I had been mentally skimming over when I read because I had an approximate understanding.

In most cases, of course, an approximate understanding is enough to get by—the continued American popularity of British writers as varied as Agatha Christie, John LeCarré, Anthony Burgess, Jeffrey Archer, and either Martin or Kingsley Amis, plus the dominance of British programming on PBS or the cable "culture" channels attest to that. But there are times when something more than approximate understanding is needed, moments when the minor misconceptions add up to complete confusion and at which the reader or viewer is likely to miss the point.

For most classics, contemporary publishers recognize the problem to some degree; Penguin and Oxford paperbacks of Dickens or Trollope often come with excellent notes, but even here the tendency is to look for the mote and miss the beam. For example, I have at hand four different popular editions of *Bleak House*, none of which explains Chancery courts or Chancery law, which leaves a considerable hole in the modern reader's understanding of that book. And, of course, the overwhelming majority of novels and stories will never be footnoted for the non-British reader. These are the works at which this dictionary is aimed. While it of course applies to the works of Dickens, Eliot, Austen, and Trollope, it is really intended to be an aid to the readers of Agatha Christie, Dorothy Sayers, Evelyn Waugh, Barbara Pym, Michael Innes, Anita Brookner, Fay Weldon, John LeCarré, Ian Fleming, Anthony Price, Alice Thomas Ellis, Keith Waterhouse, Dick Francis, P. D. James, Elizabeth Bowen, H. E. Bates, Ruth Rendell, Muriel Spark, Iris Murdoch, Noel Coward, Tom Stoppard, Alan Ayckbourn, Robert Barnard, or the hundreds of others who are clearly British and yet stimulating and entertaining to readers and audiences far from the British Isles.

Still, perhaps, the question remains: What makes this book different from or more useful than the dozens of similar works available. The answer I would offer is simple: While the information here can be found in dozens of other works, it can only be found in *dozens* of them, and then only with great difficulty. A quick glance at the Bibliography will explain what I mean. This is part dictionary, part guidebook, part history, part almanac, part gazetteer, part sociology, part literary chitchat, all combined in one single volume. It has no specialty, for it deals with British culture in general. It is intended to be a quick, easy reference for the reader or the viewer who wants a simple explanation of how much a shilling was really worth, why Becky Sharp's husband purchased his commission, whether Warden Harding was a church warden or not, why Lydia Languish had to go to Scotland if she wanted to elope, what a holiday camp is and who goes to it, whether someone who is dead chuffed is happy or angry, whether Golders Green really exists and, if so, what kind of people live there, why private schools are called public schools, whether a minister is in politics or the clergy, what the difference is between googlies and goolies, or why even a director often accedes to the wishes of a secretary.

Consequently, this book is organized as a dictionary, with entries for the terms or names that might start the confusion. Most literary "companions" are designed to save the reader the trouble of actually reading the works or to refresh the reader's memory of works read long in the past. This one assumes the reader is actually in the midst of reading (or viewing) the work and wants to clear up a point or follow a trail of curiosity, but without making a major research project of it.

Entries are arranged alphabetically, but are selected from ten basic categories:

1. titles, ranks, and honors;

2. everyday words that are not part of the typical American vocabulary;

3. words common to both America and Britain but that are used differently, including some historical changes in meaning (however, words that differ only in preferred spellings—colour/color, theatre/theater, etc.—are not included);

4. customs and activities of daily life not shared by Americans;

5. governmental and other public organizations;

6. political and legal customs and methods (including some historical references);

7. communities, buildings, and places that are often used allusively in literary works;

8. foods and common commercial products;

9. common animals and plants that are not found, or are found in a different form, in America; and

10. some longer comments on basic social practices that either differ considerably from modern American practice or that have changed so significantly over the years as to confuse many contemporary readers, such as class, marriage, village, army, party, or church.

I have laid particular emphasis on places, especially the various neighborhoods of London. Neighborhoods carry a specific image and a uniformity of residents unknown to Americans, except in New York, Boston, and perhaps San Francisco or Chicago, and British writers are very careful to situate their characters in specific neighborhoods that place them socially for the audience. This image may not always be true, just as the image of California as the land of kooks, surfers, and movie stars is not always true, but it is the accepted image nonetheless. It is important that *Major Barbara*, for example, alternates between Belgravia and the East End, that Adam Dalgliesh lives in the City, or that Harriet Vane lives in Bloomsbury. To a British audience, there is as much significant and obvious difference between a cottage in Surbiton and one in Yorkshire as there is for Americans between a home in Queens and one in Des Moines. As this is precisely the kind of information generally unavailable to the American reader, I have tried to include the stereotypical image of all places noted.

I must stress that this text is not intended to be "complete." I have selected only those entries that seem to me to have the potential to confuse a reader who knows only American English, and thus I have neither tried to include all British words nor all meanings of all the terms included. Neither have I tried to encompass all, or even the bulk, of British slang; that is for the specialists to do and of interest primarily to specialist readers. Similarly, I have included etymologies for only a comparatively few terms. The guiding principle has been to include etymologies only for words that seem to Americans to be overly quaint or for words whose etymologies help clarify meaning or usage. All other etymology is left to more specialized works.

In the same way, I have rarely tried to date terms, on the assumption that readers know when the term was used simply because they know when the book they are reading was written. However, when the term has changed meaning over the years or when the term is associated with a particular period, I have included some generalized dating, to help the reader decide which meaning is probable or to recognize the implied status or personality of the character who uses the term.

For place-names, I have indicated pronunciations, as these names are rarely pronounced the way they are spelled and are just as rarely included in other dictionaries. Even these are generalized, in that regional and class accents often give many different pronunciations for a place; where such variety exists, I have leaned toward the BBC's (British Broadcasting Corporation) preferred pronunciation, as the one most likely to be recognized if not actually used nationwide.

A handful of topics either require unusually long comments or seem to be more conveniently arranged in a handy chart, so I have also included several appendixes, dealing with: money and values, class structure, calendar of holidays and festivals, reigns and historic dates, military ranks, and the most commonly listed honours and their initials.

Naturally, there are limits to what can be included here. The most significant limitation is that, since this text is aimed at the reader and, by extension, the viewer of television or film, it is unnaturally weighted toward London, as is British literature itself. A short street in London may receive more space than an entire city or county elsewhere, simply because one has figured often in literature and the other has not. Secondly, primarily for reasons of space, all but a handful of references to Ireland have been excluded, a decision at least partially justified by the modern attempt in Ireland to develop and sustain a separate Irish culture.

Although many towns, cities, and villages are included, it is not a tourist's guide or reference. Naturally, tourists want to go to places that are known from literature—who would care about Stratford without Shakespeare?—but entries for such places are concerned only with their likely use in literature. Thus, entries will not give population data, good hotels, or unusual local history unless such information is relevant to a place's stereotyped image. Nor, for that matter, are entries concerned much with the writers themselves—they are more likely to mention where Mr. Pickwick lived than where Dickens did.

Perhaps the most difficult limitation of this book has been to eliminate the purely quaint. Britain is full of quaint customs, many of which are of interest to Americans merely because they are odd—but many of these are odd to the British as well. When one of these oddities appears in a story or film, the author is usually careful to explain it, so the reader needs no other reference. This book is concerned with the kinds of things that are comparatively normal, or at least so comparatively well known as to need little or no explanation for the work's original audience. Thus, we have no space for the Dunmow Flitch or the Pace Egging, interesting as they might be. Sadly, this has meant not only the loss of many colorful stories but also the ruthless elimination of much of the most colorful slang in all of Britain, Cockney rhyming slang. This is so incomprehensible to people who do not speak it that most writers will carefully explain any obscure terms in the course of the work; thus I have tried to focus on only those terms that have crossed the boundaries of the Cockney world and entered more general usage.

Finally, although a number of historical terms and customs are included, the work is heavily weighted toward works, customs, and language since the early nineteenth century. Shakespeare, for example, almost never appears in modern editions without copious footnotes, so the reader is unlikely to need to turn to other references except for specialized work. But from about Austen on, most works will have only limited notes, and those often quite eccentric, while practically no twentieth-century writers except Joyce are commonly annotated. So I have stressed the terminology and customs of the nineteenth and twentieth centuries.

Entries themselves should for the most part be self-explanatory. Each entry is bold-faced and is followed by a definition or explanation. However I have made no attempt to define all possible meanings or to define in the abstract; where a term has many meanings, most of which are common in both Britain and America, I have discussed only the meaning that is not common or obvious to a potential American reader, or the practice that sometimes leads to confusion for Americans.

Idioms sharing common terms are discussed within the text of the basic entry, as for example, tea shop and tea dance are included under tea; where this occurs, such related terms are in boldface. Additional related terms with a separate entry are cross-referenced by a * after the term. Additional related information not discussed in the course of the entry is indicated by *See also*. All place-names are assumed to be in England unless otherwise noted. I have tried to keep abbreviations to a minimum, the most common being WWI and WWII for World Wars I and II.

The most difficult problem concerns the use of terms within the entries themselves that have different meanings, usages, or spellings in American and British English. As a general principle, I have tried to make all explanations in American English. However, for the sake of sanity, as well as space, it was not always possible to be absolutely consistent on this. Thus, where I have used British rather than American meanings or spellings within the entries themselves, I have cross-referenced them with a * to indicate that I mean the usage as discussed under the starred term's entry rather than the common American one; if a term with different American and British meanings is unstarred, then I intend the American meaning. Note, however, that I only star the first appearance of a term within any particular entry.

There are also some personal assumptions behind the selection of entries. Fundamentally, these are the terms that I have had to look up or ask about at some time in my own life. Many of these terms are common to many Americans, particularly those who live in New England, New York City, or communities with a strong Anglo-Saxon culture in the vicinity of Washington, D.C. For example, on the day after I wrote the entry for "book" as a uniquely British verb, I read William Goldman describing an attempt to date a woman in New York who "booked" a limousine and saw a newspaper ad from a national airline encouraging us to "book" our reservations with them; thus, it is obvious that a certain number of Americans do use book as a verb in the British sense. Even so, I still include the term in this work as a British rather than an American usage, because most of the country does not use the term in that way. In these cases, I have worked from a simple assumption—if the reader uses "book" in this sense, he or she will never look the term up to begin with. The term is explained here for those people who do not normally use this term and thus might need an explanation; hence, when the definition says "What Americans call . . . ," it always carries the unspoken proviso: "unless they also use the British term."

Even more vexing is the question of what precisely is the standard American term for any British equivalent. There are numerous regional variations in terminology throughout the United States, even in this era of national media, and the more common the item, the more variants there are. *Sports Illustrated* has an annual swimsuit issue, for example, but many people actually say bathing suit, one-piece, or two-piece, or just call it a suit. American life in the 1970s and 1980s is unimaginable without the high-speed, multi-lane, limited-access highways that cover the nation and take commuters to and from work, but what is the generic term for them?—in Southern California, where they began, they are called freeways, but the traveler across the nation will hear them called interstates, expressways, parkways, beltways, by-passes, and perhaps a dozen other names. In such cases, I have had to make a decision based primarily on personal experience and have attempted to select the one or two terms that, if not necessarily used by all Americans, would at least be recognizable to almost all Americans. In most cases, this has meant the term most likely to be heard on national television, but in others, it is purely a reflection of my own personal experience.

Similarly, there are a large number of cases in which Americans have a common "public" term and an equally common "home" term. The airlines now have "flight attendants" as job titles, but many if not most people still call them "stewardesses" in casual conversation, just as most say "garbageman" in private rather than "sanitary engineer" or even "garbage collector"; most families cook on a "stove" in the kitchen, but when they go shopping, they will look for a new gas or electric "range." In such cases, I have tried to translate equivalent tones—if the term in question is a British "home" usage, then I have tried to select the American "home" usage. If there is no clear distinction, then I have tried to include both "public" and "home" American terms.

Because this is a dictionary of things that are, or once were, obvious to the British writers at time of writing, many of the entries will be obvious to the professor or critic who has long studied the writers and their culture or even to the tourist who visits Britain regularly. Most of us have to start somewhere. I hope there will be insights of interest to the most experienced student or teacher, but my goal is to make accessible what scholars and critics sometimes forget is a *foreign* culture to most of us, despite PBS programming and years of English Literature classes.

As should be clear by now, I am not myself British; nor have I lived there for decades absorbing the daily life. This distance has given me insight into those things that need explanation, but at the same time it may have allowed errors to creep in unnoticed in the course of those explanations. No one can completely or accurately explain all of a culture, particularly someone else's. There is nothing more distressing to the native than to be "explained" by a tourist after a week's visit. As a Californian, I know that feeling all too well, so I offer this as an exploratory, introductory volume rather than as a definitive work. This text will not explain "everything there is to know about Britain"; but I hope it will explain everything an outsider ought to know to make an intelligent acquaintance with the literature and entertainment Britain has given us. I have made every effort possible in the time available to have friends and acquaintances examine the entries for "clangers," but in the final accounting, this is a personal work, and mistakes, where they exist, are my own. Like that much greater pioneer Dr. Johnson, where such errors have crept in, I too must plead "Ignorance, madam, sheer ignorance."

The Dictionary

A

A. (1) Indication of a highway.* Although some have been widened and divided like American freeways, in most cases A roads are simply paved main roads used for the bulk of short-distance traffic, while freeway-style roads are called motorways.* Those most likely to figure in literature are those that begin in London,* especially the heavy commuter runs or those duplicating old long-distance coach* highways. These include: **A1**, north all the way to Edinburgh,* for the most part following the route of the Great North Road;* **A2**, to Dover;* **A3**, south to Southampton,* now a very heavy commuter run; **A5**, to the northwest and into northern Wales;* **A6**, also to the northwest but ending in Manchester;* **A10**, following a route dating back to the Roman era north through Cambridge to the east coast; **A12**, northeast through Suffolk* and Norfolk* to Yarmouth;* **A20**, southeast to Folkestone;* **A23**, a very heavy commuter run south past Gatwick* and on to Brighton;* **A40**, northwest to Oxford* and then on to Gloucester* and central Wales. The **A4** ran west through Reading* to Bristol* and into Wales but has been converted to the **M4** along its full length. In general, A roads identified with a single digit, such as A1, indicate trunk roads; those with two digits, such as A12, indicate somewhat shorter routes that connect at some point with the trunk route, and those with three or four digits, such as A113 or A1112, are short roads crossing or branching off from roads having the first one or two digits. (2) On movies, suitable only for adults, under 16 not admitted without an adult.

AA. Not Alcoholics Anonymous but Automobile Association, the equivalent of the American AAA. *See also* RAC.

abbey. (1) In the medieval era, a separate religious community, usually fairly large and wealthy; after Henry VIII confiscated the lands of most abbeys, it came to be applied to a church* that once was a part of such a community, such as Westminster Abbey.* *See also* minster; priory. (2) A large country house,* so called because it was once part of an abbey or because the owner wants to imply that it is old enough to have been part of an abbey.

abbot. The priest in charge of an abbey.*

ABC. The Aerated Bread Company, not only makers of modern, white loaf bread* but also operators of a famous chain of tea* shops from the 1870s.

abdication. Only once since Richard II was dethroned has England* had an abdication, when King Edward VIII abdicated in 1936 to marry a twice-divorced American woman, Wallis Simpson. *See also* Windsor.

Aberdeen. A port and industrial city on the northeastern coast of Scotland.* Its access to the North Sea* made it a shipping and fishing center, and since the North Sea oil development it has been a center of the British petroleum industry. Prior to that, it was perhaps most noted as the **Granite City** due to the granite quarries nearby that produce the **Aberdeen stone** used in so many British buildings.

abortion. Before 1938, abortions were absolutely illegal; in that year a case of a girl who had been raped led to some judicial relaxation, but in the 1960s estimates that at least 100 illegal abortions were performed each day led to the 1967 legalization of practically all abortions provided two doctors agreed the procedure would be safe.

about. In the vicinity, nearby, as in "Is Ted about?"

AC. In the police,* Assistant Commissioner. *See also* commissioner.

academy. (1) In general, now used to indicate an educational institution that comes after secondary school but is not a university.* Americans also often use this meaning (art academy, business academy, etc.), but a student goes to a British academy at a younger age, since the age of school-leavers* has been less than sixteen for most of the century. In the eighteenth and nineteenth centuries, however, academy usually meant a secondary school aimed toward a specific goal, such as training potential officers,* and one that did not teach Latin or Greek like the public schools;* thus it was an especially common name for girls' "finishing schools." Most of these that survived in the twentieth century have become public schools or girl's schools* but retain the old name of academy. In Scotland, this is a standard name for any secondary school. *See also* college; seminary. (2) An association or society devoted to the cultivation or promotion of the arts and sciences, such as the Royal Academy.*

accent. Before the nineteenth century, accent was understood in primarily a regional sense, with persons of various classes in an area sharing the same basic accent. Social status was related to the distance from London*— the farther away the home, the more stupid or uncouth the speaker was assumed to be, with the Irish and Scots placing at the bottom of the scale. There were of course class accents at that time; servants* often are shown in plays having crude accents, but not particularly more crude than those of country gentry* such as Tony Lumpkin. But as the country became urbanized, mixing people from various regions, as an urban middle class took social power, and as people not born to the gentry began to penetrate the public schools* and Oxford* or Cambridge,* accents came to indicate class* as well as region. In general, lower-class accents are distinguished by one of two broad factors: (1) they drop the h^* at the beginning of words and sometimes add an h at the beginning of words that begin with a vowel; or (2) they use the glottal stop* for t or d, a regionalism associated with the northern areas that became a class indicator when those areas were industrialized. Persons moving up in class tried to lose their accents and studied to sound more like the people of the class they joined, which added to the confusion for an outsider, since due to their inexperience with the higher class of people, many persons adopted an accent that never really existed, and thus revealed their gaucherie through their very attempts to hide it. This process is most obvious in the confusions over the h sound and in a peculiar accent that many Americans think is "standard" that throws all r sounds to the wind, says i sounds as ay, and pins the upper lip so firmly to the teeth that all sound is forced through the nose. Further complexity was added as many among the *nouveaux riches* hired nannies* and governesses* to train their children to speak with a different accent than they themselves used, while many members of the upper classes trained by those same nannies learned the vocal habits of the classes from which such women so often came. The basic public school accent became perhaps even more important than the education itself in opening doors to government service or professional opportunities; it also became the foundation of the standardized accent of the BBC* and of several generations of actors and thus is often thought of as an upper-class accent by Americans, although the true nobility* and gentry rarely speak with it. For a time after WWII, it appeared that the BBC might act much as American radio and TV had done to unify and standardize pronunciation. After the 1960s, however, it became fashionable among many who had escaped the working class (or who wished to embarrass their middle-class parents) to reject the various middle-class accents and adopt or exaggerate their working-class or regional accents to make a political point, and under anti-elitist pressure, the broadcast media purposely introduced announcers and programs using diverse accents. The issue has been further complicated by the large post-Empire* influx of Asian, African, and Caribbean immigrants, each with their own accents as well. When Shaw's Henry Higgins claimed to be able to place any accent, he merely codified what the average Briton could, and can, do instinctively. In a way that Americans can never really grasp, the average Briton can place any stranger into a very specific slot in the class structure very quickly and almost solely by the way he or she speaks. *See also* RP.

accumulator. In a car, what Americans call the battery.

ack emma. Morning, or A.M., used in the military since WWI. *See also* pip emma.

Act. A law as passed by Parliament.* *See also* bill; common law; reading.

action, bring an. To sue.

action group. A committee that is expected to actually accomplish something.

action replay. What American TV viewers call instant replay.

Acton. A suburb of western London* made up of several former villages, generally seen as tasteless and lower class.*

Adams, Fanny. *See* Fanny Adams.

ADC. At Cambridge,* the Amateur Dramatic Club, an extracurricular club that presents student-produced and performed plays, since WWII one of the major sources of theater directors. *See also* OUDS.

adder. *See* viper.

address. Until the late twentieth century, most British addresses outside central London operated under the assumption that anyone getting mail would be personally known to the postman.* Any freestanding house* had a name, not a street number; in or around villages, the address might not even include a street* or road* name but simply be: Name of House, Name of Village, County. This applied to very small houses, and it is still common for middle-class dwellers to give their homes names. *See also* post.

Adelphi. A neighborhood in London* south of the Strand* and west of Charing Cross* Station, originally fashionable Adam terraces,* now much replaced by offices and businesses.

administration. In business, a form of bankruptcy.

admiral. By Shakespeare's time, the rank given in the navy* to a commander of a fleet or squadron, and by the nineteenth century formalized into four specific ranks: Admiral of the Fleet, Admiral, Vice-Admiral, and Rear-Admiral. The **Lord Admiral** was originally the commander of all the navy, a rank that officially ended with the formation of the Admiralty* in 1832. *See also* Appendix V; Sea Lord.

Admiralty. The government office in charge of the navy,* formed in 1832 and since 1965 a department in the Ministry of Defence.* Although responsible for maintaining the British navy, the Admiralty may ultimately enter history as the example that prompted Parkinson's Law. The **Old Admiralty** built in 1722 housed the Admiralty offices near the **Admiralty Arch** that stands at the end of the Mall* in London,* while a major addition on the side toward the Mall in 1907 now houses the Civil Service* Department. *See also* Lords of the Admiralty; Sea Lord.

Adriatic tummy. *See* gippy tummy.

adult. *See* minor.

Advent. The period preceding Christmas,* beginning on **Advent Sunday**, which is variously defined as the Sunday nearest to November 30 (St. Andrew's Day*) or four Sundays before Christmas. The **Advent calendar** is a large stiff calendar or picture with little flaps that are opened one by one, each revealing a tiny candy, a custom that sometimes appears in the United States as well.

advert. What Americans call an ad or a commercial.

advocate. The Scottish name for a barrister.*

advowson. The right of a private person to recommend or actually appoint a clergyman to a particular living.*

aesthetic movement. The artistic and cultural ideas associated with Ruskin and Morris in the 1880s, such as "art for art's sake" and a return to handcrafted art, clothing, and furnishings to escape the horrors of the machine-made urban world, satirized in *Patience*. **Aesthetic dance**, however, was much later, a term used primarily for the kind of "modern" dance pioneered by Isadora Duncan.

affiliation order. A court order requiring a man to pay child support.

AFM. Air Force Medal, an award for air force soldiers who show unusual bravery in the air but not in combat.

afters. What Americans call dessert. *See also* pudding.

Aga. A stove, from the name of a brand that can burn either gas or coal.

AGB. Audits of Great Britain, not an accounting firm but the rough equivalent of the American Nielsens, measuring ratings for TV programs.

age, come of. *See* minor.

age of consent. For a girl, the age at which a man may legally have sex with her, currently sixteen.

age of discretion. The age at which a child is thought to be responsible, but not yet an adult, currently fourteen. *See also* minor.

aggro. Originally, aggravation, as in "not worth the aggro," but now often meaning physical violence, as in "a bit of aggro at the pub."

agony aunt. Writer of a personal advice column in a newspaper* or magazine or someone giving such advice in call-in radio programs.

agricultural show. An exhibition generally equivalent to the American county or state fair. The largest is the **Royal Agricultural Show**, a national exhibition held in a different county* annually until 1967, since permanently in Warwickshire.*

aid. *See* in aid of.

Aintree. *See* Grand National.

aircraftman. The lowest rank in the Royal Air Force,* equivalent to the army* private;* generally in three ranks: leading aircraftman, senior aircraftman, and junior technician. *See also* Appendix V.

air force. *See* RAF.

air hostess. What Americans called an airline stewardess. *See also* steward.

Air Ministry. Originally, the governmental department in charge of the RAF,* now subsumed into the Ministry of Defence.*

airy-fairy. Overly optimistic or dreamy, what Americans often call head-in-the-clouds.

aitch. A sound of an *h** spelled out.

Albany. (1) Scotland,* used only poetically, probably from the Gaelic* for mountain. (2) In London,* a mansion* of flats* just north of Piccadilly,* since 1802 one of the most fashionable addresses possible for politicians, writers, and so forth, until recently renting only to single males.

Albert Bridge. A combination suspension and cantilever bridge in London* over the Thames* to Battersea* Park (1873). In three colors and a style suggesting cake decoration and with electric lights tracing the cables at night, it is one of the most charming and eccentric bridges in the city.

Albert Hall. A gigantic round building in London* just south of Kensington Gardens,* used for large meetings and concerts, especially the annual Proms.*

Albert Memorial. The memorial raised by Queen Victoria for her husband in London* on the southern edge of Kensington Gardens,* long regarded as the quintessential example of Victorian overstatement and gaudy taste-lessness.

Albion. An artistic name for England,* from a British (but not a Greek) legend that a son of Poseidon called Albion taught the locals to build ships. **Perfidious Albion** is a French* saying from a poem of 1821.

Aldeburgh. A coastal fishing village* in Suffolk,* in the nineteenth century becoming a resort, noted primarily as "The Borough" of Crabbe's poem and since WWII home to a major music festival in June associated primarily with Benjamin Britten, whose *Peter Grimes* is set there.

alderman. Originally, the head man or men of a guild, from an Old English term used for someone acting under the king's* authority. Most cities* and towns* chartered in the medieval era were governed by the various guilds rather than by people elected from the general populace, and thus the guild aldermen often became members of what Americans would now call a city council. Most aldermen had additional authority in that they were usually magistrates* or justices of the peace* as well. Unlike the aldermen in many American cities, these men were rarely professional politicians but were rather the outstanding businessmen of the town or city, often serving for little or no pay. Numerous changes and reforms over the centuries removed these positions from the direct control of the guilds, but the title of alderman continued until the various reforms of the nineteenth century set up the modern councils,* and councillor* is now the preferred term. However, in London, the local JP* for each ward* was called an alderman until the office was abolished in 1974. *See also* mayor.

Aldermaston. A village near Reading* associated with atomic weapons, from a research lab and regular protest marches there since 1958.

Aldersgate. Originally Aldred's Gate in the wall of London,* dating to Saxon times and torn down in 1761. The modern Aldersgate is the street that continued northward outside the old gate.

Aldershot. A gigantic army* base in Hampshire.* First opened in 1855, it is used as a central training depot for the army, where most recruits do what Americans call Basic Training. Prior to its establishment, all training of recruits had been done within each individual regiment.* "Peeling potatoes at Aldershot" is a common description of life in National Service.*

Aldgate. In the medieval era, the eastern gate in the wall of London;* the gate itself was demolished in 1761, but the street through it still bears the name, now known as a Jewish neighborhood and the beginning of the East End.* **Aldgate pump** was the well, in the eighteenth century replaced by a pump, at the site of the gate.

ale. A type of beer.* Originally there were some significant differences between the two, but by the first half of the twentieth century the word ale had dropped from general use except as a euphemism for beer used by those who would not admit they drank such a common* substance; more recently, the term has made some comeback as tourists and yuppies have made minor distinctions more socially significant.

A-levels. Advanced levels, or tests, given to students at about age eighteen. Unlike the American SAT tests, which are for college admission, these dealt with specific subject matter. Students normally took these exams in three subjects, in which they specialized during their sixth form* studies; they were scored in seven grades, from A–G, with A–E regarded as passing, but common usage treated them as pass/fail tests. Thus, a student was said to "have" one, two, or three A-levels, depending on how many subject area tests he or she had passed. These were very important even if the student did not use the results to gain admission to a college.* Although not equivalent to a degree* of any kind, they were used similarly by employers, so that a person who had passed even one A-level would find far better jobs and have much greater opportunities for advancement than a student who had passed only O-levels.* Although many colleges used them for admission, until very recently those at Oxford* and Cambridge* continued to use their own tests. Since 1988 these have been officially called the GCE Advanced Tests, but most still call them A-levels. *See also* GCE; GCSE.

alight. To step down from or out of, as from a bus.

all comers. A contest open to all.

alley. The oldest meaning is a walkway in a garden* lined with trees or shrubs, and this is still in use particularly on the grounds of country houses.* In urban areas, it means a narrow street,* usually only wide enough for a person walking; what Americans call an alley, the narrow roadway behind buildings or homes used by servants, garbagemen, and so forth, is called a mews.* *See also* lane.

Alleynian. Student or alumnus of Dulwich* College.

All Fools' Day. April 1. The tradition of practical jokes on this day, in America called April Fools' Day, is older than recorded history, but it involves all levels of society; traditionally all pranks must end at noon.

All Hallows. *See* All Saints' Day.

Alliance. The political union of the Liberal* and SDP* parties in 1981, unifying the primary groups of what Americans would think of as "liberals," drawn primarily from the educated "caring" middle class.* Its primary policy seemed to be that it was against Margaret Thatcher but still wasn't Labour.* At the time, there were numerous predictions that it could become the number two party, a viable alternative that would continue public services and state industries without being dominated by the trade unions,* but so far it has not happened that way. *See also* Liberal Democrat.

all in. (1) Everything included, as in "It cost £20 all in." **All-in wrestling** means no holds barred. (2) Tired, completely exhausted, as in "I was all in that night."

allotment. A small plot of land a town dweller uses to grow things, most often food, separate from the person's own garden.* A portion of common* land is split into small plots, which are apportioned or rented to members of the local community. The practice began in the early nineteenth century as a way for town dwellers who no longer owned or worked farms to feed themselves and for laborers to occupy their free time.

all out. In cricket,* all eleven batsmen* retired in an innings.*

all-play-all. The kind of tournament Americans call a round robin.

all-rounder. In cricket,* one who both bowls* and bats well, used more generally for a person with many skills or talents.

All Saints' Day. November 1, also called **All Hallows**.

allsorts. Small candies in many colors but usually licorice flavored.

All Souls. A college* at Oxford,* since 1438 reserved only for fellows* and having no undergraduate students, thus academically of great prestige.

All Souls' Day. November 2, when special services are said for all who have died.

all square. In various sports, what Americans mean by "the score is tied."

almoner. An officer who distributes charity, usually as part of the household of royalty* or of a bishop;* sometimes used for a hospital chaplain as well. In contemporary life, this often means what Americans call a social worker. The **Royal Almonry** is the primary charity office of the monarch, headed by a **Lord High Almoner**.

almshouse. A charity home for the poor, usually aged, and supported by private donations or endowments; usually these are quite small organizations and buildings. The *l* is silent. *See also* pensioner; Poor Laws.

amenities. (1) In medicine, services beyond the basic medical service provided by a hospital on the National Health,* such as a private room for which the patient naturally pays extra. (2) In other usage, the toilet and bathroom.*

American cloth. What Americans call oilcloth.

American plan. A hotel in which meals, at least breakfast and dinner, are included in the price of the room. This practice was common in mid–nineteenth-century American hotels, but Americans of course haven't seen this in the United States for decades; even so, the term was used in Britain as in much of Europe well past the mid-twentieth century. *See also* bed-and-breakfast.

ancient. An ensign.*

and all. A lower-class* usage meaning "as well" or "etc."

Anderson shelter. A partially prefabricated bomb shelter that could be installed by the local householder in the garden,* widely used and effective in WWII.

ane. In Scotland,* one.

angel. A gold coin worth eighty pence.* *See* Appendix I.

angel cake. What Americans call angel food cake.

angle-poise. A lamp with a flexible, adjustable stand.

Anglesey. A large island off the northwest coast of Wales,* a Druid* center in the Roman era.

Anglican Church. *See* Church of England.

Anglo-. As a prefix, although now generally used by Americans to describe the participation of all of Great Britain,* the term itself means only the English and is used in this more restricted way within the United Kingdom.*

Anglo-Catholic. Not a Catholic Englishman but High Church,* a form of the Church of England* in which the rituals and the priest's dress closely resemble those of Catholic services. *See also* Oxford Movement; Puseyite.

Anglo-Indian. An English person who was born or who spent a significant amount of time in India, but never an Indian who had emigrated to or had been born in England. The term was also used among the Indian colonials* to mean a half-caste but seems not to have been used very often in this sense in England, where the more common terms were Eurasian* for women and just Indian or Paki* for men.

Anglo-Saxon. While Americans use this now (as in WASP) to mean any person not from a politically correct minority, the British tend to use it only for the basic English groups living in Anglia* and Wessex* before the Norman invasion and for their descendants. As it was assumed that these people were less civilized than the Normans, the term is rarely used except to indicate something crude or vulgar, especially vulgar forms of profanity.

Annabel's. The most exclusive and expensive night club* of London during the late twentieth century,* patronized by the wealthy and famous no longer young.

anorak. A waterproof jacket with a hood.

ante-natal. Before a child is born, what Americans call prenatal.

Antonine wall. A wall of turf and a ditch across Scotland* connecting the Firths* of Forth and Clyde, built in the early Roman era to keep out the Highland* tribes, north of Hadrian's Wall* (built around the same time), but abandoned after about fifty years.

AONB. Area of Natural Beauty. These began in 1949 under the law establishing the National Parks* but are smaller areas; an AONB is not given the same protection as a National Park, but the regulations give local authorities some controls on potential developments within them.

apartment. Originally, a set of rooms within a large house* or other building, such as a residence for a judge* in the law court building, or a portion of a castle set aside for an important guest or someone the lord* wished to reward. By the nineteenth century, this term had come to mean a single room rented out in a house (multiple-room units being called apartments or sometimes a set of apartments). The American concept of an apartment, consisting of several rooms, is usually called a flat.*

Apostles. An extremely exclusive secret society at Cambridge,* devoted to discussion and debate of philosophical questions, unique in that its exclusivity is intellectual rather than social.

Appeal Court. *See* Court of Appeal.

approved school. A detention facility for those too young, generally under seventeen, to be sent to prison,* what Americans call reform school. *See also* Borstal.

apron. Historically, this term has seriously changed in meaning, primarily to reflect class.* It appeared after the Restoration as an upper layer (often quite spectacularly decorated) that covered the front portion of the skirt, worn by ladies of wealth and fashion to protect the dress while the lady was eating. By the end of the eighteenth century, however, as layered skirts dropped out of fashion, the apron was worn only by servants,* so that by mid-nineteenth century it was associated only with servants or perhaps trades. Thus, respectable women doing their own cooking or housework often refused to use the term, usually calling it a pinafore* instead, as they still do.

arcade. *See* shopping.

archbishop. The titular head of the clergy* in the Church of England.* As might be expected in an organization of often conflicting customs, there are two archbishops in England, at Canterbury* and York,* but the one in Canterbury is the official head of the Church. Each ranks between a duke* and a marquess* and is addressed as "Your Grace"; he is titled the "Most Reverend." In theory, the monarch appoints the Archbishop, although for at least two centuries the Prime Minister has actually made the selection. Once appointed, archbishops serve for life (until retirement), but, although nominally the ultimate power and authority of the Church, Canterbury's power is primarily through influence, as the local bishops* actually ordain and assign clergy.*

archdeacon. A clergyman who supervises the rural deans* of a bishopric and also acts in other areas as a sort of assistant bishop, appointed by and answerable to the bishop.*

Archers, The. A popular BBC* radio soap opera, running since 1951 at 7:30 P.M.

Arches. In London,* a short street under stone arches that support part of Charing Cross Station.* Almost from their first construction, the space underneath the arches has been a gathering place for winos, vagrants, and the homeless seeking evening shelter.

architect. This term includes the person who designs a building, as in America, but is also used for the person Americans call an interior decorator, perhaps because in a country where people remodel rather than tear down, most of an architect's work is on interiors.

Arden. A wooded area of Warwickshire* commonly associated with Shakespeare's Rosalind and Jaques, but as most of the forest was gone by the fourteenth century, he would have known it only as a myth, and it seems more likely he had in mind the modern Ardennes on the continent.

area. Of a building, the open space outside a basement entrance below ground or street level; in urban terraces* or large houses, this serves as a lightwell but also is the servant's or tradesman's entrance.

Area of Natural Beauty. *See* AONB.

argy-bargy. A quarrel or loud fight, originally Scottish but used in most of the United Kingdom* now as well when the fight is not thought to be too serious or threatening.

aristocracy/aristocrat. Although technically only the nobility* itself, generally the terms now include members of the nobility,* the gentry,* and any others of particular wealth and social standing and are often used ironically about anyone with pretentions to grandeur.

Armistice Day. *See* Remembrance Day.

army. As with so many institutions of British life, the army grew haphazardly. After the Civil War,* Parliament* was extremely reluctant to authorize a standing army, so that only a few regiments* of personal guards for the monarch, now evolved into the Guards,* managed to survive. All other units were organized on a temporary basis as a form of private enterprise, Parliament paying a colonel* a flat fee with which he recruited his own troops. The expanding Empire* and the Napoleonic wars demonstrated that this practice was no longer feasible, so the army expanded to 109 permanent regiments of infantry and 31 of cavalry,* but the fear of a standing army kept most of these overseas and underfinanced throughout the nineteenth century. Only in 1871 did the government officially accept responsibility for the army by buying out all the commissions* of its officers,* reorganizing so that each regiment was at last given a home base in Britain with reserve and active battalions,* and standardizing pay, ranks, and duties. Enlistment was for life until 1847, at that time changed to twenty-one years for nonofficers; in 1870 this period was reduced to twelve years, part on active duty and part on reserve duty. Conscription* was used briefly in WWI and again during WWII and national service.* The present army is all-volunteer and all-professional; its volunteers sign up for twenty-two years, although some of this may be reserve duty, and, after three years most can remove themselves from active duty by giving twelve months' formal notice. *See also* Appendix V; East India Company; Home Guard; line; navy; RAF; Regular Reserve; territorials.

Army & Navy. A large department store in London,* so called because it catered originally to the families of military officers,* and for most of the twentieth century its stock and fashions were synonymous with conservative middle-class* taste. Not at all like the American Army-Navy stores that deal in military surplus and camping supplies.

Army List. A published roster of all commissioned army* officers.*

arrears. Unpaid debts or, sometimes, unfinished and overdue work, usually said as **in arrears**.

arse. What Americans call the ass, as in buttocks. Americans often assume this is a more polite way to say ass, but it is in fact crude and vulgar usage. **Ass** is normally used to indicate either the animal or a foolish person and as such raised no eyebrows at any point in literary history, while arse is rarely spelled out fully in literary works until after WWII.

Arsenal. Traditionally one of the most successful football* clubs,* playing in the northern London* suburb of Highbury.

Arthur's. *See* Carlton.

article. As a verb, to apprentice, as every apprentice agreed to a specific contract mutually binding him and his employer. An **articled clerk** was someone in a solicitor's* or barrister's* office who worked as a clerk,* copying, filing, researching, and so forth, for little or no pay in return for training in the legal profession, like David Copperfield at Mr. Spenlow's.

articles of religion. *See* Thirty-Nine Articles.

articulated. *See* lorry.

artiste. A term used since the late nineteenth century for a popular performer, originally implying one of greater quality than usual but gradually appropriated for all popular singers, acrobats, magicians, and so forth. Generally, classical music performers remain simply artists.

Arts Council. A semiautonomous institution (since 1946) that receives its funds from the government* and is appointed by the Prime Minister* but independently determines how to use the funds to subsidize arts programs throughout Britain. It formally administers the South Bank* complex and provides subsidies to other groups. As with the American NEA (National Endowment for the Arts), it is often criticized simultaneously for its support and its lack of support for particular programs; no one likes it, but no one, not even the most intense conservative, seems to really want to get rid of it.

Ascot. (1) A horse racing* track near Windsor,* noted primarily for the week in mid-June called **Royal Ascot** when, since 1711, members of the royal family* attend, taking a short ride by carriage* over from Windsor* Castle, and the most fashionable or significant members of society come down to join them in the **Royal Enclosure**, the men in full formal wear and the women in hats and elaborate dresses. Commoners* attend as well, wearing whatever they feel like as long as they stay out of the Royal Enclosure. For the rest of the racing season, Ascot is just another race track. (2) A man's tie made of two very wide sections joined with a narrow band, so that when tied, a very wide fluffy body descends from a very small knot, one of the first forms of adult long ties, first worn in the 1880s when it tucked into the top of a very high waistcoat* and almost completely covered the exposed portion of shirt. Supposedly, this first appeared at Royal Ascot, and it is still the tie traditionally worn with men's formal wear at outdoor occasions such as Royal Ascot or the monarch's garden parties,* but it is almost never seen with any other kind of suit. After WWII, the name was also given to a scarf looped around the neck so as to billow out and fill the V in an opened collar, the sign of either a bohemian* or a retired officer.*

Ashes. In cricket,* the nominal award to the winner of matches between English and Australian national teams. The name comes from a newspaper report in 1882, when England lost for the first time, that cricket was dead and cremated and its ashes taken to Australia. When England went to Australia and won the next year, the Australian ladies gave them an urn containing the ashes of a burned cricket bail.* *See also* Test.

Ashmolean. A large museum of antiquities and art in Oxford.*

aspidistra. A houseplant with large, tapering leaves, common for most of the late nineteenth and twentieth centuries in the front rooms* of respectable homes; like lace curtains and the budgie* a sign of the lower–middle class* and the respectable layers of the working class.

Aspinall's. The most select modern gambling club,* in Mayfair* in London.*

ass. *See* arse.

Assembly Rooms. *See* Bath.

assistant. *See* shop.

assisting the police. Technically, merely being questioned by the police. However, newspapers often say, "A man is assisting the police in their enquiries" to indicate he is "under arrest" because they are not allowed to publish names of the accused until they actually appear in court.

assizes. Courts* held by royal judges* on circuit, used for serious crimes, divorce,* and some appeals, meeting three times each year in at least one town per county;* after 1971, replaced by the Crown Court.* The **bloody assizes** were those conducted after the Duke of Monmouth's 1685 rebellion, in which Judge Jeffreys hanged over 800 rebels.

Association. *See* Football Association.

assurance. What Americans call life insurance, although it is more often used in a company's name than by the general public, who prefer insurance.

Astley's. An amphitheater in Lambeth* (1770–1883), first a circus, then a theater noted for its spectacular melodramas involving live horses.

Aston. A neighborhood, once a suburb, in northern Birmingham,* home to **Aston Villa**, one of the most consistently successful football* clubs,* originally formed from members of chapel* congregations in the suburb.

Atheneum. One of the oldest gentlemen's clubs* in London,* located in Pall Mall.* In many ways, this is the model for the stereotype, a club noted for the seriousness of its members, its terrible food, and a large room in which speaking is completely forbidden. Founded in 1824, it was originally literary in orientation, but for over a century it has been favored by high-ranking clergy,* academics, scientists, and senior civil servants.

athlete. This is generally used only of participants in track-and-field events; those who play cricket,* for example, are called cricketers and football* players are footballers rather than athletes. *See also* sportsman.

at home. For the middle classes* and up, in the nineteenth and the first half of the twentieth century, to be at home was to be willing to receive visitors. Thus, a butler* or maid* might tell a visitor that the mistress was "at home to no one," which was understood to mean that she was actually at home but did not want to see any guests. For much of this time, women of any social standing had formal hours during which they were at home; for example, Mrs. So-and-So might be "at home Tuesday afternoon," which meant that she held a form of open house for visitors during that time, and on other days of the week she would of course visit the same women during their "at homes."

ATS. Auxiliary Territorial Service, the women's corps of the army* in WWII. *See also* WAAC.

attendance centre. A punishment facility for juvenile offenders, where they may be confined only on weekends but are returned to home and school* during the week. *See also* approved school; Borstal; detention centre.

attorney. A lawyer, as in America, but almost never used after the mid-nineteenth century, when solicitor* replaced it in common usage.

Attorney General. Originally, the monarch's attorney, by the seventeenth century becoming an official title of the minister* in charge of government legal activities. The Attorney General need not be a lawyer, as he administers governmental activity in the field but does not try or judge any cases. *See also* Chancellor; Solicitor-General.

aubergine. The food Americans usually call eggplant.

auld. In Scotland,* old. The **auld kirk** is the old church, or the Church of Scotland;* colloquially, it is also a shot of good Scotch whisky.*

Auld Reekie. Edinburgh,* reekie meaning smoky.

Aunt Sally. Originally, a fairground figure with a clay pipe, at which people threw things to knock out the pipe; hence, an object of ridicule or target of abuse, something everyone (in American terms) tries to "take a shot at."

au pair. Beginning shortly after WWI, but becoming widespread after WWII, a young woman who looks after the children in a middle-class* household. The au pair is almost always foreign and of student age; her primary job is to look after the family's children before they reach school age or when they are home from school, although some housekeeping may also be included in her duties. She works for extremely low wages, since the chance to visit Britain* and learn or practice her English is considered to be part of her pay, and often for short term, leaving after a year or so to return to school or her home; but she offers the basic functions of a nanny* without the full expense of a nanny. As the au pair lives with the family, is usually French or Scandinavian, and is always young, her presence often raises eyebrows in the neighborhood and leads to suspicious conflicts between husband and wife, but such drawbacks are usually outweighed by the middle-class wife's belief that servants,* however minimal, must be present in order to have a true middle-class household. What has never been explained adequately by anyone is why perfectly respectable, middle-class continental girls would want to become servants in England for a year or two in the first place.

Austin Seven. The first real mass-produced car in Britain, roughly equivalent to the Model T in looks, use, and popularity (1922–38). In the 1950s, the name was revived for Austin's version of the Mini.*

Avebury. Pronounced AYVbry, a village in Wiltshire* noted for megaliths much larger and older, but far less famous, than those at Stonehenge.*

avenue. What Americans usually call a driveway, particularly one leading up to a country house.* Very rarely are streets called avenues, and most of these were built in the late nineteenth century, like Shaftsbury Avenue* in London,* as a form of slum clearance and traffic management on the Parisian model.

Avon. (1) Actually several rivers—the most famous is that which flows through Stratford* and made Shakespeare the "bard of Avon"; however, this is a relatively minor stream flowing into the Severn.* Larger and more significant is the Avon that flows from Wiltshire* through Bristol* and into the Mouth of the Severn, navigable to oceangoing vessels, which made Bristol a major port. A third Avon also rises in Wiltshire but flows south through Salisbury* into the English Channel* on the south coast. (2) Since 1974, a county* immediately surrounding Bristol and Bath,* formed from parts of old Gloucestershire* and Somerset.*

Axminster. A town in southwestern England* noted before the nineteenth century for carpets in the Persian manner; the trade died for almost a century but has been revived in the mid-twentieth century.

A–Z. The most detailed and widely used map of London,* a brand name used generically for any street map. When spoken of, called **A to Zed**.*

B

B. Indication of a paved road, but usually only what Americans would call a country road. These are the picturesque narrow lanes* tourists and movie companies think of as typically British, although some are now in the suburban environs of London* and are heavily traveled.

b——. The usual way to print bloody* before the second half of the twentieth century.

BA. *See* degree.

Babu. An Indian, but usually derogatory, from a Hindu term roughly equivalent to Mister.

baby bouncer. A device into which a small child is strapped that supports the baby for standing before the child is able to stand by itself.

baby bunting. *See* bunting.

babycham. A mildly alcoholic drink similar to a shandy,* drunk only by respectable women or children.

back. *See* cricket; football.

back, out the. *See* outhouse.

back bencher. A member* of Parliament* who has no particular standing in the party* or the government,* so called because he or she sits on one of the benches behind the front bench on which members who are in the

Cabinet* or in the Shadow Cabinet* sit during Parliamentary sessions. The back bencher is much less influential than the average American Congressman; since almost all legislation and public statements come from the party leadership on the front bench, the back bencher's only real function is to provide the votes to pass the party legislation. *See also* private member.

back chat. (1) An insolent response, similar to what Americans call "talking back to." (2) Facetious or humorous conversation, such as that between partners of a comedy team.

backfield. The players in football* who are primarily defensive.

Backs. At Cambridge,* the grounds* of the various colleges* running down to the River Cam.*

backside. What Americans call a person's bottom. *See also* arse; bottom; bum.

back stairs. The stairs used by the servants* in a large house but not by the family or guests; hence, metaphorically, anything to do with servants, such as **back stairs gossip** for gossip passed among the servants, to be treated dubiously by those who use the front stairs. *See also* below stairs.

backstroke. *See* stroke.

back-to-back. Small houses* built as duplexes, different from semidetached* houses in that they shared back rather than side walls. Generally, these were built as worker's housing in the nineteenth century in the northern areas and are associated with slums and the poorest working class.*

bacon. British bacon is cut in much wider strips, with much less fat, than American bacon, and often looks like thin ham slices to Americans. Prior to the twentieth century, bacon was often used as a generic term for pork. The bacon-and-egg breakfast* only appeared in the late nineteenth century.

Baedeker. A tourist's guidebook, from the books first published by the German Baedeker firm in the 1850s.

baggage. *See* luggage.

bagman. Not a gangster but a traveling salesman.

bagpipe. The instrument is now almost completely synonymous with Scotland,* as it was used there by the ancient clan* musicians and was adopted as the military instrument of the various Scottish regiments* formed in the eighteenth century, due to its traditional use, its portability, and its unique sound that could penetrate through the noise of movement and of battle. However a version of the bagpipe was also common in Ireland well into the twentieth century, and other variations were common in most parts of England until the nineteenth. For the Scots, it is a patriotic instrument, the aural equivalent of the kilt* and tartan,* and is heard at any and all patriotic occasions.

bags. (1) Trousers.* The usage goes back almost to the appearance of trousers in gentlemen's fashion in the mid-nineteenth century, but readers will most often see the term in stories of the 1920s and 30s, when it meant in particular a very wide-legged type of trousers with a high, wide waistband and large cuffs, called **Oxford* bags** because of their popularity among students. **Debagging**, removing a man's or boy's trousers, is a widespread schoolboy form of insult and attack. (2) As **bags of**, a lot, a great deal. (3) A children's claim to a right, like the American dibs, as in "bags first go."

bail. *See* wicket.

Bailey, Old. *See* Old Bailey.

bailie. A bailiff. In Scotland,* however, before the eighteenth century, this was the title of the officer equivalent to a sheriff* rather than to a bailiff, and after that time was applied to the equivalent of an alderman.*

bailiff. (1) An officer of the sheriff.* Although having many duties, the one most noted is enforcement of bankruptcy or eviction; a "visit from the bailiff" in literature is generally understood to mean a visit in which most of a person's goods are confiscated and the person thrown into the street or taken to debtor's prison.* A **water bailiff** is a legal officer who enforces water laws, especially those concerning fishing. (2) A manager of a nobleman's country estate, identified primarily with collecting the landlord's rents.*

Baily's. *Baily's Hunting Directory*, an annual publication about hunts and hunting in all parts of the world.

bake house. Until the twentieth century, as most cooking was done over an open fire, home baking was done in small fireside brick ovens, if at all. In many villages, the local baker would allow local residents (for a fee, of course) to use his ovens to bake their own dishes, and these ovens were often called the bake house or **public oven** rather than the bakery, especially used for joints* on Sundays* when the baker could not legally open for business. In Mrs. Gaskell's *Cranford*, the retired soldier commits a great social gaffe by helping a woman carry her basket home from the bake house; what he thinks is kindness is interpreted as an insult because it publicly acknowledges she has no oven of her own.

Baker Street. Known almost exclusively as the home of Sherlock Holmes, the London* street runs south from Regent's Park;* the address 221B did not exist when Doyle invented Holmes.

balaclava. A knitted woolen hood, similar to a ski mask with the face completely uncovered; named after the site where British soldiers first wore them in the Crimean War, they are now widely worn by civilians.

Baliol. *See* Balliol.

ball. A large, formal party at which dancing is the primary activity, held only at the upper end of the social scale. From a modern American perspective, the ball seems merely an absurd formalization of what should be simple fun, but the ball's primary function was not the dancing per se but the marriage* market that lay behind the dancing. It is no accident that when the mothers realize Bingley (*Pride and Prejudice*) has a fortune in need of a wife to spend it, they arrange a ball; that's what balls were for. From the late eighteenth century until the 1920s, the ball was practically the only place where respectable young men and women could meet, much less actually touch each other or manage a private conversation, for on the dance floor they could be chaperoned but have their conversation lost in the crowd. This function is reflected also in the types of dancing done at balls: During the seventeenth and eighteenth centuries, when the ball was an entertainment for courtiers who all knew each other, dances were large group dances with intricate movements and many changes of partners, but in the late eighteenth these began to change so that one kept the same partner throughout, until the waltz and polka swept all other dances away, leaving couples in each other's arms for the entire dance. Most balls followed a rigid format of fast and slow, long and short dances, necessitating the **dance card** on which women reserved partners to guarantee that the most eligible men got the best chances to hold her or talk to her. Balls were the primary activity of the Season,* families parading their young men and women to several every week. After the 1920s, when night clubs and later public dance halls opened in the cities, the ball lost its value for arranging marriages and became merely an excuse to dress up, often in costume as at fancy dress* balls or with admission charged and proceeds to go to charities, and young unmarried people rarely attend them any longer.

Balliol. Pronounced BAYley-el, one of the oldest colleges* of Oxford,* with a long literary tradition, featuring undergrads as varied as Southey, Arnold, Swinburne, Hopkins, and Aldous Huxley,* fellows* such as Jowett, Bradley, and Toynbee, and fictional old boys* like Peter Wimsey.

Ball Monday. *See* Easter.

balloon goes up/went up. Originally, this meant merely the start of something, from the use of a balloon in WWI to signal the start of artillery shelling, but since WWII it usually means more specifically the start of a tantrum or an angry scene.

ballot. Secret ballots were not used in elections* until 1872; before that time, all electors announced their votes in public at the polling place.

balls-up. A mess, a major foul-up, a semirespectable term used by military officers and civilians of similar class* or attitudes, similar to but not as vulgar as the American fuck-up.

bally. Rhymes with tally, a euphemism for bloody,* used since mid-nineteenth century by sporting, university, and military types.

Balmoral. The Scottish residence of the monarch, located near Aberdeen.* Built in 1856, it was a favorite place for Victoria and has since been used by the royal family* as a summer home and a place to go shooting.*

Banbury. A town about halfway between Oxford* and Coventry.* The **Banbury Cross** was a medieval cross in the town center that was destroyed by Puritans in 1602, one of many local manifestations of puritanical zeal that led to **Banbury man** being synonymous with a Puritan. For **Banbury cheese**, *See* cheese; for **Banbury cake**, *See* cake.

bandbox. A circular box such as Americans usually call a hatbox. To be **bandbox fresh** or **out of a bandbox** is to be brand new, fresh, and/or neat.

Band of Hope. A major temperance society, headquartered in London.*

bandoline. In the nineteenth century, a perfumed hair oil for women.

bandy-legged. What Americans usually call bow-legged; if the British use **bow-legged**, they usually apply it to furniture, not people.

bang. Colloquial usage in most levels for exactly, as in "bang on top," where Americans often prefer right. **Bang on** means on the spot, exactly correct; **bang off**, however, is immediately.

banger. A sausage. The term appeared just prior to **WWII**, apparently in the navy,* but quickly spread throughout all of British society. The British banger is somewhat larger than the American hot dog, with a mild taste, unusually greasy, even for a sausage, and is always fried, often until almost black on all sides. They usually burst when hot; hence the name. **Bangers and mash**, sausage and mashed potatoes, is an extremely common meal. *See also* breakfast.

bank. *See* Appendix I; Bank of England; building society; cheque; commercial bank; Exchequer; Giro; merchant bank; note; overdraft; pound; Treasury.

Bank. The Bank of England.*

bank holiday. A national holiday, not having anything particular to do with banks except that banks have been required to close on such days since 1871. These were originally passed not to increase but to reduce the number of holidays taken by the Bank of England,* which closed for numerous saints' days. The 1871 holidays were Monday after Easter,* Whitmonday,* the first Monday in August, generally known as **Summer Bank Holiday**, and Boxing Day;* except in Scotland*, where they were New Year,* the first Monday of May, first Monday in August, and Christmas.* Over the years these have been modified, but since the 1960s bank holidays have been New Year, Good Friday, May Day* (actually taken on the first Monday in May), the last Monday in May, the last Monday in August, and Christmas, common throughout the United Kingdom;* plus Easter Monday and Boxing Day outside of Scotland; plus July 12, anniversary of the Boyne,* in Northern Ireland* only.

bank manager. The manager of the local office of a bank,* similar to a branch manager of an American bank but with much more authority and much more direct contact with the depositors. He most often appears as the person who must approve an overdraft.*

Bank of England. Founded in 1694, it was operated as a private bank* until nationalized* in 1946. From the beginning, it was authorized to issue notes,* and its notes have been the official currency of England* and Wales* since 1833 (although Scottish and Northern Irish banks can also issue legal currency in those nations). It also serves as the central bank and manages the government debt, acts as national gold depository, sets interest rates and other monetary policy while still operating independently of the government itself, and holds government funds on deposit. Often called the Old Lady of Threadneedle Street (its location) partly from affection and partly for its extremely careful and conservative practices, which have also made it a symbol of financial stability and security through-out the world. *See also* pound; Treasury.

banned. In the late twentieth century, this usually means one has had one's driving licence suspended, usually for drunk driving or for multiple citations for speed or recklessness. This happens far more often than in America and to people who are otherwise often quite reputable.

bannocks. Flat oat cakes,* a Scottish dish, usually cooked on a griddle.

banns. An announcement of intention to marry. In the Church of England,* banns must be "published," or read aloud, during Sunday morning services for three successive weeks in the home parish* of both the potential bride and groom before the wedding* can be solemnized. This is done so that anyone who knows of a reason why the marriage* should not be allowed to happen has time to make that objection known (although before 1754 the practice was often circumvented by a special licence* for the wealthy or by contracts and other secular forms of marriage). The practice goes back to the medieval Catholic Church,* and the name comes from a Latin term meaning announcement, not from any suggestion of banning the wedding ceremony. Civil marriages as well as those in nonconformist* churches do not require banns.

Banqueting House. An addition to Whitehall* Palace in London* built in 1622, now all that remains after the fire of 1698; it is a large hall of great architectural significance but rather haphazardly used for state occasions.

banting. What Americans call dieting, from a popular doctor's diet pro-posed in mid-nineteenth century. The term has more recently been replaced by slimming.*

bap. A soft crustless roll, about the size of an American hamburger bun.

Baptist. A Protestant church founded in 1611 as one of many nonconform-ist* groups, named for its refusal to baptize infants, choosing to wait until the person was an actual believer. It immediately split into two main groups, the **General Baptists**, who believed in general atonement for all, and the **Particular Baptists** (1638), who took the more Calvinist road of atonement only for the saved. The two groups declined, revived under the evangelical influence of the Methodists,* and merged in the Baptist Union in 1891. Their evangelical leanings make them, for the most part, a lower-class* church.

bar. (1) In the medieval era, judges were separated from the rest of the court by a railing called a bar; those authorized to practice law were allowed to approach the bar to plead, and thus one was officially recognized as a lawyer by being "called to the bar." In England* and Wales,* all barristers* must be called to the bar in one of the Inns of Court* in London,* after passing both an examination and a residency requirement. Solicitors,* however, are not required to do so and are not members of the bar. (2) In general, Britons do not call a place that serves alcohol a bar except when it is in a hotel or restaurant. In pubs, bar is used only for the counter or to indicate separate service areas, for which *See* pub. *See also* milk bar. (3) When said of a fire,* this refers to the heating element in an electric heater. For most of the century, the British have used electric heaters with very thick straight rods rather than thin filaments to give off the heat; a small fire is a **one-bar** or single bar, and a larger heater a **two-bar** fire. In general, they have used these not as supplementary but as the sole heating for a room and do not turn them on unless someone is actually in the room, so all rooms are cold and the people huddle around what Americans see as very tiny heaters. (4) As a verb, to refuse admittance; more specifically, one is **barred** when thrown out of a particular pub.* (5) *See* colour bar.

Barbados. *See* sugar.

Barbican. A neighborhood of London* along the northeast section of the medieval city walls, called by other names, such as Aldersgate,* until it was destroyed by bombs in WWII. It is now the site of an immense urban redevelopment project of office blocks* and high-rise housing units of surpassing ugliness and complexity, buried within which is a complex of concert halls and theaters, one of which is used as the London base of the Royal Shakespeare Company.*

Barclays. One of the largest commercial banks.*

barge pole. The same as the ten foot pole Americans would not touch something with.

barley sugar. *See* sugar.

barmaid. A woman who serves behind the bar* in a pub* (but not the landlord's* wife, who is never called a barmaid, although she often was one before her marriage). She is not a waitress but rather the female version of the **barman**, the equivalent of the American barkeeper. The barmaid holds a peculiar social position in that, because she spends most of her life associated with men and alcohol and is ideally friendly, outgoing, and attractive to those men (the stereotype always has a large bosom), she is rarely considered to be respectable, but at the same time, she is almost never thought to be a part-time prostitute. The barman is always simply a worker, so the term is never used for the actual owner of the bar or pub.

barmy. Silly, bubble-headed, stupid; actually derived from barm, which is the foam on a beer.*

barn. Used almost completely for storing hay or grain; livestock stay in sheds or stables.

Barnaby Bright. St. Barnabas's Day, June 11, the longest day of the year on the old calendar.*

Barnardo's. A charity devoted to the needs of children since Dr. Barnardo opened a home for destitute children in 1870, now running children's homes and schools for the handicapped.

Barnard's Inn. An Inn of Court* for Chancery* lawyers, already decrepit when Pip joined Herbert Pocket there in *Great Expectations*; no longer in use.

baron. Originally a nobleman who was eligible for Parliament,* now for the House of Lords.* In the scale of things, a baron is the lowest rank in the nobility* but this is the rank that was actually meant by the terms "peer* of the realm" and lord.* The baron is officially called Lord (Family name), his wife is a **baroness** and is called Lady (Family name), and they are addressed as My Lord or My Lady. Their son is called The Honourable (First name), the daughter simply by her first name. No one in Britain is addressed as Baron So-and-So; if such a title is used, the person is a foreigner. It is possible for a woman to inherit some baronial titles, and if that occurs she is said to be a **baroness in her own right** (as opposed to the mere wife of a baron) and would be styled the Baroness (Family name) until such time as she married; she would then take whatever title were suitable to her husband's rank. *See also* honours; nobility; titles.

baronage. The peerage.*

baronet. Before 1611, this meant a little baron,* as Americans might assume, which in practice meant a member of the nobility* eligible for the House of Lords* but who was not actually a baron, most likely an eldest son serving while the father was still living. After 1611, it was a specific title, ranking above a knight* and below a baron. Unlike a knight, the baronet inherits his title, but unlike a baron, the baronet is not a Lord* or a peer.* The baronet is addressed as "Sir (First name)" and his wife as "Lady (Family name)," but he adds **Bart** after his surname in his signature to distinguish himself from a knight. *See also* honours.

barouche. A carriage* with four wheels and a hood over the back half that can be folded down in good weather.

barrel. Although thought of merely as a general container, this is sometimes a specific measurement, as with the American barrel of oil. A barrel of beer is 36 gallons;* of fish, 500 fish; of flour, 196 pounds; of beef, 200 pounds; of gunpowder, 100 pounds.

barrister. A lawyer who has been "called to the bar.*" Not all British lawyers are equal; only barristers may plead cases before judges* in the High Court* and the Court of Appeals;* until recently, they also had a monopoly in Crown Court* as well. **Solicitors** handle everyday legal affairs, such as contracts, wills, property exchanges, and so forth, and may represent clients in cases before justices of the peace,* magistrates,* and now in Crown Court as well if they wish. A barrister is not necessarily a criminal lawyer; he or she is assumed simply to be a specialist in some area of the law and knowledgeable in court procedure and thus may appear in civil as well as criminal cases. Another often confusing aspect of barristers for Americans is that the English have no equivalent of the District Attorney's office; the barrister for the defense in a criminal case this week may act as prosecutor in another case next week. Barristers, like judges, still wear wigs when appearing before the Crown Court or higher courts. Barristers must be members of one of the four Inns of Court* and pass an exam similar to the American bar exam; solicitors must pass a law school course. Only barristers may eventually become judges.* An **utter barrister** is an "outer," or junior, barrister, one who is not a QC* or KC* and who thus must always address the court from outside the bar; Rumpole is a quintessential example. *See also* advocate; Justice; serjeant; silk.

barrow. (1) A pushcart used by street pedlars,* now almost completely gone from daily life, although **barrow boy** continues to mean an aggressive, lower-class* businessman. *See also* costermonger. (2) In the countryside,* a mound of earth, generally covering a prehistoric burial ground, relatively common throughout Britain.*

bar sinister. *See* bend sinister.

Bart. *See* baronet.

Bartholomew Fair. A fair* at Smithfield* in London* on August 24, St. Bartholomew's Day, originally for the cloth and clothing crafts, but by Jonson's time noted as a bawdy pleasure fair, continuing until 1854.

Bartholomew's. *See* St. Bartholomew's.

basin. (1) Any large bowl. A **pudding basin** is what Americans call a mixing bowl. A **slop basin** is used not to feed the pigs but rather as a bowl into which tea* dregs or coffee* grounds are emptied at the table or on the tea tray. (2) *See* sink.

Basingstoke. Pronounced BAYzingstoke, a town* southwest of London,* once quite separate but now close enough to be a suburb* of the city, synonymous with boring, dull small town or suburban life since at least the 1880s when Gilbert used its name as the charm to calm Mad Margaret in *Ruddigore*.

Bass. One of the major brewers of beer,* located at Burton.*

bastard. Before 1754, the treatment of bastards was quite varied, due to the considerable difficulty in defining marriage* itself in a legal sense. But one point was always clear: A bastard could not inherit property unless specifically named in a will and could never inherit more than legitimate heirs. After the Marriage Act,* bastards were treated by common law* as essentially persons without rights. However, modern research indicates that bastards were actually comparatively rare: about 7 percent of births in the early Victorian era, declining to 4 percent by 1900 (in the United States in the 1980s, 20 to 29 percent of births were illegitimate). Until 1926, the child remained a bastard even if the parents subsequently married. *See also* foundling.

bat. The wooden implement used to hit the ball in cricket;* much wider than the American baseball bat, it is also flat on the side that is used to strike the ball. To **carry one's bat** is to end the innings* without being put out, which happens when the eleventh batsman is put out while one of the earlier ones is at the other wicket,* derived from the requirement that the runner keep his bat with him while running. Metaphorically, it means someone has done his duty. A **straight bat** is a bat held vertically; used metaphorically for dealing honestly or directly, or for going about a job the right way.

bath. When used as a verb, it means to take a bath, as distinct from **bathe**, which means to go swimming. Additional confusions often arise due to the habit of male nude bathing, meaning swimming, that continued until long after WWII. Since the early nineteenth century, the British middle and upper classes* have firmly believed that the bath (at least for men) should be cold, like those purposely given at public schools* to build character. **In the bath** means actually in the tub rather than merely in the bathroom.

But a swimming pool is often called a **swimming bath**. Swim suits, especially for women, are often called **bathing costumes**. *See also* stew.

Bath. A town in southwest England* noted now for its pristine Georgian architecture. In the eighteenth century, the town's ancient Roman baths, built around Britain's* only natural hot springs, were uncovered, and Bath soon became the country's most fashionable spa, where the gentry* came to soak in the hot springs and drink the warm mineral water during the day and socialize and gamble in the **Assembly Rooms** at night. For many years before and after 1800, Bath was a major center of fashion, manners, and society, figuring in some way in the work of most writers of the time, although Jane Austen's comes to the fore for most modern readers. A **Bath chair** is a three-wheeled wheelchair, often topped with a folding canopy, pushed from the rear and steered by the occupant by turning the third wheel, first popularized among invalids in Bath about 1750 but very popular among the Victorians for many purposes and common in many resort areas.

Bath, Order of the. An order of British knighthood* from 1399, named for a ritual bath taken before installation; it essentially disappeared during the seventeenth century until revived by George I in 1725 as an honor for soldiers. Now it is one of the official honours,* open to primarily the military and the senior civil service.* The order is now so large it is divided into three ranks; from the top down these are Knight Grand Cross (GCB*), Knight Commander (KB*), and Knight Companion (CB*). Only GCBs may hang their banners in the chapel* at Westminster Abbey.*

Bath bun. *See* bun.

bath cube. Bath salts sold in a cube shape.

bathe. *See* bath.

Bath Oliver. Similar to an American graham cracker, although not quite as sweet. *See also* biscuit.

bathroom. The room with the bath, not with the toilet; the latter is often called the WC,* lavatory,* the loo,* or, in vulgar society, the bog,* and except in very recent construction or remodeling is a separate room.

baths. Usually the local swimming pool rather than steam baths. *See* bath.

batman. A soldier who was also the personal servant* of a military officer.* Originally, the batman cared for a bat-horse, which carried an officer's luggage, but by the late nineteenth century, the soldier was attached to the officer, not the horse. Bunter, for example, was originally Wimsey's batman. Quite different from batsman.*

batsman. In cricket,* the batter; quite different from batman.*

battalion. *See* regiment.

Battersea. A riverside area on the south bank of the Thames,* now part of London.* Primarily industrial in nature, it is physically dominated by **Battersea Power Station**, which long supplied the electrical power for London by burning coal. It also contained **Battersea Park**, a public park from 1858, noted especially for the amusement park within it that was popular in the 1950s and 60s. **Battersea Bridge** was wooden from 1771–1881, the most dangerous of London's bridges for carriage* or boat to pass; since 1886 it has been a cast-iron structure.

batting and bowling. The sexual preference Americans often call AC/DC or swinging both ways, a term borrowed from cricket.* *See also* all-rounder.

Bayswater. A neighborhood in London* along the north side of Hyde Park,* first constructed after 1830; never as fashionable as its developers had hoped, in the twentieth century it was synonymous with bedsitters,* residential hotels, and middle-aged landladies.

BBC. British Broadcasting Corporation, the primary broadcasting organization in Britain. Beginning broadcasting in 1922, it was reorganized as a public* monopoly in 1925. It provided all English-language radio programming in the nation, and through shortwave on the **World Service**; it also broadcast to all parts of the Empire,* which in effect meant the broadcasts were available throughout the world. Due in part to its peculiar position as an official monopoly that was nonetheless independent of the government,* the BBC's broadcasts became the world standard for honest, unbiased, and absolutely trustworthy, if somewhat stodgy, news reporting, a position underlined during WWII, when other national radio services succumbed to pure propaganda. After the war, the BBC expanded into television broadcasting (which it had pioneered in 1936), where until 1955 it was the only channel. Financed entirely by a licence* fee, paid annually by owners of receiving sets, the BBC has never carried advertising. Under the onslaught of rock-n-roll and the pirate stations,* BBC radio eventually was forced to abandon its policy of a single service for all the public, and since the 1970s has been divided into four "programs:" **Radio 1**, rock-oriented popular music; **Radio 2**, conservative popular music and features; **Radio 3**, classical music and cultural programming, although also broadcasting major sporting events; and **Radio 4**, news, features, interviews, and radio drama. (**Radio 5** started in 1990, but it is still unclear what its programming pattern will be, at present being a mix of programs from the World Service and youth-oriented but not rock-oriented shows.) Only Radio 2 and the World Service broadcast after midnight. In 1962 BBC television also added a second channel called **BBC2**, somewhat more "cultural" than **BBC1** in orientation. In the mid-80s, BBC1 added a morning program and began full-time broadcasting, with its daytime educational broadcasts aimed at the schools moved to BBC2, whose general programming runs only late afternoons and evenings; neither the BBC nor ITV* broadcasts much after midnight. Although Americans, who know the BBC primarily through *Masterpiece Theater*, see the BBC as proof that television can serve the public interest without constantly appealing to the lowest common denominator, it is not so universally respected in Britain itself. During the 1950s and 60s, the BBC often came under fire for its stodgy image, its "elitist" cultural predilections, and its participation in the Establishment; during the 70s and 80s, it has been persistently attacked for its "left-wing" bias. *See also* Broadcasting House; Channel 4; Light Programme; Savoy; Shepherd's Bush; Third Programme.

beach. The British use this not for sandy seashores but for an expanse of smooth pebbles. Naturally, these are usually found along the water's edge, but whatever the water, it usually means what Americans would call gravel rather than sand. Jet travel has exposed many to the sandy beaches of the Mediterranean and the United States, so the term seems to be changing meaning, but you may still find people who dump a load of beach, meaning gravel, onto a yard* or into a hole. *See also* shingle.

Beachy Head. A promontory on the south coast of England* between Eastbourne* and Newhaven,* a sharp, five-hundred-feet high cliff, one of the major landmarks for sailors approaching through the English Channel.*

beadle. Originally an officer of a law court* whose primary duty was to see that defendants showed up in court when their cases were called; as with *Oliver Twist*'s Mr. Bumble, they often had other duties within the parish* and were usually perceived as pompous, fat, and self-important functionaries of no real value to society as a whole.

beak. (1) Since the eighteenth century, slang for a magistrate.* (2) In public schools,* slang for the assistant master* who is responsible for discipline. (3) During the nineteenth century, slang for the head or chin, related to a bird's beak.

bean. (1) Beans are much the same in British foods as in American, although the specific names for the various beans are often different. When served, they are almost always boiled until mushy. Among typical beans are: **broad bean**, much like a lima bean, but more gray in color; **butter bean**, which Americans call the lima bean; **runner** or **French bean**, which Americans call the green bean or string bean; the **flageolet**, a kidney bean. When just "beans" is used, it generally means a small bean, like the navy bean, boiled in a thick brownish sauce, much like the American pork-n-beans, and often served over something else, like **beans on toast**; this is the source of **beano**, originally a schoolboy treat and then later casual slang for a meal, particularly among the officer* class. (2) Slang for money; **without a bean** means "broke."

beano. *See* bean.

beastly. Unpleasant, awful. Use is for the most part confined to women from the middle class,* who also occasionally use it as a euphemism for bloody.*

beater. *See* grouse.

beating the bounds. An annual procession of most of the people in a parish* around the traditional boundaries of the parish. This was done in part for rogations,* which were prayers blessing the crops, and partly to guarantee that the parish had not lost any of its land to either neighboring parishes or to farmers who tried to enclose commons* without notice. The name comes from the habit of physically striking each landmark along the boundary to guarantee it had been verified.

beaver. In Shakespeare's time, the visor of a helmet. In the Restoration, a wide-brimmed hat of beaver fur worn by both men and women; it declined in popularity during the eighteenth century, returning with a higher crown near the end of the century and evolving eventually into the top hat.*

bed-and-breakfast. A small inn or hotel,* usually of modest price, that provides breakfast as part of the basic service and fee, but no other meals, common for decades before they began to appear in America.

bedding. Of the garden,* annual plants.

Bedford. The major town of Bedfordshire,* in the seventeenth century one of the most fertile breeding grounds of dissenters,* epitomized by John Bunyan. **Bedford College**, however, is in London,* in 1849 a secondary school for women but now part of London University.*

Bedford Park. A garden suburb* of London* near Chiswick,* noted primarily as a center of the William Morris esthetic movement.*

Bedfordshire. A county* or shire* north of London* and immediately north of Hertfordshire,* for the most part flat and fertile, still almost completely devoted to agriculture and often synonymous with the English farmer. *See also* Bedford.

Bedlam. *See* Bethlehem.

Beds. Abbreviation of Bedfordshire.*

bedsitter. A one-room apartment, usually rented as furnished by the landlord, so called because the bedroom is also the sitting room.* Primarily a twentieth-century term, the bedsitter was, until very recently, the basic living quarters of all unmarried urban dwellers except the wealthy. The bedsitter usually resembled the basic modern hotel room, furnished with a bed, a chair, a chest of drawers and/or an armoire. It differed from a modern studio apartment in that it had no kitchen facilities or private bath; the bath and the toilet were down the hall or out back* and were shared with other tenants. Until fairly recently, the landlady may have provided one or more meals to her tenants, who may have also shared a common sitting room, usually called the lounge,* but many lodgers simply lived on their own in the single room, occasionally cooking on a single gas or electric ring.* Modern constructions and conversions generally put in studio apartments, often called maisonettes,* but bedsitters may still be found in many areas. *See also* digs; rooms.

Beeb. The BBC.*

Beecham's pills. A patent medicine first sold in 1847, popular well into the twentieth century as a cure-all. Beecham's fortune allowed his grandson Thomas to build three symphony orchestras to conduct (London Philharmonic and Royal Philharmonic are still functioning) and an opera company that eventually became the ENO.*

beef. Long associated with the English, as in "The Roastbeef of Old England," beef has actually been something of a rarity in the British diet, so scarce before WWI that the army* often recruited not with posters but with sides of beef. When meat appeared on tables, it was usually mutton* or pork except at feasts. Until the very recent past, most families thought of it only for the big Sunday dinner* (*See* joint). When not roasted, beef was almost always boiled, and steak, in the American or French sense, was practically nonexistent until the twentieth century; it was as often called a chop* as a steak and was usually fried until black and hard, and in restaurants, until relatively recently, was often covered with unpredictable sauces. The British, however, became very adept at using the nonmeat portions of the cow, such as tripe, marrow, or kidneys. **Bully-beef**, boiled and then canned, became a standard ration of the army* and navy* by about 1900. **Salt beef** is what Americans usually call corned beef. Even when roasted, beef was more often than not cooked until dry and then served cold in very thin slices. *See also* chop; fillet; grilled; pie.

Beefeater. Technically, a Yeoman of the Guard;* the name was derived from their great strength when the unit was first formed in 1485 as a bodyguard of the monarch. Because of the "roast beef* of old England," the term is often used loosely as a term for Englishmen in general.

beef-house. In the nineteenth century, a restaurant serving primarily stew.

beef olives. A baked dish made of thin slices of beef rolled around various stuffings.

beer. The primary beverage of the British before the arrival of tea,* and still the primary alcoholic drink in all parts of the nation. The various forms of beer commonly drunk include **bitter**, a beer strongly flavored with hops; **porter**, a dark ale brewed with extra roasted malt; **mild**, darker but sweeter, smoother, and a bit weaker in alcohol than bitter; **stout**, extremely dark, brewed with extra hops, roasted malt, and also a higher alcoholic content, with **milk stout** a form of stout that is light brown in color; and **lager**, a pale beer brewed and served cold in the German manner, appearing in Britain in significant quantity only in the last half of the twentieth century. **Ale** was originally beer brewed without hops, but now the term is used generically for, or dropped completely in favor of, the word beer; however, in recent years **real ale** has made some return—this has live yeast in it and thus can only be served from the cask; **pale ale** is bottled bitter; **brown ale** is bottled mild. For a while in the early twentieth century, ale was also called **light beer**, but this described its color, not its caloric content. All British beers except lager are served at room temperature, which does not necessarily mean warm, since kegs are kept in the cellar until use and since, with rare and very recent exceptions, British rooms are always much cooler than American ones. (In Dickens's time, a **beer-chiller** was a device in which beer was held over the fire to take the chill off, not to cool it down.) Throughout history, beer served many purposes other than simple intoxication in the modern American manner; it has been a safe liquid where water was often contaminated and dangerous and local wines all but nonexistent, has served as a significant source of calories in the working-class* diet, and, through the pub,* has provided the major social focus of most village* and local, urban lower-class community life. *See also* half; licensing laws; pint; skittles; small beer.

beerage. A joke name for the large number of brewers given noble titles.* *See also* peerage.

Beeton, Mrs. *Mrs Beeton's Book of Household Management*, an extremely popular 1861 book of recipes and guides to general housekeeping that in effect defined and codified the habits and manners of the middle-class* household, in American terms a combination of Emily Post, Dr. Spock, and Fanny Farmer. (Mrs. Beeton was only in her early twenties when she wrote this.)

beetroot. What Americans call a beet. What Britons call a **beet** is similar but white and fed only to animals.

BEF. British Expeditionary Force.*

Belfast. Capital and largest city of Northern Ireland.* Its major growth began with Protestant settlers in the late seventeenth century who initiated the Irish linen industry there and later developed major shipbuilding yards, but its previous image has been completely overwhelmed by the poverty, depression, and danger associated with the civil war between Catholics and Orangemen* initiated by the Provisional IRA in 1969, and it is now always depicted as a dirty, poor, and angry city.

Belgravia. A neighborhood in London,* lying behind and to the west of Buckingham Palace.* Built in the 1830s, it was inhabited by nobility* and the wealthy, at least as fashionable as Mayfair,* possibly even more so, into the present day, although the large houses are now more often occupied by foreign embassies than by aristocrats.*

Belisha beacon. At many pedestrian crossings are little posts on the sidewalk with a small globe on top; when the light is flashing, cars are supposed to stop for any pedestrians. These were introduced in 1937 by Hore-Belisha, the Transport minister;* pronounced beLEEsha. *See also* zebra crossing.

bellringing. Not merely the ringing of church* bells for services but a pastime in which bells of several sizes and pitches are rung in complex sequences determined by mathematics rather than by melody, often called **ringing the changes**. This can take hours to accomplish, as in Dorothy Sayers's *The Nine Tailors*. It is an eccentric hobby and far less common now than it once was, but it has been nonetheless a widespread practice.

bells and smells. Lower-class* slang for religious services, especially for Catholic services.

belly. This is the oldest term for the abdomen and the bowels, but at the same time it also meant a woman's womb. For a female criminal to **plead her belly** was to claim she was pregnant, which during the eighteenth and early nineteenth centuries would postpone her hanging until the child was born or sometimes eliminate it completely. However, during the nineteenth century, people of the more respectable sort, fearing the sexual suggestions of belly, stopped using the word altogether, substituting stomach as a euphemism; at the same time, Victorian pornographers (and some contemporary writers) continued to use belly as a term for the part of a woman's torso between the bottom of her corset and her genitals, causing many modern American readers who know only the food-related meanings to think the Victorians had very strange erogenous zones. *See also* tummy.

below stairs. Anything to do with servants.* In large houses* with several servants, they spent most of their time in the basement, where the kitchen, pantry, and similar rooms were both their work space and their rest areas (although they usually slept in rooms at the very top of the house); thus, their life was below stairs, and the term was applied to anything related to that life, such as "below stairs gossip" for gossip passed among servants. A widespread alternate term was back stairs.*

belt. (1) For women, either what Americans call a garter belt, or sometimes what Americans call a girdle. (2) In the medieval era, some earls* and knights* were given belts to denote their rank, so they were sometimes called **belted earls** or **belted knights**; this belt did not necessarily denote a greater rank than other earls or knights. (3) To **belt up** is to shut up.

ben. In Scotland,* a mountain peak.

Bench. (1) Judges* in general, and the judge of each case in particular. (2) The King's Bench* prison.

bench, back. *See* bencher.

bend sinister. In heraldry, a diagonal stripe running from top left to lower right, as opposed to the normal top right to lower left, indicating a bastard;* often inaccurately called the **bar sinister**.

benefit. In the theater, before WWI this meant a performance at which all the proceeds went to a particular performer, not to a charity.

benefit of clergy. A concession made by Henry II that anyone who was a clergyman could choose to be tried for crimes in ecclesiastical rather than criminal courts,* thus avoiding a death sentence; the practice was much abused, as a common qualification was the ability to recite a single verse from the Bible in Latin, but it nonetheless continued until 1825.

benefits. What Americans are now beginning to call entitlements, various payments made under the national insurance* system.

benefit society. *See* friendly society.

Ben Nevis. A mountain in western Scotland,* the highest peak of Britain.*

benny. Stupid, from a character of that name in the *Crossroads** TV soap opera.

bent. (1) Absolutely determined; Americans know this in some idioms, such as "Hell-bent for leather," but Britons use it regularly, as in "She was bent upon doing that." Similarly, to do what you're talented in or devoted to is to **follow one's bent**. (2) Crooked, as in a bent policeman. (3) Homosexual.

berk. A fool, a nitwit. This is quite recent, since about WWI, and primarily lower class* in current use; rhyming slang*: Berkshire hunt = cunt.

Berkeley Square. A square* in Mayfair,* site of fashionable housing in the eighteenth century, now mostly modernized and surrounded by office buildings or expensive shops, which makes the nightingale of the song so miraculous.

Berkshire. Pronounced BARKsher, a county* or shire* to the west of London.*

Berry's. Berry Brothers and Rudd, perhaps the most prestigious wine merchants of London,* located in St. James's* Street.

Bertram Mills. For decades the largest and most popular circus, synonymous with the circus in general until its closure in 1967.

besom. Not a genteel* term for a woman's breasts but the kind of broom Americans associate with witches, a sweeping tool made from a cluster of small branches or twigs tied together around the end of a handle.

bespoke. Of clothing, made to order, as distinct from ready-made.*

Bethlehem. A hospital* in London* from the late middle ages, used primarily as a lunatic asylum, soon corrupted in usage to **Bedlam** and as such synonymous since before Shakespeare's day with insanity and chaos. It actually occupied four different sites: At Bishopsgate,* then Moorfields,* where it was fashionable to observe the inmates for entertainment in the eighteenth century, then after 1815 in a park near Lambeth* Road south of the Thames,* and finally in 1930 moved out of the city completely to Kent.*

Bethnal Green. Originally a separate village, by the late eighteenth century a community in the East End* of London,* like its neighbor Spitalfields* devoted to silk weaving. Like all the other East End areas, it became a dank slum in the nineteenth, and it was in an attempt to alleviate the gloom there that Victoria Park, the first park designed and constructed for general public use rather than as royal* lands, was built in 1845. This worked for a time, raising the area to at least the lower-middle class* by the time Shaw placed Candida's preacher-husband's parsonage* there, but the area declined again in the twentieth. Now it is most known for the Museum of Childhood located there.

betting shop. A bookmaker's.* Although outlawed in 1853, these have been perfectly legal again since 1960 and located in practically every neighborhood, which probably accounts for the comfortable name; many are in fact major "chain stores," such as Ladbrokes,* like any other commercial enterprise. Most gambling is related to horse racing,* and recent surveys show that about 75 percent of the British bet regularly on the horses, the pools,* or both. *See also* ring.

between maid. *See* tweeny.

bezique. A card game played by two players, most popular during the three decades before WWI, especially in the upper levels of society. The general play is much the same as in pinochle, except that the double deck uses only 7s or higher, only eight cards are dealt to each player, and scoring is on a different system.

bickie/bicky. Slang for a biscuit,* from childhood mispronunciations.

bid fair. To look promising or hopeful.

biffins. Apples first baked and then flattened into a cake* shape.

Big Ben. Technically, the large bell that tolls the hour in the clock tower at Westminster,* but generally understood by all to be the clock, the chimes, and the tower as well. The tower was finished in 1858 and the bell hung the next year; the chimes began to be used by the BBC* as a signature in 1923, and since then, the tower and the bells have been both a visual and an aural symbol of Britain to the rest of the world.

bijou. Often applied to a flat* to give some glamor to what would otherwise be seen as merely small and crowded.

bikkie. *See* bickie.

bilberry. A small blue berry found on a small heath* bush.

bill. (1) A draft of a proposed law. In Parliament,* bills are usually introduced by the government* rather than by individual members. Individuals can introduce a **private member's* bill**, but only after government policy has been implemented; it is almost never done by anyone from the opposition party.* Each bill is given three readings* before the final vote, then if passed, moves on to the other house where the process is repeated and then to the monarch for the Royal Assent,* after which it becomes an official Act;* however, many finished acts are still popularly known as bills, such as the Reform Bill.* (2) In a restaurant, what Americans call the check. (3) A policeman, possibly a variant of beak,* possibly a reference to the obsolete weapon called a bill carried by constables until early nineteenth century, possibly an import from America when the policeman's truncheon was called a billyclub. Also called **Old Bill**.

billiards. A form of the game Americans usually call pool, played with only three balls on a larger table than used for American pool. Extremely popular in the late nineteenth century when it was associated with military officers,* gentlemen's clubs,* and country houses,* its general popularity was surpassed in the latter half of the twentieth century by snooker,* which carries a much lower-class* connotation.

Billingsgate. The London* fishmarket until 1982. Besides its fish, it was widely noted for its tough-minded, and tough-tongued, fishwives,* whose language gave the name of billingsgate to any foul, abusive language.

billion. Up to a million, American and British numbers are the same. But after that, the British change names by the million rather than the thousand; thus, a British billion is 1,000,000,000,000 rather than the American 1,000,000,000; what Americans call a billion is usually called a thousand million, or sometimes a **milliard**. Similarly, a **trillion** is a million billion, (1 with eighteen zeroes) rather than the American thousand billion (1 with twelve zeroes).

Bill of Rights. Unlike the American Bill of Rights, this does not enumerate specific personal rights; passed in 1689 as a part of the Glorious Revolution,* it primarily attacked James II but also laid down the principle of parliamentary supremacy and excluded all Catholics* from the succession.*

billycan. *See* can.

Billy-O, like. A lot, very badly.

bin. This can be any container, but it is especially used for what Americans call a garbage or trash can and may be used for the container Americans call a dumpster. *See also* dustbin.

bint. Slang for a girl or woman, almost always derogatory and demeaning, from an Arabic term.

birch. A short cane,* most often made from birch wood, primarily used to beat schoolchildren. The term figures often in sadomasochistic erotica as well.

bird. (1) A pretty girl. Although the Beatles brought the term to American attention in the 1960s, it had been common military and lower-class* slang for at least a century and is still widely used without the nostalgic sense it now carries in America. (2) Hissing or booing, as in "giving the bird," supposedly from its resemblance to the sound made by geese. (3) Often used to mean a man, as in a "tough old bird."

Birdcage Walk. *See* Green Park.

Birkenhead. An industrial town across the Mersey* from Liverpool,* noted as a center of shipbuilding and shipping in the nineteenth century, in the last half of the twentieth century as a symbol of economic depression and blight.

Birmingham. Pronounced BIRmingum, although local dialects sometimes still say brummagem,* second largest city in Britain,* located practically dead center in England* in the Midlands.* Almost from its beginnings it was an industrial town, noted in medieval life for woolens and leather and in the eighteenth century spearheading the industrial revolution, including James Watt's steam engine factory. Throughout the nineteenth and twentieth centuries, it has been the site of major manufacturing plants and is generally synonymous with British industry.* Birmingham was also a leader in urban social reform and improvements during the nineteenth century, building the first public water supply, gas works, and free secondary school,* and instituting the first major efforts at slum clearance, among other innovations soon followed by other cities, and is thus also often associated with social reformers and reform movements of various political stripes. Nonetheless, it has generally been ignored in literature and other arts; when mentioned at all, it is as the home of crude working men or bluff, vulgar businessmen and for many writers has been the epitome of the kind of town you are happy to be from, as long as you are far from it, quite unlike the literary tradition of America's industrial second city, Chicago. *See also* Cadbury.

biro. A ballpoint pen, so called from the surname of its inventor.

birth. Although every person is born, only those who are born to the nobility* or to well-established families in the gentry* may be "of birth."

Birthday Honours. *See* Honours List; King's Birthday.

biscuit. Not at all like the American biscuit, this is what Americans call a cookie or a cracker. It is usually served with tea,* with sherry,* and sometimes with cheese.* A **water biscuit** is a plain cracker with little or no salt. **Sweet biscuits** or **tea biscuits** are what Americans call cookies; an **Osborne biscuit** is a brand of commercial cookies originally named for one of Victoria's residences due to her enjoyment of the product; a **marie biscuit** is a very thin, plain, mildly sweetened cookie, often eaten with cheese. **Ship's biscuit** was unleavened bread, like what Americans called hardtack, usually made in large wheels, baked on shore and then stacked and stored in casks on the ship until broken up to be eaten. *See also* Bath Oliver; cake.

biscuit, take the. To be outrageous or to be the worst possible example; Americans say "take the cake."

biscuit tin. Any container for biscuits,* including what Americans would call a cookie jar,* but most often a large metal container, like those often seen in American stores full of Danish butter cookies; most people use these to store odds and ends after the biscuits are eaten.

bishop. (1) In the clergy,* the ecclesiastical administrator responsible for a diocese. In the late middle ages, the Catholic bishops monopolized many secular government offices (memorialized on the modern chess board), giving the monarch able and educated administrators who were paid by someone else (the Church); they were rarely seen performing religious duties or even visiting their dioceses. When Henry VIII formed the Church of England,* the office of bishop remained much as before except that perhaps its ecclesiastical power increased; with the removal of the Vatican layer of administration, the bishops became almost independent rulers, subject to the two archbishops* in only a nominal fashion. Rising secular education, however, was already moving them away from the centers of political power by making secular administrators available to the monarch. This did not, however, remove them from political influence. The property that came with the title made it a lucrative position, and it was filled almost exclusively by the relatives of influential nobles or of party politicians rather than by churchmen gradually working themselves up through the ranks; in the decades before the Reform Bill,* bishops were almost universally depicted as fat, greedy, and worldly, rather like the "bloated capitalist" of later eras. This declined after reform,* as the bishops occupied themselves more with Church affairs, although they also continued to have seats in the House of Lords.* In 1878, the number of bishops given automatic seats in the Lords was limited to twenty-five: the archbishops,* the bishops of London,* Winchester,* and Durham,* and the remaining twenty with greatest seniority. A bishop is automatically a lord* upon taking the position. He is formally the Right Reverend (Rt Revd*) and his full formal title is The Right Reverend the Lord Bishop of (Such-a-place). Their peerages, however, are not hereditary but pass to the next bishop chosen. For most of the clergy,* the bishop represents Authority in all matters, as in so many of Trollope's novels. **Suffragan bishops** are clergy with some but not all of the authority of a bishop, first authorized in 1888 but officially seen only in London* after 1977, when the diocese was formally divided into five "areas," each headed by a suffragan. (2) A drink of red wine and sugar poured over oranges, so called from its purple color.

Bishopsgate. In London,* the gate to the north in the City* wall and the street that ran to it, in Roman days the main road to the north just as it is today as the start of the A10.*

bismuth tablet. An antacid tablet, taken to relieve indigestion.

bit. (1) A girl or woman, especially one who has sexual relations, as in a **bit on the side** or **a bit of the other**, which are adulterous sex, or as a **bit of ass/tail/crumpet*** equivalent to the American "piece of ass." A **bit of all right** is a great looking woman who may or may not be available for sex; however, a **bit of the rough** is a casual homosexual partner of the sort Americans often call rough trade. (2) A small coin, in the mid-nineteenth century usually applied to the groat*, in the twentieth century to the threepence* coin.

bits and bobs. What Americans call odds and ends. *See also* odds and sods.

bitter. *See* beer.

black/blacking. To shine shoes, and the shoe polish used. A **bootblack** is a servant,* usually in a hotel, who shines shoes.

Black. In common usage, this applies to any person of darker skin and may be heard about Africans, Caribbean Islanders who are of African descent, and Indians or Pakistanis. *See also* coloured; immigrant; wog.

Blackburn. An industrial town near Manchester,* in the nineteenth century the greatest textile producing center in the world.

Black Country. The industrial Midlands,* especially the area north of Birmingham,* so called from the smog and grime of all the nineteenth century factories there.

black draught. A licorice-flavored liquid laxative, common in the nineteenth century.

black economy. What Americans usually call the underground economy, business carried on in cash and without records so as to avoid the taxman.

Blackfriars. A section of eastern London* along the Thames* at the end of Fleet Street,* named for a Dominican convent there from the middle ages. Burbage had a theater in the district before moving south of the river, and it was associated with the many theater people and similar riffraff who lived there and spent time in such places as the Mermaid* Tavern. In the eighteenth and nineteenth centuries it was associated primarily with the docks, still disreputable and even dangerous. **Blackfriars Station** served the southern areas of England* but is now rarely used, its terminus replaced by Holborn* Viaduct. **Blackfriars Bridge**, connecting the neighborhood with the **Blackfriars Road** on the south bank of the Thames, was originally stone in 1760, but was rebuilt in its modern iron form in 1869 and was an extremely unpopular example of "modern" architecture when new.

blackguard. Pronounced BLAGgard, an unscrupulous villain. In Shakespeare's day, this was usually two words, black guard, used to indicate the lowest order of menial workers who were always "black" with filth; in the eighteenth century, the words merged and the pronunciation changed as the term was applied to rough villains, and by the end of the century, this had become one of the most insulting things you could possibly call a man (the term was never applied to women), in many ways much worse than calling him a villain* or a bastard.* After WWII, the term began to fade, but it may still be heard among the educated classes and perhaps older military men.

Blackheath. A common* between Greenwich* and London,* long notorious as a home for highwaymen* and cutthroats; it was also the rallying ground for Wat Tyler and Jack Cade as they approached London.

blackleg. (1) In late nineteenth and twentieth centuries, a scab or strikebreaker. (2) In the eighteenth century, a swindler, particularly associated with horse racing.

Blackpool. A resort town on the northwest coast of England.* It rose to prominence in the second half of the nineteenth century as the primary holiday site of the lower middle classes* of Liverpool* and Manchester,* expanding its clientele downward to include the industrial working class in the twentieth. It is often regarded as a vulgar, tasteless seaside resort, offering mostly "pints,* piers,* and Punch and Judy" entertainments. The vicinity is often also associated with holiday camps.* The **Blackpool Tower** is an imitation of the Eiffel outlined with lights.

black pudding. Not a pudding but a sausage,* usually made from suet, oatmeal, and pig's blood, basically what Americans usually call blood sausage.

Blackshirt. A protofascist organization led by Sir Oswald Mosley during the 1930s, formally called the **British Union**; although they made some inroads during 1934–36 with a platform combining Empire* and anti-Semitism, they never were taken seriously by much of the general public, who seemed to see them as little more than overgrown boys who liked to play about in uniforms. The outbreak of war put Mosley in prison and ended the movement, although Mosley re-entered politics after the war.

Blackstone. *Commentaries on the Laws of England* (1765–69) by William Blackstone, books so often studied by lawyers and the general public that they became synonymous with the law in general and often more specifically with the British constitution.*

black tie. *See* white tie.

Black Watch. The 42nd (Royal Highland) regiment,* the "gallant forty-twa" of the folk song. Their uniform includes a Scottish bonnet* with a red vulture feather.

Blackwell's. The largest and oldest bookstore of Oxford,* located in the Broad.*

Blackwood's. *See* Edinburgh.

blancmange. Usually pronounced bluh-MAHNJ, a particularly bland white food substance made from cornstarch, milk, and sugar* (and sometimes gelatine), much like what Americans call pudding, eaten as a dessert, for reasons understood only by the British (from the French, meaning "white stuff to eat"). Chaucer mentions it, but at that time the dish included chicken, nuts, and eggs and was considerably tastier.

blanco. A substance similar to a thick white shoe polish, primarily used in the army* to whiten uniform belts, and adopted with great relief when developed in the 1890s as a replacement for the clay powder previously used.

blanket drill. Masturbation, from the activity often done during the daily siesta required of army* troops in warmer climes during the heat of the day. As with so much military slang, it was spread to civilians by the RAF* in WWII, who sometimes also used it to mean sex with a partner.

bleeding. Much the same as bloody.*

Bleeding Heart Yard. A small courtyard in London* in the City* near Holborn* Circus; home to Dickens's Plornishes and Arthur Clenham's factory, the yard still exists, although no longer quite so depressed and depressing.

Blenheim. A gigantic palace* built by the first Duke of Marlborough* near Oxford* on the site of a royal house and park* given to him by Queen Anne, continuing in the Churchill family to the present and known as one of the grandest buildings in the country; pronounced BLENnum.

blighter. A person who acts contemptibly, similar to bugger* but used in more polite circles; another of those "standard" stereotypical terms that actually dates only from about 1900.

Blighty. Slang for England,* used by military and colonial* types in the twentieth century, derived from an Indian term for Europeans rather than from anything actually in England. In WWI, a blighty was a wound that was serious enough to have you returned home from the front but not so serious as to permanently disable you.

blimey. A Cockney* expletive since late nineteenth century, a corruption of **Gorblimey**, in turn a corruption of "God blind me."

blinding. A euphemism for bloody.*

blinking. A euphemism for bloody.*

blitz. To clean up or clean out something quickly and efficiently.

Blitz. The period of German air raids on Britain* during WWII, especially the highly concentrated period between September 1940 and May 1941 when the primary targets were the major industrial cities and the primary victims were the civilian population. For those who lived through the time, it was a period of great horror, with many nights spent sleeping in masses in the Underground* stations or in homemade shelters, only to come up in the mornings to find homes and family gone and the cities in flames. But it was also a time that has been romanticized, even as it was happening, a time when all the British for once worked together toward a common goal and there was a sense of purpose, of accomplishment, and of value to life.

bloater. A type of smoked herring.*

block. (1) A large modern building. Americans might call this a high-rise, as it is usually taller than the four or five stories of older urban construction but not as tall as a skyscraper (which, at least until the late 1980s, were illegal in London,* which outlawed any buildings taller than the dome of St. Paul's*). However, some blocks are under five stories but earn their name from the immense size of the overall construction. Generally, a **tower block** is used to mean a modern housing project, particularly the ugly square units of council housing,* although it may also apply to a multistoried set of middle class flats* as well, while **office block** indicates a similar building devoted to offices. A **mansion block** is a large building of flats* that originally were intended to be exclusive and expensive, or more recently may simply mean a building of flats like American condos. (2) In cricket,* to use the bat* simply to protect the wicket; the batsman makes no attempt to swing, merely holding the bat out, and makes no attempt to run after the ball bounces away.

bloke. An all-purpose, casual term for a man, equivalent to the American fellow or guy.

blood. From Shakespeare's time to the Regency era, an extravagant, fashionable, and wild young man, given to rakish exploits, gambling, and drink, probably so called from the noble blood such young men almost invariably had (or they couldn't have gotten away with the lifestyle).

bloody. The all-purpose British swear word, used to intensify anything, as in "bloody fool." Numerous learned theories abound as to its origins, but it has not always been disreputable. Before about 1750 it was quite respectable and was still used in all levels of society into the nineteenth century. Then, during the general urge to clean up language, the term gained a new notoriety, was assumed to be unfit for respectable ears or eyes, and was proscribed almost as intensively as the *f*-word. Shaw caused something of a scandal by having Eliza Doolittle say it in 1914, and it was only in the post-WWI spate of realism that the word crept back into literature or was spelled out in full rather than shown as b— (note however that in 1956 Lerner and Loewe still felt they could not use it in *My Fair Lady*, substituting blooming* instead). Although so widely used as to mean little more than "very, very," it still carries a connotation of vulgarity or brutality and is rarely used in the more polite reaches of society. *See also* beastly; bleeding; blinding; jolly.

bloody-minded. Obstinate or making trouble for the fun of it.

bloomer. A stupid mistake.

blooming. Late nineteenth century euphemism for bloody.*

Bloomsbury. A neighborhood in London* near the British Museum* now noted primarily for the **Bloomsbury Circle**, a group of writers and artists known for their aesthetic or, in less polite circles, their effete works in the 1920s and 30s, centering on Virginia Woolf and her husband Leonard, who lived in **Bloomsbury Square**, and from that time associated with the more bohemian* persons, like Dorothy Sayers's Harriet Vane. Prior to that it was known as a respectable middle class* area, suitable for families like *Peter Pan*'s Darlings, and in late eighteenth century was practically in the countryside.

blow. (1) Among sailors, a windy storm. (2) Also among sailors, a euphemism for damn, as in "blow me if I do" or "I'll be blowed!"

blower. Slang, especially military, for the telephone.

blow tickler. The party favor that stays rolled up in a tight spiral until you blow on it, which makes it uncurl into a long straight tube.

bluchers. Heavy, ankle-high men's boots.*

blue. (1) An indication of an athlete who competed for Oxford* or Cambridge* against the other. By American standards, collegiate sports are a ramshackle affair, most often organized and run by the students themselves without any particular attention or official support from the universities. Nevertheless, someone who "gets a blue," especially in rowing,* cricket,* or football,* is noticed by alumni and often singled out for jobs, promotions, and other honors after finishing school. The Oxford blue is darker than the Cambridge blue. (2) In the seventeenth century, the emblematic color of the Covenanters,* and since the late eighteenth century of the Tory* and Conservative* parties; hence, **true blue** for steadfastly loyal.

bluebell. In England* a plant with blue flowers clustering up a vertical stem; in Scotland* a completely different plant with a single blue flower on each stem, widely seen as symbolic of Scotland itself. In Scotland, the English bluebell is called a hyacinth.

Blue Book. Not a small blank writing notebook for college exams but rather the report of a governmental commission, usually published with a blue cover.

bluebottle. A policeman; originally used in Shakespeare's day for a beadle, the term almost disappeared until the bobbies* appeared in blue uniforms.

Blue Coat. A student of Christ's Hospital,* from the unusual uniform.

Blue Cross. Not a health insurance but a charity organization for animals, primarily paying vets to treat the pets of the poor.

blue lamp. The indication of a police* station.

blue-pencil. To edit or censor; British editors regularly used blue pencils for marking copy.

Blue Peter. An extremely popular and long-running educational TV program for children; the name comes from the **blue peter**, which was a blue flag with a white spot flown to indicate a ship was ready to sail, and on the program people go on brief adventures to find interesting things.

Blues. The Royal Horse Guards* regiment,* so called for their blue uniform tunics.

bluestocking. This is almost always assumed by Americans to mean a puritanical woman but in fact it means an intellectual woman more interested in career or intellectual pursuits than in marriage* and family. The term comes from the unusual blue, rather than black, stockings* worn at literary gatherings at Lady Montagu's in the mid-eighteenth century, but curiously enough the blue stockings were actually worn by a man, a minor poet named Stillingfleet; the color of Lady Montagu's stockings is not known, as her dresses, typical of the period, covered her legs completely.

BMA. British Medical Association, an organization for general practitioners similar to the American AMA, except that it is now one of the strongest defenders of nationalized medicine.

BNC. *See* Brasenose.

Board of Trade. A ministry* of the government responsible for matters affecting foreign trade, dating to 1696, when it was also responsible for all the colonies. It lost colonial authority in 1768 and was changed to the Department of Trade in 1974. The minister* in charge was called the President of the Board.

board school. A tax-supported primary school* administered by a local Board as authorized in 1870 and required in 1880. These replaced and expanded the old parish schools.* Most of the middle class* saw these as suitable only for the working class and avoided them.

boater. A straw hat with a flat brim and a low, flat crown, first worn in India and coming to England* in mid-nineteenth century, when it was occasionally worn by children or women. Around 1880, students took it up for boating at Oxford* or Cambridge,* from which it took its name and quickly spread through society at large until after WWII. It was always regarded as rather sporty and was associated with summer casual wear among the fashionable or with regular wear among the flashier, disreputable levels of society in general. It is still worn for boating and some traditional summer occasions and as a part of some public school* uniforms.

Boat Race. The annual rowing* competition between Oxford* and Cambridge;* it became a major social event after it began to be held annually in London* on the Thames* in 1856.

boat train. A train running each evening from Victoria Station* to connect with the night ferry to France from Dover*.

bob. Colloquial name for a shilling.* No one knows for certain how the name arose in the late eighteenth century, but by the nineteenth century it was used in almost all parts of society. After 1971, many people continued for some time to use the name for the new 5p coin. No *s* was added for the plural: People said five bob, not five bobs. *See also* Appendix I.

bobby. An English policeman, so called from Robert Peel, who organized London's* police in 1828. Initially, they were also called **peelers**, but by about 1900, bobby won out in common usage. The unusual high-peaked, rounded helmet was not part of the original uniform, which actually used a tall top hat* until late in the nineteenth century. Almost alone among world policemen, the bobbies have been unarmed from their very inception. Recent increases in general crime and particularly in terrorist and drug-oriented criminals have led to the issuance of guns to some members of some police forces, but in most cases, the typical bobby still patrols on foot and unarmed. Although the British themselves have been extremely critical of police methods in the 1980s, and although the typical bobby of literature and entertainment is slow-witted and unimaginative, for most of their existence the bobbies have been the epitome of the ideal police force, courteous, fair, dependable, honest, without either brutality or suggestions of militaristic methods. *See also* constable; PC; police; Scotland Yard; traffic warden; WPC.

Bob's your uncle. Nothing to do with the coins—although still obscure in origin, this idiom is used to indicate everything is going well or everything is fixed or finished.

Bodleian. At Oxford,* the library of the university* as a whole since 1610; publishers are required by law to provide it a copy of every book printed.

Boers. Dutch settlers in South Africa, who fought two guerrilla wars against the British who followed them into the area, in 1880 and again in 1899–1902. The British won both wars, although the second began with a number of humiliating defeats, but the Boers never really accepted British rule. Concentrated in the inland areas, primarily farmers with strong Calvinist religious beliefs, the Boers after WWII took control of the newly independent South Africa and were the primary architects of the apartheid policies that have drawn so much worldwide condemnation. The stereotype is a bull-necked, bull-headed farmer with a square beard—patriarchal, domineering, and resistant to all change. *See also* boor; Mafeking.

boff. Vulgar usage before WWII indicating masturbation but since expanded to a euphemism for our old friend the *f*-word. In public school* slang, however, it generally meant "to fart."

boffin. In WWII, someone inventing things for the RAF;* now used for any scientist or similar person doing arcane and incomprehensible things in labs and back rooms.

bog. (1) An area of wet spongy ground, usually covered in peat,* very flat with little or no drainage; these are especially common and large in Ireland.* A common English insult is **bog Irish** or **bog-trotter**, theoretically someone with no experience in the customs or manners of urban life, much the same as the American "fresh off the boat" but often used as an insult for any Irishman. *See also* fen; peat. (2) *See* bathroom.

bogey. (1) In the early nineteenth century, the devil or an evil spirit. (2) In the mid-nineteenth century, the landlord. (3) In the twentieth century, a policeman. (4) As a nickname* for people named Harris, this refers to a great cricketer* of the late nineteenth century, George (Bogey) Harris. (5) In WWII, RAF* slang for enemy aircraft. (6) In schoolboy slang, the stuff you pick out of your nose.

Bognor Regis. A resort town on the south coast of England* between Brighton* and Portsmouth,* much admired by Victoria; all in all, it is regarded as rather a dull resort by the young and the lower class,* who generally concur with George V's last words, which were "Bugger* Bognor."

bohemian. The term was borrowed from the French, who used it to apply first to gypsies,* because they were thought to have originated in Bohemia, and then in the nineteenth century to urban gypsies, such as artists, prostitutes, or day laborers, who had no fixed, stable address or life style. By the early twentieth century, the British applied this to practically anyone who could have been respectable but chose not to be so, which meant not only artists but also anyone from the middle class* or aristocracy* who frequented night clubs, listened to jazz, wore flapper fashions, socialized with musicians, actors, or writers, had sex with inappropriate partners, or simply failed to work at a job with regular hours.

boil. While it is not true that all British food is boiled until it has no taste or nourishment left, boiling has been the most common method of cooking, from the centuries when practically all people cooked with a pot of water constantly on the boil over an open fire. The most unique British boiled food is the pudding.* Meat of all kinds (except game) was also often boiled, as in the common boiled beef,* with the notable exception of the Sunday joint,* which was roasted. Until the rise of fish and chips,* which was an invention of commercial food producers, the British fried practically nothing. However, in the twentieth century, as more homes got cookers,* there was a major shift to fried foods, and only vegetables and puddings continued to be boiled on a regular basis.

boiled shirt. A white formal shirt with a heavily starched, stiff front, worn with the tail coat* and white tie,* so called because the spotless white could only be attained in previous eras by boiling the shirt rather than simply hand-washing it.

boiler. A hot-water tank, usually much smaller than implied by the similar American term.

boiler suit. What Americans call overalls, particularly the one-piece suit that Americans now call a jump suit and identify more with retirees than with laborers. The American bib overalls associated with hillbillies are generally called dungarees* in Britain.

bollocks. The testicles.

bolshie. Originally, this was slang for a radical or communist, from bolshevik, usually implying someone who needed a bath as well, but more recently it has been used more generally to mean constantly bad-tempered, rebellious, or disagreeable.

bomb. (1) A great success, the opposite of American usage. (2) Any great quantity, so that things may "cost a bomb."

bombasine/bombazine. A twilled material of silk and worsted, or cotton and worsted, the black version so often worn in mourning during the Victorian* era that bombazine itself came to be associated with both mourning and, by extension, all old ladies. Fustian* is much the same, except that bombazine has two smooth sides.

Bombay duck. Not a duck but salted and dried fish eaten in curries.*

bomber. *See* grenadier.

Bond Street. Actually two London* streets, Old and New, connecting Piccadilly* and Oxford Street,* but the name is generally applied to the neighboring streets that intersect them as well. Built mostly in late seventeenth and early eighteenth centuries, its shops have long catered to the wealthy. Now it is the center of most London luxury trade, such as jewelry, antiques, and art, the site of such companies as Sotheby's,* and is synonymous with extremely expensive goods.

bonfire. Bonfires have been significant folk customs for the English for two basic occasions. The most common since 1605 is November 5, Guy Fawkes Day,* when huge bonfires are lighted, in reference to the unlit bonfire under which Fawkes had hid his explosives, and in many places an effigy is burned on the fire. The political aspects of the holiday generally have much less importance than the excuse it provides for a great fire, and until very recently, it was often accompanied by torchlight parades and other dangerous fire-related activities. This practice may have achieved its great popularity because the date was so close to Halloween, when peasants from ancient days had built great fires to mark the end of summer and to ward off the evil spirits thought to be wandering loose at that time. By the early seventeenth century, puritanical forces had begun to try to stamp out such pagan and/or popish practices, so the Guy Fawkes holiday shifted the date of the fires in England to a more acceptable date without eliminating the practice; the Halloween fires continued, however, in Scotland* and Wales,* which do not celebrate the English holiday. The other major bonfire festival occurred on Midsummer Eve,* the night before June 24. Fires were usually built on nearby hilltops rather than in the village and were accompanied by dancing, tests for the men who had to jump through them, and vigils or wakes* to ward off evil spirits. By the twentieth century, the midsummer fires had all but disappeared throughout Britain. Thomas Hardy provides one of the best descriptions of the old practices of these disappearing celebrations in *The Return of the Native*, although he sets his story in November rather than at Midsummer Eve.

bonnet. (1) Loosely used, usually by male writers, to indicate a woman's hat. Technically, this is a hat without a brim, although in the nineteenth century it was often used for a woman's headgear meant to actually provide shade for the eyes rather than decorate the head. Thus, there were two basic kinds of bonnets, the **Quaker* bonnet** worn by farm women, usually known in America as a sunbonnet, and the fashionable bonnet, which often perched precariously on top of the head and was secured by a ribbon tied under the chin. (2) In earliest usage, before about 1700, a man's or a boy's soft cap; the usage continued until the current century in Scotland,* where the Tam,* for example, is often still called a bonnet. (3) What Americans call the hood of a car.

bonny. Good, attractive, beautiful; used stereotypically by Scots.*

Boodle's. A gentlemen's club* in London* in St. James's* Street, associated with country gentry* and known for the big bay window through which members often chat with nonmembers on the sidewalk.

book. (1) As a verb, to make a reservation. To **book in** is to register, usually after a reservation, as at a hotel. (2) Opinion, interest, attitude; a person in one's **good books**, for example, is a person one likes; something that agrees with one's plans or ideas **suits one's book**. To **bring to book** is to call someone to account for their actions. (3) In rugby* or football,* the referee may book a player, which means the player's name is recorded in his book for a flagrant foul or unsportsmanlike conduct, to be reported to the league office and possibly disciplined later.(4) In whist,* the first six tricks; as in bridge,* these tricks do not count as part of the score. (5) A **book of words** is any set of printed instructions, even brief ones.

Booker. An annual prize given for the "best" British novel; unlike most literary awards, the Booker Prize includes quite a large amount of money, and in the 1980s it was treated by the media as a major cultural event.

bookmaker. This has been a legal business since 1960. Before that, betting was legal only when done at the race track itself, where individual bookmakers were also allowed to take bets as long as they were actually at the track. *See also* betting shop; ring; Tattersall's.

Book of Common Prayer. A uniform liturgy for the Church of England,* containing standard services, creed, psalms, articles of religion, and prayers. The first version was published in 1549, but the 1552 version is still the basic form, with some revisions in 1662; major revisions were proposed in 1927, but not formally accepted by Parliament* until 1965. Used in churches throughout England, it has probably been the most significant influence on the shape and style of the English language after the King James Bible itself, even for the nonreligious. More recent revisions have caused considerable social furor, especially the "alternate services" in 1966 and the Alternate Service Book of 1980 that modernized language, substituted You for Thou in prayers, and made substantial changes in the Eucharist.

book society. What Americans call a book club.

boor. Americans often confuse this with bore, but while a boor can of course be boring, it is not essential. A boor was originally a boer, who was a Dutch peasant and thus synonymous with unlettered, crude, and thick-headed, a meaning reinforced when the British fought the Boers* in South Africa at the turn of this century.

boot. (1) Technically, a boot is different from a shoe* by going above the ankle, but the British sometimes use the two terms interchangeably. In this century the primary wearer of ankle-high boots has been the working class* male, and thus boots have generally signified the crude, clumsy, and ignorant. However, since the 1960s, many educated liberals have taken to wearing boots as a fashion statement of their solidarity with the working classes, and work boots can often be seen on young women or men who, in America, would wear running shoes instead. In recent years, boots have also implied violence through their association with punks and hooligans and the common phrase **put the boot in**, which means to fight brutally and without rules, such as kicking a person while he is down. However, most classes use boot as a verb where Americans would usually say kick instead, as in **boot him out**. *See also* black. (2) What Americans call the trunk of a car.

boots. A lowly servant* at hotels, originally the one who polished the guests' shoes and boots, often capitalized and used as the servant's name.

Boots. The largest chain of chemist* shops in England,* now often used as a synonym for chemist. Boots also ran one of the largest circulating libraries* through its shops during the late nineteenth and early twentieth centuries.

boozer. Slang for a pub* much more often than slang for a heavy drinker.

border. What Americans usually call a flower bed around the edges of fences of a yard. Often called a **herbaceous border**. *See also* garden.

Border. (1) The territory on either side of the border between Scotland* and England,* until almost the nineteenth century associated with outlaws, pillaging, and cattle raiding. *See also* Marches. (2) Since 1973, the region,* or county,* of Scotland lying in the eastern half of the country immediately north of the English border, formed from the primarily agricultural areas of the former Midlothian.*

borough. Originally, a town* that had been chartered by the monarch, which meant that it was allowed to make its own local laws and to own land communally. As parliamentary representation was regularized, a town that was allowed to elect a member* of Parliament* was also called a borough. Borough was the generic term that included both town and city,* but by the time of Henry VIII, a city was understood to be a borough that also had a cathedral.* However, city was a term of much greater status, and some boroughs without cathedrals were ultimately chartered as cities, as was Birmingham,* for example. By the beginning of the nineteenth century, the boroughs had become a significant political problem, as no new boroughs had been chartered since the Stuarts. This made existing boroughs more than 200 years out of date; major industrial towns had no representation at all, because they were technically only parishes,* while boroughs with declining or nonexistent populations still had seats in Parliament. After the Reform Bill* of 1832, many old boroughs were eliminated and many new ones chartered, and in 1835 the Municipal Corporations Act standardized the rules for local governing corporations. Most such towns continued formally to call themselves boroughs but general usage was shifting toward town or city. Finally, in 1965 Greater London* eliminated its various parishes and was divided into thirty-two "boroughs" for local administration, none of which were completely independent like the old boroughs, and then in 1972, all the boroughs outside of London were abolished, replaced by metropolitan counties* or districts.* The **Borough** to Londoners is Southwark,* long a separate borough across the Thames, but in Crabbe's poem it is Aldeburgh.* **Borough English** applies not to language but to custom, specifically the unusual practice of inheritance to a daughter or younger son, and from that is sometimes applied to any eccentric local custom. *See also* burgh.

borough, open. Before 1832, a borough* whose votes were controlled by neither party, in practice usually "open" only to the highest bidder.

borough, pocket. Before 1832, a borough* whose votes were controlled by the authority of a wealthy or powerful landlord and thus "in his pocket" during elections, allowing him, in effect, to appoint the member* of Parliament.* The pocket boroughs were often used by the party to provide safe seats for young men of promise who, for various reasons, could not be elected to represent their home constituencies.* *See also* borough, open.

borough, rotten. Before 1832, a borough* that elected a member* of Parliament* even though it had lost population and now had practically no voters actually residing in the borough; the few remaining votes were usually assumed to be for sale or were controlled by a single lord.* At least one of these, Dunwich, had been under the North Sea* for several hundred years, and many others were almost as absurd. *See also* borough, pocket; Reform Bill.

Borstal. A prison* for juvenile males, named for the prison in Borstal, a suburb of Rochester,* where juveniles were taken from 1902 after a decision to separate juveniles from adult offenders and institute serious attempts at reformation rather than punishment. By mid-twentieth century, **Borstal Boy** had become a common term for any juvenile delinquent, whether in prison or not. Currently, the official name is **Youth Custody Centre**, used for ages seventeen through twenty of either sex, but Borstal continues in common usage. *See also* approved school.

bosun. The boatswain, a person found on both merchant and navy* ships. On a sailing ship, the bosun is in charge of sails and rigging, and his whistle is the official signal calling the sailors to duty; the whistle continued in use after the rise of steam but his duties now are direct supervision of crew and equipment. In the navy, the bosun is a seagoing equivalent of the sergeant* or sergeant-major* in the army,* the highest-ranking sailor who is not an actual officer.* *See also* Appendix V.

bottle party. In the late 1920s, after the suppression of the first night clubs,* the young and the wild found a new way around the licensing laws.* A "host" would hold a "private" party which his "guests" helped to pay for; the guest would arrive around midnight when pubs* and other clubs were closed and wile away the hours of the night with dance bands and floor shows. As long as the liquor had been ordered and delivered during licensing* hours, the police* had no more authority to prevent these parties than any other private party, even though they were clearly just night clubs under another name. The fad gradually faded in the harder times of the 1930s but never completely died, and a new version in the summer of 1989 had thousands of teenagers careening across the countryside to secret addresses given by coded phone messages, occupying much police and press attention.

bottom. (1) The farthest edge, such as the bottom of the garden.* (2) What Americans once called grit, the willingness to do the right thing or to do more than one can reasonably be asked to do. (3) *See* b.t.m.

boundary. In cricket,* a score of four runs, awarded when a hit ball goes beyond the boundary of the playing field.

bounder. An ill-bred or ill-mannered person, originally Cambridge* slang in the 1880s for one who has "bounded" above his station; almost always used only for a male.

bound over. Ordered by a court* to do something. For example, someone charged with a minor offence* is often bound over to keep the peace; since everyone is expected to do that, this is more a promise that, if the person fails to do so in future, more severe punishment would follow, and it is thus essentially like being put on probation. It may also be used in civil matters to mean what Americans often call an injunction or a court order.

bourne. A stream in valleys in areas of chalk that flows only when the water table rises above the floor of the valley, which is almost always only in winter. The term occurs quite often along the south coast of England,* where it is used in a number of place names such as Bournemouth* or Eastbourne.*

Bournemouth. Pronounced BAWNmuth, a seaside town on the south coast of England,* rising suddenly in the late nineteenth century as a popular place for the middle class* to retire and live on their dividends, and thus often synonymous with the stodgy, conservative, and middle-aged, although Hardy uses it as Sandbourne where Tess lives in sin with and kills D'Urberville.

BOV. Board of Visitors. *See* prison.

Bovril. A commercial product that when mixed with hot water makes a drink like beef bouillon. Bovril had one of the most intensive advertising campaigns of the twentieth century, so its signs were found everywhere, but it is unclear how much Bovril is actually drunk.

bovver. Bother; **bovver boys**, thus, are hooligans, and **bovver boots** are boots* with metal toe caps favored by skinheads* and similar toughs.

Bow Bells. Pronounced bO, the bells of the church St. Mary-le-Bow in Cheapside;* in theory, only one who is born within hearing of the Bow Bells can be a true Cockney,* but since the late nineteenth century, most Cockneys have been born and lived in the East End,* which is well outside the range of the bells, and comparatively no one actually lives within the sound of the bells since WWII. However, the neighborhood of **Bow** is in the East End* near Mile End.* *See also* Bow Street.

bowl. In cricket,* to throw the ball toward the batsman.* This is done in a stiff overhanded motion after running up to the release point. The primary way to get the batsman out is to knock off the small wooden pin (called a **bail***) resting on top of the wicket,* but in general the bowler almost never bowls in the air aimed at the wicket; rather, he usually bowls so that the ball bounces just in front of the batsman, making it harder to hit. **Fast bowling** is bowling done with speed but little or no spin, originally regarded as unsporting but now widely accepted. A batsman* is **bowled** or **bowled out** when the ball knocks the bail off the wicket* to put him out. A number of related idioms have entered common speech: To trick someone is to **bowl a fast one**; to surprise them is to **bowl them over**, as with a wicket; and to go along smoothly is to **bowl along**. *See also* all-rounder; batting and bowling; break; chinaman; duck; googly; innings; outswinger; over; spinner.

bow-legged. *See* bandy-legged.

bowler. (1) A man's hat with a relatively narrow and stiff brim and a stiff, rounded crown. It first appeared under this name in the mid-nineteenth century, named for the hatmakers Thomas and William Bowler (or Beaulieu), and often worn by horsemen as a form of crash helmet that was shorter and more stable than the top hat,* but by the end of the century it had moved into urban fashion and had become the basic respectable businessman's hat. By the 1920s, when the top hat began to disappear from daily wear, the bowler, along with the tightly furled umbrella,* defined the stereotypical Englishman of middle and upper class,* but in the later parts of the century, as the nation became hatless in the American manner, the bowler and the umbrella were worn only by the old-fashioned and by middle-aged men in the City.* It has also been so long associated with retired military men that officers* have used the verb **to bowler-hat** as a synonym for retiring. In most literature, the bowler implies a certain amount of stodginess about its wearer, although in works set around the turn of the century it often indicates a tradesman* who is getting above his station,* thus simultaneously stodgy and pushy or tasteless, who would be uncomfortable in the top hat worn by true middle class and gentry* of the time. The bowler is also often worn by the stereotypical Cockney.* For unclear reasons, the same hat in nineteenth century America was called a derby, and derby will sometimes also appear in British writings, but the distinctions between the two are minimal, if not nonexistent. (2) In cricket,* *See* bowl. (3) *See* bowls.

bowls. Lawn bowling, unlike American bowling. The bowler attempts to roll a ball (which is not quite round and thus impossible to roll straight) closer to a small target ball than the other players are able to do, so it is similar to French boules or Italian boccie. It has been played for centuries, particularly in the country villages, but in the twentieth century has often been seen as an upper–middle class game, played by much the same people as play tennis, due to its demand for a flat, manicured lawn.*

Bow Street. A street in London* near Covent Garden,* pronounced bO. This was a significant literary neighborhood in the eighteenth century, home to many theatrical types and the site of a popular coffee house.* It is also the site of the Metropolitan Court (also called the Police Court*), where every minor literary criminal from the Dickens's Artful Dodger to Wodehouse's Bertie Wooster makes an appearance. In the early nineteenth, it was the home of the **Bow Street Runners**, what we might call licensed bounty hunters, who brought accused criminals to the court and acted as the London police* force until replaced by the bobbies* in 1829. *See also* Bow Bells.

box. (1) *See* witness box. (2) A sturdy evergreen with dark shiny leaves, fairly small and slow-growing so it is generally grown for hedges;* when Toby and Feste hide in the "box-tree" to watch Malvolio in *Twelfth Night*, they're hiding in a hedge. (3) The place where the driver sat on a horse-drawn coach.* (4) *See* hunt; shooting. (5) On streets, the intersection itself.

box coat. A heavy overcoat usually extending all the way to the ground, so called because it was originally worn by coachmen who sat in the open box* on top.

Boxing Day. The day after Christmas,* traditionally the day on which Christmas presents are exchanged, a bank holiday,* except in Scotland.*

boxroom. A room where unused furniture and personal items are stored, usually in the attic; also called a **lumber room**, even though it has no lumber.

Boyne. A river in Ireland* north of Dublin, site of a battle on July 12, 1690, in which William III's forces defeated those of James II; although not directly involving local Irish nationalists, the battle is generally treated as the date on which the English Protestants established full control of Catholic Ireland, celebrated in Northern Ireland* still as a holiday and mourned in the rest of Ireland.

Boy Scouts. The organization originated in England* in 1908, where it is most often simply called the **Scouts**; in general, its activities and organization are similar to its American counterpart, although the highest rank is not Eagle Scout but King's or Queen's Scout.* The girl's organization, modeled after but not an official wing of the Boy Scouts, is called the Girl Guides* rather than the Girl Scouts.

braces. What Americans call men's suspenders, used to hold up trousers.* When a British man mentions **suspenders**, he usually means a garter contraption worn around the calf to hook and hold up his socks or a woman's garter belt.

brackets. The punctuation Americans call parentheses. The punctuation marks Americans call brackets are generally called **square brackets**.

bradbury. Slang for a one-pound* note,* for John Bradbury, whose signature appeared on the first ones in 1914. *See also* Appendix I.

Bradshaw. *Bradshaw's Railway Guide*, a timetable listing all the railroad schedules of Britain (1839–1961), noted for its exhaustive detail and its intimidating complexity.

brain drain. The emigration of college-educated persons, particularly scientists, usually to the United States where they expect to find better pay, facilities, and support for their work. The size and significance of this have been a matter of political debate since the 1960s, but at least one historian who joined it has called it a migration to the United States matched only by the exodus of Jewish professors from 1930s Europe.

braising steak. The cut of beef Americans use to make pot roast.

brake. What Americans call a station wagon; often called a **shooting brake**.

bramble. A prickly shrub, but more specifically the blackberry.

bran tub. A tub with a number of small presents in it is then filled with bran; children reach underneath the bran to find a random gift. The activity is often associated with Christmas* and other parties for children and with village fêtes,* where it is also often called a lucky dip.*

Brasenose. A college* of Oxford,* literarily associated primarily with Pater; often called **BNC** by the students and graduates.

brass. (1) Slang for money in general, from the cheaper coins such as farthings* that were made of brass. To **brass up** is to pay a debt. (2) Slang for an impudent attitude, probably evolving from brazen; both Americans and Britons use **brassy**, but Britons tend to associate it more with impudence or putting up a good front while Americans imply noisy vulgarity. To be **brassed off** is to be what Americans usually call fed up.

brass hat. Any high-ranking military officer* with lots of braid on his hat.

breach of promise. The lawsuit for breach of promise when one had broken an engagement to be married, although occasionally seen, was not common until after 1753; before then, there had been considerable legal confusion as to what distinguished an engagement from a marriage.* Seen from a modern American viewpoint, the breech of promise suit seems almost inexplicable—why should someone owe monetary damages for getting cold feet on the way to the altar?—and has been quite rare in the United States. But in Britain it was thought a necessary device to protect women from unscrupulous men (although men did occasionally sue and win), on two basic grounds: (1) a woman formally engaged would not receive other offers, which might be "better," financially or socially, and those offers might no longer be available when her engagement ended; and (2) many couples began sexual activity upon engagement, often leaving the woman pregnant before the marriage ceremony. In either of these situations, she was thought to deserve compensation. By the mid-nineteenth century, these suits had become quite common, and the primary reason seems to have been that, even though the woman need not claim that she had had intercourse with the man, it was often assumed to be the case after the engagement was formally announced. Thus, in the more respectable parts of society, she became "damaged goods," so to speak, at the moment the engagement was official, and a broken engagement then left her unmarriageable, no matter how virginal she might in fact be. It was, in many levels of society, the same thing, and as bad, as a divorce,* often leading to a lifetime as a spinster,* and thus the breach of promise suit was in effect a form of alimony to provide the means to support herself. A number of prominent cases, in which chorus girls sued gentlemen* for huge amounts near the turn of the century, along with changing attitudes toward women owning property in their own names, caused a general public revulsion against the suits, but they did occasionally continue after WWI until finally abolished in 1970.

bread. Long a staple of the British diet, bread has taken several forms over the centuries. In Shakespeare's time, as in medieval life, bread for the upper classes* was made from wheat, but the other classes generally ate heavier, darker rye or barley breads, and the Scots made various kinds of oat breads and cakes.* By about 1800, even the working poor were able to afford white breads, and the darker and wholemeal breads were confined mostly to rural tables. By the late nineteenth century, the most common form was the loaf, like American commercial bread, which was sliced as needed at home. In the late twentieth century, most bread is called **sliced loaf**, and it is similar to American commercial presliced white bread, although many still prefer to slice their loaf themselves. As a staple, bread was eaten in many forms, including plain, with cheese,* spread with butter, margarine, or dripping,* or toasted before an open fire, and also sliced thin to make sandwiches;* a common form in early twentieth century was **fried bread**, a thick slice deep-fried in lard and eaten with a fork. For bread and butter pudding, *See* pudding.

break. In cricket,* the change in direction of the thrown ball caused by spin of the ball, something like the curveball in baseball except that it happens when the ball bounces before reaching the batsman.* A **leg break** is a ball that seems aimed toward the batsman and then bounces away from him; an **off break** is one that starts toward the outside and then breaks in toward the batsman's hands or body. *See also* chinaman; googly.

breakfast. The **English breakfast** has become a generic term, famous (or infamous) throughout the world, although by the 1980s, it was beginning to fade somewhat. Usually, it consisted of fried egg, fried sausage, kippers* (often refried), and toast or fried bread,* with a pot of strong tea.* Variations include the addition of fried tomato, fried bacon,* kedgeree,* and on occasion, scrambled or boiled rather than fried eggs. This particular

form of the meal does not seem to be particularly ancient, appearing first
in country houses* during the mid-nineteenth century, so unusual as to be
called for a time the **new breakfast**, and gradually spreading, with prosperity, to other levels of society. In the country house, the meal was casual,
each of the various dishes being placed out on the sideboard and kept
warm in chafing dishes so that residents and guests served themselves when
they rose at their own convenience (and not coincidentally, allowing the
servants* to get on with their regular work). Those who have chosen not
to eat, or have been unable to afford, the English breakfast have substituted
a number of tasteless or unpleasant concoctions, such as the traditional
porridge,* to which the Scots have remained partial, or reputedly healthy
products such as muesli* or Weetabix,* and recent inroads have been made
by American-style packaged cereals and the "continental breakfast" of
bread and coffee. Thus, in practice, one is far more likely to find the
"traditional" English breakfast in a hotel or bed-and-breakfast* than in
actual homes. In the early industrial era, the lower classes breakfasted on
little more than tea and bread for the more prosperous or gruel* for the
poorer. Before the rise of industry, the common breakfast for urban artisans was bread, butter, or cheese, and beer,* for country people porridge
or frumenty.* Coffee* has rarely been a part of the English breakfast,
except among the very wealthy and in those areas that cater to foreign
tourists, although it has recently begun to make inroads, particularly among
the English version of yuppies.

breakfast television. Television programming in the mornings, begun only
in the 1980s with programs similar in form to the American *Today*.

break-up. Of school,* the end of a term.*

breeches. To Americans, who normally pronounce the word as britches,
this is a generic term for men's pants,* but in Britain, until very recently,
the term was used more specifically to mean a form of pants that was tight
to the leg and stopped just below the knee. As such, they were the most
common form of male dress from the early seventeenth to the mid-nineteenth centuries, when long trousers* began replacing them for all but
specialized and ritualistic usage, such as court dress* and livery.*

breeze block. What Americans call a cinder block.

brevet. In the nineteenth-century army,* daily functioning often required
officers in particular to perform duties outside the regiment* at ranks higher
than those they held within their own regiment,* called brevet ranks. A
brevet major, for example, would be doing a major's job for a major's pay
but would still be listed on the regiment's rolls as a captain* or lieutenant*

and, if he returned to duty with the regiment, would resume the old rank and pay.

brew up. To make tea.*

brick. Someone dependable, reliable, and trustworthy.

brick, drop a. To say or do something indiscreet, like mentioning a man's mistress within his wife's hearing.

Bridewell. Originally an area of London* between the Thames* and Fleet Street,* location of **St. Bride's well**, one of the principal wells of the medieval city. In 1553, one of Henry VIII's old palaces* was converted into first a home and school for apprentices and then expanded into a prison,* which it remained until 1853, when it was torn down, so the name is often synonymous with any prison.

bridge. (1) The card game familiar to Americans started in India and swept Britain as it did America in the 1920s, completely replacing whist* as the middle- and upper-class* card game. A **bridge coat** was a long-sleeved black velvet jacket worn by women as evening wear for bridge parties, fading from use in the later twentieth century. *See also* cards. (2) For notable bridges, *See* (name of bridge).

bridlepath. A pathway on which right of way is legally limited to pedestrians and persons on horseback but not open to any vehicles.

Bridport. A small town in southwest England* near Lyme Regis,* once famous for its rope-making industry. A **Bridport dagger** was a noose.

brief. A set of instructions. Originally the information about a case given by a solicitor* to a barrister,* by mid-twentieth century, it was used in bureaucratic circles to mean the guidelines under which a person works and the limits of his decision-making powers, as in "that's not in my brief."

briefs. From about 1930–60, women's panties. But in the sixties the term began to be applied to men's underpants like those Americans call jockey shorts and is now rarely applied to women's clothing except for **bikini briefs**, styled like the bottom of a bikini. *See also* drawers; knickers; pants.

brigade. In the army,* before 1881, a unit containing two regiments,* usually formed as a temporary expedient for a particular campaign, such as the Light Brigade in the Crimean War. The primary exception was the Rifle Brigade,* which was in fact a regiment but contained four battalions.*

After 1881, when regiments were standardized to some extent, the term was used only in the artillery. Further reorganization followed WWI, so that a brigade became a unit of (usually) three battalions of infantry or armored troops.

brigadier. The officer* commanding a brigade,* always called brigadier rather than brigadier-general as in the United States. Before WWI, this was a temporary rank, taken by the senior colonel* in a brigade, because the brigade itself was a temporary unit, and was made a permanent rank only in 1928. *See also* Appendix V; general.

bright. Of the weather, not actually raining; **bright periods** are often forecast, meaning what Americans call scattered showers.

Brighton. A seaside town on the southern coast of England,* south of London.* It was a small fishing village until the Prince of Wales, later King George IV, began to visit the site for pleasure in the late eighteenth century. It immediately turned into a fashionable resort, particularly after the **Royal Pavilion**, one of the most playfully exotic buildings ever constructed, was completed in 1822. Railway service in mid-nineteenth century soon established it as an ideal site for a day trip from London, and amusement piers were built to provide entertainments for the masses of city dwellers who swelled the resort with short visits. Its popularity and success in turn helped establish the idea of the seaside as a place for holidays. By the turn of the century, it had lost all claim to fashion or society, becoming known instead as a place for the lower-middle class,* regarded by other groups as tasteless and tawdry. It also became synonymous with the "dirty weekend" taken with your neighbor's spouse. Numerous other seaside communities have become competitors for the seaside resort trade, but Brighton still remains the most convenient and popular, if a bit faded, for Londoners. Popular features include the wide **Esplanade** that parallels the beaches, along which visitors have paraded almost since the beginning, and the **Palace Pier**, replacing an older pier destroyed in 1896, once used as a pier and ferry dock but in the twentieth containing an amusement park.

brimstone. Sulphur. As **brimstone and treacle**,* it was an all-purpose medicine before the late nineteenth century.

Bristol. Seaport in the west of England,* a major port for exploration and trade, especially the slave trade, with the Americas until the mid-nineteenth century, when industrial growth shifted commerce north to Liverpool.* Although Dickens once called it the dirtiest place he'd ever seen, the port was so widely used that **Bristol fashion** became synonymous with shipshape, in proper order, prepared and ready for all eventualities. Bristol was the site of the first Methodist* church and a center of evangelical movements. Despite the religious associations, **Bristol milk** is sherry,* from the large trade in the product through the city since the seventeenth century. The **University of Bristol** is one of the most respected of the redbrick universities,* especially strong in engineering and medicine.

Bristols. Slang for a woman's breasts, from Cockney* rhyming slang*: Bristol City (a football* club*) = tittie.

Brit. A slangy version of Briton,* generally used to imply someone vulgar or lower class.*

Britain. Technically, Great Britain,* the island containing England,* Scotland,* and Wales.* The official name of the country is the **United Kingdom of Great Britain and Northern Ireland**, and UK is the most commonly used abbreviation. Both usages are recent, except in formal pronouncements. Individual persons tend to regard themselves as English, Scottish, Welsh, or Irish rather than as British, and until perhaps the mid-twentieth century, most natives as well as practically all foreigners referred to the country as England, since England was clearly the dominant partner, with over 80 percent of the population, and the capital was London.* **British** and Britain have come to be used to mean anything unifying or combining all the separate countries, increasingly common as the Empire* has disappeared. In actual practice, however, almost nothing in Britain is British: **British religion** does not include the Church of Scotland* and certainly not the Catholics* in Ireland; **British justice** is a different set of laws in England and Wales than in Scotland; Scotland has different legal holidays, different governmental titles, different social customs, different foods, even the right to print different money;* and of course Ireland,* now a separate country, although providing many significant writers in British literature, participates in nothing else British and is insulted if such is even implied; the **British lion** is purely symbolic, for there are no lions anywhere in Britain; and the **British public** is almost always only those with no taste, intelligence, or education. Not even the **British currency** is uniformly British, as some Scottish banks have the right to issue their own notes* for currency. (In this work, I use British in its broadest sense, to describe those things applying to most or all of the area under discussion.) *See also* British disease; British justice; British luck.

British. *See* Britain.

British Academy. An organization formed in 1901, limited to 350 members, to honor and encourage work in history, philosophy, and philology, something of a humanities counterpart to the Royal Society.*

British Battalion. A battalion of British volunteers in the Republican army of the Spanish Civil War (1936–39); participation in, or at least support of, this was one of the touchstones of British politics before and after WWII, almost a requirement for admission to left-wing intellectual circles.

British Council. A private organization since 1934 (although it now receives some government aid), intended to promote the teaching of the English language and greater understanding of British culture in foreign countries. It arranges cultural exchanges, sends arts groups on tours, and arranges teachers of language and literature for many foreign schools and colleges throughout the world.

British disease. A phrase that was common during the 1970s and 80s to describe the economic and social stagnation the United Kingdom* had been in since WWII (some said WWI) and variously ascribed to hard-headed unions,* an inflexible class* system, or cultural and political parochialism. The best summation perhaps is the common saying, "We pretend to work, and they pretend to pay us."

British Expeditionary Force. The official title given to British forces sent to France to fight the Germans in 1914 and again in 1939.

British Grenadiers. The Grenadier Guards,* who not surprisingly use the song as their regimental march.

British justice. As indicated in the entry under Britain,* there is no such thing; in addition, the term often is used ironically to mean judicial activity that violates common sense.

British Legion. A military veteran's association, similar to the American Legion.

British luck. Usually this means good luck but probably to no good purpose; to wish someone the "best of British luck" adds a touch of irony, as if saying, "It's probably a lost cause, but give it the old school try anyway."

British Museum. A massive museum of antiquities, archaeology, and history in London.* Established in 1753, it grew into its present building in Bloomsbury* in 1857. It is noted for its major examples of Egyptian artifacts, part of the Parthenon (the Elgin Marbles), Roman sculpture, Oriental materials, and manuscripts. Perhaps even more significant in literature is the vast **Reading Room**, a circular space in the center under a skylighted dome that is wider than St. Paul's, used by researchers from all walks of life, and containing a library that, by law, receives a copy of every book and magazine published. Since 1973, this has been a technically separate institution called the **British Library**, and construction of a completely new building for it is underway near St. Pancras.*

British Rail. The organization administering the nationalized railway* system.

British Restaurant. Government-run cafeterias during WWII that offered a meal for a shilling* or less, famous for tasteless, depressing foods due to their use only of unrationed items. *See also* rationing.

British Telecom. The British telephone* company. All telephone service was originally handled through the post office,* but in 1981 it was separated and then later privatized.

British Union. *See* Blackshirt.

Briton. A person from Britain.*

Brixton. A lower-class* neighborhood in south London* of little note until 1981, when the large number of minority residents from the Caribbean and Africa in the area erupted in riots. When mentioned by the British since, it is often in much the same regard as when Americans speak of Harlem or Watts. There is also a prison* there.

broad. A name used for several different coins that were larger and thinner than normal, especially the 20-shilling gold coins issued 1660–85.

Broad, the. In Oxford,* the street that passes through the central core of the university,* along which are the Bodleian,* the Sheldonian,* Exeter,* and corners of several other colleges.

Broadcasting House. Main office of the BBC,* in Portland Place in London.*

Broad Church. Not a particular sect but merely those clergy* within the Church of England* who sought to resolve or avoid the conflicts between High Church* and Low Church* by espousing the most generalized or all-inclusive statements of dogma.

Broadmoor. A hospital for the criminally insane, opened in 1863, located southeast of Reading.*

Broads. An area of Norfolk,* very flat and low and with numerous shallow lakes, sometimes interconnected. The lakes themselves are also called broads, from their shallow depth.

Broadstairs. A resort town on the coast of England* just south of Margate,* named for the stairs that run down the cliff to the sea there that, despite Hollywood's attempts to suggest otherwise, were the *39 Steps*.

broccoli. Until quite recently, British broccoli was almost the same color as cauliflower, but now it is dark green, as in Europe and America.

brogue. (1) A rough heavy shoe, usually untanned hide. Originally worn by the Irish, in the industrial era it came to be applied to workingmen's shoes. (2) A thick Irish accent, perhaps originally from people who wore brogues.

brolly. An umbrella.*

Brompton. The area of London* now called South Kensington.* **Brompton Road** is the major thoroughfare and shopping street, especially associated with antiques and near-antiques, and of course Harrods.*

Brompton Oratory. A large church in London* in the South Kensington* area. Built in 1884 in the Italianate manner, it is one of the largest and best known Roman Catholic churches in England. The name comes not from noted orations but from the Institute of the Oratory, the order that provides the priests for the services, which was reintroduced to England by Newman.

brook. A small stream, similar to what Americans in the South or Midwest call a creek. As with all terms geographical, there is considerable variation from place to place as to precisely how large or small a brook is; some are small enough to leap across, others large or deep enough for serious fishing, but the understanding is always that it is small and short, but still large enough to have water running year round. Most mills, for example, were on brooks. *See also* burn; river.

Brook's. A gentlemen's club* in London* in St. James's* Street, originally a Whig* club across from Boodle's* that in the twentieth century has become more Tory.*

broom. A shrub growing wild throughout most of Britain,* a version of which was brought to the New World and is known in America as Scotch broom. The twigs and small branches of these were so commonly used to make besoms* for sweeping that all sweeping tools came to be called brooms.

brougham. An enclosed four-wheeled carriage* pulled by a single horse, with the driver outside and in front, used in the Victorian era by the wealthy; pronounced broom, although names so spelled are often pronounced brawm.

brown. A casual name for several copper coins, most often the halfpenny.*

Brown Bess. The flint-lock musket used by the British infantry from mid–eighteenth to mid–nineteenth century.

brown paper. Before modern sticking plasters* and antiseptics, Britons commonly treated bruises and small wounds with pieces of brown paper soaked in vinegar.

brown sauce. Not homemade gravy but a generic term for commercial sauces like HP Sauce* and its many imitators, poured on practically all meats and/or potatoes.

brown study. An idle reverie or a moody dreamy state, the phrase dating back before Shakespeare's time when brown meant gloomy.

Brum. Slang for Birmingham.*

brummagem. Cheap, shoddy goods, from local pronunciations of Birmingham* where industrial manufacturing in the modern sense began.

Brummie. A native of Birmingham.*

BSI. British Standards Institute, an organization that tries to get industry to agree to standards of quality and size. *See also* kite mark.

BST. British Summer Time, what Americans call daylight saving time, first used as a war measure in 1916. For three years (1968–71), this was also used for British Standard Time, but even the British noticed that this was a bit confusing, and standard time is now officially GMT.*

b.t.m. A euphemism for bottom, itself a euphemism for bum* or buttocks, used primarily by genteel* adults with or about children during the late nineteenth and early twentieth centuries, as in Dylan Thomas's "learn him with a slipper on his b.t.m." *See also* backside.

BTU. British Thermal Unit, the heat needed to raise 1 pound of water 1° F.

bubbies. A woman's breasts, the source of the American boobs. The term was standard usage in the Restoration but became low and vulgar during the early nineteenth century and has probably disappeared in the late twentieth, except for the anachronistic imitators of the Edwardian Anon. school of pornography.

bubble. A deceptive financial scheme or an investment speculation that turns out to rise in value and then go bust as fast as a bubble. The first and most famous of these was the **South Sea bubble**: In 1711, the South Sea Company was formed to trade in slaves and gold in South America; to secure a monopoly, they bought up the national debt, also gaining a guarantee of receipt of customs duties on wine, silks, and so forth, to pay off that debt. The company was overwhelmed by investors (in spite of the fact that Spain actually controlled South American trade), stock prices rose to incredible levels, the original investors took their profits and disappeared, and the prices collapsed before the company did any business whatsoever except speculate in its own shares. The curious thing is that this was called a bubble before rather than after it burst, and that numerous other imitators calling themselves "bubble companies" sprang up at the same time with much the same result. The South Sea bubble, however, swallowed so much capital that it threatened for a while to bankrupt the entire nation.

bubble and squeak. Onomatopoeic name for a dish of cabbage and potato fried together, often with leftover meats mixed in.

Buchmanism. *See* Oxford Group.

Buck House. Slang for Buckingham Palace.*

Buckingham Palace. The London* residence of the King* or Queen.* The original house was built for the Duke of Buckingham in 1703 and purchased by George III in 1763, but it was rarely used until Victoria chose it as a primary residence. As such, it is often used as synonymous with the ruler and royalty* itself, as well as being the primary goal of hordes of tourists each year. *See also* Balmoral; Sandringham; Windsor.

Buckinghamshire. A county* or shire* to the immediate northwest of London,* still primarily agricultural in nature, with wooded hills at the southern end in the Chilterns* and rich farmland farther north.

Bucks. Buckinghamshire.*

budgerigar. A small Australian parrot, one of the most common British housepets; in general, the **budgie** is associated with petit bourgeois and respectable working-class households, much the same as the aspidistra* and lace curtains, and with lonely old women living alone in genteel* poverty.

Budleigh Salterton. A small coastal town on the south coast of England* near Torquay;* its name comes from its ancient salt industry, but in the twentieth century it has become a resort town.

buff coat. A coat of leather, usually ox, oiled and having a yellowish color, usually worn by soldiers of the seventeenth and eighteenth centuries, especially associated with Cromwell's forces in the Civil War.*

buffer. Usually an **old buffer**, what Americans call an old fogy.

buffet. Often used in the American sense; however, a **station buffet** is the café or snack bar at a train station, usually pronounced buffy and usually not serve-yourself like other buffets.

Buffs. The old 3rd Regiment* of the army,* since 1961 the Queen's Regiment. **Steady the Buffs** was first used by Kipling's Soldiers Three but has been used since by civilians as a form of "stiff upper lip.*"

bug. In general, used only for bedbugs; all other forms of what Americans call bugs are usually called insects.

bugger. In standard usage since before Shakespeare's time, this has meant one who engages in anal intercourse, and buggery is still used as a legal term for sodomy. However, parallel to this has been a much more colloquial and vulgar usage to mean a man, as in "silly bugger"; this is usually negative but with no imputation of strange sexual practices, and tone of voice can turn it into a genial or ironic greeting. When used as a verb or adjective, however, bugger is always negative: **I'm buggered** means "I'm in trouble," about the same intensity as the common American "I'll be damned"; to **bugger up** is to mess up or ruin; **bugger off** is a command to leave, used about the same way as the American "piss off"; to **bugger about** is to doodle around aimlessly or to work or act ineffectively; **bugger-all** is none. To **play silly buggers** is to act facetiously or stupidly. **Bugger's grips** are long sideburns on a man's face.

Buggins's turn. Promotion based on seniority rather than merit.

builder. The person Americans usually call a contractor.

building society. A company that provides loans primarily for home mortgages; similar to an American savings and loan.

Bull, John. *See* John Bull.

bull's-eye. (1) A large round peppermint candy, like a child's marble in size and shape. (2) A small lantern with a lens to focus the light, before flashlights usually carried by a bobby.*

bully. In hockey,* the method of putting the ball into play; ice hockey uses the same procedure but calls it a face-off.

bully beef. *See* beef.

bullyrag. *See* rag.

bum. (1) Buttocks. Curiously, this is another of those terms that has been in use since well before Shakespeare, when it was considered standard usage; by the early nineteenth century, however, it was considered vulgar and decidedly lower class,* replaced for the most part by bottom in the more genteel* circles. Then bottom came to be too explicit for some, so that in the twentieth, bum made a return among the same genteel as a cutesy substitute, in effect becoming a euphemism for itself. *See also* backside; b.t.m.; bumf; fanny; jacksie. (2) A bum-bailiff.* The term meaning a tramp or beggar is American in origin, perhaps from the German immigrants' *bummel* for a stroll, and is not generally used in Britain.

bum-bailiff. A bailiff* sent to arrest debtors, apparently so called from the habit of catching the miscreant from behind.

bumble-puppy. A game similar to what Americans call tetherball.

bumf. Worthless paper, shortened from the mid-nineteenth century schoolboy's **bumfodder**, or toilet paper.

bumper. In cricket,* a bowled ball that bounces toward the batsman's* head.

bumping. In boat races at Oxford* during Eights Week* and at Cambridge* during May Week,* the boats are started in staggered order; if a trailing boat catches and "bumps" the one in front, it moves up for the next race until a king of the river is known.

bun. A generic term for a soft roll, usually sweeter than regular bread rolls, often eaten slathered in butter or thick cream, commonly served with tea.* A **Chelsea bun** is similar to what Americans call a cinnamon roll; a **sticky bun** is a bun with frosting; a **Swiss bun** is what Americans call a Danish roll; a **Bath bun** is a sweet, soft bun served originally at the resort tea shops in Bath; a **cream bun** is a sweet bun split in half with whipped cream or its imitation and/or jam in the middle. The **black bun** is actually a fruitcake encased in pastry, made for the most part only in Scotland.* However, a **bun in the oven** has nothing to do with food but instead means pregnant; most buns rise when baked. A **bun puncher** is military slang for someone who doesn't drink alcohol, sticking instead to tea* and buns. A **bun fight** is collegiate slang for tea,* not necessarily implying any rowdiness. For **hot cross bun** *See* Good Friday. *See also* bap; cake.

bung. As a verb, to toss or throw.

bungalow. Originally a colonial house in India, gradually applied to some houses in Britain. It is technically a one-story house and generally implies something cozy, comfortable, fairly light and airy, and unpretentious, but still suitable for middle class* dwelling, and is most often found in suburbs. *See also* cottage.

bunny suit. The type of children's pajamas that have the feet.

bunter. From the eighteenth to early twentieth centuries, a thieving whore, often expanded to also indicate a woman who picked up rags and trash from the street.

bunting. (1) A term of endearment, probably from a similar Scottish word, most often used alliteratively as **baby bunting**, which was so common it was also sometimes used as a name for a child's doll. (2) A small bird similar to the sparrow or finch, most commonly found along stream banks and among reeds.

Burberry. A waterproof overcoat, so called from the most prominent manufacturer. For those who speak technically, a Burberry is different from a mackintosh* by being made not of rubberized cotton but of other waterproofed materials that "breathe."

bureau. Of furniture, usually a desk with drawers, not a chest with drawers.

burgess. Originally a full citizen of a borough,* but soon more limited to mean a magistrate* or member of a borough council,* and by the twentieth century coming to mean a man of the middle class* who, with or without office, believes he should be running things, a fat businessman of pompous attitude.

burgh. In Scotland* and some scattered parts of England,* a borough* (pronounced the same), as in Edinburgh.* The word also appears as a suffix on some village* names, signifying that in pre-Norman days it was a fort.

burial. *See* funeral.

burk. *See* berk.

Burke. *Burke's Peerage*, the standard reference on the family trees of the British nobility,* and *Burke's Landed Gentry*, which does the same for the rest of the gentry.* *See also* Debrett.

Burlington Arcade. Arguably the oldest extant shopping mall. Built in 1819 in London* near Bond Street* and still in use, it consists of a covered arcade passing between seventy-two shops arranged in two rows.

burn. In Scotland, a small stream or brook.* The term is linguistically related to bourne* but generally applies to any small stream.

Burns Night. January 25, the birth date of Robert Burns, celebrated as the primary Scottish patriotic day since the early nineteenth century. *See also* St. Andrew's Day.

burnt cream. The dessert the French call *crème brulée*, custard with a caramelized sugar topping.

burra. An Indian term meaning big or important, passing into military and colonial slang; hence, a **burra peg*** is a large alcoholic drink, a **burra memsahib*** a bossy or powerful woman, and so forth. *See also* chota.

bursar. (1) In a college,* the treasurer. (2) A student with a bursary,* that is, a student on scholarship.

bursary. What Americans call a scholarship or a student grant; unlike an exhibition,* the bursary is usually only for a single year.

Burton. Essentially, any ale or beer,* from the large number of British breweries located in **Burton-upon-Trent**, an English town near Birmingham* holding a position in English social mythology similar to that held in America by Milwaukee. Burton was also a specific brand of ale; in WWII RAF* slang said someone who was killed had **gone for a Burton**, and the usage has become common since the war.

bus. (1) Modeled on vehicles first run and named in Paris, the first English bus appeared in London* in 1829, horse-drawn, running from Paddington* to the City.* By 1834, there were several different lines operating, including at least one that was steam driven, pulled like a railway car down the street without rails, and by 1839 some were running between suburbs* such as Clapham* and the City. Similar vehicles soon appeared in most British cities. In the early twentieth century, horsedrawn models gave way to the motorized two-storied versions familiar in pictures and all but synonymous with London. For the most part, the widespread train* service meant that busses rarely were used for travel between towns, although most villages* were connected to nearby villages and the nearest train stations by local bus systems, often using the London-style double-decker. From the very beginning, busses seated some travelers on the roof, as had the stage coaches,* so the familiar red double-decker simply continues older practices, and the upper deck was not consistently enclosed until post-WWII models. In most towns and cities, the bus is the primary public transport. In London, where there is also the extensive Underground,* the bus until recently was used as a cheaper, if slower, alternative. As with so many other aspects of British life which Americans regard with envy for their efficiency, economy, and courtesy, during the 1980s moves began to change the busses more to the American model; privatisation* not only ended service for many small villages but in London and other major cities meant major fare increases and, perhaps more traumatic, elimination of conductors* on new busses, and a profusion of competitors on many routes. Some village areas now rely on the **mail bus**, a van* used to deliver mail but large enough to carry a few passengers along the delivery route. Many of the London routes have remained unchanged since the introduction of the motorbus and are commonly alluded to in literature simply by number. The most famous include: #2, north-south across Vauxhall Bridge* past Victoria Station,* Park Lane,* and on past Regent's Park;* #3 north-south along Lambeth* Road past Westminster,* Trafalgar Square,* Portland Place,* and along the west of Regent's Park; the #9 crosses the city east-west, south of Hyde park, along Piccadilly,* Charing Cross,* the Strand,* Fleet St.,* and on to Liverpool St.* Station; #11 runs east-west connecting Liverpool St. Station, St. Paul's,* Whitehall,* Westminster, Victoria Station,* and on through South Kensington;* #24 runs north-south from the Millbank* along Whitehall and Tottenham Court Road* on toward Hampstead.* Those numbered in the 500s are recent express busses between train stations. *See also* charabanc; coach. (2) Among much middle-class* males, a casual term for a car.

busby. The tall fur hat worn by Guards* and Hussars* in the early nineteenth century and still retained for ceremonial dress uniforms and when on guard at Buckingham Palace.*

Bush House. A large building in London* north of the Strand,* since 1940 home of the BBC* World Service.

business. Originally, the word simply meant busy-ness, but gradually by the nineteenth century it was being applied to commercial enterprise in general, as in America. Until late in the century, however, business was still thought to be somehow not quite respectable, in spite of Britain's world preeminence in developing modern business organizations and practices. Most Victorian writers, for example, refused to learn anything about business at all, except that they disliked businessmen; there is not the slightest hint as to what business Dickens's Scrooge, for example, or Dombey might be in, and his Gradgrind epitomizes most artists' attitudes toward businessmen in general, while Trollope, Eliot, or Thackeray hardly mention their existence. However, by the end of the century, when the wealth, power, and numbers of businessmen could no longer be ignored, the British class* structure put a number of confusing twists on the meaning in social use. For many people business came to mean something distinct from, rather than including, trade,* so that one who was in business might be socially acceptable, but one who was in trade would never be. The further removed a businessman might be from any actual sales, the more status he would have. As such, business is now often used to mean something that makes money without anyone quite understanding how exactly. *See also* City; Ltd; merchant; PLC; shopkeeper.

busker. A street musician.

busman's holiday. A holiday spent doing the same thing you always do, like the bus driver who drives on vacation.

bustard. Not a euphemism for bastard* but rather a large light brown and white bird, the largest found naturally in Britain* and extinct there since 1832. It was purely a plant-eating bird, sort of a giant partridge, and in no way similar to any of the buzzards.*

but. When used with a number, as in **but one**, this means plus; for example, next day but one means tomorrow plus one day, or the day after tomorrow. However, **last but one** means the one next to the last.

butcher's. A quick examination or look; rhyming slang:* butcher's hook = look.

butler. Originally, the servant* in charge of the wine cellar; by the mid-nineteenth century, this had expanded to charge of all valuables, such as the silver, and thus the butler became the de facto head servant in a household. However, in daily practice, he had charge of only the male indoor servants, excepting the valets,* which meant his actual authority was much shared and negotiated with the housekeeper,* who had charge of the more numerous females, and the cook, who was a law unto herself. To Americans, this is the quintessential British servant, but real butlers like *Upstairs, Downstairs'* Mr. Hudson were and are quite rare, belonging only to the largest houses whose numerous servants required considerably more organization and supervision than the mistress* could provide by herself, further limited by the luxury tax on male servants. As the number of servants has declined, people tend to call practically any male servant a butler, but this is often a sign of social pretension. Many literary characters Americans think of as quintessential butlers, like P. G. Wodehouse's Jeeves, are really valets. *See also* steward.

Butlin. Billy Butlin was the operator of the most famous holiday camp,* located near Skegness,* beginning in the 1930s; this was so popular that he started a chain and his name became synonymous with holiday camps in general.

butter boat. Before the twentieth century, butter was often served already melted; hence the butter boat, like the modern gravy boat.

butter bread. The basic food accompanying tea.* In working-class* families, this constituted the entire meal called tea until very recently, although the butter was often actually margarine. In the middle class* and gentry,* this was called a sandwich* and was often given to children as a bedtime treat, sometimes with sugar* sprinkled on the butter. *See also* meals.

buttered eggs. Scrambled eggs cooked in butter.

butter mountain. Used in the 1980s by columnists and politicians about the food stockpiled in France* by the EEC* to maintain prices artificially. *See also* wine lake.

buttery. (1) A cool room where perishables were stored, found only in large houses and now replaced by the refrigerator. (2) In the late twentieth century, sometimes used to indicate a snack bar.

buttonhole. A small flower worn in a man's lapel, what Americans usually call a boutonniere.

Buttons. A stock name for a hotel bellboy.

butty. A sandwich,* from butter bread,* which was the sandwich of the working class* from the late nineteenth to mid-twentieth centuries; used almost always only by lower-class vulgar characters, often from the north, or by slangy collegiates. A **jam butty** is bread and jam, usually only a single slice rather than a sandwich. A particularly widespread form is the **chip butty**, a sandwich filled with French fried potatoes.*

buzzard. Relatively rare now, the various types of buzzards found in Britain* look nothing like the famous buzzard of the American Southwest; most are similar to the falcon* or the hawk, and most eat nothing larger than mice and do not eat carrion.

-by. In place names, a suffix indicating a settlement that dated to at least the Saxon era.

By Appointment. A designation used by a business that has supplied a particular product to a member of the royal family* for at least three consecutive years. The royal personage pays for the goods as does any other customer, but since they can afford the best, it is assumed that the goods they choose have a unique quality, and so suppliers vie with each other to obtain the **royal warrant** that authorizes them to use the words "By Appointment to . . .", and the monarch and Lord Chancellor* regularly review such warrants so that they are current and correct.

by-blow. A bastard.*

bye. In cricket,* a run scored when the batsman does not hit the ball but the wicketkeeper* also does not catch it, allowing the batsman to run to the other wicket* before the ball is returned. A **leg bye** is scored when the ball hits the batsman* while he is batting legally and bounces so far that he is able to run before it is returned. *See also* wide.

bye-laws. Laws made by a local governmental authority.

by-election. A special parliamentary election* in only one constituency,* usually held due to the death or resignation of the member* who had previously held the seat.* *See also* general election; Parliament.

by-pass. A highway* that goes around rather than through a town. *See* also motorway.

C

C. In political and civil service slang, any official honour,* from the initials CBE* and CMG* that signify the lowest ranking within the most widely awarded orders. Someone who "hasn't got his C" is someone who has done something wrong and is behind the normal bureaucratic pace. *See also* K.

cab. This was originally shortened from cabriolet,* the earliest form of publicly rented carriage.* Throughout most of the nineteenth century, however, the most common form was the hansom,* though other larger types were sometimes to be found. When the motorcab was introduced, they had taximeters to regulate fares, which led to their being called taxis* more often than cabs.

cabaret. An entertainment, usually a variety of acts, in a restaurant, bar, or club,* performed while the food and drink are being served, what Americans used to call a floor show.

caber. A long wooden pole, usually fifteen feet or longer. One of the traditional sports of the Highland games* is **tossing the caber**, in which men lift and throw the pole for distance and accuracy.

Cabinet. The group of ministers* who comprise the government* and head the various departments or ministries* of the executive branch. Unlike the U.S. Cabinet, each minister is also a serving member* of Parliament* from the majority party* (although some few governments have been coalitions that included members of other parties) selected by the Prime Minister.* As such, Cabinet ministers are both active politicians and administrators who supervise the civil service.* They also serve as the leadership of the party in power and thus have far more influence on the course of govern-mental policy and practice than does the American Cabinet and can pres-sure or sometimes overrule the wishes of the Prime Minister.* During the years of absolute monarchy, governmental affairs were supervised by min-isters, usually nobles, appointed by and directly answering to the monarch, but the framework of the present system was in place by 1688, although the monarch still must symbolically approve the composition of the Cabinet when a new Government is formed. Individual ministers serve no fixed term and may be replaced at any time by the Prime Minister in what is called in the twentieth century a **re-shuffle**. However, most of a Prime Minister's serious rivals are usually included in a Cabinet, if only because it allows the PM to keep an eye on them; thus, Cabinets can sometimes have serious policy disagreements and political dissension, which have a way of becoming public, and Cabinet members occasionally resign over matters of principle (or politics), a practice unknown in America. The size of the Cabinet has grown, as has the number of government departments, over the years, so now only about one third of all the various ministers or department heads are actually in the Cabinet, and within the actual Cab-inet, the bulk of the influence is exerted by a handful of ministers, especially the Chancellor of the Exchequer,* the Lord Chancellor,* the Foreign Secretary,* the Home Secretary,* the Defence Secretary,* and one or two others whose personality exceeds the status of their appointments. *See also* Minister of State; Secretary of State.

cab rank. A place on a street where taxis* regularly wait for passengers.

cabriolet. A small, light carriage* with only two wheels, pulled by a single horse and driven by the rider, and with a convertible hood that could be raised or lowered as wished. In the early nineteenth century, these were the first cabs,* but were soon replaced by the hansom,* which was preferred because the driver rode outside the carriage and thus gave the riders pri-vacy.

Cadbury. The preeminent British chocolate maker, located in Birming-ham,* comparable to Hershey in America.

caddy. *See* tea.

cadge. Originally, a cadger was a small-time trader, by the mid-nineteenth century assumed to be disreputable, after which the verb to cadge came to mean to beg or to pick up occasional unguarded odds and ends. In the late twentieth century it seems to be used euphemistically among the lower classes* for begging, especially the small-time begging among acquaintances that the cadger prefers to call borrowing but which he "forgets" to pay back.

café. *See* caff.

Café Royal. A restaurant in London* on Regent Street,* in the first half of the twentieth century an artist's hangout, in the second half the BBC's.*

caff. The contemporary pronunciation of café, used to mean a cheap snack bar. However, before WWII, a **café**, pronounced in the French manner, was much more elegant, a place where the wealthy went for fancy teas* and light but expensive lunches.

cairn. (1) A conical pile of stones raised as a monument over some pre-historic burial sites in the Celtic* areas, more common in Scotland* than in England,* or any similar pile of stones used as a boundary marker or landmark. (2) In Scotland,* used as a name for some mountains.

Caius. Pronounced keys, technically Gonville and Caius, a college* of Cambridge.*

cake. Originally, a small bread, in shape, size, and baking process something like the American biscuit. In Scotland* these were made from oat flour and were a staple; in England* they were made with white flour and tended to be sweeter, with butter, sugar, or raisins, and thus by about Shakespeare's time were eaten more as a treat (cakes and ale) than as a staple. But in either case, they were small, individual-serving-sized food and in no way resembled the American cake with icing. A **teacake** is a small flat yeast-raised bun,* sometimes split and toasted like a crumpet.* An **Eccles cake** is a round, flat cake with a filling of dried fruit, while a **Banbury cake** is the same in an oval shape, and **rock cakes** are similar with a rough outer surface, often coated with currants.* A **fairy cake**, however, is a small individual-serving-sized sponge cake with icing. The **Pomfret cake** is smaller, a small round licorice sweet, originally made at Pontefract (locally pronounced pomfret) in Yorkshire.* There are also larger cakes that have to be cut into individual servings: A **Dundee cake** is a very rich fruit cake, usually topped with almonds, common particularly in Scotland;* a **tipsy cake** is sponge cake soaked with wine or liquor then generally served with custard,* but a **Madeira cake** does not have Madeira in it, instead being a basic butter cake served in the nineteenth century to accompany a glass of Madeira* but now more often with coffee* at elevenses;* a **lardy cake** is a currant cake made with lard rather than butter, raised with yeast like bread before baking, and then broken rather than sliced at tea;* **Battenburg cake** is an oblong cake made of squares of alternating colors of sponge cake and topped with marzipan. A **queen cake** lies between the two sizes, a very rich dessert cake* of flour, eggs, butter, and sugar, baked in small, often decorative pans. The larger layered cakes are served in wedged slices, like American cakes, and it's not at all clear why sometimes they are called cake and sometimes gateau* or torte*. The logical assumption is that the usage is a matter of class,* but in practice it seems instead to be related to the way they are served—slices of gateau are eaten with a fork (or very often a large spoon), usually with cream or custard poured over them, while cake slices are usually eaten by hand, like the bun-styled cakes. The **cakehole** is the mouth, primarily a lower-class* usage. *See also* biscuit; bun; hinny; scone; sponge; wedding.

Caledonia. The ancient Roman name for the northern part of Britain,* hence, a poetical or romantic name for Scotland.*

calendar. England* used the Julian calendar along with the rest of Europe during the medieval era; however, when the Gregorian calendar was adopted in 1582, all of Britain refused to accept such a Popish device. Finally in 1752, when there was a twelve-day differential with the rest of Europe, Britain capitulated and adopted the new calendar, in the process also changing New Year's* from Lady Day* to January 1. Thus, for the period of 1582–1752, British dates do not match those of the rest of Europe, and for all years before 1752, events in January, February, and most of March were considered to be in what we now think of as the previous year. Historians indicate this discrepancy by **(OS)** for Old Style.

A second, and much more significant, difference for American readers is that, having an established Church,* most Britons tend to use the church calendar as a way of dating events within the year much more often than Americans would ever think of doing, even assuming Americans knew the traditional church calendar. Although this calendar is not unique to Britain, being borrowed from the Catholic Church, I have included the more popular saints' days and festivals in this work for the benefit of (most) Americans who are unfamiliar with these celebrations.

calico. Not the cheap cotton print as in America but rather a cheap unpatterned cotton, usually what Americans call muslin; what Britons call muslin is usually called cheesecloth in America.

call. Generally, this has meant to come in person; while Americans call on the phone, the British ring or ring up. Nonetheless, the public phone booth is usually a call box.*

call box. A public phone booth. For most of the twentieth century, the call box was a fully enclosed iron and glass shelter painted bright red, as uniquely identifiable as the postal pillar box,* but after the telephone service was privatized in the late 1980s, the company began replacing these practical, comfortable, and dry shelters with wet, noisy, and awkward open air niches in the contemporary American style.

calorifier. A water heater using butane gas, from Calor, a brand name of such butane.

Cam. The river that runs through Cambridge,* even by English standards a small and gentle stream, most noted for the short stretch that runs directly behind several colleges* and is now inseparably associated with punting.*

Camberwell. An area of London* between Lambeth* and Brixton,* once a distinct middle-class* suburb.

Cambria. The Roman name for Wales,* now used only poetically or ironically.

cambric. A light, high-quality linen, originally from Cambrai in Flanders. For men, this was often synonymous with a handkerchief.

Cambridge. A town north of London,* primarily known as the home of one of the two ancient and influential universities* of the nation. Ancient rivalries between Cambridge and Oxford* continue into the present, and although they share many of the same methods and traditions, Cambridge since the nineteenth century has come to be thought of as somewhat more scientific in its leanings, especially strong in mathematics and the math-related sciences. However, it still offers the traditional humanities courses of study as well, providing the major educational influence on the Bloomsbury* group in the twenties; since WWII it has had a major impact on British and world theater through its extracurricular theatrical society, which has developed so many significant stage directors that they are often called the **Cambridge mafia**, and a dubious impact on world affairs as the school from which famous traitors and/or homosexuals like Philby and Burgess were recruited as spies in their youth. It was an all male institution until 1869, when women were allowed to study, but they were not allowed to attend lectures* until 1873, not given a specific woman's college until 1878, and not actually given degrees until 1923 (although women were allowed to take exams in 1881). For educational practices, *See* college; degree; faculty; General Admission; gown; term; Tripos; tutorials; university; University Library. For faculty, *See* chancellor; don; fellow; lecturer; master; professor; provost; vice-chancellor. For student activities, *See* blue; Boat Race; May Week; punt; rag. For campus and community aspects, *See* Backs; Cam; court; Fitzwilliam; hall; King's Parade; porter; Senate House; staircase. Individual colleges are listed under their names.

Cambridgeshire. The country* or shire* in central England* surrounding Cambridge.* The area is mostly flat fens,* although there are a few hills in the southern portions, and almost completely agricultural.

Camden Town. Originally a small town north of London,* it had some modest prosperity after the Regent's Canal* was built along it and for a time was a modest artists' colony, although the bulk remained very modest dwellings for families like Bob Cratchit's in *A Christmas Carol*. It declined into real slum by the late nineteenth century but in the late twentieth century was rediscovered as an exciting multicultural* neighborhood, still poor and slumlike but interesting to artists, musicians, and writers.

camiknickers. A woman's undergarment combining a camisole and knickers.* *See also* step-ins.

camp bed. *See* cot.

can. A container for liquids, often the same as a bucket. A **billycan** is such a container used for boiling water. A **jerry can** or **jerrican** is one with square sides, such as is used to carry a gallon or so of gasoline, from the small gasoline cans originally used by the Germans in the North African desert during WWII. What Americans call a can for foods is called a tin.* To **carry the can**, however, is to be given blame for someone else's failures.

canary. (1) A sweet white wine from the Canary Islands. *See also* hock; sack. (2) A casual name for the guinea* and sovereign* coins, from their color.

candle, hold a. Compare favorably, as in America, and generally used negatively, as in "He can't hold a candle to Ted." However, to **hold a candle to the devil** is not to compare with the devil but to work both sides of the street, to treat with both sides of a conflict, or to "cover your ass."

Candlemas. February 2, the Feast of the Purification of Our Lady, called Candlemas because its celebration included the blessing of the candles and a festival of lights. Puritanical reformers in the seventeenth century tried to crush the festival but failed. In Scotland,* it is commonly a quarter day.*

candy floss. What Americans call cotton candy.

cane. Corporal punishment, from the practice of using a switch or light stick called a cane to administer punishment to school children. In general, boys were struck across the buttocks, girls across the hand, but many masters* or mistresses* were known to use the cane as their primary instructional tool. Curiously to most Americans, the cane was, and continues to be, more common in the public schools,* where the nation's elite go, than among the poor, and although regular campaigns are mounted to outlaw corporal punishment in schools, the bulk of the public continues to support it as both useful in maintaining discipline and as "character-building" for the students themselves. In general, Britons do not carry or walk with a cane, but rather call that item a **walking stick**.

canned music. What Americans usually call elevator music or Muzak.

Canning Town. One of the neighborhoods of the East End,* generally seen as a tough slum area (Albert Campion's Lugg was born there).

canon. A clergyman belonging to a cathedral* or other large church* such as Westminster Abbey,* the staff of the church, so to speak. The canon does everything a priest in a parish* church might do, the primary difference being that, as it is a cathedral, there are several canons on staff. As members of the chapter* of the cathedral, canons may also select a new bishop.* A **minor canon**, however, assists in services at the cathedral but is not a full member of the chapter. *See also* dean; prebend.

canonical hour. The time between 8:00 A.M. and 3:00 P.M., the hours in which it is legal to perform marriages* (since 1754).

Canons, Book of. The collection of 151 canon, or ecclesiastical, laws in use in the Church of England* with only minor modification since 1604.

Cantabrian. Of or from Cambridge* University; also called **Cantabrigian**.

Canterbury. A small town in southeastern England,* noted almost completely for its religious associations. St. Augustine founded both an abbey* and a cathedral* there, and after the murder of Thomas-à-Becket, the cathedral became a major goal of pilgrims until Henry VIII formed the Church of England.* The Archbishop* of Canterbury had been head of the Catholic Church in England, and his authority and title were simply transferred to the new Church, which he continues to head, although actually operating from Lambeth Palace* in London rather than from Canterbury.

canvass. Either to campaign on behalf of a political candidate or party,* or to take a poll. Occasionally any people going door to door but not actually selling a product, such as Jehovah's Witnesses, are also called canvassers.

cap. Since the early nineteenth century, the cap has been the universal sign of the urban working class* or the agricultural laboring male. Upper classes may wear caps for specific uses, such as shooting,* motoring,* or cricket,* but until very recently men from such groups always wore hats in daily life. Thus, to go **cap in hand** is to plead as a subservient person, who would naturally remove his headgear in the presence of his betters. British caps are almost always heavyweight material, such as tweed, and take many forms except the one most common in America, the baseball-style cap.

capercaillie. A type of grouse,* also called a wood grouse, found in Scotland, locally extinct in the late eighteenth century but since reintroduced. The male was noted for an extraordinary mating call that has been compared to the sound of two cats fighting.

Cape wine. A sweet white wine from South Africa, popular in the nineteenth century.

capital punishment. This was most commonly done by hanging, with decapitation reserved for the nobility* and special cases. In London,* hangings were held from the fourteenth century until 1783 at Tyburn,* where the method was in fact slow strangulation; the noose was placed around the neck of victims standing in a cart, and then the cart was driven out from under them. Death was the penalty for all felonies until 1838, when it was limited to murder, treason, piracy, or arson; hanging for murder ended in 1965, for arson in 1971, and may now only be used for treason or piracy. *See also* Newgate; Tower.

capped. Selected to play for a select, representative cricket* team, such as a county team, the England team, or a college team.

capsicum. The food Americans call bell pepper.

captain. (1) In the army,* the officer commanding usually a company.* In the navy,* the officer commanding a large ship, roughly comparable to an army colonel* rather than a captain; in the sailing era, this would be a frigate or a ship of the line;* more recently, it would be a cruiser or larger. In merchant ships, this person was sometimes called a captain, sometimes a master,* although captain began to predominate during the nineteenth century no matter what size the ship. *See also* Appendix V; frigate; flight lieutenant; major; subaltern. (2) In cricket,* the team captain is not merely an honorary position but is more like the American baseball manager, the person who positions fielders, selects the order for the batsmen,* and otherwise supervises team play.

caravan. What Americans call a house trailer or an RV.

Cardiff. Capital and major seaport of Wales,* located on the southern coast at the Mouth of the Severn.* Because of its immediate access to the mines of Glamorgan,* Cardiff is inextricably associated with coal,* but it is also the primary cultural center for Wales and the Welsh culture.

cardigan. As in America, a sweater with buttons that can be worn either open or buttoned. While Americans see the cardigan as a sign of middle age, in Britain, it is basic wear, worn by adults, both male and female, around the home at all times of the day or the year, at least in part because homes are heated far less than in America. In winter, it is often worn under other coats or jackets. No stereotypical depiction of the British housewife or char* is without a faded, sagging cardy,* and it is seen by many as a basic signal of respectability. *See also* twin set.

cards. (1) From about the early nineteenth century, it was common for all persons of the middle class* or higher to carry cards, much like modern business cards but engraved only with a person's name. Women had their own cards, without their husband's name. These cards were "sent in" with a servant when a visitor arrived, so that the master or mistress could decide to admit the visitor or not, or were left to indicate one had called but had missed the person you came to meet. Eventually, rituals far too complex to detail here arose, with people often calling at homes not to visit but simply to leave a card, often with cryptic messages indicated by turning down corners to show whether one wished to return, to be visited in return, had a marriageable daughter, et cetera. The practice is rarely seen since WWII, perhaps because there are so few servants* left to carry the card, although American-style business cards are now widely used in business. (2) In the eighteenth and early nineteenth century, almost all card games were some form of gambling. In the mid-nineteenth century, respectable persons tried to separate cards from gambling, with not much success except for some new children's games, so cards became primarily a male pastime until in the early twentieth century bridge* swept across the nation, as it did in America, bringing women and the respectable middle classes* back to the card table, at least until television. For some card games particularly associated with the British, *See* bezique; happy families; loo; Newmarket; whist. *See also* gaming. (3) The forms showing a person's status in the national insurance* updated and held by the employer until the individual leaves a job. To **ask for your cards** is thus to quit a job; to be **given your cards** is to be fired. (4) *See* ball; Christmas.

cardy. A cardigan.*

Care Sunday. *See* Carling Sunday.

caretaker. What Americans call a janitor.

Carey Street. The site of a court of bankruptcy; thus, one who is **in Carey Street** is bankrupt.

Carfax. The center of the town of Oxford,* a crossroads named from a corruption of the Latin for four roads.

Carling Sunday. The fifth Sunday of Lent,* so called from the traditional dish of **carlings**, peas* soaked overnight then fried in butter and covered with honey or rum, served on that day as a temporary relaxation of the Lenten food rules; also called **Care Sunday**.

Carlisle. An industrial town in the northwestern corner of England.* In the Roman era, it was the western end of Hadrian's Wall.* The **Carlisle experiment** was state ownership of pubs* in the area, begun in WWI in hopes of keeping munitions workers sober and it was not discontinued until 1972.

Carlton. A gentlemen's club* in London* in St. James's* Street, central club of the modern Conservative,* sometimes called **Arthur's** because the Duke of Wellington founded it in 1832.

Carnaby Street. A small street in London* on the edge of Soho,* unnoticed until the 1960s, when it became synonymous with the youth-oriented fashions of the day.

car park. What Americans call a parking lot or a parking garage.

carr. An area of marshland, often with trees or bushes, especially common in the Fens.*

carriage. (1) Originally, this term applied to practically any kind of wagon, but in the middle of the eighteenth century, it began to specifically denote a vehicle used to carry people, particularly such a vehicle owned by a private individual as distinct from a public vehicle called a coach.* A carriage, even of the smallest type, was a significant expense, because it also demanded a horse, a place to store both the carriage and the horse, and servants* to care for the horse(s). Thus to have a carriage was to be a part of the upper class, or rather, not to have one was to demonstrate that you were not; hence, the **carriage trade** meant the desirable customers who were wealthy and socially prominent. To be a true carriage, the vehicle should seat at least four people and require at least two horses and a driver, but large numbers of people owned smaller versions that they drove themselves and also called carriages for the status. A **carriage house** was a separate building in which the carriage was stored when not in use. (2) A passenger car on a railway.* *See also* coach. (3) What Americans call a shipping charge.

carriageway. A highway.* A **dual carriageway** is one with a divider between the two directions of traffic.

carrier bag. *See* shopping.

carry on. In general, keep doing whatever you are already doing. However, in 1958 a low-budget film comedy called *Carry On Sergeant* was so astonishingly successful that it spawned a series that continues still, all called *Carry On . . .* , and the phrase now often alludes to the old-fashioned cheerful vulgarity of the humor in these.

Carthusian. Someone who attended Charterhouse.*

cartridge paper. Not paper used for wrapping bullets but quality paper used for drawing.

cartwheel. A nickname for the first copper two-penny coin, in 1797.

case. (1) What Americans usually call a suitcase. Thus, a **case bottle** is a square bottle designed to travel inside luggage. (2) In public school*/girl's school* slang, what Americans call a crush, most often on a person of the same sex.

cashiered. Fired. The term arose in the army* during the Dutch campaigns, and apparently bears no relation to the bank cashier (which has a Latin root). It is almost always used, in military or civilian life, to indicate the person has been fired for something disgraceful. *See also* redundant.

casket. A small box, and never, as in America, a coffin.

cassock. A long coat fitted to the upper torso, worn for services by most clergymen* in the Church of England* under the surplice;* the cassock, except for bishops,* is black and, until the mid–twentieth century, was often worn by clergy as a basic daily outer garment as well, especially among those with High Church* leanings.

cassoulet. A stewlike dish made from vegetables and (usually leftover) meat.

castle pudding. *See* pudding.

castor. *See* sugar.

casual. A member of the **casual poor**, who were only in poverty due to unusual temporary circumstances, or someone who did **casual work**, irregular work hired and paid by the day. Any temporary setback, such as an illness, could force such people into a **casual ward** in the workhouse* or similar charitable institution that provided aid only to the temporarily destitute.

casual shoe. What Americans call a loafer.

casualty. What Americans call the emergency room at the hospital.

cat/cat-o'-nine-tails. A whip with nine distinct thongs, used for punishment in the British navy* as late as 1948, abolished in the army* in 1881.

catapult. The former weapon and current child's toy Americans call a slingshot.

catchment area. Usually the drainage area of a particular stream, but also sometimes used to mean what Americans call a school district, hospital district, et cetera.

Catechism. Church of England* members must learn the answers to a catechism before confirmation.* This is quite brief, including a creed of belief, the Ten Commandments, and about a dozen questions about baptism and communion.*

catering. Any part of the restaurant trade, not just the special serving of restaurant food at a private function.

Catering Corps. In the army* since 1941,* the cooks.

cathedral. The home church* of a bishop* and principal church of a diocese. *See also* abbey; canon; chapel; clergy; dean; minster; provost.

Catholic Apostolic Church. Also called **Irvingites**, a sect founded by Edward Irving in 1832, originally governed by twelve "apostles" who were thought to have prophetic sight and were supposed to live until the Second

Coming. Their deaths led to doctrinal splits and reorganizations, especially in Germany where the bulk of modern members reside. This was a non-conformist* sect that gradually adopted a great deal of Catholic liturgy but was never a part of the Catholic Church.

Catholics. Following the reestablishment of the Church of England* under Elizabeth I, Catholics were methodically suppressed, as they were seen as both a political and religious threat. This suppression was total, at least in the public sphere: Priests were outlawed and executed if captured, Catholic services were banned, and no one who admitted to Catholic belief could hold any offices. Nonetheless, many of the old and rich Catholic families survived by withdrawing completely from all political activity. In the Restoration, Catholics were allowed at least to exist, but from 1661 were banned from municipal office and in 1673 from Crown* offices, including military command. Although dissenter* sects began to hold services legally in 1689, Catholics could not do so until 1791 and only in 1829 were able to hold office and run for Parliament,* but were not allowed in Oxford* or Cambridge* until 1853. Even so, the general fear and distrust of Catholics continued in the general populace, with Catholics regarded much of the way Americans regard Communists as the villains of all work, much more detested than even Jews* or Blacks,* particularly among the dissenter sects and the Scots. For the modern English, who are for the most part nonreligious, Catholic almost always also means Irish, which in turn means ignorant and lower class,* so it is often difficult to separate religious intolerance from class intolerance. *See also* Bill of Rights; Penal Code.

catsuit. A one-piece clothing item, usually applied only to children's clothes, where it is like what Americans call a jumpsuit, but also applied to a skintight version sometimes worn by young women like *The Avengers'* Mrs. Peel for physical activity, and is in the 1990s appearing in American fashions.

Cattern Day. November 25, St. Catherine's Day, a holiday in lace-making areas.

cattle. Often used not only for cows but as a generic term for all livestock.

caution. The notice given by the police* to a person under arrest, similar to the American "read him his rights." This is the "Anything you say may be taken down in writing and used in evidence" familiar from movies and TV and in use for almost as long as the bobbies* have been in existence. Also called a **warning**.

cavalry. In 1880, when the army* reorganized the regimental system, there were thirty-one cavalry regiments,* of three basic types: lancers,* hussars,* and dragoons.* The primary difference between **light cavalry** and **heavy cavalry** was training and tactical use rather than armor or size—there were both heavy and light dragoons, for example. Light cavalry was used for skirmishing, flank attacks, and pursuit of fleeing, defeated troops, while the heavy cavalry was used for concentrated shock attacks into enemy formations. All cavalry carried a sword, light units preferring a light curved sabre for slashing and heavy using a heavier straight sword for stabbing, while lancers of course used the lance as well and the dragoons were armed with muskets or carbines. The cavalry were the most glamorous units of the army* and their officers* commanded the highest social status and most expensive commissions,* so powerful and glamorous that, even after WWI showed them to be obsolete against machine guns and modern artillery, the cavalry continued until formation of the Armoured Corps in 1939. The Household Cavalry* still perform all ceremonial and guard duties on horseback. Cavalry regiments, like infantry regiments, were variable in size and organization but usually consisted of two to four squadrons,* each of two troops,* and numbered only about five hundred men total, a third to a quarter the size of typical infantry regiments. *See also* irregular; Yeomanry.

cave. Public school* slang for "watch out!" from the Latin, but usually pronounced cave-ey.

CB. Companion of the Bath, the lowest rank within the Order of the Bath.*

CBE. Commander of the Order of the British Empire. *See* OBE.

Cellotape. What Americans usually call Scotch tape or cellophane tape, a brand name used generically; also called **sellotape**.

Celtic/Celts. The languages and races of the ancient Britons, in modern Britain most associated with Scotland,* Ireland,* the Isle of Man,* and Cornwall.* *See also* Gaelic.

Cenotaph. A memorial monument to the WWI dead in Whitehall* in London,* site of the major national memorial ceremonies on Remembrance Day.* *See also* Unknown Warrior.

census. The British began taking a census at ten-year intervals in 1801.

central heat. Almost always this means what Americans call radiators, rather than a furnace that heats and circulates air.

Central Office. In Scotland Yard,* the office of detectives dealing with the most serious crimes. *See also* Flying Squad; police.

century. In cricket,* a score of 100 or more runs by a single batsman* in a single innings,* a rare and fabulous occurrence.

cess. In Scotland,* a rate.* *See also* tax.

Chad. During WWII, a cartoon character of a round head and big nose peeking over the top of a wall, drawn and used among the military much the same as the American Kilroy. Chad's principal comment was, "Wot, no such-and-such?"

chain. As a measurement, sixty-six yards.

chair. (1) During the Restoration and eighteenth century, an enclosed box on poles in which two or four men carried a passenger, often called a **sedan chair** and used in the same way as a modern cab for travel within the city. This seems perverse from a modern viewpoint, rather like the Chinese rickshaw, but although horses were of course available, the technology to make a light, comparatively cheap carriage* was not available until very late in that century when the first horse-drawn cabs* appeared, putting the chairs out of business forever. However, when Britons celebrate someone's success, they still chair him (or her), meaning that they are hoisted onto their supporters' shoulders, sometimes in a chair and sometimes simply held aloft, and paraded around a room or through the streets. (2) *See* professor.

chairman. (1) In business, the company head Americans often call the president. *See also* director. (2) In entertainment, the announcer or emcee.

chaise. A small carriage,* basically the same as a gig.* A **post chaise** could be hired* to ride between the stages also used by coaches.*

chaldron. An old measure of coal,* about thirty-six bushels.

chalk. Commonly used to record scores in games or the tab at a pub;* thus, a **long chalk** is a wide margin or great distance; to **chalk up** is to make a score, to record something, or to put it on the bill; to **chalk up to experience** is to "write it off" as a learning experience.

chalk and cheese. Two exclusive opposites; Americans usually compare apples and oranges instead. The idiom probably arose because in England both chalk and most cheese* are white.

Chalk Farm. An area of London* north of Regent's Park,* now more often thought of as Primrose Hill.*

chamberlain. Originally, a servant* of the king's chamber, which was the great hall and not a private room, gradually evolving into a single person who was in charge of the royal household.* *See also* Lord Chamberlain.

chambers. (1) The offices of a barrister.* Each barrister must be a member of chambers in one of the Inns of Court,* so all chambers have several members and many are so severely overcrowded that the barristers may have their real office space elsewhere. Ultimately, this derives from the use of chamber for bedroom, as in bedchamber, when the various Inns were actual residences for their members.

champers. Slang for champagne used by girl's school* and Sloane Ranger* types. *See also* shampoo.

chancellery. An office of a chancellor* or an embassy office, often called a **chancery**.

Chancellor. (1) Originally, the secretary of the monarch. As such, he was the primary administrator of government, and thus the name has been used as the title for some ministers* of the government: The **Chancellor of the Exchequer**,* in charge of financial affairs, is also in the Cabinet* and is generally regarded as the number-two power in the government; he is responsible for budgets, revenue collection, taxation legislation, and spending policy. The **Lord Chancellor** is in charge of all legal operations and is a member of the Cabinet;* as the speaker of the House of Lords,* he also ranks higher than a duke,* whatever his actual rank. The **Chancellor of the Duchy of Lancaster** is the nominal administrator of the Duchy of Lancaster* but is in practice a sinecure position used to put someone into the Cabinet without a major ministry. *See also* Chancery. (2) A legal officer of a bishop,* usually presiding in ecclesiastical courts. (3) Ostensibly the head of a university,* but not actually involved in day-to-day affairs. *See* vice-chancellor.

Chancery. (1) In simplified terms, the English developed two coexistent legal systems, common law* and chancery, or equity, law. Originally, a person could appeal to the King* through the King's Chancellor* for redress of wrongs that were not solvable by the common law, and by the seventeenth century chancery was well established as a place to go to cut through the red tape, so to speak, and to find a judgment based at least in theory on right and wrong rather than precedent or legal technicalities. Chancery cases were decided by a judge rather than by a jury and thus also became the place for cases of great complexity. But by the nineteenth, chancery had developed its own precedents and procedures of such complexity that it was noted for obscure procedural rules, incredible delays, and incomprehensibility to the public, and *Jarndyce v. Jarndyce* was not much of an exaggeration. In 1873 chancery was combined with common law in an attempt to regularize and simplify all legal practice and the Chancery court made a division of the High Court.* (2) *See* chancellery.

Chancery Lane. A street in London* along the Inns of Court,* synonymous with the legal profession.

change. To change clothes, as in "change for dinner," but more specifically, to dress in formal wear. It was understood that dinner, in those homes that had dinner* in the evening, was a formal occasion, and all adults and guests, unless otherwise instructed, always dressed formally for the meal until late twentieth century.

Change. The Exchange;* technically, this predates Exchange, but most usage in the last two hundred years has treated this as an abbreviation of the longer term.

changes. *See* bellringing.

Changing of the Guard. *See* Guards.

changing room. What Americans call a locker room.

Channel. The English Channel.*

Channel 4. A commercial TV channel beginning broadcasting in 1982, intended to be more "cultural" than the broadcasting on ITV* but still supported by advertisers. For the most part, it broadcasts only in the evenings and concentrates on documentaries, discussions, and somewhat more adventurous plays and movies.

Channel Islands. Several small islands in the English Channel,* much closer to France* than to England;* these include Jersey and Guernsey. Although "dependencies" of the Crown,* they are self-governing, and in the late twentieth century became widely known as a place where the British could place money in banks in order to avoid British income taxes.*

chap. A man. There is a faint tone of derogation about this, as in "this chap I know," but not nearly as strong now as in mid–seventeenth century when the term was new and quite contemptuous. When said to someone, as in **old chap**, it is intended to be friendly, but also a bit condescending, as it is most often used this way by superiors to inferiors or used ironically by an inferior who doesn't believe he really is inferior. *See also* old man.

chapel. (1) A nonconformist* church,* or the people who attend such, often a major indication of working class* origins. (2) Not a small church, as in America, but simply a church that is not the parish* church, often in the local lord's house, or a section of a church or cathedral* with a separate altar, used for private devotions or smaller services. The chapel need not be small—King's Chapel* at Cambridge,* for example, is as large as many cathedrals. *See also* chaplain; clergy.

chaplain. A clergyman who serves in a religious capacity but not at a parish* church* or a cathedral.* This could be at a chapel,* but it might also be in a military unit which, of necessity, has no fixed parish church. A chaplain is equal in rank, though perhaps not quite in status, to a rector* or vicar.* *See also* clergy.

chapter. All the clergy* of a cathedral.*

char. (1) A woman who does housekeeping, but never as a live-in servant;* also used for the cleaning woman in an office building. *See also* daily. (2) Tea,* from the term used in India, but often used among military types to mean food as well as the drink.

charabanc. A bus,* usually a bus for sight-seeing or long group trips; after WWII, the term began to be replaced by coach.*

charades. A party game as in America but played quite differently. In British charades, the team acts out a skit or scene, often with costumes, which illustrates not the phrase itself but a pun or riddle that might suggest the phrase, more complex and intellectualized than the American version in which a person simply acts out a syllable at a time until a phrase is recognized.

charge nurse. The nurse in charge of a ward. *See also* Sister.

charge room. In the police,* the room where suspects are searched and formally charged after their arrest.

Charing Cross. Originally the site of a memorial cross placed by Edward II, since the early nineteenth century this has been the center of London.* Just south of Trafalgar Square,* it is the intersection of the Mall* (leading to Buckingham Palace),* Whitehall* (leading to major government offices,

Westminster Abbey,* and Parliament),* the Strand* (to the City* and West End* theaters), and **Charing Cross Road** (leading to the major museums and London University*). Once synonymous with secondhand books, the Charing Cross Road is now also the center of the retail book trade, the site of many of the largest and most famous bookstores of the city. Also nearby is **Charing Cross Station**, the rail hub for all trains to southeastern England and a major Underground* transfer point. On a traffic island between Charing Cross and Trafalgar is a statue of Charles I where he was executed; this is the point from which all road distances in England are measured.

charlady. *See* char.

charlie. (1) Widespread lower-class* slang meaning a fool, as in "made a charlie of me." However, among Cockneys* it can mean a homosexual. (2) In the nineteenth century, **charlies** meant a woman's breasts, but the term has fallen from use in the late twentieth and is rarely met in literature.

Charrington. One of the major breweries of England.*

charter. (1) A document from the monarch granting special rights to one or more persons or incorporating a group into a legal entity. Although the Magna Carta is the most famous, most of the old royal charters are simply exemptions from certain laws, especially taxes. But English boroughs,* towns,* and cities* are also chartered, which is why their official names are not always related to their size. *See also* Chartists. (2) As a verb, often used to mean to make a short-term agreement, much as the American "charter a plane," but applied to smaller deals than in America.

chartered accountant. The accountant equivalent to the American CPA.

Charterhouse. Originally a priory,* then a house, and after 1611 a hospital and school in London.* The school in 1872 moved to Godalming,* where it continues as one of the most significant public schools.* *See also* Carthusian.

Chartists. A workingmen's attempt to get a secret ballot* and universal male suffrage, proposed in a petition ("charter") delivered to Parliament* in 1838. The movement quickly fell apart, although it sparked briefly in the 1848 troubles, but reformists of various stripes were occasionally called Chartists until late in the century.

chase. Open, unfenced forest land used for hunting.* In the medieval era, when the term appeared, this was distinct from a forest* in that it was not owned by the King,* and from a park* in that it was not fenced.

Chatham. A seaport east of London* on the Medway,* in the seventeenth century the principal naval station of the country and continuing since as a major dock and repair facility for the navy.*

chat show. On radio* or TV,* what Americans call a talk show.

chattering classes. A relatively recent term for the broad group of people in the media, advertising, education, social work, et cetera, always intended to be insulting, indicating that these groups are all talk and no action, but also usually implying a kind of knee-jerk liberalism. There is no real American equivalent, although the term carries some of the same feeling as the eighties terms "the wine and cheese crowd" or "quiche-eaters."

chat up. When said about the opposite sex, to flirt with; when said about the same sex, usually simply to have a nice conversation or perhaps to "butter up," as in "chat up the boss."

cheap. To Americans, this usually implies not only low price but also low value; to Britons, it generally means only low price. Thus, railways* might advertise **cheap tickets**, which simply means any reduced fare.

cheapjack. Someone who sells shoddy goods.

Cheapside. A neighborhood in central London,* long a home of artisans and tradesmen until being absorbed into the contemporary business* life of the City;* it was also long associated with noise, vulgarity, and immorality. The "cheap" comes from an ancient word that meant to sell or trade.

cheek. A lot of nerve or impudence, as in "you've got some cheek!"; hence, **cheeky** for someone being impudent.

cheerio. Slang generally meaning "Good luck!" or "So long," often considered by Americans to be synonymous with the British but used only by the racier collegiate types of the upper class* starting around WWI; by late twentieth century it had dropped down to the lower classes and might be considered to be completely a lower-class usage, especially Cockney.* Also as **cheeri-bye**.

cheese. Probably the basic cheese is **Cheshire**, a relatively mild, pale, cheddar-style cheese, eaten plain and used in cooking, especially admired when toasted, originally produced in Cheshire.* **Cheddar**, originally from Somerset,* is usually pale, as compared to some artificially-colored American cheddars; nowadays it comes only in "mild" or "tasty" (in America sharp).

Red Leicester is also cheddarlike and is reddish-yellow like American cheddars, the color originally arising naturally. **Double Gloucester** was so called because the milk used from Gloucester cows was so rich it was like double cream;* in the late twentieth century, the taste has been artificially enhanced and is no longer as buttery as it once was, and the cheese is a bit crumbly. **Stilton** is a buttery blue cheese, similar to Roquefort, extremely difficult to produce and expensive, considered a delicacy in all eras and eaten as a dessert, usually with port.* Even rarer is the **Blue Cheshire** which occasionally happened by accident and can't be produced intentionally. **Caerphilly** is a very mild semisoft cheese, originally developed for the miners in Wales* but now produced practically everywhere but Wales. **Banbury cheese** is very thin, about an inch thick. A cheese sandwich* will normally contain either cheddar or Cheshire. *See also* savoury.

Chelmsford. A town* in Essex,* generally associated with electronics and similar research during the twentieth century, often pronounced without the *l*.

Chelsea. A neighborhood of London* along the north shore of the Thames* and west of Victoria Station.* Originally this was a fishing village separated from London; during the eighteenth century, a number of country houses* were built in the neighborhood, and the fashionable Ranelagh Gardens* drew pleasure-seekers out from the city. In the early nineteenth, after Carlyle settled there, its reputation as an artistic neighborhood was firmly established, continuing as city grew out to surround it, although it is thought of more as a home for the wealthy with artistic interests than for poor artists themselves. During the 1960s, it was for a time a center of "swinging London" in its more upper-class form, and in the 1980s the area became yuppified. The **Chelsea Flower Show** held annually in May is the primary national event of the year for gardeners, attracting even the royal family.*

Chelsea bun. *See* bun.

Chelsea pensioners. Retired soldiers resident in the Royal Hospital* in Chelsea; 420 live there now, each wearing the distinctive uniform, red in summer, blue in winter, familiar to tourists in the area; the uniforms date only from the mid–nineteenth century while the pensioners date from Charles II. *See also* old age pensioner.

Cheltenham. A town in western England,* in the eighteenth and early nineteenth centuries a fashionable spa competitive with Bath,* but in the twentieth century perhaps more often noted as a place where you are likely to find lots of horses and retired army* officers, with a major steeplechase* race course as well. **Cheltenham College** is not a college* but a public school,* not ranking among the very top of such schools but still providing considerable status, particularly among army officers and the middle civil service.*

chemist. What Americans call a druggist or a drugstore; as with American drugstores, the chemist often sells more than drugs. *See also* Boots; dispenser.

cheque. A bank check. These were and are much more rare in British society than in American: As late as 1989 some unions threatened strikes over plans to pay their members by cheque, as most workers had no checking accounts. A **cheque card** is what Americans called a check guarantee card before most of those disappeared in favor of ATM cards and credit cards; it means the bank promises to cash any cheque you write. *See also* Giro; overdraft; pay packet.

chequers. The game Americans call checkers.

Chequers. A house in the Chilterns,* since 1921 the official home of the Prime Minister* when he or she is in the country.*

cherry. Generally used only for the fruit; **two bites at the cherry** is metaphorical for doing something the hard way or getting a second chance, as it shouldn't take two bites to eat a cherry. The multiple slang usages related to virginity are almost completely American in origin; however, **cherry-ripe** was regularly used in the nineteenth century to describe an attractive young woman.

Cherwell. At Oxford,* a river that joins the Thames* after running to the west of the town and behind most of the colleges.* Pronounced Charwell.

Cheshire. A county* or shire* (Chester shire) in northwestern England,* the area around Chester.* Until the eighteenth century, this was one of the richest and most influential areas of the nation, but its rich agricultural lands and traditions kept it out of step during industrialization, and it became a gentle backwater full of villages like the model for Cranford, despite the nearness of Liverpool* and Manchester,* and in 1974 the industrialized portions that were suburbs of the two industrial cities were separated from the county. *See also* cheese.

-chester. As a suffix of place names, a town from the Roman era, when the Romans called a major camp a *castra*.

Chester. A town in northwestern England* south of Liverpool,* until the late eighteenth century a major port, trading center, and military position near the border of Wales.* The River Dee* silted up, and Liverpool* became the dominant city of the area by the early nineteenth century, so Chester, with its continued medieval associations, such as the Chester play cycle, and its medieval constructions still intact, has since been primarily a tourist attraction.

Cheyne Walk. *See* Embankment.

Chichester. Pronounced CHITCHister, a town near the southern coast of England* south of London,* noted primarily for its cathedral* and, since 1962, a major theatrical festival.

chi-chi. Britons use this to mean overrefined, overfashionable, frilly, or pretentious, as do Americans, the term borrowed from the French; however, British colonials and military types also use the term to mean halfcaste, from an Indian word that bears no relation to the French.

Chief Constable. In the police,* the chief administrative officer of each county* police force. In London,* this person is called the Commissioner.* As such, he acts something like an American Chief of Police, but his authority covers a much wider area than a single town. Until recently, this was a political or social appointment, filled by a member of the local gentry* rather than by a policeman rising through the ranks, and the Chief Constable's duties still are administrative and political rather than related to the solution of crimes.

child. *See* minor.

child benefit. A subsidy paid by the national government to every family for each child under sixteen-years-old (nineteen if still in school*), regardless of the additional income of the family (currently the equivalent of about $15 per week per child). *See also* national insurance; single parent benefit.

child-minder. A person called a baby-sitter in America. *See also* minder.

Chiltern Hundreds. Areas owned by the Crown* to the west of London,* between London and the Chilterns.* To **apply for the Chiltern Hundreds** means to resign a seat* in Parliament;* since MPs* technically are not allowed to resign once elected, those forced out of the Cabinet* in particular usually apply for the post of Steward of the Chiltern Hundreds to disguise their defeat. The steward's job is to protect travelers from the highwaymen* in the woods there and has thus been a sinecure position since the nineteenth century, but since the steward receives a nominal salary from the Crown, the steward can no longer be allowed to vote in the House of Commons.* *See also* hundred.

Chilterns. A range of hills in Buckinghamshire,* just west and northwest of London,* with dense forests that were used in the furniture trade.

chimney piece. What Americans call the mantel or mantelpiece of a fireplace.

china. A friend, sometimes a wife; rhyming slang:* china plate = mate.

chinaman. In cricket,* a ball bowled by a left-handed bowler* that breaks* toward a right-handed batsman,* unusual because it requires an unnatural spin on the ball. *See also* googly; spinner.

chink. Since Shakespeare's day, a casual term for money, from the sound coins make in a bag or pocket.

chinless wonder. An upper-class* twit,* from the propensity of the more inbred portions of the gentry* to have disappearing chins.

chin wag. A casual talk or chat, used among military and some civil service types for a serious talk that all participants tacitly agree to pretend is casual, most often seen as "a bit of a chin wag" to underline the supposed casualness of the chat.

chip butty. *See* butty.

chipolata. A small and spicy sausage.*

chip pan. *See* chips.

Chipping. When used in town or village names, this has nothing to do with logging or lumber; rather, it is a corruption of the old "cheapening," which meant selling or trading (as in Cheapside*), and indicates a site of long-used marketplaces.

chippings. Gravel, especially **loose chippings**, which means loose gravel on the road.

chips. Not potato chips but what Americans call French fries. At home, they are cooked in a **chip pan** filled with oil for deep frying, in many lower-class* households often left filled on the kitchen stove around the clock to simplify the cooking process, because such households usually have "chips with everything." To have **had your chips**, however, is not to have eaten but to have "had your chance," from gambling chips rather than the food. *See also* butty; crisps; fish and chips.

chip shop. A local shop* selling fish and chips.*

Chiswick. Pronounced CHIZzick, a village on the Thames* west of London,* suddenly growing to a suburb after 1860. When Thackeray's Becky Sharp threw her dictionary down in the road there, it was still just another backwater village.

chit. (1) Any pass, ID card, or other document needed for authorization to do something, originally an Indian term. (2) A young girl, or a very small or frail young woman, a very old term probably from the same roots as kitten.

choc ice. *See* ice.

chop. (1) In general use, any single serving of meat; technically a piece with the bone, as in the American pork chop or lamb chop, though often used for a **cutlet**, which has no bone, as well. Chops are usually pork or mutton,* although they could be beef, and are grilled* or fried. Many people have "a chop" for the evening meal, which can mean a meal with meat and vegetables, but often is just the chop. A **chop house** is a restaurant that specializes in grilled chops and steaks. *See also* fillet. (2) Slang for being fired from a job or for dying; in general, Britons tend to say someone is **for the chop** rather than will "get the chop."

chota. A Hindi term for small, passing into much colonial and military slang. Hence, a **chota peg** is a small alcoholic drink. *See also* burra; peg.

Christ Church. A college* of Oxford,* also called the **House**. It adjoins the cathedral* of Oxford and also houses the tower for Great Tom.* One of the oldest colleges, although perhaps best known for a mathematician who wrote as Lewis Carroll, it is also among those of highest social status, with an unusually high proportion of nobles—hence Sebastian's college in *Brideshead Revisited*—and an equal tradition of poor students on scholarships.

christening. The religious ceremony in which a baby is given his or her "Christian" (and legal) name. In the Church of England,* this is part of baptism, is supposed to be done within a week of the baby's birth, and until late in the twentieth century was regularly done even by those not otherwise religious in order to have the child recorded in the parish* register. The Church also requires three godparents, two of the child's gender and one from the other (these may include the parents), who swear to supervise the child's moral upbringing and are understood to be responsible for the child, should something happen to the parents. Many nonconformists,* however, do not accept infant baptism and christenings and require that the individual be baptized again when reaching an age of personal responsibility.

Christian socialism. An intellectual movement of the mid–nineteenth century that emphasized the social aspects of Christianity, such as cooperatives, education for the working class,* and public welfare.

Christmas. Christmas has come and gone at least twice in British life. The Catholic Christmas involved many pagan customs such as the yule log,* the mummers* play, and the wassail,* and most of those celebrations in fact centered on Twelfth Night* rather than Christmas Day. Christmas itself was suppressed by puritanical Protestant groups and outlawed completely during Cromwell's reign. The customs reemerged after the Restoration, (except in Scotland,* where to this day Christmas is much less important than Hogmanay*) only to decline again during the rationalist fashions of the eighteenth century. Almost single-handedly, Dickens revived and reinvented Christmas as a time for feasts and partying, whether in Pickwick's ice-skating or Scrooge's memories of Christmas Past. At about the same time, Prince Albert's introduction of many German customs at court* made Christmas fashionable, and together the two men defined the modern concept of the holiday as a time of peace, goodwill to all, charity donations, family parties, gifts for children, et cetera. Father Christmas,* although nebulously in the background of the medieval Christmas celebrations, seems to have become the person who brings gifts only late in the nineteenth century, modeled after the American Santa Claus. **Christmas cards** appeared in the 1850s, perhaps growing out of the habit of sending boys home from school at Christmas with a fancy card of calligraphed sentiments to illustrate their progress in handwriting, and are now common throughout Britain, although their most popular visual symbol is not Santa but the robin.* The **Christmas tree** did not appear until the 1820s and was very rare until Prince Albert, originally from Germany, had one set up for Queen Victoria in 1841, after which they became a fashion that in a generation became folk custom. Prior to the tree, the primary home decoration was the "kissing bough," a garland of greenery including mistletoe. The "traditional" midnight service on Christmas Eve in the Church of England* was not in fact widely practiced until the mid–twentieth century. Christmas is now a two-day holiday, starting late on Christmas Eve and concluding on Boxing Day,* December 26; generally, Father Christmas* brings presents for the children to be opened Christmas morning, while personal gifts or gifts outside the immediate family are exchanged on Boxing Day. The traditional Christmas dinner was a goose, plum pudding,* mince pies, et cetera, but in the present, turkey has generally replaced the goose. In general, the contemporary British are about two decades behind America in the commercialization of Christmas, with decorations and sales going up in shops* weeks rather than months before, but they give every indication of following down the same path in the near future. The holiday, when it arrives, is total; for Christmas and Boxing Day, England* is closed. Puritan opposition to the holiday has continued among various nonconformist* churches, and in Scotland, which is Presbyterian,* the day was not even a legal holiday until the 1960s, so there is not quite the same total shutdown in Wales* and Scotland. For the **twelve days of Christmas**, *See* Twelfth Night. *See also* Plough Monday.

Christmas, Father. *See* Father Christmas.

Christ's College. A college* of Cambridge* since 1505, Milton's "studious cloister's pale."

Christ's Hospital. Actually a public school,* originally (1552) in London,* now in Sussex.* *See also* Blue Coat.

chuck. In cricket,* to throw the ball rather than to bowl* it properly and legally. Hence, to be **chucked out** is to be thrown out of a place or a gathering, and a **chucker-out** is what Americans often call a bouncer, someone who throws unruly people out of a club* or pub.*

chuffed. This sounds as if it means upset, particularly since it is most often heard as **dead chuffed**, but in fact it means happy or pleased. *See also* dead.

Chunnel. Popular portmanteau name for the tunnel being dug between France* and England* under the English Channel,* begun in 1989.

church. Unlike American communities, the English village* has only one church, the official church of the Church of England.* Only in the last two centuries have other religious meeting places been legalized, and where they exist, they are rarely actually called churches. The church was the center for all official life in its parish,* for it kept the records of birth, death, and marriage, until 1832 performing all marriages and funerals even for persons not officially members. It also administered many civil affairs, as religious and civil parish boundaries often coincided; the civil council* met in the church vestry* so often that its members were usually called vestrymen until 1894. In urban areas, this influence was only slightly diminished until perhaps WWII, since most people still lived and worked within a single parish all their lives, even in cities. The church was in effect the primary means by which local people were connected to national life and government and was often far more important as a social institution than as a religious one. Until about 1960, the primary service in most churches was matins* on Sunday at 10:30 or 11:00, with a sermon but only occasionally with communion;* during the sixties, many churches moved the service earlier, usually to 9:30. *See also* clergy; evensong; Registry; tithe.

Church. The Church of England.*

churching. The first visit to the parish church* by a woman after having a child. In the Church of England,* there is only a short service of "thanksgiving" for safe delivery, although most people saw it as an extension of the ancient pagan "purification" after childbirth. Traditionally, this was supposed to be the first trip the mother made out of the house after giving birth, without which she and all who came in contact with her would have bad luck. The English have never taken this quite as seriously as the continentals, but the practice still continues today in the rural north and west.

Church in Wales. Originally the Church of England* operated in Wales* as in England,* but in the nineteenth century the majority of the Welsh joined the more evangelical dissenter* sects and increasingly objected to supporting the state church. In 1920 the church was formally disestablished and reorganized under this name, with its own archbishop.*

Church of England. The official state church of England* since the religious turbulence of the sixteenth century. From its very beginning, the Church has been a compromise, retaining many of the practices and much of the theology of the Catholic Church with significant touches of Protestant theology thrown in, but never fully accepting such Protestant doctrines as Calvinist predestination; in modern America, this is the Episcopalian Church. As an established church, the **C of E** is expected to serve all of the people, whether they are active members or not, and thus at the local parish* level, even nonmembers may have church weddings, funerals, charity, and spiritual aid. At the same time, only about one third of the population claims to be Church of England in surveys, and less than 5 percent actually take communion even at Easter.* For details of organization and practice, *See* Book of Common Prayer; calendar; Catechism; christening; Christmas; church; clergy; Civil War; confirmation; dissenter; divorce; Easter; funeral; General Confession; harvest festival; High Church; Lent;

Low Church; marriage; nonconformist; parish; Thirty-Nine Articles; wedding.

Church of Ireland. The Irish version of the Church of England,* established in 1536 as the only legal religion in Ireland and from the beginning the source of intense controversy, since the overwhelming majority of Irish remained faithful Catholics.* In 1838 tithes* to support the church were eliminated, and finally in 1871 the church was disestablished, and now it continues simply as a Protestant church not specifically supported by the state.

Church of Scotland. Established as the national church in 1560, this from the beginning had no connection with the Church of England.* Although it initially retained much of the shape of the English church, it evolved into what is now usually called the Presbyterian Church, officially adopting Calvinist doctrines in 1690 after almost a century of conflict with the English Kings* over their attempts to appoint Scottish bishops.

Church of Wales. *See* Church in Wales.

church rates. A special tax, levied in addition to the tithe,* for specific church purposes, usually repairs or building. These rates were much resented, because they were levied on all persons in a parish,* no matter what their religion. In 1868, these were made voluntary, but because they came in a bill like other rates,* most modern ratepayers never realize they can refuse to pay them.

church warden. *See* warden.

chutes and ladders. *See* snakes and ladders.

chutney. A thick and chunky condiment made of fruits and spices, first found in India but by the twentieth an almost standard accompaniment to meat dishes.

CID. Criminal Investigation Department, the nonuniform branch of any police* force. Most often, however, this means the detective branch of Scotland Yard* in London* and also includes such other groups as the Special Branch* and a national Fraud Squad.

cider. A drink made from apples but, unlike American cider, always alcoholic.

Cinders. The fairy tale character Americans call Cinderella.

cinema. What Americans call a movie theater. This term is also used to indicate what is shown there, although you are more likely to hear "I saw a film at the cinema." However, in rural areas and parts of the lower class,* the **pictures** is preferred, as in "We went to the pictures last night." The American term *movie* is rarely used.

cinque ports. Originally, Dover,* Hastings,* Romney, Sandwich, and Hythe, ports on the southeast coast of England* that were exempted from certain taxes in return for providing a fleet for the king* until the sixteenth century when the modern navy* was begun.

circulating library. *See* library.

circus. What Americans call a traffic circle, as in Piccadilly Circus* or Oxford Circus,* although in London many of these are now just intersections. John LeCarré's "Circus" is thus a place where things come together as well as a clownshop where things go wrong.

cistern. The water tank on the toilet.

city. To Americans, a city is a big town, but technically in Britain a city is a community given a charter* saying it is a city,* of which for centuries London* was the only example. Borough* is actually the English term, tracing its roots back to an Anglo-Saxon word, while the Normans brought the word *city* from France. Whether called a borough or a city, the community's charter allowed it to make its own local laws and essentially govern itself, usually through a corporation.* In practice, by about Shakespeare's time people had begun to use city to indicate a town that also had a cathedral,* many of which were not actually chartered as either cities or boroughs. Size was not automatically the determining factor; after industrialization, many of the cities were much smaller than some boroughs and towns. All boroughs officially ended in 1974, except within Greater London,* and in the late twentieth century there has been a tendency among the general populace to use city more in the American sense. In the various geographical entries of this work, city has been used to indicate the approximate modern size of the community, so city without a * means a community of more than 100,000 people; city* indicates the more specific British usage.

City. Essentially, old London,* the part of that city that originally fit inside the city walls. Chartered under both William I and John, London developed its own local government under the Corporation* of London and became the primary trading center of England.* By Shakespeare's day, it was the center of all financial and cultural life of the nation, as well as center of the religious puritanism that would soon lead to the Civil War.* In the years of internal peace that followed the Restoration,* London began expanding outside the city walls, and by the nineteenth century, most of the walls were gone, but the old City retained its own governance and traditions and remained the financial center of both London and the nation. Today, it is basically the area north of the Thames* from the Tower* north to London Wall Street and west to St. Paul's,* including the Bank of England,* Lloyd's,* the Barbican,* and the old guild* halls. Fewer than 10,000 persons actually live in the area any longer, although some four million come in daily to work, and practically all major businesses, insurance firms, and financial institutions have offices there, so that references to the City generally mean much the same as American references to Wall Street or lower Manhattan. The twentieth-century stereotype of the Englishman in tailored suit, bowler,* and tightly rolled umbrella* came from the uniform dress of men who worked in the City, although the bowler at least began disappearing in the 1970s.

Civil List. Parliament's* appropriation of money for the royal household;* in 1697, this included all civil government expenses, but in 1761 George III traded the income from all land owned by the Crown* for an annual payment, and in 1831, civil government expenses were taken over directly by Parliament;* the Civil List now pays for the monarch's staff, state visits, public appearances, et cetera. *See also* Privy Purse.

civil service. The idea of a civil service was slow in developing, although obviously there had been posts of governmental administration ever since there were governments. By the early nineteenth century, these had coalesced into a handful of ministries,* supervised by sons of the nobility* and upper gentry* and staffed almost completely by people who obtained their posts by patronage. It was a gentleman's* profession, seen as more a public service than as a job and undertaken with a decidedly casual and amateurish attitude. In 1870, reform laws introduced hiring by competitive exam and promotions by merit. Such reforms hardly remade the service in any dramatic fashion—no one was actually hired as a result of the exam until 1880, and all those hired under old rules continued in office, while many of those eventually hired by exam would have been hired by patronage anyway, as they were the only ones with the public school* educations necessary to pass the exams. For the most part, it made little difference since there were very few jobs; the Home Office,* for example, had only seventy-six employees in 1876. The real explosion came with WWI, during which the civil service grew exponentially into the modern bureaucracy, the ranks filled by boys from grammar schools* or sons of merchants, lawyers, et cetera and dominated by professional managers who, if they reach high enough, are given the old gentleman's honours* and knighthoods. *See also* ministry; permanent secretary; secretary.

Civil War. In one sense, Britain has been engaged in a civil war related to religion for more than four centuries, fought primarily within England in the sixteenth century, expanding to include Scotland* until 1746, and then almost immediately shifting to Ireland* where it continues to the present. However, when capitalized as the Civil War, this almost always refers to the conflict of 1642–49, between Charles I and his supporters and the Parliamentary/Puritan forces eventually commanded and controlled by Cromwell. Religion was a factor, the rebels charging that the royalist forces were trying to reinstate the Catholic Church,* but there were also philosophical conflicts concerning the authority and rights of the monarch, and political/economic conflicts as well, with the royalists being primarily noble landowners, the rebels middle-class* businessmen. The royalist forces were convincingly defeated, and Charles I captured and then beheaded in 1649, setting up the Commonwealth;* few if any of the issues were settled however, since the monarchy was restored in 1660, the Church of England* was also reestablished in 1660 without modification, and none of the parliamentary reforms were effected for decades afterward. *See also* Glorious Revolution.

civvy street. Civilian life, used originally by the military in WWII and since often used by members of any specialized profession to talk about outsiders or retirement.

clamped. Of a car, fitted with the device known in America as the Denver boot, placed on the wheel of vehicles in flagrant violation of traffic laws to make them immovable until the owner can be fined.

clan. Basically what Americans usually call a tribe, a group of people nominally descended from a single person. The clan was the fundamental social unit of Scotland* long after such groups had been absorbed into larger communities in the rest of Britain, particularly in the Highlands,* where it reflected its feudal roots by including not only family but also tenants and followers who owed a clan chief allegiance in some way. The clans provided social organization in an area that was completely unorganized, but in many cases the clan chiefs were simply local warlords whose primary occupation was raiding their neighbors. After the Scottish and English thrones were combined, the clans continued to raid the Lowlands* and the English border towns and provided fighters in regular rebellions, including support of the Jacobites,* so that after Culloden* the English army* embarked on a concerted campaign to break up and, if necessary, exterminate the clans. This plan succeeded, and by the end of the eighteenth century, the clans were little more than a memory that has been converted into a source of romantic mythology for a modern Scot. *See also* tartan.

Clan Bogus. A tartan* from France, belonging to no real clan.*

clanger, drop a. To make a really gauche mistake that everyone would notice.

Clapham. Originally a village south of London,* it became one of the first real suburbs when wealthy Londoners built new homes there to escape the plague* and the fires of the late seventeenth and early eighteenth centuries. In 1845 regular trains began to run to the City,* joined in 1870 by the Underground* and later by busses; Clapham became so closely identified with the middle-class* commuter that lawyers and judges used **the man on the Clapham omnibus** to describe the "average reasonable man" in so many tests of legal evidence. Now it is hardly distinguishable from the city that has expanded around it, but its population is still primarily educated, suburban middle class. **Clapham Junction** continues to be the busiest train junction in Britain, possibly the world, and **Clapham Common**, once a major home for highwaymen* who preyed on travelers, is now a tame, attractive modern park.

Clare. One of the oldest colleges* of Cambridge,* especially favored with one of the loveliest gardens* in Britain.

Clare market. A market* in London* near Lincoln's Inn Fields* until 1900, for most of the nineteenth century the center of a slum; the modern street is in a slightly different place.

claret. In Shakespeare's day, a pale red wine or even a white, but since the seventeenth century, any red wine and more particularly a full-bodied red such as Bordeaux, very much an upper-class* drink.

Claridge's. A hotel in London,* frequented by celebrities from all walks of life and world-famous as one of the most luxurious of all hotels, so exclusive it was often (falsely) rumored that people could get a room there only if recommended by someone they knew.

class. (1) *See* Appendix III. *See also* accent; gentleman; goodman; Lady; meals; Mr; Oxbridge; public school; U. (2) *See* first class.

classics. In schools* and colleges,* the study of Greek and Latin literature and culture. *See also* moderns.

cleansing. In the twentieth century, this term indicates really serious cleaning, especially when the skin is involved; thus, a **cleansing lotion** or **cleansing cream** is something a woman might use to remove her makeup. **Cleansing personnel**, however, is a modern euphemism for the people who pick up the garbage, who sometimes work for the **cleansing department**, and a dirty car may sometimes go to a **cleansing station** for a wash.

Clearances. In the mid–eighteenth century, wool suddenly increased in value as the industrial textile industry grew, and in Scotland* many landlords decided to convert all their lands to sheep grazing; in order to do this, they had to evict the tenant crofters.* In a century-long process called the Clearances, paralleling the enclosures* in England,* they stripped the land of its small farmers, who, left homeless, flooded the factories with cheap labor, and not least, flooded the United States with immigrants.

clearway. A highway* with no stopping allowed, usually a portion of a motorway.* An **urban clearway** is a similar stretch of road in an urban area.

clergy. The clergy, of the Church of England* maintain many of the features of the Catholic* clergy on whom they were modeled and from whom they were drawn when the C of E was established. There are three levels of clergy: (1) at the top, the **bishops**,* who supervise large areas with many local churches and from whom are (usually) selected the two **archbishops**;* (2) the bulk of the clergy, the priests, going by the many various names discussed in detail below; and (3) **deacons**,* who are in effect priests-in-training, persons who, although selected for the clergy, are serving as assistants at various levels for at least one-year's probation before complete ordination. A clergyman was not required to have a degree in theology nor to pursue a specific course of study; however, he was expected to have at least attended a college,* (a full degree* plus additional theological studies are required since WWII) under the assumption that he would have selected at least some Biblical or theologically related subjects along the way. Thus, the English church had few of the illiterate priests that had so bedeviled the Catholic Church in many parts of Europe and instead found many historians, scientists, archaeologists, and other serious scholars among its number, while providing every village* with at least one literate person; consequently, until the mid–nineteenth century, the local parish* priest was the primary keeper of all records for the community. After his studies, the candidate simply presents himself to a particular bishop, who must be satisfied of not only his education but also his character and anything else that might be a factor before allowing him to be ordained. At present, no women may be ordained as priests, but in 1987 the first woman deacons were ordained, so it seems only a matter of time.

Among the priests, there are several different positions: In a cathedral,* there will be several priests on hand, the bulk of whom are called **canons**,* and they conduct services and perform the normal duties of a priest. Supervising them is a **dean**,* who acts as chief administrator of the cathedral for the bishop who nominally supervises not only the cathedral but all the other churches in the area. Assisting the bishop in his supervision of his area, called a see, are the **archdeacon*** and the various **rural deans**,* each of whom supervises several parishes in the see. Each church serves a parish,* and each parish church has a priest, who is usually called a **rector**. The rector might have a **curate**,* or assistant, or he might not, depending on the size and the wealth of the local church. All of this organization is relatively simple, except that each church was originally supported by a tithe,* a tax of 10 percent on lands and wages in the parish, which also paid the rector and was often called a living.* Once appointed to a living, the rector held it for life. However, he did not have to actually serve in the church to keep receiving the living; he could in effect hire a **vicar*** as his stand-in, and the vicar received either an agreed-upon salary or more often the portion of the tithe that came from wages rather than from land. Thus, many parish churches were staffed by vicars rather than rectors; they were both equally qualified as clergy, the only real difference being that one got paid considerably less than the other for doing the same job. Attempts have been made to regularize salaries and duties for more than a century, but the reforms of the tithes and declining public interest have reduced most salaries to the vicar level rather than raised the vicar up, and clerical salaries are now so low as to actively discourage new clergy.

In addition, not all ordained clergymen are expected to serve in a specific church. A **chaplain**,* for example, is simply a priest who serves in some religious capacity where there is no parish church—in a nobleman's private chapel,* for example, with a military unit, or as a special assistant or advisor to some notable person; a **warden*** supervises one of the church's charitable institutions. Many clergymen held academic positions and never served in a church; a number of the faculty positions at Oxford* and Cambridge,* although having nothing to do with theology, require their holders to be ordained, such requirements usually dating back to the medieval or Tudor eras.

None of these positions should be seen as ranks, however, except the bishops, who are in authority over all the others in their see or diocese, and to some extent deans; vicars and chaplains are not "promoted" to rectors or to canons, although of course replacements for those who die have to come from somewhere. Deacons, being assistants and trainees, eventually move to one of the other positions, but curates, who also are assistants, might not, depending on the individual circumstances. Even bishops are not necessarily promoted from the ranks of canons or rectors but are chosen by the local canons with the "direction" of the monarch (now including the government*) and might be from another bishop's staff or might even be someone who, although ordained, has never actually served as a clergyman. Once selected, however, the bishop has almost unlimited clerical powers, in the sense that the bishop rather than the church itself ordains new priests; thus, individual clergymen in effect serve the bishop for their entire lives and all matters of appointment or conflict are handled by the bishop (hence the tremendous power of a Mrs. Proudie). Until 1827, clergy were not subject to civil law.

All ordained clergy are called the Reverend, properly shortened to "the Revd*" not to "Rev."; however, this is a description, not a title, and thus all but bishops would retain any other titles they might have. Thus, one might be the Revd Mr* Smith or the Revd Dr* Smith, depending on the academic degree earned rather than the clerical position filled. Bishops, however, are the Right Reverend (Rt Revd*) and become lords* upon their selection; thus, their formal title is The Right Reverend the Lord Bishop of (name of place). For archbishops' titles, *See* archbishop.

Church of England clergy have been allowed to marry almost from the very beginning, and most do so. Within the local parish, the rector's or vicar's wife is often much more potent an influence than the clergyman himself. She is primarily, if unofficially, responsible for all the female activities of the parish and thus is the primary organizer of practically all charities and fund-raising affairs, as well as the de facto judge of local morality, even for the nonreligious. The literary stereotype of the practical, levelheaded vicar's wife has been the ideal of the clergy for centuries.

At the parish church, there might be other ecclesiastical positions, but they are not normally filled by ordained clergymen. The sexton* maintains the grounds, in particular the graveyard around the church itself, while a verger* cares for the interior of the church; a beadle,* in larger churches, would keep order during services; a sacristan* cares for the various holy vessels; a precentor* supervises the choir.

The clergy were not necessarily well-respected. Until late in the nineteenth century, most clergy were younger sons of the gentry,* often appointed by their family to a living the family controlled and leading the life of a country squire* with little time for pastoral duties. But the collapse in land values of the late nineteenth century reduced clerical income to an average of less than £250 a year, which ended the high life and remade the image of the local priest into a genial old man poor as a church mouse.

clerk. Pronounced clark, almost always applied only to an office worker; the people Americans call sales clerks are called shop* assistants. A **law clerk**, however, is more than a secretary or filer; he or she is more of an agent for a barrister,* making contacts to find cases and taking a commission from all fees earned. *See also* article.

Clerkenwell. Pronounced CLARKinwell, a neighborhood of London* northeast of the Inns of Court;* a comfortable residential neighborhood when Mr. Brownlow had his pocket picked there in *Oliver Twist*, it is now primarily commercial.

Clerk of the Closet. The clergyman who personally serves the monarch.

Cleveland. A small county* on the northeast coast of England,* formed in 1974 from portions of Durham* and Yorkshire.*

clever. This is an odd word, in that for most of the nineteenth and twentieth centuries it often had a different meaning when used by women than when used by men. For men it meant quick-witted, imaginative, ingenious, as in most dictionaries; but women often used it to mean studious, knowledgeable, profound, or dull, as in "clever books" of philosophy or a "clever child" (to mean one who studies a lot). Fowler first pointed this out, and I haven't found anything to indicate the usage has changed, nor am I familiar with any similar distinction in American usage. *See also* frightful; half.

clever dick. Someone Americans might call a smart aleck.

cling film. A brand name now used generically for a thin plastic covering for food, similar to what Americans call plastic wrap or Saranwrap.

Clink. A prison* in Southwark* from the thirteenth century until burned down in 1780, synonymous with prison in general.

clippie. A female bus* conductor. The term refers to the practice of clipping the tickets, but it's unclear why it is applied only to women.

Cliveden. Pronounced Klivden, a country house* owned by the Astors northeast of London,* significant in the 1930s for a **Cliveden set**, who were friends and acquaintances of Lady Astor noted for their fascist leanings, and prominent again in the 1960s when parties on the grounds there played a major part in the Profumo scandal.

cloakroom. Appearing in the mid–nineteenth century, a closet near the front door of a house, especially a country house,* used primarily for storing guests' overcoats, cloaks, and such; the term was extended almost immediately to the room set aside in train stations for temporary luggage storage. By mid-twentieth, however, in public areas of hotels, restaurants, and similar places, it had become a euphemism for the room with the toilet. *See also* closet; WC.

clobber. Clothes, used primarily by Cockneys,* although in WWI it was also used in the military as slang for a soldier's full outfit of gear.

clogs. Shoes with wooden soles. These were the basic footwear of peasants and working people until the early twentieth century and were occasionally worn by urban women to keep their slippers out of the dirt and mud of the streets. Even in the mid–twentieth century, some specialized workers such as coal miners continued to wear them, but they had basically disappeared after WWII until re-adopted as a political statement by many in the educated liberal, Green,* health-food groups. Some people wear them while gardening. In northern areas, **clogs to clogs** is often said to describe the life story Americans might call "rags to riches and back to rags."

close. Pronounced close rather than cloze, originally any enclosed field. The most common usage is the **cathedral close**, the open space surrounding a cathedral, usually enclosed by a wall. In addresses, it usually means a dead-end street. In some public schools, this is the playing field,* in parts of the Midlands* it is a farmyard, and in Scotland* it is the name of the passage from the street to the back of the house or to an inner courtyard or stairway of a multiple dwelling.

close season. The opposite of open season.

close stool. A toilet-like wooden box with a lid that closed over the opening. Inside was a pot to catch the excrement, emptied by servants into cesspits.

closet. *See* cloakroom; cupboard; water closet.

clot. A fool, usually implying thickheaded rather than simpleminded.

cloth, the. The clergy,* from a now obsolete use of cloth to mean a uniform.

cloth cap. Used to indicate something that would be done or liked by the working class,* whose men usually wore (and wear) caps* rather than hats.

clothes peg. Not a peg on the wall but what Americans call a clothes pin, for holding laundry on a drying line.

clotted cream. An extremely thick, tasty cream made by scalding the milk; eaten rather than drunk, often spooned over other foods. Also called **Devonshire cream**.

club. (1) The gentlemen's clubs so much a part of the English stereotype grew out of the coffee houses* of the eighteenth century and were initially commercial enterprises. Although drink and gambling were often their primary activities, they also served as political associations, and many of the oldest clubs still retain their party* image. In the early nineteenth century, however, the clubs began to take on a new function. The press of complex business, more regular Parliamentary sessions, and the revival of country house* living forced a number of men from the gentry* to stay in London* for extended periods without their families. As modern hotels and restaurants had not yet appeared, the clubs provided both meals and short-term lodging at moderate rates and, after they banned all women from the premises, with unchallengeable respectability. (A few women's clubs for independent, educated upper-class women were founded in the early twentieth century for much the same reasons, but they get little public or literary attention.) Thus, every man of any standing joined at least one club, to have a place where he knew he would be able to meet similar persons, relax in comfort, receive mail, get dependable meals, and if necessary, even sleep overnight without any of the risks associated with finding such things on the streets of London. The club thus became the center of the gentleman's* social life in the city and at the same time the very quintessence of stuffy respectability, a far cry from the kind of place an all-male preserve implies, although few were as stodgy and dull as the mausoleums so beloved of the movies. Since WWII, however, restaurants, hotels, service flats,* automobile commuting, the decline of the traditional gentry, and the relaxation of the terms of respectability have all eroded the influence of the clubs, and now they are kept alive primarily by the lunch trade and the simple status of having a club. Most now allow wives or other female guests in public areas, and some have allowed women members. Individual clubs of note are listed under their names. (2) From the late nineteenth century, a number of **private clubs** grew up that allowed members legally to circumvent many social restrictions: Gambling* was illegal, except in private gambling clubs; pornographic films were illegal, except in private cinema* clubs; private clubs could serve drinks long after the pubs* had been closed; private theatre clubs could present plays that had not passed the Lord Chamberlain's* censorship; et cetera. Many such clubs were of course private in name only, offering membership to any stranger with a stiff admission fee in hand, but they allowed London* in particular to have a cosmopolitan night life and culture while officially condemning all such activities. The nature of these clubs shows perhaps one of the finest examples of the British belief that whatever might be dangerous among the masses was perfectly acceptable among the wealthy and/or the aristocracy,* as long as it was done out of sight of the lower orders. *See also* gaming. (3) The **night club** as a particular form of private club grew up in the 1920s, under licensing laws* that allowed the serving of liquor to private members until midnight or later if accompanied by food. After a wave of publicity, this particular form of night life was suppressed by police* raids in the late 1920s and never really recovered in the way American night clubs did in the swing band era. Ironically, the form that prospered in the age of television was the **workingmen's club**, particularly in northern areas, something like a pub with restricted membership, but often holding shows or dances where most British comedians and rock bands still make their living, or simply acting as a **drinking club** that serves liquor after pub closing time.* A few private night clubs, such as Annabel's,* still prosper, but for those seeking dancing, the modern choice is the disco.* *See also* bottle party; tea. (4) Most sports teams are called clubs rather than teams, whether amateur or professional. (5) A woman **in the club** is pregnant, perhaps an ironic reference to the only kind of club she would be allowed to join. (*See also* pudding club). To **club together** is not to form a new club but to chip in to a common fund, such as that for an office present. Someone **on the club** is merely home from work for illness, from the days when workmen contributed to a "club" that paid them benefits when they were too sick to hold a job.

clubland. Generically, the place, people, and attitudes associated with the gentlemen's club;* specifically, Pall Mall.*

clutter. What Americans call junk.

Clyde. A river flowing into a firth* of the same name on the west-central coast of Scotland,* center of that nation's industries including the city of Glasgow.*

CMG. Companion of the Order of St. Michael and St. George,* the lowest rank within the order; the title is often irreverently translated by those who work for a holder as the Call Me God. *See also* GCMG; KCMG.

CND. Campaign for Nuclear Disarmament, since 1958 the major protest organization against not only nuclear arms but all nuclear development.

Co. As in America, an abbreviation for Company. However, this is often used outside of business to mean the usual friends or associates, as in "Ted and Co. robbed the shop," pronounced to rhyme with show. *See also* corporation.

coach. (1) Before WWI, any horse-drawn carriage* large enough for several people and with a permanently enclosed passenger area. The very wealthy, such as royalty,* had a coach where others simply had a carriage* or took a cab.* Public travel over a distance was done by coach, also called a **stage coach** because it traveled in fixed stages; coach passengers sat on the roof among the parcels and mail as well as inside on seats. In the twentieth century, coach has meant a bus,* but usually only a bus serving a long-distance route; thus, in London* one takes a bus from Victoria Station* to Whitehall* but takes a coach from the same point to Windsor.* (2) In the nineteenth, a railway* car was also called a coach, and the term may still be heard in a rail context; however, many, perhaps most, prefer to call the railway passenger car a carriage instead. *See also* post.

coat rail. A place to hang up clothes, what Americans call a coatrack.

Cobb. *See* Lyme Regis.

cobbler. An alcoholic iced drink, most often **sherry cobbler** of sherry, sugar, and orange slices, now rarely seen. *See also* punch.

cobblers. Nonsense, especially a **load of cobblers**.

cobbler's punch. *See* punch.

cock. *See* cocker.

cock-a-hoop. Usually, bragging or excitedly proud, from an idiom of the Shakespearean era related to drunkenness.

Cockaigne. A land of luxury and idleness, from a gypsy word and not related in any way to cocaine except by similar pronunciations; sometimes ironically applied to the East End* from its similarity to Cockney.*

cockaleekie. A Scottish soup of chicken and leeks.*

cock a snook. A vulgar and insulting gesture, roughly equivalent to the American "give the finger," made by putting the thumb against the nose and wiggling the fingers of the hand in the direction of the person to be insulted. *See also* V.

cocker. In Cockney* slang, a fellow, sometimes shortened to cock, especially **old cock**.

Cocker. Author of a widely used seventeenth century textbook on arithmetic; hence, **according to Cocker** means accurate, precise, obvious.

Cockfosters. Formerly a village, now a suburb on the northern edge of Greater London;* as the last stop on the Piccadilly Line of the Underground,* it is sometimes a metaphor for the beginning of the countryside. In recent years, it has been associated with the British version of organic, New Age life-styles, but this image is still tentative.

cockle. (1) A tiny shellfish, rarely sold in recent years, but once common from pushcart sellers; a **cockleshell** is a small boat that is almost as fragile as the shell of such a creature. (2) A small purple wildflower. (3) No one knows for certain what the **cockles of the heart** are, but if they are warm, then you are extremely happy.

cock loft. An attic room.

Cockney. Originally, a native of London,* assumed to have been born within the sound of Bow Bells* at St. Mary-le-Bow in Cheapside,* but since the population explosion of the nineteenth-century applied to the natives of the East End*. The name is generally explained as a sixteenth century insult comparing the Londoner to the cocker, a misshapen or frail egg or chicken, implying runtiness and/or effeminacy, but the locals took it as a point of pride. By the nineteenth century, Cockneys had developed a clearly identifiable accent* and a unique and all but incomprehensible local jargon built around rhyming slang.* Stereotypical Cockneys are short, thin people with combative, independent attitudes, lovers of gin, music, and small-time crime, of whom *Pygmalion*'s Alfred Doolittle is merely the best-known example. The modern Cockney is not necessarily purely English, with East End accents and attitudes now shared by Jews,* second-generation Blacks*, and numerous other groups that have squeezed into the area, but the Cockneys still tend to see themselves as a breed apart.

cock-up. A mess, a disaster, military slang in the 1920s, passing into general use after WWII.

coconut shy. A popular booth at fairs* and fêtes* in which you throw a ball at coconuts on stands in an attempt to knock them over; originally you kept the ones you hit, but now that they are less exotic, other prizes may be given, and the targets may be things other than coconuts.

cod. (1) A slang term for a parody or a hoax. (2) In Shakespeare's time, a standard term for the scrotum (hence the **codpiece** in men's dress of the time) and from that the name of a purse or sack holding valuables; it became a vulgar term in the nineteenth century and is rarely heard now.

codswallop. General slang meaning nonsense.

C of E. Abbreviation of Church of England.*

coffee. Coffee* arrived in Britain before tea* and initially had more impact, particularly through the immense popularity of the coffee house,* but by 1800 the fad had declined, and most of the coffee houses had changed into clubs* or faded away. Even at the height of the fad, coffee had been expensive and never really made any inroads among the gin* and beer* drinkers, and by the 1830s, when cheap tea first appeared and almost immediately became the respectable drink of all classes,* coffee all but disappeared from public view. It continued to be served at the tables of the wealthy, usually only at breakfast* or after meals, as even the wealthiest succumbed to the British use of tea for any and every occasion. Until very late in the twentieth century, coffee was both comparatively expensive and particularly vile, even by American percolator standards, almost always made by simply boiling the grounds in a saucepan or, even worse, boiling instant coffee when that became available. In recent years creeping Americanization as well as increasing contact with continental cuisines has put coffee on the table regularly in most middle class* households and restaurants, although it is still expensive; in another decade it is foreseeable that coffee will be yet another class divide, with tea drinking confined only to the lower classes.

coffee house. From the Restoration until the late eighteenth century, the coffee houses were the center of social life in London.* They served coffee and hot chocolate,* rarely any alcohol, but all men of wealth and/or education frequented the hundreds of these establishments, treating them almost as clubs, trading news and gossip or making political and business deals. They were the effective center of all literary life of the time. After almost a century, fashion eventually moved on to other fields, such as the resort spas, the gentlemen's club,* and the pub,* and the coffee house all but disappeared. *See also* gin; tea.

Coke. Edward Coke's numerous *Reports* and *Institutes* (1600–44) that codified common law* and were influential in establishing the English reverence for law itself as a sign of liberty.

colcannon. A version of bubble and squeak.*

Colchester. A large town in eastern England,* the oldest recorded town in Britain,* with strongest associations to the Roman era, as in *Cymbeline*.

Coldbath Fields. A prison* in London* in Clerkenwell* (1794–1889), very strict even for its time, with no speaking allowed among any of the prisoners.

cold dish/plate. A meal that is not heated before eating, usually including slices of cold cooked meat. In the twentieth century, this has been a traditional evening meal for the single person of the middle class* and above when dining at home, because it could be prepared and left by the char,* as people of that class could not be expected to cook for themselves. More recently, attitudes have changed to the extent that most single persons do at least some cooking, and the cold dish is eaten more as a matter of choice than of necessity and is often called a salad* instead.

cold store. What Americans call a freezer.

Coldstream Guards. Technically, the oldest standing regiment* in the army,* formed in 1661 from a remainder of Cromwell's army to guard Charles II, and still one of the regiments guarding the monarch, with a distinguished battle record as well.

Coliseum. A theater in London* near Trafalgar Square,* since 1968 home to the ENO* but prior to that known for relatively mindless extravaganzas.

college. (1) As with most things educational in Britain, this term is widely variable. Basically, a college is simply a community of scholars. Most often this means one of the various independent schools within the university* at Oxford,* Cambridge,* or similar institutions. Theoretically, the purpose of such colleges is study rather than education, and thus the members, or fellows,* of each college pursue their own studies and only deal with any scholars who might wish to join them by means of a tutorial system rather than in groups in classrooms; they may occasionally give lectures, but these are much more like reading research papers than the American class lecture—the lectures are open to anyone, and students are not tested on them. While a student's degree* may be from Oxford, the student always studies and lives at a specific college, each of which is independently financed and administered and operates by its own unique rules and requirements. A college can also be any other school of higher education, although before the nineteenth century these were usually called academies.* This type of college tends to be more similar to the American college, with regular classes and tests, et cetera, although as always there are exceptions. Nor does the term automatically denote higher education; many of the earliest colleges were for teen-aged boys, and thus a number of the oldest public schools,* such as Eton* or Winchester,* were (and are sometimes still) called colleges, while other public schools, such as Cheltenham,* added college to their names in the nineteenth century to imply more status, and still others, such as Dulwich* College, are ancient grammar schools.* (2) The oldest meaning is a company of colleagues, and as such the term is used for many groups unrelated to education, such as the **College of Arms**, which records the official pedigree and heraldry* for the nobility,* or professional organizations such as the Royal College of Surgeons,* and sometimes for hospitals or asylums that treated particular groups of patients.

colleger. *See* oppidan.

collywobbles. Stomach ache or a general queasy feeling.

Colney Hatch. An insane asylum north of Muswell Hill;* the village used this name before the hospital and now calls itself New Southgate.

colonel. The commanding officer of a regiment.* A **lieutenant-colonel** ranks just below a colonel and in theory commanded a battalion.* In practice, this was not always the case; for example, a regiment that consisted of a single battalion was often commanded by a lieutenant-colonel who was still called a colonel, while a regiment of two battalions was often commanded by a brigadier,* who was nonetheless often called the colonel of the regiment. In many ways, there was more status in being a colonel than in being a general, dating from the early days in which a colonel quite literally owned his regiment; when the army* was reorganized in 1881, leaving many surplus colonels, they had to be promoted to major-general, which had a much larger pension, in order to get them to retire, and many nonetheless still called themselves colonels in retirement. In addition, many regiments had a **colonel-in-chief**, an honorary commander drawn from the nobility* or royalty* who never actually served with the regiment on duty; the Royal Scots Greys, for example, fought against the Germans in WWI while nominally under the command of Kaiser Wilhelm, their colonel-in-chief. *See also* Appendix V.

Colonial. Technically, anyone from one of the colonies,* but almost always used only to indicate a person of European descent from that colony. Thus, in practice, this usually means an Australian, New Zealander, or Canadian, and never an Indian, a Chinese from Hong Kong, or a Jamaican. The term is also used to indicate people from Britain who have spent time in part of the Empire, especially India, Africa, or the Far East.

Colonial Office. The ministry* responsible for administration of all affairs in the various colonies* from 1854 to 1966. *See also* Commonwealth Office.

colony. There are technical legal differences between colony, dominion,* and protectorate,* but most usage outside the civil service* treats all overseas possessions or former possessions the same and calls them colonies. *See also* crown colony.

colour bar. Not a well-decorated pub* but rather a regulation that excludes persons from a place or activity on grounds of race.

coloured. Indicating any person not European, thus including Asians and persons of mixed blood as well as Blacks.* Currently, less than 5 percent of the British population fit into this category. *See also* immigrant.

colours. A flag. British military units carry two colours, the monarch's (the Union Jack*) and their own individual unit's colours. On the regimental colours are often **battle honours**, names of battles in which the regiment did outstanding service. These are not simply added after a battle but are real honours* granted to the unit as a whole by the monarch, often years later; the 2nd Foot, for example, did not receive its battle honour for Tangier 1662 until 1909. *See also* trooping the colour.

colour supplement. *See* Sunday supplement.

-combe. *See* coomb.

combinations. (1) For men, underwear covering legs as well as torso, similar to what Americans call long underwear or long johns. (2) For women, any underwear item combining two normally separate pieces, most commonly since the 1890s meaning a chemise and knickers* together (in the 1920s called step-ins*) but also used sometimes for a unit combining bodice and petticoat or knickers and petticoat.

come down. To leave Oxford* or Cambridge* for vacation or graduation. In general, a student says he will go down, a parent says he will come down. *See also* down; send down.

come of age. *See* minor.

come out. Used to indicate that an upper class* girl is now in the market for a marriage proposal, from the common practice of her coming out of the home for a round of balls,* parties, and similar social functions in the dress and manner of a woman rather than of a girl during the Season.* The term arose among the highest levels of society in the late eighteenth century, when the official mark of its beginning was formal presentation at court;* after 1958 even the upper class was no longer formally presented, the debut marked instead by Queen Charlotte's Ball in May. Recently, this meaning has been crowded out in general usage by "to announce one's homosexuality in public," imported from the American "coming out of the closet."

come over. As in America, Britons will say, "What's come over you?" to indicate a sudden change in mood or circumstances, but they will also use the term about themselves, as in "I come over all queasy" (in the upper middle classes "I came over all queasy"), to indicate they have had a sudden change in feeling.

comers. *See* all comers.

comforter. (1) Not a quilt or a down-filled bed covering, but a woolen scarf. (2) For a baby, the thing Americans call a pacifier.

commandant. Not an official rank in any British military* services, but used to indicate the commanding officer* of any particular place, no matter what the rank involved.

commander. In the navy,* the rank below captain,* the officer* commanding a midsized ship, now usually a destroyer or submarine, in the sailing era usually a sloop; roughly equivalent to an army* lieutenant-colonel.*

commas, inverted. *See* inverted commas.

commems. At a university,* annual celebrations in honor of a particular college's* founders.

commercial bank. This is the kind of bank* most Americans associate with the term, a place where numerous customers deposit funds, write checks, and take out loans. There are only eleven of these in all of Briton, and the business is really controlled by only four: Barclays, Midland, Lloyds, and National Westminster; each has numerous branches throughout the nation. Traditionally, these banks were extremely conservative and made no loans for longer than five years (home loans were done through building societies*), although in the 1980s they became more aggressive, taking smaller deposits, issuing credit cards, and so on. Also called a **joint-stock bank**.

commercial traveller. *See* traveller.

commission. To the modern American, one of the oddest aspects of nineteenth century army* life was that officers* bought their commissions. Basically, each regiment* was a form of free enterprise, each unit in effect "owned" by its officers. They bought in, lived on their pay (and any family income) while serving, and then sold up, using the capital returned to finance their retirement. Unfortunately, although this produced a cheap army, it did not produce an efficient officer corps, and during the 1871 reforms the government* in essence bought the army from its officers, paying out about £7 million to buy up all the commissions. Since then, promotions have been determined by a combination of seniority and merit, as in most other armies.

commission agent. A bookmaker.

commissionaire. After 1859, one of a group of men, usually ex-soldiers, licensed as public messengers and odd-job men, distinguished by a unique uniform; in the twentieth century, the term was applied to any men with similar uniforms and now almost always means a doorman at a hotel, theatre, or other public building. Not to be confused at any time with commissioner.*

commissioner. A government officer in charge of a specific job or department. For example, in the Metropolitan Police,* the chief executive is the Commissioner, an administrative post that has no direct function in crime-solving (which is why the older Appleby in Michael Innes's novels had to find so many mysteries on vacation); however, all county* police forces are headed by a Chief Constable* instead.

commissioner of oaths. Similar to what Americans call a notary public, a person who administers oaths and affidavits for legal purposes.

committee. Naturally, the British have committees within business and government who have the same functions of delay and obfuscation as in America, but they also use the term to mean a charitable organization.

commodore. A naval officer above a captain.* Unlike the American navy, this is rarely a permanent rank but is more like the nineteenth-century army brigadier,* to which it is roughly equivalent, a temporary rank which a captain might be given for particular duty, such as commanding a small squadron.*

common. (1) A piece of land held or used in common by the inhabitants of a parish* or town.* Before the Norman invasion, such land was open range where all the villagers grazed flocks, cut wood, and so on, and no one "owned" it. After the Normans came, all land was ostensibly owned by the local lord,* but the practice continued of allowing access to specific portions always treated as commons. In the burst of agricultural prosperity and commercial sheep raising of the eighteenth and nineteenth centuries (See enclosure), the commons began to disappear as the local lords enclosed, or fenced, the land. This brought great hardship to the rural poor and encouraged the revival of complex, and often quaint, customs to try to prevent the land being taken by individuals (See beating the bounds). But the commons continued to disappear even faster as suburban development grew, so that by the mid–twentieth century the common, except in the mountainous regions of the north and west, had become little more than a large public park. The Commons Registration Act of 1965 was intended to protect the commons but in practice allowed all commons not properly registered to be lost forever. Commons are usually unkempt and unlandscaped, a far cry from the neat little greens of New England villages called commons, but they are hardly wild countryside; inhabitants now fight to preserve them not to maintain food or fuel for the poor but to save some greenery and open space. Many do have some sections apportioned for food-growing in allotments.* The term is used only in England* and Wales.* *See also* green; right-of-way. (2) A term used generally by the lower middle class* or respectable working class to indicate someone or something that is not respectable, particularly applied to women who are loud, gaudy, or a bit promiscuous. The term doesn't necessarily mean lower class and may be applied even to aristocrats, but it is an epithet almost always used only by those most desperate not to be taken for common people themselves.

Common Entrance Exam. A test used jointly by most public schools* for admissions; not related to the eleven-plus,* GSE,* or GCSE* exams.

commoner. (1) A person not of the nobility.* This may, however, include persons of noble blood, as any children of nobility not having a title in their own right are considered to be commoners; thus, enormous numbers of commoners trace, or claim to trace, their family trees to the nobility without any change in their commoner status. (2) In some of the older universities,* a member of the commons.* A **fellow commoner** was a student whose wealth and social status qualified him to dine with the fellows,* especially at Cambridge;* at Oxford* these were called **gentlemen commoners**. By the late nineteenth century, gentleman commoner was also used for an empty bottle, from the assumption that these wealthy students were empty headed. *See also* fellow.

common law. The basic law of the nation, but developed from custom and precedent and thus distinct from the law laid down by specific statute. Most British legal cases deal with common rather than statute law. *See also* Common Pleas; Chancery; High Court.

Common Pleas. Courts trying cases under the common law* between two civil opponents; in 1881, superceded by the High Court.*

common room. In schools* at various levels, what Americans might call the faculty lounge or faculty room, a place where teachers may go for relaxation, conversation, and perhaps tea* or coffee.* The **senior common**

room is reserved for the senior members, at colleges* usually meaning the fellows* who may vote in the institution's self-government, but varying from one place to the next, basically what Americans would call a faculty lounge. **Junior common rooms** are for the college students.

commons. In some colleges,* meals taken in common or provided for members or students at a fixed charge. Hence, **short commons** means a shortage of food, sometimes in the twentieth century extended to any essential of which the speaker has been been deprived, especially sex.

Commons. House of Commons.*

Commonwealth. (1) A loose association of independent countries who were formerly colonies* or dominions* of Britain. The term first appeared after WWI and was formalized in 1931; most former colonies chose to remain members after gaining independence. Members pass their own laws and are in no way under British jurisdiction except that they all voluntarily pledge allegiance to the Crown.* (2) The term used for the government during the rule of Cromwell from 1649–60.

Commonwealth Games. A competition similar to the Olympics, played among athletes from Commonwealth* nations at four year intervals halfway between the Olympics.

Commonwealth Office. A short-lived ministry* formed in 1966 by merging the Colonial Office* and the Commonwealth Relations Office,* in 1968 again merged with the Foreign Office* to form the new Foreign and Commonwealth Office.*

Commonwealth Relations Office. The 1947 replacement for the Dominions Office,* administering relations with the various members of the Commonwealth.*

communion. Members of the Church of England* are expected to take communion three times a year, always including Easter.* Each parish* priest may offer communion at various services besides Easter at his discretion, but it must be announced at least one Sunday before, the partakers must notify the priest of their intent, and the priest may refuse communion to one who has "grave and open sin without repentance." *See also* matins.

community charge. *See* poll tax.

community council. In Wales,* the equivalent of a parish council.*

Companion. *See* honours.

company. (1) In the army,* a unit within a battalion.* Before the twentieth century, each battalion had eight to twelve companies, each commanded by a captain* and containing about 100 men. Major reorganizations in early twentieth century meant that battalions had only four companies, each with 200–250 men, commanded by a major* or a captain with seniority. (2) *See* livery company. (3) *See* corporation. (4) *See* Co.

Company. The East India Company.*

comprehensive. A tax-supported secondary school* that takes all students from about age eleven to eighteen and offers a broad mix of subjects like the typical American junior high and high school. These are relatively new, dating from a major overhaul of the educational system between 1965 and 1972, but by the late 1980s, about 90 percent of students in this age group were in comprehensives (almost 100 percent in Scotland*). However, this has not been an unmixed blessing, as practically all levels of society criticize the quality of education actually received in the comprehensives. The fundamental assumption behind the comprehensive movement was to avoid categorizing children at the age of eleven (*See* eleven-plus) and to provide a program of study in which students who might be behind at age eleven could still have a chance to move into collegiate preparation at a later time; the practice has been to allow many who would have been forced into the grammar schools* in the past to now avoid more academic subjects and to encourage parents with any income at all to move the cream of students to public schools.* The tensions are similar to those in America under the pressure of integration, but race is less an issue than are class* and politics: Most of the comprehensives opened in the 1960s with teachers who are perceived in many circles as sixties oriented and aggressively left-wing, more concerned with inculcating politically correct attitudes than teaching traditional coursework. Some local authorities divide their comprehensives into a "junior" comprehensive and a "senior" comprehensive, the exact dividing age varying from school to school. Some also have completely separate schools for those in sixth form* after school-leaving age, now sixteen. *See also* secondary school.

comptroller. Chief financial officer; the title is found in many government departments and in the royal household* as well.

compulsory purchase. *See* CPO.

concert party. A show, usually like a revue or vaudeville, but not put on in a regular theater.

conditionally discharged. In relation to criminals, the condition Americans call probation.

confectioner's. A shop* that sells candies.

confirmation. A rite in which a person renews and confirms the religious vows made for him or her at baptism and in effect ceases to be a child and becomes a full member of the church.* The Church of England* does this at the age of discretion,* which has varied somewhat but has always been in the early teens. Nonconformist* sects for the most part do not confirm; as they do not recognize infant baptism, the person at this age is baptized for the first time and does not need confirmation. Confirmation is voluntary and thus is a good sign of actual religious participation; by the 1960s only about one third of the English were confirmed in the Church of England.

conker. The deciding game in a three-game match of darts.*

conkers. Horse chestnuts. In the 1870s a schoolboy game appeared, played first with shells and then with horse chestnuts, in which two boys with these chestnuts on strings swung them together to see which one broke first.

Connaught. An expensive hotel and restaurant in London* in Grosvenor Square,* especially associated with wealthy Americans and as a place where TV and film producers "do lunch."

conscription. What Americans call the draft, compulsory enlistment in the military services. Despite a long history of warfare, the British have been notably reticent about conscription. The navy* used a crude form of it during its press gang* period, but it was not used in a nationally organized manner until 1916, two years into WWI, and then only by the army,* and was dropped almost immediately afterward. It was reinstituted in 1939, only for those twenty to twenty-one, expanding to include those nineteen to forty-one the next year, and the next, including single women. After the war, this plan was converted into National Service* and then officially ended in 1960.

consenting adults. Almost always used to mean two males engaged in homosexual practices, unlike in America where it often means adults of both sexes engaged in sexual activities in private.

Conservancy. A governmental authority regulating a port or a river.

Conservative. A political party* formed from the remains of the Tories* after the Reform Bill of 1832 destroyed the old parties. Its general policies have been to retain as much as possible of the traditional legal and social custom of the nation and Empire,* and from the beginning has been associated with wealth and the propertied classes.* Although the clear minority party in the nineteenth century, with very few exceptions Conservatives have controlled the government* since the Liberal* collapse before WWI, and in recent years have come to be more associated with American-style conservatism than traditional British programs through passionate adoption of monetarism, privatisation,* and "free-enterprise" solutions to social problems. *See also* Labour.

conservatory. A room or a separate building in a country house* with large windows on several sides, where plants in bloom were brought from the greenhouse for ornamental display. During the late eighteenth century, the room began to be connected to the main house, often at one end of the drawing room,* and by the late nineteenth in many large houses had come to be the main room for daytime entertainment; in the summer, when night falls very late in most of Britain, the conservatory rather than the drawing room could be used for cards* or coffee* after dinner.* *See also* orangery.

consols. The Funds.*

constable. Originally, the count of the stables and thus a major official of the monarch, usually the commander of the king's army in the king's absence; this position has been ceremonial, as in the **Lord High Constable**, since about Shakespeare's time. Local constables were responsible for raising the men for a local noble's forces, and thus the term came to be applied to local commanders, such as those in castles, and to the chief law enforcer of an area. By the sixteenth century, most parishes had a **petty constable**, such as Shakespeare's Dogberry, who was responsible for keeping the peace, supervising the night watch, and so on, within a specific parish,* and most were known more for their size than for their sophistication or intelligence. They were usually unpaid. As regular police* forces were organized in the nineteenth century, constable became the basic police rank, although parish constables on the old pattern continued until the organizing of county forces in 1872. In the modern force, there are constables in the uniformed division (the bobbies*) and **detective constables** who work in civilian clothes; detectives have the same rank and status as the uniformed branch but must also have two years of uniformed experience before becoming detectives. The literary police constable retained the stereotypes of the old parish constables: big, slow, and slow-witted. In the modern police forces, each particular force (except the London Metropolitan Police*) is administered by a Chief Constable.* *See also* PC.

constituency. Since the 1830s, the people represented by a member* of Parliament.* The British do not talk in terms of voting districts in the American manner: The member represents the people, not the place, so he or she is not required to actually live within the physical boundaries of the constituency and very often does not. Original constituencies were places, however, and had nothing to do with population; counties,* boroughs,* even the universities* elected members without regard to actual population until the Reform Bill of 1832* redefined the concept. Various changes in size and content followed each of the major extensions of the franchise (*See* voting), currently one member for approximately 65,000 voters, and since 1958 a Parliamentary Commission* is required to reconsider constituency boundaries at least once in fifteen years. However, constituencies are still identified by a place name rather than by a number as in American congressional districts, so the member is always the "Member for Such-and-Such." **Marginal constituencies** are not unimportant constituencies but rather the most important—none of the parties has a traditionally large majority in these constituencies, unlike safe seats,* and thus most election* campaigns are really fought and decided there.

constitution. The most significant point about the British constitution is that it doesn't exist. The attitudes and practices often included in the term are simply a mass of customs, habits, assumptions, and myths, most embodied in the common law.* Any new law passed by Parliament* is automatically constitutional.

constitutional. A walk taken for exercise rather than to go somewhere in particular. The gentry* have been doing this for centuries, at least since Charles II set a fashion for such walks, although the term itself seems to have originated in the universities* (the first known citation is Darwin).

Constitution Hill. Originally a path, now a road, running up a slight incline from Buckingham Palace* to Hyde Park.* The name has nothing to do with government or law but comes instead from the regular practice of Charles II, when living in St. James's Palace,* to take a morning stroll along the route for the sake of his constitution.

consultant. A doctor to whom other doctors come for advice or send patients for a second opinion, thus essentially what Americans call a specialist. In a hospital, this is the doctor who is the head of a department. **Consulting Physician** is the title formally preferred. *See also* GP; surgeon.

convalescent home. A place for rehabilitation from injuries or surgery, either private or state-operated, not yet a euphemism for "old folks' home."

convenience. A toilet, most often a **public convenience**.

conveyance/conveyancing. The transferring of deeds concerning real estate; while the estate agent* may arrange the sale, solicitors* arrange the legal paperwork of the process. Curiously, this is one of the few terms that has changed over the years from a synonym for crooked dealing in the seventeenth century into a respectable term by the late eighteenth; most such terms connected with the law move in the other direction.

coo. An interjection roughly equivalent to gee or golly, usually associated with Cockneys.*

cooker. *See* range.

cook-general. Not a chief chef but a servant* who does both cooking and other housework.

Cook's. Thomas Cook began as a travel agent arranging excursions from the provinces to the 1851 Exposition, then expanded by inventing the preplanned and prepaid tour package for continental Europe and later to the Nile that for the first time allowed the middle classes* to travel and sample foreign culture. Thus, Cook's became synonymous with travel, and **Cook's Tour** came to be applied to any quick superficial visit, from the highly organized "If it's Tuesday, this must be Belgium" nature of Cook's packages.

coomb. A small valley running up among coastal hills, also called a **-combe** in place names.

coot. A water bird related to the rail rather than to the duck, basically black in color with a white crest, found wherever there is plentiful water and reeds but for the most part living in the fens* of East Anglia.*

cop. *See* fair cop.

cop it. Americans would usually say "catch it," as in "You'll cop it when your Dad comes home."

copse. A very small wood,* usually larger than a grove.

copyholder. A person who held tenure rights on land for which he had a "copy" of the record, which generally meant he only paid money rather than services to the local lord.* Although dating from the fifteenth century, these copies became very significant in the nineteenth century, when under various Reform Bills* a copyholder was allowed to vote. *See also* yeoman.

cordial. Either a fruit flavoring mixed with water for a soft drink, or sometimes a sweet liqueur.

corespondent. In British divorce* actions, the man with whom the wife (the respondent) is accused of committing adultery. In the mid-twentieth century, when adultery was still the only grounds for divorce, most men even when not adulterous provided their wives with evidence to be used against the husband; however, some refused to do so, in which case a woman wishing to divorce her husband was often forced to provide proof of her own adultery. Some would simply have an affair, but some hired a "professional" corespondent who would, for a fee, check into a hotel with the wife and otherwise provide public evidence of infidelity, without actually having a sexual affair. There was a double edge to the divorce procedure, however: A corespondent could also be liable for damages, but if the husband was charged with adultery and his partner identified (called the woman named* rather than a female correspondent), that woman could not be held liable for damages. **Corespondent's shoes** are two-tone Oxfords,* usually brown and white, so called because of their popularity among the flashy male types who "seduced" married women.

corf. A cage or loosely woven basket used to keep fish alive under water after you have caught them.

corn. In England,* the grain Americans call wheat, a staple used primarily to make bread;* also used generically to mean all grains, as in the Corn Laws,* and in Scotland* or Ireland* to mean oats. What Americans call corn is usually called **maize** or **Indian corn**. However, in recent years, some writers have begun to call wheat *wheat*, so any casual contemporary reference is always open to confusion.

Corn, the. In Oxford,* Cornmarket Street, running north from Carfax* into the corner of Balliol.*

corn dolly. A human figure fashioned from the last sheaf of corn* harvested on a farm or in a parish.* Local custom made these figures in many different shapes and sizes, but the dolly was usually saved as a form of good luck until the next year's corn dolly could be made. As harvest practices changed with urbanization, the ancient festivities of the harvest home* disappeared during the nineteenth century, taking with them the corn dolly, so that in the twentieth century, the dollies are made only as quaint craft items for sale to tourists.

Corner House. Lyons Corner House, a paradigmatic chain of tea* shops, beginning in London in 1894. Only a handful survived into the 1980s, but from the 1920s to 1960s they were ubiquitous. *See also* ABC.

cornet. What Americans call an ice-cream cone.

Cornhill. The major thoroughfare of the City* of London,* connecting Leadenhall* with the Bank of England* and Cheapside.*

Corn Laws. A series of tariffs on wheat (and other agricultural products) beginning in the late seventeenth century, designed to keep out foreign grain and thus also protect the wealth of the country estates. The most restrictive of these were passed in 1815, widely believed to have forced up the price of bread* to a point where the urban poor faced starvation, until their repeal in 1846 following major public agitation related to the potato* famine in Ireland* and the other social unrest sweeping Europe at the time. Conservatives* long saw this repeal as the blow that destroyed British agriculture and made the country dependent on imported foods, and it was certainly a contributing factor in the conversion of many estates to country houses* and the opening of land to suburban* development. *See also* corn.

Cornwall. A county* at the tip of the southwest peninsula of England,* in the Roman era noted for its tin mines, in medieval times said to be the home of Arthur, and in more modern times one of the most independent-minded of all the English counties. Many Cornishmen spoke a form of Gaelic* until about 1900, and the Cornish dialect is still one of the most unusual of the many in the nation. The land itself, as a peninsula, has produced many sailors and smugglers, while its interior is a unique mixture of hilly terrain and fertile valleys, sustained by an exceedingly mild climate that results from the peninsula's extension into the Gulf Stream. In the last century, many of the coastal towns, such as Penzance,* have become popular seaside resorts, but the county has maintained its image of strange, forbidding, mysterious people and places, like Daphne du Maurier's Manderley. *See also* Lancaster, Duchy of.

coronation. The ceremony in which the monarch is formally crowned and thus legally recognized as the ruler. This is one of the most spectacular of public occasions and nowhere more spectacular than in England,* where it is a time of holiday-making for all. At any given time, references to the Coronation will be to the one at the beginning of the current monarch's reign; at present, this means 1953, when Queen Elizabeth II was crowned.

Coronation Street. An extremely popular TV soap opera on ITV* about working class* life in the Lancashire* mill towns.

corporal. In the army,* a noncommissioned officer ranking below a sergeant;* as the British lack the layers of sergeants common in American forces, the corporal is more equivalent to an American sergeant in duties. *See also* Appendix V; lance corporal.

corporation. (1) As in America, a company that is legally treated as a single person, but the more common term is a **limited company**. *See* Ltd. (2) In medieval life, a group of traders who monopolized or controlled their particular trade. (3) From both usages, a body chartered* by the monarch to act as a legal person and govern a borough,* town,* or city,* almost always originally the richest and most powerful traders. The most common one is the **Corporation** that still governs the City* of London.* *See also* Guildhall; Lord Mayor.

Corporation Act. Not a law concerning business organizations but an act of 1661 that made it illegal for nonmembers of the Church of England* to hold public office, not repealed until 1828.

Corpus. Technically, Corpus Christi, one of the colleges* of Oxford.*

Corpus Christi. (1) One of the smallest colleges* of Cambridge.* (2) *See* Corpus.

cortége. A funeral procession.

Cortina. From its introduction by Ford in 1962, the quintessential family car of the middle class;* production ended in 1979.

cosh. (1) A small weapon of various kinds, usually made of heavy rubber or a weighted stick or bag, but small enough to fit in a pocket, used to hit people over the head to knock them unconscious. The term is only about 100 years old and no one has any clear idea where it came from, but the item, in a nation where handguns are both illegal and very rare, has been the primary criminal weapon until very recently. (2) In Scotland,* cozy, snug.

coster/costermonger. Originally a fruit seller, but most often used for the fruit sellers who sold from barrows* in the streets. By mid–nineteenth century, this had come to mean, at least in London,* anyone who sold from a barrow, no matter what the product, and the costermongers were seen as a unique class within the Cockney* community, eventually developing the "formal" dress of suits and dresses covered in buttons called the **pearly** suit.

costume. Not a disguise but a swimsuit, shortened from bathing costume. The costumes Americans wear to parties are usually called fancy dress.*

cot. (1) What Americans call a baby crib; what Americans call a cot is called a **camp bed**. (2) A cottage,* usually only poetic usage.

cote. In Shakespeare's day, a cottage,* but by the nineteenth century this usage had disappeared except in Scotland* and northern England,* and then only in house or place names, replaced by the modern meaning of a small, crude shelter, such as a sheep cote.

Cotswolds. A range of gentle hills in the west-central portion of England,* long associated with sheep and wool and one of the most popular scenic areas of England,* especially for people who go on walking* tours, perhaps most vividly and traditionally described in *Cider With Rosie.*

cottage. (1) Originally, a small house, often of only one room, where farm laborers lived. A **tied cottage** was one that went with a specific job, sometimes rent-free, but which also meant the tenant could not leave the job without losing the cottage. By the mid-eighteenth century, the term cottage was beginning to apply to any small house in the country,* small being a relative term depending on the speaker, so that the cottage might include many rooms and even carriage* houses. By the turn of the twentieth, cottage generally meant a fully detached comfortable little house in or on the outskirts of a village,* sometimes with two floors to distinguish it from a bungalow* but just as often with as few as three rooms on a single floor, and usually partially hidden from view by a garden* on all sides. No longer associated with laborers, cottages were where old people of modest but independent means retired, or what artistic types rented for a short time to get away from it all, or where middle-class unmarried women such as Agatha Christie's Miss Marple lived. Then in the late twentieth century, cottages became fashionable, and now only yuppies and very successful businessmen can afford them. (2) As an adjective, often used to describe something small, rural, or poorly organized, such as a **cottage hospital**, which is like an American clinic.

cottage loaf. A round loaf of bread* formed by two balls of dough, the smaller one stacked on top of the larger before baking.

cottage pie. An alternate name for shepherd's pie.*

cotton wool. Cotton in the form of cotton balls or large, unshaped pads.

council. A locally-elected government unit, such as a parish* council or a county* council. Most of these continue to be unpaid, and modern ones serve a fixed four-year term. The term is also generally used to indicate anything to do with local government, in much the way Americans use City Hall.

council estates. An area of housing developed by a council,* sometimes of council houses,* sometimes apartment blocks.*

council flat. An apartment in a block,* built by and rented from the local council.* These are usually reserved for poorer members of the working class* and often are regarded in the same way Americans regard "projects."

council house. A house rented from, and usually built by, the local council,* almost always working class* housing. Usually, these are either terrace* houses or semi-detacheds.*

councillor. A member of a local council.*

council school. A school* administered by a local council,* essentially what Americans call a public school and now usually meaning a primary school* or a comprehensive,* but in the past including all of the other various forms of tax-supported schools.

counterfoil. Sometimes used for any receipt, but most often it means what Americans called the check stub before computerization eliminated those from most checkbooks.

counterjumper. A shopkeeper* or shop* assistant, almost always only a male.

countess. *See* earl.

country. Any place outside of London.* Where Americans tend to use this to mean someplace where one goes to be in the wilds, or perhaps among farms, the most common usage in Britain for at least two centuries has meant the area where the country houses* are, and thus the country very often applies only to the Home Counties,* where one is still within easy reach of London and where the countryside is anything but wild. Generally, one goes "down" to the country rather than "out" or "off," and goes back "up" to London. However, **going to the country** means holding a national election.* *See also* countryside.

country house. Originally, the country house was just "the house," the place where landed gentry* lived on their property. When the family went up to London,* they rented a house there on a temporary basis, sometimes just for the Season.* But in the late eighteenth century, this began to change. The wealthy manufacturers and professional men thrown up by the industrial revolution looked for a way to demonstrate their new status and almost uniformly chose to join the landed gentry, buying a country estate and remodeling or building a new house on it. For them it became a "country" house, as opposed to their original dwelling, and they would go down to it for weekends or holidays when business allowed, a practice made more convenient by the railroad, often moving the wife and family out to it permanently. Thus, it might have grounds* but no longer was automatically associated with income-producing property.* Thus, unlike the American country house, which is simpler than the main urban home, the British country house was a mansion by modern standards, often much larger and more impressive than the place in London. By the late nineteenth, it had once again become the center of English social life and since then country houses have been synonymous with wealth, glamor, and the life of leisure. The memoirs of people who actually lived in them, however, complain constantly of their cold drafty rooms, lack of such amenities as electricity or heating, appalling expense in servants,* and general inconvenience and isolation. Meanwhile, death duties,* maintenance, and taxes have all taken their toll; the number of old, large-scale country houses has declined with each year, and those that remain are more likely to be owned by lawyers, stockbrokers, or foreigners than by landed gentry. *See also* bungalow; conservatory; cottage; country; estate; garden; grounds; Home Counties; manor; mansion; orangery; terrace; weekend.

Country Life. A magazine since the 1890s devoted to chronicling the gentry's* way of life, possibly more popular in the towns among would-be gentry than among the gentry itself. The most popular features from the beginning were the descriptions and pictures of country houses.*

country park. A small park, usually less than twenty-five acres,* preserved in a natural or seminatural state, for use by the public; similar to a National Park* but much, much smaller.

countryside. This term rather than country* is generally used to mean the agricultural areas of the nation.

county. (1) A regional administrative entity. The name comes from Norman usage for the same thing that the Anglo-Saxons called a shire,* and most people in England* continue to prefer shire for many of the entities to the present day. These were somewhat loosely defined, related to long-since disappeared domains of earls* and/or dukes* during the medieval era, and were administered by sheriffs* and local justices of the peace.* In 1888, the boundaries were stabilized and local county councils* organized for local administration. In 1965, Greater London* was organized as a separate county. Then, in a 1972 law (effective in 1974), all the counties were reorganized, with the number slightly expanded by the formation of several **metropolitan counties** similar to Greater London; thus, currently there are forty-five counties in England* and eight in Wales.* These are in turn divided into **districts**, each of which also has its own council. County government is not centralized; that is, districts and/or parishes* within the counties do not simply administer county policies at the local level but rather have their own separate areas of responsibility. In general, county councils* are responsible for traffic, zoning, education, and social services, while district councils deal with parking, markets, housing, garbage and sewers, and enforcement of licensing laws.* The eight "metropolitan" counties are densely urbanized and governed by district councils rather than by county councils. In 1973, similar reorganization of Scotland* replaced the thirty counties there with nine "regions" and three island "areas," while in Northern Ireland* the six counties remained. London* operates by its own rules. For specific counties, *See* their individual names. *See also* cricket; Home Counties. (2) In the nineteenth century, used as an adjective to indicate the gentry,* who formed a uniform class* in rural areas, united in property* ownership and local culture; by the late twentieth century, however, county has come to be used primarily to indicate those people who claim to be part of such a culture, centered around fox hunting,* riding,* and similar practices, as a form of snobbery.

county court. A civil court established in 1846 for small civil suits, similar to the American small claims court, but now trying the bulk of civil suits with claims up to £5,000.

county school. A tax-supported rural school.*

county town. The town* that is the administrative center of a county.*

courgette. A vegetable Americans usually call a small zucchini; as the name suggests, this is an import from French cuisine and may be regarded as what Americans would call trendy food. *See also* marrow.

coursing. Hunting hares* with hounds.*

court. (1) The activities of the monarch. Thus, **at court** meant in contact with the monarch. *See* chamberlain; Chancellor; come out; Court Circular; drawing room; King; lady-in-waiting; levee; palace; Privy Council; Queen; remembrancer; royal household. (2) *See* assizes; barrister; benefit of clergy; Chancery; common law; Common Pleas; county court; Court of Appeal; Court of Justiciary; Court of Session; Crown Court; District Court; High Court; Inns of Court; judge; Justice of the Peace; KC; King's Bench; magistrate; police court; serjeant; Sheriff; solicitor. (3) At Cambridge,* the open space in the center of each college's* buildings, the same space that is called a quad* at Oxford.

Court Circular. The official daily report of the activities of the monarch.

Court of Appeal. An appeal court* of last resort. However, unlike the American Supreme Court, the Court of Appeal has no authority to overturn laws and is divided into a criminal and a civil division; civil cases are tried by permanent judges (twenty-seven who take cases variously), but criminal cases are heard by High Court* judges appointed case-by-case. *See also* constitution; court.

Court of Justiciary. In Scotland,* the central criminal court, used in major cases and as an appeals court. *See also* sheriff.

Court of Session. In Scotland,* the appellate court* for civil cases.

Court of St. James. *See* St. James's Palace.

Cousin Jack. A native of Cornwall.*

cove. A fellow, generally used only by the urban lower class,* although it has been in use since Shakespeare's time.

covenanters. In Scotland* during the mid–seventeenth century, supporters of the "National Covenant," an attempt to remove all vestiges of Catholic* influence from Scottish religious affairs. The covenanters were the wild card in the Civil War,* their extreme Protestantism at times allying them with Cromwell and at other times with the monarchy and at all times thoroughly confusing all events, with the end result that they were persecuted from all sides for the rest of the century.

Covent Garden. A square in London* in the midst of the West End.* Originally a garden of a convent, the square was first developed as a site for homes for the nobility* in the seventeenth century. A small market* was held in the square, but in 1830 special buildings were raised to house what had grown to be the major vegetable, fruit, and flower market of London. This market, and the proximity of the theaters, made the area a center of after-dark activity no longer suitable for respectable homes; the name was often synonymous with whores. In 1974 the market was closed and a "new" Covent Garden opened on the south side of the Thames;* the old area became a slum until redeveloped into a tourist shopping center. A theater has been on the site since 1732, the most recent one housing the **Royal Opera**, England's primary international opera house, which is often still simply called Covent Garden.

Coventry. A city in the Midlands* of England* just east of Birmingham,* by the medieval era one of England's largest cities and a center of the wool trade and textiles. Declining somewhat after the seventeenth century, it was most noted for its cathedral* until it revived in the late nineteenth century as a major center of armaments and motor vehicle industries, which led to the destruction of most of the city in one of the most prolonged and punishing of all German air raids during WWII. Business almost immediately revived, but the rebuilding made it perhaps the most consistently "modern" city in Britain, including a completely new modern cathedral. Lady Godiva rode here. When someone is **sent to Coventry**, it means that no one will speak to him or her; Royalist prisoners taken in the Civil War* were sent to Coventry, which may be the source of the phrase.

Coventry Street. A short street in London* that connects Piccadilly Circus* and Leicester Square.*

Cowes. A small port on the northern, sheltered side of the Isle of Wight,* one of England's finest small harbors and home to the most significant yacht racing regattas of the nation. The regatta in **Cowes Week** at the end of July is generally seen as the official end of the Season.*

cow parsley. *See* parsley.

cowslip. A small yellow wildflower, much like a primrose.*

CPO. Compulsory Purchase Order, the notice of condemnation used when a governmental authority intends to buy property through eminent domain.

cracker. A party favor of the type that makes a pop when pulled open; also called a popper.* The food Americans call a cracker is called a biscuit.*

cracking. Energetic, lively, a slang term primarily associated with the generation of the 1920s and now rarely heard.

crammer. A secondary school that teaches its students only what is essential to pass an examination, almost always a private school.* Before the age of comprehensives,* these were quite common but were only rarely used to get students into universities,* where admission depended more on fees and social class* than test scores. Instead, crammers were aimed toward various professional schools and academies,* and boys would often be sent to them to get enough information to pass the entrance exams in a much shorter time (and at much less expense) than regular schooling would take. Thus, the crammer was more often the sign of a boy on his way up out of a lower class than it was of a stupid boy who needed extra tutoring.

crazy paving. Irregular flat stones used for garden* paths or patios.

cream. *See* bun; burnt cream; clotted cream; Devonshire; double cream; single cream; tea.

cream bun. *See* bun.

cream tea. *See* tea.

crease. In cricket,* a space eight to ten feet wide behind a line drawn four feet in front of each wicket.* The line itself is called the **popping crease**; when batting, the batsman* must stand within the crease so that his body does not shield the wicket, and he is considered to be inside the crease if he has at least one foot behind the popping crease. When running, the runner is safe if at any point within the crease before the wicket is knocked over. The nonstriker at the second wicket while waiting may stand at any point in the crease but must not block the bowler; as he is considered to be legal if any piece of his equipment is inside the popping crease, he usually stands prepared to run with only the tip of his bat inside the line. The line at the back, which runs through the wicket, is the **bowling crease**, and the bowler* must not cross that line before releasing the ball. Someone **at the crease** is ready to bat, and thus the term is used metaphorically for any situation in which a person is prepared and ready to contest an issue.

crèche. What Americans now usually call a day-care center.

credit slip. At a bank, not a record of a loan but a record of a deposit.

creek. A small inlet or baylet on the seacoast. The small stream Americans often call a creek is usually called a brook.*

crempoy. In Wales,* a pancake,* usually with a filling.

crib. Not a baby bed but a translation students in language class use to cheat with. For the baby bed, *See* cot.

cricket. (1) The uniquely English summer game, with just enough suggestion of baseball to completely confuse the Americans and a unique vocabulary that almost rivals baseball's in complexity but that has penetrated all levels of the language as a source of metaphor and slang. The game itself is simple, but the vocabulary is daunting. Everything starts with two wickets* placed 66 feet apart in the middle of a field; the field may be of any size, although typically it is about 200-yards-long by 120-yards-wide (two baseball fields with foul areas included) and may be rectangular or oval, and the wickets may be placed anywhere within the general vicinity of the center. The space immediately around and between the wickets is called a pitch* (sometimes a wicket), ten feet wide, and the grass there is more carefully tended and more smoothly cut. Eleven players are on each team. The object of the game is to score more runs than the other team, which is done by hitting a ball and running back and forth between the wickets. One team bats, while the other is in the field. For purposes of identification in this explanation we will call the wickets #1 and #2, but they are not so called in the game. The bowler,* whom Americans would call a pitcher, stands behind wicket #2 and bowls,* or throws, the ball to the batsman* standing in front of the wicket #1. If the bowler hits the wicket and knocks off a little piece of wood called a bail* balanced on top, the batsman is out, or dismissed,* and cannot bat any longer. The batsman tries to hit the ball with his bat, swinging with the bat pointed down toward the ground. If he hits the ball anywhere on the field, he may run to wicket #2 and thus score one run; if the fielders have not yet caught the ball and thrown it back into the pitch, he may keep running and return to wicket #1, thus scoring two runs, and he may keep going back and forth if he so desires, scoring another run each time he changes from one wicket to the other. The batsman may also be put out if the ball he hits is caught in the air, or if the ball is thrown to a wicket toward which he is running in time for a fielder to catch it and knock the bail off the wicket before he arrives. However, unlike in baseball, the batsman is not required to run at all if he thinks he may not make it safely. There are no foul balls, and the batsman may run just as far on balls tipped behind him as on balls hit squarely to the front.

The bowler must continue to bowl to the same wicket for six throws, called an over;* thus, if the batsman stops running at wicket #2, he is now standing beside the bowler and cannot bat; a second batsman takes his place at wicket #1 and receives the next bowl. When batsman #2 hits a ball, they both run, exchanging places (but scoring only one run). This continues until one of them is out, at which point the next batsman takes his turn, and so on until all eleven players have batted. At the end of an over, the fielding team must change bowlers and wickets and then bowl to the batsman at wicket #2. Then, after six more throws, the bowlers change again and throw back to wicket #1. No bowler can throw two consecutive overs, but one bowler can bowl alternate overs for the entire match if so desired by the team captain.* The offensive strategy comes from the fact that there are two wickets; the team must plan its lineup so that batsmen can work effectively together, and each batsman must carefully judge not only how likely he is to run safely but whether he should make two runs in order to continue batting or stop at one or three to let the other man bat instead. The defensive strategy comes in using the bowlers wisely so their styles work effectively against the individual batsmen and in placing fielders. Since one player is bowling and a second, called the wicketkeeper,* is behind the batsman (roughly like a catcher in American baseball), only nine other players are available to cover the field; these players can be moved around anywhere on the entire field, depending on how the bowler intends to throw and how they gauge the abilities of the batsman, and may trade places with any other player, which happens regularly when the bowlers change.

Each team bats for an innings,* which is over when all eleven have batted, and then the teams trade places. Matches are traditionally played for two innings, which may mean several days if the teams have any significant skill. The team with the most runs wins, and play stops as soon as that point is reached in the second innings of the second batting team; thus many matches ultimately end with only a one run difference, with several batsmen* not yet batting. If after the first innings the second team is still behind, it may take its second innings immediately; if the team still does not overtake the leaders, the match ends with the winning team having only one innings. There are breaks for lunch* and for tea,* but otherwise no time outs are necessary, as the pace is set entirely by the bowlers. No pinch-hitting or substitutions are allowed. To American eyes, the game is incredibly leisurely, although the actual pace of play is, if anything, faster than baseball or American football, but most matches have scores of several hundred points for each team, which means that there is very little dramatic tension until the closing moments of play. In the late twentieth century, a number of other limits have been developed to produce one-day matches, such as playing a predetermined number of overs, but so far no attempt has been made to remake the game for television. When the game is played to a specific time limit, the match is a draw if the team that is behind at the deadline is still batting and not all players have been dismissed; to avoid this, a team with a large lead may **declare** before it is out and give the other team a chance to bat before it is that team's turn, in hopes that they will all be put out before the deadline and before surpassing the first team's incomplete score.

There is very little special equipment. Traditional uniform consists of white flannel trousers,* a white sweater,* and a small cap, but the game may be played in business suits if the players so desire. Only the wicket-keeper and the batsmen wear gloves and protective pads on the shins and knees, and the wicketkeeper wears no mask. The ball is red leather, similar in construction to a baseball but in size between a baseball and a softball. The batsman uses a bat* with a flat side to hit the ball and when running keeps the bat and pads, as he might be called upon to bat at the other wicket at any time.

There are professional cricket players but not professional clubs* in the sense of American professional teams, and there are no leagues or league standings. However, **first class cricket** is played on a regular basis by teams representing fifteen of the counties* and Oxford* and Cambridge* since 1873, eventually leading to an annual championship match played at Lord's.* Professional players have played on these teams from the beginning, but they played and may still occasionally play alongside amateurs, although most such teams except Oxford and Cambridge became fully professional in the 1960s. Since 1968, county teams have been allowed to have up to two non-British players on each team, and only Yorkshire* still insists all its players must have been born in the county. An England national team is also regularly formed from outstanding players throughout the various counties as required for matches against other national teams. Cricket is played practically everywhere in the summer, and although Americans think of it as an upper-class sport, it is in fact the only pastime (except sex) shared by all classes. The modern rules were stabilized at the public schools* in the nineteenth century, but a recognizable form of the game was played before Shakespeare's time, and the game seems to have worked its way up from the lower classes. Additional vocabulary is extensive, for the most part explained under individual entries: For field positions, *See also* crease; gully; leg; mid off; mid on; silly mid on; slip, stumps. For additional batting terms, *See also* block; boundary; century; duck; for; handle; not out; striker; stroke; willow. For additional bowling terms, *See also* bowl; break; chinaman; googly; wide. For history and culture, *See also* Ashes; Gentlemen vs. Players; match; Oval; Test; Wisden. (2) Metaphorically, fair play; something that is **not cricket** is thus outside the bounds of proper conduct.

cricketer. A person who plays cricket.* *See also* athlete.

crim. con. Criminal conversation, that is, adultery. Before 1857, a husband wishing divorce* had to sue the wife's lover for damages resulting from this before he could begin a divorce action, and the term has continued in use.

crimper. A metal device, usually hot, used to make curls in women's hair, taking various forms and heated in various ways since first introduced in the 1850s; at present, this means what Americans call a curling iron.

crimplene. Technically a particular brand of polyester fabric but often used generically for all such materials.

crisps. What Americans call potato chips.

crock. Something old or worn out; hence, **crocked** is broken down, rather than the American slang usage meaning drunk, and a **bit of a crock** is someone who is always ill, while an **old crock** is something very old, such as a vintage car driven in the Old Crock's Race.

Crockford. *Crockford's Clerical Directory*, the annual almanac of the Church of England* clergy.*

Crockford's. From 1827–43, the most fashionable gambling club* in London,* revived as a ritzy casino club under contemporary gambling laws.

crocodile. A line of schoolchildren, usually in motion. The most common form is with children walking in pairs holding hands.

croft. In Scotland,* a small farm, usually held by a hereditary tenant and providing little more than subsistence. A **crofter** is such a tenant, almost always a Highland* Scot, usually seen as extremely poor and gruff. **Crofting** is a system in which the tenants of several crofts share grazing rights on nearby space, usually the nonarable hillsides. *See also* Clearances.

crookie. Slang for a sixpence,* from the coin's propensity to bend.

cross bencher. In Parliament,* members of third parties. There aren't really any benches running across the space between government* and opposition* benches in the Commons;* cross-benchers get their name from the few such benches in the House of Lords.*

Crossroads. A popular TV soap opera.

crossword. The typical British crossword, exemplified by the daily puzzle in the *Times*, uses puns, anagrams, and allusions for its clues and is much more difficult than the American form that uses simple synonyms.

crown. A coin worth a quarter of a sovereign,* or five shillings,* gold when first issued in 1526, changed to silver in mid–sixteenth century, and in use until 1971, but remaining in circulation with a value of 25 new pence.* The

half-crown, worth 2½ shillings, was much more common. *See also* Appendix I; piece.

Crown. Not so much the person as the authority of the monarch, thus signifying the government* of the nation. The Cabinet* and Prime Minister* actually rule now, but they do so as nominal representatives of the monarch; thus those parts of the national government that represent the entire nation, traditional policies, or public services rather than party* policies or maneuverings are often called the Crown.

crown and anchor. A gambling game similar to bingo.

crown colony. A colony* ruled directly by a governor* responsible to the monarch.

Crown Court. The modern criminal court* for England* and Wales,* serving the entire nations. However, it deals only with about 3 percent of criminal cases, those involving "serious" crimes (murder, rape, robbery) and rehearings of cases on appeal and has been in existence only since 1971, when it replaced the old assizes* and quarter sessions.* *See also* magistrate; High Court.

crown jewels. The crown and regalia worn only at coronations and other large jewels owned by the monarch, kept on display in the Tower.*

crown lands. Lands actually owned personally by the King* or Queen,* in 1761, George III ceded the income* from these (with the exception of the duchies of Cornwall* and Lancaster*) to Parliament* in return for the annual payment of a Civil List,* and each monarch since has done the same at the beginning of his or her reign.

Croydon. A suburb far to the south of London,* synonymous with faceless commuters.

cruet. A set of holders or dispensers for salt, pepper, and mustard, basic outfitting for every table outside the upper class;* the lower in the social scale one goes, the more likely to find a container of vinegar as well, due to the practice of pouring vinegar on chips.*

Cruft's. The major dog show of England,* held annually in late January or early February in London.*

crumpet. (1) A flat cake,* something like what Americans call an English muffin (which does not exist in England* under that name), almost always toasted before being eaten with melted butter. (2) A sexually available girl; sometimes the sex act itself with such a girl.

crutch. Not something you use when you break a leg, but what Americans call the crotch.

cry off. To cancel an appointment.

crystallized fruit. What Americans call candied fruit.

Crystal Palace. An enormous building primarily of glass and steel erected in Hyde Park* in London* for the Great Exhibition of 1851; the symbol of modernity in its time, it was disassembled after the exhibition and moved to a park in Bromley* where it remained as an architectural curiosity and an amusement park until burned down in 1936. Most of its exhibits were used to form the core of the V & A.*

CSC. Conspicuous Service Cross. *See* DSC.

CSE. Certificate of Secondary Education, a test given students in comprehensive* schools who do not take the more traditional GCE* O-levels* at about age sixteen. *See also* GCSE.

cuckoo. A common bird in the spring and summer, somewhat smaller and more mottled brown than the American version; its song is so distinctive it has entered the language, but it is also distinguished by leaving its eggs in the nests of other species; after hatching, the young cuckoos throw the babies of the nest builder out of the nest.

Culloden. A moor* near Inverness* in Scotland,* site of a battle in 1746 in which "Bonny Prince Charlie" was defeated and with him the Highland* clans,* effectively ending not only Stuart claims to the throne but all attempts at Scottish independence.

Cumberland. A county* in the far northwestern corner of England* right along the Scottish border. The area is mountainous, containing the bulk of the Lake District,* and was primarily used for sheep grazing and border warfare with the Scots before the rise of modern tourism. In 1974, it was subsumed in the new county of Cumbria.*

Cumbria. (1) An ancient kingdom in what is now northwestern England.*
(2) Since 1974, a county* in the northwestern corner of England, bordering
on the Irish Sea* and Scotland,* made up of the older counties of Cumberland* and Westmorland,* the countryside of the Beatrix Potter books.

cup. When used as a measurement, the British cup is ten ounces, rather
than the American eight ounces. *See also* pint.

Cup. Officially the Challenge Cup, the national championship in football,*
beginning in 1871. Since 1923, the final has been in Wembley* Stadium,
usually in early May, and for most of the century has been treated with
the same national attention and semireligious fervor as the more recent
American Super Bowl. The Cup is unique, however, in that all teams in
the Football Association* play in competition without reference to their
league standings, so it works as a separate tournament that runs parallel
to but independent of the other football matches. *See also* replay.

cupboard. Originally, what Americans call a closet. However, in the twentieth century this term is also used for what Americans call a cabinet, as
in a kitchen cupboard or a drinks cupboard. **Fitted cupboards** are what
Americans call built-in cabinets. In the eighteenth century, **closet** was also
used for a small room, but this dropped from general use during the nineteenth century, probably through its constant association with water closet
(WC*). *See also* wardrobe.

cuppa. A cup of tea.

curate. In a general sense, any priest.* In England,* however, the term
usually is much more specific, since about 1700 meaning an assistant to the
parish* priest. The curate is an ordained clergyman and sometimes would
actually assume all of the priest's duties, in which case he might also be
called a vicar,* just as sometimes the vicar might be called a curate because
he assists the nonresident priest. Curates are almost always unmarried,
although they are not required to remain single, except perhaps by poverty.
Similarly, clergy are not required to serve for a few years as a curate before
becoming rectors,* although some do, and a curate may in fact stay a
curate all his life and be much older and more experienced than the priest
he assists. They are also proverbially mild and accepting, from which a
magazine cartoon in the early twentieth century showing a curate eating
a spoiled egg because it was "good in parts" led to the use of **curate's egg**
to mean anything that has some usable part no matter how small. The
curate's assistant, however, is not an assistant curate but a small cake*
stand, usually with three tiers, used during afternoon tea.* *See also* cure.

curd. *See* lemon curd.

cure. The oldest meanings of cure, now obsolete, were a charge, duty, or responsibility. Hence, a priest who was said to have the cure of a parish,* or the **cure of souls**, was not a faith healer but simply the clergyman assigned to the parish. Although by the nineteenth century curate* took on a more specific meaning, any rector was still said to have the cure of a parish.

curlew. In Britain much the same as American curlews, marsh and shore waders with long, narrow, curved bills. However, the **stone curlew** is not the same species but rather is a small land bird similar to the plover that nests in sand or chalk and feeds at night in meadows, present only in summers.

currant. What Americans call a raisin, although in recent years the term raisin is coming more into use. *See also* sultana.

curricle. A carriage* with only two wheels pulled by two horses side-by-side.

curry. Originally, a yellowish spicy powder or sauce to flavor food, particularly mutton, borrowed from the Indians by the colonists of the early nineteenth century. By mid–nineteenth century, the term had come to be used much more loosely as any spicy meat dish, often accompanied by chutney* and rice. In the twentieth, it continued in use in the original sense in Indian restaurants, but it also gradually came to mean practically any meat and sauce dish served over rice, of any color and even with mild or no spice, and is often treated as a "fast food" or a takeaway.* *See also* vindaloo.

curtain rail. What Americans call a curtain rod.

custard. This has nothing to do with what Americans or the French call custard. Since the first commercial version appeared in 1837, it has been a sauce made from cornstarch, sugar, and milk and then poured over puddings,* pies,* or (it sometimes seems) practically anything else. *See also* HP Sauce; lemon curd; salad cream.

custody suite. Modern police* euphemism for a jail cell.

custom. In trade,* customers and sales.

cut. In cricket,* what baseball players would call a foul tip, a swing in which the ball glances off the bat to the rear of the wicket;* this is, however, still in play and the batsman* can run or can be put out if it is caught in the air. A **square cut** is one that goes to the off* side of the field, while a **late cut** is one that goes almost straight back, also called a skink;* one that goes to the batsman's, or leg,* side is called a **glance**.

cutaway. A man's coat that fit the torso, sometimes single-breasted and sometimes double-breasted, and extended to about knee-length in the back, but in the front the skirt was cut back to expose all or part of the trousers beneath. These first appeared under the name in the 1840s, based on earlier riding jackets, but became standard dress during the late nineteenth century in two forms, the **swallow-tail**, in which the entire front section was cut away at the waist, and a version often called a morning coat* that was cut away in a curve that ran from the center-waist to the side of the knee.

cutlet. *See* chop.

cut-throat. An old-fashioned straight razor.

cutting. (1) A right of way dug out of a hillside, originally for railroads but now sometimes applied to roads, made so that the roadbed could be relatively flat in hilly country. (2) An item cut from magazines or newspapers,* what Americans usually call a clipping.

cut up. Extremely sad, what Americans usually call broken up; however, to **cut up rough** is to become angry or violent. The American cut-up, meaning someone who cracks jokes, is rarely used.

cyclostyle. A duplicating machine similar to what Americans called a mimeograph before the photocopier displaced it.

D

d. Abbreviation for pence* (from the Roman *denarius* on which the penny was modeled); when the currency was decimalized in 1971, this was changed to p.* *See also* Appendix I; s.

DA. A "duck's arse" haircut, what Americans in the time of Elvis Presley called a duck tail, almost always associated with the young working class.*

dab hand. Someone who is extremely skilled, used primarily in northern England* and Scotland.*

dabs. What Americans call fingerprints.

Dad's army. A humorous nickname for the Home Guard,* widely disseminated by a popular TV comedy series of that title in the 1970s.

daft. Stupid, but usually in the sense of silly or thoughtless; generally used by people from Scotland* and northern England.*

Dagenham. A town just east of London,* generally associated with the working class* and autos from the Ford factories there.

daily. A servant,* almost always a woman, who comes in daily to clean but lives elsewhere. *See also* char.

dainty. As a noun, anything small and unusually tasty, in the twentieth century usually confined to small pastries such as are served at tea* shops.

dale. A large valley without significant stands of trees or shrubbery; used particularly in northern England* to indicate such a valley with a river running through. The **Dales** are a series of such valleys in the Pennines* of the western part of North Yorkshire,* now a National Park.* *See also* dell; vale. However, "the Dales" was *Mrs. Dale's Diary*, a popular BBC* radio soap opera ending in 1969, noted for a genteel* world in which nothing serious ever happened and for its regular opening line: "I'm very worried about Jim."

Dame. (1) A female honorary rank equivalent to a knight.* This title is never used for a knight's wife, who is called Lady So-and-so rather than Dame So-and-so; similarly, while the wife of an honorary knight automatically becomes Lady So-and-so, the Dame's husband continues to be simply a Mr. *See also* honours. (2) The comic woman in a pantomime,* always played by a man. A typical Dame role might be Cinderella's stepmother.

damp course. In a building, a layer of insulation, usually over the foundation, designed to prevent rising damp.*

dampers. What Americans would call biscuits made from unleavened flour and water, favored by Scouts.*

Darby and Joan. A club for the elderly, from the idealized elderly couple in a song published in 1735; also used for any elderly couple, and in the military for a pair thought to be homosexual.

dark lantern. Not a lantern that has gone out but one that has a screen that could be dropped to temporarily hide the light.

Dartmoor. (1) A forbidding area of high moor* in southwest England* between Plymouth* and Exeter,* now a National Park.* The area is a strange mixture of rocky hills, barren wasteland of heather or gorse,* peat* bogs, and swamps, and although it was originally called a forest,* trees are relatively sparse. It is used primarily for sheep grazing, though there is also a famous breed of wild pony that lives there. Thus, it is often treated as a desert, even though it is if anything wetter than many other portions of the island. Doyle's depiction of its look and feel in *The Hound of the Baskervilles* is accurate. The prison* in the center since 1850 has been long regarded as one of the most secure prisons, due to its location, so the most dangerous criminals are sent there. *See also* Princetown.

Dartmouth. (1) A small port on the south coast of England* near Plymouth,* once quite prominent for its unique harbor that is almost completely enclosed by land, now primarily a tourist resort. (2) Technically, the Royal

Navy College in Dartmouth, the primary educational center for navy*
officers.

darts. The most common, stereotypical pub* game. However, we should
note that darts are not merely played in pubs but are a nationally televised
sport as well. Competitive darts is far more complex than the "hit the
bullseye" form played by casual Americans, with typical games played to
501 or 301 points and the winner required to zero out exactly while also
landing on a "double point" spot on the final throw.

dash. (1) When used as an expletive, as in "**dash it** all" or "**dashed** surprised," generally associated only with fatuous gentlemen* of the Bertie
Wooster type, although it has been in use since about 1810. It derived from
the dash usually printed to avoid the word damn (**d—n**) and has always
been relatively mild as swear words go. (2) In the 1930s, a drink found in
milk bars,* made from a glass of milk with a small amount, or dash, of
coffee poured into it.

dates. The British write dates in the continental manner (day, month, year),
as in 20 June or 20/6/90. For historical dates, *See* calendar.

day boarder/boy. In boarding schools,* a student who takes classes at school
but lives at home nearby. *See also* oppidan; out-college; public school.

daylight robbery. An outrageous price or service charge.

day school. A private* or public school* at which the students do not board
but rather go home to their parents each evening after classes.

day-tripper. Someone on a holiday or trip for only one day.

DBE. Dame of the Order of the British Empire,* female equivalent of
KBE.* *See also* Dame; honours.

DC. Detective Constable.*

DCA. Due care and attention; one can be arrested for driving without this,
that is, for reckless driving. *See also* banned.

DCB. Dame Commander of the Order of the Bath,* female equivalent of
KCB.*

DCI. Detective Chief Inspector. *See* Inspector.

DCM. Distinguished Conduct Medal, awarded in the military not for good conduct but for gallantry under fire, roughly comparable to the DSO* but given only to other ranks.*

DCMG. Dame Commander of the Order of St. Michael and St. George,* female equivalent of KCMG.*

deacon. (1) In the Church of England,* a clergyman who usually has not yet been ordained but who may assist the priest at communion* and who often deputizes for the priest in charitable works. In general, a deacon is a priest in training, serving for at least a year before ordination. (2) In the Church of Scotland,* a lay member of a local church* who, with other deacons, is responsible for the secular affairs of the church. *See also* clergy.

dead. Absolutely or very; Americans use it still in a few idioms, such as "dead tired," but Britons use it much more widely. **Dead slow** on street signs means drive as slowly as possible. Something extremely boring or monotonous is **dead-and-alive**; something particularly stupid or useless is a **dead loss**.

dead stock. On farms, the machinery, as opposed to the livestock.

deaf aid. The instrument Americans call a hearing aid.

deal. Since the eighteenth century, the wood Americans call pine or fir, from an older usage for a plank of specific size, most often cut from such woods. Thus, a **deal table** may be a plank table, or it may simply be a table made from pine; most often, it is both. A deal table is usually found in the kitchen; if in other rooms, it usually signifies a cheap or casual piece of furniture (oak* or mahogany are the preferred woods for dining tables and desks). However, by the 1980s, unpainted or unstained deal had become an essential part of contemporary fashionable home furnishing for the office-working, educated middle class,* although most such persons upgrade the status of the wood to "stripped pine."

dean. (1) A clergyman in charge of services in a cathedral* and some other large churches such as Westminster Abbey*; he in effect serves as the daily manager of the church. There is also a **rural dean** who presides over several parishes,* ranking below an archdeacon.* Perhaps reflecting their medieval religious origins, the title is also used for some college* administrators and at Oxford* and Cambridge* for the person in charge of student discipline. *See also* clergy. (2) In place names, a pasture. *See also* -den.

Dean, Forest of. A forest* in western England* near the Welsh border, now a National Park.*

death benefit. A state payment to widows, ostensibly for help with burial expenses, but also including a minimal pension, replaced in 1988 by the widow's benefits.* *See also* national assistance; national insurance.

death duties. A tax since 1894 on inherited property.* The tax was a major blow to many of the wealthiest noble* families, as they owned a great deal of property accumulated over centuries that produced comparatively little cash, so many were forced to begin selling off art objects, land, and even homes to pay the tax. One of the major sources of art for museums in the twentieth century and for houses owned by the National Trust* has been property offered in lieu of death duties. There were, as always, loopholes, the biggest of which was to give the property to an heir before you actually died; if you lived another five years, then there was no tax. This loophole was partially closed in 1975 by a transfer tax on gifts. Originally 8 percent of the estate over £1 million, eventually as high as 60 percent, at present the tax is a flat 40 percent on estates over £110,000.

debagging. *See* bags.

Debrett. *Debrett's Peerage*, a biographical dictionary of the nobility* since 1802. *See also* Burke.

debtor's prison. Until fairly late in the nineteenth century, the bulk of the prison* population was in prison for unpaid debts (most crimes were capital offenses), and many prisons were devoted solely to debtors. Unpaid debt was, it was argued, a form of theft, and certainly young wastrels who lived gaily on borrowed money were fixtures among the eighteenth century gentry,* although gentlemen* were rarely actually imprisoned. But the debtor's prison system never resolved the problem of how the debtor could repay the debt while being kept in prison, a problem exacerbated by the fact that unlike other crimes, debt had no fixed term—one was imprisoned until the debt was paid, and if no money appeared, it became life imprisonment. Problems increased because the prisons were all free enterprise businesses in which the jailers charged the prisoners for rent and food, and thus any money made by the other members of the family (who often lived in prison, too, but could leave) often went just to maintain the prisoner. As a result, conditions were appalling by any standards, and the world seen by Dickens's Pickwick or Little Dorrit was at the better end of the system, where the prisoners managed to find small sums to keep food coming; most fared much worse, and death by starvation or endemic diseases brought on by the squalor were the usual end of such imprisonment.

Gradually throughout the latter part of the nineteenth century, as prisons began to fill with more obvious criminals following the end of transportation* and the limitations on hanging, debtors were in effect squeezed out; by the late nineteenth century, actual imprisonment for debt no longer occurred except when tied to intentional fraud, and such prisoners joined the general prison population with fixed terms for their sentences.

decimal. The British put the decimal point in the middle of the number (6·73) rather than at the base in the American manner (6.73).

declare. *See* cricket.

decorator. There are relatively few interior decorators in the American manner who are not also architects;* the term decorator is instead applied to the actual workers who do the inside of the house, such as painters or paperhangers.

decree nisi. The legal decree finalizing a divorce.*

deed poll. A legal declaration, most often used by people changing their legal name.

deer. The basic deer found in Britain is the **red deer**, although some others such as the roe* are also found. The **stag** is the male, generally in its fifth year; a **hart** is a male six years or older; a **hind** is a female three or older; a **doe** a female under three. Deer hunting has been so important socially that large property owners set aside lands specifically for them. Before the twentieth century, deer hunting was almost always done on horseback and only by the gentry.* *See also* gamekeeper; gillie.

Defence, Ministry of. A Cabinet*-level ministry* responsible for all matters of military policy and organization. The ministry was not established until 1947, when it was a very small ministry trying to coordinate the Admiralty,* the War Office,* and the Air Ministry.* This did not work, due to inter-service rivalry, so its powers gradually expanded until reorganization in 1964 eliminated the ministry status of the individual services and made them simple departments within the MOD.

Defence of the Realm Acts. Controversial laws originally passed in 1914 giving the government* unique powers of censorship, economic control, and suspension of certain judicial rights. *See also* Official Secrets Act.

Defence Secretary. Technically the Secretary of State for Defence, head of the Ministry of Defence* and member of the Cabinet. At present, two additional **Defence Ministers** head major subdivisions of the ministry* as well.

degree. Although students actually enroll in and study at a college,* only a university* can administer the final exams and grant a degree. Thus, in practice as well as in theory, many students in the past earned degrees with only minimal college attendance, and since the Open University* began people may earn degrees with home study. Nonetheless, degrees are very rare compared with American practice; even today, less than 15 percent of school-leavers* attend higher education courses (cf. over 50 percent in the United States), and less than 10 percent of those attend one of the forty-odd universities, the rest going to polytechnics* that grant only diplomas* (although reforms in the works will allow them to begin giving degrees). Thus, it was not unusual until quite recently to see a degree listed on a person's card* or following a signature, particularly if there was no other title or honour* to list. Although the names are similar to American degrees, British degrees have different requirements and procedures: The **BA** (Bachelor of Arts) normally takes three years, and is usually further qualified by the score on the final exam, such as first,* second, third, or a simple pass; the honours* is not only a high score, like American honors, but usually also indicates a more intense course of study and exam as well. Each university has its own required basic tests in certain areas, such as math, but there are no other "general" requirements, and for the most part the student studies only one field throughout the course of study, so beginning students are more like American juniors than freshmen. Originally, the **MA** required four additional years of study, as the scholar was required to become a master of arts in general before being allowed to study the only "advanced" subjects known: law, divinity, or medicine. As such, the MA was actually the most advanced degree someone could hold in any field other than those three. The only doctorates possible were in divinity (**DD**), law (**LLD**), or medicine, until in the late nineteenth-century, Oxford* and Cambridge* began offering the **D. Phil, D. Sc.,** or **D. Litt.,** primarily to attract rich American students back from German universities that invented these degrees; the primary result was to reduce the value of the MA, and now Oxford* and Cambridge* automatically upgrade the BA to an MA after four years for a minimal fee, while some schools offer an MA for a year's post-graduate study in a different field than the BA. The doctorate itself continues to be very rare and is often awarded to scholars for years of outstanding work rather than as the result of a particular course of study; unlike the American Ph.D., it is not required for faculty positions in colleges, which even at Oxford can go to persons with only BAs. A

good degree generally means an honours and/or a first or second. **Degree day** is what Americans call graduation day.

dekko. A look, military slang from India for reconnaissance that has also now penetrated the civil service* and some civilian usage.

Delhi belly. *See* gippie tummy.

dell. A small hollow among hills, usually with trees along the sides; quite distinct from dale.*

demand. In Britain there is little euphemism about taxes; when the local council* or the Inland Revenue* decide you owe taxes, they send you a tax demand rather than a notice or request.

demarara. *See* sugar.

demarcation. In labor relations, the definition of which unions do which jobs, what Americans call job descriptions or jurisdiction, and one of the most common causes of labor unrest since WWII.

demesne. The part of a lord's* estate that he kept for his own use rather than for use by tenants. *See also* home farm.

demister. On a car, the device Americans call a defroster.

demo. What Americans usually call a demonstration or protest march.

demob. To demobilize, to be released from military service.

-den/-dene. In English place-names, a clearing in the woods. *See also* dean.

department. *See* ministry.

deposit account. A savings rather than a checking account at the bank.*

derby. *See* bowler.

Derby. Pronounced darby, the oldest of the regular horse races, officially the Derby Stakes, so-called for the Earl* of Derby who organized and supervised the first one in 1780. Run by three-year-olds on a mile-and-a-half flat course at Epsom Downs* on the first Wednesday in June, it is still one of the most prestigious racing* events. The race had tremendous impact, in part because it attracted the very best horses early in the Season* and in part because the horseshoe-shaped track open at one end allowed vast crowds to appear without paying admission, so half a million or more people often show up to see the race for free. During the Victorian era, it was an unofficial national holiday with a remarkable mix of all levels of society, as celebrated in Frith's famous painting, and Derby Day still is noted for its holiday atmosphere, accompanied by a fair* and masses of double-decker busses* that come out to line the inside of the route and provide good views for their passengers. *See also* Guineas; St. Leger.

Derby. Pronounced darby, the central town in Derbyshire,* the model for Stoniton in *Adam Bede*, now noted primarily for its Rolls-Royce* factory.

Derbyshire. Pronounced DARby-sher, a county* in the Midlands,* geographically distinguished by the mountains of the Peak District.* Although some of its towns share in the industrialization of the other Midlands areas, it is primarily agricultural still.

Derry. *See* Londonderry.

Desert Island Discs. A celebrity interview program on radio, the unique feature being that the guest brings the handful of recordings he or she would want to have on a desert island. An invitation to be on the program is generally seen as proof that you have really "arrived," and many jokes are made about aspiring nobodies who make out their list of records to take before they've done anything to be famous for.

dessert. *See* pudding.

detached. A free-standing house.* *See* semi-detached.

detention centre. A prison for juveniles, but normally only for sentences of less than four months, with "senior" centres for ages seventeen to twenty, and "junior" centres for fourteen to sixteen. Long-term older offenders serve in a Youth Custody Centre.* *See also* approved school; attendance centre; Borstal.

deuce. A euphemism for devil, as in "What the deuce happened here?"

development area. A town or neighborhood with severe unemployment and thus in fact one without business development.

devilled. Of food, with a "hot" taste. Americans often use this term for pâté-like foods, like deviled ham, but the British apply the term to foods served in fairly large pieces under hot sauces, like **devilled kidneys**, served in Worchestershire sauce, mustard, pepper, and lemon juice for breakfast.*

devolution. The return of power from a central authority to a more local one, in most cases meaning potential quasi-independence for Scotland,* but occasionally also used about Wales.* *See also* home rule; Plaid Cymru.

Devon. The county* also called Devonshire.*

Devonshire. A county* or shire* in the southwest of England* on the Cornish peninsula. Most of the interior area is moor* (*See* Dartmoor; Exmoor), but the southern coast is part of the English Riviera,* lined with small seaside resort towns, and there are pleasant agricultural areas around Exeter* where Jane Austen's Dashwoods lived. **Devonshire cream** is a local form of clotted cream.*

DFC. Distinguished Flying Cross, awarded to officers of the RAF* for bravery under fire.

DFM. Distinguished Flying Medal, awarded to other ranks* of the RAF for bravery under fire.

DHSS. Department of Health and Social Security, now split into two separate departments, the DoH* and the DSS.*

diamante. The "jewel" Americans call rhinestone.

dicky. Weak, unpredictable, usually as a "dicky heart."

different to. Although most American schoolteachers struggle mightily to get students to use "different from" instead of "different than," the preferred British usage is "different to."

digestive. A biscuit* that is rather plain and bland.

digger. An Australian, especially an Australian soldier, from WWI after the Australian troops dug themselves into the sides of the cliffs in Gallipoli.*

digs. Furnished rooms* or a bedsitter.*

diligence. A stage coach,* usually an express with limited stops except to change horses; these were common in the eighteenth century but died with the coming of the railroads.

dingle. A small hollow like a dell,* but usually deeper, with steeper hillsides and/or thicker woods.

dinky. Where Americans see this as tiny, cheap, or shoddy, Britons use it more often to mean cute and attractive.

dinner. The largest meal of the day, although the term has a completely different meaning depending on the class* of the speaker. In the working class and lower portions of the middle class, dinner is the midday meal, the meal that in America is called lunch. For the upper and upper–middle classes, dinner is eaten in the evening. Formal dinners with guests usually begin around 8:00 P.M., but family dinners are earlier; however, with many people from these classes commuting fairly large distances since the coming of the railroads, the normal meal time is rarely earlier than 7:00 P.M. In the wealthier families, children are given their own separate meal (sometimes called tea,* sometimes supper*) long before the adults have dinner. Prior to the late nineteenth century, however, all levels of society ate dinner in the middle of the day, the Elizabethans at noon or earlier, but by the eighteenth generally around 3:00 P.M.; commuting is probably the major factor in the change, as the professional classes could no longer return home in the middle of the day. Lower-class dinners of the twentieth century usually have been a pie* or meat pudding,* with potatoes and something sweet, while middle- and upper-class meals usually involved the chop* and three veg.* Sunday dinner, however, in all classes is almost always still eaten in early afternoon and is built around the roast joint.* Dinner in a restaurant rather than at home is a twentieth-century practice, since the first restaurants in the modern sense were opened in London by the wave of emigrés following the French Commune and were not considered respectable for women until at least the 1890s, and is still done only for "special occasions." *See also* breakfast; dog's dinner; dress for dinner; lunch; meal; meals.

dinner jacket. A hip-length formal jacket, usually called a tuxedo in America, so called because it was accepted as suitable wear for dinner* although not as formal as tails.* *See also* dress for dinner; white tie.

diploma. A certificate of completion of an advanced course of study but not at a college* or university,* usually given at polytechnics* in technical fields and seen primarily as a vocational qualification. *See also* degree.

direct grant school. A school,* usually a grammar school,* that received grants from the national government, in return for which it took some or all of its pupils without fees. Such schools were formally abolished in 1976, but ironically most converted into public schools* rather than comprehensives,* closing a door of opportunity for poorer students.

director. In a company, what Americans usually call a vice-president or a manager, quite different from the directors on the Board of Directors in America. *See also* chairman; managing director.

directory inquiry. The telephone service Americans call Information.

dirk. A knife with a long thin blade, often about eighteen inches, carried as a basic weapon by Scottish Highlanders* well into the nineteenth century and now worn decoratively as a part of the traditional kilt* regalia.

dirty, do the. To play a dirty trick on someone, to betray someone.

Dirty Dick's. In the 1920s, a pub* in Limehouse* popular with the upper class* when going slumming, similar to the obligatory trip to Harlem in New York of the same time.

disablement benefit. The benefit* Americans call disability, but paid from national insurance* and uniform throughout the nation.

disc. *See* penalty disc.

disco. In the 1970s and 1980s, used much more often than in America and more generically, often indicating simply any place younger people go to dance or just to hang out together. Churches* or councils* often sponsor discos as a form of youth activities, and thus the term has fewer negative associations with alcohol and the sexual meat market than in America. *See also* club.

dispenser. The actual pharmacist at a chemist's*; signs saying **Dispensing Chemist** indicate a pharmacist is on the premises.

dispute. In business, a strike. *See also* industrial action.

dissenter. A member of one of the many Protestant sects that refused to conform to the theology or practice of the Church of England,* the term particularly used during the sixteenth and seventeenth centuries but still active in the twentieth. Lloyd George, for example, was often referred to as a dissenter, even when he was Prime Minister.* *See also* nonconformist.

dissolution. (1) Of Parliament,* the act of sending the members* away and calling an election;* this is done by the monarch, although since 1694 this has been only a formality, since the monarch acts on "the advice" of the

Prime Minister.* (2) During the reign of Henry VIII, the confiscation of the lands of all monasteries in the kingdom by the Crown.*

Distaff, St. *See* St. Distaff's Day.

distemper. A type of paint made from a base of glue size rather than oil, and thus thinnable with water; by the 1980s this paint had all but disappeared, replaced by modern latex paints that are washable after drying, but it was quite common for interior walls before then.

district. *See* county.

District Court. In Scotland,* the local court for minor offenses, roughly equivalent to the English magistrate's* court.

district nurse. A nurse* paid for by the National Health* who visits or cares for people in their homes.

disused. Abandoned or closed down.

divan. In the nineteenth century, a smoking room, usually furnished with divans and adjacent to a bar. In the twentieth, divan is often used for what Americans call a sofa or couch, although Britons also use both of the latter terms as well.

diver. Before the twentieth century, a pickpocket; hence the name for Jenny Diver.

diversion. On the road, what Americans call a detour.

division. (1) In Parliament,* most laws are passed by voice vote only; since the government* is the majority party, most bills* proposed will clearly pass. Only if there are serious defections from the ranks of the majority party is a formal count taken: The members file out into separate lobbies, for and against, and are counted as they formally divide. (2) At Cambridge,* the halfway point in a term.* (3) *See* first division.

divorce. During the medieval era, as the concept of marriage* was relatively fluid in England,* so was the concept of divorce. However, once formed, the Church of England* firmly opposed divorce, and by Shakespeare's time, the only way to get a divorce was to ask Parliament* for a special act granting it. This was done when the wife was thought to be barren or had committed flagrant adultery, and of course was available only to the wealthy and influential; modern research shows an average of about five divorces per year in the two centuries before 1857. After that date, the Divorce Act allowed divorce for adultery, and the rate went up to about 1000 per year, with the wife's adultery the only one that counted in practice until 1923, when wives were at last allowed to divorce husbands on the same grounds as those on which husbands could divorce wives. Nonetheless, the social strictures against divorce continued to be significant, and the adultery requirement still forced many couples into charades in hotels to provide "grounds" that would be acceptable in court. A 1937 law allowed divorce for desertion after three years or if one spouse was certified insane, but even so the rate for the entire country, after a sudden burst that caught up with old desertions and another post-war burst that caught up with wartime infidelities, remained much the same until the 1960s, when it began to increase at a rate comparable to that in America, and since 1971 couples have been required only to show evidence of irretrievable breakdown of the marriage. Before 1857, poorer people had to resort to what was often called a **wife-sale**, because the husband took the wife to a regular market* and formally offered her for sale. The practice was not quite as horrible as it sounds, for in practice it was usually done by mutual consent of husband and wife, with the "buyer" and the price already agreed to in advance, and was seen at the time more as a divorce than as a symbol of the woman's "slavery"; records are necessarily incomplete, but modern research suggests less than a dozen a year actually happened in the entire country, except for a small increase recorded in the 1820s, when Hardy had set *The Mayor of Casterbridge*, and as the practice was never really legal, it faded away during the late nineteenth century. In Scotland,* which was not subject to English marriage laws, divorce on grounds of adultery or desertion has been legal since the sixteenth century, at a fairly constant rate of less than 2.5 percent of all couples until very recently. *See also* correspondent; crim. con.; woman named.

dixie. The small pot in a soldier's basic kit,* the name first used by troops serving in India but by WWI used throughout the army.*

DIY. Do It Yourself, a fairly recent concept in home upkeep in most of Britain. Most DIY stores are located in large suburbs,* where they replace the ironmonger.*

d—n. *See* dash.

D notice. A statement from the government* that certain information or events are an official secret, used to prevent newspapers* or other media from printing or broadcasting anything about the subject. *See also* Official Secrets Act.

do. (1) As a noun, a party. (2) As a noun, in slang, a swindle. (3) As a verb, to rob, as in "do a shop.*" (4) As a verb, to do housekeeping. Old bachelors, in particular, have women who come in to **do for** them, and no hanky-panky is ever implied by the terminology. (5) Among lower-class* males, to **do for** is to do serious harm to someone, as in "I'll do for him next time." Similarly, to **do over** is not to re-do but rather to beat someone up. However, to be **done** is to be convicted of a crime, as in "he was done for robbery." (6) **Could do with** is to need, as in "I could do with a vacation." (7) *See* done.

dock. The part of the courtroom where the criminal defendant sits, separated from the rest of the court, unlike the American practice of seating the defendant beside his or her attorney.

Docklands. A general term for the portions of the East End* of London* that lie along the Thames,* including areas on both sides of the river. Like most dockside areas in the world, this was a major slum. After it was bombed heavily in WWII, the term has been used for a vast urban renewal project that tries to provide modern housing along with revived docks and major new industries to the area. *See also* Isle of Dogs; Limehouse; Wapping.

doctor. *See* consultant; GP; Mr; surgeon; surgery.

Doctor's Commons. An Inn of Court* (until 1857) near St. Paul's* in London* that had a monopoly in ecclesiastical law cases, which included marriage licenses,* divorces,* and some probate cases, already a byword for pointless law when Betsey Trotwood sent David Copperfield there to be the equivalent of a solicitor.*

doe. *See* deer.

DoE. Department of the Environment.*

dog cart. A small, light, two-wheeled carriage* with seats back-to-back, so called not because it was pulled by a dog but because the driver so often had a dog in the space under the seats.

dog collar. Slang, generally collegiate, for a clergyman's collar, which in the Church of England* is a stiff high white collar visible all the way round the neck. Many contemporary priests wear it only for services and official appearances, but until very recently it was worn with all forms of dress; after the arrival of the modern suit, the collar was accompanied by a dark smooth dickey that covered the open area of the chest.

dog days. July and early August, so called from the rise of the "Dog Star" Sirius.

doggo, lie. To hide or to wait patiently and quietly before attacking.

dogsbody. The person at the bottom of the heap who gets all the miserable jobs no one else wants.

dog's breakfast. *See* donkey's breakfast.

dog's dinner. Originally, in the 1930s this meant fancy or attractive, used admiringly for highly ornate decoration or dress, but perhaps from its similarity to **dog's breakfast** or donkey's breakfast,* by the 1970s it was coming to mean a mess, not quite disgusting but close.

DoH. Department of Health, administering the National Health.*

dole. Originally, this was a portion or share but in the medieval era was most often applied to the portion given from the endowment of a local parish* charity. These took many forms, with many personal and local variations; **graveside doles**, for example, were distributed at the grave of the founder. However, most were extremely small (usually only once a year), and thus gradually lost their impact as the various Poor Laws* tried to standardize national practice; the term was fading in the nineteenth century except for famous curiosities like the Tichborne Dole*. Then, in 1919, a newspaper* attached the name to national unemployment* benefits in an effort to ridicule them, and the name stuck; since then, someone **on the dole** is collecting unemployment payments, which is quite different from American welfare benefits. Such benefits must be collected in person, so the length of the **dole queue*** is one of the primary indicators of economic health, or lack of it, in an area. *See also* national insurance.

doll. In Shakespeare's time, this was a nickname for Dorothy, given as well to pets and mistresses, and this actually preceded the children's toy. But by the nineteenth century, the term had been extended to mean a woman who resembled a doll, "dressed up" but empty-headed, and from that was a very short step to prostitute, especially as a **dolly**. Thus, in cricket,* a dolly is a ball that's very easy to catch. Similarly, dolly is often used as an adjective to indicate that someone or something is very attractive, so that a **dolly-bird** is a pretty young woman (*See also* bird). A **dolly bag** is a small bag with a drawstring, perhaps from the drawstring purses common in the nineteenth century. But a **dolly-mop** was a nineteenth-century maidservant, who was often assumed to be available for casual liaisons. Dolly used as nickname for a man, however, implies no effeminacy but is instead an all-but-automatic nickname* for men named Gray, from the popular song *Dolly Gray*. *See also* poppet.

Domesday Book. Usually pronounced doomsday, a survey of England* made in 1085 at William the Conqueror's orders. One of the most remarkable historical records in any country, this listed and described all the various pieces of land in the country, their use, and their populations.

dominie. In Scotland,* a schoolmaster.

dominion. Technically, a country within first the Empire* and then the Commonwealth* that had autonomy in both domestic and foreign affairs; Canada was the first (1867) and the only until in 1931 Australia, New Zealand, South Africa, the Irish Free State, and Newfoundland were given the same status, although they had sometimes been called dominions before the passage of the law granting such autonomy. *See also* colony.

Dominions Office. The ministry* that dealt with members of the Commonwealth* from 1925 until merged into the Commonwealth Relations Office* in 1947.

don. A senior member of a college,* especially at Oxford* or Cambridge.* This is not the title of a position, as is professor,* and no one is appointed Don of a college. The term apparently arose satirically after the Restoration, comparing the independence and pigheadedness of the academic to that of the stereotypical Spanish Don, and thus is still rather a generic term for someone with a stuffy or particularly academic turn of mind, for which the Oxford and Cambridge fellows* still set the pattern.

Doncaster. A town in Yorkshire,* in the nineteenth century a major construction center for railroads but now known for the St. Leger* horse race run there.

done. (1) That which is socially acceptable in upper-class* circles; something **not done** is something that proper persons do not do because they do not do such things. *See also* thing, the. (2) *See* do.

donkey. A sheet of plastic, often with handles at the corners, used to carry loose rubbish, such as gardening detritus.

donkey's breakfast. Originally, navy* slang for a straw mattress, now also applied to a type of wall covering made from wood chips used when walls are too uneven to use paint alone or other forms of wallpaper; not at all like a dog's dinner,* but sometimes now said as **dog's breakfast.**

donkey's years. A very long time. No one is quite sure how the phrase arose around 1900, but it has since been used throughout all classes.

DORA. Defence of the Realm Acts.*

Dorchester. A market town* in southwestern England,* the principal town of Dorset.* Hardy used this as the model for Casterbridge, and many of the specific landmarks and buildings Hardy described still exist there.

Dorking. A small town south of London,* now a commuter suburb, normally noted as a town with absolutely nothing of interest about it. However, the area to the north is usually assumed to be the site of Jane Austen's *Emma*.

dormitory. While Americans almost always use this for a building such as a college dorm, the British almost always still mean a single room with many beds, especially in a public school* where the building itself is usually called the house* or hall.* However, a **dormitory suburb** or **dormitory town** is a suburb where people only sleep in their homes but go elsewhere to work or find entertainment, what Americans call a bedroom community.

Dorset. A county* or shire* on the southern coast of England,* with resorts on the coast and active agriculture in inland areas. This is the heart of Hardy country, corresponding to his "South Wessex," with the town of Dorchester* the model for Casterbridge, the areas immediately north of there the settings for *The Woodlanders* and most of *Tess of the D'Urbervilles*, a village to the northeast for *Far From the Madding Crowd*, and the eastern part of the county for Egdon Heath.

doss. To sleep casually or rough,* as on the floor or sofa or perhaps under a bridge. A **doss house** is a cheap lodging that has very seamy associations.

double. In cricket,* scoring 1000 runs as a batsman* and also knocking over 100 wickets* as a bowler* in the course of a single season, a major feat that would be roughly equivalent to a baseball player hitting 50 home runs while also pitching and striking out 200 or so hitters.

double-barrel. A name with a hyphen.*

double bend. On a road, an S-shaped curve.

double cream. What Americans call whipping cream.

double first. *See* first.

double Gloucester. *See* cheese.

doughnut. Almost always used only for the kind Americans call a jelly doughnut, and often for a version baked rather than deep fried. What Americans call a doughnut was rarely seen until fairly recently.

dove. Essentially the same bird as a pigeon. The **turtle dove**, noted for its particularly pleasant repetitive sound, is smaller and brown and is concentrated in the southern English countryside* during the summer, but most other doves are gray and similar to American pigeons in size.

Dover. A town on the southeastern coast of England.* For centuries, this was the primary port for travel to France, formalized in mid-nineteenth century by regular ferries connecting to the boat train* each evening from London.* The town itself seems surprisingly small to the American tourist, given its prominence in literature and entertainment. The **Straits of Dover** are the body of water between Dover and France, at only seventeen miles the narrowest crossing of the English Channel.* The **white cliffs of Dover** are the high chalk* cliffs on the coast around the town, visible on clear days from France; they serve as an imposing obstacle against invaders coming from the continent and as the most immediately visible landmark for travelers, which makes them one of the most common symbols of home for the English, particularly during WWII when they were a landmark for returning fliers and the subject of a popular song. Dickens's Betsey Trotwood lived and chased the donkeys on the top of them, and Gloucester attempted to jump from them in *King Lear*. Similar cliffs can be found all along this coast, but these are the highest and most vivid. The **Dover Road** was the long, almost straight road from London to Dover via Canterbury,* following a road first made by the Romans, also calling Watling Street,* and now called the A2.*

Dover's powder. An eighteenth-century patent medicine, a powder made of opium and ipecacuanha root, taken for almost any pains.

dowager. Formally, a widow who still retains a title or property* from her late husband. Usually this means the mother of the current title holder, as in Dowager Duchess,* but the widowhood is the determining factor; she would still carry the title of Dowager if she were childless and the title passed to a nephew. From this it has come to mean, more casually, any woman of age, wealth, and authoritative mien. *See also* Queen Mother.

dower. Technically, this is only property* retained by a widow after her husband's death, from which she gets the name of dowager.* However, it has also often been used interchangeably with dowry,* particularly before the nineteenth century.

dower house. A small house near and on the same property as a larger one,* originally a part of a widow's dower* and thus a house that could be used by the widow to live separately from her son's household after the son inherited the main property. After the widow's death, the house would revert to the family, although usually still called a dower house.

down. (1) A large open area without trees, usually undulating hills, particularly such an area in the southern portion of England.* The **North Downs** are a rather extensive series of such areas south of London*; now broken in many places by urban developments, they run from near Basingstoke* east to the vicinity of Canterbury.* The **South Downs** lie farther south near the coast above Portsmouth* and east to the Brighton* area. There are other extensive areas of downs, particularly in Sussex.* The **Downs**, however, are in the sea, the area off the coast of Kent* between the shore and the Goodwin Sands,* used often as a safe temporary anchorage for ships approaching the Thames. (2) Away from London*; you always go "up" to London, no matter where you live, and "down" to the country.* Similarly, the **down train** is any train leaving London, while the **up train** goes to London. The primary exceptions are that you go up to the university* and down when you leave it for vacation or graduation, even if that is to London, and the Scots always say they go down to anywhere in England.* *See also* send down.

Downing Street. A very short street between St. James's Park* and Whitehall* in London.* The Prime Minister's* residence and office has been located in a rather nondescript building at 10 Downing Street (often called simply **Number Ten**) since 1735, and offices have overflowed into all the neighboring buildings, so that now Downing Street is used as a synonym for anything to do with the Prime Minister or official government* policy. Eleven Downing Street (often called simply **Number Eleven**) is the residence of the Chancellor of the Exchequer.*

down tools. To go on strike.

down train. *See* train.

dowry. The British practiced the dowry system well into the twentieth century, although it had clearly begun to decline in importance by the second half of the nineteenth century. It is important to note that this practice was not seen as a way to buy or sell daughters but rather as a way to guarantee that the daughters would be able to continue to live as well as they had in their parents' home. Through the Restoration era, the bride's dowry money went not to the husband but to the husband's father, who in return guaranteed an equivalent income, called a jointure,* for the woman should the son leave her a widow. As the custom gradually changed to provide the money directly to the husband, dowries became even more complex, like the prenuptial contracts beginning to appear in modern America, often with the dowry itself held in some form of trust for potential children or the wife's widowhood and only the income from it available to the couple for living expenses. Nonetheless the dowry remained a major target for many young men, particularly younger sons who would never otherwise get their hands on a significant lump sum that could be used to buy a commission* or a legal practice, or to gain a government or clerical position, or to allow them to live in any comfort while holding such positions. We tend to think of this as an aristocratic practice, perhaps because of all those mercenary marriage pursuits in Restoration comedies, but the practice was common all along the social scale and was the primary means by which the social class* structure was sustained. In the traditional sense, the British killed the declining dowry system in 1882, when married women were legally allowed to own property in their own name, thus negating the need for complex prenuptial property agreements, but a cynical observer of the way in which marriage within one's own class still predominates would suggest that the practice has simply gone underground. *See also* dower.

doxy. A relatively standard term for a mistress from Shakespeare's time to perhaps WWI, although usually implying a cheap or slatternly one.

Dr. British preference is without a period. *See also* doctor.

dragoon. A cavalryman who carried a carbine or light musket as well as a sword and often fought dismounted after riding a horse to get to the fight. In the eighteenth century, all cavalry regiments* were dragoons, but in the nineteenth century many were changed to lancer* and hussar* regiments. For most people a dragoon and cavalryman were synonymous, a dashing, romantic figure; Sergeant Troy in *Far From the Madding Crowd* is typical of the stereotype. The horse has long since been replaced but the name is still used by some armored regiments.* *See also* commission; hussar; lancer; trooper.

drainpipe trousers. Trousers* with very narrow, tight-fitting legs, associated with the Teddy boys* in particular.

drains. The plumbing of a building. A house on the **main drains** is tied into the town sewers and thus needs no septic tank.

drake. (1) A nickname for a shilling* before the Civil War,* when it had a bird as a mint mark. *See also* Appendix I. (2) *See* ducks and drakes.

dralon. A synthetic fabric for upholstery, a sort of imitation velvet, a brand name often used generically.

dram. Originally, a tiny measure of medicine, less than an ounce, such as the dram of poison Romeo takes. By the eighteenth century, this had been extended to other "medicinal" drinks, such as whisky.* The Scots,* in particular, use it to mean a shot of whisky, but a **wee dram** usually indicates a drink that is considerably larger than wee.*

draper. A person who sells cloth; sometimes he also sells the clothes made from that cloth. In London,* the **Drapers** are one of the great livery companies* of the City.* *See also* mercer.

draughts. The game Americans call checkers.

drawers. In general, underpants. This is a very variable term. Men go swimming in **bathing drawers**, for example, but often wear briefs* or trunks under their trousers.* In Shakespeare's time, drawers were long hose or stockings worn by men, sometimes a rough outer pair worn over the smoother softer hose underneath. But in the eighteenth century, they were either very full, ankle-length underpants worn by women or bulky loose underpants ending above the knee worn by men. By the twentieth century, the women's usage had begun to be replaced by knickers,* while the men's continued even as the underpants got smaller.

drawing pin. What Americans call a thumb tack.

drawing room. In the seventeenth century, the withdrawing room, a private room next to a public room in a house where the residents could go for privacy. By the eighteenth century, this had become the room to which the ladies withdrew after dinner.* Almost immediately it began to be associated with talking and general socializing, so that by the nineteenth it had completely reversed itself and become the most public room of the house, where women met their guests during the day and where afternoon tea* was served, as well as where the men rejoined the ladies after cigars and port* to finish the evening. In royal* circles, however, the old usage still continued, especially in the afternoon reception called a **Drawing Room**, during which women were formally presented to the Queen. These of course were not private; some of Victoria's (three per year at first, five a year after 1895) involved more than 1,000 women (men attended a levee* on different days), but the title still implied a personal touch, as if it were in the more private drawing room than in one of the rooms of state. As might be assumed, one needs a large house to have a drawing room; thus, in the late nineteenth century the middle classes,* in an attempt to increase status, began to apply the name to the basic family room usually called a parlour* and which Americans call the living room. But by the late twentieth, unless the speaker was in a very large house, the term was used only by the pretentious and had been generally replaced by lounge.* *See also* front room; levee; morning room; sitting room.

draw on. To take from storage, experience, savings, et cetera.

dresser. A cabinet, chest, or sideboard in the kitchen rather than in the bedroom; the **Welsh dresser** has open shelves on the top for displaying plates.

dress for dinner. To put on formal evening dress before eating dinner, done for social occasions and in some of the wealthier households done at every dinner,* but not nearly as often as implied in movies and TV shows.

dressing gown. Generally, what Americans call a bathrobe.

drill. The way things are usually done, as in "you know the drill," used primarily by military types and the police.*

dripping. Fat from cooked meat. In many British kitchens, the dripping is saved and used again, either for frying or as a food itself, spread when congealed directly onto bread* like butter. During the late twentieth century, dripping has begun to be replaced by margarine in many homes due to prosperity, but it still continues in many homes as a traditional dish.

driving to the public danger. A legal charge Americans call reckless driving. *See also* banned; DCA.

drought. This is officially defined as fifteen days without rain.*

drove. A right-of-way* for livestock, down which anyone may move cattle or sheep over land otherwise closed to the public.

drover. A person who drives cattle* or sheep* to market,* and thus also a livestock trader; different from a **herder**, who tends to the livestock on the farm. In stories set in the countryside,* a drover is something of a figure of romance because he travels, even if his view is only the rear of a cow.

Druids. The priests of the ancient Celtic* tribes, destroyed by the Romans. In the nineteenth century, modern "Druids" appeared, claiming pagan powers and authority, meeting for mystical rites at places like Stonehenge,* but they are purely a modern re-creation, along the lines of various American "witches" and "pagan" groups.

Drury Lane. A street in London* connecting Aldwych* with High Holborn,* synonymous with the English theater since the Theatre Royal, one of the two original "legitimate" theaters, was opened there in 1662.

dry. In the 1980s, a Conservative* who was a hard-line supporter of Margaret Thatcher's policies. *See also* wet.

DSC. Distinguished Service Cross, originally (1901) the Conspicuous Service Cross (**CSC**) given only to naval warrant officers for bravery, the name changed in 1914 and awarded to both warrant officers and regular officers below rank of lieutenant-commander.*

DSM. Distinguished Service Medal, given to sailors and marines for bravery.

DSO. Distinguished Service Order, a military medal for gallantry given only to officers* in all forces since 1886. *See also* DCM.

DSS. Department of Social Security, administrator of various social security* benefits. *See also* DHSS.

dual carriageway. *See* carriageway.

duchess. *See* duke.

duck. (1) In cricket,* a score of zero (from "duck egg"). To **bowl for a duck** is to get the batter out without a score, while to **break your duck** is to make your first score or, metaphorically, to do anything for the first time. (2) A **lame duck** is someone in need of care or coddling, unlike the American lame duck (someone finishing out a term after losing a reelection campaign or failing to be promoted), who is never coddled by anyone.

duckie. A term of casual endearment, particularly among working-class* women.

ducks. (1) Casual white flannel trousers. (2) Same as duckie.*

ducks and drakes. What Americans call skipping rocks across a pool of water. To **play ducks and drakes with** is to waste foolishly.

duck's arse. *See* DA.

duel. Duels figure rarely in English life or literature compared to the Continent, with legislation against them beginning under Charles II. Various laws tightened the restrictions until an 1837 law made shooting at a person an offence,* and the last known duel was fought in 1852. *See also* gentleman.

duff. (1) In northern England* and Scotland,* a boiled pudding,* from regional pronunciations of dough. A **figgy duff** was originally made with figs, but now may use raisins. (2) From late nineteenth century, faulty or no good. Suggestions that this was derived from the food are purely conjectural. A **duffer** is an inept person or a piece of counterfeit goods, and sometimes a person who sells shoddy goods by pretending they're really stolen. *See also* gen.

duke. The highest rank of nobility* not actually in the royal* family, although some princes* may also be **royal dukes**. Currently there are only about two dozen dukes. A duke's wife is called a **duchess**, and both are addressed as "Your Grace." Title names in most cases are derived from an area, but neither the original duke nor his family need to have actually owned land or ruled in the area (the Duke of Devon,* for example, has his estate in Derbyshire*); Mary and Elizabeth I together executed the last remaining medieval dukes, so all modern titles began during or after the Restoration when the most common qualification was great wealth and friendship with the monarch, not feudal power. Brothers and sons are given the title Lord* but use the family name, daughters are entitled Lady* and keep the title for life, unlike most other children of the nobility. To use a fictional example, Peter Wimsey is Lord Peter, but his elder brother is Gerald, Duke of Denver, or just Denver, but never Gerald Wimsey or Lord Gerald, although sometimes for convenience he would be called Lord Denver without serious objection; his signature would be Denver and nothing more. Gerald's wife is Helen, Duchess of Denver, and she would not be called Lady Helen (unless she had that title before she married) but would be Lady Denver; her signature would be Helen Denver, not Helen Wimsey. Peter's sister is Lady Mary Wimsey, but after marrying a commoner* she becomes Lady Mary, Mrs* Parker. Their mother, widow of a Duke, is the Dowager* Duchess of Denver.

dull. Of the weather, cloudy and gray.

Dulwich. Pronounced DULLidge, a village just south of London* now absorbed into Greater London, long a desirable suburb* noted for its tree-lined streets, the nation's oldest public* picture gallery (1814), and the influential **Dulwich College**, a grammar school* founded by Edward Alleyn, an actor/manager said to have been detested by Shakespeare.

Dumfries. A town and a shire,* since 1975 absorbed into the region* of **Dumfries and Galloway**, on the southwest coast of Scotland.* Many of Burns's Scottish ballads were collected here.

Dumfriess. Dumfriesshire. *See* Dumfries.

dummy. What Americans call a baby's pacifier.

Dundee. A small city on the east coast of Scotland* north of Edinburgh,* a center of Calvinist traditions during the Reformation and noted especially for the marmalade produced there (from imported oranges) and for the jute industry. For **Dundee cake** *See* cake.

dungarees. Clothing in the style Americans call overalls, usually of the bib type, but worn primarily by children, not for work clothes.

Dungeness. A small fishing port on the southeast coast of England,* famous not for shellfish but for a nuclear power station.

Durex. A condom, a brand name often used generically.

Durham. A county* and a town in the northeast of England.* The town is the site of a famous cathedral, and the town and its castle were one of the major fortresses in the long centuries of border warfare with Scotland.* The county runs from the coast inland to the Pennines* and has some of the densest agricultural land in the country, with coal* in the mountainous areas. Durham is also the site of a university,* chartered in 1837.

dustbin. What Americans call a garbage can or garbage pail.

dust cart. What Americans call a garbage truck.

dust jacket. The paper jacket on a hardback book, sometimes also used to mean the cover of a paperback book.

dustman. The person who picks up the garbage. In the nineteenth century, dustmen like Dickens's Noddy Boffin were mostly what contemporary Americans call recyclers; rather than burying the garbage, they sorted and resold the rags, bones, metal, et cetera, and thus made a profit. The modern dustman, however, is paid to just throw it in the truck and take it to the tip.*

dust-up. A fight or brawl.

Dutch, old. *See* rhyming slang.

duvet. On a bed, what Americans call a comforter. Usually pronounced DOOvay. *See also* eiderdown.

DVWP. The initials come from a part Latin, part English phrase, "Deo volente (God willing), weather permitting."

E

each way. In betting on horses, you may bet to win, to place, (meaning to come in either second or third—unlike American place or show), or each way, meaning in the first three.

Ealing. A suburb to the west of London* noted primarily for a movie studio where a number of successful eccentric comedies of English daily life were produced in the 1940s and 1950s, often called **Ealing comedies**.

earl. A member of the nobility* ranking below a marquess* and above a viscount.* The earl is the British equivalent of the continental count, the name dating back to Anglo-Saxon rulers of shires,* and the earl's wife is in fact called a **countess**. Earls are styled as the Earl of (Someplace), rather than Earl of (Family name), although a few exceptions drop the "of". An earl is properly addressed as My Lord,* the countess as My Lady,* and their son is the Honourable* (First name Family name), but curiously, their daughter is Lady (First name Family name), thus in title at least outranking her brother; for example, Lady Antonia Fraser Pinter, the daughter of the Earl of Longford now married to the commoner* Harold Pinter. Sometimes, as a convenience in newspapers or public speech, the earl may be called Lord So-and-So, but he may be distinguished from a mere Lord* by the use of the place-name in his title rather than his family name. *See also* titles.

Earl Marshal. A hereditary position held by the Duke* of Norfolk,* in charge of significant royal* occasions such as coronations,* a remainder from the medieval marshal* who supervised the monarch's military affairs.

Earl's Court. An enormous exhibition hall and the neighborhood around it, in London* west of Kensington.*

early closing. In many villages* and smaller towns,* all the shops close for the afternoon one day each week, called early closing day. The day varies from place to place, usually Wednesday or Thursday; this compensates for the shops staying open on Saturday* afternoon.

early days. Too soon to tell how things will really turn out.

earth. (1) In electricity,* what Americans call the ground; as plugs* often must be rewired every time they are plugged in, the ability to recognize this wire (green) is much more important to the average person than in America. (2) In fox hunting, an underground burrow where the fox may hide; hence, the number of spies and criminals said to **go to earth** when they hide out from their enemies, just as the fox tries to do.

East. When speaking of foreign climes, Britons have used the East to signify practically any of those countries from Egypt or Syria to China or Japan. *See also* East of Suez.

East Anglia. An ancient kingdom on the eastern coast of modern England,* after 917 a part of England. The name is still used for the general area including Norfolk* and Suffolk,* noted for its flat lands and large areas of marsh. *See also* Fens.

Eastbourne. A resort town on the south coast of England* east of Brighton,* one of the many coastal vacation spots of the south coast in the twentieth century but perhaps the most respectable and least touristy.

East End. Originally, small communities that sprang up to the east of the old walls of London* along the north bank of the Thames.* By the seventeenth century, this area had become inseparable from the city itself and was the home of the city's poor. The river was lined with docks handling most of the shipping that went through London, and by the early nineteenth the area was filled with sweatshops and similar industry, along with the innumerable pubs* and prostitutes that accompany active docks, making it a notorious slum and hotbed of crime, a perfect setting for Mr. Hyde or Jack the Ripper, and synonymous with horrific slums. Cockneys* are the major inhabitants of the East End neighborhoods. The area, due to its poverty, naturally also became the first settling place for each wave of immigrants to London, first from the English countryside and then from overseas, and has seen waves of Jews, Irish, and Chinese; currently Pakistanis, Hindus, and West Indians predominate in many neighborhoods.

The area was heavily bombed in WWII, and in recent years several development projects in the modern urban renewal manner, such as the gigantic Docklands* projects, have begun in hopes of both reviving industry and taming the poverty and crime. *The EastEnders* is a popular TV soap opera of the 1980s, portraying a mix of races around a central core of Cockney characters in the East End. *See also* Ham; Isle of Dogs; Limehouse; Shoreditch; Spitalfields; Stepney; Tower Hamlets; Wapping; Whitechapel.

Easter. Easter traditions, in addition to the religious services, have long included a brightly colored Easter egg, but usually only one, hidden and then when found eaten as part of a large meal. In England,* Easter has generally been the start of a longer holiday that includes a day of games and sports on the Monday after Easter, which led to this day's inclusion among the national bank holidays.* In the Oxford* area, the games were so prominent that the Monday was called **Ball Monday**. *See also* term.

East India Company. A private company organized in 1600 that in effect conquered India.* Beginning as traders, the company soon had its own private army that defeated the French colonial army and then subdued the bulk of the native rulers as well. After unrest culminating in the mutiny* of 1857, the Crown* took control of the subcontinent away from the company, which survived only until 1873.

East of Suez. Almost never did this include Britain's most obvious possession east of the Suez* Canal—India; instead, it usually meant the rubber plantation countries such as Malaya or Burma. Kipling used it about the road to Mandalay, "where there ain't no Ten Commandments," and the phrase always carries a similar suggestion of decadence, of "going native" in Somerset Maugham or Joseph Conrad territory, all rattan chairs, seductive native women in sarongs, and gin* at Raffles'.* *See also* East.

Eaton Hall. Before 1958, a cadet school for potential infantry officers* on the outskirts of Chester.*

Eccles cake. *See* cake.

ecclesiastical courts. Courts administered by the Church,* originally dealing with any crimes committed by clergy* and with cases related to religious questions. Until 1857, this also included many probate and divorce* cases; now they deal only with cases directly involving clergy.

Economist. One of the most influential of the national magazines, essentially conservative in tone but, despite its name, more political than economic in subject matter.

Eddystone. A lighthouse at Plymouth* Sound, in various structures since 1699, and thus one of the first (or last) sights of England* for the sailor and sea traveler.

Edinburgh. Pronounced eddin-burrow, the capital of Scotland,* located on the east coast at the tip of the Firth* of Forth. Somewhat slow to develop in relation to the English medieval towns, it was the center of trade for the eastern areas of Scotland, by the eighteenth century becoming as well an intellectual and cultural center that earned it the nickname of Athens of the North. It had a major impact on British literature as the birthplace or home for (among many) Burns, Scott, Boswell, Hume, Smith, Smollett, Crabbe, DeQuincey, Carlyle, and Stevenson, although figuring only rarely in their actual writings; and possibly even more importantly as the home of *The Edinburgh Review* and *Blackwood's*, the two dominant British literary magazines of the nineteenth century. The **University of Edinburgh** no longer has the reputation it once had, but is still perhaps the major medical school of Britain. The **Edinburgh Festival** began in 1947 to bring world-class music, dance, et cetera, to the city in tourist seasons, but since the late 1960s has been dominated in the media by its "fringe," which is full of hundreds of unofficial groups performing avant-garde and otherwise eccentric productions. *See also* Lothian; Midlothian; new town; tolbooth.

education. *See* school.

Educational Welfare Officer. A contemporary official euphemism for the person who used to be called a truancy officer,* in American a truant officer.

Education Secretary. Technically the Secretary of State for Education and Science, the minister* responsible for all government* policy, support, and subsidy for schools* and scientific research.

effing. An expletive, used euphemistically for the word fucking; also used generically to mean swearing of any kind, as in "He was effing and blinding* up and down the lane."

egg nog. Unlike the American version, this is purely an alcoholic drink, usually strong ale* and an egg, but with no milk or cream. *See also* flip.

eggs. The British tend to eat eggs in two forms: fried or soft-boiled. When soft-boiled, the egg is placed in a holder called an **egg-cup**, the top of the shell removed, and the interior either scooped out with a spoon or by dipping soldiers* of toast into it. This is another of those rough class* dividers, with upper levels preferring the boiled egg and the lower eating the fried, but boiled eggs penetrate fairly far down the scale. Fried eggs often appear in sandwiches.* Poached eggs also are eaten in the upper layers of society. **Egg mayonaise** is used in sandwiches* and is more like the American egg salad than the French dish of that name. An **egg cosy** is a small cloth bag inverted over the boiled egg and its holder to keep the egg warm until eaten.

Egon Ronay. A restaurant guide since 1959 generally seen as the authority on quality English restaurants of all types.

Egypt. Perhaps the oddest of many anomalies in the Empire,* Egypt was controlled by England through most of the nineteenth century, even though it was ostensibly still a part of the Ottoman Empire. British soldiers were stationed there, and by 1882, when the French were at last pressured out of the country, the British consul became the effective ruler of the country. An unexpected side effect was that British archaeologists became the primary authorities on ancient Egypt. After WWI, Egypt became a protectorate of Britain until given complete independence in 1936, but the British presence remained strong until the Suez* crisis of 1956. *See also* gippie tummy.

eiderdown. What Americans usually call a quilt, but lighter than a duvet.*

eight, one over the. A phrase indicating someone has had too much to drink, from the traditional assumption that any serious drinker ought to be able to handle eight pints* (more than two American six-packs) in a pub* session.

Eights Week. The end of the academic year at Oxford,* during late May, a time of parties, dances, and of course the Eights rowing races among the individual colleges. *See also* bumping; May Week.

Eisteddfod. In Wales,* an ancient contest for the poetic bards, declining as the Welsh were more completely absorbed by the English, then reviving in the late eighteenth century with pseudo-druidic trappings grafted on. In 1880, a National Eisteddfod was organized again, held annually in August, and now these are festivals of all the Welsh arts, although the central focus continues to be the poetry contests in the Welsh language. As such, the eisteddfodau have been instrumental in keeping the Welsh language alive in the face of the dominating English.

elastic band. What many Americans call a rubber band. *See also* rubber.

Elastoplast. A bandage similar to the American Band-Aid, a brand name often used generically. *See also* plaster.

election. National elections for Parliament* after the Restoration were held every three years; in 1715, this was changed to seven years, in 1911 reduced to five. However, these are not regularly scheduled as in the United States; the government* may call an election at any time, and most governments try to find a moment before the legal deadline when they seem most likely to be returned to office. Whenever one election is called, then the next must be held within the next five years. They are usually held on a Thursday, although this is tradition, not a legal requirement. Elections for various councils* are determined by local rules and procedures, but most are held every four years. *See also* ballot; by-election; voting.

electric fire. *See* fire.

electricity. The British use direct current (220 or 240 volts) for all home use. In general, light switches go down to turn on and up to turn off, opposite to American practice, although many move clockwise rather than up and down. *See also* fire; ground; mains; plug; points.

electricity board. What Americans usually call the electric company.

elephant. Of paper, sheet measuring about 23 inches × 28 inches.

Elephant and Castle. A major intersection on the south side of the Thames* for roads to and from London,* so called because of a pub* of that name located there in the sixteenth century.

eleven. A cricket* team, which is composed of eleven players, although it may also mean the football* (soccer) team, which also has eleven players. To make the **first eleven** at a school* is thus like making the starting team of the varsity in an American school sport.

eleven-plus. An exam given to schoolchildren (except in most prep schools*) at about age eleven, used for admission to grammar schools.* The test was discontinued during the conversion to comprehensives* in the 1970s and 1980s, but it was a very controversial decision. *See also* Common Entrance Exam.

elevenses. A morning snack, usually coffee* and a bun,* and the break taken to eat or drink it.

Ely. Pronounced EE-lee, a small town in the fens* north of Cambridge,* noted primarily for its imposing cathedral* on the area's highest hill, seventy feet high. The Bishop of Ely, however, lived in a palace in the Holborn* area of London* until the late eighteenth century, and it was there, not in Cambridgeshire,* that John of Gaunt died and the gardeners debated the fate of Richard II in a garden* that still exists.

Embankment. In London,* officially the **Victoria Embankment**, a major construction project (1864–70) on the north shore of the Thames* from Blackfriars* Bridge to Westminster* that built a permanent stone wall along the banks, eliminating the marshy land inside, protecting a new major sewer system and the Underground,* and producing on the surface a major roadway and promenade, whose stone railings figure as the background for practically every walk along the Thames ever taken in movies or TV shows. A second Embankment was built at the same time across the river on the South Bank,* called the **Albert Embankment**, running from Waterloo* to Westminster Bridges as a promenade only, eventually extended to Lambeth and then to the roadway of the same name running to Vauxhall* Bridge; the promenade is now a major part of the South Bank arts developments. A third embankment was built in Chelsea* in 1874 but is rarely admired except for its contribution to the traffic flow, although it followed part of **Cheyne Walk**, home to many nineteenth-century writers and artists in the Chelsea colony.

Emmanuel. One of the colleges* of Cambridge.*

Empire. Through history, England has actually won and lost three empires. The first was the bulk of modern France, finally lost in the sixteenth century. The second was on the American continent, won from France and then almost immediately lost again (except for Canada) through American independence. But the one most often meant by the term was the vast series of worldwide outposts and colonies of the late nineteenth century, including big chunks of Africa, India, and significant bases in China and southeast Asia, as well as Australia and Canada. By the time of WWI, the world map was covered with red countries, used on British maps to show British territory, and it was in fact true that "the sun never sets on the British Empire." Perhaps most remarkable of all, almost all of this territory was voluntarily surrendered by the British without bloody local civil wars, first through self-government for many in the Commonwealth* and then through independence movements for the rest in a steady process beginning with India* after WWII. *See also* army; colonial; FCO; Foreign Office; Gibraltar; Kenya; remittance man; transportation.

Employment, Department of. The government department* primarily responsible for dealing with unemployment,* administering benefits and operating the state job centres.* The **Employment Secretary** is the minister* in charge.

enclosure. In theory, all land in England* had been held in common during the Anglo-Saxon era, and although the Normans made the local lords* the actual owners, much of the land remained open for use by anyone, particularly for grazing and garden farming. Gradually, individual lords began to fence off the most valuable parts of such lands, a process that continued slowly but inexorably until the early eighteenth century. At that time, major changes in agricultural techniques and the opening of new markets for wool caused a massive increase in such fencing, called enclosure, often authorized by **enclosure acts** passed through Parliament* as a favor to a particular landlord. The economic effects, particularly as accompanied by the protective Corn Laws,* were spectacularly positive for the landlords, who became immensely wealthy, but the social effects were disturbing, as vast numbers of the rural populace were left with individual plots that would no longer support them or driven off the lands completely, sending many to the cities, where they constituted a slum-dwelling underclass of crime and disease, or in many cases to America. By about 1815, enclosure was complete and only a comparative handful of commons* remained. *See also* Clearances.

Enclosure, Royal. *See* Ascot.

endorsement. A record of a traffic violation; these are made directly onto the driver's license rather than merely filed as in America.

engine driver. What Americans call an engineer on a train.

England. Technically, only one of three nations in the United Kingdom;* however, it occupies the bulk of the island of Great Britain,* contains about 80 percent of the population and even more of the wealth and industry and thus has been the dominant partner in the kingdom since the medieval era. Because of this dominance, most people casually refer to the entire kingdom simply as England. As the bulk of entries in this work refer to the language, places, and customs of England, I will make no attempt to cross-reference items here or to provide any significant summary of history or culture. However, it should be noted that in the course of the whole work, I have tried to use England or English only when referring to aspects of England itself; when a more general term is needed, I have tried to use Britain* or British.

English Channel. The body of water between England* and France.

English Heritage. Technically the Historic Buildings and Monuments Commission, since 1984 the administrator of all state-owned historic properties (except those still owned by the Crown*), most of which are open to the public. *See also* National Trust.

English palm. The willow tree, from the habit of waving willow branches in Palm Sunday* processions.

ENO. English National Opera. *See* National Opera.

enquiries. The telephone service Americans call information.

enquiry agent. A person Americans call a private detective.

ENSA. Before 1946, the entertainment service for the British military, similar to American U.S.O. shows.

ensign. (1) A flag, especially among sailors, for whom the ensign is a specific type of flag, a solid color with the Union Jack* symbol in the upper interior corner only: white for the navy,* blue for the navy reserve, and red for merchant ships. (2) In the army,* the lowest-ranking officer,* so called because his primary duty was to carry the flag of the unit. This was usually also the youngest officer and was often regarded as something of an officer-trainee. By 1880, the rank had officially been replaced by sub-lieutenant,* except in the Foot Guards,* who retained the rank until after WWI. Before the rise of the regular army, this was a position of considerably more trust, if not authority, something along the lines of personal assistant to the commander, as can be seen by both Iago and Pistol holding the rank. Although the American navy uses the name for its lowest-ranking officer, the British navy* does not. *See also* subaltern.

entail. Legally, to bequeath property to several persons successively. Thus, the person living off the income* does not actually "own" the property and cannot sell it or bequeath it to his or her own heirs. The procedure was especially used to guarantee that property stayed with male heirs, as in *Pride and Prejudice*, where the Bennetts live off property that cannot be inherited by any of the daughters, making the search for husbands a more desperate issue than the modern reader often recognizes.

enterprise zone. An area legally exempted from some rates* and business taxes in order to encourage new industry in depressed areas; first used in 1980.

Environment, Department of. The ministry* responsible not only for aspects of the nation Americans associate with the environment, such as national parks,* water resources, et cetera, but also for all local government.

Environment Secretary. A Cabinet* minister,* technically Secretary of State for the Environment, in charge of the Department of the Environment,* much more powerful than American environmental figures.

Epping Forest. In one of those curious anomalies of English life, this is a park of the City* of London,* although it lies ten miles northwest of the City's boundaries. Henry VIII used to hunt there, and it remains primarily woodland.

Epsom. A village to the southwest of London,* for a brief period in the Restoration a fashionable spa, now a commuter suburb. **Epsom Downs** is a race course located there, most noted as the site of the Derby,* and what we now call Epsom salt was first found naturally there.

Epworth League. A fellowship and study organization for Methodist* youth.

equity. *See* Chancery.

Ermine Street. An ancient road from London* north to Lincoln* and York;* it left London from Bishopsgate* and is followed for part of its way by the modern A1* and A10.*

Ernie. Electric random number indicator equipment, the machine that produces random numbers for the premium bond* lottery.

Esher. A suburb of London* to the southwest, immediately southwest of Surbiton,* generally seen as a home for the well-to-do and stuffy.

espadrille. A rope-soled shoe, usually with a canvas upper, worn most often at the beach.*

Esplanade. *See* Brighton.

Esquire. Originally, a title used by a squire,* abbreviated as **Esq.** and written as: (First name Family name), Esq. By late nineteenth century, the title was used as a compliment for any male who gave the impression of gentlemanliness and was often used on formal announcements, invitations, or signatures for a man who had no other titles available. By the mid–twentieth century, however, Mister* (Mr*) had replaced that usage, except in the most formal situations. However, like the nebulous concept of gentleman,* one may confer it on others but never on oneself; in the contemporary world a man who signs himself Esq. is definitely not. *See also* squire.

Essex. Originally, a Saxon kingdom in the southeastern portion of England* north of the Thames,* so called from the East Saxons, as distinct from those in the kingdom of Wessex.* After the Norman invasion, the name was used for the fertile county* lying along the east coast just north of the Thames Estuary. This came to be one of the Home Counties* and, in the mid–twentieth century began to be filled with featureless housing developments for the lower ends of the middle class* and working class as London* spread its suburbs into the southwestern regions of the county; the bulk of the county, however, remains primarily a market garden* for London.

estate. A neighborhood, sometimes as small as a single block of a street, of houses developed at the same time, generally a twentieth-century term for suburban developments, although builders and salesmen have called even a block* of flats* an estate in order to give it more status. However, the rise of council estates* has taken some of the shine off the term, making it more suggestive of poor people, so it has not been used so often in recent housing developments.

estate agent. What Americans call a real estate agent, having much the same love-hate relationship with the general public.

estate car. What Americans call a station wagon.

et. The most common and most widely used pronunciation of ate; its use is not a sign of ignorance but often the reverse, a sign of upper class* linguistic usage, which is why some writers choose to spell it this way in dialogue. As with so many linguistic and social customs, you are likely to find this at the top and the bottom, but not in the middle.

et cetera. Used as in America, usually abbreviated as *etc.*, but often heard as **and etceteras**, meaning all the usual related items, as in "tea and etceteras" rather than "tea, etc."

Eton. A small town near Windsor,* known almost completely for the public school* there, founded in 1440 and since at least the early nineteenth century one of the most influential and socially significant of all such schools. *See also* Harrow.

Eton crop. A very boyish hairstyle worn by women before WWII.

Eton jacket. A jacket that stops at the waist and is open down the front, with lapels so wide they almost touch the shoulder seam, similar to the uniform worn at Eton.* This was one of the earliest fashions specifically for children and not simply adult clothes cut smaller, introduced in the mid-nineteenth century, but adult versions have since been worn occasionally by women.

Eurasian. While Americans usually think of this as a person of European and Chinese or Japanese ancestry, Britons tend to think of it as mixed European and Indian, although they also use the term for those who are partly Oriental as well. *See also* Anglo-Indian.

Euston Station. One of three different train stations practically side by side in north-central London,* built originally in 1837, rebuilt in 1968; its trains serve the western portion of the island from the Midlands* north into Scotland.* *See also* King's Cross; St. Pancras.

evangelical. This refers to the general set of religious attitudes associated in America with fundamentalism, but it is used specifically not for the nonconformist* sects but for those tending in this direction within the Church of England,* particularly in the late eighteenth and early nineteenth centuries, often still in considerable dispute with the Anglo-Catholic* wing of the church.

Evening Hymn. The Church of England* has a number of hymns specifically for Evensong,* but the most commonly meant is #267 in the 1935 *English Hymnal*, beginning "Glory to Thee, my God, this night . . . " and with perhaps the more familiar final stanza, "Praise God, from whom all blessings flow. . . . "

evensong. (1) An evening service in the Church of England,* conducted daily; the *Book of Common Prayer* lists Evensong on Sundays and Holy Days, and Evening Prayer on all others, but most usage makes no such distinction. *See also* matins. (2) Sunset, the time when the Evensong service would be conducted.

ever so. Very, as in "ever so nice" or "ever so rich." Also as **ever such a**, as in "ever such a big house."

Everton. A suburb of Liverpool,* noted for a famous brand of toffee made there and for a successful football* club.*

Evesham. A small town in the middle of the **Vale of Evesham**, a rich agricultural valley between the Avon* and the Severn* in western England.*

Excellency, Your/His/Her. The proper form of address for an ambassador or governor.*

Exchange. (1) The **Royal Exchange**, in London* in Threadneedle Street,* an institution since 1566 where merchants met to conduct major trading activities. Most cities built similar buildings, often called a **Corn Exchange** because the trading of grain was the primary business carried on there. Over the years, most businesses became more regularized, so the various exchanges, as in America, focussed only on items such as crops, metals, money, or stocks and bonds that were subject to constant fluctuation in price. (2) The **New Exchange**, built as a competitor of the Royal Exchange in 1608 in the Strand* in London,* but surrounded with shops that soon became a shopping arcade that dominated the other aspects of the exchange, very fashionable and popular in the seventeenth century but torn down in 1737. People in Restoration plays are always arranging to meet at the Exchange, which might of course be the business institution but much more likely is this one, which was the Restoration equivalent of hanging out at the shopping mall. (3) *See* Labour Exchange.

Exchequer. Originally the financial office of the monarch, so called because it reckoned accounts by counters on a checkerboard, similar to an abacus. Over the years, its functions outside pure record-keeping were taken over by the Treasury,* so that now the Exchequer is understood to mean the nation's actual bank account. However, the Chancellor of the Exchequer is still the chief financial officer of the nation. *See also* Chancellor.

ex-directory. What Americans call an unlisted phone number.

exeat. In some public schools* and colleges,* a temporary leave for a student, from the Latin for "let him go."

Exeter. (1) The major town of Devon* in southwest England,* a major center of wool trade until the eighteenth century, long noted for its cathedral.* (2) One of the oldest colleges* of Oxford.*

exhibiting. The activity Americans call exposing, done typically by a man who throws open his overcoat to "exhibit himself" to women.

exhibition. Originally, a pension or monetary reward of any kind, but since the late seventeenth century used in this sense only for very specific scholarships given to a student from a college's* own funds. *See also* bursary.

Exmoor. A rough large moor* in the northern part of the Cornish peninsula in southwestern England,* long noted for the uncivilized life lived there, best exemplified by *Lorna Doone*. It is a National Park* and a favorite vacation site, particularly for hikers and campers, due to its scenery.

expanded town. A previously small town much enlarged to cope with urban spill, sort of a new town* built on the core of an old one.

Express. A daily newspaper* that once, under Lord Beaverbrook, was a serious challenger for most popular paper, primarily read by the lower–middle class,* shopkeepers,* et cetera. The *Sunday Express* has much the same audience, with a tabloid attitude but printed in regular broadsheet format that looks much more respectable. *See also Mail*.

ex-serviceman. What Americans call a veteran; the latter term is rarely used in Britain except for the very old.

extra. In cricket,* a run scored for a team but not counted for an individual batsman's* statistics, such as a run scored on a wide* or a bye.*

extractor fan. What Americans call an exhaust fan.

-ey. As an ending on place names, this is often a shortened form of eyot.*

Eyeties. Usually pronounced eye-tize, Italians, in use only since WWI.

eyot. A small island.

F

Football Association.*

face flannel. *See* flannel.

facia. In a car, what Americans call the dashboard; a **facia pocket** would be the glove compartment. Also spelled **fascia**.

factor. In Scotland,* the bailiff* of a landed estate.

Factory Act. Any of several laws regulating working conditions. The first (1819) banned children under nine from the work force and limited those under sixteen to a twelve-hour work day. Another in 1833 limited those under thirteen to a forty-eight-hour week and those under eighteen to a sixty-eight-hour week; in 1844 limited women to twelve hours a day and children under thirteen to six and one-half hours; in 1853 all textile workers were limited to twelve-hour days, with similar limits gradually extended to other industries, continually modified in additional acts during the twentieth century.

faculty. Rarely used in the American sense of all teachers at a school, this usually means a collection of related collegiate departments, such as a Faculty of Engineering, which in American would be called a School of Engineering.

FA Cup. *See* Cup.

fag. (1) A cigarette; the **fag end** of something is the very last part, usually worthless like a cigarette butt. (2) A really dull or tiring job; **fagged out**

is how you feel after doing such a job. (3) A younger boy student who also acted as a servant to an older boy in a public school.* No homosexual relationship is implied; the American usage to mean homosexual was not known in Britain until very recently and is still very rare.

faggot. (1) In a fire, a bundle of sticks or large twigs. (2) A nonexistent person, or a dummy made from faggots to look like a person. In the eighteenth century this usually applied to civilians hired just to stand-in on a muster to make a military unit look up to full strength and in the nineteenth to voters found by the practice called in America "voting the graveyard." (3) On a dish, a ball of chopped meat (often liver) and oatmeal, baked or fried, eaten primarily in the north of England.* (4) In some regional dialects, a prostitute, but not a homosexual. *See also* fag.

fair. (1) In the medieval era, a regular gathering, usually annually, of traders who came from large distances to do major buying and selling (as opposed to a market,* which happens more often and deals with traders from a smaller area). Almost always, these coincided with religious festivals. Most fairs were devoted primarily to a single product, such as the Nottingham* Goose Fair, the Findon Sheep Fair, the Cherry Fair at Chertsey, et cetera. As might be expected, fairs also attracted purveyors of pleasures—food, drink, sex, gambling, puppets and plays, et cetera—and in many cases this came to dominate the commercial aspects, so that a number of the fairs, such as Bartholomew Fair,* became **pleasure fairs** where trading was all but nonexistent. These too were on the wane in the early twentieth century but have revived under the stimulus of the same kinds of "rides" familiar in American carnivals and amusement parks, now usually called a **fun fair**. In the modern world of urban development and department stores, there are still a few **trade fairs**, which are now more like annual business conventions than the old trading fairs. The one significant exception seems to be the **horse fairs**, which continue to be run in the old personal trading manner, the largest of which, at Appleby in northern England,* is also the major gathering of the gypsies.* *See also* fête; hiring fair. (2) As an adjective or adverb, very or completely, as in "he was fair upset," much more intense than the American fairly.

fair cop. The stereotypical criminal's saying in films and literature, this meant not that the bobby* had caught him fair and square, as if in a game, but rather that he knew he was completely trapped (*See* fair) and was giving himself up without resistance.

fair do's/dos. Act fairly.

Fairy. A popular brand of liquid dishwashing soap, sometimes used generically for all dishwashing liquids.

fairy cake. *See* cake.

fairy cycle. A child's tricycle.

fairy lights. Strings of small lights used in decorating outdoor fairs* or displays, similar to the lights Americans put on Christmas trees.

falcon. A hawk used for hunting. Technically, only the female is called a falcon, but generally falcon and hawk are used interchangeably. A trained falcon is released, looks for and kills rabbits or other large birds, and then the game is retrieved by the hunter, who has followed on horseback. Hunting with a falcon has always been done for sport rather than for food and in the medieval era was one of the primary entertainments of the nobility.* The sport has steadily declined since the Restoration and is now rarely seen. *See also* hunt.

Falklands. A brief war with Argentina in 1982 over control of the Falkland Islands in the South Atlantic, won by the British.

Family Court. *See* High Court.

family credit. A benefit* under Social Security* to families with children at home but in which the parent (or parents) work and still make less than a specified amount (currently the equivalent of about $200 a week); the amount of the benefit varies depending on family size and income.

fancy. (1) As a verb, to feel sexual desire for, as in "I could really fancy you." (2) As a verb, to like or desire in a casual way, as in "Fancy a drink?"; similarly as a noun, something you might like, as in "What's your fancy?" Americans still occasionally use this general sense, as in "take a fancy to," but never as often or as widely. (3) An exclamation of surprise, as in "Fancy that!"

fancy dress. Not fancy or expensive clothing but rather a disguise or costume to be worn to a costume party or masquerade ball.* Fancy dress parties appear in literature and films perhaps more often than in real life, since they offer such romantic possibilities for characters to meet and to eavesdrop, but they have been consistently much more popular for at least two centuries in Britain than in America and have been attended by all groups from the middle class* upward.

fancy man. This only means a male lover and has no relation to nancy* boy; simply a male equivalent of the **fancy woman**, which is a genteel* euphemism for a tart* or a mistress.*

fanny. Not a euphemism for a person's buttocks, as in America, but a much more vulgar term for a woman's genitals. *See also* bum; jacksie; pussy.

Fanny Adams. Something of little or no value. There is a sick derivation: In a famous murder case, Fanny Adams was killed and chopped into small pieces. When the navy* began experimenting with canned meat rations, the sailors jokingly called them Fanny Adams. The meat was not particularly tasty or popular, and the term came to mean something you didn't really want, and as such passed into the rest of society by WWI.

fan tan. A card game, completely unrelated to the Chinese game of that name, played both by children and, for stakes, by adults. Cards are dealt equally, first play is a seven; the next person must play either a six or eight of the same suit (or start another suit with another seven); the next plays either a five or nine, and so on in sequence until the suit is full. Winner is the first person to play all his cards. If money is involved, the usual practice is one chip every time you are unable to play a card, and one chip per card left in your hand at the end of play.

farthing. The smallest coin, worth a quarter of a pence* (the name a corruption of fourth); hence, used metaphorically to indicate the cheap or worthless. The coin was used until 1961 when it was officially recognized as worthless. *See also* Appendix I.

fascia. *See* facia.

fast bowler/bowling. *See* bowl.

Father Christmas. The person who brings Christmas* gifts, similar to but not quite as commercialized (yet) as the American Santa Claus. He has a bulky white beard and wears a red robe with a hood, but (so far) has no reindeer or elves. However, under the American media influence, many people are beginning to tell their children his name is Santa.

FCO. Foreign and Commonwealth Office.*

feast. In addition to the large meals called feasts, the term is also used for a festival, originally one celebrating the feast day of the saint of the local church.* The nature of these celebrations varied from village* to village, and most lost their religious connections during the eighteenth century when England* finally adopted the same calendar* as the rest of Europe* and the traditional dates were separated from the liturgical calendar. Increasing urbanization continued to lessen their importance, and by the early twentieth, the local village feasts had all but disappeared, remaining as a pale remnant of their former selves in the village fête.* The term feast tended to be used in the northeastern areas of England, while other areas called them wakes* or revels.*

feed store. Not the store where feed for livestock is purchased but the barn* on the farm where it is stored.

fell. High, rough, and wild terrain with numerous outcroppings of rocks and boulders, used primarily in northern England;* occasionally applied to a mountaintop, particularly in the Lake District.*

fellow. (1) At Oxford* or Cambridge,* a senior member of a college,* including but not limited to the British professor.* Technically, a college is incorporated as a self-governing institution, and the fellows are those members who participate in that self-government, usually signified by their being paid from the college's own funds, and thus in American terms might be thought of as those faculty members with tenure. In some colleges, however, full voting rights are limited only to **senior fellows**, those of higher academic rank, variously defined. A **prize fellow** is a fellow who obtains his position as the result of winning an examination rather than by the usual means of selection and is usually a recent graduate who receives a stipend for a specific period of further research (cf. the American research fellowship). An **honourary fellow** is a notable elected to such membership as an honor, like the American honorary degree; such a fellow is allowed to dine at the high table* and is expected to front for the college in political and social situations but is not really a part of the governance or teaching of the institution, and the award is generally reserved for royalty,* nobility,* or politicians, and for retired fellows. Other colleges and universities also have fellows but with more variable meanings. *See also* commoner; don; lecturer; reader; tutor. (2) A member of a professional organization that also calls itself a college or of a similar learned society, such as the Royal Society* or the Royal College of Surgeons.*

fen. A marsh or swampy area.

Fenchurch Street. A street in London* in the eastern portion of the City,* noted primarily as the home of shipping businesses. **Fenchurch Street Station** is the terminus for trains serving the areas east of London.

fender. The part of a car Americans call a bumper, probably from their original similarity in shape to the fender in a fireplace that kept falling coals from spilling out onto the hearth. *See also* wing.

Fenland. The Fens.*

Fens. A wide area of fens* in England,* south and west of the Wash* in Cambridgeshire,* Norfolk,* and Lincolnshire.* There are no specific boundaries, as the size and nature of the area has changed considerably since the Roman era, when much of it was under water. Constant silting, the formation of peat,* and (since the seventeenth century) drainage projects have reclaimed much of the area from marshland and made it suitable for farming, with perhaps the richest soil available in the nation; as the land has been drained, however, it has also sunk, and much of the area lies below sea level, behind dikes where it needs constant pumping, much like Holland, and is in continual threat of flooding. This is the visual image most often associated with East Anglia,* of which the Fens are but a part, giving the area an otherworldly quality that is used to good effect in such completely different fiction as Graham Swift's poetic *Waterland* and Dorothy Sayers's *The Nine Tailors*.

ferret. A small mammal something like the weasel, tamed and used for hunting, especially for creatures such as rabbits or rats that live in holes down which ferrets go easily, and often kept as pets, particularly by working-class* men. To **ferret something out** is to dig out the information in a devious or unseen manner.

fête. A small fair,* featuring stalls of sale items (usually secondhand or homemade), contests, and entertainment; in the twentieth century almost always for charity purposes, such as the church fête that is an annual highlight of village* life. *See also* feast; jumble sale.

FHB. Family Hold Back, a common code used in middle class* families to warn children not to eat up the food before the guests get their choice.

fiddle. To cheat, doctor the books, do something under the table, usually something small in scale. However, **fiddling** as an adjective means merely small in scale, implying no particular dishonesty, as in a "fiddling business" such as a street stall.* *See also* fiddly.

fiddler. A casual name for the sixpence.* *See also* Appendix I.

Fiddler's Green. Since the early nineteenth century, the heaven sailors go to, a place of free rum* and tobacco.*

fiddly. Thin, fussy, not worth bothering with; sometimes heard as **fiddling**.

field. When not used by a farmer, this means a broad flat expanse of grass used for games, such as cricket,* hockey,* or football.*

Field Marshal. The highest rank in the British army.* This is not necessarily the single commander of all army units, for there may be several men holding the rank at the same time, but it is similar to the American general with five stars, outranking a regular general and awarded only to generals with unique duties or unusually successful records. *See also* admiral.

Fife. A region* or county* in Scotland* across the Firth* of Forth from Edinburgh,* Scotland's most prosperous area with numerous fishing villages, rich farmland, and coal.

fifteen. A rugby* team; to make the **first fifteen** at school* would be like making a starting lineup of the varsity football team in America.

fifteen-hundred weight. Three-quarters of a ton,* used primarily to indicate the truck of that size.

figgy duff. *See* duff.

fig roll. The cookie Americans call a fig newton.

Fig Sunday. Palm Sunday,* due to the number of traditional fig dishes eaten on the day. The practice and the name had essentially disappeared by WWI.

fillet. (1) Pronounced FILLit, in theory, similar to the American filet, but in practice any steak with the bone cut out. In most restaurants this usually means what Americans call round steak, tough and thin and usually cooked well-done. For fish, it is the same as in America, a relatively large, boneless piece of the fish, but is still pronounced FILLit. (2) In figurative usage, to cut a little something off on the side, to steal in a small way.

Financial Times. A daily newspaper* similar to the American *Wall Street Journal* in its style and audience; unlike the *Journal*, however, it also covers "regular" news and the arts and is printed on pink paper. The **FT Index** is one of the paper's two basic indexes of stock prices, used like the Dow Jones Index to track the general shape of the market. Not connected to the *Times** in any way.

Finchley. A northern suburb of London* associated with the dull middle class,* in recent years known as a Jewish neighborhood.

find. *See* found.

fine leg. *See* leg.

finger out, take your. Stop standing around doing nothing and get a move on; WWII military slang that has penetrated much of society. It is never specified just where or what the finger is in, unlike the American versions of the phrase.

fingers. For the symbol made by holding up two fingers, *See* V.

finger sandwiches. Sandwiches* cut into small strips before eating.

Finnan haddie. A dish made from smoked haddock* boiled in milk.

fir. In daily life, used interchangeably with pine.

fir apple. What American call a pine cone.

fire. Anything that provides heat. The British have a deep attachment to a flaming fire in the home, and most homes were heated by an open fireplace past mid-twentieth century, although usually with coal rather than wood on the fire. After the British began to ban soft coal in 1956 for health and environmental reasons, most people converted to either central heat* (radiators), gas or electric heat, or paraffin* heaters, but they continued to call these the fire—when they come into a cold room most will say, "Switch on the fire," rather than, "Turn on the heater." *See also* bar; fog.

Fire, Great. Old London* was regularly scourged by fire and plague* but in 1666 what is now called the Great Fire burned about 80 percent of the buildings within the walls of the City.* London recovered surprisingly quickly, as there was almost no loss of life, and much positive grew out of the fire, since local regulations banned the construction of wooden buildings and Wren was put in charge of the restoration of churches and public buildings.

Fire Brigade. The organization Americans call the Fire Department. In London,* the first fire brigade was not organized until 1866.

fire office. A company that provides fire insurance. *See also* assurance.

fire-raiser. What Americans call an arsonist.

fire tender. What Americans call a fire truck or fire engine.

firewood. Since most open fires used coal,* this usually meant only the small bits of wood used as kindling to get the coal fire started. *See also* pimp.

firm. The British tend to use this for any small business, although the legal distinction is that it is a partnership. *See also* Ltd.; PLC.

first. In relation to a particular examination, the top mark, roughly equivalent to the American grade of *A*; in relation to a college* degree, a degree ranking among the top graduates, roughly equivalent to the various American degrees "with honors." A **double first** is such a degree in two separate fields of study. *See also* honours; second; pass.

first class. Many services are distinguished according to class and price. Trains, for example, have separate carriages* for first class, with wide seats and comfortable headrests, often in small compartments; second class, with relatively comfortable seats in rows; and third class, with bench-style seating; although in recent years, third class has disappeared and second has been euphemized to "standard," just as American airlines have euphemized it to "coach." In mail service, a first-class letter should be delivered within a day, and in London may even arrive in the second post*, while second-class letters should be delivered in two to three days; Americans of course are used to this, but in Britain the difference in cost is a couple of pence* while in America one-day service costs an extra $10 to $20. *See also* first rate.

first division. As a metaphor, roughly equivalent to the American major league, from the first division of the Football Association.* The FA plays in four divisions, or leagues, but unlike American sports leagues, these are neither equals nor major and minor leagues. After each season, the teams at the bottom of the first division are demoted to second, while those at the top of the second are promoted up, and so on through all four, so that the first division is not only assumed to be but also demonstrably is the strongest competition.

first foot. The first person across a threshold on New Year's* Day, thought to bring extraordinary luck (some say bad, some say good). The term is used primarily in Scotland.* *See also* Hogmanay.

First Lord. (1) The Prime Minister,* from the time in the early eighteenth century when he was the "First" Lord of the Treasury.* (2) *See* Lords of the Admiralty.

first rate. In the navy,* sailing ships were classified according to length, with the first rate the largest, usually about 180 feet or more, the **second rate** 10 to 15 feet shorter, and so on down to smaller categories. This led to the colloquial "first rate" to mean the best, top of the line, excellent, where Americans usually say "first class."

first school. A primary school* for children aged five to nine.

firth. In Scotland,* an inlet, strait, or other comparatively narrow arm of the sea. The **Firth of Forth** is the large bay on the east coast at Edinburgh* around which the bulk of Scottish towns are located. The **Firth of Clyde** is a similar bay on the west coast around which are Glasgow* and its related communities. **Moray Firth** is at the far northeast, with Inverness* at its inland point. **Solway Firth** is at the southwestern border of Scotland on the west coast. **Pentland Firth**, however, is not a bay but the strait between Scotland and the Orkney Islands to the northeast. Also called a **frith**.

fish. Very often this term is used generically to include shellfish as well.

fish and chips. One of the basic foods of the lower classes, a fish fillet* rolled in batter and deep fried, accompanied by potatoes* in the form Americans call French fries. The fish is usually plaice,* although sometimes cod or haddock is also used. Traditionally, the chips are rolled in a piece of newspaper, the fish placed on top, and then both are doused with vinegar and eaten with the fingers. Although long seen as a quintessentially English food, it only appeared during the late nineteenth century in the cities, where it was in many ways the first "fast food" and was eaten primarily by the working class,* as it still is. It is almost never cooked at home but rather brought in from the corner shop* or eaten while walking down the street.

fish fingers. What Americans call fish sticks.

fishing expedition. From mid–nineteenth century to mid–twentieth century, an annual flood of eligible young women who had failed to find husbands in Britain to India* and some other outposts along the way in hopes of finding one where the competition wasn't quite so severe.

fishmonger. A person who sells fish. In London,* the **Fishmongers** are one of the oldest of the great livery companies* of the City.*

fish slice. Originally, a utensil for cutting and serving cooked fish, something like a frosting spatula with one serrated edge. Because of the similarity in shape, this name is sometimes also given to the general utensil more often called a spatula.*

fishwife. A loud vulgar woman, from the women who sold fish in Billingsgate.*

fitments. Furniture, usually institutional.

fitted carpet. The carpet Americans call wall-to-wall.

fitted cupboards. What Americans call built-in cabinets. *See also* cupboard.

fittings. What Americans usually call fixtures, as in shop* fittings.

Fitz-. As a medieval surname, a prefix meaning "son of" (cf. French *fils*); by the eighteenth century, often used to provide a name for illegitimate children of the nobility,* and by mid-nineteenth also used by the English as a stereotype in names for the Irish gentry.*

Fitzrovia. An area in London* north of Oxford Street* and west of Tottenham Court Road,* so called from Fitzroy Square, the name surfacing in the 1930s when a number of artists and writers began to hang out in the pubs* there.

Fitzwilliam. The museum associated with Cambridge* University, a museum of antiquities and art.

five-fingered widow. Army* slang for masturbation.

Five Nations. A regular rugby* competition among the five principal nations that play the game: England, Wales, Scotland, Ireland, and France.

fiver. *See* note.

fives. Essentially the game Americans call handball, developed at Rugby* and sometimes called **Rugby fives**. It is played by two persons (or two teams of two) on a four-wall court and differs from other handball in that the serve must hit the sidewall first, and points are scored when a round is won by the person receiving rather than by the server.

five stones. A children's game similar to American jacks.

fixture. (1) Built-in or permanent furniture. (2) A regularly scheduled sporting match.

flag down. To wave down or stop someone else; no actual flag is required.

flageolet. *See* bean.

flan. What Americans usually call a pie, usually without a pastry top, as opposed to the British pie.* Usually this is sweet, with a custard or jellied filling, but sometimes it is what Americans call a quiche. Just to confuse things, a sponge* cake with a jam or fruit filling spread between layers is also called a flan. *See also* tart.

flannel. (1) What Americans usually call a washcloth or a facecloth. (2) As a verb, to whitewash, cover over, or to disguise without really lying; often used of politicians.

flannel cake. In Yorkshire,* a scone,* usually served under cream.*

flannels. Trousers* made of flannel,* worn by men only with casual jackets or sweaters in casual daytime situations or for sports such as cricket.*

flap. In WWII military slang, a crisis, probably from the tendency of people caught in them to throw their arms around aimlessly, quickly spreading afterwards to the civil service* and corporate society.

flapjack. Oatmeal, brown sugar, and butter, baked and then cut into strips, not at all like American flapjacks or pancakes.

flapper vote. The lowering of voting age for women from thirty to twenty-one, done in 1928. *See also* voting.

flash. What Americans call flashy, as in a flash suit or a flash car.

flashers. On a car, what Americans call the turn signals.

flashlight. *See* torch.

flask. Also sometimes used to indicate a Thermos bottle.

flat. What Americans usually call an apartment, a suite of rented rooms including a kitchen and private bath in a building large enough to have several such units. The name was borrowed from Scotland,* where a flat was a storey or floor* of a building, and in the mid–nineteenth century originally implied that the tenant occupied the entire floor (rooms* or an apartment* meant several tenants on the same floor, while a house* always had several floors), but by the early twentieth century the normal inflation of real estate terms meant simply that it was a self-contained unit, and it is now the generic term used for almost all kinds and sizes of rental units. A **garden flat** is in theory a flat overlooking the garden,* which in practice turns out to be what Americans call a basement apartment; a **granny flat** is a small version of the same thing, such as Americans in some cities call an in-law apartment, usually converted by the homeowner from a room or two in the basement of the family home; a **service flat** is a flat for which the building provides servants* as part of the rent; a **mansion flat** usually indicates a flat in a large building (*See* mansion). *See also* bijou; maisonette.

Fleet. A prison* in London* alongside the River Fleet* before it was covered over, dating back to Richard I but noted primarily as a debtor's prison,* which was its major use from about 1640 until demolished in 1846. Dickens's Pickwick is imprisoned there for refusing to pay the damages in his breach of promise* case but, as he is not a real debtor, manages to escape most of the misery of the squalid conditions. Through various loopholes, no licence* or banns* were required for a **Fleet marriage**, and so people who were not prisoners but who wished to be married in secret could go there to get married until the new Marriage Act outlawed it in 1753.

Fleet Street. A street in London* running approximately parallel to the Thames* from the Strand* to Ludgate Circus* but named not for the ships on the river docks but for the **River Fleet** that ran into the Thames at Blackfriars* and has now been so covered by construction that no one is absolutely sure if it is still there. It was noted for the prison nearby (*See* Fleet). From the very earliest days of printing, it was a primary site for bookshops, publishing, and the literary life, with Dr. Johnson living in a square just to the north. With so many printers in the vicinity, early newspapers* also started there, and since the mid–nineteenth century, the street has been synonymous with the British newspaper industry and journalism in general, as most of the national papers had offices and printing plants there. In the 1980s most papers moved plants to other areas, but Fleet Street is still used to mean the print media.

flesher. In Scotland,* a butcher.

flex. An electric wire or cord.

flick knife. The knife Americans call a switchblade.

flight lieutenant. *See* lieutenant.

fling. A Scottish dance similar to a reel* but with much wilder movements, often called the **Highland fling** and treated as a unique national patriotic dance.

flip. A drink made of beer,* sugar,* and some harder spirit such as gin* or brandy, heated by sticking a hot iron in the cup. An **egg flip**, however, is hot wine, beer, or cider with an egg mixed in, sometimes also called egg nog.*

flip-flops. The sandals, usually made from rubber or plastic, that Americans sometimes call thongs.

flipping. Same as effing.*

flit. To move your residence, used primarily in northern England* and Scotland.* A **midnight flit** means skipping out without paying the rent.

float. (1) Of a company, to raise the money for start-up. (2) *See* milk float.

flog. (1) Originally, to beat a person as a form of punishment (*See* cat). However, this term has spread into figurative use and is now often used to indicate that you have outdone a competitor. (2) To sell something, usually implying the item is either stolen or very hard to sell.

floor. The British number actual floors, so the bottom level of a house is called the ground floor, the second story is the first floor, and so on. *See also* shop floor.

florin. Originally a gold coin from Florence, used generically for a number of different continental gold coins and for one fourteenth century English gold coin worth six shillings.* In 1849 a new silver florin was coined, about the size of an American half-dollar and worth two shillings; it was formally dropped in the decimalization of 1971, but the coin remained in circulation as it was the same size and value as the new 10p piece. *See also* Appendix I.

Flowering Sunday. In Wales,* Palm Sunday,* from the tradition of putting flowers on family graves on that day.

fluff. *See* lint.

flummery. A dessert made from beaten eggs, flour, and honey, something like an American pudding.

flutter. A bet, usually a very small one.

fly. (1) When said about a person, smart, sharp, quick-witted. (2) A small carriage* with a double seat and pulled by a single horse, so often offered for hire* as to be synonymous with all hired carriages.

flying officer. In the RAF,* the lowest-ranking officer.* *See also* lieutenant.

Flying Scotsman. An express train from London* at King's Cross* to Edinburgh.*

Flying Squad. A small unit within a larger police* force, designed to deal with emergencies or crimes requiring unusually quick action.

flyover. What Americans call an overpass.

flyscreen. Fine wire mesh Americans call windowscreen or screen wire.

fog. London* in particular has long been associated with fog. Throughout most of the nineteenth and early twentieth centuries, it was wrapped in fog so dense and suffocating that some people actually died of asphyxiation, and fog became a cliché of stories and films set in London. Following the particularly dense and deadly fogs of 1952, the Clean Air Acts of 1956 and 1965 outlawed the burning of soft coal* and similar smoky fuels in congested areas like London, and the London fog disappeared almost immediately; the fog had in fact been smog. The city now has only the fog normally associated with ports and perhaps somewhat less of that than most other similar cities in the world due to its inland location. *See also* Smoke.

fold. A pen for livestock, almost always applied only to a sheep pen.

follow, to. When used in restaurants or describing meals, this means "for dessert," as in "with pudding* to follow."

folly. A purely ornamental building on the grounds* of a country house.* Buildings that were absurdly expensive have also been called follies, for the folly of building them, but most usage indicates this smaller building raised purely for the delight of looking at it and rarely indicates any serious disapproval, the name often used by the original builder.

fool. A dessert originally made from thick cream, sugar, and puréed fruit (especially gooseberries*), now also made from puréed fruit and custard. *See also* trifle.*

foolscap. Not a type but a size of paper, about 12½ inches × 17 inches.

football. (1) The game Americans call soccer. As this game has become familiar in recent decades in the United States, we need not go into the rules here. This is the primary professional team sport in Britain, played professionally in the Football Association* in England* and Wales* and the Scottish League* in Scotland.* The annual "season" runs August to May, with league matches* on Saturday afternoons, and star players are paid salaries that match those of American professional sports, all the more remarkable in that there are no lucrative TV contracts to augment income. *See also* club; Cup; football hooligan; terraces. (2) The game usually called Rugby* football or simply rugby to distinguish it from football (soccer). For details, *See* rugby. (3) In the 1980s, some TV broadcasting of football games from America began, with the result that some people have begun to watch and to play the American game, calling it **American football** to distinguish it from other forms.

Football Association. The organization administering professional soccer in England* and Wales.* Founded in 1863 as an amateur association, it tried to stabilize rules among public school* and club* teams, but many groups preferred to play rugby* rules and separated after a while. However, by establishing the FA Cup* in 1871, the association became the clear leader in the sport, and by the 1880s a number of working-class* clubs had been organized to compete, soon establishing complete dominance of the sport and introducing some professional players among the amateurs of the club. After WWI, the Association became completely professional. Currently some ninety-two professional teams compete in four divisions, with standings within divisions determined by total points scored in matches rather than by wins and losses, since professional soccer so often ends in a tie. *See also* first division; pools; replay; Scottish League.

football hooligan. Teenagers or young men involved in various forms of hooliganism, associated with football* because their violent binges often grow out of drunken revelry during and after professional football matches. Since the 1970s this has been a serious public concern, as outbreaks of violence produce not just local disturbance but seriously harm Britain's reputation in Europe, due to the number of fans who export such violence on trips to international matches, where British fans became a byword for mindless, drunken violence. The original assumption was that the hooliganism expressed the frustration of the poor and unemployed who used football as a release. However, the discovery by police* of organized gangs that include office workers, bank managers, et cetera, rather than the unemployed, and the large number of hooligans who can afford foreign travel have made many see them more as a symbol of the collapse of traditional British society. No solution has been found at the time of writing. *See also* lager.

footer. Schoolboy slang for football.*

Foot Guards. *See* Guards.

footpad. A highwayman* without a horse, a robber who operates on foot. Originally the footpad operated on the highways,* stopping foot travelers or slow wagons, but the term was also used for the urban robber who stole from the passing pedestrian at gun- or knifepoint; thus, the term survived into the twentieth century and was still used after WWI for the person modern Americans would call a mugger.

for. In cricket* scoring, partial scores for a match are reported as *x* for *y*, meaning number of points scored for the number of batsmen* already put out; thus, 215 for 7 means the team has 215 points already and the eighth batsman in the order is now batting. The bowler's* statistics may also be shown in reverse order, as for example 2 for 12, indicating number of batsmen put out for number of points allowed by the individual bowler.

Foreign and Commonwealth Office. The governmental ministry* formed in 1968 by combining the Foreign Office* and the Commonwealth Office,* responsible for administration of all foreign relations of the nation.

Foreign Office. The ministry* responsible for relations with foreign nations, although from its organization in the 1780s until 1919 it had no authority over the diplomatic service, which accounts for many of the eccentricities of British foreign policy over the years. Formally joined with the Commonwealth Office* in 1968, its chief minister* is still called the Foreign Secretary* and the FCO* is still casually called the Foreign Office.

Foreign Secretary. Technically the Secretary of State for Foreign and Commonwealth Affairs, head of the Foreign Office* and one of the most influential members of the Cabinet.*

forenoon. What Americans call the morning; Britons also use morning, and forenoon is now regarded as old-fashioned.

forest. In general, forest is used more technically than in the United States, meaning a particular area of woodland designated, usually by the monarch, as a preserved forest area. Other forested areas are generally called woods.* *See also* chase; New Forest; park; plantation.

for it. In trouble, likely to be punished, as in "I'm for it when I get home." *See also* chop.

fork. The British use the fork in the continental manner, keeping it in the left hand at all times while eating. Also, when picking up food with the fork, the majority use the knife to push a small portion up onto the back of the fork, on which it is lifted to the mouth. A **fork supper** is a meal needing no knife, that is, without meat or with meat in a pie* or casserole.

form. (1) A grade in school, but almost always only in a secondary school.* The exact meaning varies from school to school, but in most schools since the mid-nineteenth, there are five one-year forms starting at about age eleven, followed by a **sixth form** which is completely college-prep in nature and lasts several years. In most public schools,* where students begin at age thirteen, they start in the third form. In sixth form, most students concentrate on only three subjects, and in most places the sixth is divided into an "upper" and "lower sixth" with the upper the second year students. In other forms, however, upper and lower may be used to distinguish smarter students from slow students or classes formed by students entering in different terms,* depending on the school. *See also* standard. (2) In slang, a horse racing record, as in the American racing form, and from that, also used to mean a criminal record. (3) Manners* in the sense of doing the right thing; used almost always as **bad form** for doing something that "just isn't done." (4) The normal procedure, as in "What's the form for . . . ?" Thus, **on form** is the way it has always been done, the way things have gone in the past, usually.

fortnight. Two weeks (fourteen nights).

Fortnum & Mason. A grocer* in Piccadilly* in London,* founded in 1707 by a footman of the Queen* to supply the royal household* and famous since as one of the most expensive and elegant of grocers, where the sales clerks still dress formally and where the wealthy come for simple foods in elegant containers, elegant picnics complete in their hampers, and delicacies sold in carpeted rooms under chandeliers.

forward. (1) In hockey,* one of the five players who are specialists in offense and scoring; a girl who plays forward is thus one of the real stars of a girl's school,* not merely athletic but also lithe and intelligent and, in girl's school fiction at least, beautiful as well. There is one **center forward** who starts in the middle of the field, and two **inner forwards** who play to either side of her, and two wings* who play on the outside of the front line. (2) In rugby,* the players who form the scrum,* thus the toughest but not necessarily the fastest; forwards can be identified by a shortage of teeth. (3) In football* (soccer), the five offensive players in the forward line who were responsible for most of the scoring; in modern play, this traditional formation (with the same names as in hockey above) has been replaced by a more flexible one with only three such players, now called **strikers**, under either name the most idolized players on the team.

Fosse Way. The Roman road from Exeter* to Lincoln,* passing through Bath.*

found. Food and lodging; **all found** in relation to wages for servants* meant food and a room were included in the agreed-upon wage. Those who **find themselves** must pay for their own lodging and food.

foundation boy. A student at a public school* on a scholarship from the school's own funds.

foundling. An orphan whose true parentage is unknown. The **Foundling Hospital** in London* was founded in 1739 as a home and school that eventually accepted both foundlings and the bastards* of women who promised to "reform." It was for its time a remarkably humane institution, and the relative handful of babies admitted there, like Dickens's Tattycoram, had a good chance of actually surviving to adulthood. The school was moved to Berkhamstead in 1926, then to Hertfordshire* in 1954, where it is now the Coram Foundation, which also built a new building near the original site in 1937 to house the foundation offices and show the many paintings that had been donated to it and in the 1950s built the **Great Ormond Street** hospital, primarily occupied with children's diseases and child welfare.

four. In cricket,* a hit that results in four runs, usually a boundary.*

four-by-two. (1) The lumber size Americans call a two-by-four; British practice is to always put the larger number first. (2) In the army,* the rag used to clean a rifle, from its common size of 4 inches × 2 inches.

fox hunt. *See* hunt.

Foyle's. A bookstore in Charing Cross* Road in London,* one of the largest in the world, with a shelf stock that includes almost every book in print in England* and a shelving system that makes it impossible to find one.

France. *See* French.

franchise. *See* voting.

FRCP. Fellow,* Royal College* of Physicians.*

FRCS. Fellow,* Royal College* of Surgeons.*

free church. A nonconformist* church.

freehold. *See* leasehold.

free house. A pub* that sells several different brands of beer,* as opposed to a tied house.*

French. The English in particular have had a long love-hate relationship with France and the French since 1066, pausing only occasionally from open warfare to worship at the shrine of French fashions and customs. Thus, French has been the only "modern" language regularly spoken or studied, and people have regularly dropped French terms and phrases into their talk to demonstrate their education or gentility. At the same time, **French** is often used as an all-purpose term for profanity—the man who swears in front of a woman might say, "Pardon my French." Similarly French itself is often used to indicate anything unacceptable or foul, particularly if there is a sexual connotation: **French leave** is desertion or running away; **French prints**, like **French novels**, are pornography, while a **French letter** is a condom; the **French pox/gout/ache/crown/et cetera** are all venereal diseases (the French return the favor and call them the English pox, et cetera).

Friday, Good. *See* Good Friday.

friendly society. A cooperative association similar to an American lodge, some dating to the early seventeenth century but known primarily for providing insurance of various kinds for their members. Also called a **benefit society**.

frigate. In the navy,* the largest sailing ship still too small to be a ship of the line,* usually more than 140 feet long with 20–40 guns, noted for its combination of speed with firepower; its officer was a full captain.*

frightful/frightfully. Although dictionaries define this as likely to lead to fright or fear or shock, in practice this is more often used to mean extremely, as in "frightfully dull," or to describe anything unpleasant, as in "how perfectly frightful for you." Dr. Johnson pointed out that it was used only by women; in the early twentieth century it appeared in literature in the mouth of the public school twit* as well, but it still continues to be associated far more with women than men. *See also* clever.

fringe. The part of a haircut Americans call the bangs.

frith. A firth.*

frock. Originally, a long gown-like garment worn by men, like a monk's habit or a clergyman's cassock,* from which we get the terms unfrock or defrock when a priest loses his ecclesiastical status. The term then spread to include any long outer garment worn by men, often the same as a smock.* By Shakespeare's time the term was extended to a long woman's garment that overlay another, usually worn only indoors. In the seventeenth and eighteenth centuries it would be applied mostly to a gown-like garment worn only by children, in the early nineteenth century coming to be more associated with girls than boys. From that it seems to have worked back upward to mean a less formal dress worn by women, the kind of dress that could be worn in the mornings or in daily activities, and in the early twentieth century it suddenly became a generic term, in both Britain and America, for a woman's daytime dress. It's unclear how this meaning of the term appeared, as it seems unrelated to the French *froc* (underwear) or *frac* (the man's frock coat*) and the term was in widespread use for a dress in England some thirty years before hemlines rose to the knee length of the frock coat. The term disappeared very suddenly in the United States during WWII but continues in Britain, although used not nearly as often as before. Before the 1960s it generally meant a specific style of short dress that seemed to be both youthful in spirit and was usable as a party dress* if necessary. The "simple little frock" was more likely to be worn to be noticed by other women than by men. After the major change in fashion emphasis of the 1960s, the frock lost much of its suggestion of youthfulness and now is usually a **party frock** that is more sedate and "feminine" than the normal youthful dress, worn primarily to indicate the wearer's respectability to other women.

frock coat. A man's coat of approximate knee length. The term was used in the eighteenth century, and Robinson Crusoe had one, but by the early nineteenth century it meant a very specific kind of coat: double-breasted with lapels, the hem extending to just above the knees, almost always black or dark gray, worn with trousers,* vest, shirt, stiff collar, and tie as the basic daytime apparel of all respectable men from mid–nineteenth century through the early twentieth century. After WWI it began to be replaced, much more slowly than in the United States, by the modern suit for business wear and by the cutaway* or morning coat* for formal daytime wear.

frog. A Frenchman, but only since the late nineteenth century. During the seventeenth, frog meant a Dutchman.

front. A pedestrian walkway along the seaside, often beside a street also called the **Front** in practically every seaside resort town.

front bench. *See* back bencher.

front room. The room Americans call the living room, from the traditional arrangement of rooms in terrace houses and semi-detacheds* of two rooms downstairs; the kitchen was in back and the one in front was used for a family sitting room.* Naturally, the usage is confined to the lower classes who live in such homes, and even among them sitting room, lounge,* or parlour* has been preferred by anyone with the slightest bit of social ambition.

frost. What Americans call freezing point, 32° F, 0° C. So many **degrees of frost** means so many degrees below freezing. The frozen dew Americans usually call frost is called **rime** or **hoar frost**. Thus, **frosted foods** are what Americans call frozen foods.

fruit cup. *See* punch.

fruiter. A tree that bears fruit or the grower of such trees, not to be confused with the **fruiterer**, who sells the fruit in a shop.*

fruit machine. What Americans call a slot machine.

frumenty. An English* breakfast dish sometimes found before the late nineteenth century and that appears to have been made by soaking wheat or barley in warm water for several days until it cracked open and formed a starchy gelatin-like substance, over which was poured milk or honey. A modern version is made by boiling the wheat in milk and topping it with sugar or cinnamon.

FT Index. *See Financial Times*.

fug. Pronounced like mug, not a euphemism for fuck but rather meaning stuffy air, especially air in a hot, smoke-filled room; also sometimes used as a verb meaning to stay in such a room, especially at home, where this is a sign of coziness, particularly in the lower half of the social scale.

Fulham. An area to the west of London* along the Thames, before the mid-nineteenth century used primarily for farmland and the site of **Fulham Palace**, the home of the Bishop* of London, and afterward developed into a typical suburb.

fullback. (1) In hockey,* one of two primarily defensive players who move around on the field but stay to the rear of any attack so that they can fall back to help the goalkeeper* at any moment; hence, they tend to be large and strong girls who are much less speedy than the other players, and in stories have simple, hearty personalities. (2) In rugby,* the player who acts as a last line of defense, similar to a soccer goalkeeper* in purpose but not actually positioned at the goal line, moving around much more on the field.

full stop. The punctuation mark Americans call a period. Other punctuation marks are sometimes called stops, too, but only the period is a full stop.

Funds. The Consolidated Fund was a mutual fund that, since 1751, owned the bonds of the national debt. Paying 3 percent interest unchanged for more than a century, it was the ultimate in secure investments, the place where the capital of most nineteenth century widows and spinsters was invested. The Funds still exist, with two types at guaranteed 2½ percent and 4 percent, which in this era of staggering inflation means heavily discounted prices, and thus they are less likely to be used by small investors.

funeral. Funeral customs varied considerably before the nineteenth century, but during the early Victorian era the funeral became one of the central expressions of respectability.* Mourning* clothes became fashionable, funeral processions involving funeral coaches* for the coffin replaced the traditional procession of pall bearers, and funeral directors adopted the black suit and top hat with long streamers down the back that continues into the present. Most parish* churchyards have been used for graves for centuries, and thus the bones from very old graves are often dug up and combined into a single grave to make room, or new caskets are buried on top of the bones of previous burials. In Church of England* funerals, bodies are laid in the grave facing east toward Jerusalem, and by custom, the "worst" part of the graveyard is the northern border, which would be the last to be resurrected and hence is reserved for strangers and criminals. It is also customary for close mourners to drop a handful of dirt on the coffin at the part of the service reading "ashes to ashes, dust to dust." Although the wake* before the burial has all but disappeared, some refreshments after the funeral are still expected, almost always including cold ham.*

fun fair. *See* fair.

funk. The original meaning was smoke or smell; however, Britons also use it as a slang term for fear, perhaps from the smell of fear. Thus, to funk or to **do a funk** is to desert, run away, or act in a cowardly manner. However, someone **in a funk** is someone who is depressed, and a **blue funk** is the worst kind of depression.

further education. Much the same as what Americans call adult education or continuing education, but also sometimes including business courses.

furze. A spiny shrub growing wild on land usually too poor for any serious farming or grazing, called gorse in the rest of Europe.

fuse. To blow a fuse or to short-circuit.

fusilier. In the eighteenth century, a soldier armed with a flintlock musket called a fusil, long since replaced by rifles, but the old name has been retained by many regiments,* such as the Royal Fusiliers. In the late nineteenth century, riflemen insulted other soldiers by calling them fusiliers, but this ended for the most part when all the people who remembered what a fusil was had died off.

fustian. A material similar to bombazine,* made of cotton and flax or simply twilled cotton, relatively heavy, almost always died black or dark olive and used for linings or underwear. The material is almost always associated with old women, in part because they were more likely to favor such heavy material and perhaps in part because it sounded like **fusty**, which means old, smelly, or old-fashioned but is derived from a completely different source. *See also* bombazine.

G

Gad's Hill. A hill southeast of Gravesend* controlling the ancient road from London* to Dover* and hence a favorite place for highwaymen,* including of course Shakespeare's Falstaff and Prince Hal.

Gaelic. Among linguists, ancient Scottish and Irish languages, but in more common usage usually applied only to the ancient Irish language, which is now the official language of an independent Ireland,* even though most Irish still speak English. In Scotland*, Gaelic was confined to the Highlands* by the late medieval era and was quite different from the Irish version. Nonetheless, a **Gael** is a Scot,* not an Irishman, but **Gaelic football** is the Irish form of rugby.*

gaff. A fair,* cheap music hall,* or similar amusement; a **penny gaff** of the Victorian era was such a show that charged only a penny admission. However, **blow the gaff** is lower class* slang for revealing a secret.

gaffer. An old man. If used in rural areas the term implies considerable respect, but in urban areas it implies disrespect, indicating an old man who is rustic in appearance or manner, similar to the American old coot. The term is derived from godfather* and in some areas means grandfather.

Gaiety Girl. Originally, a chorus girl at the Gaiety Theatre in the 1890s, more than twenty of whom married English nobles;* thus often a synonym for chorus girls and/or women who use their looks to jump up in social class.*

gallery. In a theater, the top or back balcony, used since the Restoration to indicate the cheapest seats. In most modern theaters, which were built in the nineteenth century, the gallery has a completely separate entrance so that other patrons need never have any contact with the poorer types who would buy such tickets.

gallon. About 20 percent larger than an American gallon; also called **Imperial gallon**. *See also* pint; quart.

gambling. *See* gaming.

game. (1) For the landed gentry* and nobility,* game such as deer,* hares,* and numerous birds such as grouse* was often more common on the table than beef,* but in the twentieth century game has become a delicacy and is more often hunted for sport than for food. (2) Prostitution, as in **on the game**; however, within various professions, especially those of a more dubious nature, insiders often call their business **the game**—prostitution is simply the one most widely understood by outsiders as well. (3) By the late nineteenth century, many upper-class* men, perhaps from public school* influence, had taken to calling very important things a game, including life itself, perhaps as a form of the stereotypical understatement associated with that class. Thus, to **play the game** meant to live honorably, to act according to the understood code of conduct. *See also* games; gaming.

gamekeeper. A person on a country estate whose job is to protect the wildlife that lives there so that the landlord or his guest can kill it later. Thus, his primary duties are not to actually feed or care for the animals, who are living wild, but to keep out trespassers who might kill the game before the landowner does and to then organize the hunting* or shooting* so that the landlord can enjoy the sport with minimal effort. From 1831 until the early twentieth century, a gamekeeper had legal powers that included confiscation of weapons and was usually allowed to maim or even kill poachers* without legal repercussions, making him generally the single most disliked person in a typical village.*

games. At schools,* what Americans call sports; a **games master/mistress** is the teacher who supervises or coaches such activities. *See also* gaming.*

gamester. Not one who plays games* but a gambler. There was some use of the term for athletes in general before the eighteenth century, but as athletics were very rare in those eras, the concept of one who plays games of chance predominated and was the only meaning by the early nineteenth century. *See* gaming.

gaming. What Americans call gambling. Theoretically all gambling except on-track wagering was illegal after 1853, but private clubs* continued to offer games of chance to their members. Football pools* in the 1930s were the first chink, and in 1960 new laws regulating private casino clubs almost inadvertently allowed off-track betting, and betting shops* opened in almost all neighborhoods. At present, not only bookmaking but also casino gambling are legal, and surveys show about 75 percent of the public regularly play the pools or bet on races. Casinos are technically clubs* open only to members who must wait at least forty-eight hours after joining before placing bets. *See* cards.

gammer. An old woman. Similar to gaffer,* this term implies respect if used in rural areas but in urban areas often implies disrespect, although its common usage as a form of grandma limits the disrespect intended.

gammon. (1) What Americans call ham, usually sliced. (2) Nonsense, as in "don't talk gammon;" sometimes also intentional fraud, from thieves' use of such nonsense to distract a mark while a partner picked his pocket.

gammy. Crippled or weak, as in a gammy leg.

gamp. An umbrella,* from Dickens's Sairey Gamp, who went everywhere with hers.

gamy. (1) Same meaning and pronunciation as gammy.* (2) Pronounced gaymy, smelling badly, from the smell of dead game.

g and t. Gin* and tonic.

gangway. Indoors, what Americans call an aisle. In general, **aisle** is used only in a church.*

gaol. The same institution and pronunciation as the American jail.

garden. In the twentieth century, what Americans call the yard of a house. The **garden gate** is the gate on the front edge of the property, but garden includes the yards both in front and back of the house. Almost never is food grown in the garden, which is devoted to flowers, grass, shrubs and/ or trees; if the dwellers want to grow food, they obtain an allotment* away from their actual dwelling (although herbs and a few vegetables may be grown in a **kitchen garden** in a corner of the back garden). In earlier uses, only larger houses, particularly country houses,* had gardens, but these were usually a particular portion of the grounds* set aside for decorative plants and landscaping. Prior to the mid–eighteenth century, these followed the continental pattern, with complex geometric patterns, mazes,* and topiary, but after Capability Brown's work, the fashion changed to the **English garden**, a much more casual, relaxed, and "natural" arrangement without geometrical regularity. All American stereotypes about the English passion for gardening, of army officers* retiring to grow roses and middle-class* wives spending hours each day on their knees with the secateurs, are understated; what the perfect lawn is to the Midwestern American, the flower garden is to the English, only more so. Typical modern suburban gardens feature roses, chrysanthemums, and/or dahlias, wisteria, and cherry or laburnum* trees, while the more rural ones often add hollyhocks and delphiniums. **Common or garden** indicates the very ordinary, from plants found in typical gardens. **Everything in the garden** is simply an emphatic form of everything, from a catchphrase "Everything in the garden is lovely," common in middle-class* circles in the first half of the twentieth century. To **lead up the garden path** is to use sweet promises to talk someone into something they would normally refuse, from the common route a young man would take while courting. *See also* border; gnome. (2) In place names, a street or a square that, before being developed, was open space or perhaps even used for farming, such as Covent Garden.* (3) Metaphorically, since before Shakespeare's time, a woman's genitals.

garden centre. A store that sells plants and gardening supplies.

garden chair. In the early nineteenth century, a wheelchair, sometimes pushed by a person, sometimes modified to be pulled by a small donkey or pony.

garden city. *See* garden suburb.

garden flat. *See* flat.

Garden of England. Kent.*

garden party. A party or social gathering held outdoors. The most significant of these is the Queen's,* several of which are held each July on the lawns of Buckingham Palace,* each attended by up to 5000 people, all of whom regard it as a signal honour* to be invited even though most will never even see, much less meet, the Queen herself. Dress is essentially the same as at Royal Ascot.*

garden suburb. A town surrounded by a green belt* of farmland and purposely built to sustain a rural feeling, with much more open space, tree-lined streets, et cetera, than most towns. Most of these are developed and maintained by a public trust or governmental body, which strictly controls development, remodeling, and improvements to make sure certain types of dirty industry are not allowed and the rural tone is maintained. The first seems to have been **Merton Park** near Wimbledon,* built by a private developer in 1870, and other noted examples include Bedford Park* (1875) and Hampstead* Garden Suburb (1906). Several **garden cities** were built north of London* in the years following 1898, following similar guidelines but also with an industrial base intended to make them self-supporting, with all the land owned by a trust rather than individuals. The term is now used interchangeably for both types of communities and, as with anything related to real estate, has lately been applied rather loosely to any new town* or similar development that has trees and grass.

Garrick. A gentlemen's* club* in London* near Covent Garden,* founded in 1831, and through the nineteenth century the liveliest of such clubs, with most of the major literary figures and actors of the time as members, still noted as an extremely sociable and fashionable club though now with perhaps more lawyers and businessmen than actors.

garrison town. Originally a town with a fort in which troops were regularly stationed, after the 1881 army* reforms this came to mean a town with a regiment's home depot. After that time, a regiment* sent one battalion* overseas and kept a second in the garrison for training and reserve duties.

Garter, Order of the. The oldest and most prestigious of the British honours,* this order dates back to 1388 when it was given to noblemen for particular bravery, military success, or jousting skill. It is limited to twenty-six, including the monarch; membership is signified by a blue and gold garter worn below the left knee. The limited membership gives it great prestige, but the grounds for membership are nebulous, recent membership including nobles* noted only for friendship with the monarch as well as genuinely illustrious political and military figures and some foreign heads of state. A member is called a **Knight of the Garter** (KG). In addition, there are another twenty-six **Military Knights** of the Garter, originally called **Poor Knights**, impoverished persons of noble birth who are allowed to live at Windsor Castle.*

gas. Used only for natural gas, used in the late nineteenth century for lighting and in the twentieth for heating and cooking. The gas in a car is called petrol.*

gasper. Slang for a cigarette, but until recently the term was more specifically used for cheap brands. *See also* Russian; Turkish.

gateau. What Americans call a cake, usually a layered cake with frosting, served sliced and often with cream or custard* poured over the slice. *See also* cake; torte.

gated. In colleges,* slang for a punishment that confines a student to the area inside the gates.

Gatwick. An airport south of London,* in the 1970s and 1980s the primary airport for charter flights and minor airlines trying to avoid the congestion of Heathrow,* hence often suggesting something a bit second-rate when used for any allusion other than strict timetable realism.

Gaudy. A feast of commemoration, used in this sense almost completely for various annual dinners at Oxford* or Cambridge.* These dinners are usually subsidized by some bequest, so they tend to be rather spectacular, but the name comes from the Latin for joy or celebration, not from the gaudy dress or activities of the participants. Each celebrates something in a particular college's* history, but the number and the purpose of the celebrations vary widely among the various colleges. This is also traditionally a time when alumnae return to the college, and thus the dinners serve some of the functions of American class reunions.

gay. As in America, now used to describe a male homosexual, but in the nineteenth century the term when applied to a woman was a euphemism for prostitute.

Gazette, The. Technically the first English newspaper,* begun at Oxford* in 1665 to report the activities of the court.* It moved to London* with the court and soon became the official public record of governmental activity, twice each week listing appointments, military commissions, bankruptcies, and war casualties, in 1923 taken over by the Stationery Office.

GBE. Knight Grand Cross of the Order of the British Empire. *See* OBE.

GBH. Grievous bodily harm, what Americans call assault and battery.

GC. George Cross.*

GCB. Grand Cross of the Bath, the highest rank within the Order of the Bath.*

GCE. General Certificate of Education, a test given in two forms, the O-level* for school-leavers* and the A-level* for more advanced studies, from 1950–88 used primarily in state schools to determine qualification for moving to the next level and to verify actual skills and knowledge upon leaving school. Public schools* used their own tests. *See also* CSE; eleven-plus; GCSE.

GCMG. Knight Grand Cross of the Order of St. Michael and St. George,* the most senior rank in the order; irreverently known as the "God Calls Me God," from being awarded to only the most senior of civil servants. *See also* CMG; KCMG.

GCSE. General Certificate of Secondary Education, a test intended by the government to combine and replace both the GCE* O-levels* and the CSE,* beginning in 1988 with general distrust and lack of support throughout the educational community and public, many of whom saw it as an attempt to eliminate serious academic standards from all British schools.

gear box. In a car, what Americans call the transmission.

gee. Pronounced with a soft *g*, a widely used command to make a horse go, from at least Shakespeare's time, often as **gee up**; by the mid–nineteenth century, the command was so common that many children called a horse a gee or a **gee-gee**, and both words continue into the present as nouns.

gel. With a hard *g*, the upper class* or county* pronunciation of girl, in casual usage indicating any woman, no matter what her age.

gen. Pronounced like gin, knowledge or information, associated primarily with people of the WWII generation, from the phrase "for the general information of all ranks" used in military notices during the war. **Pukka* gen** was correct or reliable information, **duff* gen** unreliable or misleading. To **gen up** is to study or prepare.

general. Curiously, although colonels,* majors,* and captains* abound, generals are rarely found in British literature before the nineteenth century, in part because anyone holding such exalted rank would also have titles* of their own—no one need call Wellington General Wellington when he was also a Duke.* But this is also because the rank did not exist in the same way as colonel, for example, existed: A general commanded an army, and armies only existed when some particular and extraordinary campaign required one, the largest on-going military organization being the regiment* (hence the title itself, from "general officer," one who serves in general rather than with a specific unit). Thus, before 1871, an officer might act as a general but hold the permanent rank of a colonel or hold the rank of general but literally sit at home without any command until some war arose that brought him out. In 1871, many of the colonels were promoted to general to increase their pension and encourage them to sell their commissions* back to the government, and after that, generals became more common and permanent, with intermediate ranks established for intermediate units between the regiment and the army. In order downward, these now include: general, lieutenant general, major general, brigadier.* *See also* admiral; Field Marshal.

General Admission. The ceremony at Cambridge* that Americans would call graduation, held in late June; however, degrees* may be presented at several other times during the year as well.

General Confession. The Church of England* rejected the Catholic practice of confession, but in the regular services there is a General Confession read by all members of the congregation, beginning "Almighty and most merciful Father, we have erred and strayed from thy [*sic*] ways like lost sheep . . . ," spoken near the very beginning of the service.

general election. A national election in which all members* of the House of Commons* must stand* for their seats.* *See also* by-election.

general post. The party game Americans call musical chairs. The game Americans call post office is called postman's knock.*

General Post Office. *See* GPO.

General Strike. In May 1926, workers in railways,* docks, utilities, and other major industries went on strike in support of coal miners already on strike. The strike failed after about ten days, due primarily to a flood of middle-class volunteers into many of the jobs, but it was nonviolent for the most part. However, it frightened the middle class* and aristocracy* with potential Bolshevism and was immediately followed by strong legislation limiting the authority of unions, in turn leading to increased union activity. *See also* British disease; trade union.

Geneva. Gin* imported from Holland.

genteel. Prior to the nineteenth century, simply "of good birth.*" But during the nineteenth century, it acquired a connotation of respectability that altered the meaning to include anyone who has the attitudes or manners of the idealized gentry.* This was most often associated with women— spinsters and widows like Jane Austen's Mrs. Bates or the women of Cranford, who insisted on living like the gentry without the funds to sustain such a life. Being genteel, they can never be considered to be poor, as only the common people are poor; hence, **genteel poverty**, which is in many ways worse than real poverty because nothing can be done to alleviate it, since to work would be to lose one's genteel status. Thus, genteel often is used to mean someone who is much more interested in form than in substance, stressing rank and birth and manners* in order to sustain the illusion of their own importance. However, the term can be used admiringly about someone who acts in the way a gentleman* or, more often, a lady* ought to act. Since WWI, the term has altered again to mean those solidly in the middle class* rather than the gentry (or at least that portion of the middle class that is not in trade*), the people who live comfortably and quietly, who are well-mannered in a reserved, stereotyped way, and who never do, feel, or express anything enthusiastically. In addition, it almost always implies a heavily euphemistic vocabulary developed by people who want to sound like their "betters" but who, having no actual experience of upper-class vocabulary, substitute euphemisms and pseudo-French* terms to avoid sounding common* or vulgar; the practice is so widespread that **genteelism** is a standard term among lexicographers. In general, persons who call themselves genteel usually are, but when people use the term about others, it is almost always with a touch of irony or distaste. Also, men rarely call themselves genteel; the term is still almost always used only by or about women. *See also* gentility.

gentility. All persons of gentle birth,* which technically means the gentry* but is more generally used for anyone who is either gentry or nobility.* From this, the term is more often used for the idealized attitudes, life-style, and manners associated with the gentleman* or lady,* and thus means the type of appearance aspired to by the genteel,* who unfortunately never really are part of the gentility.

gentleman. This is one of the most significant terms in English social life, and hence one of the most difficult to define. The very nebulousness of the term has made its definition one of the fundamental themes of the English novel: from Tom Jones to Pip to Guy Crouchback and Lucky Jim, through the works of Richardson, Austen, Dickens, Eliot, Trollope, Conrad, and hundreds of others, runs the question "How are we to know the real gentleman, and how is he to live properly in these times?" In the face of such complexity, we can only make the broadest simplifications in the space available here.

Although there is some evidence that this term originally meant a younger son of a knight,* it was more widely used to mean any man of good birth,* which in practice meant from an established family that owned a country estate. By Shakespeare's time, this meant one with a life of leisure, signified primarily by horses and hunting.* However, the gentleman's leisure did not necessarily mean he did no work, but merely that he worked only for honor or duty or his own personal curiosity, not for monetary reward; hence gentlemen were found in all layers of government service, the clergy,* and army officers* (although rarely in the navy,* which required too much professionalism). However, in practice, most gentlemen, once they inherited the property,* ceased their other activities, and the civil servants, career officers, clergymen, scholars, and lawyers tended to be the younger sons of gentlemen, spreading the concept ever wider through society. With the prosperity of industrialization, landed property passed into the hands of ever newer families, and the concept of gentleman began to alter in response to this, both to distinguish the old gentleman from the *nouveaux riches* and to absorb the new money. A code of conduct modified from the idealized tales of chivalry developed, and a gentleman came to be seen as one who acts in a gentlemanly fashion, perhaps most vividly personified by the contrasts in *Vanity Fair* among Pitt Crawley, a gentleman of the old school, George Osborne of the *nouveau riche* with only the gentleman's appearance, and Dobbin, the complete new gentleman. Most importantly, this change in attitude meant that the gentleman was one whose private life and character were above reproach. Thus, by the mid-nineteenth century, many people by virtue of their respectability proudly thought of themselves as "middle-class gentlemen," an oxymoron less than fifty years earlier. The curious thing is that this ideal worked back up the social scale, so that the landed gentleman began to act more like the middle-class gentleman; the Pitt Crawleys were gradually replaced by Dickens's John Jarndyce and then eventually by John Buchan's Richard Hannay (a mining engineer) or Doyle's Dr. Watson as the gentleman-ideal.

The changing concept of the gentleman also changed the role of education in England; prior to the early nineteenth century, schooling was primarily for training the clergy, but as people began to think of gentlemanliness as something that could be learned, the English public school,* starting with Dr. Arnold at Rugby,* began consciously to train boys to be gentlemen, a process eventually continued by Oxford* and Cambridge* in what to Americans has usually seemed a most perverse type of education unrelated to the "real world." This system of course still favored the old landed families, as their children were more likely to afford this training, but it allowed the gentleman to remain an approachable ideal and in effect protected the gentry and nobility from the attacks that shattered their class on the continent. One could become a gentleman, or at the very least, one's children could, and many professions that had once been the preserve of the gentleman, such as the civil service,* retained that cachet even as the proportion of "real" gentlemen declined; the new office holders, often themselves from the public schools, simply became gentlemen in their attitudes and often in titles* and honours.* Nonetheless, the gentlemanly ideal continued to be centered on land, and the middle-class gentleman almost always eventually ended up with a country house* at least. Since WWII, the landed gentleman has fallen on hard times, reflected in the modern gentleman's role as outcast, misplaced loser, or buffoon in modern fiction, from Waugh's Sebastian Flyte to Wodehouse's Bertie Wooster, and social fluidity has confused the meaning, so that, although many of the old

ideals—the country house, the life of eccentric leisure, public school connections, et cetera—continue in force, the word gentleman in the sense of
a distinct class is now rarely heard—the term now is used primarily to
indicate one with good manners. *See also* aristocracy; gentility; gentlewoman; gentry; knight; lady; noble; walking gentleman.

Gentleman at Arms. One of a guard of honor of forty who attend the
monarch on state occasions.

Gentlemen vs. Players. An annual cricket* match played at Lord's* from
1806 to 1962, pitting in effect all-star teams of amateurs (gentlemen) against
professionals (players). Social distinctions were maintained throughout,
with separate entrances and refreshment areas for the two teams.

gentlewoman. No longer the female equivalent of a gentleman* as it was
in the eighteenth and nineteenth centuries (modern usage prefers lady*),
this now is a more ironic term, implying someone of respectable class*
who is old-fashioned, impoverished, or both. *See also* gentility.

gentry. Basically, the class* of people who owned real property* but who
were not nobility,* consisting of knights,* the country squires,* and the
few very wealthy who had left the cities to buy country estates, and their
children. Even at the height of its influence, this was a very small group:
in 1870, less than 5,000 families were accepted as gentry by Burke.* In
more general usage, this is often extended to include the wealthy of all
types, including both the nobility and what Americans would usually call
the upper–middle class, who almost always eventually end up with country
estates. However, the term implies inherited wealth or family, so the "self-
made man" is rarely accepted within the class; *nouveaux riches* can never
be gentry, although their children might be, and their grandchildren almost
always are, assuming they haven't blown the fortune completely. Although
the bulk of the old gentry declined with the aristocracy when land values
collapsed and death duties* went up, their family influence often continued
through alliances with new sources of wealth—as late as 1962 it was pointed
out that seven members of the Cabinet* and chairmen of four major newspapers and of three of the largest investment banks* (not to mention several
ambassadors and the United States President) were all related by blood
or marriage to a single family. The shift in political fortunes during the
1980s hasn't necessarily broadened the base of society; 1990 estimates
suggest that, while many of the names may be new, fewer than 6,000 people
still control the government, industry, banking, and media of the country,
and whatever their names, they look and act like the same old gentry. *See
also* Esquire; gentility; squire; trade.

geography, show you the. An upper-class euphemism meaning to tell a guest where the toilet is. *See also* wash.

Geordie. Pronounced jordie, a person from Tyneside,* in or around Newcastle,* and generally noted as a tough.

George, St. *See* St. George's Day.

George Cross. A medal in the shape of a cross given to civilians for acts of "Most conspicuous courage," established by George VI during WWII. The **George Medal** was established at the same time for "acts of great bravery."

getting on for. Nearly.

geyser. Generally pronounced geezer, a gas water heater, usually fairly small and mounted on the wall over the sink or tub for which it provides hot water. *See also* immersion heater.

ghyll. A wooded ravine, used primarily in the northern areas, in the Lake District* in particular.

Gibraltar. A tiny peninsula at the southern tip of Spain controlled by the British since 1704. Its strategic position gives it complete control of all shipping entering or leaving the Mediterranean, and as such it has been the keystone of British naval power for almost three centuries; although Spain has long disputed Britain's right to be there, it is unlikely that the navy* could relinquish the position and still continue to be the British Navy.

gig. A small two-wheeled carriage* pulled by a single horse.

gill. Pronounced jill, one-quarter pint,* a measure used primarily for liquor, although in many northern areas the gill is one-half pint.

gillie. A Scottish term for the shotgun-bearer of a hunter and often applied to all the male outdoor workers on a Scottish estate, from an ancient usage meaning an attendant to a Highland* chieftain. Pronounced with a hard *g*.

gin. The liquor came from Holland, originally called Geneva* and flavored with juniper berries, but the English quickly imitated it with different flavoring agents as soon as it appeared in the early eighteenth century. Coming at a time of very cheap grain, the new gin was often cheaper than water ("drunk for a penny, dead drunk for two"). London* was all but overwhelmed by gin drunkards, depicted with little exaggeration in Hogarth's work. Nothing alleviated the mess until a new law in 1751 managed to enforce viable taxes that raised prices and also began limiting the number of persons who could sell it, a process that would eventually lead to modern licensing laws.* Even so, gin remained much cheaper than whisky,* and those businesses licensed to sell it soon became rather magnificent **gin palaces**, especially in slum areas, during the nineteenth century. Eventually the price rose until beer once again became the primary drink of the poor, although gin continued to be "mother's milk" to more than Eliza Doolittle's aunt. In the twentieth century, gin has remained the quintessential English liquor, usually mixed with tonic (or quinine) water and without ice.* **Gin and it** is made with gin and Italian vermouth, like a martini but sweeter and usually garnished with a cherry rather than an olive; in general, this is associated with women, particularly young, loose, and flighty women. A **gin twist** is gin and hot water, sometimes with lemon juice or sugar; a **gin sling** is gin, hot water, sugar, and nutmeg; **pink gin** is gin and bitters, sometimes diluted with water. **Plymouth gin** was first made near Plymouth,* but the term is now generic for a type of gin with a sharper taste than normal, supposedly coming from sulfuric acid added before distilling; **sloe gin** is gin made from blackthorn plums. *See also* Gin Lane.

ginger. As a noun, spirit, enthusiasm. To **ginger up** someone is to put some ginger into them, to build up their spirits, make them eager to get going; a **ginger group** is a small group of activists within a larger organization.

Ginger. Practically obligatory nickname for any man named Jones, for some reason not quite clear today, no matter what his hair color, and also a common nickname in England* for red-haired Scots; red-haired Irishmen, however, are usually called Mick* or Paddy.*

ginger beer. Not the same as American ginger ale, this is a fermented drink. Made from a ginger-flavored syrup, it is bubbly and less alcoholic than beer,* so that it is usually drunk only by women and children. What Americans call ginger ale Britons usually call **ginger pop**.

ginger nut. A cookie similar to what Americans call a ginger snap. The British **ginger snap** is a snap fastener.

Gin Lane. This did not really exist, but the name was a metaphor for early eighteenth-century slums peopled with alcoholics who lived on gin, especially as depicted in Hogarth's "Gin Lane," which was the Seven Dials* area. A comparable American term is skid row.

gippo. Military slang since about WWI for gravy, sometimes extended to mean soup as well.

gippy tummy. Upset stomach or diarrhea. The term appeared in the years when Egypt* was the first land stop on the voyage to India and thus the first place British travelers met local food and water. The term has held on as a generic phrase used by people who have been nowhere near Egypt, so you can get gippy tummy anywhere, even inside Britain.* The British are, if possible, even more paranoid about this than American travelers, often refusing to drink the water even in countries like France or the U.S.A. for fear of contracting it. Equivalent phrases naturally have surfaced, most related to the local site of military activity, such as **Delhi belly**, **Malta dog**, or **Rangoon runs**; in the late twentieth century, as large numbers have begun to holiday around the Mediterranean, additional variations such as **Adriatic tummy** or **Spanish tummy** have gained some prominence. *See also* sanitary.

Girl Guide. A person Americans call a Girl Scout. *See also* Boy Scouts.

girl's school. A secondary school* for girls roughly equivalent to the public school* in subjects taught and in social status. Until very recently, all public schools were male only, as most continue to be. The first girl's school as commonly understood was the Queen's College* in London founded in 1848. By the end of the century, however, there were a number of these, with somewhat more emphasis on music, art, and modern languages than typical male public schools. They offered subjects suitable for gaining admission to one of the universities* once women were allowed to attend them or, far more important, for being a colonial administrator's or professional man's wife, going rather lightly on the home crafts taught in the older "finishing schools" and young ladies' academies.* Girl's schools were boarding schools and, like the male schools, were socially exclusive and often centered on a sports culture, hockey* in particular, and developed their own influential slang and literature. In recent years, they have been challenged, as many public schools have bowed to pressure and admitted girls for at least the sixth form* and many grammar schools* have accepted girls completely, skimming the intellectual layer from most girl's schools and leaving only the socially exclusive. *See also* class; hockey; mistress.

Giro. Pronounced like gyroscope. The post office* operates what is called a girobank, in which people deposit money that can then be transferred to banks and similar institutions; thus, it operates something like a checking account for payment of taxes, utilities, and similar bills for people who have no bank accounts or cheques,* in practice the overwhelming majority of the populace. In addition, social security* payments are mailed to recipients as giro money orders, which must be cashed at the post office, so **giro cheque/order** or just giro is often synonymous with these payments, as in "I get my giro next Wednesday."

git/gitt. A fool or worthless person.

give. In British sports of all kinds, the umpire or referee gives rather than makes a call; for example, in cricket,* the umpire "gives leg before wicket," meaning "calls the batsman* out for leg* before wicket."

give over. To stop doing something, especially to stop talking, usually heard in the lower portions of the social scale.

give way. On road signs, what Americans call yield.

Glamorgan. A county* or shire* in southern Wales.* This is the principal industrial and commercial area of Wales, where about half of all the nation's population live, with Cardiff* its urban core and the Rhondda* coal district its backbone. In 1974, it was separated into three new counties, **South Glamorgan** for the industrial area around Cardiff; **Mid Glamorgan** for the coal districts, and **West Glamorgan** for the coastal areas around Swansea.*

glance. *See* cut.

Glasgow. The largest city of Scotland,* an industrial port on the Clyde* that, with its suburbs, has contained the nation's major industries since the early seventeenth century, with large ship-building, engineering, chemical, and related industries. From the beginning of its industrial growth, it was famous for the slums in which its working class* were housed, and the city as a whole developed a great pride in the difficulty of life there, its natives noted throughout Britain for a tough, independent, and violent personality, the violence and tensions only increased by the influx of Irish Catholics* drawn to the industrial jobs. In the late nineteenth century, Glasgow nurtured a noted school of realist painters, and in the twentieth has produced a number of vivid working-class writers and theater people. *See also* Gorbals.

glass. (1) What Americans call a mirror. (2) A barometer.

glasspaper. What Americans call sandpaper.

Glastonbury. A small town in southwest England* south of Bristol.* Legend says this was Arthur's Avalon, and in the twelfth century remains thought to be Arthur and Guinevere were found and reinterred there.

Nearby is **Glastonbury Tor**, a tor* with a commanding view and topped by **Glastonbury Abbey**. The abbey* is supposed to be the oldest church* in England, in legend the site to which Joseph of Arimathea brought the Grail. Several abbeys have been built on the site, the last (from 1303) falling into neglect after the Reformation and left deserted, much of its stone stolen for other building sites, until it became the ideal picturesque ruin, much admired, visited, and imitated during the Romantic and Victorian eras.

Glaswegian. A native of Glasgow,* usually associated with the crude and rough and with a cocky attitude to life.

GLC. Greater London Council, established in 1965 as the central local government for the country* of Greater London* formed at the same time, replacing the LCC* that had governed what were now called the twelve boroughs* of Inner London.* This was the only serious attempt to administer the entire conurbation of London, and it seemed to function as well as could be expected until the Conservatives* returned to power in the Commons* in the late 1970s. The GLC at that time had become Labour* and militantly socialist, with the result that it often seemed to be a more visible and powerful Opposition* than the Labour Party in the Commons; by 1985, the warfare between the two came to a head and legislation was passed disbanding the GLC, devolving its powers back onto the individual borough councils.*

glebe. An ancient term for the soil itself, used almost exclusively now for land owned by the Church* or used by a clergyman for income.

glen. In Scotland,* a narrow, steep-sided valley.

Glenalmond. One of the most prestigious public schools* of Scotland.*

Glencoe. A glen* in the western Highlands* of Scotland,* fabled in Highland lore as the site at which the Campbells massacred the Macdonalds, most noted for its detailed use as the setting of Stevenson's *Kidnapped*.

Glorious Revolution. In 1688, general dissatisfaction with the rule of James II was so great that William and Mary, both cousins of James II, were invited by prominent statesmen and by Parliament* to assume the throne instead. Support for James was so minimal that he fled the country, thereby avoiding another round of civil warfare, although supporters and descendants of James continued to dispute the succession* from Ireland* and Scotland;* thus, this is sometimes also called the Bloodless Revolution. James's removal ended all serious threats of the restoration of Catholicism, and William and Mary both agreed to the Bill of Rights,* which formalized the concept that there were limits on monarchial power without specifying those limits, so there was more at stake than simply succession to the monarchy. Even so, it was much more a coup d'etat than a revolution.

Glos. Gloucestershire.*

glottal stop. One of the basic distinctions of regional accents* in Britain is the use of the glottal stop for medial *t* or *d*. Except for Scottish accents that use this, the stop was rarely heard by Americans in English accents until the Beatles brought it to our attention, as it occurs primarily in regional accents far from London* and thus rarely made it into films, radio, or television. The medial glottal stop is particularly strong in the industrialized areas of the northern parts of the country and since the 1960s has come to be thought of not as a regionalism but rather a working-class* usage, so it is heard primarily in entertainment aimed at people in that class and rarely if ever even indicated in print. The Cockney* accent also uses a glottal stop but in a different way: middle *t* and *d* are usually clearly said, but the glottal stop is used at the end of words that end in *t* or *k* and sometimes *p* or *l* sounds. Except for Scots, the use of the glottal stop is a clear sign that the speaker is not part of the Establishment and thus, except for the politically correct elements who often now retain or adopt it to show their solidarity with the masses, it is never heard among the London-area middle class.

Gloucester. Pronounced GLOSSter, a town in western England* near the Welsh border, one of the earliest Roman settlements and during the medieval era a major port on the Severn* until eclipsed by Bristol* in the sixteenth century.

Gloucestershire. A county* or shire* on the western border of England* astride the Severn,* famous for centuries for its dairy lands and cheese.* It contains an extremely fertile river valley, parts of the Cotswolds,* and the Forest of Dean.* In the medieval era, it was an especially rich area, accounting for the prominence of so many Dukes of Gloucester in Shakespeare's history plays and the revival of the title for modern princes.* In 1974, the primarily urban industrial area around Bristol* was separated to form the county of Avon.*

Glyndebourne. Pronounced GLINDburn, a mansion in the south of England* between Brighton* and Eastbourne,* a part of which has been converted into a theater at which a major opera festival has been held annually since 1934.

GM. George Medal. *See* George Cross.

GMT. Greenwich Mean Time.*

GMW. *See* NUGMW.

gnome. No one can quite explain why, but among the respectable classes no garden* is thought complete without a stone or plaster figure of a gnome somewhere.

go. In general, a person may **go sick** where in America they get sick, and once you are sick, you **go down with** a disease rather than come down with it. A **go-by** is the same as the American "I'll pass on it." To **go begging** is to be left over, as in a biscuit* that is "going begging." To **go down** is to leave Oxford* or Cambridge,* either by graduation or for a vacation, while **go up** means to enroll there. To **go west** is to die, especially common for the WWI generation but dating back to Shakespeare's time (*See also* Burton). To **go off** is to spoil, as in food that has "gone off;" however, to go off someone or something is to lose interest in someone or something. To **have a go** is to make an attempt or to make an attack. To **go to the country** is not to take a vacation but to hold a general election.* *See also* down; go slow; great go; little go; no go; right go; up.

goalkeeper. In hockey* and football,* the player who permanently guards the team's goal.

goal kick. In football,* this is a kick from the out-of-bounds toward the goal area of the field and not aimed at the goal itself, while in rugby* it is a kick aimed directly at the goal taken during regular play.

gob. Lower-class* slang for the mouth. To **stop your gob** is to shut up, but a **gobstopper** is not a punch in the mouth but the candy Americans call a jawbreaker.

Godalming. Usually pronounced GOD-alming, a small town southwest of London,* once an independent market town,* now primarily a well-to-do commuter suburb, noted primarily for Charterhouse* school located nearby since 1872.

godfather. *See* christening.

godmother. *See* christening.

God spot. Slang for a religious program on TV, usually (as in America) early on Sunday mornings or very late at night.

Gogmagogs. A small but distinctive set of hills south of Cambridge.*

golden handshake. A contemporary term for an extra payment made to an employee when he or she is fired in order to maintain his or her goodwill or silence or to prevent lawsuits, a practice similar to the American golden parachute but perhaps extending somewhat further down the office ladder.

Golden Square. A small square in London* in Soho,* in the eighteenth century a fashionable address, by the time Dickens's Ralph Nickleby had his office there full of boarding houses, and in the twentieth century home to some of the modern rag trade and movie business.

golden syrup. *See* treacle.

Golders Green. A neighborhood in London* northwest of Hampstead Heath,* site in the 1920s of the paradigmatic suburban real estate development, now absorbed into the city and associated with Jews,* due both to the Jewish cemetery and the large number of Jewish families living there in mid–twentieth century.

golliwog. A stuffed doll like a Raggedy Ann but with black face and kinky hair, popular for most of the twentieth century, although in recent years people have tended to call them **gollies** to avoid racial tension. *See also* wog.

GOM. Grand Old Man, originally used about Gladstone, then about the cricketer* Grace, and then passing into general usage.

gong. (1) It seems like something invented for the movies, but it really was common during the late nineteenth and early twentieth centuries in large houses* for a servant* to ring a gong to announce that meals were to be served. This was much easier than tracking down all the family and guests for a personal announcement. (2) Military slang for a medal.

Good Friday. The Friday before Easter,* in the Church of England* a solemn day, observed primarily by a three-hour "meditation" service. Although the English dropped the Catholic practice of meatless Fridays, most families traditionally eat only fish on Good Friday; for reasons long since lost in obscurity, the one traditional break from the austerity of Good Friday and Lent* as well is the **hot cross bun**, a small sweet bun* with a cross cut into the top before it is baked, traditionally served on this day throughout most of England and often a part of special charity doles* distributed at the same time.

goodman. A male head of household. In the medieval era when the term originated, individual households not connected to a local lord* were still relatively rare, so the term was a modest sign of respect, generally used by those higher in the social scale to indicate their own respect for the goodman. The term essentially disappeared in England during the wave of urbanization of the nineteenth century but held on in Scotland* into the twentieth century, where it meant simply a husband and might be used by a wife about her own husband. *See also* goodwife.

goods. What Americans usually call freight; hence, a **goods train** is one without passengers, what Americans call a freight train.

good school. Not necessarily a school* with a high academic reputation or demanding classwork, but rather a school that has a recognizable social status. Usually this is not just any public school* or girl's school* but one of a comparatively select handful of such schools. It was also sometimes said of a similar handful of grammar schools.*

good show. *See* show.

goodwife. A title for a married woman who ran her own household, the wife of a goodman.* This was a sign of respect, roughly equivalent to the modern Mrs,* often abbreviated to goody,* and used into the nineteenth century, when Mrs finally supplanted it. *See also* lady wife.

Goodwin Sands. A group of large sandbars off the southeast coast of England* just as ships turn from the Thames* estuary into the Straits of Dover,* one of the most dangerous areas in the world for ships. For ships going to and from London,* these marked a symbolic as well as physical danger, since ships could be destroyed on them as the voyage was just beginning or at the very end when home was at last in sight. They also formed the protection that made the Downs* a safe anchorage for ships waiting to enter the Thames.

goody. This means simply goodwife;* as Mae West would say, goodness has nothing to do with it.

googly. In cricket,* a throw from a right-handed bowler that looks like it will be a break* toward the batsman* but which instead bounces away from the batsman, a relatively unusual throw that requires an unnatural spin on the ball. *See also* chinaman; wrong 'un.

goolies. The testicles, probably brought back from India by the military in mid-nineteenth century, now used primarily among the lower class,* especially when discussing targets for kicks or punches.

Goon. "The Goon Show" was an extremely popular and surrealistic radio comedy series of the 1950s, and Goon is often used since then for anyone with a similar sense of humor, similar to what Americans call off-the-wall.

Goonhilly. Site in Cornwall* used by the post office* for all satellite communications.

goose. The British generally ate much more fowl than meat until the twentieth century, and goose was a common food; it was also the traditional Christmas* dish, in the same way as the American Thanksgiving turkey, until the mid-twentieth century, when turkey began to replace it in many families. Most such geese are domestic geese, of course, larger than the wild fowl of the same name that occasionally visit the islands.

gooseberry. A tart green berry, known primarily as the main ingredient in the gooseberry fool.* In many families, little boys are told they were found **under the gooseberry bush**, perhaps because such bushes are found growing wild at the bottom* of many gardens.* However, to **play gooseberry** has nothing to do with the food or the plant but rather means to be the third person who makes the crowd for a romantic couple; nobody has a convincing explanation of the origin of the phrase. *See also* parsley.

Gorbals. A slum district in Glasgow,* notorious for its poverty and lawlessness, and for the tough, brawling males who live there.

Gorblimey. *See* blimey.

Gordon Riots. Anti-Catholic demonstrations in London* in 1780 that turned into more than a week of rioting, finally quelled by the army* with more than 300 deaths among the rioters. They were sparked by a petition by Lord Gordon against the relaxation of some anti-Catholic legislation. These are the anti-popery riots described in Dickens's *Barnaby Rudge*.

Gordonstoun. A public school* in Scotland,* noted as the most physically demanding of such schools, with more emphasis on outdoor life than the classroom and the model for American "Outward Bound" programs.

gormless. No one is quite clear what gorm is, but if you're without it, you're particularly stupid.

gorse. *See* furze.

go slow. A form of labor protest in which the workers don't go on strike but do the work as slowly as possible until grievances are settled. *See also* work-to-rule.

Goswell Road. A street in London,* the northward extension of Aldersgate;* when Pickwick lived there, it was also the start of the Great North Road,* which perhaps contributed to his wanderlust.

governess. A woman in a private household who cares for other people's children. In Shakespeare's time, the governess often took care of babies as well as children, but by the eighteenth century the term was being reserved for a woman whose primary duties were more teaching than child care. By the early nineteenth century, most wealthy homes had a governess whose primary duty was to teach the children to read and write, with the nanny* responsible for physical care of the small child. As boys from such classes* were quickly sent off to boarding schools* while the girls stayed at home, the governess also was a sort of duenna for the family girls, teaching them the social graces such as basic music, watercolor painting, needlepoint, et cetera, and chaperoning them in daily life, often, like Wilde's Miss Prism, until the girl was of marriageable age. Hence, a governess had to be absolutely, irreproachably respectable. Like the nanny, she was not a servant,* but neither was she an equal member of the family nor treated as a professional teacher might be. The life of a governess was practically the only profession open to the nineteenth-century woman born into the gentry* or real middle class* and suddenly impoverished, and thus the governess like Jane Eyre became the quintessential heroine of romantic novels for more than a century. The expansion of formal schooling for girls in the twentieth century basically ended the governess's profession and few are seen today. *See also* au pair.

governess car/cart. A small cart with two seats on the sides facing each other, pulled by a donkey or pony, relatively common before WWI.

government. From the late seventeenth century, the government has meant the group of ministers* who supervise and administer all national governmental activity. Technically, the monarch asks someone to form a government; since the government must have the support of Parliament,* this is almost always the leader of the majority party* in the House of Commons,* but it does not have to be. The person so designated, now called the Prime Minister,* selects a number of persons (currently about 75) to administer the various departments* and ministries* of the executive; these must be approved by the monarch (for more than a century a formality only) and about a quarter of them are also included in the Cabinet.* These people then govern until (1) the next election,* which before 1715 was three years, then changed to seven years, and in 1911 changed again to five, although the Prime Minister may call an election at any time before the limit is reached; (2) the Prime Minister dies or resigns; or (3) the party is no longer able to sustain its majority on major votes in the House (*See* vote of confidence). Thus, there may be several different governments formed without an election being called, or several elections that result in the same government staying in office. In theory, the government can also be dissolved for displeasing the monarch, but legal limits passed in 1694 now require the monarch to do so only on "advice" of the Prime Minister. Although elected by the voters, no one in the government is actually elected to a specific position; not only may the Prime Minister remove or reshuffle ministers without an election, but also the party in power may itself remove the Prime Minister, as it did to American surprise in 1990, with Margaret Thatcher, and choose another head of the government without any reference to the voters. Where Americans tend to think of the government as the bureaucrats and regulators in Washington, the British, even when using the term loosely, tend to use it only for the politicians.

governor. (1) In a dominion* or colony,* the representative of the Crown,* originally ruling directly but in most gradually giving way to local government and now having very limited powers. Formally called the **Governor-General**. (2) The chief administrator of a prison* and sometimes of other similar institutions. (3) In schoolboy slang, one's father, never said to the father but used among friends about the father; in widespread use since the early nineteenth century but fading in late twentieth century. (4) In many businesses, employee slang for the boss. (5) Among the lower classes,* especially Cockneys,* a semi-respectful greeting for a stranger who appears to be from a higher class, in literature usually spelled **guv'nor** or shortened to **guv**. (6) In many state-supported or nonprofit organizations, a member of the supervising board, such as Americans usually call the board of directors or board of trustees.

gown. Basically, this is a garment that goes from shoulder to ankle or floor. In various forms, this has been a staple of women's clothing since the Restoration, and British and American women have generally used the term in the same way, as in nightgown, evening gown, or ball* gown. But the British have also used it to mean a number of male dress items as well, which are in America usually called robes. In particular, the academic has continued to wear a gown since the medieval era. American academic gowns or robes are like choir robes, with large loose sleeves, and are worn only at graduation ceremonies. Most British academic gowns vary at different universities* but are usually extremely loose, with a very short sleeve or perhaps even merely a slit on the side for arms and extending only to the knee; they are worn over suits or other normal types of clothing and look more like an overgrown vest than a gown. At Oxford* or Cambridge,* faculty and students are no longer required as they once were to wear these whenever they go outside their rooms* but are still expected to wear them when attending exams and other specified academic activities. Teachers wore them while actually teaching at most public schools* and grammar schools;* however, they are not worn at elementary schools or comprehensives,* and many of the public schools have moved toward more relaxed dress for teachers in recent years. Both barristers* and judges* wear full-length gowns for all court appearances, but magistrates* do not.

GP. General Practitioner, a doctor* who provides basic medicine and the first line of care, what Americans often call the family doctor. Technically every GP is a "Physician and Surgeon"; if one calls himself merely a "Physician," then he is a consultant.* *See also* surgeon.

GPO. General Post Office. This was actually only the central post office* for London,* located about a block north of St. Paul's,* but sometimes the initials are used generically for all the British postal service.

Grace, Your. *See* archbishop; duke.

grace and favour. When said of an apartment* or a house,* a dwelling occupied without rent by permission of the monarch.

graduand. In universities,* a person ready to receive a degree.*

graduate. (1) In general, the only graduates are those who receive a university* degree;* no one graduates from public school,* grammar school,* or any of the other rough equivalents of American high schools, or from any other non–degree-granting institution. (2) In Scotland* before the early twentieth century, a medical man.

graft. Hard work. Sometimes it is also used ironically to signify dishonest descriptions, as from a salesman, but it never means bribery or embezzlement in the American sense.

grammar school. Originally, a secondary school* for boys paid for by a governmental body, or sometimes by church grant, rather than by private fees and thus for poorer boys a route to college* or the professions. Since WWII these have been officially replaced by comprehensives,* which are not as academically oriented, so many old grammar schools have kept the name but converted to fee-charging public schools.* They were called grammar schools because of their concentration on the teaching of Latin grammar. Some of the grammar schools attained academic reputations that rivaled the best of the public schools, and their old boys* are often extremely proud of their educations there, in no way feeling they were deprived academically, in spite of the still significant social prejudices against grammar school boys. The grammar schools also differed in that they were rarely boarding schools and almost always taught only local boys. In some places, also called **high schools**.

gramophone. What Americans called a phonograph or now call a stereo.

Grand National. A horse race run annually in late March or early April since 1839 at Aintree course in Liverpool,* the most prestigious steeple-chase* in England,* covering a course of four-and-one-half miles with thirty jumps of hedges, fences, and streams. Steeplechase horses compete for many years, and thus several famous horses have won the Grand National more than once.

grange. Originally in the medieval era a barn for storing grain; by the Restoration this had come to mean a house* with numerous other farm buildings around it. By the nineteenth century, grange meant quite a large house with such buildings and thus indicated the home of a gentleman*-farmer rather than a mere farmer. As with all real estate, term inflation in the twentieth has applied the name to almost any house that is vaguely rural in setting.

grangerizing. Stuffing or gluing clippings, pictures, or other additions into books, from Granger's *Biographical History of England* in 1769, which left a number of pages blank to encourage people to add in their own illustrations and addenda and set off a wave of book mutilations to find things to add to the Granger.

Granite City. Aberdeen.*

granny flat. *See* flat.

grant. A government payment of a student's tuition and basic living expenses at a college,* what Americans usually call a scholarship, in theory available to any qualified student although the amount (an average £2500) is now subject to a parental means test. Before the rise of the comprehensives,* grants were also given for tuition in grammar schools* and in similar Church* schools, and these were sometimes called **grant schools**.

Grantchester. A village near Cambridge* with a long tradition in literature since Chaucer placed the "Reeve's Tale" about the miller and the students at the mill there; Tennyson wrote about the place, and it was here that Rupert Brooke placed the vicarage* where there was "honey still for tea."

Grasmere. The village in the Lake District* inseparably tied to Wordsworth, who lived and wrote many of his most famous poems there.

grass. To inform on someone to the police.*

grave marks. The skin spots Americans call liver spots.

Gravesend. A port near the mouth of the Thames.* For centuries, this has been the point from which naval expeditions for war or exploration began and the port to which all ships returning to London* actually sailed, hence Conrad's choice of it as the site where Marlow actually narrates his story *Heart of Darkness* from the safe anchorage at which civilization has at last clearly been reached. In the twentieth century it has been the official beginning of the Port of London.* The name indicates that, after this point, the sailor would see no grave but the sea.

graveside dole. *See* dole.

Gray's Inn. One of the Inns of Court* in London,* located to the north of Lincoln's Inn,* the buildings dating back in part to the fourteenth century when there was a manor* house on the site and little changed since long before Tommy Traddles had chambers there. Currently, it trains primarily provincial* barristers.* *See also* Walks.

greaseproof paper. What Americans call wax paper, although a bit heavier.

Great Britain. The island containing England,* Scotland,* and Wales.* *See also* Britain; United Kingdom.

greatcoat. A very heavy and long overcoat, usually extending down below the knee and with a collar that can be turned up to protect the face; some version has been worn at least since the Restoration, but most people associate the coats with the army* and especially with the wool greatcoats worn by soldiers in the trenches during WWI, which were not called trench-coats.

Greater London. The administrative area formed in 1965 combining the former County of London* and the suburban communities surrounding it, containing a total of thirty-two boroughs* plus the City,* administered by the Greater London Council.* The area still officially exists despite the dissolution of the GLC* in 1986, but in effect it no longer has any single central government.

Great Fire. *See* Fire, Great.

great go. At Cambridge,* the final exams for a BA degree,* similar to the Greats* at Oxford.* *See also* little go.

Great North Road. The main highway* running north from London* to Edinburgh,* route of coaches* during the horse eras and in the twentieth century followed for much of its way by the A1.* It left the City* by Aldersgate.*

Great Ormond Street. *See* foundling.

Great Portland Street. *See* Portland Place.

Great Russell Street. In London,* the site of the British Museum.*

Greats. At Oxford,* the final examination for the BA* degree,* more specifically the final honours* exam in what is called lit. hum.,* the course concentrating on classics* and philosophy. *See also* great go; moderns; Mods; Smalls.

Great Seal. The seal used to authenticate royal* pronouncements, still used on all public acts of state, held in the custody of the Lord Chancellor* since the medieval era. *See also* Privy Seal.

Great Tom. The bell in Tom Tower in Christ Church* College at Oxford.* The bell is rung each evening 101 times, for the number of original members, at 9:05 P.M. (Oxford is five minutes west of the Greenwich* meridian), which was the signal for curfew in all the colleges* in the days when curfew was enforced.

Great War. World War I.

grebe. Any of several common water birds. Only the small brown **little grebe** is common year round, living on ponds, slow streams, et cetera, while the other larger and more colorful grebes generally come only in the winter. All the grebes can fly, but they spend most of their time swimming and feeding from the water, even building floating nests for their eggs, and are noted for the suddenness with which they dive for food.

Greek. In addition to things related to history, philosophy, and art, Greek is also used as a euphemism for sodomy.

Greek Street. A short street in London* in Soho* named for the number of Greek immigrants who settled there around 1800, often synonymous with Soho and thus also for crime and vice; in the late twentieth century, it is noted primarily for its high concentration of foreign restaurants.

green. (1) A small piece of open common ground in a village.* The green is usually in the middle of the village, while the common* is larger and outside the village itself. Greens come in all sizes and shapes but are usually simply flat, grassy areas with no trees or shrubbery. Some appear to have originally been common grazing land, while others were preserved for markets,* and still others simply kept open for communication among houses. (2) A person who is green is naive or unsophisticated; however, someone who is **green about** is jealous, as with Othello's green-eyed monster.

Green. A person, group, or political party* devoted primarily to environmental issues, from the name of the most famous of such parties in Germany.

green belt. An area around a town or city where no development is allowed by law. Since 1938, a green belt is supposed to encircle London* on a radius of about twenty to thirty miles from St. Pauls',* but suburban development has encroached on it and exceptions have been made that allowed the belt to be broken, leading in turn to grass-roots political action from both Conservatives* and environmentalists to protect and save the open space.

green fingers. The skill in growing garden* plants that Americans call a green thumb.

greengage. A type of plum that is green when ripe, first imported from France in the early eighteenth century.

greengrocer. A seller of fresh vegetables and fruits. *See also* grocer.

green paper. A government* document that describes potential policies, issued for purposes of discussion and evaluation. *See also* Blue Book; white paper.

Green Park. A park in London* to the north of Buckingham Palace,* connecting St. James's Park* and Hyde Park,* noted originally for the exotic birds kept there by Charles II along **Birdcage Walk**. On the outskirts of the city until the nineteenth century, this was known as a place for duels or fireworks displays (Handel's Fireworks Music was first played here). Lacking a pond, this is the simplest of the city's major parks, consisting of open lawns dotted with trees and crisscrossed with paths. *See also* Constitution Hill.

greens. Vegetables in general, but often more specifically cabbage and sprouts.* *See also* greengrocer.

green tea. *See* tea.

Greenwich. Pronounced GRINNidge, originally a village on the south shore of the Thames* east of London* where the ships of the navy* commonly anchored, now indistinguishable from the rest of the city that has grown out around it. The core of the community is the vast royal park where originally Henry VIII and Elizabeth I had a favored palace.* The palace was rebuilt by Wren as **Greenwich Hospital**, a hospital* and home for retired sailors, that now is part the Royal Naval College* and part the major national Maritime Museum; **Greenwich Pensioners*** lived there until 1873. Also on the grounds on a hill was the **Royal Observatory** built in 1675, primarily to establish reliable data for use in navigation, which it did so successfully that the meridian passing through the observatory is used as the 0° longitude for all navigational and mapmaking purposes throughout the world, and **Greenwich Mean Time**, the time at the meridian, is the base time for all time zones in the world, as well as the standard time for the United Kingdom.* The observatory moved to Sussex* in 1957 to escape the polluted skies of the city, but the official time for the entire world is still signalled by the dropping of a ball at noon from the spire on top of the old observatory. Until 1857, two annual fairs* were held here, both noted for their wild activities. *See also* Queen's House.

green wire. In electricity, what Americans call the ground wire. *See* earth.

grenadier. In the eighteenth century, a soldier who threw grenades, but by the nineteenth century, armed like other infantrymen. The old weapon meant that the grenadiers recruited men who were taller than normal, to get better throwing power, and grenadier soon became a byword for tall, strong, and handsome soldiers. Ironically, in WWI, when grenades became a significant weapon in the trenches, grenadier had such a strong romantic association that new grenade throwers were called **bombers** instead.

Grenadier Guards. A regiment* of the Guards,* formed in 1685 as His Majesty's Regiment, with the name changed in 1815. This is arguably the single most prestigious regiment in the army, in the mid-nineteenth century its commissions* costing more even than the Life Guards.*

Gresham College. A small college* in London* founded in 1567 (by the Lord Mayor* and Counsellor to Elizabeth I, who first stated "Gresham's Law") to provide free public lectures on academic subjects. Located in the City* just north of Cheapside,* it was merged in 1966 with the new City University.

Gretna Green. A Scottish village just across the border on the main road from London* to Glasgow.* It became famous after 1754 as the nearest place eloping couples could go to be married outside the strictures of English law, particularly the English requirement of parental consent. Until 1940, marriage there required simply a declaration by the couple to practically any resident witness that the pair wishes to be married, which proverbially was the blacksmith on the edge of the village.

gridiron. *See* grilled.

grilled. Americans put meat on a grill, Britons put it **under the grill**, thus using grilled to mean what Americans usually call broiled, cooked underneath a flame or electric element. It can also mean cooked on a **gridiron**, an open frame that allows fat drippings to fall into the fire. Sometimes, however, it seems to mean fried but not in deep fat, so a grilled steak in a restaurant is always a bit of an adventure. *See also* mixed grill.

Grimsby. A port on the eastern coast of England,* for centuries the busiest port of the English fishing fleet.

grinder. Someone who operates a crammer,* and sometimes a student at one, such as Rob the Grinder.

grip. A pin or clasp such as Americans usually call a bobby pin.

gripe. Temporary, irregular bowel pains, an illness unrelated to the grip or **grippe**, which is a bad cold or flu. **Gripe water** is given to babies to relieve stomach and bowel pains.

groat. A medieval silver coin, originally worth four pence* but gradually debased over the years until worth about two pence in the seventeenth century. Hence, a **groatsworth** is a small or worthless amount. From 1836–56, a new fourpence coin was called a groat. *See also* Appendix I.

grocer. A seller of foods. Originally, grocers sold only dry foods and supplies, but more recently, in competition with hypermarkets,* the grocer may deal with all types of food. The **Grocers** are one of the twelve great livery companies* of the City* of London. *See also* greengrocer; shop.

grog. Rum and water, issued as a ration in the navy* from 1740–1971. The name comes from the admiral* who ordered it, who was called Old Grog for the cloak he wore made of **grogram cloth**, a type of coarse wool/mohair mix.

Grosvenor Square. Pronounced GROV-ner, a large square in London* in the middle of Mayfair.* Since 1959, this has been the site of a remarkably ugly U.S. Embassy. Hence, the name is often used in civil service* circles and modern spy novels as a synonym for the U.S. government.

ground. (1) A sports field. (2) In rugby,* to touch the ball to the ground behind the goal line; if done by the offensive team this scores three points; if done by the defenders, they get to start on offense from their own twenty-five yard line, similar to a touchback in American football.

groundage. A tax levied on ships arriving in a port.

ground floor. *See* floor.

grounding. Scraping an axle or other lower part of a car or wagon on a hump or bump in the roadway.

ground nut. What Americans call a peanut.

ground rent. Rent paid only for the land underneath a building. Much of British property is leased rather than sold; hence, the ostensible owner of a building that is rented or leased to tenants often in turn pays rent for the land underneath the building to someone else. This has long been one of the fundamental sources of income for the aristocracy.* *See also* freehold; leasehold; property.

grounds. On an estate or around a country house,* the part of the land surrounding the house or central building used purely for ornamental purposes and on which no crops are grown. *See also* demesne; garden; terrace.

group-captain. *See* Appendix V.

grouse. A bird similar to the partridge, somewhat larger but less rotund and mostly dirty brown in color, found primarily on the heathers* of northern England* and Scotland.* British gentlemen* shoot thousands of these each autumn, for no known reason; the bird is eaten, certainly, in pies* or roasted, but rarely in the quantities in which they are shot (in 1888, one man shot 1,070 in a single day, and many others have come close to that record). Going shooting* almost always means going to Scotland or the north of England in order to shoot grouse (although partridges are also common targets). The shoots, particularly in the late Victorian* and Edwardian* era, were massive social affairs, with numbers of gentlemen staking out separate areas and long lines of "beaters," men from the villages, walking through the woods and heather* to scare the birds, who normally stay on the ground among the leaves and seeds they eat, into the air where they could be seen and shot.

grouty dick. A pudding* made from suet and sultanas,* primarily in the Midlands.*

growler. A horsedrawn cab* similar to the hansom* except with four wheels and a side entrance for the passengers.

Grub Street. Formerly a street in London* near Aldersgate,* in the eighteenth century synonymous with hack writers who lived there; the street was renamed and then demolished to be covered over by the Barbican* project.

gruel. A watery oatmeal porridge.*

guard. On a train, what Americans call the conductor.

guardee. Slang for a guardsman.*

Guardian. Until 1960 the *Manchester Guardian*, then moved to London,* long the semiofficial voice of the Liberal* party and in the contemporary world the paper of choice for the educated "liberal" associated with the SDP,* i.e., a member of one of the "caring" professions.

Guards. Any one of seven regiments* that guard the monarch's palaces and processions and the Bank of England,* beloved of tourists for the **Changing of the Guard** ceremony at Buckingham Palace.* Originally considered the finest units in the army,* during Victoria's time these units were noted more for ceremonial drilling and the extremely aristocratic background of their officers* than for feats in the field, but since just before WWI they have once again been considered to be among the very best fighting units in the army. In the days when commissions* were purchased, the most expensive and exclusive were in the Guards, the cavalry* Guards the most expensive of all, and the Guards officers were more noted as sportsmen and clubmen than military minds. The Guards regiments are— infantry, or **Foot Guards**: Coldstream Guards,* Grenadier Guards,* Scots Guards, Irish Guards, and Welsh Guards; cavalry, or **Household Cavalry**: Life Guards* and Royal Horse Guards.* *See also* guardsman; line.

guardsman. A member of one of the Guards* regiments.* Historically, since the Guards were the regiments of highest social status, the guardsman has been the romantic ideal soldier: handsome, brave, a gambler, and a ladies' man, a dashing figure in a tight tailored uniform. Hence, the **guards-**

man's defence used when charged with killing a man, which is the claim that the dead man made homosexual advances, due to the guardsman's great physical attraction.

Guernsey. *See* Channel Islands.

guild. During the medieval era, an association of traders and artisans in similar businesses or crafts, extremely powerful during Shakespeare's time, acting as regulators of all things relating to one particular trade, including prices, wages, apprentice training, et cetera. The rise of free trade and capitalistic industry broke their power, and for the most part they are only ceremonial associations today. *See also* livery company.

Guildford. Pronounced GILLferd, a town and the administrative center of Surrey,* southeast of London;* in the early nineteenth century it was thought one of the most pleasant towns of southern England,* but in recent years it has become less independent and more a commuter suburb of London. Malory thought this was Arthur's Astolat, but for modern writers a more typical occupant is Douglas Adams's Arthur Dent.

Guildhall. In London,* the administrative center of the City* of London* since the twelfth century. Originally a place where the various guilds* and livery companies* could meet together, the modern building still retains a core of its fourteenth-century structure, despite major remodeling and expansion after the Great Fire* and again after WWII. The Hall itself is a large meeting room used for major banquets and public meetings within the City, with the statues of Gog and Magog at one end, and numerous smaller meeting rooms are used by the surviving guilds and as reception rooms for society weddings and similar events. This was the site of the Court of Common Pleas,* where cases like *Bardell v. Pickwick* were tried until 1873. *See also* Corporation; Lord Major.

guillotine. A procedure used in Parliament* to end debate and force a vote by setting a specific time at which voting on a particular bill* must begin.

guinea. A gold coin worth one pound* plus one shilling;* the last of these were minted in 1813 but continued in circulation for many years. More importantly, it became customary to state and pay fees for the professions and donations to charity in guineas; the fee or donation might appear to be £20 but in fact be 20 guineas, which was actually £21. The person paid 20 guineas was recognized to be more professional than the person paid £21, even though the amounts were the same. Thus in novels or films we often find characters negotiating about prices in pounds or guineas, which makes a difference not only in amount paid but also the status of the persons involved. Similarly a person might pay in guineas as a sort of tip for people who would have been insulted by the offer of a tip. Since decimalization* in 1971, some people still use the term to indicate 105p. *See also* Appendix I; Appendix III.

Guineas. The **2,000 Guineas**, a one-mile horse race for three-year-olds held at Newmarket* in early May since 1809, when the original prize was 2,000 guineas, one of the most prestigious races in Britain. There is also a **1,000 Guineas**, run about a week earlier since 1814, also at Newmarket. *See also* Derby; St. Leger.

Guinness. A brand name for the most widely known stout,* sometimes described as "motor oil with foam" and imported from Ireland. *See also* beer.

gully. (1) In cricket,* the area on the field of the off* side, slightly behind the wicket and near the boundary far from the batsman.* (2) In Scotland* and northern England,* a large knife.

gum. (1) What Americans call glue or paste. (2) A small candy similar to what Americans call gumdrops; **fruit gums** are various fruit flavors, **wine gums** have a red wine flavor, et cetera.

gumboots. Rubber boots with very high tops; also called wellingtons.*

gun. In the military, a cannon or other artillery piece, never a rifle or musket; among civilians, a shotgun. Only very recently has the general American use of gun for a pistol or other handgun become common, under the influence of movies and TV programs.

Gunpowder Plot. The plot by a group of Catholics to blow up Parliament* in 1605. *See* Guy Fawkes Day.

gunpowder tea. *See* tea.

Gurkha. A tribe in Nepal, since the mid-nineteenth century supported primarily by the large number who volunteer to serve in the British army,* where the Gurkha regiments* have built a reputation as the finest soldiers in the world.

gutter crawler. A man in a car who slowly drives along trying to pick up prostitutes or other women. Also called a **kerb crawler**.

gutter press. Newspapers* and magazines that concentrate on scandal and personal stories.

guttersnipe. *See* snipe.

guv/guv'nor. *See* governor.*

guy. (1) An effigy of Guy Fawkes. Traditionally on Guy Fawkes Day,* children go through the neighborhood asking for a **penny*** **for the guy,** such funds ostensibly being used to make the effigy but more often a form of trick-or-treat. (2) As a verb, to make fun of or play a practical joke on.

Guy Fawkes Day. November 5, celebrated since 1605 although not an official bank holiday,* when a band of men including Guy Fawkes were discovered with explosives in the cellars underneath Parliament.* The most common form of celebration is a great bonfire,* often with fireworks as well, on the night of the fifth, and it is probably the most exciting holiday for the children of England* next to Christmas.* *See also* guy; Ringing Day.

Guy's Hospital. One of the largest hospitals in London,* located in South-wark,* built in 1725 but much expanded and modernized.

Gwent. In ancient days a kingdom in south Wales,* now a small county* on the Severn* and the border with England.*

Gwynedd. An ancient kingdom in northern Wales,* now a county* in the northeast corner of the country, particularly mountainous and containing Snowdonia.*

Gymnosophist. A euphemism attempted by British nudists in the 1920s and 30s to stress the health aspects of nudism.

gym slip. A loose tunic without sleeves worn as outerwear by schoolgirls for physical activities.

gyp. At Cambridge,* a servant for the student rooms.* *See also* scout.

gyppo. *See* gippo.

gyppy tummy. *See* gippy tummy.

gypsy. From 1554 to 1783, gypsies were formally outlawed in England,* although there is no evidence that the law reduced their numbers. The number of real gypsies with Romany* culture has always been relatively small—Britain is after all an island—but those gypsies to be found there carry much the same reputation as on the continent: fortune-tellers, horse traders, and thieves who are never welcomed in a community. Many vagabonds of various kinds are often also called gypsies, but they share nothing of the culture but the vagabondage. *See also* fair; traveller.

H

h. One of the most significant variants in British accents* is the *h* sound at the beginning of words. One of the primary characteristics of the Cockney* accent and of various regional accents associated with the Midlands and industrial North* is that the *h* sound is not made; thus, half becomes 'alf, house becomes 'ouse, et cetera. During the nineteenth century, these accents became inextricably associated with the lower classes,* so that anyone moving upward in society had to consciously learn to put the *h*'s back in. This led to a late nineteenth and early twentieth century accent in which people attached *h*'s to words that had never had them—open became hopen, office became hoffice, et cetera—thus betraying their origins and pretensions even more clearly than the old accent would have done; writers were quick to make use of this practice, and until after WWII an accent with randomly added *h*'s was almost invariably used to signal that the character (if not a Cockney) was in trade.*

H. On movies, "horror," unsuitable for children.

haberdasher. Originally, a person who sold hats; now, a person who sells accessories for clothing construction, such as lace, pins, and ribbon, but never as in America one who sells men's clothing. The **Haberdashers** are one of the great livery companies* of the City* of London.*

hacking jacket. A riding* jacket, or sometimes a casual sport coat in similar style.

hackney. This actually means something for hire, from its original use for an average, everyday kind of horse (in America quickly shortened to hack). In the seventeenth and eighteenth centuries, hackney generally referred to a rented horse, which would be of this everyday kind. The renting soon outweighed the horse in the public mind, so there are also references to hackney chairs* or hackney coaches,* and Pepys and others of his time also used the term figuratively for any poor souls who have to hire themselves out for drudge work, including especially the more common prostitutes. By the nineteenth century, however, the term had come to be most often applied to horse-drawn carriages* for hire,* as in hackney cabs;* it seems to apply to any kind of carriage, but in most literature it means a hansom,* simply because they were the most numerous form of hire carriages. In the twentieth the term faded, although it was used occasionally for motor taxis* by oldtimers.

Hackney. One of the northern communities of the East End* in London,* in nineteenth and early twentieth centuries particularly squalid and slum-ridden, although much urban renewal has been done in the area since WWII.

haddie. haddock.* *See also* Finnan haddie.

haddock. A fish similar to but smaller than cod,* one of the principal fishes in the British diet. *See also* fish and chips.

Hadrian's Wall. A stone wall built by the Romans to keep marauding bands from Scotland* out of Roman England,* in use from the early second century until the late fourth century. It ran from near modern Newcastle* on the east coast to near the Solway Firth* at modern Carlisle.* Portions of the wall still remain and are visited by numerous tourists. *See also* Antonine wall.

haggerty. A dish of potatoes, onion, and grated cheese, shaped like a pancake and fried. Also called **pan haggerty**.

haggis. A dish now eaten only by Scots* at traditional meals,* made primarily of sheep's entrails and oatmeal stuffed into a sheep's stomach, then boiled.

haha. A big ditch, apparently named for the sound other people make when you slip and fall into it. People began to build these around the grounds* of country houses* in the eighteenth century, where they acted as a fence to keep out interlopers without interfering with the view from or to the house. Sometimes one side was sharp and the other sloping, sometimes both sloped and there was an actual wall down in the bottom, but the haha was grass-covered and never filled with water (like a moat) or with a hedge.*

haircord. Upholstery material made from horse hair or sometimes camel hair.

hairdresser. Used to indicate both a barber shop and a beauty salon.

hairslide. What Americans usually call a barrette, to hold women's hair in place.

hake. A common food fish, similar to a cod.*

half. (1) A half-pint, almost always of beer.* One of the oddities of the British pub* is that two half-pints cost exactly the same as one pint,* by law, a practice unheard of in America, where the economies of scale are devoutly practiced. A second round of drinks is thus known as the **other half**, even if the two men happen to be drinking pints (or liquor). Otherwise, the half is usually associated with women or with prim office workers, schoolteachers, and other wimpy types of males, or until very recently with the poor man in the country pub who carefully nursed his half for an entire evening. (2) As an adjective or adverb, **not half** means a lot; "I wasn't half upset," for example, means "I was very upset." However, **by half** indicates too much, as **too clever by half** means too smart for your own good, making something simple very complicated, knowing things you shouldn't know. (3) In relation to time, thirty minutes after; thus, half one is 1:30. (4) *See* halfback.

half and half. Mild and bitter beer* mixed together.

halfback. (1) In hockey,* one of three players who operate in the area between the fullbacks* and the forwards,* more defensive than offensive in strategy. (2) In football,* players in the same position, in more modern style of play replaced by midfielders. (3) In rugby,* the player, often called the **scrum half**, stationed just outside the scrum* who tries to get the ball when it appears and then pitches it to the threequarter backs* to initiate a play.

half-century. In cricket,* fifty runs scored by a single batsman* in a single innings.* *See also* century.

half-crown. *See* crown.

half-inch. Steal, rhyming slang* for pinch.

Half Moon Street. A short street in London* in Mayfair,* an extremely fashionable address, suitable for people like Wodehouse's Bertie Wooster and Jeeves.

half-pay. Paid to military officers* who have retired or who, for various reasons, are not currently on active duty.

halfpenny. Usually spelled **ha'penny** or **ha'p'ny** because it was almost immediately pronounced HAYPny, a coin worth half of a pence* or two farthings,* from early pennies that could literally be cut in half. In Shakespeare's day, this was silver, but Charles II changed it to copper, and then in 1860 it was changed again to bronze. The size and value were changed during decimalization, but inflation meant that the coin disappeared long before formally discontinued in 1985. A **ha'p'ny farthing** is not a coin but the value of a halfpenny plus a farthing, or three farthings: i.e., three-fourths of a penny. A **ha'p'nyworth** or **ha'p'orth** (HAYputh) is how much a ha'p'ny could buy, and thus, almost from the beginning, a synonym for "not much at all." *See also* Appendix I.

half-round. Half a slice of bread or half a sandwich.*

half-term. A short vacation in the middle of each school* term.*

hall. (1) Originally, a large assembly room. In the medieval era, a lord's castle or house often consisted of little more than a gigantic hall where all indoor activities took place and a few small bedrooms off to the side. By Shakespeare's time, houses had begun to grow, and many people began to use hall to indicate a house that contained such a large room, which might be used only for dances or as a large living room, and by the nineteenth century it often meant simply a large house, with or without a large hall, such as Baskerville Hall. When Britons mean the passageway between rooms, they generally say **hallway** or **passage** rather than hall. (2) In the universities,* the building set aside for residence and/or instruction of students; over the years, each of the "halls" came to be called colleges* instead, and now the usage is heard only casually if at all or in intentionally archaic announcements. However, most colleges still retain a hall, in the sense of a large room, and this room is used as the main dining room of the college and for other large meetings.

Hallé. An orchestra in Manchester,* the oldest (1858) extant symphony in the nation, predating all current London* orchestras by half a century.

hall porter. *See* porter.

halls. The music halls;* a performer with a variety act was **working the halls**.

halt. (1) On the railroads, an unscheduled stop, a station where only selected trains will stop and only then when there is a definite request. Thus, in stories, Such-and-Such Halt for a place name implies either an unpopulated district or someone with extremely high status who could get the trains to put in a special stop just for their convenience. (2) Until fairly recently, stop signs actually read "Halt," but now most have been converted to "Stop."

ham. (1) Used primarily in southern England,* this was Old English for a settlement or a single home and thus was the foundation for both the modern word hamlet* and for the tremendous number of English villages and towns whose names end in -ham. (2) The meat is quite common, although often called pork* or gammon.* It is also the meat traditionally served after funerals.*

Ham. Several neighborhoods of the East End* of London* east of the Isle of Dogs,* such as **East Ham**, **West Ham**, or **Newham**, all sharing much the same persona as the rest of the East End.*

hamlet. A very small rural settlement, distinguished from a village* by its lack of a church.*

hammer. (1) On the stock exchange, to act in the way Americans call bearish, to drive down the price of stocks* and shares. (2) In the Highland games,* a heavy iron ball on the end of a chain that competitors throw for distance.

hammer and tongs. With violence or intensity, as in "They were at it hammer and tongs;" from the action of a blacksmith.

Hammersmith. A borough* of Greater London* to the west of Kensington,* in the nineteenth century very artistic, in the twentieth becoming lower–middle class* and showing little identifiable personality. **Hammersmith Bridge** across the Thames* was London's first suspension bridge (1827).

Hampshire. A county* or shire* southwest of London,* with rolling hills (*See* down) well suited for grazing, noted for famous breeds of sheep and of pigs originating there.

Hampstead. Originally a village north of London,* a popular weekend home for writers like Vanbrugh, Addison, or Johnson. Well into the nineteenth century, it was a suburb still quite separate from London in which many artists and writers, particularly successful ones, lived, but eventually the city grew out to it. Even so, it was always associated with wealthy and independent residents, like Emma Peel of TV's "Avengers," and is now the home of the "Hampstead left," what Americans usually call "radical chic." Hampstead itself is immediately south of Hampstead Heath;* **West Hampstead**, however, moves north around the edge of the heath and merges with Golders Green* and is often seen as a Jewish neighborhood. **Hampstead Garden Suburb** was built in 1906 to the north of the health, when it could still be thought of as separate from the city; intended originally to rehouse the slum poor, it is now thoroughly gentrified, associated with politicians, economists, middle-class* artists, et cetera. Hemel Hampstead* is a completely different place.

Hampstead Heath. A heath* immediately north of Hampstead,* the bulk of it preserved in a near natural state by an 1871 law after much agitation to protect it both from developers and from governmental groups that wanted to make it a formal park. This is an enormous open space of grassy hills interspersed with trees and occasional ponds, used by many Londoners as a touch of the countryside* within the city. **Parliament Hill** between the village and the heath is the highest point in London.

Hampton Court. A palace* on the Thames* upstream from London* about half way between the City* and Windsor.* Built in 1520 by Wolsey, it was confiscated by Henry VIII and then modified and used as a regular residence by him and by Elizabeth I. Since then it has been used only occasionally as a residence but in the twentieth century has been a major tourist attraction, due to its well-preserved Tudor interiors and famous gardens* including the Maze.*

handbagged. Sandbagged* by a woman, first appearing in political circles in the 1980s in reference to Margaret Thatcher's political tactics.

handbasin. *See* basin.

handful. In criminal slang, a prison* sentence of five years.

handle. In cricket,* to touch the ball with your hands while batting, which is an automatic out.

hanger. A wood* on a steep hillside, as in Northanger Abbey.

hanging/hangman. *See* capital punishment.

Hansard. Originally, a printer who published *Parliamentary Debates*, the regular daily proceedings of Parliament;* hence, used casually for the official daily record of Parliamentary activity, even after taken over by the state in 1909, similar to the American *Congressional Record.*

hansom. A horse-drawn carriage, first built by Joseph Hansom in the early nineteenth century. It was covered but not fully enclosed, the passengers sitting facing an open front directly overlooking the horse. Since it was small and light, with only two wheels, and carried two passengers in a private cubicle with the driver perched outside, above and behind the passengers, it became the most common cab* of the century, with more than 7000 licensed in London* by 1886. *See also* growler.

Hants. The abbreviation for Hampshire.*

ha'p'ny. *See* halfpenny.

ha'p'orth. *See* halfpenny.

happen. Perhaps or probably, as in "Happen something's wrong;" its use is confined to provincial* dialects, especially Lancashire* and Yorkshire.*

happy families. A card game played mostly by small children in which the players draw cards trying to match up members of families rather than suits.

hard. (1) A road, but most often used for a road along a shore. (2) Among criminals, a sentence of hard labor, as in "six years hard."

hard by. Close to, near, as in "hard by the car park." When you are **hard done by**, however, you are treated badly.

hard lines. Americans often say "tough luck!" possibly from sailing usage about frozen ropes.

hare. (1) Similar to a rabbit, the English hare is larger and nests on the surface rather than underground in burrows. March is mating season, which is why a **March hare** is mad. Sailors consider it bad luck to mention a hare because many meat suppliers in the eighteenth and nineteenth centuries substituted hare, which decayed very quickly, for pork. The British also have rabbits. (2) As a verb, to go fast; someone **haring** down the road is running. *See also* hunt.

hare and hounds. Among school boys, a race similar to a paper chase.*

Harlech. A seaside village in northwest Wales,* site of a castle where a brave resistance during a siege in 1468 inspired the song *Men of Harlech*, an unofficial Welsh national anthem.

Harley Street. A street in London* where many doctors have offices, now synonymous with private doctors, specialists (consultants*), and expensive private medicine. *See also* National Health; Wimpole Street.

Harrods. A massive department store in London* in Brompton Road.* A small grocer's* in 1849, it had become a leader among department stores by the 1890s. A century later it still tries to live up to its old motto, "Everything, for everyone, everywhere," with over 200 departments. The **Food Halls** are actually a massive supermarket in the center of the store, with practically every kind of food available in Britain. *See also* Marks and Spencer; Selfridge's.

Harrogate. A town in north-central England,* noted as a spa as early as Shakespeare's time but gaining its greatest popularity in mid–nineteenth century, superseding Bath* as the country's most popular spa until the early 1920s, when spa-going declined.

Harrow. A village now in northwestern London,* noted for the public school* of that name there since 1572. During the nineteenth century, along with Eton,* Harrow became a model for all English public schools, and the two are still almost always spoken of in the same breath as paradigms for the entire public school system, and their old boys* carry the highest status possible.

hart. *See* deer.

harvest festival. Although the harvest festival service in the Church of England* appears to be an ancient custom, it is in fact quite recent. During the mid-nineteenth century, respectable elements of society grew impatient with both the drunken revelry and the mixing of classes* in the ancient harvest home* celebrations, and this led to a number of clergymen independently trying to substitute a church service followed by food and drink of a nonalcoholic nature. By the end of the century, the old customs had been suppressed in favor of what one rector* called "tea and cake in the schoolroom and a choral service and sermon to follow." During the twentieth century, the harvest festival has become one of the major festivals of the Church of England, although celebrated at different times in autumn in various parishes; churches are specially decorated with fruits and such, and there is much choral singing. Ironically this is often most actively observed in urban and suburban churches that have no contact at all with agriculture and is often the only time casual churchgoers make a point of attending church services. *See also* Lammas.

harvest home. Celebrations held at the end of the autumn harvest. These varied throughout the British Isles, according to local custom, but in most cases were a time of feasting and drinking. Some were held on individual farms, some throughout a parish.* *See also* harvest festival.

Harwell. A village south of Oxford,* center of national nuclear research.

Harwich. Pronounced HARE-idge, a small port on the eastern coast of England,* traditionally a major port in the trade with Holland, a relationship continuing today in regular ferries from Harwich to Holland and Germany.

Hastings. Originally a village on the southeast coast of England,* site in 1066 of the battle in which William the Conqueror defeated the Anglo-Saxons and took control of England. In more modern times, it has become a resort town, favored since the early nineteenth century by the genteel* middle class,* noted by other classes as the dullest excuse for a resort even today, almost two centuries since Charles Lamb called his holiday* there a "penance."

Hatchards. A large bookstore in London* in Piccadilly* since 1797.

hatches, matches, and dispatches. Slang for the births, marriages, and deaths columns in a newspaper, especially in early twentieth century and in the *Times*, which reported on only the most socially significant families.

hat trick. Three great things, from the hat trick in cricket,* which is to bowl* out (like a strikeout) three batsmen* in a row, for which in the old days a bowler was presented a top hat.

haulier. The profession Americans would call a trucker, although more often applied to the truck owner than to the driver. *See also* lorry.

have it off. To have sexual relations, a rather vulgar formulation.

have on. To tease or to try to trick someone.

have up. To bring someone before a judge or for an interview of some kind.

Haworth. A village in West Yorkshire,* almost completely given over to the tourist industry surrounding the Brontës, who lived there. The neighboring countryside provided the model for *Wuthering Heights* in particular.

Haymarket. A street in London* running south from Piccadilly Circus,* originally a market for farmers but now primarily associated with theaters.

hayter. A lawnmover, a brand name used generically.

hazelnut. A small nut from the hazel bush, extremely popular in British candies, especially chocolates, where it is used in much the same ways as peanuts or almonds are used in American chocolate bars.

H.E. Abbreviation for His/Her Excellency.*

head/headmaster. The teacher in charge of a school,* similar to the American principal* except that the head is a teacher who often continues to teach at least a few classes; however, in the modern comprehensives,* which are as large as American high schools, heads rarely teach any longer. In some schools called **head teacher.** *See also* private school; public school.

head boy. In public schools,* the senior student chosen by the head* as best all-round contributor to the school, whose primary duty is to set a good example for the rest of the students. Thus he is almost always a good athlete and a good (but not too good) student. He has few specific duties or powers but in most schools is allowed a tremendous amount of *de facto* authority over the rest of the boys, and thus his selection is often critical to the effective operation of the school's daily life. In girl's schools* a similar **head girl** is usually chosen.

head lad. Very different from head boy,* this is the senior stableboy, who may be and often is a mature man (and may be a woman), who exercises horses at a stable and sometimes also supervises the other stableboys.

headlamps. On a car, what Americans call headlights.

head teacher. *See* head.

heath. Originally, a hillside or large area with heather growing on it; later, a large area where plants and trees were left to grow in their natural state, but primarily an open space with only shrubs or scattered smaller trees. Some of these heaths are now urban parks, like Hampstead Heath,* treated much the same as a common,* others have disappeared to survive only in local place names, while many others are simply areas with loosely defined boundaries that have not yet fallen under cultivation for various reasons. The larger heaths are sometimes also called moors,* particularly if they are wild, forbidding, or far from urban life.

Heath Robinson. W. Heath Robinson was a cartoonist for *Punch** and similar magazines* in the early twentieth century who specialized in drawing strange and unnecessary inventions, most of which were made of incomprehensible gears and belts. Thus a Heath Robinson machine or affair came to mean anything that was more complicated than it had to be or seemed to be an amateurishly assembled contraption.

Heathrow. The major airport for London,* located west of the city, the primary airport for international flights. By American standards a fairly typical large airport, it is often seen by the British as a metaphor for all the inconvenient, incomprehensible, and ugly aspects of modern life, its waiting rooms an annex of Hell. Terminals 3 and 4, used for international flights, are especially detested.

Hebrides. A number of islands off the northwest coast of Scotland.*

hedge. *See* hedgerow.

hedgehog. A small nocturnal mammal with a snout and spines, similar to the American porcupine.

hedge-laying. Not planting hedges* but a method of trimming them so that the stripped branches can be interwoven to make the hedge sturdier and denser.

hedgerow. A natural growth of trees or shrubs used as a fence to enclose a farmer's field, most common in the Midlands* but found at times throughout Britain. Many of these were planted purposely after the enclosures,* the branches of the trees interwoven as they grew, but many others grew up naturally over the years in the area near a fence where the plow could not reach until they overwhelmed the fence. Most of these are not bush-like little hedges but are trees and undergrowth so densely grown together that they not only serve as a fence but also as a natural habitat for much wildlife. In recent years the hedgerows have come under attack from modern farming methods, spurring much of the modern conservation movement's growth in an attempt to save what many see as a uniquely English institution.

Hellfire Club. A gentlemen's club* founded in 1745 at an abbey* near Henley.* The club's motto was "Do whatever you please," and the members were widely rumored to hold orgies, engage in satanic practices, and even plan to overthrow the government,* but modern research indicates the rumors were for the most part groundless. The name was so applied to a number of earlier small clubs in London* patronized by the younger rakes* of the town.

helping the police. *See* assisting the police.

Hemel Hampstead. One of the new towns* built just outside the Green Belt* to the northwest of London,* in the 1950s the height of suburban aspiration and still a solid middle-class* commuter suburb.

Henley. A small town on the Thames* west of London,* noted primarily for the **Henley Regatta**, a series of rowing* races held annually near the first of July since 1839. When Prince Albert gave the races royal* patronage in 1855, the event quickly became a major social affair, much like Royal Ascot,* which everyone who is anyone attends. The races themselves are eccentric in length, intensely amateur in attitude, and now extend over four days; most men in the crowd wear "traditional" boating costume: white trousers, striped jackets, and straw boaters* or rowing caps.

Herald. A daily newspaper* primarily Labour* in orientation and respectable working class* in readership, once potent but declining after WWII and closing in the early 1960s.

Heralds' College. The College of Arms. *See* college.

herder. *See* drover.

Hereford. Pronounced in three syllables, a castle and town near the Welsh border, primary town of Herefordshire;* in spite of being a cathedral* town, its primary place in British life since the Roman era has been as a center of the long wars fought with the Welsh along the Marches.* It stagnated when Wales* finally was subdued and only lately has begun to modernize.

Herefordshire. County* or shire* on the western border of England,* undulating hills with fertile valleys along the Wye, primarily orchards and cattle land and source of the white-faced Hereford cattle now raised throughout the world as the primary breed of beef cattle. In 1974 it was combined into a single county with Worcestershire.*

heriot. In the medieval era, when a tenant of a noble died, his heirs had to return to the noble any military equipment, such as a horse or armour, that the tenant had used. Gradually, this changed to a payment of the best animal the dead tenant had owned, or sometimes an equivalent money payment. By the seventeenth century, the custom was seen by many as a cruel practice, a form of robbing poor widows, but it nonetheless continued well into the nineteenth.

herring. A small fish that has been a major part of the British diet for centuries. The **kippered herring** (or kipper*) is dried and smoked, eaten regularly for breakfast;* the **bloater** is also a smoked herring treated by a different process that splits and smokes it for only about four hours so it is still soft, usually from Yarmouth* where the major fishing fleets operated. The **red herring** is dried for about two weeks after several days of salting, which makes it very dry and gives it a reddish color; these were often dragged on a string to train hounds* to follow a scent, from which the term came to mean a false trail of clues in a mystery. The **herring pond** is the Atlantic Ocean, a joking reference in common use since the seventeenth century.

Hertford. Pronounced HARferd: (1) A small town in Hertfordshire.* (2) A college* of Oxford;* Waugh never specifically says Charles Ryder went here, but many of the descriptions match, and it was Waugh's own college.

Hertfordshire. Pronounced HARferdsher, a county* or shire* immediately north of London,* one of the Home Counties,* full of country homes* and market gardens* and, since WWII, expanding suburbs of the city.

hessian. A very coarse stiff cloth made from jute and hemp, in America usually called burlap.

HGV. Heavy goods vehicle, a big truck similar in size to a moving van.

High, the. At Oxford,* the high street.*

high change. Noon, from the busy period at the Exchange.*

High Church. Not a particular sect but merely those clergy* within the Church of England* who wished to retain significant continuity of belief and ritual with the Catholic Church.* This was the dominant faction of the Church from its formation until the end of the Stuarts,* when more strictly Protestant factions gained control; the Oxford Movement* revived its ideas in the nineteenth century, resulting in new growth of High Church services, also called Anglo-Catholic.* *See also* evangelical; Low Church.

High Commissioner. The equivalent of an ambassador from one Commonwealth* country to another.

High Court. The court* that deals with the more complex civil cases, as well as all slander cases, and also acts as an appeals court for some county court* cases. The modern High Court, formed in 1873, has three basic divisions: Chancery,* dealing with wills and estates; **Family Court**, dealing with adoptions, guardianships, et cetera; and the King's/Queen's Bench, dealing with commercial and maritime law. *See also* Common Pleas; Court of Appeal.

Highgate. An early suburban development of London* northeast of Hampstead Heath,* from the Restoration to the present a community of the prosperous. Steerforth's mother lived there, and David Copperfield was perhaps overreaching his income when he moved Dora into a cottage* there. **Highgate Cemetery** contains many graves of the famous, the most noted and ironic, considering the surroundings, being Karl Marx.

high jump. Serious punishment, perhaps in reference to the highest jump of all, from the hangman's* cart; someone who is **for the high jump** is in very serious trouble.

Highland. *See* Highlands.

Highlander. A native of the Highlands,* almost always a member of one of the clans* and generally seen in both the Lowlands* and in England* as a wild, savage, or ignorant person. Until mid–twentieth century, a figure of a Highlander stood, like an American wooden Indian, to mark a tobacconist.*

Highland fling. *See* fling.

Highland games. A series of sporting events held at annual clan* gatherings in the Highlands* areas of Scotland.* During the eighteenth century, these all but disappeared, due partly to suppression and partly to economic changes, but they were revived during the enthusiasm for things Scottish prompted by Scott's novels. There are now more than seventy separate games across Scotland during late summer, but the ones most generally noted as *the* Highland Games are those at Braemar given prominence by Victoria's regular patronage during her visits to Balmoral.* The games include regular track and field events plus traditional Scottish sports. *See also* caber; fling; hammer.

Highlands. Approximately the northern half of Scotland,* north of a diagonal geological fault line running northeast from the Firth* of Clyde, consisting of mountainous, rough country (although not very high by American standards, most of the peaks only 2,000 to 3,500 feet high). The area was dominated by the clans* until they were broken in the aftermath of Culloden,* and its inhabitants continued to speak Gaelic* well into the nineteenth century, but much of the population was driven out not by the English but by landlords during the Clearances.* This is the home of the stereotyped Scot,* the one with the kilt,* the thick burr, and the bagpipe.* It has always been considered to be a wild forbidding place, and only within the last century or so has the rest of the island regarded the inhabitants as anything other than savages. The name is almost always seen in the plural, except for the modern Highland region* (or county*) that contains about half of the area.

Highness, His/Her/Your. This title really doesn't exist. It was once used as the formal style and proper form of address for children of one of the monarch's daughters but was abolished in 1917. American writers and the more sloppy British writers still use it inaccurately for any member of the royal family,* but this is properly His/Her Royal Highness.*

high school. Another name occasionally used for a grammar school,* most often in Scotland.* *See also* school.

High Sheriff. *See* sheriff.

high street. The main street, usually the street* on which most of a town or village's shops are located; so called not because it is on a hill but because it was the old highway* that passed through the community. The term is also often extended to mean the businesses typically located in a high street and sometimes to mean the general public as well, in much the same way as main street or middle America is used in America.

high table. The table at which the senior fellows* of a college* dine.

high tea. *See* tea.

highway. Formerly, a public road without toll and kept up by the monarch. After WWII, it came to mean any main road where cars could go with some speed. *See also* A; alley; clearway; lane, M; ring road; road; street.

highwayman. Not a man who builds highways but a man who robs travelers on them. Essentially put out of business when the nineteenth century railroads took the travelers off the roads, the highwayman was a figure of both opprobrium and of glamor, like the outlaw of the American west, and in the eighteenth century in particular, famous highwaymen were the media stars of the day, subjects of numerous ballads and stories and drawing uncountable crowds to their hangings. In modern times, the word is heard outside historical fiction and poetry only in media reference to particularly colorful or flamboyant thieves. *See also* footpad.

hiking. The term is American, first appearing in the 1920s, but the practice is peculiarly English, growing out of the English constitutional* walk and short one-day excursions of the middle class* into the local countryside called **rambling**. As more people began to get real holidays from work during the 1920s, many people used them to tour the countryside, and many of those chose to do this on walking tours, sleeping at night in local inns, in hostels, or sometimes camping out. Many people did this as a cheap adventure, especially the young, but many others adopted it as a healthy and moral form of holiday. The practice has continued into the present, particularly among the fitness-oriented portions of the middle class, and in many ways the fad of the 1920s and 1930s is responsible for the retention of ancient public rights-of-way across farmlands and the development of numerous hiking paths in the National Parks* and AONBs* that make the English countryside so accessible to the modern tourist and perhaps for the development of National Parks themselves. This is much more casual and widespread than American hiking that usually involves going into the wilderness, and it is never associated with hunting; it is done purely for the pleasure of the walk and the viewing of the scenery. *See also* district; rambler; walking.

Hilary term. *See* term.

Hillman. An automaker known almost completely for family sedans, actually owned by Humber* after 1928.

Hillsborough. *See* terraces.

hind. *See* deer.

hinny. A cake* made from much the same recipe as scones* but baked or cooked in a single large round unit rather than the small scone size, also called a **singing hinny** because when cooked on a griddle it bubbled or hissed.

hipbath. A portable hip-deep bathtub, a saucer-like tub with a high sloped back but so small the bather's legs usually hung outside, the most common form of bathtub even among the well-to-do far into the twentieth century.

hire. To rent. Hence, a **hire car** is a rental car, a **hire firm** a company that rents equipment of various kinds, et cetera.

hire purchase. Something bought on the installment plan, also called the **never-never**. Most hire purchases are arranged with credit from special companies that exist solely for the purpose, rather than from the shop* or department store* from which the item is actually purchased.

hiring fair. Until WWI, annual fairs* at which farmers and farm workers came together to find new jobs or new hands, farm workers traditionally being hired for a full year.

hithe. A protected landing place on a river, now used only in ancient names, such as the Queenhithe* or Lambeth* (loam hithe).

hive. To **hive up** is to hoard, as with honey in a bee hive; however, to **hive off** means to separate from and is used to indicate that business has been sent to a subsidiary or a subcontractor or that a small group has gone off on its own.

HM. His/Her Majesty;* the initials are often placed in front of other names or initials, like the American "U.S.," to indicate an official possession or position in national service, such as **HMS**, meaning His/Her Majesty's Ship, for a ship in the navy,* or **HMG** for His/Her Majesty's Government, et cetera.

HMV. His Master's Voice, a major recording company using the same dog logo as the American RCA, and more recently the largest recording store in the nation, in London* in Oxford Street.*

hoarding. What Americans call a billboard, but sometimes quite small. This also is used for the temporary fence around a construction site, probably because such fences are almost immediately covered with posters.

hoar frost. *See* frost.

hob. The part of the stove where things are actually cooked, from a grating in a fireplace called a hob on which things were placed to keep warm.

hobbledehoi. Clumsy, ignorant youths; sometimes, more specifically, hooligans.

hock. White wine, originally from Germany around Hochheim but soon extended to all similar white wines from the Rhineland, now generally called Riesling.

hockey. Always "field hockey," played much like a cross between soccer and ice hockey on a flat field about the size of an American football field and with a ball about the size of a baseball. There are eleven players on a team, one goalkeeper who permanently guards the goal and ten others who may move anywhere on the field. The object, as in ice hockey, is to score points by knocking the ball with a curved stick into the other team's goal, a net at the end of the field. There are two thirty-minute halfs with no time outs. It is played without protective gear or other special equipment except for the stick. This is almost always a girl's sport (boys play football), although it's unclear why the teachers who introduced it at girl's schools* thought it was more "feminine" for girls to charge up and down a field hitting each other with sticks than to kick a ball. The **hockey stick** is one of the stereotyped signs of the girl's school student. For individual positions, *See* forward; fullback; halfback; wing. *See also* bully.

Hocktide. The second Monday and Tuesday following Easter.*

Hogmanay. In Scotland,* New Year's* Eve, one of the most significant holidays in the year, much more important than Christmas.*

hoist. Not a block and tackle but what Americans call a freight elevator.

Holborn. A neighborhood of London* immediately north of the old City.* Several of the Inns of Court* are located there, so that it is often associated with the legal profession. In the medieval era, this was the valley of the River Fleet,* site of Ely* Palace, and in the nineteenth century many solidly Victorian developments and businesses were built on either side of both Holborn and **High Holborn** roads that ran up **Holborn Hill**; **Holborn Viaduct**

was a major elevated roadway with room for buildings along either side built in the mid-nineteenth to span the Fleet valley and connect Holborn and Newgate* roads; the train station there is a terminus for trains to the southern areas, primarily commuter trains that deliver people to the insurance companies and similar businesses that now dominate the area.

hold-all. A soft-sided suitcase or briefcase.

hold-up. Not a robbery but what Americans call a traffic jam.

holiday camp. Beginning in the 1930s, a cheap but also highly organized form of vacation usually associated with seaside resorts; "campers" lived in huts like military barracks and had every minute of their day organized for them. Most camps had not only organized games and military-style meals but also included morning reveille followed by daily exercise periods led by instructors. Their pre-WWII users were the lower–middle class,* but after the war and through the 1950s, these were extremely popular among the respectable portions of the working class, for reasons that defy explanation to an outsider. Although now even the working classes think it normal to take their holidays* in Portugal or along the Mediterranean, numerous camps still survive. *See also* Butlin.

holidays. The period Americans call vacation. Holidays (always plural) is the term used by most Britons except for students, who often say vacations (in the plural). *See also* vac.

Holinshed. One of the earliest British historians, whose *Chronicles of England, Scotland, and Ireland* (1577) provided the raw material for the plays of Shakespeare and others of his day, and thus the bulk of medieval and early history as it is still understood by the general public today.

Hollands. Imported gin.*

Holloway. A prison* (1852) in northern London,* the largest women's prison in the nation.

Holloway's pills. No relation to Holloway* prison,* a popular patent medicine of the nineteenth century, taken for any and all ills.

hols. Holidays.*

Holyroodhouse. A palace* in Edinburgh* used as the monarch's official Scottish residence, although since Victoria most monarchs have preferred the country estate at Balmoral.*

Holywell. A town near the north coast of Wales,* since the seventh century the site of St. Winifred's Well, whose waters are said to heal the incurable.

homburg. A man's hat with a stiff brim like a bowler* but with a soft crown almost always worn with a single crease down the middle; this is often worn in lieu of the bowler by businessmen and civil servants and is definitely a sign of the solid middle class.*

home, at. *See* at home.

Home Counties. The counties* surrounding London,* so called because most of the influential nobility* and gentry,* wherever their estates, had homes there within easy reach of London. Originally these were understood to be Middlesex,* Surrey,* Kent,* and Essex,* but by the late nineteenth-century Hertfordshire* and Sussex* were often also included; curiously, Berkshire* and Buckinghamshire* are closer than the latter two but are rarely included.

home farm. A farm actually used by the landlord who leases or rents other portions of an estate to other farmers. *See also* demesne.

Home Guard. A volunteer, part-time, unpaid force formed in 1940 from those men too old, physically unfit for, or in occupations exempt from regular military forces, to be a last-ditch defence force against German invasion. *See also* army; Dad's army.

home help. A person sent by the local council* to aid the elderly or the ill, doing housekeeping or running errands, but not doing any nursing.

homely. Home-like or homey; thus, a homely woman is not necessarily plain or ugly as in America but is merely feminine and domestic in attitude.

Home Office. The government* ministry* that was originally in charge of internal affairs, as opposed to the Foreign Office.* Originated in 1782, it has over the years lost some of its responsibilities as departments were expanded to separate ministries, but it is still one of the four major ministries, responsible at present for police,* prisons,* fire services, immigration, and elections.* The head of the ministry is the Home Secretary.*

home rule. Authority for the Irish to govern themselves, at least in domestic affairs. This was regularly proposed during the nineteenth century, almost passing in the English Parliament* in 1886 until Parnell's downfall ruined its prospects, defeated again in 1893 by the House of Lords,* then finally passing in 1914 only to be suspended for the duration of the war but taking effect in 1920. *See also* devolution; Ireland.

Home Secretary. Chief executive of the Home Office,* officially the Secretary of State for Home Affairs. Depending on the personality of the Secretary, he or she is usually seen as the number three or four person in the ruling party.* In addition to the administrative function, the Home Secretary is also the official spokesman for commoners* to the monarch.

homosexuals. Male homosexual relations were absolutely illegal until 1967, when activities between consenting adults* over the age of twenty-one were legalized. Lesbian activity was never outlawed, supposedly because Queen Victoria refused to believe it even existed.

Hon. Abbreviation for The Honourable.*

honest. Originally, when said about a man, it usually meant someone worthy of respect; when said of a woman, it meant sexually faithful, as with Dekker's Honest Whore. Both these meanings declined in the nineteenth century, and now Britons use this much as Americans do to describe a person who speaks mostly the truth and does not visibly steal.

Honourable, The. The formal title for a number of different persons, including: sons of earls;* sons and daughters of viscounts* and barons;* judges;* and members of the Privy Council.* Often used inaccurately as a form of politeness.

honours. (1) A relatively modern form of providing some special recognition to those who have served the realm in some way. All such honours are officially bestowed by the monarch, although in recent times the Honours Lists* are initially prepared by the Prime Minister's* office. These often refer back to the ancient orders of chivalry, and thus many of the honours include the grant of a knighthood and the right to be called Sir,* and some include elevation to the peerage.* Practically all such honours are for the life of the holder only, with the last dukedom granted in 1874 and only a handful of lower ranks granted since. Within the various orders there are several ranks, usually Knights* and Companions of various titles, except in the OBE,* which uses different names. Individual ranks are discussed under their initials. Order of precedence is described in Appendix VI. *See also* colours. (2) In college* examinations, marks* ranking at the top, like an American *A* grade. In a degree,* however, this indicates a more specialized or intensive course of study than for the normal pass* degree and thus is sometimes thought to be equivalent to an American M.A. *See also* BA; first; MA; second.

Honours List. The list of people to receive honours* from the monarch. Two lists are announced annually, New Years Honours on January 1 and Birthday Honours on the June date that is the monarch's official birthday. Special lists are also made when a government* resigns.

hon. sec. Honorary secretary.*

hooha. A fight, an argument, a lot of noise usually unnecessary or pointless.

hoover. Any vacuum cleaner, or as a verb, to use a vacuum cleaner.

hop it. Not quite the same as the American "hop to it," this means "go away" more than "get going."

Hopkins. A common nickname* for a crippled person. This seems to have faded from use in the twentieth century, although **don't hurry Hopkins**, meaning go slow or take it easy, which seems clearly related, is still in use.

Horlicks. A brand of malt-flavored powder to be added to milk, marketed primarily as a health aid and often served warm as a soporific at bedtime.

horny. Almost always used to mean calloused, as in horny-handed, but sometimes heard in vulgar usage in the American sense of lustful or sexually aroused.

Horse Guards. *See* Guards.

horsey. Applied to a character type whose life seems to revolve around the horse, in modern England almost always applied only to a woman. This is not someone who works with horses but rather someone from the gentry* whose social life and vocabulary revolve around the fox hunt* in particular but also include the racing* seasons, dressage, and similar activities, with a braying voice and very brusque public manner that often seems rude or ignorant, best exemplified to Americans perhaps by Princess Anne.

hosepipe. What Americans call a garden hose.

hospital. As in America, an institution which provides care for the sick and injured, although Britons generally say a person is "in hospital" rather than "in the hospital." However, in many cases the British still use the term for other institutions, such as: a hospice or hotel for travelers (generally falling from use by the nineteenth century); a charity home for the aged or infirm, such as Greenwich* Hospital; a charity boarding school for children, such as Christ's Hospital* in London,* a usage still common in Scottish legal terminology; or, in Shakespeare's time, a lodging house.

hospital job. Originally, a small job that the workman squeezes in between other jobs when convenient, but now more often a small job that the workman stretches out forever.

hot cross buns. A small round spiced cake* with a cross cut into the top, traditionally baked and eaten on Good Friday.* No one has a convincing explanation of the practice, since Good Friday is otherwise a fast day.

hot ice. What Americans call dry ice.

hot money. Not stolen money but money used for short-term speculation in currency markets.

hot pot. A stew of mutton,* potatoes,* and onions, almost always called **Lancashire* hot pot** but eaten in all areas.

hounds. Dogs used for hunting,* almost always only the hounds used for fox hunting, although also used for deer hunting before the rifle. Other kinds of hunting dogs, such as retrievers, are generally called dogs. To **follow the hounds** is to go fox hunting.

Houndsditch. A street in London* in the eastern portion of the City,* synonymous with Jews* due to the concentration of brokers and Jewish secondhand clothing traders in the area for centuries.

house. (1) For various types of dwellings, *See* apartment; back-to-back; bungalow; country house; cottage; flat; maisonette; mansion; palace; semi-detached; terrace; villa. (2) Basically, any large, free-standing building in which people reside, thus often used to identify public buildings that include sleeping quarters, such as an almshouse* or the workhouse,* or, at a public or prep school,* the building in which a student lives and sleeps. *See also* dormitory; free house; safe as houses; tied house.

House. (1) The House of Commons.* (2) Christ Church* college* at Oxford.* (3) In business, the London* Stock Exchange. (4) In the military, Sandhurst.* (5) Historically, often the workhouse.*

house agent. What Americans call a real estate agent.

house breaker. Not a burglar but a wrecker or wrecking crew.

house call. A visit by a doctor to a sick person's home. American doctors once did this but decided it was more convenient to have all the sick patients meet and share diseases in the waiting room; British doctors still make house calls, even in the 1990s.

household, royal. *See* royal household.

Household Cavalry. *See* Guards.

householder. What Americans now call the head of household; this became a much more significant term in urban areas after the Reform Bill* of 1832, when the vote was extended from freeholders* to include householders of houses that cost more than £10 in annual rent.

housekeeper. The female servant* in charge of all female servants (except the cook) in a large house and responsible for all cleaning. *See also* butler.

houseman. In medicine, what Americans call an intern.

House of Commons. Americans like to think of the House of Commons as representing the "common people," but the name actually arose because its members represented the communities ruled "in common," the chartered* boroughs* or cities.* These were necessarily not actual lords,* but they were almost as small a portion of the general populace, drawn from the chartered guilds and the untitled gentry,* and they had no function but to give sanction to taxes imposed on them by the Crown.* They were called irregularly, only when new taxes were needed, and forced to meet in a separate place from the lords. Growing dissatisfaction over taxes and religion led to increased intractability that ultimately exploded in the Civil War,* but Cromwell had no more interest in the Commons than did Charles I before him and sent it home. The jockeying for power after the Restoration and the Glorious Revolution* gave the Commons new power, and with the establishment of regular sessions and elections, it gradually evolved into the Cabinet* system of government that we know today, with practically all new legislation initiated in the Commons, particularly after the Reform Act* of 1832 expanded the franchise and eliminated many ancient boroughs. Even so, the Commons was still dominated by the gentry, and as late as the 1860s, about 60 percent of the members were gentry or sons of nobles and one-fourth of the members came from only about thirty families. Continued expansion of the franchise, the dominance of the Liberals,* and the rise of Labour* gradually changed this situation, and since WWII the majority of the members, as in the American House and Senate, are lawyers or other professionals (although a surprising number are practicing journalists). Since 1911, when, after one of the most brutal political battles in history, the House of Lords* surrendered their veto power, the Commons has been the sole legislative power of the country, while the cabinet system and the increased powers of the parties* has meant that practically anything a Prime Minister* wants will be passed, as he or she controls the party, the party controls the Commons, and the Commons controls the country without any of the "checks and balances" of the American system.

The House of Commons meets in Westminster* in London.* Elections* are currently held at least once every five years. Sessions generally last from mid-October to late July, with daily sessions primarily in the afternoon and early evening Monday to Thursday, as the majority of the 650 members* also still hold their jobs. Technically, no member may resign; to do so, the traditional method is to apply for a position with the Crown,* such as the Chiltern Hundreds,* which makes the person ineligible. *See also* back bencher; bill; Conservative; constituency; cross bencher; division; front bench; Opposition; Question Time; reading; Tory; Treasury; Whig; woolsack.

House of Lords. This was the original Parliament,* called by the King* to "advise" him. It was a small body, barely eighty, including the twenty-five bishops* under Elizabeth I. After the Restoration, titles were given to many of the faithful, and the House of Lords began to allow any noble* to attend any session. As the Commons* grew in power over the years, the Lords* were seen as primarily a conservative, often disruptive body, able to veto practically anything that might upset their wealth and power, and there were constant clashes between the two houses throughout the nineteenth century. Then, when the Lords vetoed a new tax in 1909, the Liberals,* with the consent of the new King George V, threatened to create enough new lords to get the tax passed anyway and destroy the traditional Conservative* majority of the Lords, and the Lords surrendered, losing their veto power over legislation; the most they could do was delay legislation for two years, during which time the Commons must reconsider and re-pass the new law; in 1949, this delay was reduced to a maximum of thirteen months. The Lords were also the ultimate judicial authority, acting as a court of appeal until 1876, when jurisdiction for appeals, which had become far too numerous to be dealt with by such a body, was given to professional judges who were made peers* for their term; however, the Lords was still allowed to try cases involving peers until 1948 (the last actual case in 1935). During the twentieth century, there has been some agitation for abolishing the Lords, as its function seems no longer clear and the inheritance of its membership seems undemocratic. However, although there are almost 1200 members, 800 of them hereditary, barely 300 attend with any regularity and about two-thirds of those are life peers* who obtained the honour* for actually accomplishing something in their life; thus, they act somewhat more like the American Supreme Court than the Senate, debating the issues that are too hot for politicians to handle and applying the only brake, however minimal, to the otherwise complete legislative powers exercised by the majority party in the Commons. The Lords meet in London* in Westminster* across the lobby from the Commons. Sessions generally match those of the Commons, Monday through Thursday in the afternoons and early evenings, from mid-October to late July.

house party. Not a particular party or celebration but the group of guests staying at a country house* for several days at a time. *See also* weekend.

houses, safe as. *See* safe as houses.

Housewife's Choice. A popular BBC afternoon radio program that played music requested by listeners.

housey-housey. A game similar to American Bingo, usually played as a form of gambling.

housing estate. *See* estate.

how. An ancient term meaning a hill, found today primarily in ancient place-names.

How's your father? A catchphrase that appeared in a music hall* song, quickly spread through the trenches in WWI, and has since been used as an all-purpose nonsense phrase throughout the lower classes.* This usually implies something ribald or ridiculous or ridiculously ribald, without any particular reference to anyone's father; it's one of those phrases that, simply by being said, is supposed to be funny or "dirty." In recent years this implication of dirty talk has also made it a euphemism for sex.

HP Sauce. A commercial sauce similar to the American A-1 Sauce but, since its introduction in 1896, poured on practically all foods that do not have custard* poured on them. *See also* brown sauce; salad cream.

HRH. His/Her Royal Highness. *See* Royal Highness.

Huddersfield. A city in north-central England* between Manchester* and Leeds,* for centuries a center of the textile industry, most famous for its Choral Society since 1836, often called the "world's greatest choir."

hulks. Ships without masts anchored offshore and used as prisons.* Primarily intended as an alternative to hanging* when introduced in the 1770s, they were not the province of the navy* but merely a convenient way to isolate convicts. They were also used for French prisoners during the Napoleonic wars and as places to hold prisoners awaiting transportation.* In the mid-nineteenth century, as transportation wound down and prison reform movements led to new prisons on shore, the hulks were no longer used.

Hull. A port city on the northeast coast of England* near York,* one of the largest industrial ports of the nation. Hull is also long associated with puritanism and independent-minded locals, of whom Robinson Crusoe is the best-known example, and its refusal to admit Charles I inside the city actually initiated the Civil War.* This tradition continued later when the city was an early force in the antislavery movement.

hulme. In place-names, a small island.

humane society. Not a society to protect animals but a society of volunteer life guards along the seacoast.

Humber. (1) A large estuary in northeastern England,* site of Hull* and a number of other industrial and fishing towns, once synonymous with seagoing and more recently synonymous with unemployment and industrial unrest. *See also* Humberside. (2) An automaker declining in the 1960s, known primarily for bulky sedans for middle-class families that also became the standard police* car. *See also* Hillman.

Humberside. A new county* formed in 1974 from portions of Yorkshire* and Lincolnshire,* centering around the city of Hull* and the Humber.*

humble pie. Figuratively, as in America, a sign of personal humiliation. However, originally this was an actual pie* made from the "umbles" of a deer, which were organs such as the heart, liver, or lungs, and to eat it meant you ranked so far down you couldn't get the meat pies.

humbug. A small hard candy, usually peppermint-flavored.

hundred. An administrative division of a shire,* used from the Anglo-Saxon era into the nineteenth century. The size varied and it's not absolutely clear just what they were originally a hundred of, but the hundred was larger than the local parish.* The Chiltern Hundreds* are the last remaining such unit.

hundredweight. Not 100 pounds but 112 pounds. No one knows why, that's just the way it is.

Hungerford. An English village west of London* little noted until in 1987 a local man with a rifle shot a number of persons. This was the first mass shooting spree of the "American" type in British history and thus made Hungerford an immediate metaphor for the rising violence in British society and the need for even stricter gun control. **Hungerford Market** in London* was known for cheap goods until it was torn down for Charing Cross* Station.

hunt. From the medieval era, hunting was done on horseback and was the primary form of entertainment of the aristocracy.* With the advent of the hunting rifle and the shotgun, the horse disappeared from the pursuit of most animals, except for the fox, and a hunt now almost always means a fox hunt. When a Briton hunts for birds, he or she goes shooting,* but deer hunting may still be called a hunt. A **hunting box** is a small, usually rustic, house where the hunter lives while hunting, like a cabin in America.

The **fox hunt** itself may have begun as a way of keeping down the number of foxes, which are predators, but its primary purpose is more the horse riding;* chasing the fox adds an element of unpredictability and challenge that regular riding* does not. Typically, a set of hounds* search for the fox and then, when a fresh scent is found, chase the animal, and the hunters chase the hounds, who actually kill the fox if they manage to catch it before it goes to ground.* It was the special sport of the local squire* and his friends, since they would be the only ones who could afford the hounds and horses and also have the right to cross the local land at random. As the landed gentry* lost their wealth and power, the hunt passed to the new money of the towns, and now the overwhelming majority of fox hunters are townsmen who own little or no land and pay landowners for the right to cross their lands. The passion for the sport has been shared so widely and for so long that there is even a documented instance of a Civil War* battle pausing to allow a fox hunt to pass between the lines, although various movements to ban the sport have grown since the mid–twentieth century.

hunter. (1) A horse for fox hunting,* meaning a horse with speed, stamina, and jumping ability. To the gentry,* such horses are treasured and cannot be used for any farm work, and thus they are always a luxury. (2) A pocketwatch with a hinged metal cover that protects the glass over the face, so called because they were first marketed in the mid–nineteenth century as a watch that would not be damaged in a hunting* accident.

hunting. *See* hunt.

Huntingdonshire. A shire* in the east-central area of England,* very flat, primarily agricultural; in 1965, it was combined with the Soke of Peterborough* into a single county* and then in 1974 completely absorbed into modern Cambridgeshire.*

hunting pink. The color of red in the jackets worn while fox hunting.

huntsman. The person who cares for, trains, and supervises the hounds* in a fox hunt.*

hunt the slipper. A party game in which one person who is "it" stands in the center of a circle while those in the circle pass a slipper (or similar object) behind their backs, and "it" tries to guess who actually has the object and grab it from them. This necessarily involves a certain amount of body contact, usually decorous but contact nonetheless, and the name is thus sometimes used as a metaphor for sex.

-hurst. In place-names, such as Sandhurst,* an ancient wood.*

hussar. A member of the cavalry* unit technically distinguished by use of the saber as the primary weapon, but more noted for their devotion to dashing romantic uniforms. The boot called a Hussar is a stiff man's boot that covers the knee in front but is cut down at the sides so it allows the knee to bend easily in the saddle. *See also* dragoon; lancer.

husting. In the early eighteenth century, a temporary platform on which candidates for Parliament* were introduced to the electors. After the introduction of the secret ballot* in 1872, the practice was no longer necessary, but by then it had come to be a metaphor for the election process itself. Thus, going **on the hustings** means making an election campaign.

Hyde Park. A large park in central London,* north of Buckingham Palace.* Henry VIII used it for a deer park, but Charles II opened it to the public. For a century or so, it was rather disreputable, but by the late eighteenth century had taken much of its modern form, becoming one of the most popular areas of the city, and becoming world famous with the building of the Crystal Palace* and the Exhibition of 1851 in its southern portion. It is basically an open park, with trees widely and regularly spaced (more widely since the great storms of the 1980s uprooted so many of the old trees), circled by the Ring,* with the long straight Rotten Row* still used for riding* parallel to its southern border. A large pond called the Serpentine* takes most of its western border, although the neighboring Kensington Gardens* is no longer separated by any fence. The park is never officially closed and thus is also home to many courting couples in the darker hours; between the wars, a **Hyde Park case** was a voyeur, from the people who like to roam the park in search of such couples. Much more significant is its symbolic association with free speech, due to the Speakers' Corner* on its northeastern corner, often mistakenly called **Hyde Park Corner**, which is instead the southeastern corner where the Wellington Monument stands at the end of Constitution Hill.*

hypermarket. *See* supermarket.

I

ice. (1) What Americans call ice cream. **Water ice** is what Americans usually call sherbet. However, a **choc ice** is not chocolate ice cream but a bar of vanilla ice cream on a stick covered with a layer of chocolate; an **ice lolly** is what Americans call a Popsicle. In practice, most British ice cream is made from lard without any cream at all; if cream is used, the product is usually called **dairy ice.** (2) Although the British have long ridiculed Americans for putting ice in their drinks, the spread of refrigerators, central heating, and of American soft drinks in the late twentieth century seems to be breaking that resistance down; however, Americans should always remember that "room temperature" in most British buildings has traditionally been below 60°, even in summer, and so "warm" drinks are often quite cool. *See also* sorbet.

ice, black. A layer of ice on the roads that is too thin to be seen.

identification parade. In the police,* what Americans call a lineup.

I hear what you say. A civil service* locution that, like the American "I understand," almost always implies "but I think it's nonsense."

ILEA. Inner London Education Authority, responsible for tax-supported schools in the twelve Inner London* boroughs,* until dismantled in 1990.

immersion heater. As in America, a device that drops into the water to heat it, but in Britain these heaters are often much larger than ours (which usually only heat a cup) and are used to heat water for the home. *See also* geyser.

immigrant. In contemporary usage, this is a code word for Black* or coloured;* about 45 percent of the people so called are in fact native-born Britons, and the term is rarely applied to Australians, Irish, or Canadians who have immigrated to Britain.

in aid of. Not directly related to aid or charity, this idiom is used to indicate purpose, function, or point; "What's this in aid of?" means "What's the point of this?" or "Why are you doing/saying this?"

In and Out. *See* Naval and Military.

incapable. Drunk but no particular trouble; English police* distinguish between "drunk and incapable" and "drunk and disorderly."

inclosure. Enclosure.*

income tax. The British have had a form of income tax since 1799, when it was levied to help pay for the Napoleonic Wars, except for a brief period between 1816–42. Originally a flat rate of two shillings* per pound,* in 1907 two rates were established, with the lower for "earned" income. After WWI, progressive rates began to be introduced, and later various surtaxes were added, until eventually a top category of 98 percent was reached, but by the 1980s this was being replaced with the current simple 25 percent tax on all income below £19,300 (excluding various allowances) and 40 percent for everything above. *See also* Inland Revenue; rates; tax.

incumbent. Used almost always for a parish* priest, who is appointed for life, and not for a member of Parliament.*

indent. A requisition or order, originally used in the East India Company* and now much more widespread.

Independent Labour Party. A socialist political party* founded in 1893, connected to the Labour* Party in 1906, but separating again in 1932 over policy disagreements and losing its last seat in Parliament* in 1959.

Independents. Members of non-conformist* sects that when begun in the seventeenth century refused to participate in either the Church of England* or the Presbyterian,* extremely active in Cromwell's army during the Civil War.* In America they are known as Congregationalists.

index-linked. Since the 1970s, many pay scales have been "linked" to one of the various economic indices, which means automatic pay raises to keep up with inflation.

India. India's position in both the practical wealth and the mythology of the Empire* was so important that, as with Ireland,* we can provide only the briefest sketch here. The British presence began in 1623 when the East India Company,* driven out of the East Indies by the Dutch, established trading posts in Bengal, almost by accident. These posts led to a series of wars with French traders, fought by the company's own mercenaries, until the French were driven out in 1763. The company directly controlled some areas and held monopoly trading rights with most of the independent rajahs,* and, after the introduction of tea* plantations in the early nineteenth century, became immensely wealthy. However, as tea and cotton for the English mills became more important, the British government took more interest, and in 1858 after the Mutiny* rescinded the Company's monopoly and took over direct administration of the colonies. Contrary to common mythology, the British did not actually occupy and control all the country, about half of it staying under the direct control of local princes over whom the British still maintained considerable influence. Local governors, called viceroys, and colonists increasingly lost contact with the locals, and by WWI independence movements had begun in earnest, centered eventually around Gandhi. This movement led to some self-government in 1936 and then to independence in 1947, without significant violence between the British and Indians, although a major civil war between Muslims and Hindus broke out as soon as the British left. *See also* army.

industrial action. Any action taken by workers or unions to try to force employers to change the way work is done or paid; this includes not only strikes but also such British variations as go-slow* and work-to-rule.* Also called an **industrial dispute**.

infant. *See* minor.

infant school. The first stage of school, ages five to seven; in many areas, these are not separate from the primary school,* which teaches ages five to eleven. *See also* nursery school.

injury time. In football* and similar games, the referee allows play to go over the scheduled time limit to compensate for time spent dealing with injuries; sometimes used metaphorically for any extra chance.

Inland Revenue. The rough equivalent of the IRS, collector of taxes* for the central government.*

Inner Circle. A circular carriage* road that circles the garden and open air theater in the center of Regent's Park* in London.*

Inner London. Since 1965, the twelve central boroughs* of Greater London,* from Greenwich* to Wandsworth* south of the Thames,* from the Tower Hamlets* to Fulham,* on the north bank, but not including the City.*

Inner Temple. *See* Temple.

innings. In cricket,* a time at bat, always used with the plural ending; unlike in American baseball, a batsman* and a team each has an innings. Similarly, **good innings** is used metaphorically for any fair opportunity; "I had a good innings," for example, could mean "I had a good life," "I took my best shot," et cetera. *See also* chips.

innit. Working class* usage for "isn't that right?" "doesn't it?" or even "haven't I?"; always used as an intensifier as the last word in the sentence.

Inns of Court. Since the medieval era, the controlling organizations for the legal profession in England.* Only members of one of the Inns of Court may become barristers.* The Inns were originally a combination of school and residence, with both students and practicing barristers actually living in each of the inns and sharing meals in the great hall.* In the modern era, the press of business has ended most residencies, but all potential barristers must study there at least twelve terms* and all practicing barristers are still required to have at least an office in one of the Inns. At present there are only four, all in London* near Chancery Lane*: the Inner and Outer Temples,* Lincoln's Inn,* and Gray's Inn.* In the past there was also a Serjeant's Inn, which disappeared when the serjeants* lost their exclusive rights, as well as Staple Inn, Clifford's Inn, and Barnard's Inn, portions of which still remain but are no longer used by barristers.

inspector. In the police,* the rank above sergeant* and below **chief inspector**; the rank exists in both the uniformed and the detective branches. *See also* constable; police; superintendent.

instructor. A teacher in an institution of further education* that is not a college* or university.* However, when a solicitor* **instructs** a barrister,* he does not teach him anything but rather retains his services and fills him in on the background of the case.

insurance. Generally used in the same way as in America, but mostly for health insurance or for the national insurance.* Life insurance is often called assurance.* For **insurance stamp**, *See* stamps.

intake. In northern England,* a piece of land taken from the moor* or common* and fenced off, or enclosed,* for individual use.

interval. In the theatre, what Americans call the intermission; most cinemas* insert an interval into film showings as well.

invalid carriage. A small, three-wheeled electric vehicle used primarily by the handicapped but often seen in the past on small roads where speed is not significant.

invalid chair. A Bath chair,* or sometimes what Americans call a wheelchair.

invalidity benefit. An extension of sickness benefit* for workers with major illnesses who do not qualify as disabled. *See also* national insurance.

Inverness. (1) A town and port in northeastern Scotland* at the mouth of the famous Loch Ness. Before the 1975 reorganization, there was also an **Inverness-shire**, now a part of the Highland region.* (2) A coat first introduced in the 1880s, usually worn by men. The coat was almost always made of plaid material, came to the mid-calf and buttoned, but had no sleeves; instead, sewn to the collar was a cape that fell to about the elbow. Most people know this today as the coat used in the traditional Sherlock Holmes outfit.

inverted commas. The punctuation Americans call quotation marks.

invigilate. To supervise or monitor students during an examination.

Ipswich. A port on the east coast of England,* most noted in Shakespeare's day as a center of both trade with Holland and Germany and the wool trades, in the late seventeenth century a whaling center, in following centuries declining in importance and interest.

IRA. The Irish Republican Army, not the military of the Republic of Ireland* but an underground organization founded in 1919 for armed resistance to British occupation of Ireland. After the Irish Free State was formed in 1921, the IRA continued the civil war against the new Irish government, was formally outlawed in 1923, and seemed to be defunct until suddenly resurfacing in Northern Ireland* in 1969, when the **Provisional IRA** split off and launched the wave of resistance, bombings, assassinations, and general terrorism against the Protestants and/or British that continues to the present.

Ireland. The English initially invaded and conquered the island in the thirteenth century, but resistance ebbed and flowed afterward. By the early sixteenth, the English had been driven out of all but the Dublin area (*See*

Pale), but Henry VIII proclaimed himself king of Ireland and began trying to resubdue the island, a process continuing under practically every monarch who followed. English settlers occupied many areas, particularly in the northeast corner, and these were not only Protestant but militantly so, especially after the Battle of the Boyne* brought the Orangemen* to power. In the rest of Ireland, the English colonists were fewer in number, but they soon took the bulk of the land. For most of the eighteenth, Ireland had a parliament for local affairs, although only Protestants could vote, but this was disbanded after the rebellion of 1798, when Ireland was officially absorbed into the United Kingdom.* In 1829, the local Irish were given the vote and immediately began pressure for home rule,* which was ultimately granted in 1920. However, as the Protestant north refused to leave the United Kingdom, yet another civil war broke out, this one perhaps the bloodiest, until the treaty of 1921 that organized the Irish Free State,* which remained a member of the Commonwealth* while Northern Ireland remained a part of the United Kingdom. Over the following years, the Irish simply took additional powers for themselves and the English declined to notice, so that the formal declaration of independence in 1949 was hardly noted, much less opposed, in London.* Since independence, Ireland has tried to maintain the Catholic religion, enforce very conservative social legislation, and revive the Gaelic* language, but the nation's general poverty has continued, with thousands of residents emigrating, usually to the United Kingdom, each year. Numerous Irish writers have made significant contributions to British literature, but for reasons of space, in this work I have focussed only on those who in effect became British and did not write particularly about Ireland itself; Irish culture and its writers will have to be discussed in another work. *See also* IRA.

Irish famine. *See* potato.

Iron Duke. Wellington.

ironmonger. A hardware store or the shopkeeper* of such a store.

irregular. Cavalry* units formed in nineteenth-century India, similar to the Yeomanry* units in Britain in that they provided their own horses and equipment and were used as reserves for use in local action; they were commanded by Britons but almost all the rest were Indians. *See also* regular.

Irvingites. *See* Catholic Apostolic Church.

I say. A stereotypical ejaculation for a gentleman* when upset by something. However, the practice is perhaps more literary than genuine, used as a convenient tag for the public school twit* or the vacuous military mind; when someone says "I say," it is usually a sure sign he has nothing to say.

Isis. At Oxford,* a name sometimes used for the Thames* above its junction with the Cherwell.*

Isle of Dogs. In the East End* of London,* not really an island but a peninsula almost cut off by a sharp curve in the river Thames* and numerous dock basins; a primary shipping and industrial area, now the core of the modern Docklands* development project.

Isle of Man. An island about halfway between northern England* and Ireland.* This is a rough, mountainous island, and its inhabitants (the Manx) have long been associated with a primitive and difficult way of life almost completely devoted to fishing and sheep, although its mild climate made it a resort site in the late nineteenth century. Technically, the island is owned by the Crown,* bought from a duke* in 1765, and it retains its own parliament and is not subject to British laws except by its re-adoption of them.

Isle of Wight. An island off the southeast coast of England* near the harbors of both Portsmouth* and Southampton.* Its picturesque views and mild climate made it a popular winter resort for royalty* and others in the mid-nineteenth century, but it also often figures in literature as a major landmark that indicates ships have reached England.

Islington. The *s* is pronounced. Originally a village quite separate from London* where Henry VIII liked to go hunting, now a borough* of London just north of the City.* The village was popular as a resort after the Restoration, due to its springs and entertainments at Sadler's Wells,* and in the later part of the eighteenth century it became a popular suburb, still far enough away for Londoners like Johnson to treat it as exotic and unsophisticated. Industrialization changed the area into a neighborhood for poor office clerks* and similar workers, and only very recently has the gentrification process begun to revive the status of the area.

ITA. Independent Television Authority. *See* ITV.

ITV. The broadcasting channel used by commercial broadcasters, operating since 1955. Programming is provided by several different "networks," which are companies that provide programming for only a few days each per week. In general, they operate like American television, interrupting programs regularly for ads, but the programming itself is not noticeably different from or worse than that on the BBC.* In 1982, ITV was allowed to add another channel, known as Channel 4,* which would be somewhat more "cultural," but as yet this has not eliminated the documentaries, discussion programs and dramas from ITV as has happened with American commercial TV, and in fact much of *Masterpiece Theatre* and similar programming Americans see on PBS and credit to the BBC is produced by ITV networks. They are supervised by the ITA,* whose members are appointed by the Postmaster General.

J

Jack. A common man, as in Jack and Jill; **Jack Nasty** is a nasty man, **Jack Sauce** is a saucy fellow, and so on. Sometimes used as an intensifier, as in **every man jack** to mean everyone. A **jack-in-office** is a petty official who is a stickler for his or her position, status, rights, or procedures. **I'm all right, Jack** always carries the implicit "so I don't care what happens to you." *See also* Cousin Jack; johnny; lance corporal; Union Jack.

jacket potato. *See* potato.

jacksie. Lower-class* slang for the buttocks, in the northern areas sometimes more specifically a woman's genitals. Sometimes spelled **jaxy**. No one is certain, but possibly derived from jakes.*

Jaeger suit. Dr. Jaeger, a German, proposed a health system in the 1870s based on the use of undyed wool for all clothing, including underwear, and for men knee breeches* and no collars or ties. The system was brought to England in 1884 and quickly picked up in artistic and socialist circles in Britain, and the Jaeger suit was worn by G. B. Shaw, for example, until he died.

jaffa. An orange, especially a thick-skinned type originally imported from Jaffa in Israel.

jakes. A privy or toilet, standard usage in Shakespeare's day but becoming vulgar by the late eighteenth century.

jam. (1) Of food, what Americans call both jam and jelly. A **jam sandwich** is not bread and jelly but sponge cake with jam* spread between two layers. (2) Any treat or good thing. Hence, **jam tomorrow** is that which never comes, like the American "pie in the sky." **Money for jam** is money that took little effort to get; to **want jam on it** is to want things to be easy, to **have jam on it** is to have them easy already. For bread and jam, *See* butty; for **jam tart** *See* tart.

jam and Jerusalem. *See* Women's Institute.*

jankers. In the military, slang for punishment.

jannock. A loaf of oat bread, used primarily in northern England.*

jar. A glass of beer,* as in "Come have a jar with us."

Jarrow. A shipbuilding town near Newcastle.* In 1936, a march by unemployed shipworkers from there to London* made news throughout the world.

jaxy. *See* jacksie.

jelly. A gelatin dessert, such as Americans usually call Jell-O. The sweet fruit spread Americans call jelly is usually called jam.* **Marrowbone jelly** is a gelatin flavored with marrow from a meat bone. However, a **jelly baby** is a small, bite-sized candy molded in the shape of a baby.

jerk. In cricket,* to bowl* illegally, usually meaning with the elbow bent.

jerks. Physical exercises.

Jermyn Street. A street in London* near Piccadilly,* originally the central shopping district of a fashionable suburb built north of St. James's Park* during the Restoration and continuing to this day as a site for expensive antiques, wine, specialty shops, and especially men's shirtmakers.

jerry. A chamber pot, primarily lower-class* slang.

Jerry. A German, first used during WWI and generally preferred over various other nicknames for the Germans during WWII. Its derivation could be from German, but a strong case could be made for the German soldier's metal helmet, which looked very much like a jerry.*

jerry can. *See* can.

jersey. What Americans call a heavy pullover sweater, usually bulky, warm, and high-necked, thick enough to be worn as an outer garment by sailors and other outdoor workers.

Jerusalem. A hymn that has been an unofficial national anthem of England,* from Blake's poem *Milton*, concluding with the lines: "Till we have built Jerusalem/In England's green and pleasant land." *See also* Women's Institute.

Jesus. (1) A college* of Cambridge.* (2) A college* of Oxford,* often thought of as the Welsh college.

Jew. In 1290 the Jews were expelled from England.* Although Shakespeare and Marlowe may have known a few who hung on by converting to Christianity, Shylock and Barabas was drawn mostly from hearsay and imagination. Jews had begun to trickle back into London* by way of Holland about the time of the Civil War,* after being expelled from France and Spain; their English expulsion was formally withdrawn by Cromwell, but they received real protections from Charles II, who seemed to be happy to find one group that did not want to convert him to their religion. However, there were still significant legal restrictions on Jews until the mid-nineteenth century, and well into the present they have been regarded with much the same stereotypes as in the rest of Europe. Anti-Semitism has been a constant among the bulk of the populace, more persistent perhaps for not being overt, and most Britons, even among the educated, still seem to think they can recognize a Jew on sight, but there have been no legal formulations of that prejudice for most of the century, and there have been no modern public outrages of the types that occurred on the continent.

jiggery-pokery. Deceit, tricks, manipulation, fraud, underhanded activity.

jim-jams. Not pajamas but rather a feeling of fear or dread.

jink. Slang in many sports for what Americans call a fake or a feint.

jobber. *See* stock jobber.

job centre. A state-run employment office. *See also* Labour Exchange.

jobs for the boys. Hiring or promotions through contacts and friends rather than by ability; the term is not necessarily sexist and may be applied to women as well. *See also* Buggins's turn; old pals act.

Jock. An inevitable nickname for a Scot, from the common Scottish pronunciation of Jack.

Jockey Club. Since 1750, the governing organization for British horse racing.* Its headquarters are at Newmarket,* its fifty members self-elected.

Jodrell Bank. A huge observatory devoted to radio astronomy located south of Manchester,* Britain's largest and one of the most significant observatories in the world since its construction in 1945.

Joe Miller. A hoary old joke, such as might have been included in *Joe Miller's Jest Book* in 1739.

joey. Slang for the groat* coin introduced in 1836, from the MP* who proposed it. In the twentieth century, when this coin was no longer in use, Cockneys* gave the name to the threepenny coin instead, which also disappeared with decimalization in 1971. *See also* Appendix I; thruppence.

John Bull. The typical Englishman, from a character in a satire of 1712, originally depicted as bluff, hearty, country gentry,* but sometimes since expanded to include less pleasant character traits such as drunkenness and pigheadedness, not really equivalent to the American Uncle Sam because it personifies a national personality rather than the government or nation as a whole. **John Bull's other island** is Ireland.*

John Innes. Standard formulae for various fertilizing compounds, so called for their originator but now used by all agricultural firms.

johnny. A fellow, almost always derogatory, as in "some head office johnny." *See also* Jack.

John o'Groat's. The northernmost tip of Scotland,* so called because it was said to have been the site of the sixteenth-century trader John o'Groat's octagonal house. "John o'Groat's to Land's End*" is the British equivalent of America's "Maine to California."

John Thomas. The penis. Lady Chatterley was rather fond of the term, and the term is used more often by women than men, especially by many quite respectable mothers who so call it when talking to their male children. Why this name seems to have been chosen is a complete mystery, although the name was also a generic name for a servant; many mothers prefer **Willie** or, more formally, **John Willie.**

joiner. (1) A carpenter, as was Shakespeare's Snug the Joiner, but usually in cabinet work rather than construction. (2) In clothing, what Americans call a zipper.

joint. Not marijuana but a roast, usually eaten at Sunday's* main meal, as likely to be mutton* as beef,* accompanied by potatoes, cabbage, and fruit pies;* this usually must be "carved" at the table by the head of the family. In the later twentieth century, the joint has been replaced in many homes by roast chicken, with chips* and peas* and commercial sweets.*

joint-stock bank. *See* commercial bank.

joint-stock company. A form of company developed in the seventeenth century similar to the modern corporation; a number of prominent failures of such companies, especially the South Sea bubble,* led to legislation that changed them to limited liability companies. *See* Ltd.

jointure. A sum of money left to a widow. Among the gentry,* this was usually a guaranteed income that the inheriting son was required to pay rather than a lump sum or a specific piece of property* and was often guaranteed in the widow's original marriage settlement in return for her dowry.* Occasionally also used for sums left to younger sons and daughters. *See also* portion.

jolly. (1) As an adverb, this was standard usage meaning very in a positive sense, as in "jolly good," from about Shakespeare's time until the nineteenth century, at which point it dropped out of favor to some extent and was used primarily in colloquial situations, especially in schoolboy and schoolgirl literature. It apparently never was a euphemism for more vulgar words such as bloody* or damn,* although by the early twentieth century, it often seems to have been understood as such, particularly **jolly well**, as in "You'll jolly well go when I say," used almost always only in the respectable middle class* where other classes would use something more blunt. (2) As an adjective, primarily girls' school* slang meaning good, wonderful, fun, as in "That was jolly." (3) As a noun, in the nineteenth century, a marine. (4) As a noun, in the late twentieth century, an expense-paid trip with little or no real work to be done on it. (5) As a verb, to encourage someone or, more often, to help or to play along with someone in hopes they'll do you a favor later.

JP. Justice of the Peace.*

JT. John Thomas.*

Jubilee. This usually refers to Victoria's Diamond Jubilee in 1897, which celebrated her sixtieth year on the throne and was accompanied by lavish celebrations and public spectacles, often portrayed as the peak of the Empire.* However, there were also significant celebrations for the Silver Jubilee of George V in 1935.

judge. Distinct from magistrates* in that they are professionals, appointed for life from the ranks of barristers* and paid regular salaries. They serve only in the higher courts* on complex civil or the most serious criminal cases; most trials are tried before a justice of the peace* or a magistrate, who are never called judges. *See also* ordinary.

judge's rules. Rules governing how the police* may treat suspects and prisoners.

Jug. A nickname of Joan and related names, used until the early twentieth century as a nickname for an ugly woman.

jugged. Of meat, such as hare* or birds, cut into large pieces and cooked inside a pot or jug set into boiling water, thus stewed in its own juices.

juggernaut. A large truck; this has become fairly standard usage now, rather than a joking allusion.

juggins. A stupid person.

jumble sale. A sale of secondhand goods and clothing, much like what Americans call a rummage sale, almost always for charity. *See also* fête.

jumped-up. A description of people who have gotten above their station* in life. A common insult directed at Margaret Thatcher was that she was "a jumped-up grocer's* daughter" and thus not the proper type to be a Prime Minister.*

jumper. A woman's lightweight garment of soft knitted wool, pulled over the head when put on or off; thus, essentially what Americans call a woman's pullover sweater. *See also* cardigan; overdress; pullover; sweater; twin set.

junction. An intersection of roads or highways.*

junior. *See* leader.

junior school. An alternate name used for what is more generally called the primary school,* usually attended from ages seven to eleven. There are also some "junior" comprehensives,* which teach those above age eleven.

junket. Of a food, sweetened curds, often with fruit flavoring as well; the consistency looks rather like soft lumpy ice cream, but curds are partially formed cheese, so no freezing is involved. In the recent past, American stores offered a mix for an imitation ice cream called Junket (brand name), but that is quite different.

jury. Americans developed their jury system on English models, so the two are quite similar still. It has been twelve in size for centuries, although in 1967 new law allowed decisions to be made by a ten-to-two majority. Juries sit primarily in criminal cases, and then only in serious ones such as murder or robbery, and make no decisions concerning sentencing; most civil cases are also tried without juries, although litigants may ask for one. In Scotland,* criminal juries are fifteen persons.

Justice. (1) A Justice of the Peace;* in Scotland,* Justice is the official name. (2) As **Mister Justice**, the formal manner of address to a judge* when using his or her name, as "Mr Justice So-and-So."

Justice of the Peace. An unpaid magistrate* who deals with criminal cases at the local level. Appointed by the Lord Chancellor,* the JP can try relatively minor criminal cases. The original justices in the medieval era, such as Justice Shallow, were responsible for keeping the peace within their jurisdictions, acting both as supervisors of the constabulary and as judges, so they knew everyone and had significant authority over them, which is why Falstaff comes to Shallow to find recruits. This was gradually modified during the nineteenth century through the establishment of modern police* forces headed by Chief Constables.* The modern JPs still continue as socially prominent persons of the local community, if only because they would not be able to try cases without pay if they were not independently wealthy.

Justiciary, Court of. *See* Court of Justiciary.

juvenile. In law, a person less than seventeen years old, thus under a different set of laws and punishments than an adult. *See also* minor.

K

K. Slang for a knighthood, as in "got his K." *See* honours; knight.

Kaffir. A native tribe in South Africa; the term is used in South Africa as an equivalent of nigger* and as such appears in some British use, especially in the Rider Haggard/Buchan school of fiction.

Karno's Army. Fred Karno was a music hall* star who headed a troupe of slapstick comedians, at one time including the young Charlie Chaplin, prior to WWI. At the outbreak of war, the raw recruits' awkward drills earned them the name of Fred Karno's Army from the regulars,* and the name was adopted by the soldiers themselves in the trenches as a bitter commentary on the absurdity of the way the war was being fought by the command.

KB. Knight Commander of the Bath, the middle rank of the Order of the Bath.*

KBE. Knight Commander of the Order of the British Empire. *See* OBE.

KC. King's Counsel. *See* Queen's Counsel.

KCMG. Knight Commander of the Order of St. Michael and St. George,* the middle rank within the order; often irreverently known as the "Kindly Call Me God," from its being awarded to so many senior civil servants. *See also* CMG; GCMG.

kebab. Basically the same as what Americans usually call shishkebob, but pronounced kebab and often used generically for any Greek takeaway* food.

kedgeree. A dish of rice and shredded fish and eggs, generally eaten only at breakfast* in country houses.*

keep company with. To be engaged to marry.

Kelly's. A series of directories since 1799 of London* and various counties* and towns.

Kenilworth. A small town near Coventry,* noted primarily as the site of the castle built first by John of Gaunt and then later given by Elizabeth I to Dudley and celebrated in Scott's novel; the castle fell into ruin in the seventeenth century, although the ruins are now a significant tourist site.

Kensal Green. Not a green* but a Catholic cemetery in London* northwest of the Paddington* area.

Kensington. Originally a village west of London,* it became a suburban site of homes for the wealthy after William and Mary established a palace* there. Over the years, the open spaces have been filled in, but in general the neighborhood, lying to the west of Hyde Park* and Kensington Gardens,* is still only for the prosperous and prominent, and it is held in such high esteem socially that nearby neighborhoods try to gain status by association, with Brompton,* for example, now calling itself South Kensington,* and the areas to the north that are part of the Bayswater* and Paddington* areas often claimed by real estate agents and tenants to be really a part of Kensington. Kensington became a self-governing borough* in 1901, and in 1962 combined into the new borough of Kensington and Chelsea.*

Kensington Gardens. Originally the western end of Hyde Park,* used by Queens Mary and Anne as the gardens* for the new Kensington Palace.* Victoria finally opened them to the public, although they were fenced and open only on a schedule until very recently. Now they are the part of Hyde Park west of the Serpentine,* but they still retain a somewhat different feel, much cozier and with a sense of public privacy about them that makes them ideal for the lovers' meetings in *Wings of the Dove*, for example. Near the palace is Queen Anne's famous Orangery,* and Barrie's love for the park is reflected in its choice as the site for the Peter Pan statue.

Kensington Palace. A palace* in London* at the west end of Kensington Gardens,* bought by William III and rebuilt by Wren in the 1690s. This has been the "comfortable" London home of the monarchs since its beginning, associated in history more with their childhood and family life than with state occasions. Currently part is open to the public, and the rest is a residence for the princes* and their families. **Kensington Palace Gardens** are not the gardens* of the palace (which are Kensington Gardens*) but a street to the immediate west, once called Millionaire's Row for the wealthy who lived there, now primarily the site of embassies.

Kent. The southeastern-most county* or shire* of England,* running from London* to the Channel.* Historically, this is the core of English history, with Dover* the principal access to the continent, Canterbury* the home of the English Church,* and the Thames* ports on its north border the center of sea power and trading prosperity. It is one of the Home Counties* and is often called the Garden of England both for its agricultural riches and for the lovely rolling hills in the North Downs* that for many are the visual image of England itself, figuring in numberless works of literature.

Kentish man. A native of Kent* born west of the Medway;* one born east of the river is a **man of Kent**.

Kentish Town. Originally a village north of London,* now a suburb north of Regent's Park,* railroad slums in the late nineteenth, gentrified since the 1960s.

Kenya. A former colony in East Africa, independent in 1963 but still retaining a significant British influence. In the first half of the twentieth century, Kenya was known throughout the Empire* as a place where the colonists—many of them remittance men* but with an unusually high proportion of British women for a colony—lived a particularly decadent lifestyle.

kerb. What Americans call a curb.

kerb crawler. *See* gutter crawler.

kettle. The tea* kettle; all other items for boiling water are called pots, although occasionally there is a special oval pot for boiling fish called a **fish kettle**. In most modern homes, the tea kettle is electric.

Kew Gardens. The Royal Botanical Gardens located at Kew, now in the western portion of Greater London* along the Thames,* the first and largest of such gardens and still the model for all others of the genre in the world, begun in 1759 and initially stocked by Captain Cook's voyages.

KG. Knight of the Order of the Garter.*

khaki election. An election* called in 1900 to take advantage of government* popularity due to the Boer War, since used for any similarly timed election.

kibosh. Pronounced KYE-bosh, ruin, disaster, hurt, most often seen as **put the kibosh on** someone or something, very common in WWI but in use for at least a century before and still in use since, although associated more with upper-class* and military types.

kidney pie. *See* pie.

Kilkenny cats. People who can't be left together without fighting. The cats ostensibly fought until nothing was left but their tails, themselves a metaphor for the warfare endemic around Kilkenny in Ireland* since the first English arrived there in the thirteenth century.

kilt. The traditional costume of the Scottish male. Originally, the kilt was a long rectangular piece of cloth wrapped around the waist with the end thrown over a shoulder. After Culloden,* the kilt was outlawed, except in Scottish regiments* of the English army,* at which time kilt began to mean only the lower portion, which slowly evolved into the modern version similar to a pleated skirt. Once the power of the clans* was broken, the kilt returned, spurred by the Scottish revival led by Scott's novels, but it is now almost completely a costume worn only on holidays and patriotic occasions, while trousers* are regular daily male wear. *See also* dirk; sporran.

kindergarten. A school for children age two to five, generally a private, fee-paying school as opposed to the tax-supported nursery school.*

King. Britain is generally called a constitutional monarchy, meaning that there are recognized limits on the power of the King or Queen.* In the law itself, however, these limits are minimal, dealing primarily with religion, marriage, and succession. The monarch still must formally approve actions taken by Parliament,* as always; the difference is that, for about two centuries, no monarch has dared to exercise a veto. At this point no one knows what would happen if he or she should suddenly try to do so. Thus, in a political sense, it is not quite clear what function the monarch serves. But in a cultural sense, he or she still serves as the single unifying symbol of all the nation, the one person above party* or class,* and has immeasurable diplomatic value, as any reader of American supermarket magazines knows. The monarch's activities are very expensive and regular calls are made to reduce these, but in practice the nation makes a profit; since George III the monarch has ceded royal lands (with some exceptions) to the government in return for a fixed salary and expense account called the Civil List* and Privy Purse,* and many expenses are paid from the monarch's extensive private fortune not related to those lands. For family titles and relationships, *See* prince; princess; Queen; royal family; Royal Highness; royal household; succession. For homes, *See* Balmoral; Buckingham Palace; Hampton Court; Richmond; Sandringham; Windsor. For activities, *See* Ascot; drawing room; garden party; honours; Queen's Speech; royal; Royal Maundy. *See also* Appendix II; HM.

King George VI. A steeplechase* run on Boxing Day,* possibly the only public activity open in England* on that day, demonstrating if nothing else the importance of racing* to English culture.

King's Bench. From the medieval era, a court of common law* at which the King (or Queen) might preside. This in practice dealt primarily with criminal cases until 1873, when it was combined with the Court of Common Pleas* and of the Exchequer* into a single court, now a division of the High Court.* Called the **Queen's Bench** during the rule of a Queen, it now deals primarily with the bulk of the more complex civil cases, such as defamation, personal injury suits, or breach of contract, although its judges may serve in criminal cases in Crown Courts.* Prisoners of King's Bench criminal cases were sent to the King's Bench prison in Southwark,* although by the late eighteenth century it was reserved for debtors; hence Mr. Micawber's residence there in *David Copperfield*. It was demolished in 1880. *See also* county court.

King's Birthday. A national holiday celebrated on a date chosen for its suitability for ceremonial purposes, usually in June, with no relation whatsoever to the monarch's actual birthday. Queen Elizabeth II's is in June, usually a Sunday, although her real birthday is April 21. This is, among other things, the date on which summer honours* are formally bestowed.

King's Chapel. The chapel* of King's College,* built by Henry VI and VII, as large as some cathedrals and often regarded as the last great medieval building.

King's College. (1) A college* of Cambridge* founded in 1411, its age giving it considerable status within the university. (2) A college* in London,* originally intended as a Church of England* college to balance the nondenominational University College,* now a part of London University.*

King's Counsel. *See* Queen's Counsel.*

King's Cross. A rail station in London* alongside Euston* and St. Pancras,* the terminus for trains that serve the eastern portion of the island north into Scotland.*

King's English. This is no different from anyone else's English. Unlike France, for example, England has no person or body that dictates usage, spelling, or anything else related to language; the phrase simply means a version of the language that most listeners can understand, which, given the profusion of accents* and dialects, is not always as simple as it appears. The royal family* have never been arbiters of pronunciation (for much of the time the phrase has been in use, the King spoke German).

King's Parade. In Cambridge,* the street that runs past the entrances to a large number of the various colleges.*

King's Road. Originally Charles II's private road from London* to Hampton Court,* this is now a major street of Chelsea,* in the 1960s a center of "swinging London's" night life and still housing quite fashionable and popular shops and restaurants.

King's Scout. *See* Queen's Scout.

King's Speech. *See* Queen's Speech.

King Street. A street in London* just off Covent Garden* known for the headquarters there of the British Communist Party.

kiosk. (1) A telephone call box.* (2) A small shop or stall selling newspapers* and/or candy.

kip. As a verb, to sleep; as a noun, a nap, or sometimes a place to sleep.

kipper. A herring,* so called because it is dried and smoked, a process called kippering; generally eaten at breakfast.*

kirk. In Scotland* and northern England,* a church.*

kissing gate. A small gate that allows people but not livestock to pass through a fence. The gate itself swings within a U-shaped enclosure, and the name comes from the fact that when the gate is negotiated by two persons, the first must turn back to face the second, at which point they are so close together they can easily kiss.

kit. Clothing or outfitting, sometimes for a specific activity, such as "full riding* kit," sometimes any full outfit, such as a soldier's kit, carried in a **kit bag**, which is like the American duffel bag.

kite. A large bird of prey similar to the falcon,* once extremely common but in the twentieth century quite rare, killed due to its attacks on chickens.

kite mark. A label on a product that says it meets the standards of the BSI.*

knacker. (1) A horse butcher. (2) As a verb, to be very tired or worn out, perhaps like a horse ready for slaughter.

knees-up. A lower-class* slang term for a party, not as sexually suggestive as it sounds, from a popular music hall* song.

knee trembler. Sexual relations, specifically done standing up, but often used generically.

knickers. Women's underpants. Originally, these were loose and baggy and reached below the knee, like the outer trousers for men that were called knickerbockers in America. American women called the undergarment bloomers; curiously enough, whatever their name, respectable women of the mid-nineteenth century opposed them because no one was supposed to be able to see under their skirts to begin with. Changing fashions, however, eventually made underpants necessary, and then made them much smaller and lighter, but although specific names for fashion variations came and went and American women opted to call them other names, knickers became the generic British term no matter how brief or flimsy the garment. To **get your knickers in a twist** is to be upset, but in an extreme, illogical, or unjustified manner, said mostly to or about women and implying "feminine" illogicality when said to a man. *See also* nicker; pants; plus fours; step-ins; trousers.

knight. In the medieval era, a knight was basically a man who fought for a lord* while on a horse and in armor, as distinct from yeomen.* One did not become a knight by accident, as it required considerable skill acquired through years of apprenticeship, usually as a squire,* and thus, unlike nobility* was not an inheritable rank. However, knights were often rewarded with land, and the sons of previous knights were of course those most likely to be accepted into service as squires and thus become knights in their own right, and, not coincidentally, retain the family land. As feudal service declined, the land eventually became permanently owned by the families of the earlier knights, thereby establishing the families of the gentry* who maintained coats of arms but were not themselves noble. Many of their children were eventually made knights again themselves, but by about the mid-sixteenth century the rank could be granted only by the monarch and was given for some particular service to the crown.* The knight was entitled to style himself Sir* (First name Family name), his wife Lady* (Family name). However, the rank and the title remained noninheritable and is not part of the peerage,* with all knights technically considered commoners.* Today, knighthoods are still given in many of the modern orders of honours.* *See also* baronet; Dame.

Knightsbridge. A street in London* immediately south of Hyde Park* and Kensington Gardens,* sometimes also used to identify the immediate neighborhood leading to the museum areas of South Kensington.*

knobkerrie. A stick cut so that one end seems to have an enlarged knob on it, used as a walking stick* or a potential weapon.

knobs on, with. An intensifier, similar to the American "with bells on," meaning absolutely, completely, or with all possible emphasis.

knock. To impress someone, the opposite of the American colloquial usage, as in "That'll really knock them."

knock down. To sell, from the auctioneer's knock on the table at the end of a sale but also used in other situations.

knocker, on the. Slang for doing door-to-door selling, but definitely not selling door-to-door sex.

knocking shop. A house of prostitution.

knock-on. In rugby,* a ball that has bounced forward off the hands or arms of a player. This is illegal, so only the opposing team is allowed to touch it. If the referee decides it was intentional, the opposing team may be awarded a penalty kick as well. *See also* rebound.

knock up. (1) To wake up or to call on the phone. This is one of the classic illustrations of the two different languages, and many tourist jokes revolve around hotel clerks offering to knock up female guests, but unfortunately for humor, the phrase now seems to be disappearing from British usage. (2) To collect in a total, as in "he'll knock up about 50 pounds* this week." (3) To put together quickly or haphazardly, as Americans often say "throw together."

Knole. A large house* southeast of London,* given to the Sackville family by Elizabeth I, remodeled and expanded into one of the largest and best preserved seventeenth century houses in the country. Now a tourist attraction, it has figured largely in the literature of Vita Sackville-West, who grew up there, and her friend Virginia Woolf, who set *Orlando* in a fictionalized version of the house.

knoll. A small hill, almost always with a rounded top.

knotted, get. Roughly equivalent to the American "go fuck yourself." *See also* stuff.

knuckle, near the. Off-color or tasteless, just on the edge of obscenity or profanity.

KO. The start, from football* kick-off, rather than the end as in America, from the boxing knockout.

KT. Knight of the Order of the Thistle.*

kyle. In Scotland,* a narrow strait or channel between two islands, or between an island and the mainland.

L

L. On a car license plate, notice that the driver is a "learner."

£. The standard abbreviation for a monetary pound,* from the Roman libra. *See also* Appendix I.

Labour. A political party* formed in 1906 from several different smaller parties, reorganized in 1918 as a completely independent party with a socialist agenda and representing the unionized working class* in particular. By the mid 1920s it was the number two party of the country, participated in several minority governments* before WWII, and became the majority party in 1945 and in several subsequent governments since. The party's strength and weakness has been its strong ties to the trade unions,* which provide it with a solid base of support but which frighten away middle class* supporters in times of union unrest. It has also had some difficulty deciding what its goals are since nationalizing many industries, organizing the National Health,* and changing the factory acts* in its first burst of power after WWII, and in the 1980s much of its middle class and intellectual support was siphoned off by the SDP.*

labourer. In spite of the Labour Party, this term is almost always used only for an unskilled worker, almost always outdoors. *See also* navvy.

Labour Exchange. A state employment office. *See also* job centre.

laburnum. A small tree with a short trunk and rather gnarled branches, similar in looks to the American mimosa; not a wild tree, it is so popular in suburban gardens* that it is synonymous with the suburban middle class.*

lace-up. A shoe with laces.

lack of moral fibre. In the military during WWII, the official formulation for cowardice. Officers so charged often had their records stamped **LMF**.

lacquer. What Americans call hair spray.

lad. Although used to indicate a boy, and similar to the use of fellow, as in a "likely lad," especially in Scotland,* this is also a generic term for a helper, such as a plumber's lad or the lads on a construction crew. Around a stable, this is the stableboy/girl. Occasionally it implies a ladies' man, as in **a bit of a lad**. *See also* head lad.

Ladbroke's. The major chain of betting shops.*

ladder. A tear in stockings,* what Americans usually call a run or runner.

Lady. (1) A title used by a countess,* marchioness,* viscountess,* or baroness,* who may be called Lady (Husband's–Title name). Lady is also used by the wife of a baronet* or a knight,* but in their cases they are called Lady (Husband's–Family name). If a woman is properly called Lady (First name), this means that she is the daughter of a duke,* marquess,* or earl;* upon marriage, she would take her husband's title, whatever it might be. *See also* My Lady; Sir; Your Ladyship. (2) Without the capital letter, a female equivalent of a gentleman.* The term held this meaning for quite a long time and was rarely expanded to mean "any respectable woman," as it did in America during the nineteenth century; however, after WWI, the English began to use lady more in the American sense, just as Americans were beginning to sense something derogatory in the term and switch to woman. *See also* gentlewoman.

lady, good. *See* lady wife.

ladybird. Not a bird but the insect Americans usually call a ladybug.

Lady Bountiful. A wealthy woman doing charitable work, used as an ironic and insulting term to suggest that her charity is insincere or self-serving.

Lady chapel. A chapel* dedicated to the Virgin Mary in a large church* or cathedral,* usually to the east of the main altar; the practice was Catholic but the name usually remained after the churches became Church of England.*

Lady Day. March 25, the Feast of the Annunciation. For most of Britain, this was treated as the first day of the year from about the thirteenth century until the official adoption of the new calendar* in 1752, making some dating from original records quite complicated. It is a quarter day* in England.*

lady-in-waiting. A woman from the nobility* or gentry* who personally attended the queen* or a princess.* *See also* maid of honour; waiting woman.

Lady Margaret Hall. The first women's college* at Oxford* (1878).

Lady Muck. Slang for a pretentious woman. *See also* muck.

Ladyship. *See* Your Ladyship.

lady's maid. *See* maid.

lady wife. Simply a wife. The term is not used as a formal title, as no one says, for example, the Lord* and his Lady* wife; rather it is used by middle-class* fogeys, ex-colonials,* or military types, most often as "your lady wife" or "my lady wife," both to show respect by suggesting she is a lady in all but name and yet somehow still to imply the woman's inferiority. "Your **good lady**" is used in much the same way.

lag. A person who has spent much time in prison.

lager. A pale, golden beer* brewed in the German manner, in looks much the same as American beer, almost always served cold. Its use did not become widespread until late twentieth century, and it is often associated with women, tourists, "sophisticates," or the namby-pamby drinker. **Lager and lime** is a mixture of lager and what Americans call limeade, similar to a lemon shandy,* and almost always drunk by women only. Recent years have seen "superstrong" lagers with more than double the alcohol of regular lager, sold in cans and the primary fuel of the **lager lout**, a drunken hooligan, generally under thirty and from working-class* origins.

laird. In Scotland,* a lord.*

Lake District. An area in the northwest corner of England* containing a concentrated mixture of mountains, valleys, and picturesque lakes. Before Wordsworth the area, if noted at all, was treated as the epitome of the savage wilds to be avoided by civilized persons, but Wordsworth's poetic evocations of "nature" in the area caught the public imagination and since about 1800 this has been perhaps the most admired, visited, and avidly protected natural countryside in Britain. To an American familiar with the Rockies or the Sierras, it seems both tiny and tame, but this has been part of its charm for the British; while providing some of the last glimpses of "undeveloped" nature, it is readily accessible to the hiker and as such has been one of the primary spurs to the vacation sport of walking.* Throughout the nineteenth century, one was hardly allowed to claim the name of poet without at least an extended visit there, and some, such as Wordsworth, Coleridge, de Quincey, Ruskin, Arnold, and Beatrix Potter, lived there for extended periods. It became the artist's *sine qua non* of beauty and naturalness, and in the rest of society it became almost a pilgrimage site; no respectable person could be counted civilized without at least one holiday walking in the Lake District to remove the cobwebs and cares of modern urban existence, and it is often used in literature to symbolize the possibility of escape from the strictures of civilization. It is the largest of the National Parks* (1951). *See also* Grasmere; Windermere.

Lambeth. The name originally was loam hithe,* or muddy landing, for a place on the south side of the Thames,* now a well-developed area across from Westminster* that for most of the nineteenth and twentieth centuries has been an industrialized area. The **Lambeth Walk** was a popular song about a dance step from a pre-WWII musical and had nothing to do with Lambeth except that the colorful lower-class* characters who lived there were supposed to do this dance. **Lambeth Palace** is the residence and offices of the Archbishop* of Canterbury, located in Lambeth since the thirteenth century (You thought he would live in Canterbury,* didn't you?); this is often shortened to Lambeth and used synonymously for the Archbishop of the Church of England.* A **Lambeth Conference** of all Anglican bishops worldwide is held here every ten years.

Lammas. August 1, celebrated in the Church of England* until the eighteenth century, when it gradually faded in importance. In the nineteenth, its rituals were transferred to the various harvest festival* services. In Scotland,* this is a quarter day.*

lamp. Often used for what Americans call a light or a light bulb, especially **head lamps** or **tail lamps** on a car.

Lanarkshire. A county* or shire* in Scotland* along the Clyde,* inseparably associated with coal mines and with heavy industry in the Glasgow* area; in 1975, absorbed into the new Strathclyde* region.*

Lancashire. A county* or shire* on the northwestern coast of England,* wealthy from the wool trade in the medieval era. In the late eighteenth century its coal fields encouraged its industrial growth, particularly along the Mersey* in Manchester* and Liverpool.* The area was synonymous with cotton mills, fed by cotton from the American South and from India through Liverpool. In 1974, Manchester and the Merseyside* areas were separated to make two metropolitan counties, and the primarily rural areas remained in Lancashire, with Lancaster* remaining the county administrative center.

Lancaster. A town in Lancashire* prominent during the medieval era, its wealth and influence surpassed by Liverpool* and Manchester* although it remained the administrative town of the county.*

Lancaster, Duchy of. Lands owned by the monarch but not ceded to Parliament along with all the other royal lands in return for the Civil List* at the beginning of each reign; instead the income, along with that of the Duchy of Cornwall, is used for the Privy Purse* and the Prince of Wales's* expenses.

lance corporal. In the army,* the lowest ranking of the NCOs, more equivalent to the American corporal than the PFC. In practice, he is an "assistant" corporal,* doing a corporal's dirty work or sometimes his whole duty for less pay, often called a **lance jack**. A **lance sergeant** was a provisional or "assistant" sergeant.*

lancer. A cavalryman whose primary weapon was the lance. Although the spear was an ancient cavalry weapon, it had disappeared by the seventeenth century, but was revived among regiments* fighting in India and did not completely disappear until long after WWI; several modern armored regiments still call themselves lancers. *See also* dragoon; hussar.

Lancs. Abbreviation for Lancashire.*

land agent. A real estate agent.

landau. A large carriage* with four wheels; the top separates in the middle and may be lowered in either direction.

land girls. During WWII (and briefly in 1917), young women from urban areas sent to the countryside* as farm workers to replace men who had gone to war.

landlord. In addition to American usages, the owner and operator of a pub.*

Landrover. *See* Rover.

lane. A very narrow roadway or path, distinguished from other types of roads by having some kind of wall, usually hedges or banks in the country or close buildings in a town, along its edge. *See also* alley; highway; road; street.

language. Vulgar or profane language, in the same way as the American "watch your language," but often said as a single peremptory word, "Language!"

lapwing. *See* peewit.

larder. What Americans call a pantry, a place to store food.

lark. (1) A common songbird, much the same as the American lark, noted for its lovely song. The constant association of the lark with rising comes from the fact that the lark usually sings as it is flying upward, and it is also associated with the dawn, as the bird begins singing very early. (2) Any kind of pleasant activity, as in "what a lark!" but sometimes used ironically as well. To **lark about** is to act foolishly.

lashings. Lots, as in "lashings of butter."

lass/lassie. In Scotland* and northern England,* a standard term for a girl, but often used poetically by more southern writers to mean a female sweetheart. By the early twentieth century, this was well established as one of the stereotypical Scottish words and was used there for practically any woman at practically any time.

last call. In a pub,* this is given just before closing time,* leaving just enough time for everyone to order one more round. *See also* time.

Last Post. In the army,* the bugle call that signals the end of the day, a different melody but the same function as the American Taps.

laudanum. A medicine widely used from Shakespeare's day through the nineteenth century to relieve aches and pains and to provide general relaxation. The fact that it was a mixture of alcohol and opium made it quite successful at these tasks, and in the nineteenth century, it became a common drug for respectable women, who dosed themselves with it for any and all problems, making a large number of them unwitting opium addicts.

Laugharne. *See* Llaregyb.*

launderette. What Americans call a laundromat; these often combine coin-operated machines and an attendant who may do part of the laundry for customers. Also spelled **laundrette**.

laurel. An evergreen tree with tiny yellowish flowers, usually grown as a garden* hedge and often trimmed and shaped.

lav. A lavatory.*

lavabo. A washing basin, especially one with its own stand, from the basin used in the ritual washing of the hands in the Catholic mass.

lavatory. A toilet. In the scale of euphemism, this seems to rank above loo* and below WC,* and is currently the most commonly used term. *See also* bathroom; littlest room.

laver. A type of seaweed, once fairly common as a boiled food in south-western England* and Wales.* **Laverbread** is laver boiled and then fried in an oatmeal batter, found mostly in Wales.

law. *See* barrister; bill; Chancellor; Chancery; common law; Common Pleas; constitution; court; county court; Court of Appeal; Court of Justiciary; Court of Session; Crown Court; High Court; Inns of Court; judge; Justice of the Peace; KC; Law Courts; magistrate; Parliament; police; prison; QC; serjeant; solicitor.

law agent. In Scotland,* a solicitor.*

Law Courts. The building in London* in the Strand* housing the High Court* and Court of Appeal.*

law hand. The careful, clear handwriting used in legal documents before the typewriter; the term is often used still for any clear, precise handwriting.

lawn. As in America, a small field of grass, but the term is not much used except for the playing area in sports such as lawn tennis, bowls,* or croquet. When around a small house* the grass is usually called the garden,* and around a large house* it is the grounds.*

Law Society. An association for solicitors* only, similar to the American Bar Association.

lay. Americans set the table, Britons usually lay the table.

layabout. A loafer, more specifically someone who chooses to live off welfare payments of various kinds.

lay-by. A place beside a highway* where cars can pull off and stop.

lay clerk. One who sings in the choir of a cathedral* or a collegiate church.*

lay on. To plan or to order.

l.b.w. In cricket,* leg* before wicket.

LCC. London County Council. *See* GLC.

lea. A meadow. *See also* -leigh.

lead. (1) Pronounced leed, an electric cord. *See also* mains; plug; points. (2) What Americans call a leash, as for a dog.

lead, swing the. *See* swing the lead.

Leadenhall. In London,* a street and a market* in the City,* primarily for poultry but also with fruits and vegetables; the market is now more like a shopping arcade,* located in Gracechurch rather than Leadenhall itself.

leader. (1) In a newspaper,* what Americans call an editorial. (2) In a court* case, the chief barrister* of a team representing a client. In practice, this is almost always a QC,* who must always be accompanied by a "junior" barrister, although the junior often actually conducts the case.

Leader. In the House of Commons,* the member of the government* who officially introduces and guides all government proposals.

Leamington Spa. Pronounced Lemmington, a town near Coventry* whose mineral springs brought it considerable popularity as a resort community in the early nineteenth century, given the official name of **Royal Leamington Spa** by Victoria. For the Victorians, particularly of the upper–middle class,* this was a favorite resort, the kind of place where Dickens's Dombey could meet a beautiful Edith Granger and be sure that she would also be socially suitable as a second wife.

leasehold. The bulk of British real property* has been owned by a relatively few persons, and until quite recently, this meant that most housing was built to be leased rather than rented or sold. In the leasehold an individual would buy the use of a property rather than the property itself, usually for ninety-nine years. Although you would become the nominal "owner" of the property for the term of the lease, could build on it, remodel, sublet, or resell the remaining years of the lease at any time, you might still owe a ground rent* for the land underneath. At the end of the lease, not only the original property but any of the buildings and equity added to it would revert to the original owner. Some of the houses in the burst of development after WWI and most of the houses since WWII, when not council houses,* have been built to be sold permanently, which is called a **freehold** and includes all rights to both building and ground beneath forever. But many of the older houses, often the most fashionable and elegant, especially in London,* are still leaseholds.

lecture. At traditional colleges* and universities* like Oxford* or Cambridge,* attendance at lectures is completely optional; the student attends tutorials* but may skip all lectures or attend those in subjects which he or she is not officially studying. At many of the redbrick* schools and at polytechnics, however, classes are run more on the modern American manner, with regular class lectures, tests, and required attendance.

lecturer. At a college* or university,* the primary rank of what Americans would call the faculty. The lecturer ranks below a reader* or a professor*, and lecturers themselves are usually separated into three ranks: **senior lecturer**, **lecturer**, and **assistant lecturer**. The lecturer is a fellow* and thus has considerably more rank and status than lecturers at American colleges who are usually just graduate students themselves who teach undergraduate courses to cover their tuition fees.

Leeds. A city in Yorkshire,* a major industrial and commercial center, especially for the textile industries of the eighteenth and nineteenth centuries. Major slum clearances in the 1920s began to improve the lot of workers there, but the city, if mentioned at all in literature, is still generally seen as yet another of the tough, dirty, and soulless Midlands* industrial towns. The **University of Leeds**, founded in 1904, was one of the redbrick universities,* with particular strengths in technological fields. **Leeds Castle**, however, is nowhere near the city but is instead located near the tiny village of Leeds in southeast England; standing in the middle of a lake, the castle, although mostly nineteenth century restoration, is a favorite tourist site as it epitomizes the fairy-tale conception of the medieval castle.

Lee-Enfield. A manufacturer of weapons; the term most often means the basic bolt-action rifle used in WWI and II.

leek. A food that looks like an overgrown green onion, somewhat milder in taste than a regular onion, eaten raw or boiled. The leek has been the symbol of Wales* for so long no one is quite sure why: One story says St. David, the Welsh patron saint, was a vegetarian and ate a lot of them; another says Welsh troops wore them as a badge in a seventh century battle with the English; another says it relates to a battle in a leek field in France, described in *Henry V*, in which the Welsh troops distinguished themselves. However, none associate it with the Welsh as a primary food in the way that oats are linked with the Scots* or the potato with the Irish. Whatever the cause, by Shakespeare's time, the leek and the Welsh are synonymous.

leftenant. *See* lieutenant.

left luggage. A place to check luggage, as at a train station.

leg. (1) In cricket,* the quarter of the field on the batsman's* side of the wicket, extending from midfield back behind him;* for the right-handed batsman, this is the left side of the field. Various fielding positions on that side include: **fine leg**, just behind the batsman; **short leg**, close to and level with the batsman; **long leg**, far behind the batsman in the corner; **square leg**, somewhat farther away than short leg, about halfway between the batsman and the boundary on the leg side; and **deep square leg**, near the boundary and about the middle of the field lengthwise. A **leg break** is a bowled ball that starts toward the batsman and then bounces away; a **leg cutter** is an extremely fast leg break. A **leg hit** is a hit ball that goes to the leg side, while a **leg glance** is a hit ball that goes almost directly behind the batsman to his leg side—this is still in play, for there are no foul balls in cricket. A **leg bye** is a run scored when the ball bounces and hits the batsman, then bounces away so far that he may run to the other wicket. However, if the batsman is ruled **leg before wicket**, he is out for blocking a ball that would have hit the wicket with any part of his body (not just the leg) rather than with his bat. (2) A **leg up** is any kind of assistance, from the practice of making a step with your hands for someone else to climb up with, but a **leg over** is an indication that you want to have sex. To **show a leg**, however, is not to undress or to prepare for sex but to get out of bed and get moving, like the American "shake a leg."

legal aid. Publicly funded lawyers for people who can't afford them, available in some specific criminal cases since 1907, but in 1964 made widely available, subject to a means test.

legless. Drunk.

Leicester. (1) Pronounced LESter, a small city in the Midlands.* Long associated with the hosiery and stocking trade, it was also a center of Protestant power during the Civil War.* Legend says it was the home of King Lear. (2) *See* cheese.

Leicestershire. A county* or shire* in central England.* There is mining and considerable industry in the western portions near Birmingham,* but the bulk of the county is agricultural and traditionally associated with fox hunting.* In 1974, Leicestershire* was expanded to include Rutland* as well.

Leicester Square. A square in Soho* in London;* since several large theatres were built around it in mid–nineteenth century, it has been the figurative center of London nightlife, with first-run cinemas,* most West End* theatres, and dance halls or discos* within easy walks down various side streets.

Leics. Abbreviation for Leicestershire.*

-leigh. In place names, indicating an ancient lea.*

leisure centre. An area or building with space and equipment for various leisure activities, often including a swimming pool, sometimes council*-run, sometimes private enterprise. Sometimes called a **leisuredrome**.

lemon curd. A mixture of lemon juice, eggs, sugar, and butter, about the same consistency as soft cream cheese, used as a spread on bread* or as a filling in cakes* or inside what Americans call jelly rolls.

lemon squash. A lemon-flavored soft drink.

lending library. A circulating library. *See* library.

Lent. The forty days before Easter,* but not observed with the same care or intensity in the Church of England* as in the Catholic Church. In the medieval era, such foods as butter, eggs, and meat were strictly forbidden during Lent, which led to the traditional Shrove Tuesday* pancake* tradition to use up existing stores; the Church of England does not require fasting, although it still keeps all the points of the calendar during Lent and many people still "give up" something for the duration. Nonconformist* groups do not observe Lent at all, and it is barely noticed in Scotland.*

Lents. Inter-college* boat races held at Cambridge* during the Lent term.*

lesson. In the Church of England,* a selection from the Bible read at a service; one each from the Old and New Testaments are read at each service.

let, to. For rent.

levee. (1) In the eighteenth and early nineteenth centuries, a group of guests whom you met shortly after rising from your bed. For upper-class* women, this was a significant social function, a morning session for gossip or chat conducted while *déshabillé* and a demonstration of close friendship with both male and female guests (though more often male, as the other women were also at their levees and could not yet leave their homes); from this, applied also to any morning meeting with an important person. (2) For royalty,* an afternoon public reception attended only by men; women attend the Drawing Room.*

level. An especially flat area of land; several parts of the Fens* have been given this name.

level crossing. Where a road crosses a railroad track.

Lewisham. A suburb of London* to the southeast, near Blackheath,* still firmly middle class* just as when it was the home of Nesbit's Treasure Seekers.

Liberal. A political party that replaced the Whigs,* the name becoming common in the 1860s as a contrast to the Conservatives.* Under Gladstone in particular, they were the party of free trade and social reform and were the clearly dominant party until WWI, when in an amazing sequence of events and personal animosities, the party fell apart within less than a decade and lost almost all influence in British political life, the new Labour* party becoming the number two party. The Liberals still exist, but for most of the 1980s only as part of the Alliance.*

Liberal Democrat. In 1989, another version of the Alliance.*

Liberty. A large department store in London,* one of the first such stores in the world, in the nineteenth century having a profound influence on fashion through its introduction of Japanese designs and materials and its commercial championing of the fashions and materials of Morris and the Pre-Raphaelite movement. The current version of the store is in Regent Street.*

Liberty Hall. An imaginary place (actually first used in Goldsmith's *She Stoops to Conquer*) in which all do just as they please; hence a synonym for chaos as well as casual live-and-let-live attitudes.

library. (1) Although an 1850 law allowed local authorities to levy a tax for public libraries, not many communities took up the option until after WWI. Most people who borrowed books actually rented them from commercial companies called **circulating libraries**. The first of these began in Edinburgh* in 1726, and the concept slowly spread to London* and to the major resort towns, where patrons paid a fee to local shopkeepers for each book borrowed. Although many village shops* operated small libraries among their other goods, by the mid-nineteenth century, the field was dominated by major chains such as Mudie's,* W. H. Smith,* or Boots,* who purchased books in the thousands and rented them to members all across the nation. These bought the overwhelming majority of novels published and had a profound impact on the types of fiction printed by publishers, concentrating on entertainment fiction, usually the romantic but morally uplifting three-volume novel so attractive to the middle-class* women, who made up the overwhelming bulk of customers. But the gradual spread of public libraries, the establishment of national book clubs in the 1920s, and the arrival of the Penguin* paperback in the 1930s eventually put the circulating libraries out of business. Many of the public* libraries are in fact subscription libraries open only to members who pay an annual fee, but since WWII, most boroughs* and counties* have opened free public libraries similar to those found in America. *See also* British Museum; London Library. (2) In private homes, the library was sometimes a room from which the business of the estate was handled but more often was simply the husband's equivalent of the wife's morning room* or drawing room.* *See also* country house.

licence. (1) A permit allowing the serving of alcohol; an **occasional licence** is one that allows liquor sales only at limited, specified times, while an **off-licence** can sell liquor all day long but the buyer must carry it away to drink it. *See also* license; licensing laws. (2) An annual fee charged to owners (or renters) of televisions (originally radios), used to pay for BBC* programming. In 1991, this was £77 per year. (3) *See* marriage; road licence; special licence.

license. To issue a licence.* **Licensed premises** are those that have a licence to sell alcoholic beverages.

licensing laws. The laws governing operations of pubs* and other stores selling liquor. The modern forms of these were instituted during WWI to limit pub hours so the boys in France wouldn't think the folks back home were having too much fun. Basically, pubs were allowed to open for about nine hours total with a closed period in the middle, which in practice became, with local variations, open from 10 A.M. to 2 P.M. and again from 6 to 10:30 P.M. Individual pubs could, in special circumstances, open at different hours, as long as they stayed within the same overall limits, and pubs near places such as Covent Garden* might open after midnight to meet the early morning trade. In 1988, pubs were allowed to stay open for more consecutive hours during the day, but many continued to close in the afternoon and almost all close by 11:00. Off-licence* stores may sell bottled beer and liquor when the pubs are closed, except on Sundays,* when they can sell only when the pubs are open. Prior to 1914, things were different: The first restrictions of 1830 forced pubs to close between 10 P.M. and 4 A.M.; in 1872 open hours changed to 5 A.M. till midnight in London, until 11 P.M. in other towns, and until 10 P.M. in the countryside.* Children under fourteen may not enter a pub, and may not be served alcohol until eighteen.

lido. An outdoor, public swimming pool.

lieutenant. Pronounced lefTENant. (1) In the army,* the lowest ranking officer,* usually in two ranks, lieutenant and sub-lieutenant,* in the modern army commanding a section but before WWI usually commanding a platoon.* In the navy,* this is also the lowest rank, but the next higher is a lieutenant commander,* not a captain.* The RAF* does not use the rank, its equivalent being flying officer;* a **flight lieutenant** is more nearly equivalent to any army captain.* See also Appendix V; ensign; subaltern.

life belt. See life preserver.

Lifeboat Service. A rescue service along the sea coast run by volunteers and private charity.

Life Guards. One of two cavalry* Guards* regiments,* formed in 1661 from Charles II's household cavalry.

life peer. See peer.

life preserver. What Americans usually call a blackjack; what Americans call a life preserver is called a **life belt** or **life vest**. See also cosh.

lift. What Americans call an elevator.

lighting-up time. A half-hour after sunset, when drivers are required to turn their headlights on.

Light Programme. The general entertainment radio service of the BBC* before the division into Radio 1/2/3/4. *See also* Third Programme.

like. For much of the twentieth century, this has been a verbal space-filler and modest intensifier among the lower classes,* as it has been in America since at least the 1960s; but whereas Americans use it in the same ways as "uh," as in "I was, like, all alone," Britons will say, "I was all alone, like."

li-lo. A portable air mattress, a trade name used generically.

Limehouse. A neighborhood in the East End* of London,* alongside the Thames* and west of the Isle of Dogs.* In the eighteenth century, a number of Chinese settled here, making Limehouse a synonym for Chinatown and giving it a popular image of opium dens, inscrutable crimes, and the Yellow Peril capitalized on by the Fu Manchu and Bulldog Drummond school of popular fiction. The Chinese area was never more than a few blocks square, and almost all of the Chinese had moved on by WWII.

limit. *See* speed limit.

Limited Liability Company. *See* Ltd.

Lincoln. (1) A town in eastern England;* although well inland, its river access to the North Sea* made it one of the major ports of medieval England. Today, it is most noted for its cathedral,* which Ruskin thought the "most precious" in all of England, and for its high concentration of extant medieval architecture. **Lincoln green** was a very bright green material made here, associated with Robin Hood and commonly worn by English hunters. (2) A college* of Oxford.*

Lincolnshire. A county* or shire* on the eastern coast of England,* from the Wash* to the Humber.* Most of the shire, like its neighbor Norfolk,* is flat with extensive fens,* but in the north it rises to chalky upland, called the Wolds,* and to hills. In 1974, the northern area along the Humber was transferred to the new county of Humberside.*

Lincoln's Inn. One of the Inns of Court* in London,* located south of High Holborn.* **Lincoln's Inn Fields** is a large square nearby, used as a park by the legal profession and the passing public, with the Royal College of Surgeons opposite the Inn and residences of lawyers, like Dickens's Tulkinghorn, along the other sides.

line. (1) In the army,* *See* regiment. (2) In the navy,* large sea battles were fought with the largest ships sailing in a line so as to bring the maximum number of guns into play, with smaller ships scattered around to guard flanks and harry the enemy; hence, a **ship of the line** was one of the largest armed ships. From mid-eighteenth century, this generally meant a ship over 160 feet in length with sixty or more guns. In the modern navy, this is a battleship, cruiser, or aircraft carrier. (3) *See* Underground. (4) *See* lines.

line-out. In rugby,* a play used to bring the ball in from out of bounds; the forwards of both teams line up side by side at right angles to the out-of-bounds line and a player tosses the ball in between the two lines over their heads, something like a basketball jumpball with twelve players jumping.

lines. At school,* the punishment in which the child has to write things, such as "I will not throw chalk," many times, each repetition called a line. *See also* hard lines; marriage lines.

linesman. A man on the railroad who walks the tracks to inspect them.

links. In Scotland,* a narrow strip of coastal land with coarse grass and sand dunes, basically so worthless that even the Scots could not find any use for it, so they played a game on it instead, which is how the name came to be applied to golf courses throughout the world.

linnet. A small bird related to the swallow and finch, found in the wild on heaths* and other furze* areas, noted for a variety of coloring and a pleasant song.

lino. Linoleum, but pronounced line-o.

lint. The cotton Americans call a dressing for a wound. What Americans call the lint on a suit, for example, is usually called **fluff**.

list, short. *See* short list.

listed. Protected from real estate developers; a **listed building** is a building of historical interest or architectural merit that cannot be remodeled or torn down without permission from some governmental body.

Listener. A magazine of the BBC,* originally (1928) to publish talks broadcast on the radio and literary/cultural news and reviews, different from the *Radio Times** that concentrated on schedules and radio publicity, gradually becoming a general interest magazine until going out of business in 1991.

lit. hum. *Literae humaniores*, the school* more casually called Greats* at Oxford,* dealing with classical language, literature, and philosophy.

litter bin. *See* bin.

little go. *See* Responsions.

littlest room. An extremely genteel* euphemism for the room with the toilet. *See also* back; bathroom; bog; lavatory; loo; WC.

Little Venice. In London,* the neighborhood fronting onto the triangular western terminus of the Regent's Canal,* developed in the early nineteenth century, very small and not at all like Venice but now with a high concentration of artists.

Liverpool. A city and port on the northwest coast of England,* the city no one wants to know. Liverpool hardly existed until docks were built there in the natural harbor of the Mersey* in the early eighteenth century, but it quickly established itself as the major port for trade with America, especially importing cotton for the mills in surrounding Lancashire.* By the mid-nineteenth century it was England's major port. Thus, it was also the primary port from which emigrants left for America and through which Irish immigrants came to England. Its wealth is reflected in the solid Victorian architecture of the city. But in the twentieth century, the mills began to close and trade declined, so that since WWII Liverpool has become symptomatic of the industrial decay and unemployment associated with all the north of England. In spite of, or perhaps because of, its economic prominence, Liverpool is all but ignored in British literature; no one wants to live there, and no one wants to write about it; "The Leaving of Liverpool," as the folk song says, is its primary literary association. *See also* Everton; Toxteth.

Liverpool Street. A street at the eastern edge of the old City* of London, site of a train station that serves as terminus for trains running to the eastern areas of England* and a major transfer point for the Underground.*

Liverpudlian. A native of Liverpool.*

livery. Originally a badge or uniform given by a lord* to his followers and thus the precursor of military uniforms. In the late nineteenth century this began to be applied to servants' uniforms, almost always to those worn by male servants only, and in the twentieth is used only for male servants dressed in out-of-date fashions, especially breeches* and powdered wigs. However, it is also used for uniforms such as those worn by the livery companies.*

livery company. In London,* a guild of associated merchants* or artisans who were entitled to wear distinct livery* and to vote in elections for local government of the City.* Originally, there were twelve of these, growing to the present eighty-four. The twelve "great" companies, in order of precedence, are Mercers,* Grocers,* Drapers,* Fishmongers,* Goldsmiths, Merchant Taylors,* Skinners, Haberdashers,* Salters,* Ironmongers, Vintners, and Clothworkers. As such, they provide a clear view of the significant trades of the medieval city.

living. The right to the income from property used to support a church* and its clergyman. The money usually came from a combination of endowments and parish property subject to the tithe.* Depending on the nature of this property, two clergymen holding ostensibly the same positions could live one in poverty and one in great wealth. Sometimes the living was controlled by the church authorities, and sometimes it was still in the control of the local squire,* who could thus in effect appoint the local clergyman. A priest who "had the living" would be called a rector.* However, there was no requirement that the person receiving the income from the living actually had to serve in the parish* involved. Someone might live quite comfortably on the living and leave the clerical duties to a vicar* or curate,* as did Dr Vesey Stanhope in *Barchester Towers*, who lived in Italy for twelve years on the income from several livings. Thus, the living was often used to support the younger sons, or illegitimate sons, of various gentry* (and sometimes of the local squire himself) who never went near a church. The number of livings "in the gift of" individuals has declined in the twentieth century, but even so, about 20 percent of current clerics have livings to which they were appointed by lay persons. The bulk of the rest are appointed by the monarch, the Lord Chancellor,* or Oxford* or Cambridge,* and only a relatively few appointments are made by the bishops* or archbishops.* This is particularly significant in that a living is for life; once in possession of it, the clergyman cannot be removed for any reason short of defrocking, which contributes to the unusually broad range of theological opinion in the Church of England. *See also* advowson; clergy.

Llaregyb. A small town in southwestern Wales,* also called **Laugharne**, often assumed to be Dylan Thomas's Llareggub, although the latter is in fact bugger-all* spelled backwards.

LLD. Doctor of Law; *See* degree.

Lloyd's. Synonymous with insurance since its members began insuring ships from Lloyd's Coffee House* in the late seventeenth century, Lloyd's is different from an American insurance company in that each underwriter is an individual who puts his own money personally at risk when writing a policy. In 1986, they moved to a new building, the unrelenting "modernity" of which has caused furor among the general public. **Lloyds** (*sic*) **Bank** is completely unconnected to the insurance company but is one of the largest banks in Britain.

LMF. Lack of moral fibre.*

loads. What Americans usually call lots, as in "loads of money," casual usage but heard in practically all classes.

loaf. (1) Slang, usually lower class,* for head or brain. (2) *See* bread; lump.

lobby. When used specifically, it means the lobby of the House of Commons,* and thus a **lobby correspondent** for a paper is a political correspondent. To lobby originally meant to meet with a member* in the lobby, but now of course it may be done in any other place as well.

local. The favorite neighborhood pub* of an individual. This implies more than just nearness; the local is the one where the person feels most at home, not necessarily the one closest to home, and is thus treated by him (or her) more like a club or community center than just a place to get a drink.

local authority. The local governmental body, usually a council.*

loch. In Scotland,* a lake; however, most of the lakes are formed in geological fissures, making them long, narrow, and deep, and the term is also often applied to similar bodies of water that actually open onto the sea. Thus, **Loch Ness**, with the famous unconfirmed monster and the uncharted bottom, and **Loch Lomond**, fabled in song, are both lakes, but **Loch Nevis** or **Loch Long** are bays similar to fjords. *See also* lough.

lock-up. Not the jail but a garage or storage facility located at a different site than one's home; sometimes also applied to a small shop* when the shopkeeper* lives elsewhere.

locum. A professional who stands in temporarily for another, usually a doctor who looks after the patients of another doctor during vacation or illness, but sometimes also a lawyer or a clergyman.

lodger. A tenant, almost always a tenant in a bedsitter.*

lodgings. Rented housing, usually rooms* or a bedsitter,* almost never applied to a flat.*

lollipop lady/man. Not a seller of children's candy, but what Americans call a school crossing guard, from the stop sign carried on a stick.

lolly. (1) Money. (2) A shortened form for lollipop. *See also* ice.

Lombard Street. A street in London* near the Bank of England,* long associated with banking since representatives of the Italian private bankers, called **Lombards** by the English, took offices there in the early Renaissance and often used as synonymous with all banking.

London. Since well before Shakespeare's time, London has been the political, economic, and cultural center of England* (and of Britain*), in a way that no U.S. city could ever manage. It dominates all aspects of life in modern Britain, in American terms as if Washington D.C., New York City, Boston, and Los Angeles were all combined into a single city. From the mid–eighteenth century to the mid–twentieth century, it was the largest city in the world; by the time of Fielding or Dr. Johnson there were over a million inhabitants, over 2.5 million when Dickens was describing its complex life, 5 to 6 million when Sherlock Holmes walked its streets.

Technically, London is only the ancient medieval town, called the City,* little more than a mile square. Everything else is a set of independent parishes* and boroughs* whose borders gradually merged with those of London as population spilled out of the confines of the old walled city. Everyone refers to the mass as London, but there is officially no such place, except at the post office. In 1855, a central board was established to build sewers, but this was the first and only such governmental body until 1888, when London was officially formed as an independent county,* administered by the LCC*. The population kept spreading, however, and in 1965, Parliament* faced the facts and enlarged the county into the new unit called Greater London,* comprised of thirty-two individual boroughs plus the City, administered by the GLC,* and eliminated the old county of Middlesex.* But political conflicts eventually led the Conservative* government to dissolve the militantly Labour* GLC with legislation passed in 1986, and now once again, the thirty-three individual boroughs are basically independent cities with no central government for the metropolis. Not even the Metropolitan Police* from Scotland Yard* serve the entire urban area.

As London's impact on British life and literature is immeasurable, no attempt will be made here to try to summarize that impact; nor will I try to cross-reference related items, as they can be found in entries on practically every page of this work. As any Briton will tell you, London is not Britain or even England; it is a world unto itself, self-absorbed in its culture in a way that perhaps only New York is in America. But for the outsider who knows Britain through books and films, almost everything we know is filtered through the interests and sensibilities of London, for London sets the images and stereotypes and decides what is important about all the rest of the nation. In that sense, this entire work is about London.

London, Museum of. A museum in London* located along the old City* wall, devoted to the history of life in London (personal aside: one of the best-organized and most pleasant and informative museums anywhere).

London, The. The largest music hall in London* (1856–1934), located in Spitalfields.*

London Bridge. Not the drawbridge with the neo-Tudor towers on it, which is perhaps why it could be sold to an Arizona millionaire in 1971 without too much complaint. There has been a bridge on the site crossing the Thames* from the City* to Southwark* since the Roman era, and until 1729 this was the only bridge; it was lined with buildings and shops,* an entire community living on the bridge from the twelfth century until that bridge was replaced in 1831 by the one that was shipped to Arizona. The new one is a bland concrete structure offering no relief from the unrelentingly modern architecture of the redeveloped areas on both banks around it. *See also* Tower Bridge.

London Clinic. Perhaps the most fashionable private hospital in the country, located in Harley Street.*

Londonderry. A county* and a port on the northern coast of Northern Ireland,* known primarily from the "air" associated with it. The countryside is primarily mountainous, the inhabitants poor. Both county and town were originally called **Derry** until 1609, when the O'Neills were driven out by the English and their lands granted to the Corporation* of London.*

London Library. The first and still the largest public library* in London,* located in St. James's* Square, established in 1840; the library is not public in the American sense but requires a yearly membership fee from its members, currently the equivalent of about $150 per year if you take books home. *See also* British Museum.

London pride. A small plant with small pink flowers that is noted for growing in rocky or unpromising soil.

London School of Economics. *See* LSE.

London Town. *See* Town.

London University. Founded in 1836 as an institution with no official religious requirements, it affiliated with the existing University College* (which had previously called itself London University) and King's College.* Over the next decades, it gradually affiliated with a number of other existing institutions in the immediate London* area. The main building of the university* is in Bloomsbury* near the British Museum,* but the individual schools* and colleges* are still scattered all over London. It has gained a high academic reputation and is spreading its social influence as well, if more slowly, due to its willingness to except large numbers of students who could never afford to attend or would never be accepted by Oxford* or Cambridge,* exemplified by its being the first university to admit women (1878) on an equal basis. Of all the eccentric universities, it is the most eccentric, each of its individual components operating as if *sui generis*. *See also* Bedford; LSE; Slade; St. Thomas's Hospital.

London Zoo. Located in Regent's Park,* one of the oldest and largest zoos in the world, basically the model that all zoos followed since its opening in 1830 with animals brought by members of the Zoological Society and from royal menageries formerly at Windsor* and the Tower.* In the nineteenth century its star was Jumbo the Elephant, whose name coined the term, and in the twentieth its pair of pandas, but its quantity of animals is rivaled by few other world zoos. In 1991, budgetary and political constraints began to threaten its very existence, and its future suddenly has come into serious doubt.

long odds. In racing,* the odds for the heavy favorite, very different from the American long shot.

long off. *See* off.

long on. *See* on.

long stop. In cricket,* the fielder at greatest distance directly behind the wicketkeeper;* his primary role is to prevent any balls the wicketkeeper misses from rolling so far away that runs can be scored. From that it is often used to mean the last chance or last resort to block something, such as a law or a project.

long vac. (1) Long vacation; specifically, the three and one half month break between summer term* and winter term at Oxford* or Cambridge.* Many other students use the terminology for their summer holiday, which is not so long. Also called **long hols**. (2) In law courts, before 1873 the long break between law court terms from June 12 to November 2. The idiom is still used by legal people for the summer vacation, but it is no longer so long.

Long Water. The portion of the Serpentine* contained within the boundaries of Kensington Gardens* in London.*

loo. (1) A toilet, and the room with the toilet, a respectable euphemism probably corrupted from the French "l'eau," simultaneously a bit pretentious and a bit cutesy, but nonetheless probably the most widely used spoken term in use for the object in the twentieth century. *See also* bathroom; lavatory; outhouse; littlest room; WC. (2) An apparently simple but potentially very expensive gambling card game. Any number can play, but usually five or six participate. Each player is dealt only three cards, plus one blind hand; players starting on the left can play, drop out, or exchange for the blind hand. All that do not drop out must follow suit or trump whenever possible, and winners of any tricks split the pot according to the number of tricks taken. The pot of any size is initially paid in by the dealer, but it is replaced by (a) any player who doesn't follow suit properly; or (b) anyone who didn't drop out and yet didn't win a trick (is looed). As there are only three tricks, games of many players may have many losers, each of whom must match the previous pot; when this has happened a few times, the pot may soon grow to many times its original size, and a game that started out with minor stakes could become quite expensive. The appearance of simplicity and the wild swings in size of the pot made this an extremely popular game from the Restoration until at least WWI, especially in gentlemen's clubs.* Those playing at house parties for recreation, as they do in *Pride and Prejudice*, kept the competition friendly by setting a limit so that pots couldn't get out of hand, in which case it served much the same function as the modern American penny-ante poker. (The name has nothing to do with #1 above but rather comes from the French *lanturlu*, an interjection indicating scorn or contempt, perhaps often spoken by losers from whom the pre-Restoration exiles learned the game.)

look-in. An opportunity or chance to participate, as in "I couldn't get a look-in for that job."

loop, up the. Military slang for crazy.

Lord. Technically, the title of a baron,* who is always referred to as Lord Such-and-So, never Baron Such-and-So; also used for a bishop,* who is officially the Lord Bishop of Somewhere. The title is also given to sons or brothers of a duke* (as Lord Peter Wimsey) or marquess,* and also for some special cases such as Lord Mayor* of London.* This is properly a form of address, as in Lord Frilby, and not an identification, as in "Frilby is a Lord;" for this, the actual rank is preferred. A Lord is a peer* of the realm and as such automatically has a seat in the House of Lords,* which includes all persons of the rank of baron or higher. This is all complicated somewhat by the form of address **My Lord**, which is used when speaking to any baron, earl,* viscount,* or marquess, or to a bishop. In addition, it is accepted usage in newspapers and daily conversation to refer to any nobleman as Lord So-and-So, no matter what his actual rank. Thus, references to Lord Argyll, who is a duke, or to Lord Norbury, an earl, may be seen alongside those to Lord Olivier, who was a life peer* or baron; the distinguishing point between the baron, who is always Lord Something, and others who are called Lord in this journalistic and spoken convenience is that the higher ranks never use family names but are always Lord (Place name of their official title). *See also* Honourable, The; Lady; noble; peer.

Lord, First. *See* First Lord.

Lord Chamberlain. The official who supervises the royal household* and is responsible for all ceremonial functions. Until 1968 he also acted as official censor for all plays before their public productions.

Lord Chancellor. *See* Chancellor.

Lord Chief Justice. The chief judge* of the High Court.*

Lord Haw-Haw. Not a comic stereotype but rather the name used for William Joyce, actually an Irish-American, who during WWII did radio propaganda broadcasts for Germany in English. The name comes from the peculiar accent he affected based on American perceptions of upper-class* speech.

Lord High Steward. In the medieval era, a representative of the monarch who presided over his own court of justice. After Henry IV, they were appointed only for special cases. *See also* Lord Steward; steward.

Lord Lieutenant. Originally, a nobleman who acted in place of the monarch for specific duties, most often commanding the county* militia. Under Elizabeth I he became the official representative of the Crown* in all county affairs; with the growth of modern county councils* and a standing army,* the position has declined into an almost completely ceremonial role.

Lord Mayor. The mayor* of the City* of London,* not actually a Lord.* The title is also now used in more than a dozen other cities but is purely ceremonial and carries no more powers than a plain mayor.

Lord Privy Seal. *See* Privy Seal.

Lord's. Britain's largest cricket* stadium, located in London* just west of Regent's Park,* the site of most significant matches. The name comes not from the number of Lords* who played there, but from Thomas Lord, who built it. *See also* Oval.

Lords. The House of Lords.*

Lordship. *See* Your Lordship.

Lords of the Admiralty. The heads of the Admiralty* in a system unusual even by British standards. There were six of these operating in committee: One was a member of the government,* usually called the **First Lord** (and like Sir Joseph Porter he need never go to sea); one was an actual Lord;* the other four were naval officers, called the **Sea Lords.*** They held responsibility for the navy* but none of them actually commanded anything.

Lord Steward. The officer of the royal household* responsible for the servants* within the household, in modern days a sinecure whose functions are actually carried out by a professional administrator. *See also* Lord High Steward.

lorry. What Americans call a truck. Something stolen is often said to have **fallen off a lorry**. An **articulated lorry** would be what Americans call a semi or a semi-trailor truck.

lost property. What Americans call the lost and found.

Lothian. The region* or county* of Scotland* around Edinburgh,* formed from the primarily urban and suburban areas of the former Midlothian* in the reorganizations of 1973.

loud-hailer. What Americans call a bullhorn.

lough. In Ireland,* a lake. *See also* loch.

lounge. A room for sitting and relaxing, originally used in the nineteenth century in public buildings such as hotels for the room just off the main lobby where guests could meet and chat, but quickly applied to a communal parlour* used by lodgers in boarding houses. By the late twentieth, however, this had transferred into the home, where it is now used to mean the room where the family sits to relax, watch television, et cetera. This seems to be in process of replacing parlour or sitting room* completely, except in those homes large enough to have two separate rooms, one for family and one for guests, in which case the lounge is what Americans usually call the den or family room.

lounge bar. *See* pub.

lounge suit. A nonformal men's suit; originally in the late nineteenth century implying something casual as might be worn in the lounge,* it has remained in the twentieth as a general term for almost any suit.

Low Church. The clergy within the Church of England* who tend to downplay or ignore church ritual and decoration and thus tend toward the more puritanical or fundamentalist interpretations of doctrine. *See also* evangelical; High Church.

lower-class. This is primarily an American term, not a British one; I have used it as a matter of convenience in many of the entries to indicate the large number of groups that lie at the lower end of the social scale, generally including all levels of the working class and the several lower reaches of the middle class as well, such as low-ranking office workers, shop assistants,* traveling salesmen, minor shopkeepers,* et cetera, who would consider themselves middle class but who share many working class customs and linguistic habits and who are generally looked down upon by other members of the genuine middle class. For more details, *See* Appendix III.

Lowlands. In Scotland,* the southern and southeastern portion of the country, so called because it is somewhat less elevated and much less rough and rocky than the Highlands.* While most of the paraphernalia of Scottish romance comes from the Highland clans,* the bulk of Scottish life and culture has grown up in the Lowlands, which over the centuries fought with both the Highlanders and the English in the border country in about equal proportions. *See also* Border; Dumfries; Fife; Lothian.

Low Sunday. The Sunday* after Easter,* so called because nothing much happens.

Loyal Opposition. *See* Opposition.

£.s.d. Money, from the old method of listing prices or accounts in three columns of pounds* (£), shillings* (s), and pence* (p). Pronounced like the drug LSD. *See also* Appendix I.

LSE. London School of Economics, founded by the Webbs in 1895 and from the first associated with economists of a socialist bent.

Ltd. Limited Liability Company, a business in which the personal liability of its investors is carefully limited by law, similar to the American corporation. Recent laws have made PLC* the more common contemporary term. *See also* corporation.

lucky dip. A form of the game Americans call grab bag, usually played at fêtes* and similar charity bazaars; small gifts or toys are hidden in a large tub of bran, and people reach in to find one. Hence, used metaphorically like the American "luck of the draw."

Ludgate Circus. Originally a gate in the western wall of the medieval City* of London,* named for the ancient King Lud, now the east end of Fleet Street.*

Ludlow. A small town in Shropshire* near the Welsh border, with some medieval fame in the wool trade but declining into a reasonably typical small town; the Ludlow fair* made famous by Housman's poem had nothing to distinguish it from hundreds of other such fairs, except the Shropshire Lad's proximity.

ludo. A children's board game similar to Parcheesi.

luggage. This is never used interchangeably with baggage; to the British, a **baggage** is a loose young woman. The **luggage van** is the railway carriage Americans called the baggage car.

lumber. As a noun, useless stuff that you cannot bring yourself to throw out. The wood pieces Americans call lumber are usually called timber.* To be **lumbered** is to be stuck with, as in "lumbered with a mother-in-law."

lumber room. *See* boxroom.

lumme. Pronounced lummy, a corruption of love me, used as a general interjection of surprise, primarily among Cockneys.*

lump. (1) Originally, a lump of sugar* was simply a small piece broken off the large lump called a **loaf** in which all sugar was sold, and thus was relatively random in size. The spread of tea* shops encouraged a standardized size and shape, which is like what Americans call sugar cubes. (2) Modern labor slang for casual workers, perhaps from lumpen proletariat.

lunch/luncheon. As in America, a meal eaten at midday. However, there is a significant class* factor to the usage, as most people in the lower portion of the social scale refer to the midday meal as dinner.* Before about 1850, however, lunch was used for what is now called elevenses,* a light snack (such as the ploughman's lunch*) taken between breakfast and dinner, which was usually around 3:00. When, for various reasons, people at the upper end of the scale moved their main meal to the evening in mid–nineteenth century, lunch became somewhat mc:e than a snack and moved to a time near 1 P.M.. In the twentieth, many pubs* also offered food, now called a **pub lunch** and usually consisting of sandwiches and pies,* accompanied of course by beer.* *See also* meals.

luncheon voucher. A benefit given by many employers, a voucher (or coupon) that can be exchanged for restaurant meals.

LWT. London Weekend Television, one of the TV networks sharing ITV.*

lying-in hospital. A hospital or clinic devoted primarily to maternity care.

Lyme Regis. A small port and seaside resort on the southeast coast of England,* especially popular in the nineteenth century. Louisa is injured jumping from a long harbor wall there called the **Cobb** (which still exists) during an excursion in Austen's *Persuasion*, and its continued popularity throughout the century made it a logical primary setting for Fowles's re-creation of Victorian mores in *The French Lieutenant's Woman*.

Lyons. *See* Corner House.

M

M. Indication of a motorway,* similar to the American freeways. On some routes, M roads duplicate or widen the A* roads and take their number, while in other cases, they are completely new roads with new numbers. Speed limit on M roads is currently 70 mph. The ones most likely to be mentioned are those that emanate from London,* which include: **M1**, the principal route north through the Midlands* to Leeds;* **M3**, southwest to Southampton;* **M4**, west to Bristol;* **M11**, northeast to Cambridge;* **M25**, a giant ring road* that circles Greater London;* **M40**, west to Oxford.* The other principal route is the M5/M6 running the length of the western border of England,* with **M6**, from Gretna Green* on the Scottish border through Manchester* to Birmingham* and **M5** continuing south from there to Exeter.*

MA. *See* degree.

Ma'am. Originally, this shortened form of madam* was used as a respectful form of address to any woman of equal or superior rank who was entitled to be addressed as My Lady. By mid-to-late nineteenth century, however, it had been dropped from much daily life and was said mostly by servants.* Nonetheless, it continues to be the proper way to address the Queen* or a princess;* after the initial address of "Your Majesty" or "Your Royal Highness," one continues by saying, "Yes, Ma'am," et cetera.

mac. A mackintosh.*

Mac-. As a prefix, in Scotland* and some parts of Ireland,* this theoretically means "son of." However, in practice, it means "descended from"; Donald MacDougal's son is still MacDougal, not MacDonald, the prefix indicating that they are both descended from the original Dougal who founded the MacDougal clan.*

macadam. *See* tarmac.

machair. On the western shore in Scotland,* light sand that is arable.

mackerel sky. High, small, and fleecy clouds, a sign of good weather coming.

mackintosh. What Americans call a raincoat; technically, this is a raincoat made of rubberized cotton, named for its inventor, but few people are technical when using the term. *See also* Burberry.

mad. Almost always still used to mean crazy or insane rather than angry. However, someone who is **mad on** something is what Americans call "crazy about" and is not really insane, just enthusiastic.

madam. A title of address for an elderly or married woman, used as a sign of respect rather than of genuine social rank, and declining during the twentieth century into something a salesclerk would say, often pronounced moddom, to flatter a customer or that people in general would use sarcastically about someone who is stuck-up. *See also* Ma'am; Mrs.

made to measure. Of clothing, made to the customer's measurements, as opposed to ready-made.* *See also* bespoke.

Mafeking. A small town in South Africa, unknown until the siege during which a British army* unit was trapped there during the Boer* War. The **Relief of Mafeking** (when reinforcements finally released the British, on May 17, 1900) was not particularly significant in a military sense, but the siege had been so played up by the newspapers* in Britain's first media-covered war that it was greeted by the British public with celebrations and rejoicing unmatched in British history, making **mafficking** a new term for drunken celebrating.

magdalen. Pronounced magdalin, a fallen woman who has repented and reformed, an especially common term in the nineteenth century. **Magdalen Hospital** in Southwark,* now defunct, aimed to reform prostitutes.

Magdalen. Pronounced maudlin, a college* at Oxford,* generally seen as one of the more progressive. **Magdalen Hall** was a separate college* until it burned down in 1820; its students were absorbed into Hertford.*

Magdalene. Pronounced maudlin, a college* at Cambridge.*

magistrate. A judge in a local court* dealing with minor criminal offenses, equivalent in the courtroom to a Justice of the Peace* but with no other ceremonial or political duties outside the court. In practice, they deal with as much as 97 percent of the criminal cases of the nation (from theft and assault down to traffic offenses, drunk cases, etc.) and refer more serious crimes to a higher court; most of their cases are decided by three magistrates together and without a jury.* Magistrates are unpaid, although they do receive expense money; thus, they are usually from the local gentry* (often women—about 35 percent currently) or retired officers* rather than lawyers or other persons with legal training. In London* and some other areas with very active courts, some magistrates are paid to serve full-time and try their cases alone. Magistrates also have some minor civil law duties, primarily issuing local orders to enforce county court decisions. *See also* judge; justice; petty sessions; police court.

Magna Carta. A charter* signed by King John in 1215 guaranteeing certain "rights" to the barons* and to the churchmen. It was for the most part ignored and nearly forgotten until the seventeenth century, when it was rediscovered as a precedent for limiting the rights of the monarch; it has since come to be seen as one of the fundamental documents of English freedoms.

magpie. A black and white bird similar to a small crow or a jay with a long tail, living year round in Britain as in much of Europe, with a song that sounds like a loud chuckle; hence, the common association with chattering.

maid. (1) An unmarried woman or teenaged girl, more specifically a virgin, same as a **maiden**. Hence, a **maid of honor** is the same as a lady-in-waiting* except that she is unmarried. (2) A female servant,* probably from the general requirement that such servants would be unmarried. A **lady's maid** is the personal servant of a woman, a female equivalent of the valet.* Most other maids take their title from their place of principal duty; thus: A **chamber maid** works in the bedrooms of a house* or hotel; the **parlour maid** works in the parlour* (in its dining room sense), waiting on table at meals when no male servants are available for such duty; the **scullery maid** works in the scullery* and thus cleans pots and pans. A **housemaid**, however, works in any part of the house but the kitchen, in larger establishments working only in the non-bedroom areas; a home with only one servant would usually call that servant a housemaid rather than just a maid, but she is also sometimes called a **maid of all work**, with both kitchen and household duties. *See also*; nurse; skivvy; slavey; tweeny.

Maida Vale. A street in London* to the west of Regent's Park,* developed with villas* during the nineteenth century, since augmented by numerous blocks* of flats* but continuing its association with the upper–middle class.*

maiden. (1) A female virgin; *See* maid. (2) In cricket,* an over* in which the bowler* prevents any runs from scoring.

Maidenhead. A small town on the Thames* to the west of London,* during the 1930s the most fashionable of all riverside resort spots and still a popular resort area for people coming out from the city for sports along the river, due to the idyllic riverside scenery in the area.

Maiden Lane. A short street in London* parallel to the Strand,* since at least the seventeenth century containing restaurants and pubs* popular with the literary and theatrical communities.

maiden speech. The first speech made by a new member* of Parliament.* In the House of Commons,* this is the one speech all members present agree to actually listen to.

maid of honour. *See* maid.

mail. *See* post.

Mail. A daily newspaper,* generally read by the lower–middle class;* the paper has bragged that its politics have not changed since its founding in 1900, a combination of jingoism, union-bashing, and social conservatism. In the 1980s, a *Mail on Sunday* also began publishing, aimed at the same market.

mains. The electricity supplied through the socket in the wall. The term is also used for the main lines of all utilities, such as the gas mains or water mains, but in these cases it applies only to the large pipes outside the house. With electricity, it is used as a general term for all electric power, as in "plug it into the mains," and a home that has electric power is said to be **on the mains**. *See also* drains; plug; points.

maintenance. A payment to an ex-spouse after a divorce,* what Americans usually call alimony.

maisonette. Technically, an apartment sharing a building with only one other apartment. In general, this originally meant an apartment in a house, the remainder of which was used by the householder, but occupying parts of two floors (as opposed to a flat*) and with its own private entrance. In

recent years, however, it might be applied to almost anything, the French*
sound implying something a bit more attractive than a mere flat.

maize. *See* corn.

Majesty, Her/His/Your. Formal title and proper form of address when
speaking to or of the King* or Queen;* no one else is ever properly called
Your Majesty. *See also* Highness, His/Her/Your.

major. (1) Before WWI, an army* officer* who acted as an aide and
assistant to the regimental colonel,* a person with much responsibility but
little authority as he still ranked below the lieutenant-colonel(s). In reorganizations just before the war, however, companies* were expanded and
most were commanded by majors rather than captains.* Thus, the major
was something of an anomalous character—in the days of purchased commissions* he was not quite the social cream; after the 1870s reforms he
was a frustrated failure, a man without a real command. In WWI, however,
this changed somewhat, as the new command structure clearly identified
him with actual fighting and any self-respecting member of the gentry*
who was not a career soldier could be expected to reach the rank if he
survived long enough. Thus the major has had a strange career in literature,
where this is the most common rank found among ex-military gentry. Most
bogus officers in stories claim to be majors (as in the American South they
claimed to be colonels), as do ex-officers of dubious character, from Dickens's Major Bagstock to the present, because it was a rank high enough
to impress civilians but not so high anyone important might be expected
to know him personally or check his claims. After WWI, however, writers
liked to make their heroes majors, as it implied just the right touch of
authority and heroism in the trenches (Peter Wimsey was a major). But
perhaps most often the major is the pigheaded opinionated blusterer, the
epitome of the retired military man whose recommendation for every social
ill is a "spot of discipline," a man frustrated by a career that stopped dead
only part way up the ladder. (2) *See* minor.

majority. In British elections,* a simple plurality. In elections for Parliament,* there are often candidates from three or more parties,* but there
is no requirement that the winner get 50.1 percent of the vote; if he or she
does, this is called a **clear majority**.

make over. Not to completely re-do but rather to leave in a will.

make up. Prepare, as in "make up a prescription." In general, it is not
used in the American sense of imagining or inventing, as in "make up
stories."

Mall. In London,* the large avenue running from Buckingham Palace* to Trafalgar Square.* Pronunciation usually rhymes with pal rather than with ball. It was first laid out by Charles II as a site for the game of Pall Mall,* hence its name; actually completed as a street* only in 1910, it is most often associated with ceremonial processions related to royalty.* Most of the social and governmental buildings along it actually front on the older parallel Pall Mall. This is the only common usage; at least so far, the British have not yet succumbed to the American shopping mall, although by the late 1980s more than 200 were under construction around the country, most including and financed by Sainsbury's.*

Malteser. A chocolate candy, small and round, similar to American chocolate malted milk balls.

Malvern. A small range of hills in western England* near the Welsh border, noted primarily for a number of clear springs, attractive scenery for walkers, and a modern music festival devoted primarily to Elgar, who lived in the area. In the eighteenth century, it was a popular spot to "take the waters."

Man, Isle of. *See* Isle of Man.

man, my. A manservant, usually a valet;* never just man or the man, always my.

managing director. What Americans now call a CEO. *See also* director.

Manchester. A major city in northwestern England* just inland from Liverpool.* There was a medieval settlement here, but it had no impact until Arkright applied steam to his cotton mill there in 1783. The port of Liverpool provided the raw material, surrounding Lancashire* provided the coal, and almost overnight Manchester was "Cottonopolis," the world center of cotton milling; cotton textiles, for example, were **Manchester goods**, no matter where they actually came from. In the nineteenth century, it was amazingly rich, while also housing some of the worst slums in the world, the stimulus for Engels and practically all other English socialists. In the mid-twentieth century, however, it began to decline, as the mills faced worldwide competition, and it is now most often spoken of as a depressed area of high unemployment and no future, like all the rest of the North.* At its height, it was the epitome of Victorian independence, hard work, and self-help, exemplified by some of the first genuinely public art galleries, schools,* libraries, and the *Guardian** newspaper that managed to hold out against the London dailies until late in the twentieth century. Despite that, writers and artists have concentrated on the dark side of the city, and when it is mentioned, it is almost always as an illustration of the evils of industrialized society. **Manchester Grammar School** has a record of academic success for its pupils matched by only a handful of public schools* in the nation. **Manchester University** is perhaps the ugliest of all the redbrick universities,* but it is also one of the most respected; its students are nearly all commuters, but it has from its beginnings been especially strong in mathematics, economics, astronomy (*See* Jodrell Bank). *See also* Hallé; Peterloo.

Manchester School. (1) Not an educational community but a loosely connected group of economists and political theorists emerging from the Manchester* area during the 1840s. Their writings stressed the fundamental importance of free trade in economics and rejected imperialist aggrandizement in foreign policy; they had significant influence in the Liberal* party* at least until WWI. (2) A group of regional playwrights of the early twentieth century who concentrated on working class* and Midlands* subjects, the most noted being Brighouse, Houghton, and Monkhouse.

Manchester United. *See* United.

Mancunian. A native of Manchester.*

mandolin/mandoline. A vegetable slicer, usually a frame with several taut wires that make several slices at once.

mangel-wurzel. A beet but with a much larger root than the beet that is normally eaten, yellowish in color and used primarily as feed for livestock.

mangle. (1) A wringer, such as for squeezing water out of wet clothes. (2) A large presser for ironing clothes, in American laundries usually called a steam press.

man jack. *See* Jack.

mannequin. Not only a dummy in a store window but also a human fashion model. *See also* model.

manor. (1) In the medieval era, the land under the control of a particular lord;* part was the demesne* used for the lord's own cultivation and the rest those lands apportioned to tenants. Thus, the **lord of the manor** was the local lord with almost total authority in the life of the local resident, the idiom continuing into the present for someone in any field who has, or claims to have, wide-ranging authority. The **manor house**, naturally enough, was the lord's house on the manor, the largest house in the local area; as the manors declined in legal authority by the nineteenth century, manor house gradually came to mean any large country house* with significant grounds, although the term is still for the most part reserved for such a house owned by an actual nobleman and as such is often used symbolically for all the remains of the British class* system. (2) In slang, often used to mean the equivalent of the American "my turf," especially by policemen who unofficially refer to their districts as beats or manors.

manse. In Scotland,* the home of a minister,* like a vicarage* but usually implying even greater frugality and restraint.

mansion. Originally, a separate part within a larger house, like apartments,* and as such used in the King James Bible: "In My Father's house are many mansions." But even by then, mansion was beginning to change to mean a large expensive house, as it is commonly used in America. But the older meaning held on in some specific usages, so that during the Victorian* era, developers of very large buildings with multiple flats* called them So-and-so Mansions, implying both separate apartments and something swank. As with all real estate terms, the name immediately was cheapened, but it is still used in the twentieth century, as in mansion block.*

mansion flat. *See* flat.

Mansion House. Since 1753, the official residence of the Lord Mayor* of London,* located across the street from the Bank of England.*

Manx. Native of or to the Isle of Man.*

Marble Arch. A triumphal arch in London,* built in 1828 near Buckingham Palace* then rebuilt in 1851 at the northeast corner of Hyde Park* on the old site of Tyburn* gallows. Cars drive around it rather than through it.

Marches. Technically, any border, but usually this identifies the territory along the border between England* and Wales,* subject to much rebellion, warfare, and outlawry, as in *Henry IV*, and noted as a place for wild people, primarily along the borders of modern Shropshire.*

marchioness. *See* marquess.

mare's tail sky. Long, thin cirrus clouds, indicating a coming storm.

Margate. A resort town at the far eastern tip of the southeastern knob of England* that points to France. One of the very first seaside resorts, it became fashionable in the eighteenth century when a local resident invented the first "bathing machine" and the gentry* sailed down the Thames* from London* to visit there. It continues to be one of the most popular of all English seaside resorts, with gentle seas and pleasant temperatures as well as convenience to London, but that very popularity gives it something of a low reputation; Baedeker* called it "Cockneyfied" in 1906, and it is still known as a place for lower-class holiday making.

marie biscuit. *See* biscuit.

mark. (1) In cooking, a temperature indication. Many British ovens, made to be sold in both Fahrenheit Britain and in Centigrade Europe, come with a series of standardized temperature markings rather than detailed gauges; mark 6 is 400°F., for example, 7 is 425°, et cetera. Sometimes stated as **Regulo** 6, et cetera, from a brand name for the thermostatic control. (2) There was never a coin of this name, but until at least 1770 the term was used in many financial transactions, based on the standard European weight of a mark (reflected in modern German currency), which in England was generally understood to be 160 pence.* *See also* Appendix I. (3) *See* marks.

mark, beside the. Not to the point, not relevant.

market. A regular gathering of sellers of various items, usually in the open air. Traditionally, this was the place at which the producer sold direct to a wholesaler or to an individual customer, so most were agricultural in nature, selling produce, animals, et cetera. However, many markets also developed for trader's goods, such as cloth or manufactured items. Eventually, of course, most towns with markets managed to support shops* that are open daily, so markets shifted their emphasis to bargains, and now the term generally means a regular open air collection of trader's stalls;* some of these, such as Portobello Road* or Petticoat Lane* in London,* have become major tourist attractions, while others simply allow the small independent trader to squeeze a living from cheap clothes, secondhand goods, and novelty items. In village names, such as Market Deeping, this indicates a medieval site of a regular market, which may no longer exist in the modern village. *See also* fair; market town.

market cross. A stone cross erected at the site of a market* rather than in a churchyard. Sometimes these were simply crosses but in many places they were rather elaborate affairs erected underneath a stone canopy that could also be used for temporary shelter.

market garden. What Americans usually call a truck farm.

market town. In England,* a town* legally authorized to hold a market.* Such authorization usually dates to the medieval era.

marks. What Americans call grades, as in school reports.* This can be used the way we use points, as in "6 marks out of 10," or as **full marks**, meaning the highest possible grade or, metaphorically, praise or credit of any kind. Similarly, Britons tend to say mark when Americans would say point, as in "You get one mark for trying."

Marks and Sparks. Slangy nickname for Marks and Spencer.*

Marks and Spencer. A chain of department stores begun from a single stall* in 1884, now with hundreds of stores all over the nation. Like many British department stores, they also sell food, especially an extremely popular line of frozen meals and party foods, as well as clothes. They are as ubiquitous as Sears in America but serve a clientele a notch or two up the social scale, the primary store of the modern British middle class* and for certain basic items not subject to fashion whims, such as underwear, almost the only retail outlet trusted by the general public. *See also* Harrods; Selfridge's.

Marlborough. Technically **Marlborough College**, a public school* founded in 1843 in the town of Marlborough in Wiltshire.*

Marmite. A brand of spread used on toast or in sandwiches, something like apple butter in looks and consistency but made from yeast essence.

marquee. A very large tent, used particularly for wedding* and garden parties* and for refreshment areas at fêtes.*

marquess. Pronounced MARkwiss, the rank of the nobility* between duke* and earl.* His wife is a marchioness. As a practical matter, the Marquess of So-and-so is usually called Lord* So-and-So; thus the Marquess of Marchmain in *Brideshead Revisited* is also Lord Marchmain, his wife Lady Marchmain. Sons are called Lord (Family name), daughters Lady, so Sebastian is Lord Sebastian Flyte, the sisters Lady Julia and Lady Cordelia. (The eldest son is however usually given a courtesy title* of some other minor title also held by the father, so Sebastian's brother is called Brideshead, as the Earl of Brideshead). Marquesses are quite rare, less than forty still remaining.

marquis. An alternate spelling of marquess.*

marriage. Marriage customs and legal arrangements have been quite complex over the years, reflected, often to the confusion of the modern reader, in the literature. In the medieval era, marriage was a property* exchange or a simple agreement between couples with no property, did not require

either church or state validation, and could be dissolved by either party.
Only slowly did the Catholic Church introduce the idea of marriage for
life, and it formally required a priest only in 1563, by which time Henry
VIII had already formed the Church of England,* so the English paid little
or no attention to such Popish practice. In Shakespeare's day and during
the Restoration, the primary purpose of marriage was widely understood
to be the production of an heir and protection or increase of the family
property. A church marriage normally required several steps: a legal contract between parents; the spousals, an exchange of oral promises between
the couple in front of witnesses; banns,* which could be avoided by a
special license* for the wealthy; the wedding* itself; consummation. But
the couple was considered to be legally bound at the spousals stage, and
many, if not most, people, never bothered with any of the other steps,
except of course, the consummation. Thus, many Elizabethan and Restoration plays end without the appearance of a priest—Shakespeare's Rosalind is legally married to Orlando when she gives herself before the
witnesses, as are, for all practical purposes, Congreve's Mirabell and Mil-
lamant when they agree to her contract. In addition, it was illegal for the
clergy to perform marriage except at certain times and places, but since
there were so many exceptions, and since any public formal promise was
considered binding anyway, many poor or unscrupulous clergy performed
quick marriages for money, particularly in London where there was also
a tax on wedding ceremonies. Shakespeare's Martext may be one of these
(or his willingness to act so suddenly may be a leftover from the medieval
habits of the countryside).

These practices all changed in 1753, when Parliament* at last passed a
Marriage Act, binding in all points only in England* and Wales.* The most
significant points were the requirement of a Church of England* wedding,*
its recording in the parish* register, and parental consent for all persons
under twenty-one. This removed the validity of all "secret marriages," as
the parish register made them public. It also made the threat of disinher-
itance for marriage without parental consent quite genuine, providing one
of the major themes of eighteenth- and nineteenth-century literature. Since
Scotland* was not covered by the Act, it still accepted many of the older
forms of marriage; until 1940, two persons could be married there (after
1856 subject to twenty-one-days residence for one of the pair) by simply
declaring to witnesses their desire to be married, which almost instantly
made the elopement to Gretna Green* for young people without their
parents' consent a part of English folklore. The new law also closed most
opportunities for divorce.* The Marriage Act of 1837 moved the actual
registration of the marriage to a Civil Registrar, also called the Registry,*
in effect legalizing marriages performed in Catholic or nonconformist
churches, which had been legally nonbinding prior to that date unless
repeated in a Church of England service, and also allowed nonreligious

weddings at a local register office.* Currently, almost half of all marriages
are performed at register offices. In 1971, the age at which parental consent
was no longer required was changed to eighteen.

As Americans have come to see marriage as an arrangement for personal
gratification and fulfillment, with family as a postponable by-product, it
becomes harder for us to understand the British attitudes that continued
well into the 1980s. Even in the twentieth century, British marriage has
been aimed primarily at economics and children—men did not and do not
marry until able to independently support a family at the levels required
by their class* and, despite the modern belief in nineteenth-century child-
brides, analyses of parish records show the mean age for first-time brides
has never dropped below twenty-five. The long courtships of nineteenth-
century literature are not so much the result of sexual reticence as purposeful economic delay. One unusual by-product was the large number of
women who spent ten or more years in the workforce, in the mills or as
servants.* The curious thing from a modern view is that sex seems to have
been postponed through all levels of society; illegitimacy rates in the nineteenth century in a society without contraceptives or abortion ran between
4 percent and 7 percent (by comparison, in the United States currently
about one in four children are born out of wedlock), although about one
in five brides were apparently pregnant at the time of the wedding.

Within the marriage, in theory, all property belonged to the husband.
However, almost all parents with significant property arranged not only
dowries* but also made **marriage settlements**, which were like modern
prenuptial agreements that provided guaranteed income and property in
trust for the woman independent of her husband's wishes. In 1870, a law
allowed wives to keep all wages earned for themselves, and another in
1882 allowed them to keep property owned prior to the marriage and to
acquire property in their own name after marriage. However, as divorce
initiated by the woman was, for all practical purposes, impossible until
1937, these changes made little difference in the daily life of most married
couples. *See also* wedding.

marriage lines. What Americans call a marriage certificate.

marron glacé. Chestnuts glazed with sugar.

marrow. What Americans usually call a squash or a large zucchini; sometimes called **vegetable marrow** to distinguish it from bone marrow.

marshal. An officer of the royal household* in the medieval era, originally
supervising military affairs. *See also* Earl Marshal; Field Marshal.

marshalling yard. On the railroads, the large yard where trains are assembled or disassembled, the main rail yard.

Marshalsea. A prison* in London* from the fourteenth century, actually on two different sites. The first, on Borough* High Street in Southwark,* was used for the prisoners convicted in the court of the Marshalsea (for crimes committed within twelve miles of the monarch's residence), after 1601 used primarily for debtors; it was burned down in the Gordon Riots,* rebuilt and renamed the King's Bench* in a site farther down the street, used until 1860. Meanwhile, a "New" Marshalsea Prison primarily for debtors was opened in 1811 on the site of the old county* jail, also on Borough High Street, and used until 1842; this is the Marshalsea of *Little Dorrit*.

martin. A bird closely related to the swallow, often called a **house martin** because it nests under the eaves of houses.

martini. Vermouth, from a popular brand, drunk straight; no gin* is mixed with it. However, pressure from American films and tourists has brought the American version of gin and vermouth into some use in the late twentieth century, and of course James Bond drinks a mixture of vodka and martini.

Martinmas. November 11, the Feast of St. Martin of Tours. In most parts of Britain, this was a quarter day* and thus was a major date for hiring fairs,* particularly since it also came near the end of harvest season. It was also a date on which livestock were slaughtered for curing for winter food to avoid the problem of feeding them through the winter months and thus was often associated with feasts and festivals. The feasting declined as the country became urbanized and stopped after other associations of Nov. 11 destroyed the desire for celebrations. *See also* Michaelmas; Remembrance Day.

Mary, little. A popular euphemism for the stomach, appearing in polite society before WWI and found for some time afterward among the more prim and proper. *See also* belly; tummy.

Marylebone. Actually **St. Marylebone** and usually pronounced marry-bun, the area of London* north of Oxford Street,* developed in the early eighteenth century and, although continually remodeled and rebuilt, a relatively expensive area of the city for all its life, including as it does Harley Street,* Lord's,* and some of the city's most attractive small squares. **Marylebone Road** runs through the center of the area, and **Marylebone Station** is a railway* terminus used primarily for short commuter runs to the west and an Underground* station in the area. *See also* Baker Street; Regent's Park; St. John's Wood; Wimpole Street.

mash. Mashed potatoes.*

master. (1) As a title, *See* Mister. In many homes with servants,* the son was often called the "young master," so that by the nineteenth century master was almost exclusively a formal title for a young boy; now that usage too has all but disappeared except in the most formal or pretentious occasions. (2) As a formal title, someone in charge, as in **Master of Hounds** for the person who runs a fox hunt;* at colleges* at Cambridge,* the person equivalent to a Provost,* Principal,* et cetera, at other colleges. (3) A teacher, especially in a public school.* (4) On a merchant ship, the captain; on a navy* ship, the person in charge of navigation. (5) In Scotland,* the eldest son of a baron* or viscount,* as in *The Master of Ballantrae.*

Master of the Rolls. The number two judge* in Chancery,* so called because he kept the actual records on rolls of parchment; in 1881, he became a judge on the Court of Appeal.*

masters, our. An ironic term used in the civil service* for the politicians in the government,* and sometimes also so used in the military.

match. In sports, a contest or game; there are football* or cricket* matches rather than football or cricket games. *See also* test.

mate. (1) A friend or associate, but implying much more: Used in the twentieth-century working class,* this indicates a man's buddy who shares all the same background and attitudes. This can be a lifelong friend, but it can also be "one of the guys" at the pub,* at the works,* on the football* club, or any other place where serious male bonding is supposed to occur. (2) On a ship, an officer ranking just below the ship's captain* or master.* Most merchant ships would have three mates—first, second, and third, with the second and third commanding specific watches* and the first either assisting or alternating with the captain in overall command. In the navy,* the rank is not used for officers,* with the persons carrying out similar duties usually called a lieutenant;* however, various assistants to warrant officers are called mates, such as the gunner's mate or the carpenter's mate, and the bosun* will have several mates who act as non-commissioned officers for each watch, like sergeants,* in the army.

matelote. A dish of fish in a sauce of onions and wine, usually pronounced MATalote.

matelow. A sailor, from the French, in use before 1900. Associations with Noel Coward's song often gave the term a suggestion of homosexuality of the "Hello, sailor" type, but the term also was used by navy* sailors themselves (usually pronounced matlow) as late as WWII without any such subtext.

mater. Pronounced mayter, mother, used only by the public school* class* and for the most part disappearing after WWII.

maternity benefit. British employers are now required to pay pregnant women for up to eighteen weeks of maternity leave (at less than full salary); maternity benefits are paid by the state to women who take maternity leave but have not worked for a single employer long enough to qualify for these payments. *See also* child benefit; single parent benefit.

maths. What Americans call math, anything to do with mathematics.

matinee jacket. A short coat or cardigan* for a baby.

matins. A morning service in the Church of England,* performed daily, but rarely attended except on Sunday, usually at 10:30 or 11:00. *See also* evensong.

Matron. (1) In a school,* the woman in charge of the daily care of resident children, almost never also a teacher. To whatever extent would be possible, she was expected to stand in for nanny,* if not for mother, when the children were at school and is usually depicted as a middle-aged woman of forbidding features and attitudes, much given to regimentation. Very few public school* or prep school* stories or memoirs speak of Matron as a warm, kindly woman; most depicted could be army* sergeants* but for their gender. (2) In a hospital, the senior female supervisor, probably from the earlier public school usage. Sometimes this seems to be used interchangeably with Sister.* Neither of these is ever called *the* matron or matron So-and-so but is always addressed or discussed as if Matron were her only name.

Maundy. *See* Royal Maundy.

mavis. In Scotland,* a thrush.*

May Day. (1) May 1, the major spring festival in Britain as in most of Europe. Local customs varied enormously but generally included two basic points: trips to the woods before dawn, usually by maidens* of marriageable age, to collect flowering branches and make the garlands worn throughout the day (and sometimes hung on homes as well); and dancing and revelry among the whole village, often around a **maypole**, a tall straight tree trunk cut for the purpose and decorated with garlands and ribbons. The con-

nection with pagan spring fertility festivals was obvious but traditions were
so strong that neither the Catholic Church nor the Church of England*
made any serious attempts to stamp them out. However, the puritanical
Protestants saw them as pagan revelry, complaining in particular that the
number of virgins was considerably reduced between the time the girls
went to the woods in the morning and the dancing ended at night; Scotland*
outlawed them, despite large riots, in 1555, and England* followed suit in
1644. The maypole and May Day festivities were immediately reinstituted
after the Restoration, but declined again during the industrialization of
the eighteenth century, probably given their major death blow by the
calendar* change in 1752 that moved May 1 almost two weeks earlier,
making it almost impossible to find the flowers that motivated the celebrations to begin with. Curiously, the Victorians, in their search for a folk
past, revived the maypole and May Day celebration but converted it to a
children's festival carefully supervised by parish* parsons* and teachers
and purified of all alcohol, sex, and fertility symbols, preferring to see it
as a revival of the "Merrie Olde Englande" of popular fantasy. Modern
festivals follow this pattern, their separation from the ancient past underlined by their celebration on convenient Saturdays rather than on May
Day itself. The schoolgirl crowned as **May Queen** traces back only to
Ruskin; in the old days, she was a nubile young woman, often accompanied
by a young male **May King**. (2) In 1889, the Second Socialist International
designated May Day as an international Labor Day, and as such it is often
observed by Britain's more militant unions.* (3) The May Day bank holiday* was a reference to the old May Day, not to the labor celebration; it
is currently actually celebrated on the first Monday in May rather than
May 1 and, in recent years, has been formally called Spring Bank Holiday
to avoid suggestions of governmental support of socialism.

Mayfair. Since its first development in the early eighteenth century, the
most expensive and fashionable neighborhood of London.* Before that,
Mayfair named a site near modern Park Lane* that held the most licentious
and uncontrolled fair* in London. The area was first developed with great
mansions for wealthy aristrocats,* and by about 1800 the spaces were filled
in with a number of elegant terrace* houses occupied by practically all the
people who came from their country houses* for the Season* in town;
thus, Mayfair "Society" and English "Society" have been virtually synonymous for almost three centuries, with a Mayfair address the most prestigious a person could have. In the twentieth, many of those large houses
have been divided into flats,* and the stables in the mews* behind also
converted into housing, but these all remain extremely expensive. This is
the area east of Hyde Park* and north of Green Park,* including the areas
around Grosvenor Square* and Berkeley Square,* also containing some

of the most expensive and fashionable shops in the city in such areas as Saville Row* and Bond Street.*

mayor. The chairman of a council* in a borough;* as such, he (or sometimes she) is politically and socially significant at the local level but with little or no independent executive authority. *See also* alderman; Lord Mayor.

maypole. *See* May Day.

May Queen. *See* May Day.

May Week. In typical Cambridge* fashion, this is in fact two weeks in June, a time of parties, boat races, and general celebration marking the end of the academic year. *See also* Eights Week.

Maze. At Hampton Court,* a famous garden* with hedges planted in the form of a complex maze; although associated by most tourists with Henry VIII or Elizabeth I, it was actually added by William and Mary.

MBE. Member of the Order of the British Empire. *See* OBE.

MC. Military Cross.*

MCC. Marylebone Cricket Club,* the ruling body of cricket* since 1814. *See also* Lord's.

McNaughten rules. Sometimes **M'Naghten**, the guidelines used in criminal cases to determine insanity, based on the questions first used in the case of Daniel McNaughten, who tried to assassinate the Prime Minister* in 1843. The specific rules were changed in 1957, but the term is still often used.

MD. Mentally deficient, what Americans used to call retarded.

meadow. Technically, this is a field used to grow grass that will be mown for hay, almost always lying along a stream, as distinct from a pasture, which is grazed. Americans occasionally use the term, too, but for the most part mean a natural open area in the woods and instead use field where hay is grown.

meal. As in America, something to eat involving meat and a vegetable at least, but almost always used only in reference to an evening meal (for specific meals in the day, *See* meals). Since WWII the term has been used primarily by people on the cusp of a class,* as if unable or unwilling to risk calling the meal dinner,* supper,* or tea,* or by people cooking for themselves or eating alone. Also, the term is sometimes used to imply casualness—a man might ask a woman to join him "for a meal," which implies it is more a casual get-together that happens to include food than an official date for the entire evening, which would usually be called dinner. Or, in households with servants,* the servants would have only "a meal" when the master and mistress are away, thus signifying something simple like a chop* and a vegetable or two. To **make a meal** of something, by contrast, is to exaggerate it or magnify its importance by turning it into something complex or extensive. In restaurants, of course, meal continues to mean any full serving of food except breakfast, while a **set meal** is either a particular combination of foods and drink served at a fixed price or a single meal served to all customers. *See also* ordinary.

mealie. What Americans call corn; the term appeared in South Africa and is normally used only in African stories or for dishes brought back from there.

meals. Although most Britons eat on approximately the same schedule, the names used for the various meals vary significantly among classes,* especially in the twentieth century. In middle- and upper-class homes, the schedule has been: breakfast*—8:00 A.M. (earlier for schoolchildren or if father had a long commute); elevenses* at 11:00; luncheon* or lunch— 1:00; tea*—4:30; dinner*—7:30 (later for company; with young children given their own meal, often also called tea, earlier). In lower–middle class and working-class homes, the schedule is typically breakfast (timed to get father off to work), lunch or elevenses around 11, dinner about 1:00, and tea 5:30 to 6:30, timed to happen as soon as father gets home from work; some also have a snack called supper* before bedtime. Before the mid– nineteenth century, however, all classes ate their main meal in the middle of the afternoon, calling it dinner, and this was very often the only meal of the day; the army, for example, did not offer three meals until almost 1900, and even then the afternoon tea was little more than a snack. By American standards, the British have always eaten very frugally, despite the reports of Edwardian gluttony; since the early nineteenth, going hungry has been thought to "build character" at all levels of society, an attitude encouraged by twelve years of rationing.* *See also* meal.

mean. As in America, this can mean wicked or nasty, but it is used much more often to mean cheap or miserly.

means test. A check of personal finances made before certain governmentally paid benefits may be given to a recipient. The one causing the most political furore was the means test introduced in 1931 that paid unemployment* benefits only to those who had first exhausted their own savings, ended at last under the post-war Labour* government. However, some modern benefits, such as the family credit* and supplementary benefits,* are subject to means tests.

measure. As a noun, what Americans call a measuring cup.

meat safe. A cupboard for storing meat, usually distinguished from other cupboards by the screening on the doors.

Mecca. One of the largest chains of betting shops.*

meccano. A child's toy similar to the American Erector set.

mechanic. While Americans tend to use this only for repairmen, such as car mechanics, the British apply it to anyone who works with machines and thus to most factory workers as well.

Medical Officer. A public servant in charge of community health services.

Medway. A river in southeastern England* that forms a broad deep natural channel through the marshes and sandbanks of northeast Kent,* which made the towns along it natural harbors for the navy* until the mid–twentieth century. Although the river flows through the North Downs,* almost all references to it are to the harbors and the flat mysterious marshland around it that figures so vividly in the childhood portions of *Great Expectations*. *See also* Chatham; hulks; Rochester.

meet. Technically the gathering of riders and hounds* before a fox hunt* but usually meaning the hunt itself.

meeting. In horse racing,* several consecutive days of races at a single track.

member. (1) Although formally called a Member of Parliament,* this term is used only for the elected representatives in the House of Commons,* never for the members of the House of Lords,* who are, after all, Lords. A **private member**, more often called a back bencher,* is one who is not given a ministry* post and thus does "nothing" but serve a constituency* and provide dependable votes for the party.* Unlike American representatives, the members are first and foremost responsible to their party; there is no requirement that they reside in their constituencies or even know where the constituencies are. Nominations come from the party headquarters, and members thus do not establish themselves with the local public by working their way up from local elected offices as they do in America; similarly, members who are popular locally may be replaced by the party at the next election or moved to a completely different constituency. Unlike American congressmen, most MPs continue to hold an independent job, in part because the Commons itself still meets primarily in the evenings and in part because MPs are paid less than congressmen pay their aides (in 1991, less than £22,000, roughly $36,000 to $40,000). (2) At a college,* one of what Americans usually call the faculty. Technically, this also includes all graduates, as their degree* is their admission into membership in the community of scholars, but in practice the term is usually confined to the permanent scholars and teachers who are allowed to participate in the self-government of the college.

memsahib. *See* sahib.

menaces. In police charges, threats; thus, **demanding money with menaces** would be extortion.

ménage. (1) Like so many French* terms, often used to imply something not quite respectable. Technically, this is a household and is often used to mean just that, but it implies usually the household of an unmarried couple, a homosexual couple, or a married couple who lead wild or unconventional lives.

mend. As in America, this means to repair, but it is used far more often; where Americans tend to use mend only for small items, like clothing, the British may mend even something as large as a road.

Mendips. A small range of hills, noted for limestone caves, near the southwest coast of England* in Somerset.*

mental. In the early twentieth century, insane, but gradually also used to mean slow-witted, simpleminded, or particularly stupid as well; most commonly used with a modifier, as in "a bit mental," but can be used alone, as in "Don't go mental on me now."

mentioned in dispatches. A military honour* that involved no medal but was nonetheless highly prized. The term came from doing something so unusual or valuable that the commanding general* would mention the soldier by name in his official report. This was sufficiently rare to be noted permanently alongside an officer's* name in the Army List* and was (and is) an honour particularly cherished by the soldiers themselves.

Merc. Common nickname for the Mercedes automobile.

Mercantile Marine. Commercial shipping, what Americans call the Merchant Marine.

mercer. A dealer in textiles, particularly expensive textiles such as silk. In London,* the **Mercers** are the oldest of the livery companies* and first in precedence in City* activities. *See also* draper.

merchant. (1) A businessman who deals with business* rather than trade.* In general, this means either a large wholesaler or one who is engaged in foreign trading. Thus, merchants may be socially acceptable to those who shun all others in trade, so many shopkeepers* try to designate themselves as merchants, and the more successful retailers may be "promoted" to merchants for social events and honours.* (2) In slang, someone who is intensely involved in a particular activity, such as a **speed merchant**, who drives fast.

merchant bank. A private bank* that deals with securities and exchange, commercial loans, et cetera, rather than with checking and savings accounts, in America usually called an investment bank.

Merchants Adventurers. A trading company founded in 1407, by Shakespeare's time controlling the overwhelming majority of English foreign trade; the monopoly became so oppressive that it lost its charter in 1689.

Merchant Taylors. A livery company* in London,* one of the original twelve that governed the City,* noted now for its large guild hall dating to 1345. Merchant taylors (or tailors) are distinct from tailors in that they supply the goods used by the regular tailor to make clothing. The **Merchant Taylors' School** is one of the more significant public schools,* since 1561 educating urban boys not from gentry* families, with two branches, one moved from London* to the suburbs in 1932 and the other near Liverpool.*

Mercia. An ancient kingdom occupying the south-central area of modern England;* the term sometimes is used to refer to the general area.

mere. A small lake or pond, especially common in Norfolk.*

Mermaid. In Shakespeare's day, a tavern in London* noted primarily as a hangout for Shakespeare, Beaumont, Fletcher, and Sir Walter Raleigh. A modern theatre uses the name now, located in a converted warehouse in the City* near Blackfriars* Station, but the name is more significant to readers for the **Mermaid Plays**, the series of carefully edited, uncut reprints of sixteenth, seventeenth, and eighteenth century plays that changed these forgotten works into classics for modern readers, begun by Havelock Ellis in 1887.

Mersey. A river in northwest England,* with a particularly broad and deep mouth forming an estuary on which is the port of Liverpool.* The Mersey is lined with industrial communities, most either in cloth mills or the coal trade. Since WWII, as British industry has declined, the Mersey is often used symbolically for all the industrial decay and unemployment associated with the northwestern areas. *See also* Lancaster.

Merseyside. Since 1974, the urban county* containing Liverpool* and its immediate environs. *See also* Lancaster; Mersey.

Merton. A college* of Oxford;* this was Beerbohm's college, although *Zuleika Dobson* is set in an imaginary college.

Merton Park. *See* garden suburb.

mess. A group of people who regularly eat together. Originally, this meant the four people who shared the same dish at a banquet table and as such is still used among members of the Inns of Court.* The meaning expanded to mean any group, most commonly seen in the military but also used in such groups as judges* and barristers* on circuit,* public school* dining halls, et cetera. In the army* in particular, the mess is one of the most important social instruments, carefully dividing classes, with separate messes for officers,* sergeants,* and private* soldiers. For officers in particular, this was far more than just a place to eat; it was the place providing the major entertainments of daily life and the protector of all the regimental traditions and history. A **mess jacket** was originally a military uniform jacket worn for formal dinners* or balls in the mess, introduced around 1930 as an alternative to tails* in formal wear for civilian men. It was usually white or colored rather than black, cut like a tail coat with no tails and worn with a cummerbund; it was a fad only briefly, soon replaced by the white dinner jacket* for summer or more casual formal occasions, and is now associated in the popular mind primarily with stewards* and waiters. The **mess kit** was actually the kit,* or uniform, to be worn in the regular mess;* thus, a semiformal uniform, often a variation of the mess jacket for officers. However, mess kit has also been used as in the American army for the eating utensils carried by individual soldiers.

messrs. Abbreviation (usually without a period) of messieurs, which, though French,* is often used in business correspondence as a plural for Mr,* especially when referring to a partnership. When spoken, pronounced messers.

metalled. Of a road, paved. The term comes not from what is commonly thought of as metal but from a term for crushed stone used in the macadam* process.

metals. On a railway,* the rails.

Meteorological Office. The government service Americans call the Weather Bureau.

meter. (1) Until late in the twentieth century, most homes and flats* had coin-operated meters for gas and/or electricity. The individual dropped a coin, usually a shilling,* into the meter and received the service of the utility for a fixed number of watts or cubic feet, at which point the meter would shut off and the tenant would have to feed in another coin to restore service. Instead of reading the meter, the man from the utility would empty it. By the 1970s, the utilities began to convert most residences to American-style meters and bill the tenant on a regular basis. (2) *See* metre.

methadone. The British have used methadone as a legal substitute for heroin, providing it to addicts on prescriptions since the 1950s. While the program is criticized in some quarters because the methadone addict is not cured, just transferred, the majority of such addicts are able to maintain jobs and a normal-appearing daily life, and drug-related crime was non-existent by American urban standards until very recently.

Methodist. A nonconformist* sect growing out of the evangelical movement begun by John and Charles Wesley in 1738; it was often opposed by the Church of England,* although its ministers* did not formally withdraw from the Church of England until 1795. From the very beginning, the Methodists aimed at the lowest portions of society who had, for the most part, been ignored by the established church of the time, and they continue strongest among the working class* and in industrial areas. Over the next century Methodists separated into a number of different smaller sects, most of which recombined into the Methodist Church in 1932. They are still the largest of the nonconformist denominations and are thus the group most often meant by the term chapel.* In Wales,* the Methodist church developed simultaneously but independently, led by Anglican clergy who converted to evangelical forms of Presbyterian* worship, officially leaving the Church of England in 1811 and for most of the time since the largest denomination in Wales. Both groups are associated with evangelical conversions and a tradition of fine hymns and hymn singing.

meths. What Americans call wood alcohol, or sometimes Sterno; most commonly used about a **meths drinker**, an alcoholic so far gone he drinks this.

metre. The British have resisted the conversion to metric measurement perhaps even more emotionally than have Americans, but it hasn't helped. Further integration into the European Community will certainly mean eventual conversion to kilometre, litre, and metre, and most scientific and military applications have already converted in the years since WWII.

Metropolitan Board of Works. A central authority in the London* area from 1855, the first to attempt some kind of coordination among the various parishes* of the city, especially in sewage planning and control and in street lighting, paving, and cleaning. Eventually, it became obvious more was needed, and it was superseded by the London County Council* in 1888.

metropolitan county. *See* county.

Metropolitan Police. The police* force of London* (except for the City,* which has its own force organized at the same time). Organized in 1829, it was headquartered in Scotland Yard,* by which name it is much more often known, and its methods and organization were used as a model for all the other police forces eventually organized throughout the rest of the nation. *See also* bobby; commissioner; constable; inspector; PC; superintendent.

Metropolitan Water Board. From 1903–74, the local authority responsible for water supply and sewage in London,* replaced by the Thames Water Authority.*

mews. Originally, the alley that went behind a house to the stables in back. Since the appearance of the automobile, the stables and servants'* quarters overhead have been converted to housing, but as they were always in wealthy neighborhoods, it is quite fashionable to have a mews address. Some new developments that never saw a stable are now being called mews, particularly if they are in a cul-de-sac, to share in this status. *See also* alley.

Michaelmas. September 29. In the southern portions of England,* this is a quarter day,* somewhat earlier than in the northern areas that preferred Martinmas,* and as such, often accompanied both by hiring fairs* and by various local festivals. Traditionally, these feasts feature geese,* which are at their fattest in this season. A **Michaelmas daisy** is an aster that flowers about this time. For **Michaelmas term**, *See* term.

mick. An Irishman, from the ubiquity of Michael as an Irish name, for the most part not seen as particularly derogatory, except of course by the Irish.

mickey, take the. To tease or, more nastily, to insult in order to humiliate; often heard as "take the mickey out of." No one knows who mickey was, although the idiom only surfaced in the 1950s, but in the 1930s Cockeys* sometimes said **take the mike**, so it may ultimately be related to outdated rhyming slang.*

midday. Often used for noon.

midden. A garbage dump. Archaeologists in all countries are particularly fond of the term, as it makes the source of most of their findings sound better, but the British in general have been using the term since the medieval era and sometimes even mention a midden in the garden* that Americans would call a compost heap. *See also* tip.

middle class. This is a much more specific term in Britain than in America, where it usually means anybody with a job who earns less than a million dollars a year. For details as to this more specific meaning, *See* Appendix III. In the course of this work I have tried to use middle class in the British sense throughout.

Middle East. *See* East.

middle school. This is a tax-supported school* for those students in the middle, but there is no consistency about the ages taught. In some areas, the middle school follows infant school* and teaches ages eight to eleven, in others it is an early secondary school* that teaches those age eleven to thirteen, in others still it is a variant of these. Thus, it is never a clear equivalent of the American middle or junior high school. Relatively few exist and the number is in general declining. *See also* comprehensive; grammar school.

Middlesex. Originally, the home of the Saxons in the middle between Sussex,* Wessex,* and Essex.* After the Norman invasion, this became a county* or shire,* of which London* was the center. As the county of London, it was the most central of the Home Counties* but it was also most subject to London's suburban expansion, so that by the mid-twentieth century, most of the countryside* of Middlesex had disappeared, its villages now suburbs of the city. In 1965, Parliament* bowed to reality, and Middlesex formally disappeared, reorganized as Greater London.*

Middlesex Hospital. A hospital in London* in the Marylebone* neighborhood, in use on the same site since 1754.

Middlesex Street. *See* Petticoat Lane.

Middle Temple. *See* Temple.

midge. A tiny insect, similar to but not exactly like a mosquito, generally found in large swarms around ponds and streams at sunset; some of these bite, but most don't. Also called **no-see-ums.**

Mid Glamorgan. A county* in Wales* formed in the reorganizations of 1974, the mountainous area just north of Cardiff,* including the coal areas of the Rhondda.*

Midland. One of the largest and most visible commercial banks.*

Midlands. The central area of Britain.* As always, precise boundaries are unclear, but it generally starts around Birmingham* at the south, runs up to the western portions of Yorkshire* in the north, east to Leicester* and west to about the Welsh border; sometimes the term also includes the Manchester* area, other times that area is included in the North.* The term is inseparably associated with industry and factories, as the bulk of the nation's industrial development took place in this area beginning in the eighteenth century. *See also* Black Country; Potteries, the; shire; Watford.

Midlothian. The ancient Scottish county* around and to the south of Edinburgh;* in 1973, it was split into two new regions,* Lothian* and Border.* For **Heart of Midlothian,** *See* tolbooth.

mid off. *See* off.

mid on. *See* on.

midshipman. In the navy,* a sort of officer-trainee. Midshipmen were almost always boys rather than young men; some (now all) had gone to naval school of some kind but others were simply the sons of gentry,* and they were primarily on a ship to serve an apprenticeship, gaining sea and battle experience and learning to sail properly under the eye of real officers,* and often performing menial chores for the other officers. They might also be given command of small parties of men for specific duties but were not in the normal chain of command. By the end of the nineteenth century, the system had somewhat standardized, with the midshipman expected to serve at sea for at least three years before taking an exam that made him a sub-lieutenant* and a real officer.

Midsummer. June 24. The date is actually the assumed birth of John the Baptist, six months before Christmas,* rather than the actual summer solstice, but the celebrations accepted most of the old pagan midsummer activities, particularly the ideas of spirits loose in the land, used to such effect in Shakespeare's *A Midsummer Night's Dream*. Many communities held major bonfires* and celebrations on **Midsummer Eve**, the night before, which was understood to be the most dangerous time.

midwife. A woman who specializes in delivering babies. This was a traditional and respected occupation in ancient times and, although the modern United States does not recognize or accept them, they are still considered a valid part of the British medical profession, with a Royal College of Midwives in London,* founded in 1881, that trains modern practitioners.

MI5. Military Intelligence department 5, although now run by the civilian government* rather than the military, in charge of security within the confines of Britain,* roughly comparable to the FBI. *See also* MI6.

Milady. *See* My Lady.*

mild. *See* beer.

Mile End. A point on the road exactly one mile east of the east gate of the City* of London;* in the late eighteenth and early nineteenth centuries, this was the point at which a toll road began and marked the end of free travel. Since the mid-nineteenth, it has been part of the East End.*

Militant Tendency. A group of 1960s left-wing radicals that in the 1970s made a serious attempt to take over the Labour* Party. They did not completely succeed, but they remain an extremely influential radical wing of the party, applying the primary pressure to push it toward more socialistic stances.

Military Cross. A military award for bravery, given only to officers.* The **Military Medal** is awarded to other ranks* for similar bravery.

Military Knight. *See* Garter, Order of the.

military ranks. *See* Appendix V.

milk bar. A rather odd fad of the 1930s, a bar that served only milk and milk shakes along with sandwiches* and buns* or rolls. This was not a temperance idea but was rather an attempt to be "modern," an English imitation of the American soda fountain, and was extremely popular among young adults until the war brought rationing* and sent most people back to the pubs.* The fad died, but a few milk bars continued at least through the 1960s.

milk float. A small truck used primarily for home deliveries by milkmen, generally with a one-person driving cabin and a small open flat bed behind, the whole thing often electric-powered.

milk stout. *See* beer.

Millbank. A street in London* along the Thames* from Vauxhall* Bridge to near the Houses of Parliament.* **Millbank Penitentiary** was a prison opened there in 1821 on a site now used by the Tate Gallery;* in its time it was considered a model prison on liberal humanitarian lines, with individual cells for each prisoner, but the swampy site led to regular epidemics until the prison was torn down in 1896.

millboard. What Americans call a clipboard.

Miller, Joe. *See* Joe Miller.

milliard. *See* billion.

millions. In Britain, it has been common practice to say millions or "millions of" for more than one million; where Americans would say three million, the educated Briton would say three millions, particularly when talking about money. *See also* billion.

mill pond/pool. The pool of water formed by a small dam at a mill.

Mills, Bertram. *See* Bertram Mills.

Mills and Boon. A publisher since the early twentieth century, originally in hardback but beginning widespread paperback publication in the 1950s, synonymous now with the sentimental romance novel that Americans associate with the Harlequin romances (the two companies are in fact related).

Milord. My Lord.*

Milton Keynes. A new town* built in 1967 northeast of London,* now with more than 150,000 people and projected to reach 250,000 by the year 2000. This is one of the most successful of the new towns, and as such it symbolizes both the good and bad aspects of modern urban developments, alternately a modern, comfortable, clean, and safe place or a soul-less, cultureless, personality-less blank space where the middle classes* go to hide.

mimosa. Not a tree as in America but a shrub similar to the acacia.

mince. (1) Either chopped meat of any kind (minced meat), or chopped apples, suet, currants,* et cetera (mincemeat). In recent years, the term has also been applied to what Americans call ground beef, since it is made in a mincer.* (2) To **mince words** is not to be so angry you chop them up but rather to choose the words very carefully so as not to insult someone. Thus, someone who "doesn't mince words" speaks bluntly and honestly.

mincer. The tool Americans call a meat grinder.

Mincing Lane. A street in London* near the Tower,* primarily associated with the tea and wine trades. The name probably comes from minchens, a term for the nuns of a nearby convent founded in the fourteenth century, not from any peculiar steps practiced by the merchants* in the lane itself.

mind. To watch out for, as in "mind the steps."

minder. Among criminals, in spy novels, et cetera, a bodyguard; in other walks of life a babysitter.

minerals. Mineral water.*

mineral water. Sometimes used to mean not only mineral water but any carbonated nonalcoholic drink.

minge. Female sexual organs, vulgar usage roughly equivalent to American pussy, originally rural but now lower-class, probably from a gypsy* term; **mingy**, however, is miserly, a portmanteau word combining mean* and stingy.

Mini. A popular little car from 1959, like a tiny box with windows on 10-inch wheels but still somehow holding four people, a British answer to the Volkswagen bug in price and simplicity, made by Morris* and Austin; 1980s models are styled more like other brands of subcompacts. The **Mini-Cooper** was a sportier version in the 1960s that could reach 100mph. *See also* Austin Seven.

mini-cab. A taxi* that legally can only pick up people who have phoned for it, as opposed to the regular taxi that picks up fares from taxi stands or when waved down on the street. Also, these are usually regular-sized cars rather than the standard taxis.

minister. (1) An elected member* of Parliament* who is also made the head of a ministry* or department* of the civil service,* before the nineteenth century almost always from the House of Lords* but since almost always from the Commons.* Formal titles may vary, some being called Secretary of State,* some Minister of State, but the general practice seems to be to address either as Minister. In theory, daily operations are run by a civil servant called a Permanent Secretary* while the Minister gives direction and policy, but in practice, as with bureaucracies the world over, the Minister often has little control or influence over his ministry. (2) The clergyman of a nonconformist* church,* a title chosen originally to indicate no connection with the Catholic priest. Occasionally, the Church of England* will refer to anyone who actually conducts a service as a minister as well, but only occasionally and only as a generic term, never as a specific title or rank.

Minister of Defence. *See* Defence Secretary.

Minister of State. The formal title of a number of ministers* appointed by the Prime Minister* to form the government.* *See also* Secretary of State.

ministry. A unit of the civil service.* Some of these units are officially called departments, some ministries, and some offices, and some ministries have departments within them, but most are called ministries and all operate like American bureaucratic civil service departments. Each ministry is headed by an administrator from the civil service, usually called Permanent Secretary,* and by a member* of Parliament* called a Minister,* appointed by the Prime Minister,* who is supposed to set the policy for the Permanent Secretary and the ministry to implement.

minor. (1) Since 1969, the legal term for a person under the age of eighteen; before that date, a person became a legal adult at age twenty-one, but until then was legally called a child* or an infant. To turn eighteen is to **come of age**. *See also* age of discretion; juvenile. (2) The younger son, particularly used in schools* where two boys from the same family would be called, for example, Jones Major and Jones Minor. In some schools, this term was used for any younger boy with the same surname, even if the two boys were unrelated. (3) *See* Morris.

minster. A church* once connected to a monastery. Sometimes this is really a cathedral,* as is the York* Minster, at other times just a church.

minute. What Americans call a memo, but generally only used for "official" memoranda that actually contain a decision or clear instructions.

Mirror. A daily tabloid newspaper,* noted for its generally cheeky attitude of opposition to any government,* from the 1930s to the 1960s the primary paper of the London working class* with the largest daily circulation in the world but sliding into decline as it became more clearly associated with the Labour* party and its market dominance was challenged by the greater vulgarity of the *Sun** and its imitators. However, the *Sunday Mirror* (formerly the *Sunday Pictorial*) continues as the only serious challenger to the *News of the World*'s* Sunday circulation dominance.

MI6. Military Intelligence department 6, although now run by the civilian government* rather than the military, in charge of intelligence operations overseas, also called **SIS**, roughly comparable to the CIA. *See also* MI5.

Miss. (1) As in America, an unmarried woman, but with some significant distinctions. Technically, the eldest daughter was addressed as Miss (Last name) while all other daughters were addressed as Miss (First name); thus, in *Pride and Prejudice*, letters arriving addressed to "Miss Bennet" go automatically to Jane, the eldest. The *Oxford English Dictionary* treats this as common knowledge before WWI, but such a fine distinction has surely disappeared by the late twentieth century and of course never applied in the lower portions of society. The use of miss as a general form of address, as in "Be careful, miss," is primarily a trade* usage, addressed to women too young to be automatically called madam.* (2) In schools,* the formal address used by a student speaking to a female teacher, equivalent to sir.* Although she is actually titled a mistress,* such as a maths* mistress, the students always address her as Miss,* as in "What page, Miss?" no matter what her marital status. (3) Originally, the abbreviation for mistress* and thus a concubine, still seen until the mid-nineteenth century, a rare instance of a vulgar meaning being crowded out by a more respectable one.

Mister. In the medieval era, mister was a craft or occupation, or the tools of such a craft, so a man with a craft was called a "man of mister." By Shakespeare's time this meaning was declining; however, since the "man of mister" was usually a "master" of his mister, a respectful title of Master* was coming into common use for such men. In writing, Master was abbreviated as Mr.* As might be expected, considerable confusion developed in the public mind (see modern American confusion as to the precise pronunciation or meaning of Ms. and Mrs. for a way in which this happens), since master was also being used to mean a servant's* boss, and by the eighteenth century people who might put Mr in front of their name found that the Mr was more often than not pronounced Mister instead of Master. Gradually Mister became a generally respectful title for a man who has no other title, which is how it is used now. When the person has another title, the Mr is usually dropped: John Smith, Esq;* the Hon.* John Smith, et cetera; however, if Revd* is used properly, the clergyman would be called the Revd Mr Smith. *See also* Esquire.

mistress. (1) A female equivalent of master* and thus used for the wife in charge of a household or for any woman who has authority over servants* or other employees. Since WWII, this usage has declined except in the abbreviation Mrs* used, as in America, as a title for a married woman. (2) A female instructor at a school,* the female equivalent of master.* *See also* Miss. (3) Almost equally ancient is the usage of the term to indicate a paramour or concubine; however, by about the 1830s it was generally unacceptable for a respectable man to keep a mistress in the continental manner, which together with the late ages for marriage* perhaps encouraged the high level of open prostitution* during the century.

mixed grill. A plate of several kinds of meat, sometimes fried, sometimes broiled, usually served with tomatoes, also often fried. *See also* grilled.

m'lud. My lord,* a pronunciation usually heard only in law courts.

MM. Military Medal. *See* Military Cross.

M'Naghten. *See* McNaughten rules.

mo. A moment; **half a mo** is a very brief time or signal to wait for a brief time.

MO. Medical Officer.*

mockers on, put the. To spoil or mess up, as in "That put the mockers on it."

MOD. Ministry of Defence.*

mod cons. Modern conveniences, gaining general usage from its common appearance as an abbreviation in real estate listings. Originally, this meant indoor toilet, electric lighting, and perhaps a gas cooker,* but as with most real estate terms it can mean most anything. It is used in general speech as a sarcastic or ironic term for anything modern or fashionable.

model. This is very often a euphemism for prostitute,* used by prostitutes on their notice* cards and by the media. American media tend to prefer actress. Clothing models are generally called mannequins.*

Moderations. *See* Mods.

Moderator. *See* Mods.

moderns. In universities,* any subject in the general humanities not about the Greek or Roman era; thus, in literature, modern may begin as early as Chaucer and almost always includes Shakespeare, and in history always includes the Renaissance and may include the medieval era. Thus, at Oxford,* **Modern Greats** is the final examination in economics, political science, and philosophy. *See also* Greats; PPE.

Mods. (1) Moderations; this is one of three required exams at Oxford,* concentrating on mathematics, so called because it is supervised by the Moderators. *See also* Greats; Smalls. (2) During the 1960s, gangs of young men distinguished by overly-stylish dress and motor scooters, assumed to be at perpetual war with the Rockers.* *See also* skinheads; Teddy boy.

moggy. A pet cat.

money. *See* Appendix I.

monger. A store or the shopkeeper* in such a store, as in ironmonger* or fishmonger.

Mongol. A mongoloid, a person suffering from Down's syndrome. Generally, the British tend to use less euphemism in dealing with disease or handicaps than do Americans; thus, a term such as this that Americans would find unnecessarily brutal or cruel, the British tend to see as simple description of fact. Similarly, *See* NN; spastic.

monkey. Slang for £500.

monkey engine. The machine Americans call a pile driver.

monkey jacket. The short jacket worn by sailors; in recent times, also applied to the safety vest, which is a glowing green rather than the American orange, worn by road workers and others in similar situations.

monkey nuts. Peanuts, usually still in their shell.

Monmouth. A town and a shire* on the border of England* and Wales,* primarily a coal area. As with all such border areas, it was the site of raids and battles for centuries. In 1830, the shire was officially returned to Wales, and in the county* reorganization of 1974, **Monmouthshire** disappeared, parts going to Gwent* and Glamorgan.*

Monmouth Street. A short street in London* near Covent Garden.* It is bisected by Seven Dials* and thus was also included in the notorious crime-ridden slum area associated with the latter. Later it became synonymous with secondhand clothing but now is relatively nondescript.

monologist. In the music halls,* a comedian who, rather than telling jokes, did a monolog as if playing a particular character in a dramatic situation.

monopoly. In the late medieval era, a monopoly was thought to be a positive situation, providing stability for prices and employment. In particular, the monarch issued charters* granting monopolies in certain commodities, in return for a fee, which in effect imposed the equivalent of a tax without asking Parliament* for a tax law. The monopolists recouped their expenses by controlling the market for their goods. The bulk of monopolies within Britain lost their charters by the early eighteenth century, when theories of free trade began to dominate economic discussions, but much of the Empire* was built not by military conquest but by companies such as the East India Company* operating under monopoly charters.

Monument. A large column just northeast of London Bridge,* built in 1677 to commemorate the Great Fire.* Recent developments of high-rise office buildings on all sides have almost obscured its 202-foot height from view, but until very recently it was a major landmark on the London skyline.

moonraker. A native of Wiltshire.* The story says that some locals were discovered trying to rake the moon's reflection from a pond, but the alternate is that they were trying to rake in kegs of smuggled rum that had fallen out of a boat; so many Wiltshire people were engaged in smuggling (when the county* still extended to the coastline) that the term also was used to mean a smuggler.

moonshine. Not homebrewed whiskey but rather nonsense, usually more dreamy and unrealistic than senseless.

moor. A large open area, usually both flattish and somewhat elevated. In general a moor usually has neither good grazing grass nor any significant stands of trees to break the visual monotony. Although to American eyes accustomed to the deserts of the West they seem more like picturesque open space, to the British these are almost always associated with wild nature and semi-savage inhabitants, the ideal setting for fantasy like *The Hound of the Baskervilles* or the play of uncontrolled passion like *Wuthering Heights*. The poor soil means the areas are only sparsely inhabited, and their open nature leaves them subject to extremes of wind in particular. Most are found in the northern areas, particularly in Yorkshire,* but other similar areas are scattered around the country, such as Dartmoor* in the southwest. In general usage, moor and heath* are sometimes used interchangeably.

Moore's. *Old Moore's Almanack*, known for its predictions since 1699.

Moorfields. A small street in the City* in London,* in the eighteenth century the site of Bedlam* Hospital.

Moorgate. The northern gate in the wall of the City* of London,* torn down in 1762, so called because it opened onto the moor* that stood immediately outside the walls in the medieval era. The street that ran to the gate still exists and is now a center for the insurance business.

moorhen. Sometimes used to mean a female grouse,* at other times a different species of bird, but dark brown to black in color and living in meadows and marshes, also called a **water hen**.

Moray Firth. *See* firth.

morning coat. A man's knee-length coat with the lower portion cut away in a curve from the front waist to the center behind the knees. Worn with trousers* (usually not matching material), waistcoat,* stiff collar, shirt-front, and tie,* this was common wear for formal daytime gatherings until at least WWII, but is now seen only on formal occasions such as weddings, diplomatic gatherings, or royal garden parties.* When the trousers are of matching material, called a **morning suit**.

morning dress. Male dress that is not formal enough for evening dress, worn at any time during the day time, in practice meaning either a morning coat* or a frock coat.* The term is not often used since WWII.

morning room. A small, comfortable sitting room* in a large house, so called because it was placed so as to catch morning sunlight. Thus, it was usually comfortable and cheery and was associated almost always with the wife rather than the husband, the room she used to meet close friends or to write letters and from which she organized the daily life of the household.

Morning Star. The daily newspaper* of the Communist Party.

morning suit. *See* morning coat.

Morris. An English auto maker at Oxford,* by the 1920s the largest outside of the United States. The flat-topped Morris Oxfords of the 1920s and 30s were as ubiquitous as the American Model A, while the Morris **Minor** was the basic family car of post-WWII society. In 1951, the company merged with Austin to become British Motors, but the name continued until 1984. *See also* Mini.

morris dance. A folk dance performed by adult males. The exact history of the morris dance is shrouded and controversial, but most of Britain apparently had some form of regular, ritualized male dancing long before the medieval era. This often was related to the mummers* and frequently involved "disguises" and blackened faces, which may explain why it earned the name morris, or "moorish," although the dances clearly predate the name. The dancers wore odd hats, ribbons, garlands, and/or bells, and sometimes danced with toy horses or dressed as women. What precisely the dances meant or celebrated remains unclear, but they were banned by Cromwell and held on only in distant rural areas. In 1899 the folklorist Cecil Sharp saw one of the last remaining groups in a village near Oxford,* learned the version they did, and taught it to other intellectuals involved in the folklore revival movement. They in turn passed it on, until after WWI it came to be taught in most schools and thus became the "official" English folk dance known by everyone; no modern "English" celebration seems possible without at least one set of men dressed in white with ribbons and bells dancing in geometric patterns, varied by waving handkerchiefs, clicking sticks, or interweaving swords. The sword dances* of the north-eastern areas are not technically morris dances, but they have been blended into many of the modern versions of the dance and are inseparable to all but purists.

Morrison shelter. A small bomb shelter that could be used as a table the rest of the time, used during WWII.

Morton's fork. Any proposal to raise taxes; a Bishop Morton told Henry VII he could raise taxes because some on the one hand clearly had the money to pay and those on the other who seemed to have no money were merely hiding it.

Moss Bros. Often pronounced Moss Bross, now a generic term for rented formal clothes, from the name of the most common dealer of such in London.*

MOT. (1) Ministry of Transport.* (2) The certificate from the MOT that says a car has passed the standard yearly safety inspection.

Mother, be. When tea* is served, to pour the tea; commonly used no matter what the gender of the persons drinking or pouring and in no way implying effeminacy.

Mothering Sunday. The fourth Sunday in Lent,* a church holiday unconnected with biological mothers except that students and apprentices were allowed to go home to visit parents; commercial inroads made since WWII by the American "holiday" have caused some people to call this day **Mother's Day** and send cards or presents to their mothers.

mother-in-law. Until the twentieth century, used to mean stepmother.

Mother's Pride. A commercial brand of white bread, having much the same impact among British families as Wonder Bread in America, now something of a generic term for store-bought white bread.

motor. Often used to mean an automobile, and, as a verb, to travel by car.

motorist. A car driver.

motorway. What Americans generally call a freeway. Britain has few of these, identified by their M* designation, as in M1. *See also* clearway.

mourning. In the late twentieth century, the British rarely go into mourning after deaths, adopting for the most part the modern American attitude of "let's get back to normal as quickly as possible." But in the surge to respectability of the mid-nineteenth century, the middle classes* adopted mourning rules for women that rivaled the Sicilians: Black dress was absolutely required for the funeral,* and then expected for a year and a day for widows, daughters, and mothers, then grey or purple trims were introduced over the next eighteen months, during which time the women were essentially confined to home and immediate family. Many widows, like Queen Victoria, never wore anything but black for the rest of their lives. This continued until a governmental ban on public mourning clothes during WWI, for fear the whole nation would be in mourning and recognize the true number of casualties, but older women continued some form of visible mourning dress until at least WWII. Men expressed mourning much more simply, with a black arm band on the left sleeve (from about 1840, almost all men's coats were already grey or black).

mousse. Used to identify what Americans call both pudding and mousse. *See also* pudding.

mouth and trousers, all. All talk and no action.

moving stairs. What Americans call an escalator.

MP. Literally, Member* of Parliament,* but in practice only used for a member of the House of Commons.*

Mr. This is actually an abbreviation for master* but has gradually come to be pronounced as mister (discussed under Mister). British preference is without a period. Its most confusing usage in modern life is that it is also a title indicating a specialist surgeon,* used in place of Dr.*

Mrs. Pronounced mistress until at least the mid-nineteenth century, then pronounced missez as in America. During the Restoration, this term was used for any adult woman, married or unmarried, but by the early eighteenth century, common usage had begun to use the abbreviation for the married woman to distinguish her from the other kind of mistress,* and gradually polite society also evolved a different pronunciation to cement that distinction. British preference is without a period. Curiously, Mrs was also used as an honorary title for housekeepers* and female cooks, who were rarely if ever married, by both the family and the other servants.*

much of a muchness. No difference between them.

muck. As a noun, dirt or filth; as a verb, to do something that will leave you dirty, as in "muck about in the garden." *See also* Lady Muck.

muddle. A mess, but usually only of the kind made by disorganization or distraction. To be **muddled** or **in a muddle** is to be confused. To **muddle through** is to get through without any plan or organization, just by keeping on keeping on, so to speak; this is often said to be the British way of life and is applied to politics, military action, social programs, business relations, and practically any other aspect of social life.

Mudie's. One of the largest circulating libraries* of the nineteenth century, beginning in London* in 1852, perceived as the most strictly moral and uplifting of these in its selection of books on offer.

muesli. Originally a Swiss concoction of oat flakes, raisins, and nuts, something like granola without any oils or sweetness but eaten cold with milk as a breakfast cereal. It was first associated with the health fanatic, particularly of the kind who goes walking* on vacations, or the naturist,* but more recently has become a stereotyped part of the fitness/feminism/college-liberal life-style.

mufti. Military slang for civilian clothes.

muggins. A fool or sucker, apparently not an allusion to anyone in particular named Muggins.

Muggletonians. A tiny nonconformist* sect begun by Muggleton in 1651, with strong emphasis on the prophecies of *Revelations*.

mull/mulled. Originally, this described a common punch* made from wine, sugar, and spice, heated (or mulled) by submerging a hot poker in the full mug. Since the decline of open fires,* the term describes any hot wine, cider,* or punch, no matter how heated.

multi-cultural. Technically, containing persons of various ethnic or racial backgrounds, but like the American term integrated, in practice it usually means Black.* Neighborhoods with Italians, Greeks, Jews,* or even Chinese are almost never classified as multi-cultural, and as far as I can find, no one has ever applied the term to Northern Ireland.*

multiple stores. What Americans call chain stores.

mum. Mother, usually lower class* in usage, roughly equivalent in tone and respect to the American Mom. Girls and women from the higher end of the middle class* and up generally say **mummy**, while men of that class, having been separated from her almost at birth, generally call her Mother or, before WWII mater,* if they call her anything at all.

mummer/mumming. Dances, mimes, or short plays, usually performed in some kind of disguise that hides the face, either a mask or face-blacking, and dating in content and form far back into the medieval era. These are traditionally performed at Christmas* and involve some form of death and resurrection story, the most common being St. George,* who kills a number of enemies who are at the final moment revived (and reformed) by a doctor. Hardy's description in *The Return of the Native* is one of the most complete we have, and many modern attempts to revive the mummers' plays start from the novel, as traditional versions had all but disappeared by the time Hardy wrote.

Murray. Murray's *English Grammar* (1795), the standard Victorian school text.

muscular Christianity. The form of general Christian attitudes associated with Dr. Arnold of Rugby* but shared by most of Victorian society. There is no fixed theology but rather a general attitude that God may want you to be good, but that does not mean you have to be a wimp, too.

Museum of London. *See* London, Museum of.

mushy peas. *See* pea.

music centre. All the electronic equipment that in America is usually lumped under the generic title of the stereo.

music hall. A form of variety entertainment, in the late nineteenth and early twentieth centuries, similar to the American vaudeville, with singers, comics, and variety acts, wounded in 1902 when licensing laws* outlawed the selling of liquor and beer* at them, and killed by radio and the movies. *See also* cabaret; concert party; variety.

muslin. *See* calico.

Muswell Hill. A hill north of London* with a famous well, now a working-class* neighborhood north of Hampstead* perhaps more known as the site of Colney Hatch.*

Mutiny. While there have been many individual mutinies, the Munity generally means either the mutiny that swept through the navy* in 1797 or the mutiny of 1857–58 in India,* during which the local troops mutinied after the introduction of a new cartridge they were required to bite and which was believed to be greased with pork fat; it was followed by widespread uprisings throughout the general populace.

mutton. Although Americans tend to call meat from sheep lamb no matter what its age, the British tend to call it mutton, unless absolutely certain it is lamb. This is usually eaten as a chop* but is also quite common in joints* and in stews such as Lancashire hot pot,* and in the nineteenth century was the basic meat of all middle-class* life. **Mutton dressed as lamb** is someone or something pretending to be better than they are, most often said of a middle-aged woman who tries to dress and act like a young woman.

muzzy. The way you feel the morning after the night before.

MVO. Member of the Royal Victorian Order.* *See also* honours.

My Lady. The proper form of address to the wife of a baron,* viscount,* earl,* or marquess.* *See also* Lady; Your Ladyship.

My Lord. The proper form of address to a baron,* viscount,* earl,* or marquess.* *See also* Lord; Your Lordship.

myrtle. A shrub very popular in gardens* for its white flowers and fragrant leaves.

mystery tour. A one-day holiday trip in which the passengers on the tour do not know the destination until the trip is underway, a common form of coach* holiday for people seeking a bit of cheap adventure in their own neighborhood.

N

NAAFI. A canteen for military servicemen, an acronym of Navy, Army, Air Force Institute. Organized in 1921, in WWII it entered the language as an adjective as well, usually spelled as pronounced—**naffy: A naffy sandwich**, for example, was a hand of cards, alluding to the typical thickness of the real thing. The naffy was also the place where those avoiding work hung out, so that the letters were often read as "No aim, ambition, or fucking initiative," and thus naffy attached to any noun would make the noun ironic, such as a **naffy hero** or a **naffy romeo** or the **naffy medal**, the basic service medal given to all participants in WWII.

nabob. An Indian title for a Muslim prince, applied in Britain in the late eighteenth century to a man who made a fortune in India, in the late nineteenth spreading occasionally to any very wealthy person.

naffy. *See* NAAFI.

nail varnish. What Americans call fingernail polish.

NALGO. National and Local Government Officers, the union of most government office workers and similar white-collar jobs in local bureaucracies, one of the five largest unions of the country. *See also* NUGMW; NUPE.

nance/nancy. A homosexual. *See also* fag; poof; poofter.

nankeen. Buff-colored cotton cloth, originally from China.

nanny. A child's nurse, but not really a nurse.* The nanny was in practice a surrogate mother; she cared for the child from as early as the age of one month until it went away to school* or until, if the child was female, it was old enough to need a governess* instead. Nanny, not mother, played with the kids, tucked them into bed at night, told them stories, fed them, taught them manners and morals, and in general was the formative influence on their lives. Yet she was a hired worker, not quite a servant* but certainly not part of the family. The name isn't recorded until mid-nineteenth century, probably a childhood corruption of nurse, but the great wealth of the industrial era made the nanny affordable throughout a broad range of society, and wealthy women took advantage of that wealth to pass along responsibility for their children whenever possible, especially for all the dirty parts of child-rearing like weaning, potty-training, food manners, and bed wetting. From the mid–nineteenth century to the mid-twentieth century, the number of nannies remained relatively constant, about half a million, which meant that, since nannies only stayed where there were young children, nannies were not restricted to the nobility but were used quite far down into the middle class,* but the universal conscription of WWII and post-war taxes effectively ended their reign, replacing them, if at all, with the au pair.* Most upper-class boys hardly saw their mothers, passing from nurse to nanny to prep school* to public school* with only the briefest of visits with their parent; thus, it often happened that the adults, like Sebastian in *Brideshead Revisited*, would go visit Nanny and avoid meeting Mother. Curiously, unlike governesses who were always from the impoverished upper class, nannies almost always came from the respectable portion of the working class* and coped by being unutterable snobs,* often dropping their own surname and adopting that of the most prestigious family they worked for. They were usually called Mrs* by the other servants and by the mistress even though married women were never hired as nannies.

nap. The best bet available or a bet so sure that all the bettor's available funds are wagered, from a whist* term for a hand that seems a sure winner.

napkin. Although used as in America for a table napkin, this also can mean something much larger, like a towel or a baby diaper, or much smaller, like a handkerchief. *See also* nappy; serviette.

nappy. A baby's diaper, from napkin.*

NAS/UWT. National Association of Schoolmasters and Union of Women Teachers, a union primarily of public school* and girl's school* teachers. *See also* NUT.

national assistance. A system of national financial aid to the poor, in 1934 replacing the various parish* aids required under the poor laws,* in 1946 itself replaced by national insurance.* *See also* dole; National Health; social security.

National Front. A right-wing party* formed in the 1960s with strong anti-Semitic, anti-Black* policies, generally getting far more media attention than success at the polls.

National Gallery. An enormous art museum begun by national purchase of a private collection in 1824 and moved into a new building on the north side of Trafalgar Square* in London* in 1838. The collection covers all of European painting, with the bulk of English paintings now in the Tate,* and is of extremely high quality in a very approachable setting.

National Health. The National Health Service, a system of universal medical treatment, authorized in 1946, initiated in 1948. The system is paid for by a combination of pay deductions and general taxation and is available to everyone without means tests.* Medical personnel in hospitals are salaried and in individual practices are paid by formulas based on the number of patients on their panel* rather than by individual treatments done, with bonuses for factors such as night duty and regional variations. Individuals may also opt for private* care in addition, in which they pay for their own treatments, on the assumption that they get more personal care or, in hospitals, more amenities, such as private rooms, but no one is required to pay "deductibles" or pay extra for some treatments that are not "covered" by the national plan, as with American Medicare or private insurance plans. However, some charges are made for glasses, dental work, and prescriptions. During the last decade, there has been much criticism of the National Health Service, primarily because there have been significant increases in delays in some services and shortages of beds in some hospitals, which the health service itself usually blames on Conservative* attempts to cut costs.

national insurance. A governmental insurance plan, paid in part by the employer and in part by deductions from pay, covering not only retirement pensions but also unemployment, injuries and illness, welfare benefits, and a portion of the National Health.* The first step was a means-tested old-age pension in 1908, with unemployment and illness benefits added in 1911, gradually modified and then combined into a single system with the same basic shape as at present in 1946. The national insurance scheme at present includes: child benefit;* death benefit;* disablement benefit;* family credit;* invalidity benefit;* maternity benefit;* various retirement pensions;* sickness benefit; SSP;* supplementary benefit;* unemployment;* widow's benefit.* *See also* dole; national assistance; social security.

nationalisation. The British began nationalizing industries immediately following WWII through a process of compulsory purchases, starting with the Bank of England* and the aviation industry in 1946, followed in 1947 by coal mines and electricity, in 1948 by railways* and gas,* in 1949 by iron and steel (privatized in 1953, re-nationalized in 1967). *See also* privatisation.

National Opera. Three different companies operate as "national" opera companies with comparatively large subsidies from the government. The English National Opera (**ENO**) is based in London* at the Coliseum* since 1968, before which it was the company at Sadler's Wells* (1931) and at the Old Vic* (1900). Since occupying the Coliseum,* it gives almost a year-round season, all sung in English and for the most part using British singers. The **Welsh National Opera** has been based in Cardiff* since its organization in 1946 but tours for much of the year throughout Britain; it too sings almost always in English. The **Scottish Opera** is based in Glasgow* since 1962.

National Park. In England* and Wales,* areas authorized under an act of 1949 as areas of natural beauty that should be protected. Unlike American National Parks, however, the areas designated are not necessarily owned by the nation, and much of the land within them continues to be used for farming, industry, or housing, as well as the recreational visits we would expect, but development and changes are much more strictly controlled than in other areas of the nation. *See also* AONB, country park.

National Portrait Gallery. An unusual museum of paintings (and some photographs) founded in 1856 and located just behind the National Gallery* in London,* a collection of some 4500 portraits of the significant persons in British history.

national school. One of a series of schools* founded in 1809 to teach basic literacy and religious principles to the poor, after 1832 administering the first government grants* for education.

national service. Compulsory conscription* for the military in peacetime, what Americans would call the draft, from 1947–62. Every male had to serve for two years, unless physically unfit.

National Theatre. A nationally subsidized theater company and complex originally organized in 1962 in the Old Vic* and moved in 1976 into a modern building on the South Bank* of the Thames* beside Waterloo

Bridge.* The modern complex houses three separate stages, all of which produce plays year round. *See also* RSC.

National Trust. A private, nonprofit organization that cares for houses of architectural or historic interest and some lands of particular beauty. The trust is paid for by a combination of donations and entrance fees charged at many of the homes now open to tourists. It acquires new property primarily from donations or purchase, though occasionally it acquires property from the government that has been accepted in lieu of death duties.* The National Trust in Scotland* is a separate organization with similar functions. *See also* English Heritage.

natter. Idle talk, chatter, or gossip, often used by lower-class* women in particular about a comfy chat over tea.*

Natural Beauty, Area of. *See* AONB.

naturist. What Americans call a nudist. *See also* Gymnosophist.

Nat West. National Westminster, one of the largest commercial banks.*

naughty nineties. The 1890s, naughty in Britain, gay in America.

Naval and Military. A gentlemen's club* in London* for military officers,* usually called the **In and Out** because these are the only visible signs on the driveway in Piccadilly,* model for Sayers's Bellona Club.

navvy. Not a sailor but a manual laborer, in the eighteenth century on a canal, in the nineteenth on a railroad, and in the twentieth on a road. *See also* labourer.

navy. The navy has existed in a recognizably continuous form since the Cinque Ports* in the eleventh century chose to provide ships for the King* rather than pay taxes. This was formalized into a navy administered by the king's ministers* under Henry VIII, although the ships, ranks, and methods were randomly organized and operated until the mid–eighteenth century. As such, the navy became the symbol for the British of their independence and power and was the primary means by which it controlled and sustained its Empire;* until WWII, when the U.S. navy surpassed it in size and power, Britannia really did rule the waves in practically all parts of the world. Curiously, the navy men themselves have had a peculiar relationship with the rest of British society. In particular, navy officers* never had quite the social cachet the army* officers had, perhaps in part because they were at sea for months or years at a time but perhaps even more because commanding a ship required considerable technical knowledge that carried more than a taint of trade.* Officers could and in fact did work themselves up to considerable commands after starting among the other ranks,* a situation almost impossible in the army, and many others became officers by attending naval academies* rather than by purchasing commissions,* so that the navy was somewhat more clearly middle-class in its composition and orientation, with its officers much more likely to actually live on their stipends, plus whatever capital could be gained by the taking of prizes (common navy practice until mid–nineteenth century). This situation was further underlined by the change to steam, as daily operation of the ships as opposed to their use in combat required numerous engineers who were not quite officers but required an education and an authority that clearly separated them from the seamen. Perhaps this is why, despite the tremendous patriotic status of the navy, it plays such a small part in British literature, with the notable exception of the boys' adventure books epitomized by Captain Marryat.

Marines were soldiers on large ships who guarded landing parties or in battle served as marksmen but did not engage in actually sailing the ship, evolving into a modern commando-like force. In the modern navy, non-officers enlist for twenty-two years of active service, although they may leave at any time after three years upon eighteen months' formal notice and complete the term in the Naval Reserve, and some selected specialists may enlist for a further ten years. For organization, *See* Admiralty; Sea Lords. For ranks, *See* Appendix V. *See also* Gibraltar; Medway; oak; Portsmouth; Scapa Flow.

NBG. No bloody* good.

Near East. *See* East.

nearside. *See* offside.

Neasden. A suburb of London* near Wembley,* so often used by *Private Eye** as a synonym for the town where nothing ever happens that many people think it is purely mythical.

neb. In Scotland* and northern England,* a nose, beak, snout, et cetera; thus, someone who is **nebby** is too curious or nosy.

needful, do the. To do whatever is necessary.

neep. In Scotland,* a turnip.

Nelly, not on your. Not on your life; this phrase seems to have been used only since WWII, appearing as rhyming slang:* "Nelly Duff" for "puff," itself slang for "life." American uses of Nelly implying weakness or effeminacy, such as a nervous Nelly, seem not to be related and are rarely used in Britain.

nem con. From the Latin *nemine contradicente*, no one contradicting; hence, unanimous.

net ball. A game similar to American basketball but with seven players per team and no dribbling, played only by girls.

never-never. *See* hire purchase.

Newbury. A town west of London,* site of a horse racing* track.

Newcastle. There are two Newcastles of note: **Newcastle Upon Tyne** is the one most commonly meant by the word Newcastle; a city in the northeast* on the Tyne* with shipping access to the coast, it has been synonymous with both coal mining and the coal trade since the medieval era, from which **carrying coals to Newcastle** became a common phrase for absurd or unnecessary activity. In the nineteenth century, it expanded into all aspects of industrialization, especially shipbuilding and related iron and steel work, but since WWII it has suffered most heavily from collapsing economic conditions so that it is now often synonymous with industrial and urban decay. *See also* Tyneside. The second, and smaller, **Newcastle-under-Lyme** is in the Midlands,* one of the major towns of the Potteries,* fictionalized as Oldcastle in Bennett's Five Towns novels.

New Church. *See* St. Mary-le-Strand.

New College. One of the oldest of Oxford* colleges* (1379).

New Covent Garden. *See* Covent Garden.

New Exchange. *See* Exchange.

New Forest. A royal forest* in southern England* near the coast west of Southampton,* so called because it was not officially designated as a royal forest until William the Conqueror. The area is not really a forest in the American sense at all, with only about a quarter devoted to growing timber. The rest is heath* used for grazing by livestock still exercising common* rights and a unique, indigenous wild pony; there are some farms, although the poor soils have kept agricultural pressure at a minimum. The area is known especially for its oaks, which were farmed for several centuries to build navy* ships, and is one of the last areas of English vegetation still in something approximating its original state.

Newgate. Once the prison* for the city of London.* Originally in the gatehouse of the city wall, it was moved in the fifteenth century to a separate building on the site now occupied by the Old Bailey,* where it was burned in the Great Fire* and again in the Gordon Riots* (the sack of the prison vividly described in *Barnaby Rudge*), to be rebuilt in 1782. For the next century, it housed the convicted criminals of London in conditions of appalling filth and squalor, so that it was synonymous not only with prison but with the worst of Victorian degradations. Public executions were held at the prison gates from 1783–1867 and continued inside the prison until 1901. Prison reform movements and the construction of new national prisons relegated Newgate in 1880 to simply a local jail used for remand* prisoners, and it was torn down in 1902. The **Newgate Calendar** was an occasional publication of histories of the most famous criminals in Newgate.

Newmarket. (1) A small town east of Cambridge,* the center of English horse racing* since races began there during the reign of James I. The bulk of the stables and trainers operate in this area, most using the local heath* as a common exercise ground. *See also* Guineas. (2) A simple gambling card game. Four cards are dealt face up, and all players divide up a standard number of chips among those cards. Remaining cards are dealt equally to all players and to a blind dummy hand. Player to left leads lowest card, the person with next lowest in same suit then follows, et cetera, until either the ace is reached or no one has a card because it is in the dummy hand; then play passes to the lowest card of another suit. The person to play all his or her cards first collects a chip from each player, and any person who turns up a card to match one of the four dealt face up collects all the chips on that card. Americans play a version usually called Michigan.

Newnham. A women's college* at Cambridge,* founded in 1875.

newsagent. A person who sells newspapers* and magazines, usually in a little stall or shop* that also sells candy or tobacco. Practically all newspaper sales are done through newsagents; subscribers, for example, order through the local newsagent, who either reserves issues until the subscriber passes by each morning or evening or has his lad* deliver them.

New Scotland Yard. *See* Scotland Yard.

News of the World. Throughout most of the twentieth century, the most popular Sunday newspaper,* aimed primarily at a working-class* and lower–middle class audience, with particular emphasis on crime reporting.

newspaper. For Americans there are four major oddities of English newspapers: (a) Although there are local papers in many towns, the overwhelming majority of sales are of national newspapers published in London* but delivered and sold all over the country. Local papers deal only with local news, and all national and international news comes through London, with local London news also treated as national news, one of the primary means by which London dominates cultural and political life. (b) These London national papers (still numbering over a dozen) have readerships very strictly divided along class* and party* lines. Although journalistic standards generally include accuracy, there is no pretense of objectivity in the choice of stories or facts to include or stress. This means that someone seriously seeking news must regularly buy more than one paper. But the papers are not so much official spokesmen for parties in the French manner as spokesmen for class attitudes; a person's newspaper marks his or her class status perhaps more clearly and obviously than even accent,* and although some of the names have changed, this has been true since newspapers became widespread in the mid-nineteenth century. One of the resulting peculiarities is that, even in the age of television, all levels of society still read newspapers; the navvy* stopping off for a pint* or two at the local* is as likely to have a paper under his arm as is the executive commuter in his three-piece suit on the train—but they will always be different papers. (c) The papers themselves by American standards are very small—all the London daily morning papers together would rarely match the size of a midweek New York or Los Angeles *Times*—usually with only one section, relatively few ads, and, even in the most popular papers, no funnies pages, and with sports pages rather than sports sections. All the papers aimed toward the lower end of the scale are tabloids in size. (d) The Sunday papers are not just Sunday editions but separate weekly newspapers; these are, for the most part, large and multisectioned in the American manner, with colour supplements,* but are completely independent of the dailies, even when the dailies carry the same name, as with the *Times** and the *Sunday Times*,* and cover not just the news that happened on Saturday but all the week's news, and as a result there are few news magazines in Britain. Individual papers of note are discussed under their names. *See also* agony aunt; Fleet Street; leader; page three; silly season; strip cartoon.

newsreader. What Americans call a news anchor.

New Statesman. A small but influential magazine, noted primarily for socialist viewpoints.

new town. (1) Beginning in 1946, government policy allowed, or encouraged, developers to build towns from scratch rather than grafting housing onto existing towns* and villages,* particularly in suburban London;* these were called new towns, the most famous or symptomatic of which was Milton Keynes.* In some ways these are similar to the American Levittown and its imitators, but great effort was made to manufacture village- or town-like centers to make them seem traditionally English and to provide the urban amenities that would prevent their being simply dormitory towns.* *See also* expanded town; garden suburb; Hemel Hampstead. (2) In Edinburgh,* the area north of the medieval central city, built primarily in the eighteenth century.

New Year. In Scotland,* where *Auld Lang Syne* originated, this is a major holiday, more significant than Christmas;* New Year's Eve is called Hogmanay.* In England,* this never quite seemed significant, in part because the English continued to celebrate Christmas after the more puritanical Church of Scotland* had outlawed it there and in part because, before the new calendar* of 1752, most of the country treated Lady Day* as the first day of the year and concentrated its new year activities around that date instead. In some rare areas, January 11 is celebrated, as that was January 1 in the old calendar. However, in the more secular world after WWII, New Year's Eve in particular has become a more significant party time throughout modern Britain,* not quite as excessive as in America but in similar fashion, particularly among those without families.

NF. National Front.*

NI. National Insurance.*

nick. (1) To steal. (2) The police station or jail; also, to be taken there, as in "I was nicked." (3) Condition or health, as in "in good nick."

nicker. (1) In the twentieth century, slang for £1, generally in criminal and racing circles. (2) In the Restoration, a card sharp or cheat. *See also* knickers.

nicknames. As with all peoples, the British use many nicknames. In general, these fall into three types: (1) those used at home or among close personal friends, similar to American practice but very unpredictable and unique;

(b) those picked up at public school,* which usually have something to do with physical appearance or some embarrassing habit or social gaffe made when quite young but never forgotten. To Americans, the peculiarity of these nicknames is that they are not confined to close friends and the owners never seem to outgrow them; the most powerful members of the government* or civil service* may be known to, and addressed by, their associates as Bunny or Stinky or some such equally childish or demeaning name right up to their death. Use of such nicknames, however, seems not to be any attempt to lessen the power or authority of their holder but rather to underline the long-standing ties within the ruling groups that go back to childhood days when they were all together at the same schools; (3) nicknames that Partridge calls "inevitable," given to comparative strangers and having nothing whatever to do with personal habits or history. Most of these have to do with ethnic background or appearance (Mick,* Taffy,* Jock,* Ginger,* etc.) popular catchphrases, celebrities, or products (Dolly* Gray, Johnny Walker, Pincher* Martin, Nobby* Clarke, Nosy Parker, etc.) or trade associations (Dusty Miller, Chip Carpenter, etc.). Curiously, almost all such "inevitable" names seem to derive originally from navy* slang in the late nineteenth century and have been in use in the general population only since WWI spread them from the military to all levels.

nigger. Slang used in all levels of society for dark-skinned people; curiously, the earliest usage in the *Oxford English Dictionary* is from Robert Burns. Since Britain* never had Negro slavery, the term was used much more loosely there than in the United States and by the late nineteenth century was used more often for Indians than for Africans, sometimes so loosely as to apply to anyone with slightly darker skin. As such, it was used in "polite" society far later than in America, as can be seen by Agatha Christie's *Ten Little Niggers* published in 1939 and still sold under that title in the 1980s. The term was pejorative but in a somewhat less specific sense than in America, meaning simply the darker versions of the "inferior" peoples, which in general included everyone in the world not British. For example, in 1926, Fowler thought it an insult only if the person wasn't really a nigger, and the 1965 revision listed it as insulting only in America. *See also* wog.

niggers in a snowstorm/in the snow. Military slang for a curry* of rice and raisins or prunes, passing into some general use after WWI.

nightingale. A small bird, rather plain and drab brown in appearance but much loved in daily life and among the poets because it prefers to sing at night; found primarily in the south and Midlands* of England.*

Nightingales. Nurses trained at St. Thomas's Hospital,* home of the first nursing school, founded by Florence Nightingale.

nightjar. A mottled bird that is active mostly at night, so called from a unique song like a loud whirring noise, sung only in the dark.

nignog. Sometimes a synonym for nigger,* sometimes army slang simply meaning a fool, although the latter may have been derived from the number of recruits of the former in colonial forces in the late nineteenth century.

nil. Zero; used primarily in scores, as in three-nil for three-to-nothing.

999. The standard phone number to dial in an emergency.

ninepins. Skittles.*

nines. A corruption of eyne, medieval English for eyes; hence, **dressed to the nines** is perfectly, fashionably dressed.

nip. To go, usually implying something quick or brief, as in "I'll nip out for a drink," or "She nipped over to see her mum." In general, the British do not use this to mean a drink of alcohol as in America.

nipper. A boy, usually one not yet a teenager. This seems to have been common only since the late nineteenth century; in the early nineteenth century, pickpockets like the Artful Dodger were called nippers, and the term seems to have spread to include any boys of similar size. There are indications that in very recent usage this is changing to include little girls as well as boys.

nit. A fool or stupid person, actually an Australian term adopted by many Britons after WWII.

NN. Neurotics Nomine, a charitable organization that tries to help mental patients readjust to life in general society. *See also* Mongol; spastic.

nob. Since the early nineteenth century, slang for someone wealthy or noble, probably from an eighteenth century slang use of nob for head, and now also used sarcastically for the kind of people who try to lord it over others.

nobble. To influence surreptitiously (but not necessarily illegally).

nobby. Fashionable or elegant. As a nickname,* almost automatic for anyone named Clark, because of the habit of City* clerks* (pronounced clarks) in the late nineteenth century wearing top hats* to work like the nobs* to signify their self-importance.

nobility. The ranks, in order from the top are: Duke* (Duchess); Marquis or Marquess* (Marchioness); Earl* (Countess); Viscount* (Viscountess); Baron* (Baroness). The King* and Queen* and any princes* and princesses* are royalty* and not part of the nobility. Americans, and many British, see this as a holdover from the medieval era, but in fact practically all the nobles* gained their titles after the Restoration; only fifty-three medieval noble titles were still in use when Elizabeth I took the throne, but there are now more than 850. *See also* aristocracy; gentry; House of Lords; Lady; Lord; peer.

noble. (1) Technically, someone with a title of nobility,* but in common usage also including the sons and daughters who will not actually inherit titles. (2) A gold coin, generally worth about 80 pence* and used in various forms until the eighteenth century. *See also* Appendix I.

noddy. A fool, usually simple-minded and provincial.

noggin. In the eighteenth and early nineteenth centuries, about a quarter of a pint* (more than half a modern American cup), and thus a pretty sturdy serving of gin* or whisky,* and a miserly serving of beer* or ale; also the cup or mug in which a noggin was served.

no go. Something not likely to happen, not possible.

noise. As a verb, to give out information, as in "noise it about," which means "tell everyone about it."

nonconformist. A Protestant sect not connected to the Church of England,* also called dissenter.* They were suppressed, both before and after the Civil War,* almost as intensely as the Catholics and, for example, until 1829 they were not allowed to hold public office of any kind. Lloyd-George was the first Prime Minister* from one of these groups. The primary sects involved are the Presbyterians,* Methodists,* Baptists,* and Quakers,* with some growth in the late twentieth century in such American-style groups as the Jehovah's Witnesses. *See also* minister.

non-striker. *See* striker.

non-U. *See* U.

noodle. A simpleton or fool; sometimes also used to mean the head or brain. The term has been used widely since about 1750, but why is unclear, as noodles were unknown in the British diet until much later.

Nore. A large sandbank in the Thames* estuary near the mouth of the Medway* and the protected waters behind it that were often used for safe anchorage for navy* ships.

Norfolk. A county* along the eastern coast of England,* named for its ancient position as the "northern folk" of East Anglia.* It is noted for its low coast land, fens,* and extremely fertile flat farmlands; Noel Coward's "Very flat—Norfolk" is its most representative and concise description. The **Norfolk Broads** are a series of shallow lakes formed by rivers creeping through the flatlands. A **Norfolk dumpling** is not a food but a slow-witted person, ostensibly like a typical native of the area. *See also* Suffolk.

Norfolk jacket. A men's jacket of about hip length, primarily distinguished by an adjustable belt across the back, popularized in the 1890s by Prince Edward and worn only for sporting purposes, especially shooting* or golf.

norland. North land, that is, the north of England.*

Norland. Perhaps the most prestigious training academy* for nannies.

North. The northern part of England,* but usually more to the west than east, and more specifically used to indicate the industrialized areas around Manchester,* Liverpool, or Leeds.* Very often in the 1970s and 80s it means anything north of the Greater London* area and implies decline, depression, and industrial squalor as well as rude manners,* rough accents,* working-class* culture, and crime. Although more of the North than of the South* is rural, the term now almost never applies to anything but urban areas. Before industrialization, however, it was used to indicate any of the areas in the vicinity of the Scottish border, from about Yorkshire* on.

Northampton. A small city northwest of London,* a significant site during the medieval era, much used and fought over in the various dynastic wars of the time, but since noted primarily as a center of the shoe trade.

Northamptonshire. A county* or shire* in central England,* basically rolling hills and still agricultural in nature.

Northants. Abbreviation for Northamptonshire.*

Northeast. Generally, the areas around Newcastle;* compare North.*

Northern Ireland. Six counties* in the northwestern portion of the island of Ireland* that remained a part of the United Kingdom* after the Irish Free State was formed in 1921. Settled largely by Protestant Orangemen,* its inhabitants by considerable majority refused to participate in a Catholic Ireland. It is now governed and administered by Parliament* in London,* although a local assembly was organized in 1982 which can propose new laws subject to the approval of Parliament, replacing a provincial parliament for domestic issues that had been disbanded in 1972. The six counties are divided into twenty-six districts* whose councils* form the real local government. However, the region is notorious only for the festering civil war that has continued since the Provisional IRA* began terrorist activity in 1969, following generations of tension and conflict between the Protestant majority and the Catholic minority, which has led to the regular presence of troops from the British army* and continued economic distress for the whole region. Further complicating the religious issue is that most of the Protestants are Presbyterian* rather than Anglican.* Most of its courts,* schools,* and social security* systems are basically the same as those in England.* *See also* Belfast; Boyne; RUC; Ulster.

North Riding. *See* riding; Yorkshire.

North Sea. The ocean off the east coast of England* and Scotland.* In the 1960s oil was discovered there within the territorial limits of Britain; before that, its major contribution to British life was fish.

Northumberland. The county* of England* on the northeast coast and the border with Scotland,* before the 1974 reorganization including Newcastle* as its principal town. Site of Hadrian's Wall,* the county spent most of its history subject to border raiding and open warfare with the Scots, its rough hills and high moors* providing little prosperity to its inhabitants beyond sheepherding until the industrialization of the Newcastle area.

Northumberland Avenue. In London* a broad street running from Charing Cross* down to the Embankment.* Built in the late nineteenth century as a form of slum clearance on the model of Parisian avenues, it is something of a disappointment; it connects a major center with the river, but since there is no bridge at its river end, it is simply a broad street that goes absolutely nowhere. *See also* avenue.

Norwich. Pronounced NORidge. The principal town of Norfolk* and one of the oldest urban sites in the country, with a cathedral* since 1096 and about thirty churches* predating Henry VIII. Surrounded by rich flat farmlands, particularly good for livestock grazing, it was a major center of the woolen cloth trade in the medieval era and the source of most of England's beef* after the coming of the railroads.

no-see-um. *See* midge.

nosh. One of the few Yiddish terms to penetrate general use, now widely used slang for a snack or even a meal;* also used as a verb, to snack.

not at all. Used as Americans use "you're welcome," a response to "thank you" that means "no thanks are necessary" or "don't mention it."

note. In general use, paper money. Technically, a bank note is a promissory note payable to bearer on demand but paying no interest. The Bank of England* is the only bank* authorized to issue such notes, except in Scotland* and Northern Ireland,* where some local banks may do so for local currency. Thus, in a technical sense, the bank and not the government* issues the money for the nation. Originally, the only note was the five-pound* note, or fiver,* all other transactions using coinage, but a one-pound note was added in 1914. The one-pound note has since been replaced with a coin as post-WWII inflation has forced the issuance of tens, twenties, and fifties as well. *See also* Appendix I.

notecase. A holder for monetary notes* rather than for memos, what Americans call a wallet or billfold.

not half. *See* half.

notice. (1) A written announcement; hence, a **notice board** is what Americans call a bulletin board. Most local shops* have a notice board in the window, a board with small notecards thumbtacked to it advertising rooms for rent, small items for sale, thinly disguised ads from prostitutes,* et cetera, for which the shopkeeper* makes a small weekly charge. (2) To **give notice** is to fire an employee; employees may also give notice, meaning that they quit a job. In either case, notice usually means there is some warning given before the job actually stops. *See also* sack.

not on. *See* on.

not out. In cricket,* said of the batsman* who is still at bat and has not been put out for various reasons when the match ends (or in announcement of partial scores, when play pauses, as for lunch or overnight); thus, "36 not out" means the batsman has scored 36 runs and has still not been put out.

Nottingham. A town in central England.* Noted primarily for its association with the Robin Hood legends, it was also a center of support for the royalists in the Civil War.* In the sixteenth century a center of lace-making, it was quickly industrialized and became a major textile center, depicted particularly in *Sons and Lovers*. *See also* sheriff; Sherwood Forest.

Nottinghamshire. A county* or shire* in central England,* famous in legend as the site of Sherwood Forest* and the Robin Hood legends. The land is primarily moor* and fen* used for pasturing, and during industrialization it became one of the Midlands* counties focussed primarily on textiles. The borders were somewhat modified in 1974.

Notting Hill. An area of London* northwest of Hyde Park,* site of major developments after WWII and more than a little déclassé, noted primarily for the antiques market in Portobello Road;* the area around **Notting Hill Gate** is often associated with Caribbean Blacks, as in 1958 it was the site of the first modern race riots in the country.

nought. Zero.

noughts and crosses. Zeroes and *x*'s, the game Americans call tic-tac-toe.

nous. Intelligence, good sense. Curiously, although a fairly common casual term, it is quite intellectual in origin, from the Greek for intellect; thus the terminal *s* is usually pronounced, except by those who confuse it with the French for we/us.

nowt. Nought;* a common usage in northern dialects to mean "nothing" or "no one," but rarely heard elsewhere. *See also* owt.

NSPCC. National Society for the Prevention of Cruelty to Children. Many people find it significant that this was founded in 1884, sixty years after the RSPCA,* and almost as significant that it has never officially become the RSPCC, although people often mistakenly call it that.

NUGMW. National Union of General and Municipal Workers, the union representing primarily manual workers in various governmental jobs, such as dustmen* or road repair crews. *See also* NALGO; NUPE; TUC.

NUJ. National Union of Journalists, a union representing the bulk of newspaper* and magazine reporters and writers. In the 1970s, the NUJ was particularly aggressive, trying to control not only wages and working conditions but in some cases content, but the many changes in the newspaper* business of the 1980s left the union with considerably less power.

NUM. National Union of Mineworkers. Probably no union* in post-WWII Britain had more power or a worse public image than the NUM. A coal strike in 1926 initiated the General Strike,* and its failure only proved to miners the need for more militant action, although they did not form into a unified NUM until nationalization* of the coal fields forced it on them. Coal was, and still is, Britain's energy lifeblood, and the NUM strikes in the 1970s practically closed the country, brought down at least one government, and made union-busting a primary goal of the Conservative* party when it resumed power during the 1980s. NUM continues to be the most aggressive and most class-war oriented of the TUC* unions, but North Sea* oil, clean air acts, and the automobile have lessened its overall influence.

number. In addition to numerical uses, this is also used for an issue of a magazine or newspaper. A **back number** is an old issue, and hence, metaphorically, a retired or useless person.

Number Eleven. *See* Downing Street.

number nine. A laxative, from the code used on a type issued by the army.*

number plate. What Americans call a car or truck license plate.

Number Ten. *See* Downing Street.

NUPE. National Union of Public Employees, primarily government office workers. *See also* NALGO; NUGMW.

NUR. National Union of Railwaymen, the largest union of railroad workers, primarily made up of porters,* guards,* et cetera.

nurse. (1) Historically, the child's nurse was quite different from what modern Americans mean by the term. The original nurse was a **wet nurse**, a woman who was hired to allow another woman's child to nurse at her breast; this was common practice among the nobility* and other wealthy wives well into the twentieth century, and until mid-nineteenth century it was also common for the nurse to actually take the baby to her own home. When in novels we read of nurses who slept in the nursery,* they did this not to be sure the baby didn't fall from its crib but to keep themselves convenient to the child for breastfeeding and to prevent the child from waking its parents. In general, once the child was weaned, usually by eighteen months but often much earlier, care passed to the nanny.* A **nursemaid** was not a nurse but rather a maid* assigned to the nursery,* to clean the room and clothes and serve foods and help nanny* with menial chores; most nannies started as nursemaids and then were hired away by other families after several years' experience. *See also* governess; pap. (2) For medical nurses, *See* district nurse; Matron; National Health; Sister.

nursery. The children's area of a home. These were rare until the nineteenth century, but when the Victorians built or expanded houses, they always added two things: a servant's* wing, to get them out of sight, and a children's wing, to make them almost as invisible. The nursery itself was a largish room in which all daytime activities—play, meals, lessons, et cetera—took place, supervised by nanny*, and was connected to sleeping rooms for nanny, perhaps for a nursemaid* or two, and sometimes for the children as well, although they often slept all together in what was called the night nursery.

nursery school. A school* that precedes infant school,* generally ages two to five; sometimes called a **play school**. Official school-starting age is five, so only part of the nation's children attend these, although they are tax-supported institutions. In many places, their classes are held within the primary school* structure. *See also* junior school; kindergarten.

nursing home. Not a residence for the elderly but a private hospital where surgery as well as other treatments are available. What Americans call a nursing home is usually called a **rest home**.

nut. To be **off one's nut** is to lose one's head in anger; to **do one's nut** is to be either very angry or very worried. *See also* nutter.

NUT. National Union of Teachers, the largest and most active of the teachers' unions, chiefly representing teachers in comprehensives* and primary schools* and generally seen as a militant union and a driving force not only in obtaining better pay but in changing the entire educational structure of the country. *See also* NAS/UWT.

nutter. General slang for someone acting in a crazy manner.

O

oak. The oak has been symbolic of England* and the English since the very beginning of its navy*, as oak was the wood from which the ships were built. Thus, those who were brave, steadfast, and strong, like the wood and the ships, had **hearts of oak**, which phrase has remained current long after the ships became steel. Much British furniture was also made of oak, especially tables and desks, a sign of stability, sturdiness, and some wealth in the home; **fumed oak** was oak which had been artificially darkened by exposure to ammonia fumes, extremely common in late nineteenth and early twentieth centuries for the heavy furniture favored by the stultifyingly respectable of the time. To **sport the oak** is university* slang for studying, that is, staying behind a closed oak door. *See also* deal; timber.

Oaks. A race for three-year-old fillies run at Epsom Downs* in early June since 1779, similar to the Derby* in importance.

oakum. The loose, individual fibers of a rope, which when separated were sometimes used as a caulking material. **Picking oakum** was a common activity in prisons* and workhouses* before the twentieth century, which meant that people had to take worn and broken ropes apart into individual threads.

OAP. Old age pensioner.*

oat. The primary grain grown in Scotland* and northern England*. For the Scots,* oats appear in practically all national dishes: *See* haggis; oat-cake; porridge. For the English, as Dr. Johnson said, it was used primarily as feed for animals, except in gruel,* until the contemporary oat bran and health food fads.

oatcake. A small unleavened bread made from oatmeal, like a thick cracker.

OBE. Order of the British Empire, the honour* with the broadest base, used to recognize members of the general public and used for everyone from civil servants to businessmen to actors and rock stars. This has five categories, from the top rank down: Knight (Dame) Grand Cross (GBE); Knight (Dame) Commander (KBE), both of which carry the title Sir as for any other knight; Commander of the British Empire (CBE); Officer of the British Empire (OBE), in the civil service* often known as the "Other Bastards' Efforts" because it is given so often to retiring administrators; and Member of the British Empire (MBE).

obligatory. What Americans would call token, as an obligatory female board member or an obligatory Black* given a position that is important primarily for its visibility.

oblique/oblique stroke. The punctuation mark Americans call a slash (/).

Observer. A Sunday newspaper* of unchallengeable probity and detail, the oldest Sunday paper, originally appealing to Liberals* as opposed to the Conservative* *Sunday Times*, and as that party declined still espousing more "liberal" viewpoints, particularly in foreign affairs, which have been its editorial strength throughout its life.

obtain by deception. Legal phrase for fraud.

OC. In the military, Officer Commanding; American forces say CO, for Commanding Officer.

occupier. Many British use this to distinguish the person occupying a house,* from the **occupant** who temporarily sits in a room or railway carriage*.

och. In Scotland* and Ireland,* an interjection, used much the same as "Oh!"

oche. The line behind which a darts* player must stand to throw a dart.

OD. Technically, Ordnance Datum, the mean sea level at a site in Cornwall* from which all British elevations are measured.

odds. *See* What's the odds?

odds and sods. A miscellaneous group, odds and ends, a mixed bag, from WWI military slang for the soldiers with no useful function who were nonetheless assigned to a unit; now used casually in most layers of society. *See also* bits and bobs; sod.

odd sizes. In shops,* indicating not that the sizes themselves are weird but that the store has only some sizes available.

off. (1) In relation to food, gone bad or spoiled; in relation to a person, away or leaving, as in "I'm off" or "off you go." However, to **go off** is to no longer like something or someone. Something **a bit off** is something unpleasant or unreasonable and usually applies to a situation rather than a thing. To **have it off** is to have sexual intercourse. (2) In cricket,* the large portion of the field on the side of the bowler* and to the side of the wicket on which the batsman* is not standing. Thus, an **off break** is a ball bowled so that it starts to the off side of the wicket but bounces toward the batsman, and an **off drive** is a ball hit to the off side. **Mid off** is the area to the off side in the approximate middle of the field, **long off** is the part farthest away from the batsman. *See also* spinner.

offal. Most any internal organ (and the tongue) of an animal, an accepted part of the British diet; Americans almost never knowingly eat this, so we really have no comparable term.

Offa's Dyke. An earthen wall built in the eighteen century by King Offa to keep raiders from Wales* out of Mercia;* it ran from the Wye in the south to the Dee in the north, and significant portions of it still remain.

off colour. In general, this is used to mean sickly. What Americans call off-color, such as a dirty joke, is usually called "near the knuckle.*"

offence. Where Americans tend to use this (as offense) only for traffic violations, if then, the British tend to use it for most crimes and misdemeanors.

offer. Sale; hence, **on offer** means on sale, for an **offer price**, until **offer closes** at the end of the sale. A **special offer** means things are on sale at reduced price.

offices. In real estate, as in "usual offices," and sometimes in conversational slang, an indoor toilet.

Official Secrets Act. Passed in 1911, this provides for severe penalties for anyone who signs the act and then reveals any governmental secret, thus making practically all government* papers secret for thirty years.

off-licence. *See* licence.

off-load. Americans usually say unload; when used figuratively, this is what Americans usually mean when they dump on someone.

off-putting. Repellent, disturbing; used primarily by the middle class.*

offside. The right side of the car, the side toward the center of the road and the driver's side since the British drive on the left side of the road; the left, passenger side near the curb is called the **nearside**. The terminology comes from the pre-auto era, when people led animals from the left side, mounted horses from the left, et cetera.

off the peg. Ready-made* clothes, such as Americans often call "off the rack."

oiks. Public school* slang for the people in the local town, thus sometimes expanded to mean the hicks, the common people.

old age pensioner. What Americans call a retiree or senior citizen, an example of the British tendency to be several decades behind America in the development of euphemisms. Since under national insurance* every worker is now entitled to a pension, the term or its abbreviation, **OAP**, is used to mean any visibly old person. *See also* almshouse.

Old Bailey. Officially the Central Criminal Court, its nickname coming from the street on which it has been located in London* since 1834, originally the site of Newgate* prison,* the current buildings completed in 1907. This is the court for crimes committed in Greater London* and thus, through the national media, has become synonymous with criminal courts. Although Court #1 is often reproduced in films and television, there are eighteen different courtrooms in the building, the bulk of them modern, carpeted, and hardly distinguishable from contemporary American courtrooms.

Old Bill. *See* bill.

old boy. (1) Technically, a former student of a school, but more specifically, he attended one of the public schools* or one of the colleges* at Oxford* or Cambridge*. Thus, he is a part of the **old boy net**, or network, part of what Americans call the Establishment and on the inside track for appointments of power and influence. There is a similar network of **old girls** for graduates of the girl's schools*, but necessarily much smaller and with much less influence. It is unclear at the moment whether the females who have recently been enrolled in and graduated from many of the formerly all-male public schools will be called old girls or old boys. *See also* Appendix III; tie. (2) Occasionally, many men in the middle class* and gentry* use old boy as a synonym for old chap* or old man.*

old-fashioned. Not "living with the attitudes of another time" but precocious or mature beyond one's years; hence, Dombey's son grows "more and more old-fashioned" until he dies.

old girl. *See* old boy.

Old Lady. *See* Threadneedle Street.

old man. Essentially the same as old chap.*

Old One-Hundredth. A hymn beginning "All people that on Earth do dwell," which was #100 in the 1563 psalter and is based on the 100th Psalm, actually #365 in the 1935 *English Hymnal*.

Old Pals Act. Not a specific law but rather a slangy idiom for the idea that friends should give each other extra help when they can.

old school tie. *See* tie.

old stager. Someone with lots of experience.

old thing. Used as a casual address, much like old chap* but usually with more genuine affection; often used between married couples.

Old Vic. A theater in London* in the South Bank* area, for most of the twentieth century synonymous with serious artistic endeavor. This was a commercial theater that in 1912 began regular seasons of Shakespeare mixed with regular seasons of ballet and opera. After 1931 the ballet and opera moved to Sadler's Wells* and the theater expanded to full time, developing the legendary generation of English actors like Olivier, Richardson, and Gielgud. When Parliament* finally authorized a National Theatre,* it rather naturally operated in the Old Vic until the new buildings were ready, and the companies that had moved to Sadler's Wells grew into the English National Opera* and the Royal Ballet*.

O-levels. Ordinary levels, a test given from 1950–88 at about age fifteen or sixteen, and used to determine admission to sixth form* and to indicate a general level of education in job applications (but not technically required for school-leaving). Scores were given in eight specific subject areas, so a person would say he or she "had" (rather than "passed") "five O-levels" rather than any particular score or grade. *See also* GCE; GCSE.

OM. Order of Merit, a unique honour* limited to only twenty-four living persons at a time. This carries no knighthood or other title, but because of its exclusivity carries extremely high status.

on. When used without an object, this means acceptable, practical, or going ahead as scheduled, as in "the invasion is on for tomorrow morning." **Not on** means the opposite: wrong, unacceptable, or impractical, as in "It's just not on." (2) Talking, as in **on about**, which is talking endlessly or senselessly, or **on at**, which is nagging. (3) In cricket*, the large portion of the field on the side of the bowler* and on the same side of the wicket as the batsman* is standing; **mid on** is the area to the on side in the approximate middle of the field; **long on** is the portion farthest away from the batsman near the boundary* corner.

oncer. Pronounced WUNser, slang for a £1 note*, disappearing when the note did in 1983.

one-off. Something unique, not intended to be part of a series; used of TV programs, fashion, and other similar items.

open-cast. What Americans call strip mining. *See also* pit.

opening time. The time when the pub* opens. *See also* licensing laws.

Open University. A national educational program operated through TV, radio, and various publications, since 1969 designed to allow adults to gain a university degree* without enrolling in a regular university.* The bulk of BBC* TV broadcasting in the daytime is devoted to open university courses, and there are additionally more than 250 "study centres" where students may come for lectures, discussions, testing, or questions.

opera hat. A version of what Americans call a top hat, the style that is collapsible. *See also* silk hat.

operating theatre. In a hospital, what Americans call the operating room, with or without places for students or other observers to watch.

opera top. Not an opera hat* but a woman's slip designed to be worn under an evening gown.

oppidan. Originally, at public schools* or university*, a student who went to his or her own home at night. The term is rarely used since the seventeenth century except at Eton*, where it means one of the normal fee-paying students who live in various boarding houses in the town, as opposed to the seventy "foundation scholars" (on scholarships) who live in the college* itself and are often called **collegers**. *See also* day boarder; out-college.

opportunity shop. What Americans call a thrift shop or a secondhand store, usually such a shop run for charity.

Opposition. The largest political party* not participating in the government,* formally the **Loyal Opposition** to indicate their loyalty to the monarch despite their opposition to the government. *See also* Shadow Cabinet.

Orange. The House of Orange was the dynastic family of William III before he became King,* but practically all references are related to Northern Ireland,* where Protestant groups adopted this in their names after William's troops defeated the Catholics at the Battle of the Boyne.*

Orangemen. Officially the Orange Order, a political society founded in Northern Ireland* in 1795, named after William of Orange (William III of England). Interested primarily in maintaining a Protestant succession* for the monarchy, it was relatively unnoticed until the 1880s, when the rise of home rule* movements raised the possibility of Irish independence. At that point, the Orangemen began very public agitation to promote and protect Protestant interests and maintain the union with England, and in contemporary Northern Ireland they remain the principal force for Protestant political action. *See also* IRA.

orangery. A room or building with large windows on several sides, first appearing in country houses* during the Restoration, used during winter to shelter the ornamental orange trees so fashionable in that era. The orangery was sometimes separate from the main house, sometimes a room added on to the rest of the building; in later years it contained many other plants, or even no plants at all, and was often used as a sun room for members of the household. The most famous orangery is in the gardens of Kensington Palace* in London*. *See also* conservatory.

orchestras. Testicles; rhyming slang*: orchestra stalls* = balls.

orderly. A soldier who records and carries orders for an officer.* The **orderly book** is the regiment's* or company's* daily journal in which all orders are recorded, kept in the office of the unit, called an **orderly room**.

ordinary. (1) In Newgate,* the chaplain,* the usage disappearing when the prison* did. (2) A basic or standard meal* served at a fixed price in an inn* or tavern, and the inn or tavern where such meals were served. The term faded during the nineteenth century and has been replaced by set meal* or the French *prix fixe*. In the seventeenth, many of these inns in the City* also offered gambling, so that the term was often used for a gambling house.

ordinary shares. What Americans call common stock. *See also* shares.

Ordnance. In 1805 England* began an attempt to map the entire country accurately and in detail; finally concluded in 1873, the **Ordnance Survey** mapped every foot of England* and Wales* at a scale of one inch = one mile. The Ordnance maps became the standard for everyone and continue to be revised and used today for military and legal purposes and by the general public, especially hikers and cyclists.

Oriel. A college* of Oxford.* The Oxford Movement* was centered here, especially associated with Newman.

ornamental pond. An artificial pond, usually very small, in a garden*.

OS. (1) Ordnance* Survey. (2) *See* calendar.

Osborne biscuit. *See* biscuit.

osteopath. What Americans usually call a chiropractor.

OTC. Officer Training Corps since 1908, similar to American ROTC programs but confined to selected public schools* and universities.* *See also* Appendix V.

other, the. *See* bit.

other place. At Oxford,* Cambridge*; at Cambridge, Oxford. At Harrow,* Eton;* in the House of Commons,* the House of Lords,* et cetera.

other ranks. Members of the military who are not officers.*

OU. (1) Oxford* University. (2) Open University*.

OUDS. Oxford University Dramatic Society. This is not, as in the American manner, a university department or major but rather a student extracurricular club that produces full seasons of plays each year, using students in most or all capacities, and as such has been one of the major training grounds for British actors. *See also* ADC.

our. When preceding a person's name, this means a relative or friend, as in "how's our Johnny?" or "What are you doing there, our Ted?" However, this is almost always a lower class* usage, and if heard in the mouth of intellectuals or the upper classes is always a joke or an insult.

out-college. A student at a college* who attends classes but lives in the town or at home. *See also* day boarder.

Outer Circle. In London*, a carriage* lane that circles Regent's Park.*

outfitter. A shop* that concentrates on men's clothing.

outgoings. Regular or predictable expenses.

outhouse. On farms or estates, the outlying buildings, which could include the barn, stables, tool sheds, smithy, and occasionally perhaps even the workers' cottages,* but not the outdoor toilet meant by the American outhouse. However, in urban areas, once water-operated toilets began to replace the chamber pot, they were often placed in a separate building at the back of the garden* or in a separate shed touching the back wall of the house, because it was much easier to lay the water pipes there than to put them into buildings that had been built centuries before. Sometimes these were called outhouses, but very often people simply went **out the back**, particularly in working class* areas, where the term is often still used even if the toilet is now inside. *See also* lavatory; mod cons.

out of. Not connected with; to be **well out of** something is to have no part in it and glad of it.

out-relief. Charity given by a poorhouse* to a person not resident.

outsize. When used about clothes, large sizes.

outswinger. In cricket*, a ball thrown so that it curves away from the batsman* while still in the air rather than after bouncing.

out the back. *See* outhouse.

Oval. A major cricket* field in London,* located on the south side of the Thames* near Vauxhall* Bridge, in use since 1845. *See also* Lord's.

oven cloth. What Americans call a pot holder.

over. In cricket*, one round, usually six throws, by a single bowler;* the six bowls* must be within reach of the batsman* or the wicket*, so the bowler may make more than six actual throws if some of them go wide.* No single bowler may throw two consecutive overs, so the team must use at least two different bowlers; if the batsmen change places following a hit ball, the bowler may bowl to two or more different batsmen in the course of a single over. As the batsman is not required to run when the ball is hit, a bowler may go through an over without giving up a single run. Some matches* may be played for a predetermined number of overs rather than for full innings* in an effort to keep them within a single day. To have **had your overs** is used metaphorically to mean you have had your turn or opportunity.

overall/overalls. (1) Any simple garment worn to cover regular clothes while working, such as a lab coat or smock, but often meaning full coverings such as a boiler suit* or dungarees.* (2) In the army*, a type of tight-fitting uniform trousers,* first used in the cavalry.*

overdraft. To Americans, perhaps the single most amazing aspect of British banking. Operating apparently under the assumption that the customer must be the right sort of person or the bank would never have given them cheques* to begin with, the customer is allowed to write cheques for amounts greater than the amount actually on deposit, which the bank nonetheless pays. This does not last forever (*See* RD), as the amount and length of the overdraft is at the manager's option, and interest is charged on what is in effect an unsecured loan, but for temporary problems there are no bounced checks to ruin the customer's credit rating and no surprise fees greater than the amount of the check as in American banking.

overdress. Usually not a dress worn over another one but a jumper.*

overlook. (1) To provide a view from; for example, in Britain a window overlooks the pond while Americans often say it looks over the pond. (2) Modern Britons generally use the term the way Americans do, meaning to casually examine or pay little attention to, as in "overlooked the small print," but before the twentieth century, they often used it to mean the exact opposite: to examine carefully.

overset. To upset.

overtake. On the road, to do what Americans call passing.

owd. In the northern areas, old.

Owenite. A supporter of Robert Owen, who tried to reform mill practices in the early nineteenth century and was associated with socialism, utopianism, and "free love."

owt. Ought, meaning something or anything, a common usage in northern dialects but rarely heard elsewhere. *See also* nowt.

Oxbridge. From Oxford* or Cambridge.* Until very recently, graduates of the two universities so completely dominated political, social, and cultural life that the term is sometimes used to indicate the entire Establishment structure. *See also* class; United.

Oxfam. The Oxford Committee for Famine Relief, one of the largest charitable organizations, since 1942 providing not only food but also clothing, medicine, and some educational programs throughout the world. Oxfam shops* are found in cities and towns throughout Britain, primarily selling secondhand clothing in the manner of American Goodwill or Salvation Army stores.

Oxford. A town in central England* on the Thames,* itself a significant trading and industrial center for centuries but more often known for the university* there, which is arguably the oldest in Britain and one of the oldest in the world. Unlike American universities, Oxford (and its competitor in age and status, Cambridge*) is not a centralized institution but a loose cluster of all-but-autonomous colleges,* each with its own students, its own rules, and often duplicating the courses of study at others nearby; it is also incredibly small, even today having only about 13,000 students. Students are in a sense by-products, as most of the colleges were originally founded as institutions where scholars could think and research, like modern think tanks, particularly in theology, and the fellows* were treated much like monks, not in fact allowed to marry until 1880. Students were accepted primarily to replenish the ranks, which led to a system of tutorial rather than classroom instruction followed by a single examination to determine full admittance to the ranks of the fellows. The primary subject matter was religion and the Greek and Latin authors, and thus it continued well into the twentieth century, with Greek dropped as a required subject only in 1920 and Latin in 1960. The university rarely affected "real life" after its ranks were decimated during the Catholic* purges of the late sixteenth century and again after the fall of Charles I, and during the eighteenth and early nineteenth centuries, both Oxford and Cambridge were seen primarily as places in which to train clergy* or headmasters* and to hide eccentrics. But the revitalization of the public school* in the mid-nineteenth century suddenly gave new impetus to college educations, and it became important to go up* to Oxford in order to be a real gentleman.* Since then, Oxford and Cambridge together have had a profound impact on public life, producing the overwhelming majority of senior civil servants, politicians, and media powers, so powerful that the term Oxbridge* is used to signify the entire British Establishment. Women were admitted in 1879 in women's colleges, allowed to sit for exams in 1894, and given actual degrees in 1920; now two all-women's colleges remain, but all the rest also admit women. In general, Oxford has an image that is more literary and humanistic than Cambridge, which is more associated with science, but most of the famous writers who attended there in fact failed to get a degree.* For the town and environs, *See also* Broad, the; Carfax; Cherwell; Isis; Morris; Oxfordshire; Woodstock. For faculty and organizations, *See also* Chancellor; common room; hall; lecturer; proctor; professor; reader, tutor; vice-chancellor; warden. For calendar, *See also* Eights Week; hols; term. For student life, *See also* blue; bumping; down; gown; Great Tom; oak; OUDS; punt; rooms; scout; staircase. For academic matters, *See also* BA; Greats; honours; MA; moderns; PPE; Schools; Smalls. Colleges are listed under individual names.

Oxford bags. *See* bags.

Oxford Circus. The intersection in London* of Oxford Street* and Regent Street,* thus one of the central traffic interchanges and a center of the shopping district of the city.

Oxford Group. A religious revivalist group of the 1930s, not in any way associated with Oxford* except by its leader, an American named Frank Buchman who used the term for the intellectual status it implied. The group had no particular theology but was primarily a self-help form of Christianity that attracted members of the middle class* who could have their personal problems solved by "giving them to God."

Oxford Movement. A religious movement associated primarily with Newman and Pusey in the 1830s to move the Church of England* more toward Catholic practice, leading eventually to Anglo-Catholic* clergy and services. *See also* Tractarian.

Oxford Road. The old highway* from London* to Oxford,* following the route of modern Oxford Street* and along the north of Hyde Park.*

Oxfordshire. The county* or shire* in south-central England* surrounding Oxford.* Despite the university* and Oxford's industry, the county itself is full of small agricultural villages* like the one in *Lark Rise to Candleford*, which is set here.

Oxford Street. Originally the road to Tyburn* gallows, this London* street was built up as part of the city in the mid–eighteenth century. By the nineteenth century, it had become an area of shops,* cemented by the opening in the early twentieth of Selfridge's* and Marks and Spencer,* and continues to the present as the primary shopping district of London, its full length from Hyde Park* to Charing Cross* Road lined with shops and department stores, and its many side streets connecting with the more fashionable and expensive shops of Bond Street* and its environs. It has also served as the unofficial border of Mayfair* since the mid–nineteenth century, so that addresses north of it are decidedly more bourgeois and of less status than those to the south. Pedestrian traffic here is some of the densest to be found outside the Orient, in spite of Londoners' claims that locals never go there.

Oxon. Oxfordshire* or Oxford,* from the Latin Oxonia for Oxford.

Oxonian. Of or from Oxford* University.

P

p. Since 1971, the abbreviation for pence.* However, most people say "50 pee" rather than "50 pence." *See also* Appendix I; d; £; s.

PA. Personal assistant, in practice what Americans usually call a secretary; we of course are not above any number of similar euphemistic promotions.

pace. Pronounced pah-chay, a Latin term used by the educated classes for polite disagreement, meaning "by your leave," or "although I know so-and-so does not agree," as in "pace Darwin." However, it often appears in literature in the mouths of shopkeepers* and politicians, often used inaccurately, to illustrate their pretensions to education.

packdrill. Retribution or punishment, from a common army* punishment in which the offender had to do regular drill while carrying a loaded pack, sometimes filled with stones. The term is a part of general usage, particularly in the phrase **no names, no packdrill**, used when one wishes to give information without naming specific names for fear of retribution.

packed up. In relation to machines, broken down.

packet. (1) A small parcel or package of practically anything. (2) A great deal of money, as in "it cost a packet." (3) *See* pay packet. (4) To **stop a packet** is to have a major wound.

pad. In fox hunting,* the fox's foot, cut off as a trophy.

Paddington. An area in London* north of Hyde Park,* open country until the nineteenth century when first a canal and then the railroad terminating at Paddington Station made it a major transportation hub of the city. From

Paddington Station trains run to the western parts of England,* Wales,* and the southern Midlands,* and from the station originated the first busses* in London, followed by the first line of the Underground.* Additionally, the Regent's Canal* extended canalboat traffic from there to the Thames* in 1820. The residential area growing up around these was primarily lower–middle class,* as it continues today, but artist colonies have grown up at Little Venice* just north of the Station.

paddle. In water, not to swim but to wade in the shallows; hence, a **paddling pool** is what Americans usually call a wading pool, most often the small, portable, plastic one set up in the yard for small children.

Paddy. An Irishman, from Padraic, the Irish form of Patrick, and implying an Irishman fresh off the farm or in the working class.* *See also* mick.

padre. There is no clergyman officially called a padre in the Church of England.* In the late nineteenth century, the term was military slang for the unit chaplain,* by WWI so widely used as to be almost standard in the trenches. Since then, it has been used, especially at the upper end of the social scale, as a casual but respectful term of address for any priest.

page three. In 1970 *The Sun*,* a tabloid-style newspaper,* began running daily photos of females with bare breasts on page three. The feature was so successful that others have imitated it, and the term **page three girl** has come to mean a nude model or a pretty girl who might qualify if she wanted, especially one with large breasts.

pair. In a building, a floor,* as in "third pair," implying, not always truthfully, that there are only two flats* per floor.

Paki. A person of Pakistani origin, although used very loosely and often applied to Indians as well. *See also* Black; nigger; wog.

palace. The term is reserved only for residences of the monarch, with the single exception of Blenheim* granted by Queen Anne.

Pale. A wall of stakes built around English colonists in Ireland* in the fourteenth century, beyond which lived the "uncivilized, savage" Irish, from which we get **beyond the Pale** to mean anyone who is outside the bounds of proper society or socially acceptable behaviour.

Palestine soup. A cream soup made from Jerusalem artichokes.

Palgrave. Technically, Palgrave's *Golden Treasury* (1861, revised 1895), for generations on the shelf of even modestly educated persons as the repository of the poems "everyone" was supposed to know; probably supplanted in this function by the *Oxford Book of English Verse* although editions of Palgrave continue to be published by other hands.

Palladium. A large music hall* in London,* opened in 1901 and regarded as the top spot for variety performers; an American equivalent would have been the Palace in New York City. *See also* London, The.

Pall Mall. A street in London* running from St. James's Palace* to Trafalgar Square.* There is still disagreement as to pronunciation, but the upper-class preference is to rhyme with pal rather than with bell or ball. Although the site of numerous governmental offices, it is synonymous with the gentlemen's club,* as most of the oldest and most influential are located along the street. The name comes from a game which was played over a long straight course; the players tried to hit a ball from one end through a hoop suspended at the other, the winner taking the fewest strokes. The game was very popular in the Restoration, and Pall Mall apparently gained not only its name but its unusually straight nature from having been a site for the game. *See also* Mall.

palm. *See* Palm Sunday.

palm court. Between the wars, the lounge* or tea* shop of a swank hotel, almost always decorated with potted palms and with a string ensemble providing music, all modeled after the famous Winter Garden, or Palm Court, of the Ritz* Hotel in London.*

Palm Sunday. The Sunday* before Easter,* celebrated before the Protestant era with processionals of people waving "palms" in reference to the palms waved when Jesus entered Jerusalem; palms being foreign to Britain,* the local substitute was the willow, sometimes called an **English palm**. Puritans suppressed such processions, but folk customs kept them alive in many areas outside the church,* and they were reinstituted with special hymns in High Church* services during the mid–nineteenth century. *See also* Fig Sunday.

pan. What Americans call the toilet bowl. The term is also used as Americans do to identify a cooking utensil.

pancake. What Americans call a crêpe, almost always eaten for dessert with sugar or wrapped around a fruit filling, not for breakfast.* What Americans call a pancake does not exist outside tourist restaurants; the flapjack* is not at all like the American pancake either. *See also* Shrove Tuesday.

pancake race. A race for women run on Shrove Tuesday* in which they have to run a course while flipping a pancake* in a frying pan several times. The oldest is at Olney in Buckinghamshire,* claimed to date back to the fifteenth century; although there may have been others, they died out over the years, and all others run today are actually imitations begun following some publicity given to Olney after WWII.

Pancake Tuesday. Shrove Tuesday.*

Pancras, St. *See* St. Pancras.

panda car. A police car, once black and white; contemporary ones are usually white with variously colored stripes but are often still called pandas.

pandie. In Scotland,* a blow on the hand, especially one given in school* with a cane,* strap, or ruler.

p & p. Postage and packing, what Americans call p & h, postage and handling.

panel. For a doctor, not a list of advisors but rather a list of patients, more specifically, a list of patients on the National Health.*

pan haggerty. *See* haggerty.

pannage. A right of a tenant to let his pigs graze in the woodlands of the local lord* and the name of the rent paid for that right.

pantechnicon. In the early nineteenth century, a large warehouse in London* near Belgrave Square* used this term as an advertising name for the bazaar inside; it converted to furniture storage when the bazaar failed. Vans used to pick up or deliver furniture to it were naturally called pantechnicon vans, with the result that in the twentieth century, this was shortened, and pantechnicon came to mean the large truck that Americans call a moving van.

panto. A pantomime.*

pantomime. The British pantomime is not done in silence. It is basically a children's play, usually based on a fairy tale, with songs and dance and fancy scenic effects much more like a musical comedy that what Americans call pantomime. Since the mid–nineteenth century, these have been done primarily at Christmas.* Among the unusual traditions is that the male hero's role, called the principal boy,* is played by a woman while the comic woman, called the Dame,* is played by a man. A **pantomime horse** is the kind played by two people inside a horse suit.

pants. More likely to apply to underwear than to outerwear, which is called trousers,* and most often to women's underwear rather than men's, although more common usage is knickers* or drawers.* Since women regularly wear whatever pants might be worn in the family, the British couple argue over who wears the trousers.

pap. A substance fed to nineteenth-century babies as a substitute for breast-feeding as early as a month after birth, made of bread, water, and sugar, with a touch of milk.

paper chase. A cross-country race, usually in public schools,* in which the racers follow a course marked by dropped pieces of paper; metaphorically, any project requiring complex research.

paper hats. Americans still use these occasionally at New Year's Eve parties, but they have otherwise disappeared from adult festivities; the British seem to find them an essential part of practically any family or holiday party for adults, such as Christmas* and birthdays, along with poppers.*

paper knife. What Americans call a letter opener. The name comes from the time when these were used to cut the pages of regular books, which before WWI were almost always published with uncut pages.

parade. In addition to the American usage, the British also use this for a street or area intended for pedestrians, usually lined with shops.

paraffin. (1) Not melted wax but a petroleum product used primarily for home heaters, basically what Americans call kerosene. A **paraffin burner** is a stove using paraffin, either for heat or cooking. Although paraffin comes in a liquid state, **liquid paraffin** is something else, not burned but drunk, a mild laxative that Americans call mineral oil. (2) In Glasgow,* fancy clothes, most likely a shortened form of paraphernalia.

parish. (1) In the medieval era, the local area under the care of a single priest and a single church.* The practice and parish names carried over into the Church of England.* *See also* clergy; village. (2) In the sixteenth century, civil governmental authorities were instituted within the boundaries of the church parishes, usually called the Vestry until 1894,* primarily responsible for administering the poor law* and maintaining highways.* As the nation industrialized and new towns grew up, the civil parish boundaries changed so that most no longer matched those of the ecclesiastical parishes, and the establishment in 1888 of county* councils* and more rationally organized borough* and town councils took away most of their authority, so now the parish councils do little more than maintain rights of way, organize allotments, and supervise parking and streetlighting. Until the development of national assistance in 1934,* the parish was responsible for all relief of the destitute within its boundaries; thus, someone **on the parish** is someone receiving such relief, still occasionally used for people taking charity of any kind although the parish is no longer involved. *See also* beadle; beating the bounds; constable; dole; Justice of the Peace; vestry.

parish magazine. These were actual magazines, with articles, serials, etcetera, provided for the entire diocese by the bishop's* office but with a locally printed section of parish* news and calendars; thus, they were sold rather than distributed free, usually the duty of the priest's wife.

parish pump. Used as an adjective, what Americans would call "over the back fence" or "main street," meaning local gossip, politics, or deal making at the small, provincial level, like that done around the old parish* pump, where all the local people gathered for water.

parish school. In the eighteenth and nineteenth centuries, a school* run by the local parish,* almost always by the Church* but occasionally independently; these were elementary schools that taught reading, writing, and basic math, as well as church-related topics, for all the children of the parish. Most charged a small fee, and few were compulsory, but they provided the basic education for the bulk of the populace until the formal authorization of school boards and the board schools* in 1870. After free compulsory education was established in 1891, most parish schools were replaced by primary schools.* *See also* Sunday schools.

park. In urban areas, open space with grass, trees, and/or ponds, just as in America. In the country, however, park originally meant an area where deer were protected from all but noble* hunters. By the eighteenth century, this term had come to mean any parts of the grounds of a country house* where no crops were grown and where deer might graze freely, and by the nineteenth century had shrunk to mean any extensive ornamental grounds around a large house. *See also* AONB; chase; country park; forest; National Park; plantation.

Park. In London* in the eighteenth century, this meant only St. James's* Park, in the nineteenth it usually meant Hyde Park.* But in the twentieth, it usually means all three (St. James's, Hyde, and Green Park*), which are now interconnected.

Parkhurst. A prison* on the Isle of Wight* used only for male prisoners serving long terms or under special security restrictions.

parkin. A flat cake,* like a biscuit or gingerbread, made from oatmeal, molasses, and spice, common in the north of England.*

Park Lane. The street in London* on the eastern edge of Hyde Park.* Since first developed in the eighteenth century, this has been one of the most expensive and fashionable addresses in the world, site of fabulously large and expensive mansions for the nobility and others of great wealth. For Hercule Poirot to have a flat* there, his fees must have been considerable. In the late twentieth century, most of the old mansions have been converted to expensive hotels or offices, while the street has been widened into a dual-carriageway* to deal with a heavy flow of traffic.

parky. Chilly.

Parliament. In theory, this term means both the House of Commons* and the House of Lords,* but in practice, particularly in the twentieth century, it has increasingly meant only the Commons, as that is where the real power abides.

Parliamentary train. In the nineteenth century, all railroads were required by law to offer one train a day to each destination with a fare no greater than one pence* per mile, often also called the slow train.*

parlour. This term has a complicated history. Originally, a parlour was a room in a monastery where the monks were allowed to talk to outsiders (cf. French *parler*) and from that was applied to the small room off the main hall in a mansion* or castle where a small-scaled discussion or conference could take place. From this, parlour came to be used for the room in a home where the family sat and talked, similar to a drawing room* but not as fancy; thus it was used one notch down the social scale from people who had drawing rooms or, in those houses that had both a parlour and a drawing room, used for the more private family-oriented room. Thus, among the wealthy, an invitation into the parlour would imply admission into more intimate circles. However, among those not quite so rich, the parlour would be used only for important guests and special occasions and often the family would not be allowed to enter it during daily life. At the same time, the name was also often applied to what is now called the dining room, and George Grossmith's quintessential middle-class* average man Pooter was extremely proud that his house had a breakfast-parlour; thus, a **parlour maid** was not the maid* who dusted the furniture in the parlour (drawing room) but rather a maid who served at table in the parlour (dining room) in those households that had no menservants to do such work. In terraces and semis* that had three rooms downstairs, there was often a **front parlour** used only for company and a **back parlour**, a dark room in the middle between the front room and the kitchen, where the family actually lived. In those areas of the country with little Norman influence, parlour had a completely different meaning: it was the second room in a two-room cottage,* the room without the kitchen fireplace, and thus sometimes a "best room," sometimes a bedroom, and sometimes the room in which the family "lived" while work was done in the main room. In the nineteenth century, many inns* and pubs* set aside a small, plush room where guests could drink and talk in some comfort (and at higher prices) and called this a parlour as well. At present, most of these usages are disappearing, and in most homes the room that would have been called the parlour in the past is now called the lounge* or, reflecting American influence, the family room.

parsley. The same herb as in America, but many English parents tell little girls who ask where they come from that they were found **in the parsley bed**; little boys, however, are usually found under gooseberry* bushes. **Cow parsley** is larger, the plant usually called in America Queen Anne's lace.

parsnips. A kind of yellowish turnip, eaten regularly and occasionally used to make homemade beer or wine. To **butter parsnips** is to try to disguise the truth with fancy words.

parson. Originally, a parish* priest. The term is generally used casually and somewhat ironically for any clergyman, while more formal usage tends to be more specific and identify the clergyman as either vicar* or rector.* *See also* clergy.

parsonage. A home for a parish* priest, often more specifically called a rectory* or vicarage.*

Parson's Pleasure. At Oxford,* a site on the river Cherwell* until 1992 used for nude swimming by male students.

party. Although political parties historically accreted more by accident than by conscious design, by the late eighteenth century party had become as much a factor in parliamentary elections* as personality or status, and after the Reform Act* of 1832 realigned all political relationships, the modern system was recognizably in place. To Americans, the major difference in British parties is their control of membership. In America, politicians establish supporters and personal constituencies at local levels before moving on to state and national arenas, and the party they align with is more a matter of geography, family traditions, luck, or opportunism than conscious doctrine; most contemporary American politicians may wear a party label but they are in fact semiautonomous spokesmen for their own personal constituencies and, once elected, can be removed by little short of earth-shattering scandal. In Britain, the national party, not the local branch of it, approves or often actually selects candidates for the Commons;* there is no requirement for the candidate to have ever held office, nor even to actually live in the constituency* served. Thus, the members of parties when elected are both more in debt to the central party and much more consistent in their ideology than American party members, a factor further enforced by a system that requires a new election whenever any significant number of the majority party fails to vote as instructed, which in turn often means loss of the job for those members voting against the Prime Minister* when candidates are selected for the new election campaign. However, the winner-take-all nature of elections* means that the number of parties is kept down; unlike most continental countries with ideological party lines and dozens of parties represented proportionally, Britain for the last century or so has had only three effective parties: Conservative,* Liberal,* and Labour.* *See also* Whip.

party piece. Something a person does regularly in public, from the days before stereos and TV when guests at a party had to provide their own entertainment and most had at least one song they could sing or play.

party political. Not a political party but a program on TV or radio produced by a political party* to explain its positions, usually during elections.*

pass. At university,* a basic BA* degree. *See also* first; honours; poll; second.

passage. What Americans call a hall, hallway, or corridor.

passing out. Not falling unconscious but rather graduating from a school,* originally used in military academies* but sometimes used in others as well.

pass the parcel. A children's party game. The players are given a package with many layers of wrapping. Each tries to unwrap the package but must stop and give it to the next when the music stops. The one who finally unwraps the last layer before the music stops gets whatever is inside.

paste. In relation to food, a pâté, as in fish paste.

pastille. A small lozenge-like candy.

pasty. Pronounced PAHsty, a pie* the size of a single serving that can be eaten by hand, filled with either meat* or sweet fillings. A **Cornish pasty** has meat and vegetables and looks like a turnover.

patch. A territory or area of responsibility, similar in tone and meaning to what Americans call turf, as in "Keep off my patch." A **bad patch**, however, is an unlucky or unfortunate period of time rather than a place.

Patel, Mr. A euphemism for Paki* or wog,* from the surprisingly large proportion of Indian immigrants* actually named Patel. This often implies a small shopkeeper,* from the number of such immigrants who run corner shops.*

pater. Pronounced payter, for father, used only by the public school* class who had studied Latin; disappearing after WWII except in ironic references. *See also* mater.

Paternoster Row. A tiny street north of St. Paul's* in London,* in the eighteenth and nineteenth centuries the center of English publishing.

patience. The card game Americans call solitaire; when Britons play **solitaire**, they usually play it with marbles.

paved. Topped with brick, stone, or metal;* what Americans call paved (covered in asphalt, concrete, etc.) the British call sealed.*

pavement. Not the street but the sidewalk.

pawky. Funny in a very dry way associated with the Scots.*

pawpaw. What Americans call a papaya; the American pawpaw is an entirely different fruit from an entirely different tree.

Pax Britannica. The British Empire,* from the peaceful law and order assumed to have been given to the areas colonized. The assumption was often true, up to a point; the locals usually stopped fighting among themselves, but the British army* was nonetheless in regular action for two centuries.

pay bed. A bed in a hospital not paid for by the National Health* but paid for by the patient privately.

PAYE. Pay As You Earn, what Americans call withholding tax, which includes income tax* and national insurance* deductions.

paying-in. Making a deposit at a bank or similar savings institution, usually accompanied by a **paying-in slip**, which is a much more complex process than in American banks.

pay packet. The overwhelming majority of British workers have always been paid weekly and in cash; as late as 1989 some unions* threatened strikes when employers wanted to change to paychecks, as most workers still have no bank accounts. The money is received in a small envelope, along with a receipt for any tax and insurance deductions; hence the pay packet. Those on salary or now being paid by cheque* still use the term to refer to what is left after deductions.

pay round. A period of labor negotiations over wages.

PC. Police Constable. This is the basic bobby,* the policeman of lowest rank walking the street in dark blue uniform and funny helmet or patrolling in a car. A policewoman was a **WPC** until 1975; since then, she has been simply a PC. *See also* constable; Metropolitan Police; police.

pea. Not for nothing is it called an English pea. For most of the twentieth century, this has been the vegetable served with almost every meal but breakfast* (I once found a pile of them underneath restaurant spaghetti), but more recently, improving tastes and incomes has led to more variety. Although it seems that all peas in Britain are cooked till mushy, **mushy peas** are puréed peas. *See also* pease.

Peak District. A mountainous area southeast of Manchester,* a National Park* since 1951. Although the highest peak is only about 2,000 feet, the area was much admired in the nineteenth century for its romantic and craggy vistas and continues to be popular both with walkers and climbers.

pearly. *See* costermonger.

pease. The pea.* The term is for the most part no longer used except in traditional names and sayings; **pease pudding** or **pease porridge** of the nursery rhyme is what Americans usually call pea soup, although sometimes pease pudding is also used to indicate mushy peas.

peat. A layer of soil and decomposed plants, basically the same material as soft coal but not yet hardened into coal, found on the surface of moors* and fens* in two somewhat different forms. It was dug up, cut into brick-like shapes, dried, and then burned for fuel, but except in remote parts of Scotland* and Ireland* it has now been replaced by gas or electricity.

pebbledash. A stucco or concrete wall surface purposely roughened by mixing in small pebbles, appearing in the late nineteenth century and, despite its unsurpassed ugliness, remaining popular until at least the 1960s.

pebble glasses. Eyeglasses with very thick lenses.

pecker up, keep your. Keep up your spirits. The idiom appeared in mid-nineteenth century with pecker a play on beak or bill, words themselves slang for head, nose, or chin. The phrase is used casually in most levels of society and among both sexes, unlike the American version, which uses the phrase to mean much the same thing but locates the pecker considerably lower on the body.

Peckham. A neighborhood in southern London* near Brixton,* usually associated with the textile industry; **Peckham Rye** is the large open common* there.

peckish. Hungry, but only a little.

Peculiar People. A religious sect founded in 1838 (the name is their own choice, from a reference in the Bible), similar to American Christian Scientists in that they reject medicines in illness and similar to Quakers* in many other practices.

pedlar. The person Americans called a peddler; **pedlar's French** is the jargon of small-time thieves.

peeler. *See* bobby.

peep-bo. The childhood game Americans call peek-a-boo.

peer. A member of the nobility,* which means someone of the rank of baron* or higher who can serve in the House of Lords.* In 1957, Parliament* created a rank of **life peer** as a major honour;* this peer has all the privileges of a real peer except that he can not pass the title along to his heir. Because the United Kingdom* began as separate kingdoms, some peers are more equal than others: After 1707, all English peers continued to sit in the Lords, but only sixteen of the **Scottish peers** were given seats until 1963. Any newly created peers were British peers and also given seats in the Lords. Similarly, after 1801 only twenty-eight **Irish peers** were allowed in the Lords, and after 1921, of course, no new Irish peers could be created as Ireland was independent. In 1963, hereditary peers were allowed to renounce their titles, but this has rarely happened except among politicians who wanted to stay in the Commons* in hope of becoming Prime Minister,* and almost all were made life peers again anyway.

peerage. All the peers.*

peevers. In Scotland,* the children's game Americans call hopscotch.

peewit. A smallish bird related to the plover but more colorful, with greenish feathers and a crest, also called a **lapwing**.

peg. (1) What Americans call a clothespin. (2) A place to hang clothes; hence, **off the peg** is ready-to-wear clothing. (3) Among colonials in India, an alcoholic drink. *See also* burra; chota.

pelican crossing. What Americans call a crosswalk, distinct from a zebra crossing* in that it has a traffic signal that the pedestrian operates.

Pelmanism. A system of memory training and self-improvement widely popular in the lower–middle class* in the 1920s.

Pembroke. (1) A college* of Cambridge.* (2) A college of Oxford,* Dr* Johnson's college until he ran out of money.

pen. An ancient term for a hill, now found primarily in place names and in the range of small mountains called the Pennines.*

Penal Code. In America, this refers to all the criminal laws, but historically in Britain this applied to a specific set of laws passed between 1695–1727 that restricted the rights of Catholics,* making it illegal for them to vote, hold public office, or even buy land from Protestants.

penalty disc. The disc that pops up in a parking meter to indicate time has expired.

pence. Technically the plural of penny* but also used for only one. After decimalization in 1971, there were only 100 pence in a pound, and the new pence was abbreviated with a *p* rather than the old *d.** But curiously most people quit calling it a pence, and now you are much more likely to hear that something costs "50 pee" than "50 pence," even though no one ever said "50 dee" in the past. *See also* Appendix I.

Penge. A suburb of London* south of Dulwich,* dully middle–middle–class.*

Penguin. Not the first but certainly the most significant publisher of paperback books in Britain, since 1935 publishing a broad range of nonfiction and fiction both serious and entertaining that has made them synonymous with the paperback in Britain and made the imprint perhaps the most consistent sign of quality publishing in the English-speaking world. Penguin Classics began in 1946. *See also* puffin.

Pennines. The mountain range of England,* running from the Peak District* in the south through western Yorkshire* and Northumberland* to the Scottish border area. The **Pennine Way** is a hiking path that follows the ridges from the Peak District to the Scottish border.

penny. A coin worth one pence.* The penny has been basic currency in England since the Roman era, when it was silver and called a denarius, from which came the abbreviation *d* for pence. In 1971, when the currency was decimalized, the penny officially disappeared, replaced by a new coin called the one-pence which was worth 2.4 pennies, but many people still use the term penny for that coin. To **spend a penny**, however, is not to buy something but to urinate, something of a cutesy euphemism now but dating from the time when women who used public toilets* had to pay a penny to get a closed private stall. **The penny dropped**, meaning that suddenly everything became clear, seems to come from the release of the lock on the toilet stall door after the penny was inserted. *See also* Appendix I; farthing; halfpenny.

penny-a-liner. A journalist or hack writer, from the days when they were paid this way.

penny black. *See* penny post.

penny dreadful. A sensational paperback book or comic, like the American dime novels of the nineteenth century, from their original prices.

penny-farthing. (1) Cheap, slapdash, amateurish, as in a "penny-farthing business" that must always make do or do things clumsily due to lack of funds. (2) A bicycle with one large wheel and one small one, comparable to the size relationship between the two coins, very popular in the late nineteenth century. *See also* penny; farthing.

penny post. Mail using a standard postage of one pence* for any address within the United Kingdom* from 1840–1918. The **penny black**, the first self-adhesive stamp, was issued at the same time. *See also* post office.

penny reading. In the nineteenth century, a show with comedians and skits charging a penny* admission.

pension. Under the national insurance,* all employed persons are eligible for a national pension plan, similar to the American Social Security, with a basic rate supplemented by amounts paid based on previous deductions from paychecks and with no penalties for additional earned income.

pensioner. (1) *See* Chelsea pensioners; old age pensioner. (2) At Cambridge,* a student who pays his own fees and expenses.

Pentonville. A prison* built in 1842, its plan of small individual cells used as a model by most of the Victorian prisons; it is still in use, located in London* in the Islington* area. The neighborhood was a prosperous suburb in the early nineteenth but had deteriorated to a slum by the end of the century.

Penzance. A popular resort town at Land's End* on the southwest coast of England.*

peppercorn rent. Rent so small as to be a mere token payment.

pepper pot. What Americans call a pepper shaker.

perambulator. A pram.*

perch. *See* rod

pergola. What Americans usually call a trellis, primarily for roses.*

perishing. (1) An all-purpose modifier, used to intensify anything, as in "a perishing idiot." (2) Of the weather, very cold, as in "it was perishing outside."

periwinkle. *See* winkle.

permanent secretary. Technically, Permanent Undersecretary of State, the professional administrator of a governmental ministry* or department.* The PS* is a civil servant (hence "permanent"), and in theory his or her job is to administer the department under the policy direction of the politically appointed Minister.* As in all government bureaucracies, the PS wields enormous influence and authority. In almost all cases, he or she has also received several honours,* if not while in office then upon retirement; the overwhelming majority of people called Sir* are not national heroes but civil service* executives. *See also* PPS; secretary.

perry. A cider* made from pears rather than apples.

Persil. A brand of laundry detergent often used generically; something **persil white** is equivalent to American advertising's "whiter than white."

Perspex. A brand name often used generically for a plastic similar to what Americans call plexiglass. *See also* polystyrene.

Peter, Blue. *See* Blue Peter.

Peterborough. A town north of Cambridge,* associated primarily with an abbey* and cathedral, * portions of which date back to the seventh century, until the development of the brick industry there in the nineteenth. The **Soke of Peterborough** was the surrounding area originally controlled by the abbey* in Peterborough, treated as a county* until 1965, when it was absorbed into Huntingdonshire.*

Peterhouse. The oldest college* of Cambridge.*

Peterloo. On August 16, 1819, a mass demonstration on St. Peter's Field in Manchester* against the Corn Laws* was broken up by a cavalry* charge than led to at least eleven deaths, earning it the name of the Peterloo massacre in ironic reference to the great victory at Waterloo.*

petrol. What Americans call gasoline, the fuel for a car. The **petrol feed** is a gas line in the car, the **petrol gauge** a gas gauge, et cetera. Octane grades are indicated by stars (**); **two star** is approximately what Americans call regular, **four star** ethyl or super, et cetera.

Petticoat Lane. Actually Middlesex Street in the eastern portion of the City* in London* but almost always called by this nickname. A street market* devoted primarily to old clothes in Shakespeare's time, by the Victorian era it had become the largest street market in the city, still concentrating on clothing. It was held on Sundays (in significant part because so many of the traders were Jews* from the East End*), and thrived despite numerous attempts to close it down in keeping with other Sunday* closings, finally in 1936 given a special licence* to operate on Sundays. It remains an extremely varied and lively market popular with both locals and tourists.

petty sessions. In the legal system, a magistrate's* court, used to try minor offenses. Prior to 1949, these were sessions held by two or more justices of the peace* as an augmentation of those held at the regular quarter sessions.* *See also* police court.

Pevensey. A small village* on the English Channel* where William the Conqueror landed in 1066.* Although generally pronounced as spelled, locals often called it Pemzy.

PG. Paying guest, a euphemism for the lodger* in a bedsitter.*

phaeton. A light carriage* with four wheels and no roof, pulled by two horses.

pheasant. A moderately large bird with long tail feathers, one of the major sport birds that English gentlemen go shooting* for, often treated as something of a delicacy when roasted. *See also* grouse.

physical jerks. *See* jerks.

pibroch. A type of bagpipe* music in Scotland* used for military or funeral occasions, usually variations on a theme.

Piccadilly. A street in London* on the north edge of Green Park.* The name comes from a house* built on it in 1612 called Piccadilly Hall because its owner was a tailor who had become very rich selling picadils, the stiff collars with notched or laced borders common to early seventeenth century fashions. It serves as an unofficial border to Mayfair* and as such in the eighteenth and nineteenth centuries it was lined with expensive houses and was a very fashionable address. In the twentieth, it has been developed, so that many of the houses are hotels, offices, or expensive shops.

Piccadilly Circus. The intersection in London* of Piccadilly,* Shaftesbury Avenue,* Regent Street,* Haymarket,* and Coventry Street.* Traffic moves around a miniscule triangular island on which is a statue of Eros. Its location makes it the logical starting point for shopping, West End* theater, and the nightlife of nearby Leicester Square* and Soho.* For years, all the buildings around it have carried enormous lighted billboards, making it one of the liveliest corners in the world at night. For tourists and for locals, this has long been the emotional center of London, of England,* and of the Empire,* for reasons that defy explanation. It is small, crowded, ugly, and tasteless, it has no plan or organization, the traffic island is unreachable (although dozens of young people at a time somehow manage to gather on it), the traffic is a threat to life, no famous shops or buildings front on it, no major historical events took place here, and yet it is a rare English native for at least a century whose throat hasn't choked up at the thought of Piccadilly Circus as a symbol of all that is home, and it is a rare visitor who hasn't immediately felt all the vibrancy of a great metropolis as soon as he or she stepped into the area, day or night.

Pickford's. The most famous firm of furniture movers in London.*

Picts. An ancient tribe in Highland* areas of Scotland,* generally disappearing in the ninth century, but the term is occasionally used for modern Scots, especially Highlanders.*

picture hat. A woman's fancy hat with a very wide, round brim, apparently so called from their first appearances in portraits by Reynolds and Gainsborough but used to describe any similar hat into the present day. For the most part they are now actually seen only at Royal Ascot* and other outdoor royal occasions.

Picture Post. A news and photo magazine similar to the American *Life* magazine, having its greatest impact from WWII into the 1950s, gradually killed off like its American counterpart by television.

pictures. *See* cinema.

pie. A filled pastry, more often filled with meat than with fruit fillings. What Americans call a pie, eaten for dessert, is usually called a flan* or a tart.* A **pie dish** is not the dish on which it is eaten but the pie pan in which it is baked. A **raised pie** is made with a meat filling and with a crust on top as well, usually eaten cold. A **pork pie** is a pie with a filling of chunks of pork or ham, round with vertical sides and a flat top, usually made large enough for several portions, sliced and almost always eaten cold. **Yorkshire pie** is a meat pie made predominantly from fowl. Perhaps the most common is the **kidney pie**, made with a filling of kidneys, carrots, et cetera, so ubiquitous that the visitor sometimes wonders if the English throw away the meat to get the kidneys; this is also found as **steak and kidney pie**, with chunks of beef added, but somehow the kidney always predominates. Most meat pies are usually made in large dishes and scooped out to be eaten warm, but in recent years they have also appeared in the form of individual pot pies. A **shepherd's pie** or **cottage pie** is made of chopped or ground meat, originally ground mutton but now usually hamburger, topped with mashed potato.* A **woolton pie** is meatless, the bulk of the filling being potatoes and carrots, popularized during rationing.* *See also* pastry.

piece. (1) A woman or older girl; the term has been vulgar, low, and sex-related, similar to the American piece of ass, since the late eighteenth century. Thus, a **fancy piece** is a man's mistress,* but the term is usually said only by other women or by men who disapprove, implying she is also lower class and tarty, and is not used by the man himself. Before that, however, it was standard usage since well before Shakespeare, who once called Queen Elizabeth a "mighty piece," and was used in a generally complimentary sense, as a shortening of a "piece of work," which at the time was also occasionally applied to men as in Hamlet's famous comment. (2) The half-crown* coin; thus, **two pieces** equaled five shillings,* et cetera. (3) In Scotland* and northern England,* bread and butter, and from that occasionally any tea*-like snack between regular meals.*

pig/piggy-in-the-middle. A children's game like keep-away; when used metaphorically, it means a victim caught between two opposing sides and unable to do anything about it.

piggery. A farm that raises pigs; sometimes also a pig sty.

pigs fly. *See* when pigs fly.

pi-jaw. A pious jawing, or talking-to, the kind of talk you receive "for your own good."

pilchard. Another name for what Americans call a sardine.

Pilgrim's Way. A series of roads in use before the medieval era, running from near Winchester* to Canterbury.* It's not clear now that the route ever was complete, for the title is relatively modern, connecting a number of possibly separate paths. The pilgrims who came through London, such as Chaucer's, used Watling Street,* a completely different route.

pillar box. A mail box, so called because it is tubular like a building pillar. The red pillar boxes, about five feet tall, have been a fundamental landmark since their appearance in the 1850s, installed, as it happens, by the writer Trollope when he was in charge of the post office,* although in the late 1980s, plans were bruited to replace these with mailboxes more of the American type.

pillion. A light saddle used primarily by women in the sixteenth century. By the nineteenth century, this had become a pad behind the regular saddle on which a second person, usually a woman, could ride or on which things such as the mail might be carried and in the twentieth was transferred to the space for a second person behind the driver of a motorcycle.

pillock. In northern England,* a stupid person.

Pimlico. A neighborhood of London* between Victoria Station* and the Thames,* developed in the 1850s as South Belgravia,* with terrace* houses to be homes for the almost-successful and nearly rich. Rather quickly it became just the tiniest bit down at heel, a personality it has carried into the present day, along with a reputation for independence and individuality among its inhabitants. In the present day it is noted for its concentration of bed-and-breakfast* hotels, for Dolphin Square, one of the largest apartment developments in the world, and for quiet residential byways.

Pimm's. A brand of premixed alcoholic drinks in several different varieties, usually drunk in summer as a "refresher" but nonetheless quite potent.

pimp. In southern England,* a small bundle of kindling used to set a coal fire alight. The meaning of pimp related to prostitution* is used throughout the nation, but the origin of and relation between the two meanings is unclear.

pimpernel. A small wildflower, more common in continental Europe than in Britain;* the **scarlet pimpernel** of the novel is a form of primrose.*

pinafore. Originally, in the mid–nineteenth century, this was simply a piece of cloth pinned onto the front of a child's, usually a girl's, clothing (hence the name), to keep the dress from being soiled. Naturally, these were soon fancied up for the more well-to-do, tied behind the waist and attached behind the neck or over the shoulders; Alice in Wonderland, for example, is always shown wearing a pinafore. Thus, by the end of the nineteenth, the name was applied to two completely different garments, one simply a bib apron* that hooked over the neck and was tied at the waist, and the other a sleeveless dress or smock worn over another dress and tied in back, rather like a modern hospital gown, worn for heavy housework or by women in factories or similar dirty jobs. *See also* apron.

pinch. (1) To steal. (2) To arrest someone, used for any crime.

pinchbeck. An alloy of copper and zinc that looks like gold, named for its inventor, and thus also a synonym for the deceptively cheap or shoddy.

Pincher. All but automatic nickname* for a man named Martin, from an admiral* Martin who was noted for strict discipline.

pine. *See* deal.

pink. When said about a motor, the sound Americans call a ping.

pink, strike me. A working class* expletive indicating surprise or shock, although why pink would be a cause for alarm is unclear; other pink idioms, such as "in the pink," are positive.

pink gin. *See* gin.

pinny. A pinafore.*

pint. (1) A generic term for beer,* due to the practice, now required by the licensing laws,* of serving beer in pubs* only in pint or half-pint glasses. *See also* half. (2) As a measure, larger than the American pint, twenty ounces rather than sixteen.

pinta. A pint of milk.

pipe cot. In the navy,* a hammock.

pip emma. The afternoon, P.M., military usage since WWI. *See also* ack emma.

pipe rolls. Official financial records itemizing income and sheriff's* expenses in each county* of England,* from 1130–1832; the origin of the name remains obscure.

pips. (1) Fruit seeds, as in the oranges in Sherlock Holmes's *Five Orange Pips*. (2) The metal insignia worn by officers* on the shoulder of a uniform. (3) Spots on dice, dominoes, or other similar gaming tools.

pirate stations. When rock'n'roll began to arrive from America, the BBC* had little time or inclination to broadcast the records. In the 1960s, a number of commercial stations set up on ships just outside the territorial waters where they could escape the BBC monopoly and broadcast both music, usually rock'n'roll, and commercials. The BBC eventually expanded its radio service, and private stations were also authorized (now about seventy total), and the pirate stations no longer exist, although the powerful Radio Luxemburg from the continent continues the style and competition.

pish. Since Shakespeare's day, an all-purpose exclamation indicating: don't be silly, what foolishness, et cetera; not in any way related to piss.* However, it is generally associated with the old speaking to the young or the upper speaking to a lower class,* and in the twentieth century is often put into the mouth of dominating upper-class women. **Pish and tosh** is roughly equivalent to "stuff and nonsense," or "don't be so stupid."

piss. As in America, to urinate; however, this was standard usage (cf. French, in which the root word *pisser* is still standard) until the late eighteenth century, when suddenly it was thought to be vulgar and crude and thus disappeared from respectable vocabularies. But it continued to figure in much popular slang: Someone very drunk is **pissed**, and a night of heavy drinking is often called a **piss-up**; the dandelion was called a **piss-a-bed** until the nineteenth century, for what eating them would make one do; to **piss off** means to leave in a hurry and is often used as a command for get out; before the nineteenth century, it was common to use **pissing** to describe anything small, brief, or worthless, and a very short time was often called a **pissing-while**. In the twentieth century, pissing reappeared as vulgar slang for a heavy rain, first surfacing among the Cockneys* after WWI. Someone who is despicable or worthless is one who should be **pissed on from a great height**, while someone who has been made the scapegoat for someone else's mistakes has already had this done to him.

pit. A coal mine, almost always the tunnels underground rather than an open pit. *See also* open-cast.

pitch. (1) In cricket,* the part of a field* where most of the game is actually played, basically the central wicket* area, although sometimes used for the entire field as well. (2) In football* or rugby,* the playing field. A **plastic pitch** is one covered with what Americans call artificial turf. (3) A barrow* or market* stall; thus, to **queer the pitch** means to mess up someone's business.

pitch and toss. A gambling game in which players toss coins at a target; the closest throws all the coins in the air and keeps those that land heads.

pitcher. A granite paving stone.

pit pony. Before complete mechanization of the mines, a pony that pulled loaded carts of ore. These were lowered down into or born in the mines and lived their entire lives underground.

place. Not only geographical but also social; hence to **know your place** is not to know where your house is but to understand exactly where you fit into the social class* system, to know who you must be respectful toward and exactly how much respect you should show them. Similarly, to **put someone in his/her place** is to remind them of their position and stop them from acting in the way Americans call uppity. *See also* station.

place man. A person given a government job for political reasons and using such a position only for private profit.

plaice. A flatfish, when whole about a foot long and similar to a flounder, used as the basic fish in fish and chips.*

plaid. Technically, in Scotland,* the plaid is the piece of cloth worn draped over one shoulder when wearing the kilt,* made of wool in one of the many patterns that are now called plaid by most people; the Scots usually called the pattern itself a tartan.*

Plaid Cymru. Not a Scottish tartan* but a Welsh nationalist, encouraging Welsh language and culture and from the 1930s advocating nationhood for Wales.*

plaits. Pronounced plats, what Americans call braids.

plane tree. A tree with very broad leaves, similar to the American sycamore, rarely found growing naturally but widely planted in parks and along streets, especially the "London plane" that is resistant to smog.

plantation. An area growing trees that have been planted, as opposed to a forest,* which is natural growth.

plant pot. What Americans call a potted plant or a house plant.

plaster. Shortened from **sticking plaster**, used for almost any small bandage held by adhesive tape. *See also* Elastoplast.

plasticine. A soft modeling material used as a children's toy, something like American Play-Doh, a brand name often used generically.

platform ticket. In most railroad stations, tickets were collected as the traveler left the platform; people who came to meet someone had to have a ticket to surrender as well, to prove they had not stolen a ride on the train. Thus to go onto the platform to meet or to say farewell to someone they were required to buy a separate ticket.

platoon. In the army,* a portion of a company. By the mid-nineteenth century, the platoon had disappeared, replaced by the section,* but just before WWI regiments were reorganized, with the number of companies reduced and size increased, at which point platoons returned, now having three sections, with four platoons in a company. The new platoon was commanded by a subaltern.*

playing field. An outdoor space in which sports are played, especially associated with schools.*

play school. *See* nursery school.

PLC. Public Limited Company, a company whose liability is limited by law, basically the same as an American corporation. *See also* Ltd.

pleached. With the branches of several plants woven together, done to make hedges* or sometimes to form alleys.*

pleb. A common person, from plebeian but pronounced plehb rather than plebe, generally intended to be insulting.

plimsolls. A soft shoe, usually with canvas top and rubber soles.

plonk. A casual term for any cheap red wine.

plough. In collegiate slang, to fail an exam, usually expressed as "he was ploughed" rather than as "he ploughed."

Plough. In the sky, the constellation Ursa Major, usually called by Americans the Big Dipper. The **Plough and the Stars** was the flag used in the 1916 Irish rebellion, with the constellation superimposed on a plow.

ploughman's lunch. Bread and cheese, usually accompanied by beer.*

Plough Monday. The first Monday after Twelfth Night,* thus the day on which farm work in the medieval era officially began after the long Christmas* holidays and festivities. This was often the start of early spring ploughing and hence was often accompanied by special festivals or customs designed to bless the plough and encourage a good planting season, including in some places dancing and mummers.* The bulk of such practices faded in the mid-nineteenth century. Some of the religious aspects were revived in many parishes* following WWII as part of the urban urge to reconnect with agricultural roots, best exemplified by the harvest festival,* and thus many churches now hold **Plough Sunday** services on the day before.

PLR. Public Lending Right—writers love this, a royalty paid by funds from a Treasury grant* and based on the number of times a book is borrowed from a public library,* passed in 1979, first paid in 1984.

plug. Britain was very slow to standardize its electric sockets, so there is no uniform size and shape of plug for appliances; most houses have wall sockets (called points*) requiring plugs with either two round pins or three flat blades, or often both. Thus, most appliances are sold with bare wires, so that the buyer has to put on a plug at home to match the wall socket he intends to use, and in many cases, if the appliance is moved, the plug has to be changed. Plugs also require a fuse, with different amperage needed for different appliances, and the sockets themselves have a switch, so plugging in a toaster can be a complex operation. *See also* earth.

plug hole. The drainage hole in a basin* or bathtub.

plum in his mouth. *See* plummy.

plummy. Said of a voice, rich and rounded in speaking tone, often implying an artificial speaking voice in which certain sounds have been exaggerated either for resonance or to imply higher social class.* Said of other things, it generally means something desirable.

plum pudding. *See* pudding.

plus-fours. Loose trousers* that stop below the knee, worn by gentlemen since late nineteenth century for sporting activities such as shooting* or golf. The name comes from their having four more inches of length than breeches* or the American knickerbockers.

Plymouth. A major port on the southwest coast of England,* used by many ships sailing for America, of which the *Mayflower* is only the most famous, and home of the English fleet that sailed out to meet the Armada.* The city was a major embarkation point for both D-Day in 1944 and the Falklands* War and continues to be a major port for the navy.* It was also long a center of puritan groups and is often associated with various chapel* religions. The natural harbor, called **Plymouth Sound**, is additionally protected by a breakwater built in 1841. *See also* Eddystone.

PM. Prime Minister.*

po. Euphemism for a chamber pot, from the French* pronunciation of pot, disappearing now, as is the item.

poach/poacher. The English country gentleman* was passionately devoted to hunting and shooting and resented anyone interfering with his pleasures in this area. After the enclosures,* his attempts to gain exclusive use of the game on his land became a major source of social conflict. Locals, who had formerly hunted or trapped small game for food or grazed their pigs on the common* land to which they were now denied access, turned to poaching to get meat. This was not the quaint game of hide-and-seek Americans like to see it as, but a source of serious social conflict, particularly after the gentlemen managed to make poaching a criminal offense; poachers were liable to transportation* for a single rabbit, and after 1831 local gamekeepers* in effect had the powers of policemen.

Poet's Corner. A portion of the south transept of Westminster Abbey* used for memorials to persons of primarily literary reputation; some of the poets are buried there, such as Chaucer, but most simply have memorial plaques or statues.

po-faced. A blank, smug, or disapproving expression; the term was first noted among the educated in the 1930s and is now used throughout almost all levels of society, but curiously there is no generally agreed upon source.

point duty. Of police,* duty as traffic cops.

points. What Americans call the electric socket. Unlike American sockets, these usually also contain a switch. Sometimes called the **point**. *See also* electricity; mains; plug.

poky. Cramped, confining, almost always said as "poky little."

pole. *See* rod.

police. Until the early nineteenth century, the British had no police forces
as we understand the term. In the rural parishes,* the constable* was
responsible for keeping the peace; in urban areas, particularly London,*
the citizen was on his own, required to identify and often to capture a
criminal himself to get him before a magistrate.* Henry Fielding established
the Bow Street* Runners as licensed bounty hunters, with the army* the
only recourse for any large public disturbances like the Gordon Riots.*
As industrialized urban areas grew, these methods were dismal failures,
and in 1829 Robert Peel was authorized to organize the Metropolitan
Police* in London, whose members eventually used his nickname as their
own and became the famous bobbies;* City Police, serving only the City,*
were founded at about the same time. They were not welcomed, fears of
a "police state" being widespread, but after the bobbies dispersed major
political demonstrations in 1833 without injuring any of the protesters, they
gained national respect for their methods and in 1835 other boroughs* and
in 1839 the counties* were allowed and in 1856 required to form similar
forces. The Metropolitan Police serving Greater London* naturally got the
most publicity, and Scotland Yard,* the site of their first main offices,
became synonymous with police activity, but the police forces themselves
remain decentralized and semiautonomous into the present, although national pay scales and ranks were standardized in 1919. Since 1964, about
half of the county and borough forces were amalgamated into regional
forces, now numbering just over forty, but although all such forces report
to the Home Office,* each force is still in practice independent of the
others, each headed by its own Chief Constable.* Since the beginning, all
the police in Britain have been unarmed, carrying only truncheons* if they
carried any weapon at all; in recent years, some have been authorized to
carry pistols, but the overwhelming majority are still, by American standards, unarmed. For ranks, *See* commissioner; constable; inspector; sergeant. *See also* CID; Flying Squad; SAS; Special Branch; traffic warden.

police court. The popular name for petty sessions,* the basic magistrate's*
court, dealing with minor crimes without juries.

Police Medal. An award for policemen and policewomen for bravery.

policy. In Scotland,* the grounds around a country house.*

polka dots. What Americans call chocolate chips.

poll. At Cambridge,* a basic BA degree,* pronounced like Polly. *See also*
first; honours; pass; second.

polling day. What Americans call election day. *See also* ballot; voting.

polling station. Where polling, or voting, takes place.

poll tax. A tax on heads, a uniform tax paid by all individuals regardless of other income* or property.* The British have tried this twice. The first time, attempts to actually collect it in 1381 led to open civil war, and it was abandoned until 1989, when the national government* abolished rates* and substituted a poll tax (effective 1990), which was officially called a **community charge**. The theory of this tax was that people who actually received local government "services" should pay for them, with the added justification that when they did so, they would quit demanding the services in order to reduce the local tax, the rate of which was set by each local council.* However, the community charge was immediately recognized as a poll tax and widely opposed by the general public. After one year, following riots, lost by-elections,* and the downfall of a Prime Minister,* it was dropped (effective 1993).

polony. What Americans call bologna.

Polos. A brand of small circular mint-like candies, similar to American Lifesavers.

poly. Polythene.*

polyethylene. Polythene.*

Polyfilla. A substance for filling cracks in wood or plaster, sold as a powder that is mixed with water to make a putty-like consistency.

polystyrene. A strong clear plastic; when expanded with gas, molded into what Americans usually call styrofoam.

polytechnic. An institute of higher learning, but distinct from the college* or university* in that it is usually relatively new (the first were formed in 1967 by reorganizing the older technical colleges*), has some part-time or adult students, is attended by locals with few if any students living on the campus, and is generally associated with technical or vocational courses, although still offering various arts and humanities, rather like an American junior or community college. The polytechnic grants diplomas* rather than degrees* and is also popularly assumed to be filled with comparatively stupid students, although they in fact come from the top sixth of all school-leavers* and constitute about 90 percent of all higher education in the country. Legislation under way will allow polytechnics to offer degrees in the late 1990s, and only a Pollyanna would think that they will not shortly start calling themselves universities as well.

polythene. Plastic sheeting of various types. The plastic bags so common now in all parts of modern life are usually called polythene bags, and for many people polythene is used generically for almost all plastics.

polyurethane. What Americans usually call foam rubber.

Pomfret cake. *See* cake.

pommy. This is really Australian slang, used for any person from Great Britain,* though the origin is unclear. The Australians often use it with an implication of effeminancy, and when it is used in Britain itself, this is the meaning intended.

ponce. (1) As a verb, to walk in an affected, effeminate manner. (2) As a noun, a pimp.

pong. Unpleasant odor.

pongo. In the late nineteenth century, this was a common term for an orangutan. Thus, it was often used as a nickname* among schoolboys, continuing in mid-twentieth century probably as a reference to pong* instead, and thus the nickname is equivalent either to Monkey or Stinky.

pontoon. A card game Americans call blackjack or twenty-one.

pony. £25. There is no coin or note* for this amount.

poof. A homosexual male.

poofter. A poof.*

Pool. In London,* the section of the Thames* between Tower Bridge* and Limehouse,* for all but the smallest ships the limit of their trip upriver.

pools. Beginning in the 1930s, a form of lottery in which players ostensibly picked combinations of winners and scores of football* matches, thus squeezing around the gambling laws. This quickly became a regular part of working class* life, and even after other forms of gambling were legalized, the pools remained the most widespread form of gambling in the nation. *See also* betting shop.

poorhouse. *See* Poor Laws; workhouse.

Poor Knight. *See* Garter, Order of the.

Poor Laws. A series of laws that authorized and regulated government aid to the indigent. The English have had a long understanding that government had some responsibility for basic maintenance of its citizens, but they have struggled almost as long for a way to help the needy without helping the lazy as well. The first poor law in 1536 was adapted from the medieval practice of the local church* providing temporary aid to the needy, and it authorized relief administered by the local parish* but funded only from individual donations. In 1563 and 1597 justices of the peace* were authorized to levy local taxes to fund such relief, standardized throughout the kingdom in a rate* in 1601. After 1662, the poor could obtain relief only in their home parish. All of these efforts were overwhelmed by the movement of the poor during the enclosures* and early stages of the industrial revolution, and in 1723 the poor were required for the first time to enter **workhouses**, although in 1782 the able-bodied were supposed to be given outdoor work instead. Increasing urbanization made this practice impossible to sustain, so that in 1834 the parishes were replaced by larger regional councils,* and all who sought relief were forced into workhouses again, with the workhouses themselves purposely made as miserable and prison-like as possible in order to discourage all but the genuine poor from applying for relief. Readers of *Oliver Twist*, for example, should note that Oliver grew up in one of the old workhouses, before they got really bad, with families separated and the inmates given prison-style uniforms and haircuts, silent exercise periods, and hours of pointless labor, like picking oakum.* These practices worked to the extent that practically no "able-bodied" people applied for relief, but then neither did the bulk of the genuinely needy, as most preferred to starve in the gutters rather than go into the workhouse. In 1934, the workhouses were at last closed and a uniform system of national assistance* begun, leading to the complex web of modern government services and benefits. *See also* almshouse; dole; national insurance; poll tax.

poor rate. A rate,* or tax, imposed locally to provide specifically for relief of the poor, first authorized in 1563 and standardized nationally in 1601, in the twentieth century replaced by other forms of taxation. *See also* Poor Laws.

pop. (1) As a verb, to visit casually or briefly, usually as **pop in**, which equals the American "drop in" in both meaning and general tone. (2) As **in pop**, slang meaning an item has been pawned, lower-class* slang for in pawn. (3) In the eighteenth and nineteenth centuries used to mean not the father but the daughter, a shortened form of poppet.*

poppadam. A thin, crisp, and spicy form of bread, originally from India.

popper. (1) A party favor that the user pulls an end out of, making a pop and revealing a favor, noisemaker, streamer, et cetera, popular for adults as well as children. Also called a cracker.* (2) On clothes, what Americans call a snap.

poppet. The old term for a doll (cf. modern puppet), and hence often used for a cute small child. *See also* doll; pop; popsie.

popping crease. *See* crease.

pops. *See* top of the pops.

popsie. A cute young woman. This probably began in the mid-nineteenth century as a variation on poppet* and was used in nurseries, along with **popsie-wopsie**, and in the twentieth century, was gradually applied to older girls who were still cute like the small ones. Thus, the term rarely, and only recently, implies any sexual relationship.

pop-wallah. Someone who refused to drink alcohol. *See also* wallah.

porch. In general, the British only use this term about public buildings, such as a church,* where it means a covered area just outside the main entrance, or sometimes a vestibule just inside the entrance. On a house, what Americans call the porch is called the **step** if small and the **veranda** if large.

pork pie. (1) *See* pie. (2) A soft felt hat with a brim and with a flattened crown, and thus shaped like a pork pie.

pork scratchings. A snack food like American fried pork rinds.

Porlock. A small town in Exmoor* that would be without note were it not for the person from Porlock who interrupted Coleridge's *Kubla Khan*.

porridge. Essentially what Americans call oatmeal. Long a basic food for all meals, not just breakfast,* particularly in Scotland* and northern England* where oats* are the most common grain, the name and the food has declined in the twentieth century and is regarded now as a peculiarly Scottish national food. For unverifiable reasons, it was the habit until well into this century in Scotland to eat porridge at breakfast only while standing up.

port. A red wine originally from Oporto in Portugal, fortified with brandy so that its alcoholic content is about twice that of regular red wine. Similar to sherry* but much more masculine in image, it was the standard drink of the eighteenth century gentlemen*; by the late nineteenth century, however, port was drunk almost completely as an upper-class* after-dinner drink, traditionally only by the men while they smoked and the ladies retired to another room.

porter. (1) A doorkeeper or gatekeeper. (2) Someone who carries, now confined mostly to railway* stations or hotels. A **hall porter** in better hotels acts something like the French concierge, taking orders, arranging errands, et cetera. (3) *See* beer.

portion. A sum paid out to children from an estate upon the father's death. British gentry* almost always passed the property* itself to the eldest son along with the title, so younger sons rarely got estates. Rather, they would be given a lump sum (considerably less than an equal share) with which to set themselves up in another career (such as buying a commission*), after which they received nothing except as agreed upon by the eldest brother. Daughters generally were given their portions as part of dowries upon marriage* before the father died, but unmarried daughters would usually be left a portion in trust to become a dowry* later. *See also* jointure.

Portland, Isle of. Not an island but a peninsula with a very narrow neck on the southern coast of England* west of Bournemouth,* made of limestone quarried for the famous Portland stone. The **Portland Bill** is the rocky tip of the peninsula.

Portland Club. A club* in London* in Mayfair* inextricably associated with the game of bridge* since its club rules were adopted as the official rules.

Portland Place. A street in London* south of Regent's Park.* Originally intended as a close* for wealthy tenants in the late eighteenth century, it was extremely wide (125 feet), with a dead end at the south. In the early nineteenth century, the street was extended south with an odd little jog into Regent Street.* It now houses several embassies and the headquarters of the BBC* and is sometimes used as a synonym for the BBC. Ironically for such a fashionable area, **Great Portland Street** parallel to the east is London's car-dealer row.

Portobello Road. A street in the Notting Hill* area of London,* synonymous with the market* in antiques and would-be antiques carried on in stalls* and permanent shops* along the road. Stalls appeared for a Saturday night market around 1890, but the present market didn't really grow up until after 1948. You can now shop there on any day but Sunday,* but the traditional Saturday is still the time when it is most active.

Port of London. The portion of the Thames* from the first lock west of Richmond* to a sandbank called the Nore* offshore of the mouth of the Medway,* all administered by a single Authority since 1909.

Portsmouth. A coastal city and harbor on the south coast of England* at the eastern end of the Solent.* Henry VII built the first dry dock there, and it has been the major port of the navy* since. *See also* Isle of Wight.

posh. Swank, well-dressed, expensive; university* slang before WWI, very widely used in all classes during the 1920s, and then suddenly falling out of fashion except among schoolboys and the urban lower class,* who are not necessarily complimentary when they use the term.

post. As a noun, what Americans call the mail; as a verb, to put something in the mail. The word mail is also used, as in the Royal Mail,* but most people post rather than mail a letter, and they receive a letter in the **morning post**. A **post code** is similar to the American zip code but is a combination of letters and numbers that seems considerably more complex. Something mailed **post free** has the postage prepaid. The person Americans call the mailman is a **postman**, and a mail bag is a **postbag**. However, what Americans call a mail box is not a post box but a pillar box.* The afternoon mail delivery is called the **second post**; amazing as it seems to Americans, the British have had two mail deliveries a day for decades and still manage it Monday through Friday in urban areas even in 1990. They also generally deliver first class* mail within twenty-four hours, and it is not unusual to put a letter in the post in the morning and have it delivered to an address in the same city in the second post for the same day. *See also* post office.

postal order. What Americans call a money order.

poste restante. What Americans call General Delivery, mail using the post office itself as an address where it is held for a period of time until the addressee personally comes to pick it up.

posting. A job or assignment that requires the person to move to another place, used most often in the military and government service.

postman's knock. A party game similar to the American "playing post office," in which imaginary letters are delivered after payment in kisses.

post office. Government mail service began in 1635, but all letters were charged according to the distance sent and had to travel through London first, making mail service prohibitively expensive. The addition in the 1780s of mail coaches* that also carried up to four passengers between London and major cities improved the service but did little to reduce the cost, and thus in novels and plays of the period most letters are still sent by the hand of someone traveling in the same direction. Within London, private postal services grew up, at a rate of 1d* in the City* and Westminster,* 3d within a ten-mile radius. In 1840, taking advantage of the new technology of the railway, England initiated the world's first modern postal system, with a fixed rate of 1d for a letter, payment indicated by an adhesive stamp. Quickly the post office became the one governmental institution trusted by all, and thus almost any new service aimed at the broad general populace was introduced and supervised through the post office: It handled telegrams,* introduced and operated the telephone system, later supervised TV broadcasting (and collected the licence* fees for radio and TV), handled many social security* payments, and for the vast bulk of the populace even acted as a bank, with both savings accounts and the Giro.* Thus, "money in the post office" means a savings account. In the 1980s the telephone service was privatized, but other services mentioned are still under post office supervision. The **Post Office Tower** is the highest structure in London, built in 1965 as an antenna tower for microwave and TV but with a revolving restaurant near the top. *See also* British Telecom; first class; GPO; ITV; penny black; penny post; pillar box; postal order.

pot. As a measure, a half gallon.*

potato. The potato came to Britain from America in the eighteenth century and was an instant success. It is associated more with Ireland,* where for economic as well as dietary reasons it was eaten as a substitute for bread* among almost all the native populace, but the English also quickly made it a major part of their diet. It is most commonly eaten in two forms: **chips**, which Americans call French fries and which in homes from the middle class* down are served at practically every meal except breakfast; or **mash**, which is mashed potatoes, served at practically every meal not accompanied by chips. **Creamed potatoes** are mashed potatoes with a higher price on the menu. Significant variations include: **jacket potato**, a baked potato still in its skin; **straw potatoes**, very thin fried potatoes, such as Americans sometimes call shoestring potatoes; **croquette potatoes**, mashed potatoes formed into a ball or small oval, rolled in bread crumbs, and fried. *See also* crisps; pie; rationing.

pot boy/man. In a pub,* the person who washes glasses.

pot house. A pub.*

potted. (1) In reference to food, what Americans call canned, especially potted meat. (2) In reference to plants, growing in pots or containers. (3) In relation to other things, brief or abridged, as in a "potted history."

potter. As a verb, to work or to seem to be working, but with no specific goal, deadline, or often visible result, as in "pottering about the garden."

Potteries, the. The region of the Midlands* around Stoke-on Trent,* so called because of its intense concentration on the manufacture of earthenware and china since the sixteenth century, home of Wedgwood, Spode, and numerous other products, even though the clays ran out locally in the eighteenth century and now are brought up from Cornwall.* This is the area fictionalized in Bennett's novels about the "Five Towns," although it actually has six.

potty. Crazy, but not so much slang as euphemism, used among the respectable classes to imply that what appears to be insanity is merely eccentricity or harmless quirks.

pot-walloper. (1) A heavy drinker. (2) In some boroughs* before the 1832 Reform Bill,* a test of eligibility for voting was that the householder could boil a pot on a fireplace owned by himself alone; thus pot-walloper was a casual term for a voter, continuing after later reforms changed the requirements.

pouf. *See* poof.

pound. (1) The basic monetary unit of England,* and now for all of Britain.* Technically, this was not a pound of silver, despite being called **pound sterling**, but a value of 240 ancient silver pennies that were called sterlings or starlings from a star design on one face. Pounds were so valuable they were essentially merely a notion except in very large transactions, for which gold was used, and the Elizabethan sovereign* and the earliest gold guineas* were rarely seen in commerce. However, by the late eighteenth century a pound coin became essential, and the modern sovereign was introduced, almost always called a sovereign, not a pound. Larger amounts were paid in £5 notes,* the only paper money most people would ever see until £1 notes were introduced in 1914 to replace the sovereign. After 1971, the pound remained standard, but with a value of 100 new pence.* In 1983 a new pound coin was issued, gold-colored but actually cupro-nickel. *See also* Appendix I; guinea; oncer; quid.

power point. *See* points.

PPE. At Oxford,* a degree course of philosophy, politics, and economics, also called Modern Greats.*

PPP. At Oxford,* a degree course of psychology, philosophy, and physiology, often considered the most demanding exam at the university.*

PPS. Principal Private Secretary or Parliamentary Private Secretary. Neither of these is a secretary* who types and files but is rather an assistant or aide to the minister* or permanent secretary.* The Parliamentary Private Secretary is more political, maintaining contacts with the back benchers* and advising on political matters. The Principal Private Secretary is more of a general aide for the minister but is a salaried member of the bureaucracy. *See also* civil service; secretary.

Praed Street. A street in London* outside Paddington* Station, almost since its inception a somewhat shabby street associated with dubious shops.*

prairie oyster. A hangover cure made from a raw egg seasoned with Worcestershire sauce, pepper, et cetera.

pram. What Americans call a baby carriage, short for perambulator.

prang. To crash or run into, as with a car.

prat. Widely used slang for a fool. From Shakespeare's time until about WWI, this also meant the buttocks—hence, pratfall—and that may have something to do with the development of the modern term.

Pratt's. A gentlemen's club* in St. James's* Street in London,* noted for its custom of serving meals at a kitchen table in the basement, a practice initiated when the club's founder was regularly visited by his former master, a duke* who liked to carouse with his old steward in the kitchen.

prawn. Essentially the same food as in America, but where Americans tend to call both prawns and shrimp "shrimp," the British tend to call both prawns and shrimp "prawns." Large shrimp or prawns are often called **scampi**.

prebend. The salary paid to a canon,* or the land or tithe* used to provide the income for that salary. A **prebendary** is a person with a prebend, which may be a canon but, as with a living,* may be someone not even a clergyman.

precentor. The person in charge of a church choir or other church music; in a cathedral, this would be a clergyman, usually a canon,* but in parish* churches it might be a layman.

prefect. In a school,* someone who enforces discipline; in public schools,* this is almost always another student.

Prefect. One of Ford's most popular cars from 1936 until well into the 60s, a relatively low-priced family car.

preggers. Pregnant; originally collegiate slang of the 1920s, this usage has bounced around the social scale, but for the most part is now concentrated in the upper portions of society.

preliminary hearing. In the legal system, a hearing before a magistrate* to determine if there is sufficient evidence to have a trial.

Premier. Former name for Prime Minister,* used mostly during the eighteenth century.

premium bond. A rather odd device, a bond issued since 1956 by the government for one pound,* which can be redeemed for one pound with no interest; the "premium" is that all holders of such bonds are automatically entered in weekly and monthly lotteries. *See also* Ernie.

prep school. A fee-paying school* that prepares boys for a public school,* technically by preparing them for the Common Entrance Exam used by such schools. Traditionally, these are for ages seven or eight through twelve and are almost always boarding schools. Before that age, the wealthy depended on governesses* at home; but for the most part in the upper classes* the boys were shipped out as soon as possible. Traditionally, prep schools were and are horrors for their students, run essentially on the same lines as the public schools. Even today there are still about 600 of these.

Presbyterians. The Protestant sect most closely exemplifying Calvinism, so called for their control of parishes by committees of lay elders called presbyters. Although established as the Church of Scotland,* the Presbyterians had little success in England,* where they were most often a form of nonconformist* protestantism patronized only by the wealthier middle class,* much as they continue today in the United States, until they all but disappeared after the rise of the English Unitarians. In 1876 a new Presbyterian Church was formed in England, essentially as missionary activity from Scotland, merging in 1972 into the United Reform Church.

presenter. On TV, what Americans call the anchor or the emcee.

press button/stud. On clothing, what Americans call a snap.

press gang. In the eighteenth century, there was no conscription* and no way to enforce it if it existed; the navy* depended for its sailors entirely on volunteers. When volunteers were not sufficient, the navy authorized patrols, called press gangs, to go ashore and kidnap likely sailors to fill up a ship's complement. Once the men were at sea, they could not desert, and all training was actually done at sea anyway, so it seemed logical and efficient to the navy. This was one of several causes of the Mutiny,* as well as of other individual ship mutinies, and one of the primary reasons why so much navy training and discipline was enforced with the lash. The army,* operating on land where desertion was easier, in theory did not press recruits; however, all recruits were required to swear before a JP* that they enlisted voluntarily, which suggests people feared similar kidnappings. The practice gradually faded away as the navy was regularized during the nineteenth century. In the modern world, press gang is sometimes used as a verb to indicate someone else has volunteered you for an unpleasant job, as in "My wife press-ganged me into this."

press-up. The exercise Americans call a push-up.

Preston. A small city in northeastern England* near Blackpool,* one of the most successful and depressing industrial towns of the nineteenth century, model for Dickens's Coketown.

Preventive Service. A department of the Customs Service concerned with prevention of smuggling.

Previous. *See* Responsions.

pricey. Expensive.

prig. Americans also use the term but associate it more with prudishness about sex, while the British tend to associate it more with self-righteousness about anything and everything. Dickens's Mr. Pecksniff is certainly a prig, but hypocrisy is not necessarily included in priggishness. Prigs may in fact live exactly as they claim to do; what makes them prigs is their insistence that everyone else adhere to their standards.

primary school. A generic term for basic schooling from about age five to eleven; what Americans usually call elementary school, required for all children. In some areas, enrollment allows the use of separate infant schools* for those five to seven, and some primary schools for ages five to nine are called first schools. Primary schools are now almost always tax-supported. *See also* day school; junior school; middle school; parish school; prep school; school.

Primate. Actually, the Church of England* has two archbishops* and thus two primates: York, who is the "Primate of England," and Canterbury, who is the "Primate of All England," presumably including some mysterious portion of England* not otherwise in England.

Prime Minister. The executive head of the government,* but not at all like the American President. Fundamentally, Britain is ruled by whoever can rule. Over centuries, the monarch gradually ceded authority in return for taxes, until in 1688 Parliament* clearly established itself as the ultimate authority. Prior to that time, the monarch had appointed ministers* to deal with the daily business of government at his or her own desire; after that date, these ministers were appointed with the clear understanding that they must have the approval of the majority in Parliament, and from that practice it was only a short step to appointing actual members of Parliament. Political parties* gradually emerged, with the ministers appointed from those who controlled the most powerful party. Of these ministers, reflecting the traditional power of the purse, the one with the most influence was the First Lord of the Treasury.* Beginning with Pitt, this First Lord was often called the "prime" minister (or for a time Premier*), but it was not until 1905 that the title officially became Prime Minister, although his or her official title still also contains "First Lord of the Treasury." In theory, then, the Prime Minister is first among equals, a person holding the office through influence or control of the majority party in the House of Commons.* The Prime Minister (often shortened to PM) is not elected in a national vote; voters select only a local member,* and then the Prime Minister is selected by the party after the election is finished (although of course everybody knows who is in control of a party and most local elections are decided on the nature of the party and the potential PM rather than on the nature of the local candidate himself). The PM may be removed and replaced at any time by the party members without a general election. The Prime Minister appoints the Cabinet,* but since posts must be given to others with influence in the party, the Cabinet is often in opposition to the PM's wishes. In practice, the Cabinet, acting as the government,* both proposes laws and administers them, and as recommender of judges,* is significant in the judicial branch as well; thus the PM as head of the Cabinet has potential authority that would be inconceivable to the most power-hungry President. But that authority is only potential; checks provided by the monarch's influence, by custom, and by infighting within the party itself often make it difficult, if not impossible, for the Prime Minister to exert that authority.

primrose. Not a rose at all but a wildflower common throughout England,* usually yellow, blooming in early spring and long associated with youthful dalliance that wells up in the same season; hence the **primrose path** is one that looks attractive but will lead to trouble. The **Primrose League** was a conservative political organization formed in 1883 in memory of Disraeli, named for his admiration for this "typically English" flower.

Primrose Hill. A hill in Regent's Park,* from the top of which, before modern high-rises, one could see across London and into the hills of Kent* and Surrey,* in the modern city popular with walkers and kite fliers in particular. The neighborhood of the same name north of the open space dates from the early nineteenth century and in recent years has become a popular neighborhood for the fashionable but eccentric, such as successful writers or Tara of the *Avengers* TV series.

primus. A portable stove using kerosene (paraffin*) for fuel, common in caravans* and in homes or rooms without natural gas.*

prince. A son of a reigning monarch. Unlike many other European countries, England* has always reserved this title for this one specific use, and it is not inheritable; that is, Prince Charles's sons will be princes, because he will inherit the crown, but Prince Andrew's will not be princes, for they will not be the sons of the monarch. However, if and when Charles succeeds to the throne, Prince Andrew will still be a prince, for once the title has been given it cannot be lost, except by becoming King.* *See also* princess.

prince consort. The husband of a ruling queen;* however, it was first used for Albert and was so completely associated with him that it has in fact never been used for Prince Philip, the only other candidate since, who is officially only the Duke* of Edinburgh.

Prince of Wales. A title since 1301 reserved for the male heir apparent to the throne. However, the title is neither hereditary nor automatic but is conferred only if and when the prince's father (or mother in the present case) decides to do so. If the Prince of Wales should have a male child before he succeeds to the throne, that boy is also called the Prince of Wales but is distinguished from his father by being called Prince (First name) of Wales; thus, Charles is Charles, Prince of Wales, while his son would be Prince William of Wales.

princess. The daughter of a reigning monarch. Unlike many European countries, England* has always reserved this title to this particular usage. Thus, if Princess Margaret or Princess Anne had children, they would be neither princes or princesses. Neither do wives of princes become princesses, with one exception: The wife of the Prince of Wales becomes the Princess of Wales. Thus, "Lady Di" became Diana, Princess of Wales, as she will presumably become Queen Diana, but "Fergie" became merely the Duchess of York when she married Prince Andrew.

Princetown. The official name of the prison located in and popularly known as Dartmoor.*

principal. At some colleges,* the head or chief executive. The term in general is used only in colleges at the redbrick universities,* although it is used at Cambridge* and Oxford* for the head of some halls* within colleges and for the head of some of the women's colleges. The American principal of an elementary or high school is in Britain called a headmaster.*

principal boy. A male lead in a pantomime,* always played by a young woman. Completely different from a head boy.*

principle, on. As a result of a principle or moral scruple; quite different from "in principle," which in both countries means "only in theory."

priory. In the medieval era, a separate religious community, smaller than, and often still controlled by, an abbey.*

prise. To lever up or out; Americans tend to say pry.

prison. Prior to the nineteenth century, prison was a random affair; they were few in number and each operated by its own local rules. Conditions were appalling even by medieval standards, in part because few criminals ever stayed in the prison longer than to await their trial or their hanging, or later their transportation.* The only significant exception was the debtor's prison,* where those in debt could be imprisoned for unspecified terms until the debts were paid. The dependence on bribery among literary jailers, as with Gay's Lockit or the various Dickensian turnkeys, was not so much corruption as necessity; all prisons were originally run as a form of free enterprise, with the jailers themselves paid only what they could get in "tips." This changed as the concept of prison itself changed in mid-nineteenth century. After the death penalty was severely limited in 1838 and transportation ended, local councils* built new prisons to hold the criminals; almost all the modern prisons still in use were built in the 1840s and 50s, but the central government did not accept responsibility until 1877. In general, conditions continued to shock visitors, and prison reform was a constant item on the agenda of all reform movements well into the twentieth century. Juveniles were at last separated into the Borstal* system in 1895. Generally, modern British criminals serve shorter terms and have somewhat more privacy than American counterparts, but prisons are still overcrowded and every few years a new scandal emerges to raise cries for new reforms. A **prison visitor** is not a friend who visits a prisoner but an independent person who reports on prison conditions, provides a legitimate contact for a prisoner, etc. *See also* Bridewell; Brixton; capital punishment; Dartmoor; Fleet; Holloway; hulks; King's Bench; Marshalsea; Millbank; Newgate; Pentonville; Tower.

private. Originally, this term was used only to mean that someone had withdrawn from public life or had never had any distinction within that public world, and thus it had nothing to do with privacy in any modern sense; implications of privacy (in the sense of alone) were carried by the word privy* instead. A **private gentleman**, for example, was a gentleman* with no title, just as a **private soldier** was, and still is, a soldier with no rank, the soldier at the bottom of the military scale, a **private member** of the Commons* still represents a constituency* but holds no Cabinet* position or other similar official public distinction, and a **private trader** is one who has no other shareholders or partners. This is the sense in which public schools* are different from **private schools** in Britain, as public schools charge fees like private schools but are governed by some board, with any profits used to further future educational activities, while a private school is actually run for the profit of its owner. Similarly, **private medicine** is medicine conducted for the profit of the doctor or clinic owner (*See* National Health). Americans for the most part have never used any of these senses of private, except for private enterprise, as we defined public* differently.

private bill. In Parliament,* a bill* applicable only to a particular locality or small group of persons. *See also* private member.

Private Eye. A contemporary satirical magazine with a small but extremely influential circulation and a sophomoric sense of humor; also possibly the world leader in number of libel suits filed against a single magazine.

private member. In the House of Commons,* a back bencher.* His or her importance can be illustrated by the fact that all of them together are only allowed to offer twenty **private member bills** in an entire session, and debate on these is limited to ten minutes each. *See also* bill.

private school. *See* crammer; private; public school.

privatisation. A reversal of nationalisation* in which the government* sells state-run services into private ownership. The term and the practice belong primarily to the 1980s and are almost invariably associated with Margaret Thatcher, who made this one of the foundations of her time in office, privatising not only many industries that had been previously nationalised but also privatising many basic utilities that had long been assumed throughout Europe to be the normal province of state activity.

privy. Originally, this meant personal or not public, so there were privy gardens* as well as Privy Councils.* Because it meant out of the public eye, privy also came to be applied to secret negotiations, spying, and such. The **privy chamber** was simply a room where the owner of the house might go and expect not to be disturbed by the general public of the household and had nothing to do with the usage of privy as a term for a latrine, except that it had the same linguistic root. The privy chamber was rarely private in the modern sense, for a lord's privy chamber often had not only servants* but also other nobles in it constantly, but they were always persons who were being shown special favor by having access to such a room. All usages of privy, except in formal names dating back to the medieval era and some legal terminology, have disappeared in the twentieth century and have been replaced by the newer term private.* *See also* public.

Privy Council. The inner council of advisers for the monarch; during the sixteenth and seventeenth centuries they actually governed the country, gradually losing their authority to the Cabinet* in the eighteenth, so that their power has declined as has the monarch's. The titles remain, and they also have some formal and ceremonial duties.

Privy Purse. Money allocated by Parliament* for the personal expenses of the King* or Queen.* *See also* Civil List.

Privy Seal. The seal of the monarch used to authorize activities of Chancery* or Exchequer.* The **Lord Privy Seal** was originally the person, usually a noble,* who kept the Privy Seal,* but since 1884 this has been a sinecure that is used to put someone into the Cabinet* without giving them a specific ministry* to administer. *See also* Great Seal.

prize day. *See* speech day.

prize fellow. *See* fellow.

prize-giving. An annual ceremony at most schools* in which various student achievements and academic honors are announced and prizes awarded, usually accompanied by a speech from a local worthy, similar to an American graduation ceremony except that there is no formal graduation of the students and no awarding of diplomas or degrees.* *See also* speech day.

PRO. (1) Public Records Office.* (2) Public Relations Officer, a person with the same duties as an American press agent or "official spokesperson."

proctor. An adult at a university* responsible for student discipline.

procurator. An agent, especially one in law.

Procurator Fiscal. In Scotland,* the coroner and public prosecutor combined.

professor. At a university,* there is only one professor per field of study. Other teachers are called fellows,* lecturers,* or readers* of various individual colleges,* but the professors are professors of the university as a whole. A professor is said to **hold the chair** in his subject, because the position usually has an endowment that pays his or her salary, including his chair at the high table;* sometimes the chair has a name, such as the So-and-so Chair of Philosophy. A **Regius Professor** is a professor who holds a chair established by a reigning monarch, most often Henry VIII at Oxford* or Cambridge;* as Henry set up only five of these (other monarchs have added a few since), they are the professorships of greatest status in the nation within their respective fields.

promenade. A street or walkway along the seashore at a resort. *See also* proms.

proms. Promenade concerts, which are concerts that include standing room. **The Proms** are an annual festival held for about eight weeks that include August at the Albert Hall,* long the focal point of classical music in London* for the middle classes* who do not regularly frequent other such music performances and for students who respond to the ample cheap tickets, now sponsored by the BBC.*

proofed. Of cloth, waterproofed.

propeller shaft. In a vehicle, what Americans call the drive shaft.

propelling pencil. What Americans call a mechanical pencil.

property. No matter what dictionaries say, for the overwhelming majority of Britons the only real property is real property—land.

proprietary name. What Americans call a trademark.

prorogation. Termination of a session of Parliament.*

prostitute/prostitution. Technically, prostitution has always been legal in Britain. However, it is illegal for prostitutes to solicit on the street; hence the carefully phrased card on the newsagent's* notice* board.

Protectorate. The period (1653–59) during which Cromwell was Lord Protector (in modern terms, dictator) of England.*

provinces. Any place not London.*

provincial. Not from London.*

Provisional IRA. *See* IRA.

provo. A member of the Provisional IRA.*

provost. (1) In Scotland,* the equivalent of a mayor.* (2) In a handful of colleges* at Oxford* or Cambridge,* the head of the college; at Eton,* the headmaster.* (3) In a cathedral,* the head of the group of canons* in a cathedral, in the medieval era outranking a dean* but in more modern times equivalent to, and often replaced by, a dean, so that not all cathedrals have a provost.

prunella. (1) A plant with pink, purple, or white flowers, once thought to be medicinal; the flowers made it a woman's name, still relatively widely used and in no way implying the looks or attitudes associated with prunes in America. (2) A very sturdy silk or (later) worsted cloth, used in the gowns* of clergymen and barristers* in the eighteenth and nineteenth centuries and sometimes for women's shoes, leading to the idiom **leather or prunella** borrowed from Pope, meaning there's no different between two things.

PS. (1) Permanent Secretary.* (2) Parliamentary Secretary, generally a deputy minister.*

pseud. Slang for a pretentiously intellectual or artistic person.

pub. Americans see the pub as the quintessential quaint cozy British institution, but it has had a checkered history. Most villages* had alehouses where the local ale* was brewed and served, and many were called public houses in that they also served as inns for travelers. But in the eighteenth century, beer* took a back seat in the towns to gin,* wine, and coffee,* and the new urban poor of the early nineteenth patronized the gaudy gin palaces that grew up at the time. But in 1830, a special licence* was required to serve liquor, and the beer-only pubs began to grow in popularity until in 1872, they too were licensed, which meant that most pubs also began to serve liquor as well as beer. For the most part, the pub continued to be the domain of the working class* in the towns and the farm workers in the villages, as the middle class and higher simply did not leave home for food or drink. The social mixing caused by WWII began to break down these divisions, and the local pub in the years afterward grew into a meeting place for the neighborhood that all classes, and later, both sexes, could use. Until very recently, pubs had several separate serving areas: The **public bar** was the basic pub, with minimal or very plain furnishings and few entertainments other than a dart board, where prices were cheapest and the primary business was drinking. The **saloon bar** (sometimes a **lounge bar**) was more comfortable, with tables or booths, more games, and perhaps other entertainment, but the same drinks were served in exactly the same amounts as in the public bar but at higher prices; usually, women were allowed only in the saloon bar. Some also had a **snug**, like a private booth that backed onto the bar and was served through its own private window. As more women have frequented the pubs, many in the 1980s eliminated the separate areas and prices, but most continue either the plain simple decor of the old public bar or the Edwardian coziness of the old saloon bars, and few have modernized along the lines of dark American bars. Many pubs, particularly in the country, kept a few rooms as a reminder of their old duty as inns, but as hotels and the bed-and-breakfasts* have become more common, most pubs have now eliminated this part of their business. For the odd pub hours, *See* licensing laws. *See also* free house; local; lunch; tied house.

pub-crawling. Drinking in several different pubs* in one evening.

public. This term is one of the most confusing for Americans to deal with, as Americans tend to use it almost exclusively for things that imply or actually have governmental participation or supervision while the English in particular have tended to use it to mean those things carried on outside of governmental activity. This is historical, in that most governmental activity in England* before the nineteenth century was carried on out of view of the general public, as the business of the monarch and his or her councillors, and then later "made public," so most terms having public in them apply more to the "general public" rather than to the public as a formal unit. Thus, for Americans, public property is only that property actually owned by some governmental body, while much public land in Britain is either privately owned but with long-standing rights of access for the general public or, like commons,* is not "owned" by anyone. Similarly, public schools* in America are schools operated by a governmental body, while in Britain they are schools operated by nongovernmental bodies. A public house* is privately owned but used by the public, and a public company* is not one that has been nationalized but rather one that has shares traded on an exchange.* The only significant similar American usage is public television. More recently, however, American usages have been creeping in, further confusing the issue. *See also* library; private; privy.

publican. Landlord* of a pub.*

public bar. *See* pub.

public convenience. A public lavatory.*

public house. A pub.*

public lavatory. A public toilet. Yes, Virginia, these actually exist, and they are open to the public, in public places, in the cities and towns of all sizes. Not too long ago, they were also clean.

public oven. *See* bake house.

Public Record Office. Since 1838, the national archive in which all governmental records are open to the public, with the general proviso that some governmental documents can be kept from researchers for thirty years.

public school. A fee-charging secondary school for boys. Technically, public schools require parents to pay tuition fees, while the school itself is governed by a board of directors (hence, "public*" rather than "private,*" which also requires fees but is operated for profit by an individual.) The practical distinction is that most public schools are boarding schools, while students at most tax-supported schools, grammar schools,* and private schools tend to still live at home.

The oldest public schools began in the medieval era to train promising boys for work in the clergy* or clerical government work and had comparatively little social or cultural impact; most of the gentry* were educated at home. But a major change occurred in the nineteenth century, when two cultural factors came together—the concept of the gentleman* changed, and the Empire exploded outward. The Empire builders needed boarding schools back home to which they could send their children, and the would-be gentry* of the industrializing nation needed to train their sons to become proper gentlemen. Under the influence primarily of Dr. Arnold at Rugby,* the public schools promised to build character as well as to educate, introduced sports, adopted a comparatively standardized curriculum based on Greek and Latin classics, and increased their boarding facilities. By the end of the century, a public school education was *de rigueur* for the gentry and for anyone in the professions or government service and the foundation stone for all other careers in anything related to the Establishment, the old boy* network and the old school tie* becoming the most important contacts a boy could ever make in his lifetime, far more potent even than Ivy League connections in American life.

One of the most curious aspects for Americans is that, although the schools were and are the very epitome of wealth and privilege, serving only the peak of the class pyramid, for the students themselves the schools were and are hellholes. The boys were anything but pampered. They were shipped off from comfortable homes to live in open dormitories, with practically all discipline maintained by the older boys, which in turn meant institutionalized bullying was a way of life. Classroom discipline was maintained by corporal punishment, with the cane* the basic educational tool. Food was appallingly bad in quality and purposely delivered in small quantities, rooms had no heat, and cold baths were required even in midwinter, all in the name of "building character." And, all in all, the education was hardly anything to brag about—success on the playing field was always more important than success in the classroom, with top athletes pampered in ways that Americans would find appalling even for small-town football heroes, while the coursework was primarily Greek and Latin translation, even after Arnold introduced modern languages and history. It is almost impossible to find a memoir or a novel in which the public school experience was positive. Americans would not in general tolerate such conditions in a prison, and yet generation after generation of the most privileged classes sent their boys off to endure the same misery. And, in the late nineteenth century, a number of girl's schools* opened to offer the same treatment and methods to young ladies from the best families as well. Whatever you read in fictional accounts of public school, evidence indicates that reality was and often still is worse.

Although students have attended public schools at almost any age and first form* begins at around age eleven, in most schools since the mid–19th century, pupils generally begin at age thirteen and, if they go through sixth form, stay until about eighteen.

Since WWII, the public schools have come under increasing political attack as the home of privilege. They have not only withstood the attack but have thrived, particularly since the introduction of comprehensives,* which encouraged many of the most academic grammar schools* to convert to public schools. At present, they now teach about 6 percent of all the students in Britain. Although there are several hundred such schools, the ones that really count socially are the same as they were one hundred years ago, the oldest ones: Eton,* Harrow,* Winchester,* Rugby, Westminster,* Charterhouse,* and Marlborough,* and the graduates, or old boys, of each form mini-mafias within the larger "public-school mafia" that is the British governmental, intellectual, and business* community. Recently many began to admit some girls, although most limit the girls to a small minority in only the sixth form.* *See also* foundation boy; term.

pud. A pudding,* but usually a sweet kind.

pudding. (1) A frustrating term for Americans, as it applies to any number of different dishes which share little in common except that they rarely resemble what Americans call pudding. Some puddings are sweet, but many are main dishes for meals, made with meat. Most, but not all, puddings are made in one of two ways: either the mixture is wrapped loosely in a cloth, tied securely, and then boiled, usually called a boiled pudding; or the mixture is placed in a pudding bowl,* covered with a cloth, and the bowl is then placed in boiling water that comes partway up the side, usually called a steamed pudding. **Kidney pudding** is a main dish, basically the same ingredients as a kidney pie,* boiled rather than baked, also made as a **steak and kidney pudding**. **Blood pudding** or **black pudding** is what Americans usually call blood sausage. **Yorkshire pudding**, however, is baked— a simple mixture of flour, water, and egg poured onto the hot drippings from the roast beef and baked until it rises. **Plum pudding** is like a very dense fruitcake, but steamed, so closely associated with Christmas* meals that it is also called **Christmas pudding**. **Roly-poly pudding** actually starts as pastry dough, rolled flat, spread with fruit or jam, rolled up, and then boiled, and **Queen pudding** is like a custard, usually with a citrus flavor. **Sponge pudding** is a generic term for a pudding that starts from the same basic ingredients as sponge cake; **castle pudding** is a sponge pudding then served warm with a jam sauce on top. **Bread and butter pudding** is bread and butter covered with a milk and egg mixture and baked, called bread pudding in many American families. **Hasty pudding** was originally something like what Americans call pudding—mild, eggs, butter, and flour boiled until it thickened and could be eaten with a spoon—but in the twentieth century the mixture was often steamed like other puddings. **Summer pudding** is alternate layers of bread, fruit, and sugar molded in the pudding bowl but left cold until the bread has soaked up all the fruit juices, then unmolded and eaten.

In addition, pudding is often used as a generic term for dessert, with some class* distinctions: In the nineteenth century, the upper class preferred dessert, the middle classes sweet,* and the lower classes pudding or afters; somehow in the early twentieth this shifted, and now pudding tends to be used in this generic sense by the upper end of the social scale, while the middle prefers afters,* and the lower sweet, and some use **dessert** only for a fruit dish. *See also* grouty dick; spotted dick. (2) In many sports, a playing field* that has been thoroughly soaked by rain.

pudding basin. *See* basin.

pudding bowl. A large crockery bowl used for making shaped steamed puddings;* the mixture is placed in the bowl, the top covered with cheese-cloth or similar material tied securely around the top of the bowl, and the whole seated in a large pot of boiling water, the water below the top of the bowl. The resulting heat and steam cook the pudding, which is turned out of the bowl in molded form onto another plate.

pudding club. Someone in the pudding club is pregnant (most puddings* expand as they are cooked); also shortened to **in the club**.

Pudding Lane. A small street near the Monument* in London,* said to be the starting point of the Great Fire.*

puffin. A cute arctic sea bird that nests in the shore cliffs of Scotland* and northern portions of Ireland.* It is black and white and on land stands erect, so that it resembles a short fat penguin, but the bill is lined with red and yellow stripes. Penguin* Books have used the bird as a logo for a line of children's books, which causes many people to think of the puffin as a baby penguin, but the two birds are unrelated, and the puffin flies rather than swims.

pukka. A military slang term meaning real, solid, trustworthy, from an Indian word brought back during the nineteenth century. After WWII it has been used among civilians with a touch of irony, still meaning sound or solid but implying something dull, old-fashioned, or simple-minded, especially **pukka sahib**.* *See also* gen.

pull. Some common idioms include: to **pull a face** is to grimace; to **pull a pint** is to fill a beer glass; **pull the other one** means "You don't expect me to believe that nonsense, do you?"; **pull up your socks** is "Straighten yourself out and do better."

pull-in. On the road, what Americans call a truck stop.

pullover. What Americans usually call a light sweater,* generally used only for the type worn by males. It often has no sleeves, in which form it may also be called a slipover,* and in recent years the name has also been used for what Americans call a sweatshirt. *See also* jersey; jumper.

pull-up. A roadside caff.*

punch. A drink of wine and fruit juices, almost always served hot. The cool nonalcoholic drink Americans call punch is usually called a **fruit cup**. A **cobbler's punch** is made from gin instead of wine. *See also* cobbler.

Punch. A popular English comic weekly magazine (1841–1992) noted especially for its cartoons but also featuring comic stories and satirical essays.

punch-up. A brawl or fist fight.

puncture. What Americans call a flat tire. A **slow puncture** is a slow leak in the tire.

punnet. A small basket; when used as a measure, either a pound or a half-pound of berries.

punt. (1) A small, flat-bottomed boat used on streams, propelled by pushing with a long pole against the stream bed. These are especially associated with Cambridge,* where punting on the Cam* is one of the stereotypical student summer activities. (2) A bet.

punter. Technically, a bettor, but often used in a derogatory sense for the general public, people who are suckers in some sense.

Purdey. A brand of shotgun, regarded among the gentry* as the finest.

purpose-built. Made specially for a place or a unique function.

Puseyite. A member of the Oxford Movement,* so called for E. B. Pusey, a prominent member.

pushbike. A regular bicycle, to distinguish it from a motorbike.

pushchair. What Americans call a baby's stroller, the kind that can be folded up into a small compact unit for carrying.

puss/pussy. (1) A cat. Americans use the term in this sense, of course, but not nearly as widely. (2) A woman. Curiously, puss and pussy were vulgar and disrespectful during Shakespeare's time and the Restoration but by the nineteenth century had become not only respectable but also cute, a pet name suitable even for one's own daughter. (3) Vulgarly, as in America, female genitals. Thus, the actual meaning intended often has to be determined more from the speaker than from the statement itself, and some of the hoariest double entendres (still heard on TV comedies) involve an apparently respectable woman talking about the state of her pussy.

Puss-in-the-corner. A children's game in which one stands in the center and the others stand in corners (or on other clearly marked bases); two on the outside try to exchange places before the one in the center beats one of them to the empty corner.

put. Something **put by** is saved; **put up** is raised or increased; **put paid to** is ended, finished, stopped; **put right** is repaired or straightened out. In a shop,* to **put it down** is not to put something back but to put it on account in effect to "charge it."

Putney. A neighborhood of London* on the south bank of the Thames* across from Fulham* associated with rowing due to the number of rowing clubs and the start of the annual Oxford-Cambridge Boat Race* there; in earlier days, a haunt of highwaymen on **Putney Heath** astride the highway* to Portsmouth.*

pye-dog. What Americans call a mongrel.

pyjamas. Pajamas. The term and the style comes from India, where it technically applied only to loose pants worn as outer wear by men and women both. As in America, when combined with a loose jacket of the same material, these are used as sleepwear, but they did not actually appear until late in the nineteenth century as a convenient item to wear during weekends* when going to the bathroom* down the hall. American men adopted these very quickly at all levels, but in Britain they were primarily an upper class* or semi-bohemian* garment until WWII; most men continued to wear what Americans called nightshirts until the Blitz,* when the likelihood of being driven into the street during the night converted the men and many women as well to pajamas (perhaps because of the cold houses, British women from the beginning have been almost as likely to sleep in pajamas as men). During the 1930s, the first women's slacks* were often called pyjamas or pajamas, made with much heavier materials than sleeping pajamas and with wide flaring legs, worn only at the beach or for similar casual wear and among bohemians.*

pylon. A pole or tower carrying electric or phone lines.

Q

QC. Queen's Counsel.*

quad/quadrangle. At Oxford,* an open courtyard inside various colleges* with buildings on four sides. The same space at Cambridge* is called a court.*

Quadragesima. The Sunday six weeks before Easter* and thus the first Sunday during Lent,* so called because it occurs about forty days before Easter.

Quadrant. In London,* the curving southern end of Regent Street* just off Piccadilly Circus,* designed in 1817 as part of one of the few real city planning projects in London's history. The street was originally lined with columns and fashionable shops, but most of the columns have gone as the shops and offices expanded and modernized over the years.

Quakers. In theology and church practice, British Quakers and American Quakers are much the same, but the Quakers have had a much stronger impact on British society than American. Much persecuted along with all the other nonconformists,* their status was changed by their willingness to set up their own schools, which were much more open to science, leading to a tremendously high proportion of eighteenth century scientific and industrial discoveries among their ranks which, combined with their reputation as impeccably honest businessmen, made a disproportionately high number of Quaker fortunes and gave them influence far beyond their numbers. Thus, when they turned to humanitarian causes, such as the antislavery, prison* reform, and social welfare movements, they had tremendous impact.

quango. A quasi-autonomous nongovernmental organization, meaning usually a special committee or commission appointed to produce a detailed study and report about a problem that will then be ignored by the government,* like an American Presidential Commission.

quart. Larger than an American quart, 40 ounces. The dry quart measure is even larger, about 1.3 U.S. pints. *See also* pint; gallon.

quarter day. Traditionally, one of four days in the course of the year when quarterly payments and rents came due and when agricultural tenancies or work contracts began and ended. At present, the common quarter days are Christmas,* Lady Day,* Midsummer,* and Michaelmas.* In many of the northern areas, Martinmas* is the autumn quarter day rather than Michaelmas, and in Scotland, where these are called **term days**, they are commonly Candlemas,* Whitsunday,* Lammas,* and Martinmas. At various times and in various places throughout Britain,* these have been observed at different times, the most common variation being Easter* or Hocktide* rather than Lady Day. The practice harks to a time when the vast majority of people knew no calendars* in the contemporary sense but marked time by the festivals of the Church,* so all rents and job contracts were tied to the church calendar.

Quarterly Review. A significant and influential literary magazine published in London* from 1809–1967, primarily Tory* in its tone and theory.

quartern. One quarter of a pound of something. However, a **quartern loaf** was a four-pound loaf of bread,* now rarely if ever seen.

quarters. On shoes, what Americans call taps, the metal pieces placed on heels to prevent wear.

quarter session. A court usually held only quarterly, used for appeals and some specific civil and criminal trials, replaced since 1971 by the Crown Court.* Unlike magistrate's* court, quarter sessions always had juries.* *See also* assizes; petty sessions; recorder.

Queen. Usually, the wife of the King.* However, a woman may succeed to the throne if there are no direct male heirs; thus succeeded Mary I and Elizabeth I when their brother died childless; Anne when James II had been deposed and her sister Mary died childless; and Elizabeth II in our own time when George VI had no male children. This is something of an anomaly, since no other ranks in the nobility* may be inherited by a woman. If Queen in her own right, she is simply the Queen and exercises all the rights and powers that the King would. If Queen by marriage, she may be called the Queen but formally is a Queen Consort* and has no authority of her own, nor may she assume the crown if her husband dies. If she outlives her husband, she becomes Queen Dowager or, if her child takes the throne, Queen Mother.* *See also* Cabinet; constitution; Crown; government; prince, royalty; succession.

queen cake. *See* cake.

Queen Consort. A woman who is Queen* only by virtue of being married to the ruling King.* Should the King die, she could not inherit the Crown.* Nonetheless, she is always styled Queen (First name), even after her husband dies. Thus, the nation may have two or more Queens, as it does in 1991 with Queen Elizabeth II on the throne and Queen Elizabeth, the previous Queen Consort, still living.

Queen Dowager. *See* Queen Mother.

Queenhithe. A dock in London* in Blackfriars,* in use for more than ten centuries; the area itself is now primarily offices with very few residents.

Queen Mary's College. A college* of London University* in Mile End* and quite distinct from Queen's College.*

Queen Mother. The mother of the current monarch who was also wife of the previous King;* thus a Queen Mother is always a **Queen Dowager**, which means she is the dowager* widow of the late King, but a Queen Dowager is not always a Queen Mother unless her child actually takes the throne. *See also* Queen Consort.

Queen's Bench. The King's Bench* when a Queen* is on the throne.

Queensberry rules. The basic rules for boxing,* first drawn up in 1867 and supervised, though not actually written, by the Marquis* of Queensberry. The term almost immediately passed into general use as a synonym for fair play and honest competition in any arena.

Queen's Birthday. *See* King's Birthday.

Queen's Chapel. A chapel* in London* near St. James's* Palace, built by Inigo Jones in 1625 and something of an anomaly in that it was a Catholic* chapel, intended for use by the Spanish Infanta, the Catholic betrothed to Charles I, and used by his eventual wife Henrietta Maria. Over the years it has remained the official church of the Queen* and thus has changed religious affiliation several times according to the current Queen's religion.

Queen's College. (1) A college* of Oxford.* (2) A girl's school* in Harley Street* in London,* the oldest such institution in England,* dating to 1848, originally founded to train governesses.*

Queens' College. A college* of Cambridge,* punctuated differently from the one at Oxford* because it was founded twice by two different Queens.

Queen's Counsel. A barrister* with at least ten years of experience, in theory available to the monarch to provide legal advice, although most QCs never go nearer the monarch than the Changing of the Guard.* To be a QC is an honor, but the individual barrister applies for it and is rarely denied if his record is not unsound.* The QC may enter inside the bar* to address a judge,* and practically all judges ultimately come from the ranks of the QCs. The QC is said to take silk*, meaning he or she is allowed to wear silk* robes, and protocol demands that no QC take a case alone but must rather always act as leader* for a "junior" barrister who nominally assists but in practice often conducts the case, for which the QC fronts and takes credit. Called a **King's Counsel** (or **KC**) when a King* rules.

Queen's House. A house* at Greenwich* designed by Inigo Jones for the wife of James I but not finished until Charles I's reign, particularly known for the highway that passes through the center of the house, bridged by a furnished room. Due to the Civil War,* the house was rarely occupied, although as the first Palladian building, its style was widely copied. In the twentieth century it became a picture gallery for the National Maritime Museum*, and in 1990 was restored to a controversial "original" state.

queen's pudding. *See* pudding.

Queen's Scout. A Boy Scout* who has reached the top rank; what Americans call an Eagle Scout. When a King* is on the throne, called a **King's Scout**.

Queen's Speech. The speech read by the monarch at the formal opening of a new session of Parliament,* similar to the American State of the Union address in detailing or avoiding the problems and programs Parliament will need to deal with, but no longer actually written by the monarch but by the Prime Minister's* staff to explain the government's* plans.

Queen's University. The university in Belfast;* from 1849–1908, the university was located in Dublin while the Belfast unit was only a college,* but in 1908 the name was moved to the Belfast unit.

queer. Primarily this means sickly, not homosexual. Thus, someone **come over queer** has gotten sick rather than changed sexual preference, and someone in **Queer Street** is one whose finances are sick, on the verge of bankruptcy. However, American usage of the term to mean a male homosexual has entered recent usage as well. For **queer a pitch**, *See* pitch.

query. To ask, actually used quite often in conversation or writing, as in "Shall I query this?"; however, almost always an educated usage only. Some places have a query department for information or query box for complaints.

Question Time. In Parliament,* a daily afternoon session (2:30–3:30) in which individual members* are allowed to question directly members of the Cabinet* about actions and policies; the most amazing and lively Question Time occurs when the Prime Minister* appears to answer such questions personally, usually on Tuesday and Thursday at 3:15.

queue. Pronounced cue, a line of people. In the twentieth century, the British are noted for forming orderly queues for everything without direction or command from any authority. No one quite knows when or why the practice began, as the British of previous centuries were never known for their willingness to wait their turn for anything, but rationing* for twelve years during and after WWII may have had something to do with the habit. *See also* dole.

quid. Casual usage for a pound.* Plurals add no *s*, so 10 pounds = 10 quid.

Quinquagesima. The Sunday seven weeks before Easter,* so called because it is approximately 50 days before Easter. As this is also the last Sunday before the beginning of Lent,* it is also called Shrove Sunday.*

quite. When used alone, quite means yes, or I agree. When used as an adverb, its meaning depends on tone of voice; it can mean very, or it can just as often mean not so very or partially, as in "quite well." The usage is similar to rather,* only in the middle class* and upwards. *See also* right.

quit-rent. A rent paid in lieu of services owed to a lord.* These are usually quite small, paid not as rental for the value of the land but rather as a symbolic demonstration of the continued sovereignty of the lord over the tenant who otherwise owns the land in question, and some quit-rents have achieved fame through their eccentricity.

quod. Slang for a prison.*

quondam. Former or formerly, a Latinism that is still used in educated speech due to the teaching of Latin in the public schools* and grammar schools.*

R

RA. (1) Royal Academy.* (2) Royal Artillery.*

rabbit. (1) Of a person, someone not good at sports, especially those played on lawns, such as cricket* or tennis.* (2) Before mid-nineteenth century, a newborn baby; hence, a midwife* would be a **rabbit catcher**. (3) *See* hare. A **running rabbit** is a type of clay pigeon that, instead of being shot into the air as in skeet or trap shooting, is rolled along the ground.

RAC. Royal Automobile Club, different from AA* in that it is also an actual club* (1897) in London* and, while providing road advice and service to its members, also regulates auto racing in Britain.

race ball. A ball* held in conjunction with a race meeting.*

racecourse. What Americans call a racetrack.

race glasses. What Americans call binoculars.

Race Relations Board. Since 1966, a governmental body enforcing various laws concerning the prevention of racial prejudice in society at large, especially the **Race Relations Acts** of 1965, 1968, and 1976.

Rachmanism. Crude exploitation of tenants by an unscrupulous landlord, from a famous slum landlord of the 1960s.

racialist. What Americans call a racist.

racing. Horse racing is a sport followed, and bet upon, throughout far more of society than in the United States; off-track betting is legal and betting shops* are found throughout the country. Flat racing season runs from March–November, while the steeplechase* is also extremely popular in numerous races from August–May. *See also* Ascot; bookmaker; Derby; Epsom; Grand National; Guineas; Jockey Club; Newmarket; Oaks; punter; ring; St. Leger.

RADA. Royal Academy of Dramatic Art in London,* the most prestigious training school for British actors.

Radcliffe Camera. Not a camera but a small round domed building at Oxford* across the road from the Sheldonian,* now part of the Bodleian* library.

radiogram. Not a radio-(tele)gram, but rather a radio-gram(ophone)— that is, a radio and turntable combined. Also called a **stereogram**.

Radio 1/2/3/4. *See* BBC.

Radio Times. The BBC's* magazine and program guide, originally (1923) for radio broadcasts but continuing into the present and including TV program schedules and reports as well. *See also TV Times*.

RAF. Royal Air Force, organized in 1918 from the separate flying corps of the army* and navy,* and in 1964 at last unified with the other forces under the Ministry of Defence.* The RAF's greatest glory came in the Battle of Britain* in 1940, and it has far and away replaced the navy in popular glamor. The RAF's primary unit is the squadron* of ten to twenty planes, organized into wings of variable size as needed, and larger units called groups for strategic operations. Although interservice rivalry is intense, the RAF has generally accepted a role of support for army and naval action, and thus, unlike in the United States, the navy and army have not been forced to develop their own air corps to do the jobs the air force refuses to do. Modern enlistment is for twenty-two years, with options for early release similar to those of the army.* For ranks *See* Appendix V.

Raffles'. A hotel in Singapore whose bar was the acknowledged central meeting place for all Britons in the Far East before WWII—sooner or later, "everyone" could be expected to pass through there.

rag. (1) To play jokes on, or to tease rudely. The term seems to have been used, especially as **bullyrag**, in the late eighteenth century in various parts of society, but then shortened at Oxford* and Cambridge* in the mid–

nineteenth century and used so regularly there that it became a slang term used only by the university-going classes.* By 1900, it was also used as a noun for any display of student hi-jinks at any college,* unofficially institutionalized in an annual **rag week**, a concentrated time of pranks and stunts, often to raise money for charities. (2) In slang before mid–nineteenth century, a farthing,* a coin of about as much value as a typical rag of material.

rag and bone man. Someone who collects trash in order to resell some or all of it, and thus one of the lowest of all businessmen. *See also* bunter.

raid. Usually, a burglary with no violence.

rail. What Americans call a rack, as in a **clothes rail**; or a rod, as in a **curtain rail**.

railway. What Americans call a railroad. As in America, the railways were the glue that held together the industrialized nation in the nineteenth century, but they continued to be a major form of transportation into the late twentieth century, as cars were adopted by the general public much more slowly than in America and practically all travel within the island of Britain was done on the railways. British railroads were all developed as private businesses, and by WWI there were 123 separate railway companies; following the war, the government forced them to amalgamate into four large units, still privately owned, but in 1947 they were nationalized into British Rail.* An **overhead railway** is what Americans call an elevated train. *See also* Clapham; coach; Euston Station; first-class; halt; King's Cross; Liverpool Street; Paddington; St. Pancras; Underground; Victoria; Waterloo.

rain. It doesn't rain everyday in Britain, it just seems that way. *See also* bright; drought; umbrella.

raj. Pronounced rahj, any kingdom in India* that would have been ruled by a local prince called a **rajah**. By late nineteenth century, **the Raj** was British rule itself, used particularly for the half-century before Indian independence; in literature running from Kipling to Rumer Godden and Paul Scott.

RAM. Royal Academy of Music.*

rambler. A walker, but most often used to indicate a person who walks for sport and/or a member of a hiking* club, many of which are called **Ramblers**.

RAMC. Royal Army Medical Corps.

Ramsgate. A small port and seaside resort on the southeastern tip of England.*

ramstam. In Scotland* and northern England,* inconsiderate or headstrong.

Ranelagh Gardens. From 1742–1803, an amusement park complete with orchestras, fireworks, outdoor restaurants, and a famous Chinese pavilion, located in Chelsea,* at that time outside of London,* and competing with the Vauxhall Gardens.* After the Ranelagh Gardens closed, the grounds were added to those of the Royal Hospital* and in 1860 modernized to remove all traces of the old amusement park.

range. In the nineteenth century, an iron, coal-fired cooking stove, with ovens, griddles, and usually a water boiler; the modern gas and electric versions are usually called cookers.*

Rangers. (1) A Girl Guide* organization for those age fourteen to eighteen. (2) A common name for football* clubs.*

rasher. A slice of bacon,* thicker and wider than a typical American bacon slice.

ratafia. A liqueur flavored with fruit kernels, usually peach, apricot, or cherry, or sometimes almonds; in the nineteenth century, also a cookie flavored with such a liqueur.

ratatouille. Usually pronounced RATaTOOey, a vegetarian stew, primarily eggplant, zucchini, tomatoes, and peppers. Originally a French farm food, it only recently began to be eaten among the middle-class* less for its French background than for its vegetarian health food connotations.

rate. (1) *See* rates. (2) *See* first rate. (3) *See* rating.

rates. The basic local tax, similar to the American property tax except that the tax was technically based not on the property's total value but on its potential rental value. This tax was discontinued in 1989 in favor of the poll tax.* The **ratepayer** is someone who pays rates, generally used to mean the general public in much the same way as Americans use taxpayer.

rather. (1) When used as an adverb, although it implies something limited or partial, in fact it usually means very, as in "rather happy" or "rather well," and is one of the stereotypical signs of British understatement. Often used with "a," as in "rather a mess, I'm afraid." (2) When used alone, this means yes, usually pronounced with both syllables stretched and stressed equally. Dickens uses it in the mouths of lower-class* characters, but by about 1900 it was concentrated in girl's school* slang, and it has continued in literature and entertainment as one of the most obvious and stereotypical signs of the hearty girl's school type of woman, the country gentry,* and others who would also say, "Oh, I say, what ho!" Both usages are so closely identified with the upper classes that the word is used among the lower classes only as a form of ridicule signalling affectation in the target. *See also* quite.

rating. In the navy,* a common sailor below the rank of bosun.* The term comes from the captain's "rating" of sailors on their skills, as **ordinary seaman, able seaman**, or **leading seaman**. *See also* Appendix V.

rationing. The British began rationing of food and practically everything else in January 1940 as part of the war effort. Meat, butter, sugar, tea, fats, eggs, coffee, and fruit were as tightly rationed as gasoline, and about the only foods available "off the ration" were potatoes,* carrots, oatmeal, and some fish. Each person had an individual **ration book** that he or she was required to carry that contained coupons for each allowable ration. The shortages did not end with the war, and rationing continued on most items, especially meat, until 1954. It was this generation-long rationing that, more than anything, gave Britain its worldwide reputation for tasteless foods and terrible cooking. **See also** British Restaurant; pie; queue.

rattle. Used both for the small noisemaker given to babies and for a much larger device that looks like a box with a handle (you will see Andy Capp carrying one when dressed in his club* scarf), used primarily among fans at football* matches*—the handle is shaken in a circular motion so that the box rotates around the handle, making a loud noise used as part of the cheering. *See also* zigger-zagger.

Rayburn. A brand of cooking stove, often used generically.

Raymond's. Raymond's Revuebar, a nightclub/theater in Soho* in London,* successor to the Windmill* and specializing in nude revues more complex than simple strip shows. The nightclub has been so successful that both Paul Raymond, the owner, and Raymond's are regarded in Britain in a way comparable to the way Hugh Hefner and the Playboy Clubs once were in America, as either the personification of fleshly sin or a symbol of sexual freedom and pleasure.

razzle. A spree, especially a drunken one, a shortening of the American razzle-dazzle, since the 1920s and usually seen as **on the razzle**.

RC. Roman Catholic.

RCA. Royal College of Art.*

RCM. Royal College of Music.*

RCP. Royal College of Physicians. *See* GP.

RCS. Royal College of Surgeons. *See* surgeon.

RD. Refer to drawer, written on a cheque* at the bank* when it bounces.

RDC. Rural District Council. *See* county.

RE. In the military, Royal Engineers.

reach. A part of a river between two bends; on canals, a level portion between two locks.

reach-me-down. Not the same as American hand-me-down, but rather ready-made,* clothing that a shop* assistant can reach down from a shelf to sell to the customer without alteration.

read. At school,* especially at college* or university,* to study a particular subject, what Americans call majoring; for example, "He's reading classics" means that classics* is his primary field of study.

reader. In colleges* and universities,* a teacher, from the medieval practice of the teacher reading from his book to students who transcribed his words. The rank is second only to the professor.* *See also* don; fellow; lecturer.

reader's ticket. What Americans call a library card.

readies/ready. Cash.

reading. In Parliament* a formal presentation of a bill;* these were originally formally read aloud in each case, but that may on occasion be dispensed with. Three readings are necessary in both the Commons* and the Lords* before the bill becomes law: The **first reading** introduces the bill and sends it to be printed; the **second reading** formally begins consideration, with debate on general principles, after which it is sent to committee for study and amendment; the **third reading** leads to the actual vote, usually without further debate. Bills are almost never amended by members on the floor as is so common in the U.S. Congress.

Reading. Pronounced Redding, a city east of London.* Hardy's depiction of it in *Jude the Obscure* as Aldbrickham, an anonymous large city, continues to be its typical image, and even as a modern industrial/corporate city it seems to project no particular personality.

Reading Room. *See* British Museum.

ready-made. Of clothes, what Americans usually call ready-to-wear. *See also* bespoke; made to measure; off the peg; reach-me-down.

ready-steady. A signal that something is about to start. In races, the British say "Ready, steady, go," when Americans say, "On your mark, get set, go."

rebound. In rugby,* a ball that bounces forward off any part of the player's body but his hands; this is a legal play. *See also* knock-on.

recce. Pronounced recky, military slang for reconnaissance so widely used after WWI that it became standard British military terminology in WWII and is used since then in civilian life to mean "a quick look."

receipt. In addition to normal business usages, this also means what Americans call a recipe. **Recipe** is the Latin for "take" and regularly headed medical prescriptions (hence, the Rx symbol) and thus has been associated more with medicine than cooking; both terms were (and are) used for food dishes in Britain, but receipt is generally preferred.

reception room. A room into which you would normally allow outsiders, as opposed to the rooms of the house that are reserved for family and close friends; the term is generally only found in real estate ads, but it is sometimes used pretentiously in parts of the middle class* for the room Americans usually call the living room, or the dining room.

recipe. *See* receipt.

recommend. In general usage, someone does not recommend a business or service to you but rather recommends you to the business or service.

recorder. Originally, a legal official who was responsible for maintaining the legal customs and precedents of a local court. By the mid–nineteenth century, this had become the judge* of a city* or borough* court who held the quarter sessions.* After 1971, this is a barrister* or solicitor* with at least ten years of experience who is authorized to act as a judge part-time in the Crown Court.*

recordist. A person who makes sound recordings.

rector. In the Church of England,* the parish* priest when he is actually serving in his assigned parish. The difference between a rector and a vicar* is in their pay, not their duties; a rector receives the full tithe* or living* for the parish, while a vicar is technically a stand-in for the rector who receives only a part of the tithe as salary and thus is paid much less for the same work. *See also* clergy; curate.

rectory. A home provided for the use of a rector.* *See also* vicarage.

recusant. A person who refuses to attend Church of England* services. Before 1791, this was punishable by fines and other legal limitations of rights, designed to suppress Catholicism but also applying to the various nonconformist* sects. In the nineteenth century, the term came to mean Anglican clergymen who dissented from current church policy, so that it was possible to speak of recusant bishops,* and it has long been used metaphorically in other fields for anyone who refuses to bow to a current authority.

red biddy. A drink made of cheap red wine and meths* mixed together; also called **red Lizzie.**

Red Book. Any of Debrett's* publications.

redbrick university. A university* not Oxford* or Cambridge* so called because most were begun in the nineteenth century and were built of red brick. These carry less status and also tend to be noted for their science, engineering, or other more practical disciplines, or for such sixties-style fields as sociology. Among the most significant are Manchester,* Leeds,* Bristol,* and Edinburgh.* The term is also often applied to the new universities built in the 1960s, and London University* is also sometimes considered redbrick. *See also* college; polytechnic.

redcap. Not a person who carries luggage but a military policeman.

redcoat. (1) An infantryman, from the red army* uniforms worn until 1902; thus the "thin red line of heroes." (2) A staff member of a Butlin* holiday camp,* so called for their red blazers.

red cross. The cross of St. George. *See* St. George's Day; Union Jack.

reddle. Red ochre, and more specifically the dye or paint made from this. The paint was used like a red whitewash before more modern paints replaced it, particularly on hearths, and the dye is traditionally used to mark sheep, which provided the profession of Diggory Venn in *The Return of the Native*.

red ensign. The identifying flag of the merchant marine. *See also* ensign.

Red Flag, The. The official song of the Labour* Party.

red herring. *See* herring.

Red Indian. Used to distinguish the American Indian from the Indian from India.

red Lizzie. *See* red biddy.

redundant. Unemployed because the job has been discontinued. Contemporary businesses are required to make **redundancy payments**, similar to American severance pay, to any worker laid off; the workers are said to have been **made redundant**. *See also* cashiered.

reel. A dance for groups of people in lines, its movements built on circular figures. The Scottish reel is in 2/4 time; the English or Irish reel in 3/8 or 6/8 time.

Reform. In the mid–nineteenth century, the term was used for all kinds of social reforms, but the dominant meaning was the nature of the voting* franchise, as reform of this would necessarily lead to other obvious and necessary social reforms. Hence, the various changes in voting rules were called Reform Bills.*

Reform Bill. (1) (1832) After much public disturbance and opposition from the House of Lords,* the law eliminated the rotten boroughs* and redistributed parliamentary seats* to new boroughs* and the counties* and extended the franchise so that the number of voters increased by 50 percent overnight, although still limited to the wealthy portion of the middle class* and above. In the process, it effectively destroyed the old Tory* party, eliminating its traditional bases of power, and led to the formation of the new Conservative* Party as an attempt to replace it. Both *Middlemarch* and *Felix Holt* are set in the period of disturbance leading up to this law, although written many years later, and reflect accurately the divisions in society over the issues involved. (2) (1867) A major extension of the franchise and redistribution of parliamentary seats to include not only freeholders* but also a significant proportion of rentpayers. (3) (1884) A major extension of the franchise that allowed residents of counties* to vote under the same requirements as in boroughs,* increasing the potential voters from three to five million men, with seats* redistributed in a further act of 1885 to match representation with population. *See also* voting; Whig.

Reform Club. A gentlemen's club* in London* in Pall Mall,* established by Whigs* in 1832, still the primary club of the Liberal* party and one of the few to currently offer full membership to women; generally associated with "modern" ideas, so appropriately the club of Phileas Fogg, although in contemporary life often associated with judges* and Treasury* officials.

refresher. In legal circles, an additional fee paid to a barrister* when the case takes longer than expected.

refuse collector. A contemporary euphemism for dustman.*

Regent's Canal. A canal in London* opened in 1820 to connect a canal that previously terminated at Paddington* to the Thames* in Limehouse.* Its western basin came to be called Little Venice* and portions of the canal are sometimes quite fashionable, particularly near Regent's Park,* the northern edge of which it passes through, and sometimes nearly derelict slum as it progresses through the East End.*

Regent's Park. A large park in London,* on the northern edge of the city when laid out in 1817–25 but now well within the urban area just north of Marylebone* Street. Its enormous grounds easily contain a botanical garden, an open air theatre, a large decorative boating lake, and the London Zoo,* with further green space provided by the Park Square jutting out to the south and Primrose Hill* to the north. *See also* Inner Circle; Outer Circle; Portland Place; Regent's Canal.

Regent Street. A street in London* running north from Piccadilly Circus,* a very classy neighborhood for shops.*

regiment. The fundamental unit of the British army.* The size and composition of this unit has varied not only over the years but also from one regiment to another at any given time, because each regiment essentially functioned as an independent and self-sufficient force. An officer* or a private soldier* enlisted not in the army* but in a particular regiment and expected to spend his entire military life in that same regiment. The army as such was merely a convenient name for referring to the bulk of regiments, and any time military requirements demanded the use of coordinated regiments, new commanders and organizations had to be invented. British generals* held ranks without units under their command until sent into combat, at which time such regiments as might be available were assigned to their command.

Regimental independence dates back to their very beginnings during the late seventeenth century, when a regiment was recruited personally by its colonel.* The monarch or Parliament* paid the colonel a fixed sum, which he then used to pay and equip his own private force, theoretically keeping the remainder for his own profit. Thus, many of the oldest regiments had names taken from their original colonels, such as the Howards, who were originally formed by a Colonel Howard. This is also the source of the practice, so odd to modern Americans, of purchasing a commission* in a regiment, which was in effect a share of ownership. In 1881, all the regiments were reorganized and many names changed, but the regimental traditions continue strongly into the present, even after numerous other reorganizations since 1958 eliminated more than seventy old regiments and titles. Until conscription and national service,* each regiment conducted the training of its own recruits.

In theory, a regiment consisted of about 2,000 men, each regiment containing two **battalions**,* and each battalion containing eight to twelve companies.* The companies were commanded by captains,* the battalions by lieutenant-colonels,* and the regiment itself by a colonel.* Cavalry regiments numbered only about 500 men total and were divided into about four squadrons,* each with two troops.* Artillery was normally formed in batteries, usually of six guns each; in the late nineteenth century, brigades of three batteries each were formed, but separate artillery regiments did not appear until the twentieth century. This organizational theory was sorely stretched in practice, however, as each regiment made its own rules. The value of the system was that it could be modified to fit the circumstances, so some regiments had several battalions (in WWI as many as forty-five) and others (before 1881 the majority) consisted of a single battalion. After 1881, many of the smaller regiments were reduced to battalion status within new regiments, but they still insisted on using their old regimental names or numbers. Some regiments, such as the Rifle Brigade,* refused to call themselves regiments but were regiments nonetheless. In addition, the command structure also varied: The commander might often be a brigadier* rather than a colonel and many battalions might be commanded by colonels. This structure was further complicated by the practice of a single person holding different ranks within the regiment and within the army itself (*See* brevet). Under the combat conditions of WWI and WWII, the army operated under the divisional system, with the chain of command running from division to brigade to battalion, as in the American army, but where American soldiers saw themselves as members of a division, the British still saw themselves as members of regiments.

In addition, the army consisted of several different types of regiments. The "regular" army was made up of volunteers, either in cavalry or foot (infantry) regiments. First in status among the regulars were the Guards,* who were the personal guards of the monarch. Next among the foot regiments were the regiments of the **line**, by mid–nineteenth century numbering about 100. These were numbered, before 1881, in the order of their organization. They were called line regiments because, in theory, if they were to be paraded, they would all be placed in a single line of equal status, in order of their numbering. Each line regiment also had a formal name it used in place of its number, and many also had proud nicknames used instead of the formal name, such as the Black Watch,* which was officially the Royal Highland Regiment and in the line was the 42nd Regiment. After 1881, the numbering was officially dropped, but as with most regimental traditions, most regiments paid no attention to this decree and continued to use their old numbers. This became even more confusing as many "new" regiments consisted of battalions that had been independent old regiments, and the new regiment would often be referred to by both numbers; thus, the 1881 Royal Regiment of Wales was composed of the former 24th and 41st regiments, but instead of receiving a new number it was called the 24th/41st Foot. Cavalry regiments were also regarded as separate from the line regiments and had their own independent name and numbering system.

Not a part of the "regular" army were the territorials.* Before the twentieth century, local militia had been in place as Yeomanry* or Volunteers,* each of which had their own regimental names and organizations. In the 1881 reforms, these units were reorganized (although often retaining their old names) as reserve battalions of the line regiments that had their depots in the local areas, and in 1921 were reorganized into the Territorial Army, roughly similar to the modern American National Guard. Finally, before the mid–nineteenth century, the East India Company* controlled India with its own private army; when the Crown* took administration out of the company's hands, it also took over its army. But the regiments of the regular army never accepted these units, which were often made up of Indian soldiers with British officers, and they never officially joined the line; however, after 1857 many of the line regiments saw duty in India, so Kipling's Tommy* is a member of a line regiment.

Many regiments carry the name of an area from which its original members were recruited. However, over the years, the composition of such units often changed, so that, for example, the Argyll Highlanders were eventually mostly Irish and English. In the 1881 reorganization, many of the new regiments were given a new regional or county name by fiat, given a permanent depot within the county,* and in the years following, most such regiments did the bulk of their recruiting among the locals. However, they did not necessarily reside there—the 22nd Foot (Cheshires), for example, stayed overseas continuously until 1989.

As noted above, most military men expected to spend their career with a single regiment. Thus, an officer in particular was always listed among his regiment. Army affairs often required officers to serve elsewhere, but they were almost never transferred, as in the modern American army, but were instead merely seconded* to other units, with the understanding that they would eventually return to their original regiment. In addition, many officers might be put on inactive status, or half pay,* for various reasons but still be officially listed as part of the regiment. Thus, each regiment often had many more officers than those physically present at the barracks.

region. *See* county.

register. *See* Registry.

register office. A local office of the national Registry;* birth and death certificates are issued here, and civil marriages may be performed here as well. Many people call this a **registry office**, but register office is the official name.

registrar. (1) In a hospital, not the nurse who registers patients but rather one of the more prominent senior doctors, yet one with not quite as much status as a consultant;* Americans often call this a resident. (2) The Civil Registrar. *See* Registry.

registry. Different from the Registry,* this is (or was) an agency providing domestic servants.

Registry. Since 1836, all births, deaths, and marriages have been required to be recorded by the Civil Registrar in the Central Register Office, located in London* just north of the Strand* and generally called the Registry. Prior to this, all such records were kept in the parish* **register**, the record journal of each individual parish church* kept by the local parish priest. *See also* register office; Somerset House.

registry office. *See* register office.

Regius Professor. *See* professor.

regret. Generally the same as in America, but the exception is striking; when a Briton often "regrets his youth," he means not that he is sorry for the things he did when young but that he misses the good times he had then.

Regt. Regiment.*

regular. A soldier in the "regular" army, that is one of the regiments of the guards,* the cavalry,* or the line.* *See also* irregular; territorials; Yeomanry.

Regular Army. *See* army.

Regular Reserve. The reserve units of the army* normally filled by volunteers who are completing part of their original enlistment and liable to immediate call-up and service overseas in an emergency, similar to the American Army Reserves. *See also* territorials.

Regulo. *See* mark.

relict. A widow. The term is from Latin and only loosely related to relic, but the association of the two made relict distasteful to many women, so it is now almost never used except in legal documents. *See also* spinster.

remand. To send an accused person back into custody while further investigation takes place. A **remand centre** is a temporary detention site for such persons while they are awaiting trial.

Remembrance Day. November 11, the day WWI ended, also called **Armistice Day**. Memorial services are held, wreaths are laid on various memorials, especially the Cenotaph,* and before WWII, there were two minutes of silence nationwide at 11 A.M. Most people buy a poppy, for the poppies of Flanders, to wear in remembrance of the dead, the money going to various charities; until very recently, participation was so universal that Dorothy Sayers could build an entire mystery novel around the clue of the missing poppy in the lapel. Since WWII, it has been a day honoring all British war dead. However, as distance from that war has increased, the uniformity of observance has noticeably declined, and most of the memorial services are now held on **Remembrance Sunday**, the Sunday nearest to the eleventh. *See also* Martinmas.

remembrancer. An official who collects debts owed to the monarch. Originally there were three of these, but the remembrancers of the treasury and of the first fruits were abolished in 1833 and 1838 respectively, and the King's (or Queen's) Remembrancer is now primarily a ceremonial post, the remembrance of such debts much more efficiently handled by the computers of the Inland Revenue* and similar offices.

remission. Time reduced from a prison* sentence as a reward for good behavior.

remittance man. In colonial areas, a person living on money sent from the family back home. This was almost always a member of a wealthy or noble* family who had done or was expected to do something scandalous, so the family shipped him off with the promise that the money would keep coming out so long as he didn't come back home. Thus, the remittance man was almost always the kind of person who could be expected to "go native" or to engage in other degenerate activity in the new place, which was okay since it wouldn't matter so much there. With the end of Empire,* the remittance man has disappeared, at least in name.

remould. Of a tire, what Americans call a retread.

removals. What Americans usually call furniture moving; hence, a **removal van** is what Americans call a moving van.

remove. (1) As a noun, a metaphorical space that separates, or allows you to be separated from, someone or something. This is used in a wide variety of situations, as in "one remove from" or "several removes from," and so forth, each indicating that there are one or more steps between one thing and the other; especially common in implying or indicating that the speaker is not actually responsible for events. (2) At Eton* and Charterhouse,* a form.*

removing cream. What Americans call cold cream or cleansing cream.

rent collector. As the majority of the working class* are still paid in cash, rents are still collected personally, often weekly, by a person who goes to each home for the money. He often still carries the same leather bag that Mr. Pancks carried, to be seen in the *Andy Capp* comic strip, and to Americans, the most remarkable thing is that the rent collector is rarely robbed.

rep. In the theater, a repertory company, but almost always used to mean only **provincial rep**. Before the early twentieth century, all theaters in England were run as a form of repertory company, meaning that the theater hired a group of actors to perform in several different plays for a fixed season. By the late nineteenth century, a number of shows had achieved long runs that lasted for a full season or even longer, so London theaters (like Broadway in New York) began to hire actors for individual shows rather than for seasons. Only a handful of cities outside London could sustain theatrical production in this manner, so they made do with touring productions until the early twentieth century, when many followed the lead of Manchester* and reorganized a local repertory company. In most places, this would be the only local theater company and thus would have to change its show regularly to keep audiences coming. The smaller the town, the more often the show changed. Thus, actors in rep would have to learn and rehearse a new show anywhere from once a month to as often as once a week, while of course playing performances in the evening. Although popular productions could be returned to the repertoire on a regular basis, such hurried schedules nonetheless made for less than meticulous production standards. Rep thus became a training ground for young actors, who went there to learn their craft under fire, so to speak, and a home for second-rate actors who could not make it in London. Nevertheless, it was through the rep system that small towns that in America would be unable to sustain a community theater of amateurs, in Britain could sustain professional theater companies practically year-round until at least the early 1980s. Since the large subsidized companies such as the National Theatre* and the RSC* also use a rep system, Americans tend to think of rep as a subsidy system doing classics, but outside London it was primarily a commercial enterprise.

repeat. Of food, to cause indigestion.

replay. In the Football Association,* games played for the FA Cup* eliminate the loser from the competition, as opposed to normal league play in which ties are accepted and league standings are determined by total points scored rather than wins. As football* often ends in a tie, many Cup matches* must be replayed, and fans find these especially exciting, both because they are played on days when normally there would be no game and because they must continue play until someone actually wins.

report. At school,* what Americans usually call a report card, but in public schools* always including an additional written comment from a master.*

reset. In Scotland,* to receive stolen property or to give aid or shelter to an outlaw.

re-shuffle. *See* Cabinet.

resident. In foreign affairs, an agent of a governor* who resided at a semiautonomous court, particularly common in India* but found in many other parts of the Empire.*

re-sit. *See* sit.

Responsions. The first exam at Oxford,* informally called the Smalls,* variously used as a way to weed out students during the first year, as an admissions test (before 1960), or as a qualifier for grants.* The similar

Cambridge* exam was formally called the **Previous**, informally the **little-go**.

rest home. *See* nursing home.

return. What Americans call a round-trip ticket.

Reuters. An international news reporting service, similar to the American Associated Press, used since 1849 by most British and Commonwealth newspapers.*

revally. The pronunciation used for the word spelled reveille.

Revd. Reverend. Technically, this is an adjective describing the clergyman, not a title, so Church of England* priests are properly called the Reverend Mr So-and-so, not Reverend So-and-so. Few outside the church remember to make this distinction any more, but those that do generally use "the Revd" (no period) while those that don't distinguish go for the American-style "Rev." (with period). In the Church of England, the **Most Revd** is an archbishop,* while a bishop is the **Rt Revd** and the **Very Revd** is a dean.*

revels. *See also* feast; wakes.

revise. To study or to cram for an exam; hence, a cramming session is a **revision**.

Revolution, Glorious. *See* Glorious Revolution.

RFC. Royal Flying Corps. *See* air force.*

RGS. Royal Geographical Society.*

RHG. Royal Horse Guards. *See* Guards.

Rhondda. An area of southeastern Wales* synonymous with coal and coal mining, now part of the county* of Mid Glamorgan,* in literature perhaps most vividly depicted in *How Green Was My Valley*.

RHS. (1) Royal Historical Society. (2) Royal Humane Society.*

rhyming slang. One of the most colorful versions of English slang, developed by London* Cockneys* during the mid-to-late nineteenth century. Apparently, when the East End* (was flooded with Irish immigrants, the

Cockneys fought back by developing a form of the English language that the Irish could not understand; for the most part, neither can anyone else, as it has a most complicated foundation. As with all slang, it requires a substitution of one word for another, but in rhyming slang, the substitution has nothing to do with actual meaning. In place of the normal word, such as wife, you substitute a three- or four-syllable clichéd phrase, in one case Duchess of Fife, whose last syllable rhymes with the word intended. Then, if the phrase is really common, you actually say only the first word or syllable, so that many Cockneys might call their wife "my old Dutch." This code is almost impenetrable to the outsider, not only because being Dutch has nothing to do with the meaning intended, but also because it requires a familiarity with both the language itself and the culture so that both clichés and rhymes can be understood instantaneously. Because it is based on popular clichés, the slang changes constantly. Nevertheless, in this work I have included only a few examples of rhyming slang, for a simple reason: The slang is so convoluted that when writers use rhyming slang in works intended for non-Cockney readers, they almost always find a way to explain it as they go. I have included here only those terms that have penetrated general use so far that they are used by many non-Cockneys (Bristols,* half-inch,* tart,* etc.), often without even recognizing their roots in rhyming slang.

RI. A designation used after the name of the monarch meaning *rex et imperator* or *regina et imperatrix* in Latin and thus either King and Emperor or Queen and Empress.

RIBA. Royal Institute of British Architects, a professional organization for architects also supervising various training programs.

ribbon development. The building of shops* and businesses in a strip along an existing highway,* ostensibly outlawed in 1947.

Richmond. (1) This was the site of one of the primary homes of the English kings* and queens* since the twelfth century, on the Thames* upriver from Fulham* and figuratively just around the corner from Hampton Court.* The last **Richmond Palace** was built by Henry VII and was perhaps Elizabeth I's favorite home, but after the Civil War* it was no longer used for royal dwelling. It fell into ruins, from which separate dwellings were rebuilt in the eighteenth century. **Richmond Park** was the king's private chase* and is now the largest park* in the Greater London* area, so large that it still sustains large numbers of wildlife, and **Richmond Hill** has a panoramic view of both countryside and city that has been celebrated by numerous artists, most notably Turner. (2) Another, and older, Richmond is a castle and small town in northern Yorkshire.*

rick. A pile of hay or grain, usually then thatched* to protect it from the winter rains. *See also* ruck.

riding. (1) To go riding on horseback was the primary entertainment of the nobility* and gentry* until the twentieth century, and although it has declined somewhat in recent years, it is still done regularly by most people in that class* for pleasure rather than for transportation. To **ride out**, however, was to become a thief, especially in the days of the highwaymen,* but also very common along the Border where most persons on horseback were engaged in some kind of raiding for centuries before 1800. One rarely "rides" in a car or on a train, only on a horse. (2) An administrative division of Yorkshire,* sort of a shire within a shire,* dating back to the early medieval period. Until 1974, there were three ridings: East, West, and North, with the city of York* at the junction of their borders; the term seems to be a corruption of thirding. In the county reorganization of 1974, Yorkshire was divided into several separate counties, but not along the old borders of the ridings, so the ridings disappeared except that locals still use the terms for the general areas. The term is used in no other shires.

Rifle Brigade. A regiment* of infantry, formed after the American Revolution as skirmishers armed with rifles rather than muskets; in 1815, it was formally taken out of the line* and its number eliminated so that it is always the "last" regiment, placed on the left of all formations, traditionally the most dangerous flank in battle, as a reward for its gallantry at Waterloo.*

right. When used as an adverb, it usually means very, as in "right glad" or "right stupid"; when used as an adjective, it means complete or thorough, as in "a right mess." When used alone, it means yes or sometimes "that's it!" or "that's enough!" In effect, this is the working-class* equivalent of quite* or rather.* **Too right** is a working class idiom used similarly to the American "You'd better believe it!" or "You bet!"; when used in a sentence it is always at the beginning, as in "Too right you will."

right go. A verbal attack or tongue-lashing.

right ho. "That's right," or "absolutely correct." This is primarily upper class* usage in the early twentieth century, stereotypically associated with the public school twit* character. Also **rightio** or **right-o**.

right of way. A public* pathway across otherwise private property, such rights usually maintained by the right of custom. *See also* common.

right you are. Used not to mean that someone else is correct but rather to indicate that the speaker understands what is desired; thus, a cabbie might say "right you are" when given an address.

rime. *See* frost.

ring. (1) In cooking, what Americans usually call a burner, the gas circle or electric element over which a pan is placed for cooking. Many of these are made to be used independently of a range and thus are what Americans call a hot plate; however, unlike American hot plates, these can be either gas or electric in nature. (2) As a verb, to call on the telephone. (3) At the racetrack, the area where the bookmakers* stand to take bets. Since 1897, individual bookmakers could take bets there at different odds than those of the track's tote system. Often called the **silver ring** as bets there would be in silver rather than the gold coins more common in Tattersall's.*

Ring. In Hyde Park,* a carriage road that circles the park, one of the principal social gathering places of fashionable London* from the opening of the park until the automobile finally eliminated the carriage.* Until then, however, everyone who was anyone appeared regularly either in a carriage on the Ring or riding* on Rotten Row* nearby.

ringing. *See* bellringing.

Ringing Day. Guy Fawkes Day,* so called in some parts of England* because part of the celebration decreed by Parliament* was the ringing of church* bells.

ring road. A major road that circles a town with a limited number of exits onto the town's roads. *See also* A; by-pass; M.

Riot Act. A law passed in 1715, after some violent Jacobite rioting, that defined a riot as twelve or more persons who refused to disperse if ordered to do so, on penalty of death. Before taking action, the local officer was required to officially order dispersal by reading the Act to the group, from which we get the idiom **read the Riot Act**.

Ripon. A small town in northern Yorkshire,* an ecclesiastical center since the seventh century.

ripping. Terrifically good, as in a "ripping yarn"; schoolboy slang of the early twentieth century, now practically extinct.

rise. What Americans call a raise, as in a **pay raise**.

rising damp. Condensation of moisture inside walls.

rissole. A meat or fish pattie rolled in egg and bread crumbs and then fried. Pronounced RISSsole.

Ritz. A hotel in London.* When built in 1906, it was twice as expensive as even the Savoy* and attracted the most famous and fashionable clientele of pre-WWI social life. The words ritz and ritzy quickly entered the language as synonyms for luxury and expensive taste, and its Palm Court* was much imitated in other hotels for decades.

river. In formal identifications, where Americans generally put river after the name, as in Mississippi River, the British put it before, as in the River Thames* or River Severn.*

River. In London,* the Thames.*

Riviera, English. The western portion of the south coast of England,* so called because it has a mild, semitropical climate sustained by the Gulf Stream and is lined with resort towns such as Torquay.*

RL. Rugby League. *See* rugby.

RM. (1) Royal Mail. (2) Royal Marines. *See also* navy.

RMA. Royal Military Academy. *See* Sandhurst.

RMC. Royal Military College. *See* Sandhurst.

RN. (1) Royal Navy. *See* navy. (2) *See* SRN.

roach. Not the bug but a small freshwater fish.

road. (1) While Americans tend to use road to mean a roadway outside of urban areas, the British tend to use it to mean any roadway, including a street, no matter what its official designation; thus John Lennon's "Why don't we do it in the road?" indicates the middle of the street. **Roadworks** are what Americans call street or highway repairs; **road sense** is what Americans call highway sense or traffic sense, the ability to drive well. **Any road** is anyway, anyhow, or in any manner, a lower class* usage, rural more often than urban. *See also* high street; highway; ring road; street. (2) Usually the **roads**, the sheltered portion of a coastline or estuary where ships can safely anchor. The **rules of the road** are not the highway code but the rules of right of way on the sea.

road tax. A regular tax on automobiles that a driver must pay to operate a car legally. Also called a **road fund** licence.*

robin. One of the most popular and common birds of Britain. The British version of the bird is a type of thrush* and is much smaller than the American robin. The bird is also a popular symbol of Christmas,* especially on Christmas cards.*

Robinson, Heath. *See* Heath Robinson.

Rochester. A town with a twelfth century cathedral,* significant since the Roman era as it controls both the ports of the large inlet made by the Medway* on the south side of the Thames* estuary and the road from London* to Canterbury* and Dover.* Readers know it best from *Great Expectations.*

rock cake. *See* cake.

rock candy. Peppermint sticks.

Rockers. Gangs of young men of the 1960s, distinguished by motorcycles and a passion for rock'n'roll. *See also* Mods; skinhead; Teddy Boy.

rocket. A severe reprimand or censure, usually delivered in person; originally military slang, it is now widely used in most levels of society.

rod. A measurement of five-and-one-half yards in length, in use since the fifteenth century; in area, a square of a rod in length on all sides, 1/160th of an acre.* Also called a **perch** or a **pole**.

roe. (1) A species of small deer,* found now only in very limited and wild sites. (2) Fish eggs, such as Americans usually call caviar, often called **hard roe** or roes; **soft roe** is the reproductive organ of a male fish, also eaten like caviar on toast or crackers, most often at breakfast.

Roedean. A girl's school* near Brighton,* since its founding in 1885 considered one of the most intellectually oriented of such schools.

rogations. In the Church of England,* special prayers, especially those offered up during **Rogationtide**, the Sunday through Wednesday before Ascension Day.* Coming five weeks after Easter,* the prayers often deal with crops as well as with the souls of the dead, and church services are often accompanied by processions that are in turn related to beating the bounds.*

roger. To have sex with, fairly vulgar but not necessarily lower-class usage.

Rokeby. An eighteenth century country house* in northern Yorkshire.* Scott liked to walk in the area and chose its name for his *Rokeby* poem and described the local vicinity, but Scott's Rokeby Castle is imaginary, perhaps modeled on other castles in the general area.

Roller. A Rolls-Royce,* used by people of the Sloane Ranger* type who are prone to cute nicknames ending in *-er*.

rollmop. Pickled herring* rolled up before canning or bottling.

roll neck. On clothes, what Americans call a turtleneck.

roll on. Used to indicate you are looking forward to something or some time, as in "roll on the holidays."

Rolls-Royce. As Americans know, the worldwide epitome of the luxury car, but also the major British manufacturer of aircraft engines.

roly-poly pudding. *See* pudding.

Romford. A quiet and prosperous suburb to the northeast of London.* Usually pronounced RUMferd.

Romney Marsh. Formerly a large marsh* on the southeast coast of England,* drained and now rich pastureland, much of it below sea level and very flat.

roneo. An office duplicating machine, a brand name often used generically.

rook. The British version of the crow, black, noisy, and feeding on crops as well as insects.

rookery. A slum, so called from its resemblance to a nesting site for rooks*—crowded, noisy, and full of people stealing from each other as rooks do when nest-building.

rooms. (1) Until mid–twentieth century, the moderately well-to-do urban individual rented rooms rather than a flat* or a full house.* These were a suite of rooms, usually consisting of one or more bedrooms and a sitting room,* but with no kitchen, which meant the tenant was spared the expense and trouble of maintaining a full complement of servants.* Some meals were provided by the landlady, who cooked them in the kitchen for the entire building, while others were taken at restaurants or at the club;* the landlady or one of her servants did all housekeeping. Sherlock Holmes and Dr. Watson lived in rooms, for example, as did most students at Oxford* and Cambridge,* where a servant called a scout* was shared among the students in several different sets of rooms. (2) In a house, *see under* names of specific rooms, such as drawing room,* sitting room,* and so forth.

rooty gong. The good conduct medal; rooty was army* slang in India* for bread, so the name implied the medal was given out with the bread, but in fact it required a spotless record for eighteen years and was thus quite rare in a hard-drinking army.

rose. *See* garden.

rosette. A large artificial flower, usually made of ribbon, looking rather like an overgrown version of the prize ribbons Americans give in county fairs. These are worn on the chest or lapel by supporters of political candidates, football clubs,* and so forth, and are made in the color of the political party or team being supported.

RoSPA. Royal Society for the Prevention of Accidents, something like the American National Safety Council.

rota. A list, usually a list assigning duties.

Rotherhithe. Once a village on the south bank of the Thames* used for mooring boats, across the river from Stepney,* long since merging into the industrial and dockland areas of Southwark.* *See also* hithe.

rotten borough. *See* borough, rotten.

Rotten Row. In London,* the mile-long bridle path along the southern edge of Hyde Park,* the primary site for social and recreational riding* in the city since it was built by Queen Anne. All eighteenth- and nineteenth-century society met each other along either the Row or the Ring.* Polite etymology suggests that the name comes from *route du roi*, which would make sense except that neither end connects with a royal residence and it was a *reine* who built it; a more cynical etymologist might suggest it came from the smell provided by the concentration of horses.

rotter. An untrustworthy person, generally used only by members of the upper classes.*

rough. (1) Outdoors, or without a regular home; thus to **live rough** is to be a vagrant, a wanderer, or a homeless person, who often has to **sleep rough** outdoors. (2) To **do the rough** is to do heavy housework. (3) *See* bit.

round. (1) A route, usually for regular deliveries, such as a milk round or a paper round. (2) Of bread, what Americans call a slice, or a whole sandwich* made from two full slices. *See also* half-round.

roundabout. (1) What Americans call a carousel. (2) What Americans call a traffic circle.

rounders. A children's game played with a ball and a stick, usually credited as the source of American baseball.

roundsman. A person who makes regular deliveries on a round.*

rout. In the eighteenth and nineteenth century, a fashionable evening party.

route march. In the army,* a long march taken for training or punishment.

Rover. A brand of car. The most successful model was the Land Rover, similar to the American Jeep, an indestructible vehicle used in the countryside* and in the colonies* following WWII; in recent years, the Range Rover has upgraded this into a car that still looks like a Jeep but has become one of the most expensive and highest status luxury cars, perhaps because it implies an active country house* life.

Rovers. A Boy Scout* organization for boys sixteen to twenty, more recently changed to Venture Scouts* and opened to girls as well.

row. A short, narrow street, usually one originally lined with terrace* houses.

Row, the. Rotten Row.*

rowing. At British colleges,* particularly at Oxford* or Cambridge,* rowing is the preeminent sport, especially the eights. To row for your college, or even better to row for one university against the other, is the greatest sporting achievement a student can hope to have. But all of this activity is student-organized, more like American intramural games than American collegiate team sports. *See also* blue; Boat Race; bumping; Eights Week; Henley; May Week.

Rowland's. A men's hair oil from the early nineteenth century, made from the oil of trees in Macassar, ending forever the men's fashion for bear grease.

Rowland Ward. The *Records of Big Game*, since 1892 the official record of outstanding kills made by big game hunters.

Rowton Houses. Projects begun in 1892 to provide hotel-styled accommodation for poor working men who before then could find only dormitory-like lodgings.

royal. (1) *See* royalty. (2) When used as a prefix in place names, officially patronized by a King* or Queen.* This patronage can have been long in the past, as for example Royal Leamington Spa,* or ongoing, as with the Royal Academy.* *See also* royal warrant. (3) A casual noun used in late twentieth century newspaper* headlines for any member of royalty,* as in "The royals miss the boat."

Royal Academy. Technically, the **Royal Academy of Arts**, an association of artists founded in 1768. The academy was not instructional but rather a society intended to recognize and encourage the finest British artists, and thus its membership was open only to those already recognized as accomplished artists. Membership is severely limited, selected by vote of current members; thus, the initials **RA** behind a painter's name generally has indicated considerable social status as well as artistic skill. As membership is for life and the numbers are limited, the Academy has tended toward the conservative, delaying membership for the more avant-garde until they were well established, its most noted "scandal" perhaps being the delay of Constable's full membership until he was past fifty. Although influential and conservative, it never had the kind of dead hand laid on art by the Academy in Paris during the nineteenth century. In the late twentieth century, the Academy has come to be seen as an honor but one not terribly important to the career of a modern British artist, and the annual Academy exhibitions are generally noted more for technical polish than for experimentation or serious influence on the direction of contemporary art. The Academy also operates an art school for "advanced" students, which has in fact trained a number of significant British painters. The Academy was originally in Pall Mall,* then moved to Somerset House* in 1780, again in 1837 to the National Museum,* and then in 1869 to their present building in Piccadilly.* *See also* Slade.

Royal Academy of Dramatic Art. *See* RADA.

Royal Academy of Music. The first professional music conservatory in England,* established in London* in 1822 (reviving the name used by Handel's concert society in the eighteenth century), now located just south of Regent's Park.* *See also* Royal College of Music.

Royal Agricultural Show. *See* agricultural show.

Royal Air Force. *See* air force.

Royal Almonry. *See* almoner.

Royal Arsenal. *See* Woolwich.

Royal Ascot. *See* Ascot.

Royal Assent. Approval by the monarch of any legislation passed by Parliament,* required before it becomes law; the assent has not been withheld since Queen Anne. *See also* bill; constitution; government.

Royal Ballet. A ballet company formally chartered as such in 1956, formed from the company that had begun at the Old Vic* and moved to Sadler's Wells,* playing regular seasons in Covent Garden* since 1946.

Royal College of Art. An art academy* originally founded as part of the V&A,* inclined more toward design than pure art, especially known for its fashion design program. *See also* Slade.

Royal College of Music. A music conservatory in London* since 1883, located near the Albert Hall.* *See also* Royal Academy of Music.

Royal Court. A theatre in London* in Sloane Square,* synonymous with the theatrical avant-garde for two eras, the earlier when it was the first to produce Shaw, Granville-Barker, and others; and the second under completely different management when it introduced Osborne, Wesker, and Jellicoe.

Royal Enclosure. *See* Ascot.

Royal Engineers. An engineers unit of the army,* similar to the American Corps of Engineers but rarely involved with building dams.

Royal Exchange. *See* Exchange.

royal family. The immediate family of the monarch, for example, the King* or Queen,* their spouse and children, and their brothers or sisters, plus, if she is still living, the Queen Mother.* *See also* Highness, His/Her/Your; royalty.

Royal Festival Hall. In London* the primary concert hall of the South Bank* development.

Royal Geographical Society. A private society founded in 1830 to encourage world exploration; in the nineteenth century, sponsor of many of the famous explorations of Africa and Asia and, in the twentieth century, encouraging accurate mapping and nature studies.

Royal Highlanders. *See* Black Watch.

Royal Highness, His/Her/Your. The formal title and form of address for children of the monarch; many writers inaccurately shorten this to His/Her Highness.* The title is also given to the children of the monarch's sons, but not to the children of daughters, as the title implies possible succession to the throne. The standard abbreviation is **HRH**.

Royal Historical Society. A society* founded in 1868 to encourage historical research, primarily through regular publication of research papers and reference works.

Royal Horse Guards. One of the two regiments* of the Household Cavalry* that guard the monarch, nicknamed the Blues.* They still perform guard and ceremonial duties on horseback, but in WWII and since, when not on ceremonial duties, they are an armored regiment. *See also* Guards.

Royal Hospital. Also called **Chelsea Hospital**, a hospital and home in London* in Chelsea* since 1686 for about 400 retired soldiers called the Chelsea Pensioners.* A similar hospital for sailors at Greenwich* was also called the Royal Hospital. *See also* Ranelagh Gardens.

royal household. The retinue of the monarch, originally the government of the nation. The rise of parliamentary power and a Cabinet* government left this primarily responsible only for the monarch's personal safety and well-being, headed by a Lord Steward* below stairs* and a Lord Chamberlain* above.

Royal Humane Society. *See* humane society.

Royal Institution. An organization incorporated in 1800 to further the cause of scientific knowledge in the nation, sponsor of research laboratories and educational programs in the sciences.

Royal Leamington Spa. *See* Leamington Spa.

Royal Mail. *See* post office.

Royal Maundy. In the medieval era, the reigning monarch of England* participated in a ceremony on Maundy Thursday, the day before Good Friday,* imitating Jesus' washing of the feet of His disciples. Representative poor people met the ruler, had their feet personally washed by him or her, and were given gifts of food and clothing. Elizabeth I substituted money rather than give up her own clothes, and William and Mary discontinued personal participation by the ruler, but the Royal Almonry* officers continued it until 1932, when George V began to participate personally, and George VI and Elizabeth II continued the practice. However, the recipients are no longer the poorest of the poor but elderly persons chosen for their long service to the Church* and community, and although symbolic gifts are still given, feet are no longer washed; four orphans are also included.

Royal Mile. In Edinburgh,* the main street of the Old Town, connecting Edinburgh Castle to Holyroodhouse.*

Royal Military College. *See* Sandhurst.

Royal Observatory. *See* Greenwich.

Royal Opera House. *See* Covent Garden.

Royal Pavilion. *See* Brighton.

Royal Personage. A member of the royal family;* such people are personages rather than persons in most journalistic and bureaucratic usage.

Royal Scots. The 1st Regiment* of Foot (infantry) in the army.*

Royal Shakespeare Company. Although Shakespearean productions had played regularly at Stratford* since the early twentieth century, the RSC was not organized in its modern form until 1960. It is one of the two principal subsidized theaters in England,* concentrating on the work of

Shakespeare but also regularly producing classics from other eras and nations as well as new plays, performing year-round at Stratford, but also performing in London,* currently at the Barbican,* and touring the nation regularly.

Royal Society. The principal scientific society,* formally organized in 1660, including among its members the finest scientists of the nation since its beginnings. It is an honorary society that encourages research through its publications and meetings and provides scientific advisors to the government,* for which it now receives some subsidies, but which conducts or funds little research directly.

Royal Society of Arts. A society* formed in 1754 in London* to encourage the application of science to arts and commerce, providing lectures, exhibits, and so forth, to encourage quality design.

Royal Tunbridge Wells. *See* Tunbridge Wells.

royalty. In Britain, royalty means only members of the royal family.* Many persons may have royal blood and be able to trace lineage to some member of the family in the past, but nonetheless they are not royalty. *See also* King; nobility; prince; princess; Queen.

Royal Victorian Order. An honour* given personally by the monarch for personal services to the Crown,* abbreviated VO.

royal warrant. *See* By Appointment.

rozzer. A policeman, used primarily by the lower classes.*

RP. Received pronunciation; this is a linguistic term for what is often called the public school* or Oxbridge* accent, one of the primary indicators of social status. Practically alone among nations, the British "standard" accent* is not regional—despite London's* cultural dominance, all of the London accents are considered regional accents—but is consciously learned, sometimes from parents who speak with the accent but just as often at school, and then becomes a badge of entry into the Establishment.

RS. Royal Society.*

RSA. (1) Royal Society of Arts.* (2) In Scotland, Royal Scottish Academy.

RSC. Royal Shakespeare Company.*

RSM. In the army,* Regimental Sergeant Major.*

RSPB. Royal Society for the Protection of Birds.

RSPCA. Royal Society for the Prevention of Cruelty to Animals, generally equivalent to the American ASPCA.

RSPCC. *See* NSPCC.

RTA. A road traffic accident.

Rt Hon. The Right Honourable, the formal title of an earl,* countess,* viscount,* viscountess,* baron,* or wife of a baron.

Rt Revd. The Right Reverend, the formal title used for a bishop.* *See also* Revd.

RTU. In the military, returned to unit, meaning sent back to one's original unit, but also almost always implying failure, as at a special course or training facility.

RU. Rugby Union. *See* rugby.

rubber. What Americans call an eraser.

rubbers. Waterproof shoes or boots, what Americans usually call galoshes or rain boots. Practically never used like American slang for condoms.

rubbish. What Americans generally call garbage or trash.

RUC. Royal Ulster* Constabulary, the police* of Northern Ireland.* By the late 1960s, the RUC was widely believed to be conducting a campaign against the Catholic residents, which led to the use of troops from the regular army* to keep the peace and to major reorganizations of the RUC, which nonetheless continued to be overwhelmingly Protestant in its composition and which has still failed to gain the confidence of the local Catholics.

ruck. (1) Originally, a northern term for a hay rick;* from that it gradually evolved to mean the horses in a race that "also ran," and from that by the twentieth century became a colloquial expression for the common crowd or ordinary people. (2) In rugby,* a loose crowd of players surrounding a dropped ball.

ruddy. A euphemism for bloody.*

rude. Sometimes also used to mean indecent, suggestive, or pornographic, as in "rude noises" or "rude pictures."

rug. More likely to mean a heavy blanket than a carpet; most carriages* and open cars, for example, had a rug inside them to protect passengers from the cold. Rug is occasionally used for the floor covering, as in America, but carpet is generally preferred.

rugby. A uniquely British form of football, begun at Rugby* school in 1823 when a boy, "with a fine disregard for the rules," picked up the ball in a soccer match and ran with it. It is played with almost a religious fervor but curiously is played in only two mutually exclusive parts of society: the public schools* and universities* and the lower portions of the working class* in the northern part of the country. The rest of the nation in fall and winter plays and follows soccer, called football.*

Rugby is played on a field about one-and-one-half times an American football field, with a ball that looks like an overgrown American football. Points are scored by either carrying the ball over a goal line or kicking it over a goalpost shaped like a large wide H. A player advances the ball until he is tackled, but before he is tackled, he may give the ball to another player on his own team by kicking it or by throwing it underhand; however, all such passes must be to a player behind the runner. Play does not stop when a player is tackled, for he must immediately release the ball, and it becomes a free ball that can be kicked or picked up by either team. When play stops for other reasons, such as fouls, a **scrum** is formed: Eight players from both teams form a circle with arms linked over shoulders, a player tosses the ball into the middle, and the players in the scrum shove each other around until someone manages to kick the ball out to one of the other players, who then begins the play by passing or running. No blocking is allowed, and in fact, the person with the ball must be the farthest advanced person on his team.

If a player runs with the ball across the goal line and touches the ball to the ground there, called a try,* his team gets four points, and he is allowed a free kick that, if it passes through the upper half of the goal, scores another two. At any time a player may drop-kick the ball toward the goal; if it goes through, it scores three points. Play continues with no time-outs and no substitutions (except for real injury, in which case the substitute must finish the game) for two halves, each usually forty minutes;

the play is fast and violent. The players play in shorts with no protective pads or helmets.

The game is played under two related sets of rules: **Rugby Union** is basically original rugby as played in most schools and in most of England, with fifteen players, usually amateurs. **Rugby League** uses only thirteen players, played professionally primarily in Wales,* Scotland,* and northern England,* with some differences in scoring: All kicks score two and a try only three; also, when a player is tackled, instead of releasing the ball, he is allowed to kick it back to one of his own players, until the fourth consecutive tackle. For playing positions, *See* forward; halfback; three-quarter back. For other vocabulary, *See* knock-on; line-out; rebound; ruck.

Rugby. An industrial town near Coventry,* much overshadowed by the nearby school also called Rugby. The school was established in 1567 but did not move to national prominence until the early nineteenth century, when the methods of the headmaster,* Dr. Arnold, redefined the nature of the British public school,* particularly with its emphasis on sport* as a major character builder for boys and the concept of muscular Christianity* that fueled so much of the nineteenth-century Empire.* The game of rugby* was invented here. Since Dr. Arnold's time, Rugby has been one of the dominant public schools in British social life, easily ranking among the top five or six in influence of its graduates.

Rugby fives. *See* fives.

rugger. A casual name for rugby.*

Ruislip. Pronounced RIZElip, a suburb to the far northwest of London,* synonymous with middle-class* boredom.

Rule's. In London,* an extremely expensive and conservative restaurant near the Strand,* popular with the noble, wealthy, and famous since Dickens was a regular, still very exclusive about whom it allows to dine there.

rum. (1) The spirit entered Britain only in the seventeenth century after it began to be brewed from the sugar grown in the Caribbean; it could not compete with gin* at home, but it quickly became the sailor's drink. Grog* made from rum and water was issued as a navy* ration until 1971. (2) A casual term meaning unusual, weird, or dangerous, surfacing in this sense in the eighteenth century; no one quite knows why or how, although it is probably related to Romany (gypsy*) rather than to the liquor. A **rum go** is a mysterious or dangerous set of circumstances, while a **rum co** or **cove** before mid-nineteenth century was a sharp rogue and afterward was an oddball. Similarly, a **rum duke**, a **rum doxy**, or a **rum duchess** are all fine examples of humanity, while a **rum customer** is someone not to be meddled with.

rumble. To come to understand, to catch on.

rump steak. What Americans usually call round steak.

run. To own and use, especially a car. A new car is **run in** for several hundred miles in order to break it in.

runner bean. *See* bean.

running knot. The knot Americans call a slip knot.

Runnymede. A site along the Thames* near Windsor* where King John signed the Magna Carta.*

run-up. The preparation time before an event.

rural dean. *See* dean.

rushes. Long grasslike plants with hollow stems that are used for weaving mats or chair seats. Since earliest times, rushes have also been strewn across earthen and stone floors for insulation and for cushioning. They were not necessarily a sign of poverty, for their use was common from castle to hovel. Of course, the poor cottage* dwellers continued to use rushes much later than wealthier persons, as they were more likely to continue living on an earthen floor.

Ruskin. The first college* at Oxford* (1899) to provide residence and study for working men (founded by an American, subsidized by various unions*).

Russell Square. A large square* in London* behind the British Museum, once the home of wealthy businessmen like the Osbornes and Sedleys of *Vanity Fair* and still favored by lawyers and similar professionals.

Russian. A cigarette, not made from Russian tobacco but rolled in brown rather than white paper, popular from the Edwardian era into the 1930s as part of an exotic or bohemian* pose. *See also* gasper; Turkish.

rusticate. To suspend a student from a college.

Rutland. Once the smallest county* in England,* just north of Northamptonshire,* almost completely agricultural in nature. In the 1974 reorganization, it was completely absorbed into Leicestershire.* The **Rutland Water**

is an artificial lake begun in the area in 1971, one of the very few man-made reservoirs in the American manner in Britain.

RWV. Robbery with violence, a criminal charge that Americans usually call mugging.

Ry. Railway; used like the American RR.

Rye. A port town in East Sussex,* known to Americans as the home of Henry James and the setting for many episodes of E. F. Benson's *Lucia* series.

S

s. Abbreviation for shilling,* no longer used after decimalization in 1971. *See also* d; p.

sack. Dry white wine, originally from Spain, the name apparently a corruption of the French *sec.* Canary* was a sweeter form of the same wine, but sack was often used generically for whites until the late eighteenth century. *See also* hock.

sacristan. A church* functionary who cares for the vessels used in communion* and on the altar. *See also* clergy.

Sadler's Wells. A well of mineral water in London* near Islington,* at the time of its initial development as a spa during the Restoration some distance outside the city. It soon lost its fashionable status to such attractions as Ranelagh Gardens* and Vauxhall Gardens* and to spa towns such as Bath* or Leamington Spa* but remained a popular place for entertainment among those not quite in fashion, having at various times a popular theater, music hall,* boxing ring, and skating rink, until rebuilt as a theater in 1931 housing the companies that would ultimately turn into the Royal Ballet* and the English National Opera.*

SAE. What Americans call SASE, a stamped self-addressed envelope.

safari park. A park with wild animals, usually African animals such as lions, like a zoo except that the animals are not in cages. The visitors either drive through or are driven in busses. These are almost always associated with country houses* that have been opened to the public by their owners and often have amusement parks as well.

safe as houses. Without risk; the origin of the idiom is unclear.

safe seat. *See* seat.

Saffron Hill. A street in London* north of Holborn,* in the late nineteenth and early twentieth centuries notorious as a crime center.

sahib. Pronounced sahb, in India* a title of respect used by Indians for almost any Europeans, roughly equivalent to sir; a European woman would be a **memsahib**. However, when the term is used by the British outside of India, it usually is ironic, especially memsahib, indicating a person who likes to order others around. *See also* pukka.

Sainsbury. The largest supermarket* chain in Britain.

St. Agnes's Eve. January 20, the night before St. Agnes's Day; in folklore, the girl who dreams of a man on this night will marry that man, as widely known from Keats's poem of that name.

St. Alban's. A town northwest of London,* its settlement dating to the Roman era and its name from the first English martyr executed there in the third century. It is the site of a cathedral* and was home for Dickens's Bleak House, but now it is primarily a commuter town.

St. Andrews. A coastal town in Scotland* north of Edinburgh,* site of an ancient university* but more known for its golf course, treated as the spiritual home of golf itself.

St. Andrew's Day. November 30. St. Andrew is the patron saint of Scotland,* and his day has been both a religious and patriotic festival there from the medieval era. When Scotland became Protestant, the religious celebrations necessarily disappeared, but patriotic celebrations continued until in the nineteenth century they were gradually overshadowed by Burns Night* festivities. In England,* the date was little marked outside the church except by lacemakers in the Midlands,* who called it **Tanders** and often celebrated on the old calendar* date, the modern December 11, in rather raucous, drunken celebrations, gradually suppressed with the rise of nineteenth century respectability. *See also* Advent.

St. Bartholomew's. In London* two churches* carry this name: **St. Bartholomew's the Great**, in Smithfield,* founded in the twelfth century, London's oldest church, going into decline after dissolution of the monasteries, then restored in the late nineteenth century; and **St. Bartholomew's the Less**, the church of **St. Bartholomew's Hospital**, also dating to the twelfth century. Affectionately called **St. Bart's**, this has always been London's most significant hospital, now much modernized from when Dr. Watson first met Holmes there, and treating half a million patients a year.

St. Bartholomew's Day. *See* Bartholomew Fair.

St. Bart's. *See* St. Bartholomew's.

St. Blaise's Day. February 3, celebrated primarily in wool-growing areas such as Yorkshire* and East Anglia;* such celebrations died out by the early nineteenth century, due in part to enclosure* and urbanization and in part to proximity and confusion with Candlemas.*

St. Botolph's. Many London* churches* located at the major gates from the City* carried this name, since St. Botolph was the patron saint of travelers. St. Botolph's **Aldgate**,* -**Aldersgate**,* and -**Bishopsgate*** still remain at the sites of their respective (now demolished) gates.

St. Bride's. A church in London* in Fleet Street;* rebuilt by Wren after the Great Fire,* it had the highest spire* in London and was long regarded as the parish* church for the press.

St. Catherine's Day. November 25, also called Cattern Day.*

St. Clement Danes. A church* in London* on an island in the Strand,* a Wren church that since WWII has been the official church of the RAF.*

St. Clement's Day. November 23, a date marked by feasts and drinking in northern portions of England* before the early nineteenth century.

St. David's Day. March 1, of particular interest in Wales* as St. David is the patron saint of the Welsh.

St. Distaff's Day. A joking reference to January 7, the day after Twelfth Night* when women returned to regular household duties.

St. Dunstan's. Three churches* in London* have this name: **St. Dunstan's in the East**, near old Billingsgate* Market; **St. Dunstan's in the West**, located in Fleet Street,* dating from the thirteenth century, the current 1830 version the church in Dickens's *The Chimes*; and **St. Dunstan's and All Saints**, dating from the thirteenth century, in Stepney.*

St. George's. Two major London* churches bear this name, but with significant distinctions: **St. George's Church** is in Mayfair* and is the church used for many society weddings; **St. George's Cathedral**, however, is Catholic, built in 1848 in St. George's Circus.*

St. George's Circus. A major intersection in London* in Southwark,* junction of Blackfriars,* Lambeth* and Waterloo Roads,* the first planned traffic circle in England* (1769).

St. George's Day. April 23. St. George is the patron saint of England,* and the day was marked by significant religious festivals since the medieval era, intensified with patriotic processions after Agincourt* when it was declared a national holiday as well. These celebrations died or were suppressed under Puritan control in mid–seventeenth century, but revived in the years of Empire* before WWI, when it was a halfday school holiday. Since then its observance has declined again and is now little marked except that each parish church* displays a flag with the red cross of St. George.

St. George's Hospital. A hospital in London* located near the southeast corner of Hyde Park,* founded in 1733 and noted for the medical school associated with it but moved to Wandsworth* in 1978.

St. Giles. The **St. Giles Circus** is the intersection in London* of Oxford Street* and Charing Cross* and Tottenham Court Roads.* **St. Giles High Street** is nearby, but not actually connecting with the circus* and is the site of **St. Giles-in-the-Fields**, a church* that originally stood in open fields outside the City* but in the seventeenth century was surrounded by squalid slums in which the 1664 plague* first appeared; the church was rebuilt in 1733, but the neighborhood continued to be squalid for further centuries. The **St. Giles Fair** is September 1 at Oxford,* a major market* and fair* for the area. *See also* Seven Dials; Shaftesbury Avenue.

St. Ives. Two small towns have this name: One is near Cambridge,* and is the home of the man with seven wives in the rhyme. The other is a small resort on the northern side of the Land's End* peninsula, since the 1930s also known as an artists' colony; Virginia Woolf's descriptions of her Lighthouse, although supposedly set in the Hebrides,* all fit the one here.

St. James's. A neighborhood in London* to the north of St. James's Park,* centering on **St. James's Square**, developed during the Restoration as an elegant suburban site, retaining its fashionable cachet into the present day. Since the nineteenth century, when it became the center of the club* world, it has been the center of London upper-class male society, not only for its clubs but also for its elegant traditional shops. **St. James's Church**, a block north of the square, was built by Wren in 1676. *See also* Jermyn Street; London Library; Pall Mall.

St. James's Palace. Built by Henry VIII as a country alternative to White-hall,* the palace was used only occasionally until, after the fire in Whitehall, it became the monarch's official London* residence, on the north of St. James's Park,* from 1697 until Victoria opted for Buckingham Palace* instead. Now it is regularly used only for ceremonial occasions, but ambassadors to the United Kingdom* are still officially designated ambassadors to the **Court of St. James**.

St. James's Park. The large park* in London* lying between Buckingham Palace* and Whitehall.* It was an enclosed royal park containing deer for hunting when Henry VIII built it along with St. James's Palace* on its northern side. Charles II considerably modified and expanded the park, which he often used for exercise and entertainment, adding what is now called Green Park,* landscaping it in the French manner, adding several ponds and the long space that would eventually become the Mall* and also opening the space to the public. In the nineteenth century, it was land-scaped again in its modern shape with the ponds connected into a long lake, the paths curved irregularly, and numerous trees planted. Sometimes references to the park imply a dubious reputation—since it is nearest to the Guards* barracks and has shrubbery, it is often associated with sexual assignations, in the nineteenth century heterosexual ones and in the mid–twentieth century, homosexual.

St. John's. (1) A college* of Cambridge.* (2) A college* of Oxford.*

St. John's Ambulance Brigade. A volunteer nursing and ambulance service that also provides emergency first aid at football* matches* and similar public gatherings.

St. John's Wood. In London,* a street and neighborhood to the west of Regent's Park,* quite well-to-do.

St. Katharine Dock. A dock basin developed for shipping in 1828, im-mediately east of the Tower* of London,* until WWII the most active and successful of such developments, due to its proximity to the City.* After its bombing in the war, shipping moved to other sites, and the basin was derelict until urban renewal turned it into a yacht harbor in the late 1960s and the immediate area was converted to offices and expensive flats.*

St. Leger. A horse race of one-and-three-quarter miles for three-year-olds, run at Doncaster* in mid-September, named for its founder in 1776; the race has status similar to the Derby* or the 2,000 Guineas.*

St. Lubbock's Day. Any bank holiday;* a joking reference to John Lubbock, the MP* who introduced the first bank holiday law.

St. Luke's summer. A period in mid-October, similar to American Indian summer as a time of unseasonably warm weather. *See also* St. Martin's summer.

St. Martin-in-the-Fields. A church* in London* originally sitting in open fields at the end of the Strand.* The current building opened in 1726 and was surrounded by slums until the development of Trafalgar Square* across the street. As the largest church near the Strand, it has long been a favored site for memorial services of famous actors, while its backing onto the old slums has made it a leader in aid to the poor for centuries, its crypt left open all night since the 1930s for use by the homeless. The **Academy of St. Martin-in-the-Fields** is an orchestra that played concerts there from 1959, but by the 1980s had become so renowned that it now has its headquarters and its own recording studio on the Isle of Dogs.*

St. Martin's summer. A period of unseasonably warm weather occurring in mid-November. *See also* St. Luke's summer.

St. Marylebone. *See* Marylebone.

St. Mary-le-Strand. A church* in London* on an island in the middle of the Strand,* the current building (also called **New Church**) built in 1717, known as the cabby's church since the first cab rank in the city was established on its north side in 1634.

St. Michael and St. George, Order of. A ceremonial order used as an honour* for diplomats and civil servants since its founding in 1818. This order has grown to an enormous size, and the honour is now assumed as a matter of course for the upper civil service.* The ranks from the top down are: Knight Grand Cross (GCMG*), Knight Commander (KCMG*), and Companion (CMG*).

St. Monday. The "holiday" used as an excuse when workers don't show up on Monday.

St. Pancras. The rail station next door to King's Cross* has been since 1864 the London* terminus for trains serving the Midlands,* and the station with its hotel, completed in 1872, is one of the most striking examples of Victorian Gothic architecture to be found anywhere.

St. Paul's. London's* cathedral,* located in the center of the old City.* The building on the site in Shakespeare's time was at least the third, and it was much neglected, with portions used as a prison.* Attempts to refurbish were short-circuited by the Civil War,* and most of it burned in the Great Fire.* The present building was built by Wren, finished in 1708 after thirty-three years of work, and is widely regarded as not only Wren's but one of architecture's great masterpieces. Topped by a noble dome at 365 feet, it was the most visible landmark in London and quickly became its visual symbol; in WWII it became the symbol of all British war effort as well, as it miraculously escaped the German bombing that leveled its environs. As the cathedral for the diocese of London, it is an active church for locals, in spite of the vast number of tourists who visit it, a site for both regular services and massive ceremonials. Other churches naturally use the name St. Paul's, but these are almost always followed by the name of their neighborhood, as in **St. Paul's, Covent Garden,*** also known as the Actors' Church due to its proximity to the theatrical community since the eighteenth century; or **St. Paul's Shadwell** in Wapping,* the "Church of the Sea Captains" in the eighteenth century; references to St. Paul's without modifier always mean the cathedral. **St. Paul's School** was a public school* (1509) connected with the cathedral, and moved in 1884 to Kensington* and in 1968 to the suburbs near Richmond.*

St. Stephen's. (1) The chapel* of the Palace of Westminster* in London,* used from the time of Henry VIII until the fire in 1834 as the meeting place of the House of Commons,* in the rebuilt palace still used as the entranceway to the Commons. (2) A church in the City* south of the Bank of England,* often called Wren's finest building.

St. Swithin's Day. July 15. Folklore treats this somewhat like the American Groundhog Day—if St. Swithin's Day has good weather, it will be followed by forty more days of good weather.

St. Thomas's Hospital. A hospital in London,* originally in Southwark* near Southwark Cathedral* since the thirteenth century, closed by Henry VIII, bought by the City* of London and reopened. By 1868, when it moved to new buildings on the Thames* at Westminster Bridge,* it was both a major hospital and the nation's principal medical school, a position further strengthened by Florence Nightingale's founding of the first nursing school there; both doctors and nurses continue to train there as part of London University.*

salad. To the complete confusion of both American and continental visitors, salad in general use is applied to any cold dish eaten with a fork. Thus, while it may mean the lettuce-and-tomato-based dish of mixed raw vegetables everyone else calls a salad, it more often means something else entirely, such as cold cooked beans, corn, peas, macaroni—or practically anything but lettuce or tomatoes—covered with a gooey substance called salad cream.* Sometimes it is a cold slice of meat with a couple of spoons of other salads to accompany. In previous eras it has meant many different things: in Shakespeare's day it was an herb dish, in the early seventeenth century it was a boiled vegetable, in Pepys's time it was mixed raw vegetables with olive oil as in France. In the mid–eighteenth century, Gulliver used the term for boiled vegetables again, but later in the century it had apparently come to mean raw vegetables of any kind, yet by the 1840s Miss Acton's popular cookbook showed "salads" of mixed boiled vegetables. Modern dictionaries will tell you it is still raw vegetables, but that is not what you will get in a British restaurant or buffet,* where the operable word is cold, not vegetable or raw.

salad cream. A gloppy, pale, commercial substance similar to mayonnaise but thinner and with less identifiable taste, poured liberally over any and every cold food to make it a salad.* As far as can be ascertained, this comes in only one flavor. *See also* custard; HP Sauce.

Salad Days. The phrase of course comes from Shakespeare and is still commonly used to mean youth, but reference in this form is to a phenomenally popular musical comedy about couples who find love through a piano that makes people want to dance. Opening in 1954, it ran for almost six years in London, played in the provinces for years more, and epitomized the silly little English musical and the light unchallenging theatrical fare of the time, as well as exerting a tremendous nostalgic pull on today's older generation for a time when entertainment, and life, was simpler and more beautiful.

Salcombe. A small resort town on the English south coast between Torquay* and Plymouth,* a small but significant shipbuilding center and now the center for much recreational sailing.

sales assistant. A shop assistant.*

Salisbury. A small town in south-central England,* known primarily for its cathedral* begun in the thirteenth century and the subject of many paintings, especially by Constable. This is the heart of Hardy country, and his description of it as Melchester in several works, especially *Jude the Obscure*, is detailed and generally accurate. The **Salisbury Plain** extending to the north, a large grassy but otherwise barren plateau, has a rather forbidding and mysterious image, emphasized by Stonehenge,* and in the twentieth century has been used primarily for military maneuvers and weapons testing.

Sally Ann/Army. The Salvation Army.*

Sally Lunn. A version of Bath bun,* named for its original seller.

saloon. (1) A car with four doors. (2) *See* pub.

saloon bar. *See* pub.

saloon carriage. On a train, what Americans call the dining car.

saloon pistol. A pistol modified for indoor target shooting; similarly modified rifles are **saloon rifles**.

Salop. Abbreviation for Shropshire,* from the ancient name Salopesberia. A **Salopian** is a Shropshire native.

salt beef. What Americans call corned beef. *See also* beef.

salter. A dealer in salt. The **Salters** are one of the twelve great livery companies* of the City* of London.*

saltings. An area of marsh covered regularly by high tides, what Americans often call a salt marsh.

salt pot. What Americans usually call a salt shaker. *See also* cruet.

salts. Usually Epsom* salts, drunk in solution as a laxative; hence, the old saying about going through something like a **dose of salts**.

Salvation Army. Founded in London* in Whitechapel* in 1865 as a revivalist movement, it adopted the army name and attitude in 1878; it operates within Britain in much the same way and appearance as its American version.

sal volatile. A saltlike form of ammonia; depending on context, this was a powder used as a rising agent in baking before the existence of baking soda; or, a liquid (also called smelling salts*) made by diluting this in alcohol.

Samaritans. A charitable organization (1953) that provides counseling, either by phone or in person, especially concerned with the prevention of suicide.

samosa. A triangular pastry with meat and/or vegetable filling, different from a pasty* or pie* in that it is deep fried; from India originally, these usually have lots of pepper or spice.

sanctuary. In the medieval era, a person could take refuge from civil authorities within a church* or churchyard. In England,* this refuge was never permanent; the person could stay for forty days, after which he or she must swear "abjuration," which meant a promise to go into permanent exile in another country. Sanctuary continued in practice for a while under the Church of England,* but it was banned for criminals in 1623 and for all persons in 1723.

sandbag. Used not only for the military trenching bag full of sand but also for a type of cosh* filled with sand, favored as a weapon because the sand gives on impact and leaves no mark. Hence, to be **sandbagged** is to be mugged or beaten without any marks, often used metaphorically in politics when you are caught by surprise and defeated by someone you trusted.

Sandhurst. Founded in 1799 as the **Royal Military College**, located near the village of Sandhurst west of London,* in 1946 becoming the **Royal Military Academy** after merging with programs from Woolwich.* It took some time for the nineteenth century British army to accept that officers needed any training, except perhaps in artillery (which was done at Woolwich), so Sandhurst was a way into the infantry and cavalry officer corps for men who were not quite gentlemen* and who often used crammers* rather than public schools* to prepare them for entry exams. By the twentieth century, however, Sandhurst, like the American West Point, had become the primary route to promotion and major commands.

sandpit. What Americans call a sandbox where children play.

Sandringham. The English country house* of the royal family* since the 1870s, located in the northern portion of Norfolk.* *See also* Balmoral; Buckingham Palace; Windsor.

sand sugar. *See* sugar.

sandwich. In general, these are far simpler than American versions and the names given are very literal: A cheese sandwich, for example, will often be only a slice of cheese between two pieces of white bread. The legendary **cucumber sandwich** of afternoon tea* is bread with butter and sliced cucumber. The multilayered American-style concoctions with several meats and cheeses, lettuce, and assorted other trimmings are very rarely found anywhere. *See also* butty; half-round; jam; round.

sandwich student. Not a student who brings his own lunch but a student who alternates periods of college-level studies with periods of practical on-the-job training or internships.

Sandy. An almost obligatory nickname* for a Scotsman, similar to Jock* in use and attitude; probably based on Alexander which was (and still is) a common Scots* name. *See also* sawney.

sanitary/sanitation. Used to mean not only clean and cleanliness but also healthy or anything connected to health and health-related issues. *See also* gippy tummy. A **sanitary towel** is what Americans call a sanitary napkin.

sardine. Similar to the American sardine, canned in oil or tomato sauce and usually eaten on toast as a snack or savoury.* *See also* pilchard.

sardines. A party game in which one person hides and everyone else tries to find him or her. Rather than exposing the hider, the finder then also goes into the hiding place, the goal being to cram all but the final searcher into one hiding place. The game is still popular among children, but it was often quite eagerly played by teenagers and young adults before the 1960s, as it provided an excuse for physical contact between males and females.

sark. In Scotland,* a shirt.

sarky. Sarcastic.

SAS. Special Air Service, the army's* crack commando regiment* since WWII, sometimes serving within Britain as an antiterrorist unit.

Sassenach. A Scottish term for the English, now used ironically or facetiously.

satin paper. Quality writing paper with a glossy finish.

Saturday. In 1850, law required textile mills to close at 2 P.M. on Saturday, and gradually other businesses were covered by the law. Thus, given the strictures of the English Sunday,* practically all entertainments for workers happen on Saturday afternoon and evenings—sporting events, especially football* matches, are played on Saturday afternoon, and Saturday night compresses the activities of American Fridays and Saturdays into one brief span. *See also* bank holiday; early closing; weekend.

sauce. British foods depend on sauces as much as do French; the difference is the kind and quality of the sauce. In Britain they are almost always commercial preparations. Cold vegetables are smothered in salad cream,* anything mildly dessertlike in custard,* and everything else in brown sauce.*

sauce boat. What Americans call a gravy boat.

sausage, not a. Nothing whatsoever.

sausage roll. Small sausages or pieces of sausage meat baked inside a pastry cover.

Savage. A club* in London* (1857) just north of Pall Mall,* the most bohemian of the major clubs, favored by actors and TV people.

saveloy. A smoked and dried pork sausage, usually quite spicy.

Savernake Forest. A large forest,* primarily of oak,* near Marlborough.*

Savile. A club* in Bond Street* in London,* generally associated with writers and performers.

Savile Row. A street in Mayfair* in London* parallel to Regent Street,* synonymous with quality men's tailoring since the late nineteenth century when tailors in the street revolutionized the fitting of men's suits.

savoury. A dish that is basically salty or tangy and comes either as an appetizer or after (or in lieu of) the dessert; examples would include sardines, anchovies, or perhaps mushrooms on toast, or even Welsh rarebit.* Cheese* often figures in savouries, but the "cheese course" is not a savoury.

Savoy. Originally in the medieval era the site of a palace* on the bank of the Thames* in London* south of the Strand,* it became the site of the **Savoy Chapel** in the sixteenth century, and the church* is still in use. The site holds its modern renown, however, from the **Savoy Theatre**, built on the old palace grounds by D'Oyly Carte in 1881 to house the Gilbert and Sullivan productions, the first English theatre with electric lighting and still in use, and the **Savoy Hotel** built around the theatre by D'Oyly Carte in 1889, an immediate by-word for luxury in the hotel business. **Savoy Hill**, the bank running down to the Thames, also housed the first studios of the BBC* before 1932 and was synonymous with radio broadcasting at the time.

sawney. (1) In England,* a nickname for a Scotsman, usually derogatory in intent, thought to be a corruption of Sandy.* (2) A fool, although generally a good-hearted simpleton. This seems to be derived from zawny or zany rather than from the Scottish nickname but probably has a great deal to do with the negative connotations of the nickname.

SAYE. Save As You Earn, a form of savings plan with automatic deductions from a person's salary. *See also* PAYE.

say fairer. Be more truthful or honest, as in the common "You can't say fairer than that."

SC. Special Constable.*

scampi. *See* prawn.

Scapa Flow. A protected body of water within the Orkney Islands,* in World Wars I and II the largest naval base of the country.

Scarborough. Originally a fishing village on the North Sea* coast of Yorkshire,* its pleasant bay and nearby mineral springs made it the first seaside resort; bathing* in the sea was "invented" here, much to the confusion of people like Humphry Clinker, who "rescued" his master when he was trying to enjoy the sea. Fashion eventually moved on, but the resort continued to be popular with the newly industrializing northeast, and it is still one of England's most popular summer resorts, noted in recent decades also as the site of the playwright Alan Ayckbourn's home theatre.

scarper. Slang for running away, usually lower class.*

scatty. Silly, scatterbrained.

scent. What Americans call perfume.

scheme. A plan or program, such as a **pay scheme** or a **pension scheme**, without any of the American connotations of deviousness. A **training scheme** is a course of study used to train people for a job.

scholar. A student with a scholarship.

school. When Americans ask an adult, "Where did you go to school?" we almost always mean college, as we assume that all other schooling was done in the local schools where a person lived. But if Britons ask the same question, they mean a secondary school; if they want to know about collegiate education, they will usually ask, "Were you at university?" Elementary education is rarely mentioned, usually called **schooling** when it is.

   Anyone who claims to understand the British school system would be exaggerating, to say the least. As with so many things British, there never has been a "system" as such. Schools of various types grew at random to meet specific momentary needs, and each made their own rules. Until the late eighteenth century at least, practically no one went to school as such. Members of the gentry* hired tutors* and governesses* for their children as needed. There were only two universities—Oxford* and Cambridge*— and these were almost completely devoted to training the clergy. A handful of schools, often called colleges* although they taught only young boys, had grown up over the centuries, primarily to prepare children of talent from nongentry families for clerical careers. Most people learned their professions through apprenticeships. The primary impetus for general schooling came from the nonconformist* sects who wanted their members to read the Bible and thus often encouraged small elementary classes in reading and writing. By the early nineteenth century, all this had begun to change. Perhaps the most significant factor was the Empire*; the colonializers needed someplace to teach and take care of the kids back home in England, and thus the public school* reshaped itself into the familiar boarding school for the gentry, generally teaching boys aged thirteen to seventeen or so; these were what Americans would call private schools, requiring a substantial fee, and concentrating on the training of gentlemen* from the families of the gentry, teaching primarily Greek and Latin classics. During the social upheaval we call the industrial revolution, the Church saw basic education as a way to maintain social stability, and most parishes* organized local elementary schools, usually called parish schools* or day schools,* teaching reading, writing, and maths* from about age five until as late as twelve, depending on the local parish. In many areas, where the children often worked at regular jobs, this basic education was done through Sunday schools* instead. These too charged fees, although very small by comparison with the public schools. The rising middle class of the time was somewhat left out, as they felt they could not allow their children to attend the parish schools but had neither the status nor money to send them to the public schools; for these a number of makeshift private schools* grew up, such as the dame school,* which was run by a woman and taught basics to the very young, or various private day schools or boarding schools run in the teacher's home, like Mr. Creakle's, often followed by an academy,* a secondary school aimed at a specific profession or goal. There also were a handful of local grammar schools* that taught the same curriculum as the public schools to students who lived at home, including some poor but talented boys on scholarships. These too were fee-charging schools; there were no free public schools in the American sense until the 1890s, for even the parish school usually charged students at least a penny* a week. All these schools except the parish schools were aimed at boys only; there were a handful of secondary schools for girls, but they tended either to be dumping grounds for orphans like Lowood or "finishing schools" like Miss Pickwood's Academy. By midcentury a few girl's schools* modeled on the male public school began to appear to educate the teenaged girls from much the same kinds of families.

The demands of Empire management and industrialization eventually made it obvious that such chaos and individual choice were not necessarily in the nation's good, and in 1870 a law authorized the establishment of local school boards to set up elementary schools where none already existed or in addition to the Church's parish schools. In 1880, attendance at an elementary school of some kind became compulsory between the ages of five to ten, and local boards were required to open such schools if they had not already done so, now generally called board schools* rather than parish schools. In 1891, fees for such schools were abolished. But for the most part, these schools were attended only by the working class;* the middle class and gentry continued to deal with education through fee-charging institutions, and the range of these was extended with prep schools* that were often boarding schools designed to prepare elementary students from about age eight to twelve for entry into the public schools.

In 1904, the Boards were replaced with local "Education Authorities" who were authorized to also run secondary schools as well as the old board schools, now generally called primary schools.* The secondary schools took two forms, the old grammar school for classical education, and secondary* or secondary modern* schools for vocational training, and these became much more significant when compulsory education was extended to age fourteen after WWI. In 1944, technical schools* were added, to teach the science and higher math that had been ignored in all but very specialized academies, with students assigned to one of the three secondary schools on the basis of tests called the eleven-plus* taken at age eleven at the end of primary school.

Essentially, this arrangement held until increasing pressure from the Labour* governments* that followed WWII led to the introduction of comprehensive* schools in the 1960s and a complete reorganization of all local school authorities. The new comprehensives put all the courses of the old grammar, secondary modern, and technical schools under one roof and allowed students to move back and forth between them without the eleven-plus exam. Now the tax-supported area of education is reasonably standardized, with: nursery school* (optional) for ages two to five; primary school (required), ages five to eleven, sometimes broken into separate infant schools* and middle schools;* comprehensives,* eleven to eighteen, with the bulk of students leaving when legally allowed at about age sixteen. Although basic guidelines are laid by the central government, these schools are financed and administered by local councils,* and they were financed by the rates* until 1989 when the national government agreed to pay for them in an unsuccessful effort to make the poll tax* more palatable. Parents may opt to send their children to tuition-fee schools at any point along the line, but those schools for the most part continue to use their traditional names, such as prep school, public school, and so forth, and each continues its own independent age and course requirements, the most significant difference being that most public and girl's schools still start at about age thirteen, while the state comprehensives begin at eleven to twelve. Scotland uses basically the same organization with slight local variations in vocabulary and is somewhat more standardized, with far fewer private schools, than are England and Wales.

Most schools, even comprehensives, still require students to wear a uniform, which almost always includes a jacket or sweater and tie for boys and a jacket or sweater and standardized skirt for girls; boys wear shorts until secondary school. For education beyond age eighteen, *See also* academy; college; further education; polytechnic; university. For other names of schools, *See also* approved school; first school; good school; high school; junior school; play school; voluntary school. For school organization and practice, *See also* form; grant; master; mistress; school-leaver; term. *See also* A-levels; GCE; GCSE; O-levels; school certificate.

school certificate. A certificate of a test taken by school-leavers,* replaced by the O-levels* in 1950.

school house. Not a one-room school but the house used by the headmaster.*

school-leaver. One who has finished the legally required schooling, which only very recently rose to about age sixteen. The school-leaver has no diploma as such, but he or she does take a series of tests, formerly O-levels* and now GCSE,* and the results of those tests provide somewhat more information to potential employers than a simple diploma. The school-leaver is assumed to have finished a normal education, so the term is much closer in meaning to the American high-school graduate than to drop-out. Since the 1960s, the British have made some attempt to keep more students in school longer than the legal minimum, both through the comprehensive* secondary school and through grants* to qualified students to attend college-level courses of some kind, but the overwhelming majority of teenagers still choose to leave as soon as it is legal to do so. Thus, in recent years, the term has taken on a tinge of the pejorative. However, when public figures say "most school-leavers can't read," they mean what Americans mean when they say "most graduates can't read." Historically, the school-leaving age has risen from ten in 1880, to eleven in 1893, twelve in 1899, fourteen in 1918, fifteen in 1944.

school pence. The fee charged for local parish and board schools* before 1891, not a tax but a fee of one to four pence a week paid by the parents for each child.

Schools. At most universities,* what Americans would call a department or a major is called a **school**; thus one is not "at school" but "studying a school" or "studying for a school." The final exams given for each such school are generally known as the Schools. *See also* faculty.

school tie. Technically, a man's necktie in the pattern and colors of his school's (usually a public school*) uniform tie.* Figuratively, however, this indicates the tie, as in interrelationship, founded on social class* and school attendance that is so intricately bound up in the various parts of the Establishment. Also called the old boy network.*

schooner. Of a glass, a larger than normal glass for sherry,* much smaller than the American beer schooner.

Scilly, Isles of. An archipelago of tiny islands southwest of Land's End,* site of many bitter shipwrecks tragically close to home until well-marked by nineteenth-century lighthouses, now a tourist area much admired for its unusually mild climate. Romance says they are the tops of mountains from the land where King Arthur died.

scone. A small cake* much like an American biscuit, although usually somewhat larger and sweeter, sometimes with currants,* usually eaten at tea* with butter or thick cream. These may be baked or cooked on a griddle.

Scone. Pronounced skoon, a palace* in Scotland* near Perth, the coronation site for Scottish kings* before the thrones of England* and Scotland were joined by James I. The **stone of Scone** was ostensibly the stone seat on which these kings sat, although it was in English possession since 1296 and is now in Westminster Abbey,* so not many actually sat on it.

Scot. The stereotypical modern Scot is characterized by the English much as he is by Americans—dour, cold-natured, repressed and repressive, and such a miserly and crafty businessman that canny and Scot are all but inseparable terms. However, until the romantic infatuation with Scotland initiated by Walter Scott, Scots were often associated with the Highlanders* and seen as wild, uncontrollable, and unpredictable savages.

Scotch. The whisky* only, not things or people from Scotland,* for which the preferred term is Scot* or Scottish. Nonetheless, many people still use the term Scotch, and many specific items go by traditional names such as Scotch egg* or Scotch terrier. The usage is not vicious or insulting, in the way that wog* or Paki* would be; it lies more in the realm of daily irritation, as Frisco would be to a native San Franciscan.

Scotch Corner. A major intersection of ancient roads in northern York-shire,* nowhere near Scotland.*

Scotch egg. Sausage meat wrapped around a hard-boiled egg and deep-fried.

Scotch fir. What Americans usually call a pine tree.

Scotch woodcock. Anchovy paste* and scrambled eggs on toast.

Scotland. Technically, Scotland is one of the two "united kingdoms" of Great Britain, still maintaining its own identity and customs while partic-ipating in a unified Crown* and Parliament;* for outsiders, this contributes a wealth of confusions, as Scotland has its own, different, established Church, its own school system, its own laws and legal system, and even in some circumstances its own money, although English pounds* are still the basic currency. Historically, the Scots were seen by the English as trou-blesome barbarians, since the Roman era when Hadrian built his wall to keep them out, and border warfare was a constant into the eighteenth century. In 1603, James VI of Scotland became James I of England, but the two nations continued as independent kingdoms in other ways, ancient divisions further exacerbated by the retention of Catholicism among the Scottish nobility and the adoption of fundamentalist Presbyterianism by everyone else, making it an extremist threat on both sides of the Church of England.* In 1707, the two kingdoms were formally united, with the Scots gaining membership in Parliament, but this led to more rather than less warfare, culminating in the fatal campaign of 1745 when Bonnie Prince Charlie lost at Culloden* and the clans* were for all practical purposes destroyed. From that point, Scotland assumed a place in British culture similar to that of the South in America—a defeated nation living in poverty, never fully accepted and never wishing for full acceptance. Like the Amer-ican South, the Scots became more patriotic than their conquerors, nu-merous regiments of the army* filled completely with Scots, and a mythology of vanished glories grew up, fed by the Ossian frauds, Burns's poems, and Scott's novels, while the facts of daily life drove vast portions of the populace to the more prosperous industrial cities of their former enemy. While the Scots saw themselves as a noble breed, driven by cir-cumstances to a life beneath them, to the English they gradually changed from a nation of savages to a nation of poverty-stricken farmers, miserly tradesmen, or engineers (from the Scots who flooded into that profession as the most open opportunity of the nineteenth century). Queen Victoria's fondness for Balmoral* popularized the scenic beauties of the nation, and it became a fashion that has lasted into the present to vacation or go shooting* and fishing in the semiwilderness of the Scottish countryside.

Every generation or so, new Scottish independence movements arise, the most recent spurred by the prosperity related to North Sea* oil drilling, but they usually founder on questions of practicality: Scotland has 10 percent of the population of England, barely two-thirds that of London* alone, with the countryside outside of Edinburgh,* Aberdeen, and Glasgow* practically uninhabited and Glasgow itself severely depressed. Moreover, even with today's oil money, a significant proportion of Scotland's young emigrate to England, Australia, or the United States in search of jobs. *See also* Clearances; Lowlands; Highlands.

Scotland Yard. A street in London* off of Whitehall,* in 1829 site of the first offices of the Metropolitan Police* and thus used as a nickname for the Metropolitan Police since, although they have not had offices in Scotland Yard since 1891. **New Scotland Yard** was used as the name for the headquarters on Victoria Embankment* just east of Westminster* Bridge from the 1890s, and the name was transferred in 1967 to new modern offices actually located in Victoria Street about halfway between Parliament* and Victoria Station.* Readers of mystery novels often get the impression that Scotland Yard is the center of a national police* force, rather like the FBI, but this is not true; the various county* police forces may ask Scotland Yard for help in areas requiring unique expertise or when the crimes involved may cross boundaries of jurisdictions, but this does not happen nearly so often as mystery writers would have us believe. The overwhelming majority of criminal investigations are handled by local police forces, and only the Special Branch* has a national mandate. Similarly, although fiction usually treats only Scotland Yard detectives, it includes both the uniformed bobbies* and the detective branches. For organization and ranks, *See also* constable; commissioner; inspector; PC; sergeant.

Scotsman, The. The morning newspaper of Edinburgh* and generally the most influential Scottish newspaper.

Scottish League. The league of professional football* in Scotland,* currently containing thirty-eight teams in three divisions. *See also* Football Association.

Scouse. A native of Liverpool,* almost always used to mean someone from the working class* of the area (from lobscouse, a local version of hot pot*), and the dialect spoken by such persons.

scout. At Oxford,* a student's servant.* *See also* gyp; rooms.

Scouts. *See* Boy Scouts.

scrape. In food, an especially thin layer of butter or margarine on bread.*

scratch meal. A meal* put together from what Americans call leftovers.

scree. Either a steep mountain slope or the loose gravel that slides down such a slope.

screw. (1) A small piece of twisted paper, used to hold a small quantity of something, such as tobacco. Also called a spill* or a twist.* (2) In England,* a casual term for a salary. (3) Occasionally, a prison* guard.

scribbling block/paper. What Americans call scratch pad or paper.

scrubber. A promiscuous girl.

Scrubs. Wormwood Scrubs.*

scrum. (1) *See* rugby. (2) Colloquially, any crowd milling around in close quarters or any tough in-fighting, from the scrum in rugby play. (3) In girl's school* slang before WWII, wonderful or great, from scrumptious.

scrumpy. Apple cider,* usually quite potent, made from withered apples; this is a West Country* version, often home brew.

scrutineer. One who watches; in particular, one who watches the procedures and counting of votes, what some Americans call a poll-watcher.

scug. At Eton* or Harrow,* an ill-kempt or ill-mannered boy.

scullery. A room beside the kitchen used for rough cleaning. The **scullery maid** was thus the lowest of the low, the servant* who cleaned the pots and pans. The room and the servant have pretty much disappeared from modern buildings.

Scunthorpe. An industrial town, primarily iron and steel factories, in eastern England.* The mere mention of the town's name will instantly reduce most modern English audiences to laughter, although no one seems to know why; most jokes refer in some way to the town's dullness, but why Scunthorpe should have been singled out over all the other dull towns of the nation is apparently inexplicable.

scurf. What Americans call dandruff.

scuttle. A shallow basket, usually meaning a **coal scuttle**, which was used in most homes in the nineteenth and early twentieth century to carry and store a small portion of coal beside the fireplace or cooking stove. The scuttle was usually metal with a lip through which coal could be poured onto the fire.

SDP. Social Democratic Party, a moderately liberal party* founded in 1981 by moderates from the Labour* Party. It has had little success, even after its Alliance* with the Liberals* in 1981, which is at least in part due to its public image as the party of social workers, college-educated office workers, and similar namby-pamby do-gooders.

seal. *See* Great Seal; Privy Seal.

sealed. Of a road, topped with macadam;* roads that are paved* are topped with brick, stone, and so forth.

Sea Lord. One of four naval officers* serving in the Lords of the Admiralty;* the First Sea Lord, for example, is responsible for naval military planning but, although the highest ranking officer in the navy,* is not actually in command. Before 1964, the four Sea Lords shared authority with two civilian "lords," but when the Admiralty was absorbed into the MOD* the board was expanded to include four Sea Lords and seven civilians.

seaman. In the navy,* *See* rating.

Season. The period in the year when the wealthy and fashionable find it necessary to be in London,* the time of most upper-class* events, parties, debutante balls, and so forth. There are no precise dates, but in general, the Season begins with Queen Charlotte's Ball in May, since 1958 the substitute for presentation at Court* for young girls who come out,* and ends with Cowes* Week in late July or early August. The Victorian Season started earlier, usually in March, and ended in late July.

season ticket. A commuter's ticket for a specified period on the train,* bus,* or the Underground.*

seat. (1) In Parliament,* an individual member's* position, from the seat supposedly available to him in the House of Commons* (it's really a bench, and there aren't even enough of them to seat everyone if they all show up), also applied to the member's constituency.* A **safe seat** is a constituency that votes for a particular party with an overwhelming majority in election after election, no matter who the candidate. These are often used as constituencies for party leaders, no matter where they might reside, so that there is no chance that the Prime Minister,* for example, might not be reelected along with the party he or she heads. (2) The ancestral home of a landed family, as in a **family seat** or **country seat**. This is from a Latin root, while other meanings of seat are Germanic in origin. (3) The ability to stay in the saddle on a horse; thus, to say a woman has a **good seat** is not a comment on her figure but on her riding technique.

Seccotine. A brand name for a type of liquid glue, often used generically.

second. (1) Pronounced seCOND, to send on temporary assignment, primarily in the military or government service, but occasionally used in business. One is usually **seconded**, sent by order of someone else. (2) Pronounced SECond, a university degree* with scores not as good as a first.* Test scores are often placed in either **upper second** or **lower second**. *See also* honours.

secondary school. Originally this meant a school* for students after age eleven that required passing a test for admission but that concentrated on practical or vocational subjects. Also called **secondary modern school**. Most of these have been replaced by the comprehensives* since the late 1960s, and now the term secondary school is used more generically (as in America) for any school with children between the ages of eleven and eighteen. *See also* eleven-plus; grammar school; public school.

second class. *See* first class.

second post. *See* post.

second reading. In Parliament,* the second formal reading* of a proposed bill,* when the major debate on the issue occurs.

secretary. While this term may be used for a typist and note-taker, it is also used to mean the person in charge of daily administration. This useage developed from the early meaning of secretary as a personal assistant to a nobleman, the person who handled correspondence but also took care of the little details of that correspondence that the nobleman need not bother with. Thus, various ministers* were originally called secretaries, such as the Secretary of State for the Home Department (*See* Home Secretary). Within the daily operation of government, various "permanent" secretaries were appointed who were theoretically assistants to the ministers but who in fact were (and are) the professional bureaucratic administrators of a department. In clubs and societies* the secretary is not merely the person who keeps the minutes but is the actual practical administrator, responsible for all activity of the organization; an **honourary secretary** is one who does this without pay. The principal administrator of many businesses is also called a secretary. All these secretaries may also have their own secretaries, in the sense of typists and note-takers, as well. *See also* permanent secretary; PPS; PS.

Secretary for War. *See* War Office.

Secretary of State. The technical title of many of the various members of the Cabinet.* In most usage, however, people drop "of State" and refer to the minister* as the "Secretary of" whatever the ministry might be, or even more simply as the "(Name of Ministry) Secretary," such as the Foreign Secretary.*

section. In the army,* a unit of a company;* in the nineteenth century, there were usually four sections per company, about twenty to twenty-five men, each commanded by a subaltern;* in the twentieth century, after the organization into larger companies, there were usually three sections, still about twenty to twenty-five men, in a platoon.*

sedan chair. *See* chair.

sedge. A grasslike plant with triangular stems common in marshes.

see off. As might be expected, to watch someone leave or to escort; you can see someone off at the airport, for example. However, there is more often an implication of force behind the word; if you are "seen off" the premises, you are escorted off despite your desire to stay.

see out. (1) To escort to the door, almost always friendly and much more sociable than to see off.* (2) To outlive someone.

see over. To inspect; Americans usually say look over.

see right. A lower-class* term meaning to do what is fair or to pay properly, as in "Our* Ted'll see you right when he gets home."

Seidlitz powder. A popular laxative of the nineteenth century.

seize up. To jam up or come to a stop; traffic that has stopped moving has seized up, for example.

select committee. A committee in the House of Commons* with specific oversight duties that is disbanded when their particular job is finished.

self-catering. Cook-it-yourself, used primarily for tourist lodging where the vacationers do not only all their own cooking but also most cleaning as well, a real home away from home.

Selfridge's. One of London's* oldest and largest department stores, in Oxford Street* since 1907, and surpassed in reputation only perhaps by Harrods.*

self-service canteen. What Americans call a cafeteria.

Sellafield. *See* Windscale.

sellotape. *See* Cellotape.

semi. Not a big truck but a type of house. *See* semi-detached.

semi-detached. What Americans call a duplex, a building containing two separate homes side by side. This is the most common form of twentieth century housing, occupied by both the working class* and the lower portions of the middle class. Semi-detacheds have completely separate gardens, plumbing, kitchens, and so forth, in each side, are often owned rather than rented, and are different from a detached house only in that the two units share a central wall. *See also* back-to-back; council house; terrace; two up and two down.

seminary. Before the nineteenth century, the term was often used as synonymous with academy* for a school aimed at a particular profession. The most notorious of these were the Catholic seminaries that trained priests for undercover missions to England during Elizabeth I's reign, with the result that the Church of England* refused to use the term and simply required clergy* to attend a college.* In the early nineteenth century, many a **ladies' seminary** appeared to train girls for the "profession" of lady,* and thus the term came to mean a finishing school such as that attended by the three little maids from school, and in the twentieth century, the term disappeared as did most such schools.

Senate House. At Cambridge,* the central meeting house of the university* as a whole, used for degree* presentations, meetings, and exhibitions.

send down/sent down. To expel/he expelled from university,* especially Oxford* or Cambridge.* *See also* go; up.

send off. In soccer and rugby,* to eject a player from the game, done by the referee for an egregious foul. If this happens, the team cannot make a substitution but must play the rest of the match* shorthanded. The term is often metaphorically used for any social situation in which a person is punished for doing something unacceptable. However, to **send off for** something is to order through the mail.

send up. To make fun of or to parody.

senior service. The navy.*

sennight. Seven nights, a week. This is archaic now, heard only in more rural dialects and in historical fiction.

Septuagesima. The Sunday nine weeks before Easter,* so called because it is the one before Sexagesima.*

sergeant. (1) As in the American army, the senior noncommissioned officer rank; however, the British army has rarely made the number of gradations within the rank that Americans have, so there really are only sergeants and sergeant-majors.* *See also* Appendix V; corporal. (2) In the police,* the rank just above constable,* with equal status in both uniformed and detective branches. In the modern force, the sergeant must pass a test and have at least two years experience; thus, in stories, a young sergeant is usually a real go-getter, promoted very quickly, but a middle-aged sergeant is almost always portrayed as stupid because he has stuck at what is still a comparatively low level. (3) *See* serjeant.

sergeant-major. In the army,* the senior sergeant in a company* (or troop* of cavalry*). The **Regimental Sergeant-Major** is the senior sergeant of the regiment* and thus the highest possible rank for a nonofficer.

serjeant. A barrister* of higher status than the simple barrister, also called a **serjeant at law**; from the fourteenth century, serjeants had their own separate Inn of Court* and judges for the courts of common law* could be selected only from their ranks. Eventually superseded by the King's (Queen's) Counsel* as a means of distinguishing senior barristers during the eighteenth century, the serjeants nevertheless continued to practice until the order was abolished in 1870. Pickwick's use of Serjeant Buzfuz, for example, indicates he has hired one of the "best" and most expensive barristers available, which perhaps accounts for the serjeant's own condescending attitude to his client. Sometimes spelled sergeant. *See also* Inns of Court.

Serpentine. A long curved lake crossing Hyde Park* and Kensington Gardens* in London,* built by combining several smaller ponds in 1730. From the beginning, it has been popular for swimming (some insist on swimming there every morning of the year) and boating, and for skating when frozen, even though sewers from the western portion of London emptied into it until 1860, and it has been perhaps the favorite city site for suicide (next to the Thames itself, of course). *See also* Long Water.

servant. Prior to the nineteenth century, servants had been a rather fluid group; in some way, practically everyone in the country was a servant to someone else for at least part of life, even the nobility who often spent years as pages and squires* in their youth. Visitors from Europe to England* were regularly surprised by the number of families who shipped their children off to be someone else's servant as soon as they reached age eight or so. In rural areas, practically all people in a local village would put in some time in the local squire's house or grounds. But almost all of these people eventually left service to go on to other work; the old family retainer who served a family all his or her life was in fact very rare.

In the nineteenth century, this practice began to change, as the rise of an urban middle class increased the demand for servants. At the same time, the Victorian drive to respectability insisted that the servants also be respectable, which eliminated most men and practically all members of the new working class,* leaving primarily country girls escaping village* poverty. The ultimate result was that servants became overwhelmingly female, a factor further encouraged by a "luxury tax" on male servants from 1853–1937. Respectability required that servants must not have sexual relations with anyone, and any servants of childbearing age who chose to marry immediately left service. Service thus became the primary way in which country girls supported themselves until they found a husband. Census reports indicate that about one in seven females over the age of ten were servants at any given time during most of the nineteenth century, reaching a peak of about two million in 1891; ultimately 80 percent or so would leave service, mostly to get married, so that the only family retainers were a handful of valuable males, such as butlers* and carriage drivers, and those women who did not or could not marry, who eventually became the housekeepers* and cooks and at retirement age perhaps married the butlers. Mythology says this world was destroyed in WWI, but again census figures show that there was practically no change in the actual number of servants from 1901 until WWII, when conscription* took away both men and women and an urbanized society at last ran out of respectable country girls.

Household servants were regarded both by their employers and by themselves as a separate class of society, not a part of, and in fact ranking above, the working class. When servant women married, it was to men in trade* or perhaps to farmers, practically never to working-class men, and the men, if they married at all, almost always married other servants. Within that class, other class distinctions were made, between servants of gentry and servants of middle class, indoor servants and outdoor servants, and so forth. Status was indicated by their names: senior servants, such as butlers, housekeepers, cooks, or nannies,* were called by their surnames by their masters (Hudson, Jeeves); the women almost always with an honorary Mrs* attached (Mrs Bridges); while lower servants such as maids* were always called by Christian names (Rose or Albert), often given by the masters upon employment (Tattycoram); and junior servants always called the senior servants Mr or Mrs (Surname).

Contrary to myth, servants were not plentiful because they were cheap; in fact, by 1900, female servants were the highest paid females in the country. Rather, servants were plentiful because the demand was so great. For Americans in the twentieth century, servants have been what separated the middle class from "rich people" (even if those rich people still called themselves middle class); in Britain, servants separated the middle class from the working class. To have no servants was to cease to be middle class. Thus, no matter how the servants cheat the household nor how little income he makes from his articles, it never occurs to David Copperfield that perhaps Dora and Aunt Betsey together might manage to do their own housekeeping. Better to live in genteel* poverty with servants who get more of your income than you do than to live in comfort if that meant doing your own cleaning, cooking, or child-rearing.

This attitude has been slow to adjust to the decline in available servants in recent years; most middle-class households have had to resort to the daily* or the char* who comes occasionally, and the au pair* rather than the nanny, but these households have continued to demand at least the semblance of servants long after American-style labor-saving devices have in theory made them unnecessary. The truly rich, of course, often used servants as a way to demonstrate that wealth. The large country house* became a curious self-sustaining machine. While the family itself might "need" only three to five servants, the house itself demanded more, as cleaners, groundskeepers, and so forth. These servants, in turn, required food, lodging, and cleaning services, too, which meant the house had to be enlarged, in turn requiring more servants to maintain it, so that the large households eventually developed servant staffs of twenty-five to fifty, whose own wings, rooms, and services dwarfed those required by the family; in a very real sense, the servants owned and used the country house far more than did the nominal owners. *See also* do; governess; man, my; nurse; scout; skivvy; slavey; tweeny; valet.

servery. In some pubs* and snack bars, the counter where one orders food.

service, in. Not in the military but rather earning a living as a servant.*

service flat. *See* flat.

service lift. What Americans call a dumbwaiter. The British **dumbwaiter** was a nineteenth-century device similar to what Americans usually call a Lazy Susan.

services. What Americans call the utilities.

serviette. What Americans call a napkin. The term is usually used only by the respectable portions of the lower-middle and working class,* often about a paper napkin, and appears to have developed as an attempt to sound more genteel* by using a French* term.

servitor. *See* sizar.

sessions. Either quarter sessions* or petty sessions* of law courts.

set. At Oxford,* rooms.* A **set of apartments** is not an apartment building but rather what Americans would call a single apartment; *See* apartment.

set meal. *See* meal.

set tea. A standardized afternoon tea* served in hotels and tea* shops.

settee. A sofa or couch. The term was fairly common in the eighteenth century, but faded in the nineteenth, and is generally seen in more recent time as a pretentious usage.

set up. Almost exactly opposite to American usage, this means to give people a good start or put them in a good position, rather than place them where they'll be a better target.

Seven Dials. In London,* an intersection of seven streets to the east of Charing Cross Road* that took its name from a column built in the center with a clock facing each street during an attempt at urban renewal in the 1690s. The area resolutely resisted improvement and remained a notorious slum, the model for Hogarth's *Gin Lane* and a crime center in Dickensian London, and after the construction of Shaftesbury Avenue* took away the traffic, it settled into the dull, depressed backwater area that it continues today. The column was torn down in 1773 by a mob following rumors of a treasure beneath it and re-erected in 1820 on the green* in Weybridge, now in the southwestern suburbs of the city.

Severn. The major river rising in the northern border area of Wales* and running through the western part of the Midlands* of England to Bristol,* where it joins a large estuary called the **Mouth of the Severn**. Before railroads, this was the major trading route for all the western portion of Britain,* navigable for practically all its length and later connected by its tributaries and by canals to the Thames,* Mersey,* and Trent* in the transportation system that made Midlands industrialization possible.

Seville orange. A type of orange used primarily for marmalade, due to its bitterness.

sewer. *See* soor.

Sexagesima. The Sunday eight weeks before Easter,* so called because it is about sixty days before Easter.

sexton. A person, not usually a clergyman, who takes care of the church* building and its grounds, such as the graveyard. Different from the verger* in that he takes care of the exterior portions of the church, he is also usually depicted as robust, due to his traditional duties as gravedigger and bellringer.

Shadow Cabinet. The members of the Opposition* party* in Parliament* who specialize in the same subjects as those of the Cabinet.* In theory, they are the persons who would assume the Cabinet roles if their party came to power, although appointments in practice rarely turn out that way; their primary purposes are to demonstrate the Opposition's capability to govern and to irritate the specific members of the existing Cabinet by questions and public comments challenging their expertise in their fields.

Shaftesbury Avenue. A wide curved street in London* running from Piccadilly Circus* to the east end of Oxford Street,* built in 1886 in a major urban renewal project through the slums of Soho* and the Seven Dials* neighborhoods. It didn't really eliminate either of the slums, but it did provide a much needed traffic thoroughfare that was quickly lined with theatres,* for which it is primarily known today. *See also* avenue.

shake down. Not to rob but to give someone temporary lodging.

shambles. (1) In WWII military officers' slang, any confused mess, quickly adopted by the general public. (2) Originally, a butcher's shop or meat market. The term is rarely used in this sense since the eighteenth century, except to mark specific areas that once included a shambles, such as the well-preserved Shambles in York.*

shampoo. A nouveau riche slang for champagne. *See also* champers.

shandy. A drink of beer* and ginger beer* mixed together, first appearing around 1850; **lemon shandy** is made from beer and lemonade. For most of the twentieth century, shandy was what a woman would drink in the pub* to indicate that she was respectable and not a serious drinker, but lately women drink more openly, so shandy is drunk primarily by older children.

shares. *See* stocks.

-shaw. In place-names, a grove or small wood.*

sheepfold. *See* fold.

sheepwalk. A pasture where sheep* graze.

Sheffield. A large city in South Yorkshire.* Already a major town in the medieval era, it was known for its silver tableware and its fine knives, a renown increased by the eighteenth-century origination of silver plating and development of high-quality modern steel works, which by 1760 had already earned Sheffield the reputation of the "foulest" town in England. In the twentieth century, it began an enlightened policy of urban renewal and environmental cleanup that now makes it a model for such programs throughout Europe.

Sheldonian. At Oxford* a large central hall used for degree-giving, speeches, and large meetings. Wren's first building, it has an unusual shape, half rectangular, half circular, with an octagonal cupola; on the railings around it are thirteen busts (no one is sure who they represent) recarved in 1970.

Shepherd's Bush. A street and a green* in London* in Hammersmith,* since 1960 synonymous with the BBC* as the site of the BBC Television Centre.

shepherd's pie. *See* pie.

sherbet. *See* sorbet.

sheriff. (1) In the medieval era, the chief representative of the Crown*
within each local county* or shire,* supervisor of all royal* lands and
responsible for all tax collection; hence, never a very popular figure, even
outside of Sherwood Forest.* As most needed various assistants (also called
sheriffs) to actually carry out their duties, the official sheriff was usually
called the **High Sheriff**. During the numerous social changes of the sixteenth
century, the sheriffs lost much of their local authority and, although they
continue into the present, they are responsible primarily for calling jurors
and executing writs, while the High Sheriff's post is largely ceremonial.
Sheriffs within boroughs* had different functions, varying within each borough, and were appointed by local authorities rather than by the Crown.
See also viscount. (2) In Scotland,* the medieval sheriff was similar to that
in England, although the job was hereditary until 1747, at which point the
title formally passed to the sheriff's assistant, who had done the real work
for centuries, and by the nineteenth century was used to indicate the chief
judge of a county. A **Sheriff Court** is the court* that deals with criminal
cases involving a three-year sentence or less and also tries many civil cases.

sherry. A dry wine, originally from Jerez in Spain, fortified with brandy
so that it has about twice as much alcohol as regular wines and drunk not
as a table wine but as an aperitif or as a separate drink. It is the traditional
drink of vicars,* schoolmasters, and respectable women who might take a
"sip" or a "small glass" of sherry but would never touch "hard" liquor.
See also cobbler.

Sherwood Forest. A forest* in central England,* this covered almost the
western half of Nottinghamshire* at the time of the Robin Hood stories.
Over the years, however, the oaks* were cut down as the land was enclosed
and converted to farming or dug up for coal, and now only a tiny strip of
ancient oaks remains, just north of Nottingham,* mostly on private ducal
estates. Curiously, despite its place in legend and the presence of some of
the oldest oaks in the country, no serious attempt seems to have been
made to preserve them in a National Park.*

shieling. In Scotland,* a rough hut used as a temporary lodging by hunters
or shepherds.

shift. To move.

shilling. An English coin worth twelve pence;* there were 20 shillings to a pound.* The name dates to the Anglo-Saxon era, related to the ancient Roman solidus, and the value was stabilized by William the Conqueror, so until decimalization in 1971, the shilling was a fundamental unit of the English monetary system, abbreviated as *s.* The basic silver coin was first issued by Henry VII, and its size, about the same as an American quarter, remained consistent although the silver content varied as the value of the currency fluctuated into the present day. The shilling was formally discontinued in 1971, but many people still used the name for the 5p coin, which is the same size, and old shillings stayed in circulation with a value of five new pence. To **take the shilling** meant to enlist in the army,* as a shilling was exchanged to seal the enlistment contract, although an additional "bonus" was usually paid as well. To **cut off with a shilling** is to disinherit, due to the common practice of leaving a relative a shilling to demonstrate that the relative had not been simply forgotten. *See also* Appendix I.

shilpit. In Scotland,* weak.

shingle. Small round pebbles, especially when in large groups along a sea shore or lake; often used to mean a beach.*

shire. A regional division of the kingdom used during the Anglo-Saxon era. The Normans officially replaced them with counties* in the eleventh century, but most continued to be called shires. In 1974, many of these again had their names officially changed to drop the *-shire* suffix, as with Devon,* for example, but many people still affix the suffix to the official county name, as in Devonshire. The old shires ran in a wide band from Devonshire* in the southwest to Hampshire* and then north through Yorkshire.* However, as London* drew many of these shires into its suburban net, the term **the Shires** arose, meaning mostly the Midlands,* and in the late twentieth century it is often used to indicate the strongholds of fox hunting,* especially Leicestershire* and Northamptonshire.*

shirty. Angry, upset, obnoxious, as in "don't get so shirty."

shoeblack. Someone who polishes shoes or boots.

shoestring straps. The thin shoulder straps on a dress that Americans call spaghetti straps.

shooting. Hunting with a gun. To have **the shooting** means that you have the rights to hunt on a piece of property that you do not otherwise own. A **shooting box** is not a blind from which the hunter shoots but rather is a small house in the country where he lives while shooting. Neither is a **shooting brake** a hunting blind but rather what the hunter uses to get there, what Americans call a station wagon. British hunting* is almost always done with a horse, usually after a fox. In general, shooting is seen to have even more status than hunting, since—unlike Americans—the British have very few guns and only persons with second- or third-generation wealth have the land or opportunity to learn to use them well. *See also* deer; grouse.

shop. (1) The basic term for almost all retail establishments. The most basic of these is the **corner shop** (in towns or cities) or the **village shop**, a small shop that serves the immediate neighborhood with a little bit of everything but concentrates on tinned* foods, sweets,* cigarettes, newspapers,* and other odds and ends. Most other shops specialize, as the butcher, the grocer,* or the stationer.* The village shop also often served as the local post office.* Traditional modern shop hours are 9 to 5:30, with shops in small towns and villages often all closed for lunch from 1 to 2:00, but tobacconists* and small corner shops often stay open later, and in recent years suburban supermarkets* and related stores have extended hours into the early evening. In most small shops, the shopkeeper* lives upstairs over the shop. "Shop!" is the standard call used to indicate a customer has entered and needs help. The people who work behind the counters in the shop are called **shop assistants*** rather than sales clerks, while a **shop walker** is the department store functionary Americans called a floorwalker. To **do the shops** is to go shopping,* and in most levels of society one goes **down the shops** rather than down to or around the shops, while **shop gazing** is what Americans call window shopping. *See also* business; lock-up; market; newsagent; trade. (2) In criminal slang, to inform on someone to the police.*

shop floor. Not the floor or main area of a shop* but rather the production area of a factory. Hence, a **shop steward** is a union* official at a factory, and **shop floor politics** is union-related politicking or labor negotiations.

shopkeeper. A person who owns and operates a shop.* *See also* trade.

shopping. Some unique usages include: a **shopping arcade**, two rows of shops* with the walkway between them covered with a roof; a **shopping parade**, a street devoted specially to shops; and a **shopping precinct**, one or more streets lined with shops but closed off to motor traffic. To contemporary American readers, it sometimes seems that twentieth-century British women in literature do nothing but shop for the things that aren't any fun, like food, in absurdly small quantities. Perhaps because even the middle class* had servants,* there was little interest in labor-saving devices, and pay for the average worker was, by American standards, very low, so home improvements that had penetrated American life by the 1920s, such as refrigerators, did not penetrate British homes on any significant scale until the 1970s, and even then in very small models. As a result, the housewife purchased most of her family's food in such small amounts that she needed a daily trip to the shops. As a by-product, practically no British woman of the middle class or lower was seen in the daytime without an enormous bag, called a **carrier bag** or **dolly bag**, into which the various small purchases of the day would be placed until she returned home. Suburban life with automobiles and refrigerators is in the process of breaking this custom, for now a week's shopping can be done at once, carried home, and safely stored, but even so the shopping bag is still commonly seen in larger urban areas and used constantly for non-food purchases; only very recently did many stores begin the American practice of providing a paper or plastic bag for everything, often charging extra when they did.

Shoreditch. A neighborhood in London's* East End,* north of Spital-fields.* Lying along the road that left the ancient Bishopgate,* this was still a separate village as late as Shakespeare's time, when Burbage built England's first permanent theatre there to attract audiences from the nearby City.* Overflow population quickly filled the gap; it was the center of London's furniture manufacturing but became much more notorious in the nineteenth century as part of the sprawling East End slums, the model for Morison's *Child of the Jago*. Some of the earliest and most successful council estates* were begun here in 1900, and the area, though hardly rich, is no longer a major slum. *See also* London, The.

short. (1) Without something, almost always meaning money, as in "I'm a bit short right now." (2) Of liquor, what Americans call straight, without water or a mixer. However, a **short drink** usually means a small one, such as Americans call a shot. (3) To be **caught** or **taken short** is to be caught by surprise, and often more specifically to have a sudden desperate need for a toilet.

shortcrust. What Americans call piecrust.

shorthand typist. The person Americans call a stenographer.

short leg. *See* leg.

short list. The names of persons or things left at the start of the final round of consideration, as in a short list of job applicants. As a verb, to make such a list.

shorts. Only applied to outer wear; underwear is usually called pants.*

short slip. *See* slip.

shot of. *See* shut of.

shout. In a pub,* a person's turn to buy a round of drinks, as in "It's your shout, Ted." The buyer almost always still walks over to the bar to make the order rather than shouting it across the room.

shove-ha'p'ny. A game played by sliding half-penny* coins (or any other coin now) along a board, something like bowls* or shovelboard* with coins, usually played only in pubs.*

shovelboard. The game Americans call shuffleboard.

show. Military slang appearing after WWI for any happening or event; **good show** is especially widespread, meaning "well done."

show a leg. Not to get undressed or wear skimpy clothes but rather a casual phrase used to tell someone to get out of bed and start getting dressed.

Shrewsbury. Pronounced SHROHZbry, a large town near the northern Welsh border, much involved in the border wars and most noted as the site of the battle in which Hotspur was defeated; many of its Tudor houses remain, making it a popular tourist area in the modern day. *See also* Shropshire.

Shropshire. A county* or shire* on the Welsh border, primarily hill country; this is the quintessentially English countryside* of Housman's poems. Wodehouse's Blanding's Castle, and the countryside romances of Mary Webb.

Shrove Sunday. The Sunday before Shrove Tuesday,* also called Quinquagesima.*

Shrovetide. The three days ending with Shrove Tuesday.* *See also* hurling.

Shrove Tuesday. The Tuesday before Ash Wednesday, the last day before the beginning of Lent;* also called **Pancake Tuesday** due to the tradition of making pancakes* on this day to use up stores of butter and sweet foods that were being given up for Lent. It is generally still quite cool at this time of year, so none of the British nations developed traditions similar to the carnival or Mardi Gras, even when the nations were Catholic,* and the period is little noted except in isolated communities with unusual local customs. *See also* pancake race; Shrovetide.

shufti. A look or an examination, military slang picked up in the Arabic countries.

shut of. Rid of or free from, common usage since Shakespeare's time; also as **shot of**.

shy. (1) To throw something. (2) To avoid, usually as **shy off**. (3) As a noun, a game in which one throws at something, such as the coconut shy.*

sick. Almost always used only to mean vomiting or the vomit itself; all other sickness is called being **ill**, except in the army,* where you **go sick** to be excused from duty.

sickening for. Showing the onset of an illness; the American colloquial equivalent is "coming down with."

sickmaking. This is a slangy exaggeration, beginning in the 1930s in girl's schools,* used not to indicate that you are ill but rather that someone or something is boring or unlikeable. *See also* sick.

sickness benefit. A national welfare payment for workers with illnesses lasting more than twenty-eight weeks (currently equivalent to about $60 a week). *See also* SSP.

side. (1) Conceit or pride, particularly false pride or arrogance; primarily used in upper layers of society or in northern England* and perhaps derived from **putting on side** in billiards,* which is what Americans call putting on English. (2) What Americans usually call a team.

sidelights. On a car, what Americans call parking lights.

sidesman. (1) Not a jazz saxophonist but a deputy warden* in the Church of England.* (2) In bowls,* a player.

side turning. A street* that turns off another, usually a smaller street off a main or more heavily traveled road.

Sidney Sussex. A college* of Cambridge.*

silencer. What Americans call the muffler on a car.

silent number. An ex-directory* phone number.

silk. King's/Queen's Counsel* barristers* are entitled to wear silk robes rather than the normal wool stuff;* hence, a barrister is said to **take silk** when granted this honor.

silk hat. What Americans call a top hat.

sillabub. Syllabub.*

silly beggars. A euphemism for silly buggers.*

silly buggers. *See* bugger.

silly mid on. In cricket,* a fielding position very close to the batsman* on the on* side of the field; this position seems to be so named because you have to be a bit silly to play so close to the bat. Similar close versions of other positions, such as **silly mid off**, are sometimes played.

silly season. August and September, when Parliament* is in recess and families are on vacation during the long vac* of most schools,* and thus the time when little "serious" news occurs, so that newspapers* (and now TV) give much more attention to frivolous or scandalous stories than they normally would.

silver paper. What Americans call aluminum foil or tin foil.

silver sand. The fine grade of sand used for decorative purposes.

silver streak. The English Channel.*

simnel. A traditional fruitcake with almonds or almond paste, originally served on Mothering Sunday,* now more often at Easter.*

simple. Slow-witted, as in the American simpleminded, but in late twentieth century often used more legalistically to identify those persons with mental deficiencies who are nonetheless thought to be able to care for themselves and to live outside institutions.

Simpson's. A restaurant in London* in the Strand,* originally in 1848 a tavern for chess players, by the late part of the century becoming world-renowned for its roast beef,* patronized by the wealthy and fashionable as well as numerous tourists since.

sin-bin. Slang for a separate classroom at a school* where disruptive students are confined.

single. A train or bus* ticket for one direction only. *See also* return.

single cream. Regular cream used at table for pouring into tea* or coffee.* *See also* double cream.

single parent benefit. A governmental subsidy for single women with young children at home, in 1991 £12 (about $20) a week. *See also* child benefit; national insurance.

singlet. A knitted man's undershirt, usually wool. *See also* vest.

sink. Used only for the one in the kitchen or scullery;* all others are called **basins**.

Sion College. A college* founded in London* in the seventeenth century for educating clergy,* located along the Thames* west of Blackfriars* Bridge, home to a major theological library.

sippet. A small piece of toast, now often the size Americans call a crouton.

Sir. (1) As a title, Sir is used by only two ranks, baronet* and knight,* and despite common American assumptions, is not a sign of nobility.* The baronet, however, also adds Bart* after his surname to distinguish himself from a knight. The baronet's Sir is inheritable by his eldest son, the knight's is not, so most modern Sirs are middle-aged men who have received the rank as an official honour.* A Sir's wife automatically becomes a Lady,* but while, for example, a Robert Griswold is called Sir Robert, his wife is Lady* Griswold, not Lady Margaret. *See also* Dame. (2) As in America, Sir has been widely used as a respectful form of address for men without any implication of a knighthood. This has declined somewhat in recent years, but not nearly so much as in America; practically all students still address male teachers as Sir, salesclerks still address male customers as Sir, and most workers still say "Yes, Sir," to the boss. *See also* madam; Miss.

SIS. Secret Intelligence Service, the "official" name of what is commonly called MI6,* although just as officially it doesn't exist. *See also* SOE.

Sister. Technically, this is the head nurse in a particular ward in a hospital, but most Britons use it as a generic term; when in doubt, Americans say nurse, the British say sister. The nurse is usually addressed simply as "Sister," not as "Sister so-and-so." *See also* Matron.

sit. In addition to usual meanings, it also means to take an examination.

sitting. (1) In Parliament,* a daily session. (2) In law, a period of several weeks during which sessions are held; a term.*

sitting room. A room* with furniture for sitting, as opposed to dining or sleeping. The term does not appear, curiously enough, until the early nineteenth century and was used primarily in the lower–middle class* for the comfy little room where the family gathers and into which guests could be shown. By the twentieth century, this term was being replaced in most usage by drawing room,* front room,* parlour,* or lounge.* In some large houses,* especially those built during the nineteenth century, a sitting room would be one used in the daytime, and in very large houses, in the afternoon (as distinct from the morning room*), primarily by the lady of the house and any of her more intimate friends who visited at that time.

situations vacant. What Americans call the help wanted ads.

six, hit for. In cricket,* to hit the ball out of the field, which scores six runs, similar to the American home run, and used off the cricket pitch* to mean to do something wonderful. To **hit someone for six** is to hit him as hard as possible or leave him speechless with surprise.

Six Counties. Northern Ireland,* so called because it was formed from six of the old counties of Ireland: Antrim, Armagh, Down, Fermanagh, Londonderry,* and Tyrone.

six of the best. In school,* corporal punishment, usually but not always six strokes with the cane,* given to boys on their bottoms, to girls usually on the hand. Such punishments were so common in public schools* as to make the term synonymous with all punishment. Also called **sixers** or a **quick six**.

six over six. Normal eyesight, what Americans call 20–20.

sixpence. A coin worth six pence* or half a shilling,* mostly silver and smaller than a penny.* After decimalization, the sixpence coin continued in use until 1980 with a value of two-and-one-half new pence. *See also* Appendix I; crookie; penny; tanner.

sixth form. *See* form.

sizar. At Cambridge,* a student who paid only partial fees, serving out the rest in menial work; a similar student at Oxford* was a **servitor**.

skate. A sea creature that Americans usually call a ray, sometimes eaten as the fish in fish and chips.*

Skegness. A coastal resort town in England* on the east coast just north of the Wash,* made famous by the original Billy Butlin* holiday camp* in the 1930s and still a popular resort.

skerry. In Scotland,* a rocky island or reef.

sketching block. What Americans call a sketchbook.

skilly. A soup made with oatmeal and meat, very thin and watery. Although the term sounds Scottish, it was used in England* during the nineteenth century for the gruel* served to prisoners and to people in the workhouse.*

skinhead. A young tough distinguished by a closely cropped or shaved head; America began to see these in the 1980s, but they appeared in the 1960s in Britain,* where they have been associated with working-class* bullies, football hooligans,* and aggressive racism. *See also* Mods; Teddy boy.

skip. A large container for trash, similar to what Americans call a dumpster.

skirl. In Scotland,* the sound made by a bagpipe.*

skirlie. Fried oatmeal and onions.

skirting board. What Americans call the baseboard.

skittle. In cricket,* to put out a number of batsmen* relatively easily (as easy as knocking down pins in skittles*).

skittles. A game played usually in pubs.* Nine wooden pegs are placed in a diamond shape at the end of an alley (twenty-one-feet long) and then a ball or flat disk (or sometimes a small stick) is bowled at them, each player getting three consecutive throws in a turn called a **leg**; the winner is the person or team that knocks over the most pegs in two legs. A popular variation, sometimes called **table skittles**, is played without an alley—a short post with a ball on a string is placed beside the pins, and the player swings the ball in a circle to knock over the pins. **Beer and skittles** was the usual activity in the pub and hence is used, especially in the lower half of the social scale, to mean pleasure without responsibilities, as in the common mother's adage, "Life isn't all beer and skittles."

skive. WWI military slang for avoiding work, spreading into widespread lower-class* use for the rest of the century.

skivvy. A maid* who does the heavy work.

Sky TV. A satellite broadcasting system begun in 1989, operating much like American cable TV with many narrow-interest channels but received through small satellite dishes and decoders rather than a cable.

slack. In northern England,* a shallow valley, usually a very small one.

slacker/slacking. To avoid work, and a person who does this.

slacks. Almost always a women's garment only; men wear trousers.*

Slade. The Slade School of Fine Art, the art school in University College* in London,* founded in 1871 and generally seen as the most influential art school in the nation during the twentieth century, much more associated with "modern" art and the youthful bohemian* than the Royal Academy.*

slag. (1) A coarse, sluttish woman, usually of some years. (2) As a verb, a working class* term meaning to slander or to insult. (3) Among the police* in the late twentieth century, a habitual criminal.

slanging match. A loud argument or quarrel, usually one full of insulting names and vulgar suggestions, somewhat more often used of women's arguments than of men's.

slap and tickle. A casual term for sex, generally found throughout all levels of society. Although the term is based on foreplay, it almost always means the consummation as well, but it always indicates something done for fun, a casual or light-hearted sexual interlude. Husbands and wives can engage in it, particularly if spontaneous at an unusual time or place, but the term more often implies a one-night stand or similar short-term relationship carried on purely for sexual pleasure and with no other bonds.

slap-up. Grand, terrific, wonderful.

slate. (1) A gray rock that splits into flat straight pieces, used as a common roofing material. (2) What Americans usually call the tab, as in "put it **on the slate**." Hence, a **clean slate** is one with all debts erased, metaphorically a fresh start.

slattern. A woman of slovenly appearance or morals, also often implying someone revealing her lower class* origins unintentionally.

slaver. A genteel* form of slobber.

slavery. Despite participating in a major way in the slave trade between Africa and America, the British had no significant slavery within their borders, ancient serfdom and slavery disappearing by the twelfth century and the importation of Africans being very minimal in the early eighteenth century. Slavery was officially abolished in 1772, but the trade was not outlawed until 1807, and slaves within the Empire* were not freed until 1833, primarily under pressure of the Anti-Slavery Society, which still exists with interest and investigations in Third World countries.

slavey. A casual name for a maid* of all work, usually for the only maid in a boarding house.

SLD. Social and Liberal Democrats, a political party* usually called the Alliance.* *See* Liberal Democrat.

sledge. What Americans call a sled or a sleigh.

sleeping partner. What Americans call a silent partner in a business.

sleeping policeman. An obstruction in the road that forces traffic to slow down, what Americans generally call a speed bump.

slimming. The activity Americans call dieting.

slip. (1) In cricket,* the quarter of the field behind the batter and on the off* side of the wicket; **short slip** is the position very close to the wicket on that side, also called **first slip**; second and third slips are respectively farther back in the same direction. (2) In local names, a narrow alley* or passageway.

slipover. A sleeveless pullover;* sometimes, any pullover.

slipper. As in America, this is a light shoe with little or no raised heel that can be slipped on without ties or buckles, intended primarily for indoor wear. However, this term is often still applied to the shoes for men Americans call slip-ons or loafers, with no implication of effeminacy; **dancing slippers** in particular usually indicates a man's leather shoe suitable for formal dress but light and supple for dancing (women usually wear dancing pumps rather than slippers).

slipper bath. A bathtub with part of the top covered over so that the bather slides through a hole and has most of the body hidden from view.

slip road. What Americans call an on ramp or off ramp from a freeway type of highway.*

slips. In a theater, the end of the gallery* seats, usually curved around near the stage wall with almost no view of the stage itself.

Sloane Ranger. A person of wealth, more likely a woman than a man, with county* attitudes, so called during the late twentieth century for their tendency to live and shop in the Sloane Square* area when in London.* The rough American approximation is preppie, meaning relatively young people with old money, traditional fashions, and a kind of "young fogy" mindset, but seen as much pushier than preppies; very different from yuppie, but just as negative.

Sloane Square. In London,* a square* roughly on the border between Belgravia* and Chelsea,* built in 1741 and long a site of expensive homes and shops that act as a center for the contemporary Sloane Ranger* lifestyle.

sloe gin. *See* gin.

slop basin. *See* basin.

slope away/off. To sneak away.

slops. Basically, anything thrown away; more specifically, secondhand clothing or new clothing so cheap it might as well be, especially sailor's wide-legged pants.

slop stone. A hollowed-out stone used for washing, primarily heard and used in the north of England.*

slot machine. What Americans call a vending machine; the gambling device Americans call a slot machine is more often called a fruit machine.*

Slough. Rhymes with how, a large suburban town west of London,* synonymous with all the dreary, dull aspects of suburban life.

slow train. A passenger train that provides service to all the small stops along a route. *See also* Parliamentary train.

slyboots. A person who is devious or sly.

SM. Sergeant Major.* *See also* Appendix V.

smacker. £1.

small beer. A type of beer with less alcohol than regular beer, now used figuratively for anything weak or worthless.

small clothes. *See* smalls.

smallholding. A small farm not large enough to actually be a commercially viable farm.

smalls. (1) Underwear, either men's or women's but usually women's. (2) In mid–nineteenth century, after trousers* had become fashionable, men's breeches,* also called **small clothes**. (3) In ads, what Americans call the personals.

Smalls. A test at Oxford* usually given in the first year, also called Responsions.*

smarmy. Going overboard in flattering someone else.

smart. In addition to intelligent or elegant, this also is used to mean quickly, as in "move smart."

smarty boots. A know-it-all, someone who tries to tell others the answer for every question, usually called in America a smarty pants.

smash and grab. A quick, clumsy burglary, such as smashing a shop* window to steal the items displayed there.

smashing. Excellent, wonderful; used in this way only since late nineteenth century and generally confined to the public school*/girl's school* class.

smelling salts. Not a salt or powder but a liquid, made from sal volatile* diluted in alcohol and thus smelling primarily of ammonia. Hold a bottle of kitchen ammonia under your nose and you'll get a good idea of why Victorian ladies who had "fainted" suddenly woke up after a whiff.

Smiles, Samuel. The author of *Self Help*, an extremely popular Victorian guide to self-improvement synonymous with Victorian self-improvement attitudes.

Smith, W. H. Beginning as a single bookshop in London* in 1792, the firm was the first to grasp the need for reading materials on the new railways,* opening a stand at Euston Station* in 1848 to sell newspapers, magazines, and light fiction and soon expanding to railway stations across the nation. Shortly thereafter, they also opened a circulating library* that became extremely successful and influential. The library finally closed in 1961, but the news and book stands are still ubiquitous. *See also* library.

Smithfield. Originally smooth field, just outside the walls of the City,* in the thirteenth century a horse market, by the seventeenth century, the site of London's major cattle and meat market, as which it terrified Oliver Twist. It was also the site of Bartholomew Fair* until that was outlawed in 1854, and in 1855, the live cattle were moved to Islington* and a permanent set of buildings erected for what still serves as a vast butcher shop for the modern city.

Smith Square. A square in London* south of Westminster Palace,* home to headquarters for Labour,* Conservative,* and Liberal* parties.

Smoke. London,* used by people from the Midlands,* a classic case of the pot calling the kettle black; during WWII, the RAF* called London the **Big Smoke**.

smokeless zone. Not a place forbidding cigarettes but an area where burning of material that produces smoke, such as soft coal,* is not legally allowed. These are primarily in dense urban areas such as London* or Manchester* and were first begun in the 1960s. *See also* fog.

smoking jacket. A hip-length man's jacket, often of silk or velvet with quilted or fancy lapels, similar to but much shorter than a dressing gown,* worn from about the mid–nineteenth century. The man remained fully dressed underneath the jacket, although sometimes substituting an ascot* for the collar and tie. Its name came from the practice of wearing it when smoking to prevent ashes or burns on one's real coat or jacket. It was worn only at home alone or among the closest friends in casual situations.

snakes and ladders. A children's board game in which players move up "ladders" according to the throw of a die but can also "slide" back down to the bottom by landing on a snake; also called **chutes and ladders**.

snap. (1) A card game played by children who have to be the first to shout "snap!" when two identical cards appear; hence in adult use, snap often means identical things have appeared or that someone has recognized the obvious. (2) A photograph, from snapshot.

snick. In cricket,* a ball that just nicks the bat and goes straight back, what Americans would call a foul tip except that the ball is still in play.

snipe. Although generations of American boys have been convinced after being lured onto "snipe hunts" that no such bird exists, the snipe is extremely common in Britain. It is a small brown bird that lives primarily in marshlands or along streams, closely related to the plover and the sandpiper (but generally smaller). Snipes also frequented urban areas, feeding from the open gutters as if they were marsh streams, and thus were often called **gutter snipes**, from which we got the term for a street urchin.

snob. This word has seen almost a complete reversal of meaning. In the 1830s it was Cambridge* slang for a vulgar low person, the opposite of a nob.* It soon came to mean a person who tried to ape and associate with his betters, from which Thackeray wrote a *Book of Snobs*. Not until the twentieth century did we see the modern snob, a person who despises "inferiors" and obsessively dwells on his or her own social distinctions. *See also* Appendix III.

snob screen. In a pub,* a screen separating the public bar* from the lounge.*

snogging. RAF* slang during WWII for kissing or cuddling, still used occasionally by the general public.

snook. *See* cock a snook.

snooker. A form of the game Americans usually call pool, played on the same table as billiards* with a white cue ball, fifteen red balls, and six balls of other colors. The player must alternately put the red balls and the other-colored balls into pockets, getting one point for the red and variable amounts for each of the other colors. If the player fails to sink the required ball he loses the turn; if he fails to hit the next ball required, he loses all points made in the turn. The game has become immensely popular during the second half of the twentieth century, all but replacing billiards except among the most traditional and upper class* players, and is regularly broadcast on network television, sometimes nightly during major tournaments. To be **snookered** is to have your plan thwarted.

snout. Slang for a police* informer.

Snowdon. A mountain peak in northwestern Wales,* one of the highest in Britain. **Snowdonia** is the area of northwestern Wales* around it, a mountainous area now a National Park,* extremely popular with hikers, campers, and mountain climbers.

snug. *See* pub.

snuggery. A small, cozy room at home.

SO. A sex offender.

social ownership. A 1980s political euphemism for nationalization.*

social security. Not government pensions for the elderly but rather a form of general public assistance, usually considered as part of the national insurance* but technically including only: child benefit;* family credit;* death benefit;* disablement benefit;* and supplementary benefit.* *See also* DHSS; dole; DSS.

society. Britons use this term for organizations that Americans would more often call clubs, companies, associations, and so forth. *See also* building society.

sock suspender. *See* braces.

sod. One of the basic expletives and insults. The expletive comes from sodomite, rather than from the soil, and hence all common usages, such as **sod it!** or **sod off** or **sodding mess**, are about the same as when formed with bugger.* When applied to a person, as in "old sod," this generally is either a friendly, if vulgar, term or a derogatory insulting term, depending purely on tone of voice. **Sod all** is nothing or none. **Sod's law** is the same law Americans call Murphy's law. **See also** odds and sods.

SOE. Special Operations Executive, a sabotage and infiltration unit during WWII, in 1946 subsumed into the SIS.*

soft goods. In a store, cloth.

soft sugar. *See* sugar.

Soho. The area of London* now generally thought of as lying within the boundaries of Regent Street,* Oxford Street,* Charing Cross Road,* and Leicester Square.* The name is ostensibly derived from so-ho, the old hunter's cry when a hare* had been seen, because it was an area of open field used for hunting, developed with scattered great houses* in the seventeenth century. However, the spaces between began to fill with immigrants, starting with the Huguenots, and the slums of the Seven Dials* and Covent Garden* areas soon spread, driving out the wealthy and making the area, by the nineteenth century, a center of vice and other crime, given particular spice by the various foreign communities. By the late nineteenth century, Soho had become a significant core of London nightlife, following the spread of the theater district along the new Shaftesbury Avenue,* and after WWI it began serving the greater city with both the exotic, exemplified by countless restaurants featuring the cuisines of the world's immigrants, and the illicit, as the center of prostitution, gambling, drugs, and pornography. *See also* Piccadilly Circus.

soke. A small area with its own local legal authority and jurisdiction; many of these areas predate the Domesday Book* and were gradually absorbed into other units such as counties,* but some survived as independent units into the second half of the twentieth century. *See also* Peterborough.

soldiers. (1) *See* army. (2) Toast cut into strips, usually dipped into something, such as a soft-boiled egg, before eating.

Solent. The protected channel lying between the Isle of Wight* and the south coast of England,* leading to both Portsmouth* and Southampton.*

solicitor. What Americans call a lawyer. *See* barrister.

Solicitor-General. The government's* attorney, ranking just below the Attorney General.* *See also* Chancellor.

solitaire. *See* patience.

solo. Whist* played not solitaire but rather with only two players.

Solway. *See* firth.

Somerset. A county* or shire* in England* on the northern portion of the southwestern peninsula, primarily rich agricultural valleys noted for apples and cheese,* although also including the Mendips* and Exmoor.*

Somerset House. A gigantic building in London* south of the Strand* at Waterloo Bridge,* built in 1790. This replaced a Tudor palace begun by Lord Somerset and used as a private residence by each of the Stuart Queens.* The current building originally gave space to the Admiralty,* the Royal Society,* and several other organizations, but these groups have long since been squeezed out by the Inland Revenue.* In one wing is the probate registry, where all wills in England* and Wales* by law must be recorded after deaths and are available for public scrutiny; this is the portion of the building intended in most literary allusions, especially in mysteries, although before 1970 it also housed the Registry.*

Somerville. A woman's college* of Oxford* (1879).

sonsy. In Scotland,* robust, healthy, cheerful.

soor. An insulting term indicating a worthless person, from a Hindu term meaning pig, usually upper-class or military in use.

soppy. The term arose around 1900 as schoolboy slang for the way young people act in their first romance and has since been applied to anything similarly sentimental or foolish, such as Americans might call mushy or sappy. To **be soppy on** is to have what Americans call a crush on someone.

sorbet. Pronounced SORbay, what Americans call a sherbet. British **sherbet** is a sweet powdery substance that kids suck up through flavored "straws" or sometimes dissolve in water to make a drink.

sorbo. A type of hard sponge rubber used inside balls and rubbery toys; often used to indicate a type of eraser.

sort out. To clear up or to straighten out, as in "sort things out" or "He'll sort you out."

Sotheby's. One of the world's most significant auction houses for art and antiques, located in London* in New Bond Street.*

South. This can mean anything south of the Midlands,* but most often it means only the coastal areas from about Brighton* to Land's End,* sometimes called the **Sunny South** for its mild climate. *See also* Riviera, English; Southeast.

Southampton. A city on the south coast of England,* a major port since the Roman era. Protected by the Isle of Wight* and with the great natural channel of the Solent,* this rather than the Thames* was the primary port for the great English exploration and military expeditions. It declined under competition from Portsmouth* in the eighteenth century, but completion of a railroad to London* in 1840 revived it as a harbor first for mail boats and then for the great passenger liners. Sea travelers in literature and films dock at or sail from Southampton so often that it seems to be just across from London Bridge,* but in fact it is some eighty miles away, which makes modern airports like Heathrow* seem models of convenience.

South Bank. The south side of the Thames* in London,* basically the area on either side of Waterloo Bridge,* a contemporary term for what urban renewal has turned into an arts center, with the National Theatre,* Royal Festival Hall,* film archives, and screening rooms, smaller concert halls, art galleries, and a TV center used by commercial producers.

Southeast. The southern portion of England* that includes London* and the Home Counties.* This term is generally used to mean the prosperous, dynamic portion of contemporary England as opposed to the stagnant industrial areas of the North* or the Northeast.* *See also* South.

Southend. A port and popular resort town on the *north* coast of the Thames* estuary,* one of the final landmarks for ships sailing from London* and a resort developed purposely in imitation of Blackpool,* with much the same types of attractions and clientele.

South Kensington. *See* Kensington.

South Sea bubble. *See* bubble.

Southwark. Pronounced SUTHuck, since the medieval era an independent borough* on the south side of the Thames* across from the City* of London,* now a borough of Greater London.* The Roman road to London from the southeast coast came there, making it a focus of all the travel and transportation trades and the site of notable inns, such as the one in which Chaucer met the other pilgrims, well into the nineteenth century, when railroads put most of them out of business. Shakespeare's theatres were built there, outside the jurisdiction of the City, when the area was noted for lax laws and even more lax residents as well as the home of trades too vile for the close quarters of the City. In more modern times, Southwark grew into a major industrial area, much damaged by WWII bombing and later industrial decay, in recent years reestablishing itself as an arts area with the South Bank* developments and the Old Vic* but still undergoing major reconstruction. Curiously, except for the Elizabethan theaters, the overwhelming majority of literary associations with the borough are with the prisons there, in which writers, their characters, or both often found themselves (*See* Clink; King's Bench; Marshalsea). **Southwark Cathedral**, just south of the modern London Bridge,* dates in part to the thirteenth century. **Southwark Bridge**, first built in 1819, was Little Dorrit's Cast Iron Bridge; rebuilt completely in 1921, it is immediately west of London Bridge.* *See also* Watling Street.

Southwest. The Cornish peninsula, generally including Cornwall* and Devon* and Somerset.* *See also* West Country.

sovereign. A gold coin worth one pound.* From 1914–1971, a £1 note* was used for most transactions, but the sovereign remained legal tender and was, after 1817, the only gold coin. Since 1971, the £1 coin is a different size and shape and is no longer called a sovereign. *See also* Appendix I; crown.

sozzled. Drunk; the usage faded by WWII.

spaghetti. This usually means the canned variety, which is commonly thought to be children's food and is served on toast for their tea.*

spaghetti junction. What Americans call a freeway interchange or cloverleaf.

Spanish Sunday. A name used in the Midlands* for Palm Sunday* until early in the twentieth century. The name comes not from any historical event associated with Spain but with ancient customs in which children collected the water from holy springs or a saint's well early in the morning; the water was then flavored with Spanish licorice before the children drank it.

Spanish tummy. *See* gippy tummy.

spanner. What Americans call a wrench.

spare. Since WWII, slang for mad or angry.

spares. Spare parts.

sparking plug. What Americans call a spark plug.

sparrow. Probably the most common British bird, a small brownish bird related to the finch and linnet.* The **tree sparrow** nests in holes in trees, but the **house sparrow** will nest almost anywhere, even in recesses in house walls. The **hedge sparrow** is from a different species and nests in the hedgerows of the countryside.*

spastic. Suffering from cerebral palsy; Americans have long since substituted so many euphemisms that this term is now out of existence, but it continues in Britain in both colloquial and formal use, as in the charitable Spastics Society. *See also* Mongol.

spatter dashes. A style of men's leggings buttoned around the calf, worn as a protection for stockings or trousers* in inclement weather.

spatula. As well as the kitchen utensil, this also means what Americans call a tongue depressor. *See also* fish slice.

Speakers' Corner. The northeast corner of Hyde Park* in London,* world renowned as a symbol of free speech due to the number of people who make speeches there to whoever will listen. This practice is actually quite recent, dating only from 1872 when laws of public assembly were changed, and occurs only on Sundays,* but it is nonetheless cherished as a living demonstration of both the freedom and the eccentricity of the English. Often mistakenly identified as Hyde Park Corner.

speaking clock. A phone service that provides the correct time.

Special Area. An area for which certain business laws and taxes are modified or dismissed in order to encourage new business, in hopes of improving employment in especially depressed districts.

Special Branch. The department at Scotland Yard* with special responsibility for solving or preventing terrorist activity and other political crime, organized in 1887 to deal with the Irish.

Special Constable. A part-time or reserve policeman. In Northern Ireland* this has a different implication than in the rest of the United Kingdom, for the **Specials** there were a paramilitary force that attacked only Catholics. *See also* constable; police.

special licence. A marriage* licence that allowed a couple to wed without publication of banns* or at an otherwise illegal time or place.

spectacles. (1) Still commonly used for what Americans call glasses. (2) A **pair of spectacles** is a complete failure, from a batsman* in cricket* who fails to score in either innings*, and thus scores 0–0.

speech day. A day near the end of the school year at which various honors are awarded to students, with parents and usually a guest speaker invited. Also called a **prize day**.

speed limit. These limits vary depending on place and conditions, but generally contemporary limits are 70mph on M* roads and dual carriageways,* 60mph on other highways,* and 30mph in towns.

SPG. The Special Patrol Group, a unit of the London* police* that deals with potentially violent situations, similar to an American riot squad.

spill. A sliver of wood or a piece of twisted paper used to light a fire, candle, cigar, and so forth; also used for any similar piece of paper wrapped around a small quantity of something, such as candy or tobacco, with the ends twisted to hold it closed. *See also* screw; twist.

spine-back. What Americans call a loose-leaf notebook.

spinner. In cricket,* a ball that is bowled* with spin. When the spin is done well, the ball changes directions sharply when it hits the ground; thus, **off spin** makes the ball bounce from the off* side toward the batsman,* while **leg spin** causes it to bounce away. *See also* chinaman; fast bowler; googly.

spinney. A small group of trees, what Americans sometimes call a thicket.

spinster. A legal term for an unmarried woman; now rarely used outside legal situations, but quite widespread until the 1960s. *See also* relict.

spire. Technically, a spire is the tapering point on top of a **steeple**, but in general use, both terms are often used interchangeably; however, the British tend to say spire first, as Americans tend to say steeple.

spirit lamp. A lamp that burns alcohol rather than oil- or gas-based fuel.

Spitalfields. The area immediately to the east of the walls of the medieval City* of London,* named from the fields surrounding St. Mary Spital (hospital). The major food market of the East End* was there from 1682–1991. Large numbers of Huguenots settled there, bringing with them silk weaving skills and making the area prosperous for a time, synonymous with silk cloth in the eighteenth-century. Other immigrants, especially Jews,* shifted the industry to the cheaper end of the garment trade as the area slipped into overcrowded slums, a perfect setting for Jack the Ripper. Borders are very loosely defined, and portions of the neighborhood are often included in Whitechapel* or Shoreditch.* The slums have been cleaned up to considerable extent, but it is primarily inhabited by a new wave of immigrants still in the garment trade, this time from India and Pakistan.

spiv. This term gained prominence during WWII, meaning a black marketeer, and from that usage was applied to the flashy looks and personality associated with such people; since then it has been used to mean a male engaged in petty crime or a fancy dresser or more often both.

spliff. What Americans call a joint of marijuana, a term brought from Jamaica.

split ring. What Americans call a key ring, particularly the spiral type.

splodge. A colloquial term for a stain or a spot.

sponge. As a food, what Americans call sponge cake.

sponge bag. A bag for personal toilet articles.

sponge pudding. *See* pudding.

spool. What Americans call a reel (of film) or a cassette (of recording tape).

sporran. In Scotland,* a leather or fur pouch worn with the kilt,* hanging in front from a loose belt.

Sporting Times. A newspaper popular in the late nineteenth and early twentieth century, considered very daring in its day, printed on pink paper.

sports centre. A community center with various sports facilities and meeting rooms used by the general public.

sports day. A day at schools* on which parents are invited, featuring some team sports competitions, refreshments, and meetings with teachers.

sportsman. Used for almost anyone engaged in any sport or game on a regular basis, unlike American usage that usually confines this term to hunters and fishermen. *See also* athlete.

sports saloon. What Americans call a sportscar, but not a convertible.

spot. Just a bit, a small amount, as in a "spot of tea.*"

spot on. Absolutely accurate.

spots/spotty. What Americans call pimples.

spotted dick. A flour and suet pudding* with currants* or raisins, a very common schoolboy dessert or treat. Sometimes **spotted dog**.

spout, up the. Slang for: (1) Pregnant. (2) Lost, ruined, wasted, from the traditional chute into which pawned goods disappeared. (3) The bullet in a gun loaded and ready to fire.

sprat. (1) A small fish similar to a herring.* (2) In the nineteenth century, slang for a sixpence,* from its small size.

spring greens. Cabbage picked early in the season when the leaves are especially tender.

spring onion. What Americans usually call a green onion or scallion.

sprinting. What Americans call drag racing.

sprouts. What Americans usually call Brussels sprouts, one of the most common vegetables on the British dinner plate.

spud. As in America, a common slang term for a potato,* but particularly associated with the Irish. Thus, it is an inevitable nickname* for a Murphy or a Donovan. In the military, **spud bashing** or **spud practice** is what Americans call KP duty, from the common job of peeling them.

spyhole. What Americans call a peephole in a door.

squab. A young pigeon.*

squaddie. In the army,* slang for a recruit who is not yet properly trained.

squadron. (1) In the navy,* a unit of several ships of variable size and composition sent on a specific temporary duty, usually commanded by at least a rear admiral.* (2) In the air force,* a unit varying in size between ten and twenty aircraft. (3) In the cavalry,* a unit of usually two troops,* varying in size between 100 and 200 men, usually commanded by a lieutenant-colonel*.

squadron leader. In the RAF,* the rank of an officer* commanding a squadron. *See also* Appendix V.

square. (1) In the army,* the open space in the middle of the barracks area, where drilling is done. Hence, **square bashing** is slang for marching drill. (2) In the army, before WWI, a common battle formation; soldiers in open country would be formed in a rectangle, weapons facing outward on all four sides. This was primarily a defensive formation, developed by pikemen to defend against cavalry attacks by eliminating the flanks and rear and continued after the infantry was armed with muskets or rifles. In general, the square was particularly effective in the various colonial wars, a perfect tactic for repelling waves of attacks from ill-organized opponents. However, the square was also very difficult to maintain, as it required the bulk of the unit to hold their positions while the enemy was shooting at their backs; to have the square "broken" is one of the great humiliations for a regiment,* because it implied not merely a battlefield defeat but also a weakness of spirit in the unit. (3) In cricket,* the section of grass in the center of the pitch,* cut much closer than the rest, and used for placement of a wicket.* Also, a fielding position approximately level with the batsman. *See also* cut; leg. (4) Most European squares are open public areas of stone or concrete, the central gathering place for the community, but English squares, especially in London,* are simply small parks. These were built by property developers, who put such parks in front of terrace* houses to give them more status and more attractive entrances. They give residential London a unique visual attractiveness, in many neighborhoods providing grass and trees every few blocks, but most are closed to the public, fenced off and only open to residents who have keys to the gates. (5) What Americans usually call a scarf.

square brackets. *See* brackets.

square eyes. What you get if you watch too much TV.

Square Mile. The City* of London,* approximately one square mile in size.

squash. A fruit-flavored drink, if homemade with fruit juice and water, but more often made by diluting a commercial concentrate with water.

squashbox. An accordion or a concertina.

squashed fly. Childhood slang for a shortbread cookie with raisins or currants.*

squat. Although there have been squatters in Britain since the mid-nineteenth century (the term apparently coming back from the U.S. frontier) the squat, an unoccupied house that is taken over by people who break in and live there illegally, is a quite recent development. Americans tend to see this practice as a form of "homelessness," but current law, as well as ancient parish* practice, requires the local council* to provide housing to anyone who demands it. Squats first appeared as a part of the drug culture and in the 1970s were also used by members of radical political groups as a way of thumbing the nose at bourgeois society, and thus squats tend to be inhabited more by people whose habits get them thrown out of other housing than by what Americans call the homeless. Squats are notoriously vile, as they have no utilities, and can usually be identified by the smell of garbage and feces left in rooms and in the garden.*

squib. A firecracker.

squiffy. Drunk, primarily girl's school* slang.

squint. Although used to describe a look with narrowed eyes, as in America, it more often describes eyes that do not focus properly, the condition usually called wall-eyed in America.

squire. Originally a son of a baronet* or a knight* who was in service with another knight or noble,* part personal servant and part knight-in-training. Many squires never got titles of their own, but they did continue to bear arms and received land of their own, retaining the family coat of arms and often using the title Esquire* to denote their gentle birth. By the mid–seventeenth century, the term was applied to a country gentleman,* a man who both came from a good family and owned sufficient property to live a life of comparative leisure; and in particular at the village* level, the term was applied to the local landowner who was the dominant power in the immediate area, living in the manor.* As the most numerous part of the gentry,* squires provided the bulk of the younger sons who became army* officers, lawyers, government administrators, clergy,* and Empire-builders, but the stereotype of the local squire himself remained stable almost from the beginning of the usage: a basically good-hearted but not very bright man devoted to hunting,* fishing, and shooting;* most genially represented by Squire Allworthy, Tony Lumpkin, Bob Acres, Mr. Wardle or the owners of country houses* of numberless modern mysteries. Reality was perhaps better depicted by Pitt Crawley, at least until the Victorian concept of the gentleman took hold, but in general, the country squire's life and status has continued to be an ideal to which the newly wealthy of the modern urban era aspire, although in late twentieth-century literature, the squire is seen as an anachronism which, genial though he might seem, has little or no impact on modern urban life.

squirearchy. A portmanteau word to describe the people and attitudes of the land-owning gentry.*

squitters. Diarrhea.

SRN. State Registered Nurse, basically the same as the American RN.

SSP. Statutory sick pay, which is not full salary but is required by law to be paid by employers for up to twenty-eight weeks of a worker's illness, after which time the sickness benefit* takes over. *See also* national insurance.

stack. Of wood, a specific measure, approximately 80 percent of the American cord.

Staffordshire. A county* or shire* in the western Midlands,* primarily associated with the pottery industry in the north around Stoke-on-Trent* but also associated with coal, iron, and steel, as well as beer* in the Burton* area.

Staffs. Abbreviation for Staffordshire.

stag. (1) *See* deer. (2) In business, what Americans call a bull, a person who buys stocks to resell shortly on the assumption that prices will go up.

stage/stage coach. *See* coach.

stager, old. An old hand, a person with lots of experience; almost never is there any other kind of stager than an old one. The usage predates Shakespeare's era and has nothing to do with acting; rather it seems to come from an old French term for inhabitant or resident.

Staines. A suburban town along the Thames* west of London,* sometimes used metaphorically as the official border of the country* but also the site of the enormous Shepperton film studios.

staircase. Used to mean not only the stairs themselves but also any rooms,* offices, or flats* served by a particular set of stairs; especially common usage at the old universities,* where addresses are noted by staircase rather than by room or floor number.

staithe. Primarily in northeastern England,* a wharf used for loading coal onto ships.

stall. A booth, table, or wagon used by a seller in an outdoor market.*

stallage. The space, the rent or tax, or the right to a space for a stall* in a market.*

stalls. In a theatre, the seats on the ground floor, in America usually called orchestra seats. The first to use the name were at the Lyceum in 1828, when the front third of the pit* was blocked off and the old benches replaced by individual seats inside boxes that looked like horse stalls. It took several decades, but eventually the whole ground floor area was converted to such individual seats, but without the box walls, which changed the ground floor from the cheapest to the most expensive area in the house. *See also* gallery.

Stamford. A small town northwest of Cambridge,* once a significant market* and educational center, but now noted as one of the best preserved eighteenth-century towns, due to the railroad by-passing it in the nineteenth century, and mostly a tourist center.

stamps. (1) Before 1975, all working persons were required to contribute to the national insurance,* each payment signified by a stamp applied to the person's cards;* after 1975, the stamps were discontinued as part of the computerized PAYE* program, although the deductions of course continued. (2) *See* penny black; penny post; post office.

stand. Numerous idioms include: **stand for**, meaning to campaign for political office, while **stand down** is to drop out of the race, also used in the same sense in sporting contests. In the military, to **stand to** is to go on duty, especially in readiness for action, while going off duty is **standing down**, and **stand easy** is the command for the position called in the American army "at ease." **Stand and deliver** was the highwayman's standard command, meaning stop and give up your valuables. To **stand off** is to lay off an employee, but someone who is **stand-offish** is a person who gives off signals that they don't want to be friendly with others, almost always implying that they think they're "better" than others rather than that they are shy.

standard. In schools,* what Americans call a grade, but usually only in primary schools.* *See also* form.

standard lamp. Not a lamp of uniform design but a lamp on a standard, what Americans usually call a floor lamp.

standing committee. A permanent committee of the House of Commons,* similar to an American congressional committee but with considerably less authority. It can not initiate legislation, for example, because this comes from the government,* and it meets only when Parliament is not in session.

stane. In Scotland,* a stone.

Staple Inn. *See* Inns of Court.

star. *See* patrol.

starkers. Naked.

star prisoner. In prison,* not a model prisoner but rather a first-timer.

start. A surprise or shock, as in "gave me a start."

starters. What Americans usually call appetizers or hors d'oeuvres for a meal.

stately homes. From a poem *The Homes of England* (1830) by Felicia Hemans, a cliché for the English country house,* thought somehow to personify the English spirit.

state school. Any school supported by government grants,* although these are actually administered by county or district councils.* *See* school.

station. In life, one's social position as determined by birth* rather than by personal achievement. *See also* class; place.

stationer. One who sells office supplies or stationery; such shops* also often sell newspapers,* and the **Stationers' Company*** is a guild* of both office supply and book sellers, the charter in 1557 giving it a complete monopoly on book publishing. This monopoly was superseded by the copyright law of 1709, but all copyrighted works were required to be "registered" with the Stationers.

Stationery Office. The government's official printing office.

station sergeant. In the police,* what Americans call the desk sergeant, the policeman at the front desk in a station.

stay-press. What Americans call permanent press or no-iron materials.

STD. Subscriber (or standard) trunk dialing, long-distance phone service that in America is called direct dialing.

steak and kidney pie. *See* pie.

steak and kidney pudding. *See* pudding.

steeple. *See* spire.

steeplechase. A horse race in which the horse must not only run but also jump a number of hurdles, such as fences, hedges,* or water jumps. In Britain these are still very popular, run in a regular season during fall and winter. Courses run from two to five miles, and because the races involve stamina and skill as well as speed, horses compete well into their teens. The name comes from the time when such races went cross country and the church* steeple was the landmark used to guide the racers. *See also* Grand National.

Sten. An ugly but efficient WWII submachine gun, identifiable by the clip jutting out to the side, never as ubiquitous as movies would suggest.

step-in clothes closet. What Americans call a walk-in closet.

step-ins. When first used in the 1920s, a woman's undergarment that combined a chemise and knickers,* but as underwear fashions changed the term was revived for various other items and was often applied to any knickers* with an elastic waistband. *See also* combinations.

Stepney. Originally a community along the Thames* just to the east of the walls of the City* of London, this became the home of most of the dock-workers in the eighteenth and nineteenth centuries, as well as thousands of immigrant Jewish garment workers, both groups crowded into stifling slums. Much bombed in WWII, it has been rebuilt with numerous council flats.*

steps. A ladder used around the home, usually what Americans would call a stepladder; also called a **pair of steps**. *See also* tread.

stereogram. *See* radiogram.

sterilized milk. Milk that has been boiled before packaging, sold in stores primarily to persons who have no refrigeration for storing other milk.

sterling. Money, from the pound* sterling, which in turn derived from the silver penny of the medieval era with a star in the design on one side rather than a particular weight of silver; Britain in fact was on a gold standard from 1814–1931. *See also* Appendix I.

Stevenage. A new town* north of London* built in the 1950s on the site of an older village that was E. M. Forster's home fictionalized in *Howard's End*, now primarily a commuter community.

stew. What Americans would call a sauna or steam bath. These were open to the public and were used much more often than water for personal cleaning. Naturally they attracted proponents of other forms of relaxation, and by Shakespeare's time, the **stews** was not only an area with such bath houses but also brothels; although by the mid–nineteenth century the bath-houses may have disappeared, any concentration of brothels continued to be called stews.

steward. (1) Originally, the person supervising a lord's* household, similar to and replaced by the more modern butler;* from this, the term continued into the modern era for the person in charge of catering in colleges,* clubs,* ships, and so forth. *See also* Lord Steward. (2) An official of a noble who supervised the financial affairs and the local manorial court. *See also* Lord High Steward. (3) From the usage cited in the first definition, in the twentieth century came the use of this term for any waiter on a ship, which in turn passed to the airlines when they began commercial flights. The British airlines were for many years the only ones to use significant numbers of male stewards on their flights, from conservative tradition rather than liberal concepts of "equality of opportunity."

stewing steak. Tough beef used for making stew.

stick. (1) As a noun, ridicule, abuse, as in **took some stick** or **given the stick**, probably from corporal punishment. *See also* birch; cane. (2) As a verb, to put up with or endure, as in "He couldn't stick his mother-in-law;" often also said as **stick it**. (3) *See* hockey.* (4) In cricket, *See* stumps. (5) *See* cane. (6) A woman **up the stick** is pregnant.

sticking plaster. *See* plaster.

stick-jaw. Candy that sticks your teeth together when chewing, such as caramels or toffee.

sticks. Colloquial term for furniture. *See also* up sticks.

sticky bun. *See* bun.

sticky tape. Any adhesive tape, often what Americans call masking tape.

sticky wicket. In cricket,* a pitch* that is soggy from rain, making it difficult for the batsman* to judge how the ball will bounce; used metaphorically to indicate a difficult situation.

stiffener. An alcoholic drink, generally used in the sense of something to give you courage.

stiff upper lip. To Americans, this is the quintessential British stereotype, the ability to deal with almost any situation without any sign of emotion, probably growing out of ancient nursery and school injunctions to little boys with quivering lips in order to prevent them from crying.

stile. Many fences in the countryside do not have gates; rather, there are small steps called stiles that animals cannot negotiate but that allow pedestrians to step over the fence. While this seems quaint, it is in fact the primary means by which the public paths and rights of way* are kept open, as pedestrians using stiles cannot be accused of leaving gates open.

stiletto heels. On shoes, what Americans call spike heels.

Stilton. *See* cheese.

stinks. School* slang for chemistry and similar subjects.

stirrup cup. Not a particular drink but rather simply any drink offered before a rider leaves on a horse, especially before a fox hunt.*

Stir-up Sunday. The Sunday before Advent,* when the collect in Church of England* services begins, "Stir up, we beseech Thee, O lord, the wills of thy faithful people." This day was also traditionally the one on which the Christmas pudding* was mixed.

stoat. A small mammal somewhat like, but larger than, a mink, now raised primarily for its fur, which changes from brown to white in winter, when the fur is called ermine.

stock. A type of wide necktie, wrapped several times around the neck with both ends hanging down the front to about the breastbone, widespread in the eighteenth century but after the early nineteenth century worn only by some clergy and in traditional riding* outfits.

stockbroker. *See* stock jobber.

stockbroker belt. Suburbs for the professional classes, generally toward the southwest of London* in Surrey.*

stockings. What Americans usually call socks; however, women also continued to use the term for what Americans usually called hose or nylons until the appearance of pantyhose, which the British generally call tights.*

stockist. A supplier, a shop specializing in a particular kind of product.

stock jobber. The person who handles the initial sale of stocks* or shares,* similar to the American underwriter; distinct from the **stockbroker**, who (like the American stockbroker) acts as the intermediary between the ultimate purchaser and the jobber for new issues, or between buyers and resellers of existing issues.

stocks. (1) What Americans call bonds. What Americans call stocks are called **shares** and issued as either **ordinary shares** (common stock) or **preferred shares**, which have no voting rights. However, stockbrokers* handle both stocks and shares. (2) Breeches-like garments that covered the hip area and extended down to the vicinity of the knee rather than up from the foot like stockings;* these gradually evolved into underpants and the term disappeared for the most part by the nineteenth century, except in some provincial areas.

stodge. Heavy, starchy foods, from late nineteenth-century public school* slang for any big meal.*

stoke. In place-names, as prefix or suffix, an ancient term meaning "place," sometimes used to indicate an ancient religious site. *See also* stow.

Stoke-on Trent. The central town of the Potteries* area of England.*

Stoke Poges. A small village in the Chilterns,* site of Gray's country churchyard.

Stokes. The mortar used by British soldiers in both World Wars.

stone. A measurement of weight: When said of people, fourteen pounds; of cheese, sixteen pounds, of meat, eight pounds.

Stonehenge. Concentric circles of enormous stones located on Salisbury* Plain. They date from before recorded time, and there is no certain explanation, except that they are related to the astronomical calendar. But the stones have inspired considerable mystical speculation, and the pseudo-Druid* revival of recent years claims them as a religious site. Tourist pressure has been so great that in recent years they have been surrounded by fences to prevent both vandalism and accidental damage.

stone the crows. An exclamation of surprise, originally from Australia.

stony. Without money.

stook. In northern England* and Scotland,* a shock of grain.

stop. (1) Stay, as in "stop at home." (2) To hold out or deduct from wages. (3) *See* full stop. (4) At the dentist, to fill a cavity.

stoppage. A work stoppage, euphemism for a strike.

store. Storage. Hence, **stores** is a warehouse or similar large storage facility. What Americans call a store is usually called a shop.*

Stourbridge. A town near Birmingham* known for its glass industries.

stout. *See* beer.

stow/stowe. An ancient term found in many place-names, meaning "place," often used for an ancient religious site. *See also* stoke.

Stowe. Former family seat* of the dukes* of Buckingham,* in 1923 converted into a public school.*

straightaway. Immediately.

straight bat. *See* bat.

straight fight. A political campaign with only two candidates.

Strand. Originally a track westward from the City* of London,* by the Tudor period this had become a road lined with great houses* running from Fleet Street* to Charing Cross;* during the seventeenth and early eighteenth centuries, it housed a version of what we would call a shopping mall, the New Exchange,* that increased its fashionableness. In the nineteenth century, most of the great houses disappeared, replaced by theaters, restaurants, and other entertainment, and today it continues as one of the city's busiest thoroughfares, mixing expensive hotels and restaurants with offices and the southern edge of the West End* theatre district. *See also* St. Mary-le-Strand.

Stratford. (1) Technically, **Stratford-upon-Avon**, a town in central England* south of Coventry,* known primarily as the birthplace and retirement home of Shakespeare. In Shakespeare's day it was a very typical market town* and continued as such until the late nineteenth century, when Bardolatry reached its peak and the tourist industry began to grow, so that now more foreign tourists visit it than any other town outside of London.* *See also* RSC. (2) A neighborhood in London's East End,* originally a village and Chaucer's **Stratford-atte-Bow**, used since his poem to mean overly precise, schoolbook French* from the language learned at the school there by the Prioress.

strath. In Scotland,* a valley, usually a wide one with a river.

Strathclyde. An ancient kingdom in the southwest of modern Scotland,* now used for a region,* or county,* in the same general vicinity, centering on the River Clyde* and Glasgow.* *See also* Lanarkshire.*

strawberry leaves. A sign of a duke,* marquis,* or earl;* the conventional heraldic leaf looks like a strawberry leaf.

straw potatoes. *See* potato.

stream. What Americans call a traffic lane.

street. Originally, this meant any paved road, which in practice usually meant a highway remaining from the Roman era such as Watling Street.* However, street also was applied to a road or part of a road with houses or shops* along both sides and included not just the roadway but also the buildings; thus, high street,* for example, is often used to mean the shops rather than the street. As it included both the shops and the roadway, the term also included what Americans call the sidewalk; hence, the average man was the "man in the street" and a prostitute was "on the streets," both of which are still common idioms in America as well.

streets ahead. Far ahead, superior.

strike a light. A very mild expletive.

strike off. To remove from a list, most often said of lawyers or doctors who are being thrown out of professional associations.

striker. (1) In cricket,* the batsman* on the field who is actually receiving the bowler's throw; the **non-striker** is the other batsman who is at the second wicket.* (2) In football,* *See* forward.

string vest. *See* vest.

strip cartoon. What Americans call a comic strip. These are still relatively rare, and newspapers* run only one or two on a regular basis, never the full page or more that most American papers run.

strip lighting. What Americans call fluorescent lighting.

stroke. (1) What Americans call a slash (/); also called **oblique stroke**. In money and prices before 1971, a stroke was always placed between shillings* and pence;* probably, this was a remnant of the large *s* of the eighteenth-century script *f* that got increasingly straightened in sloppy writing until it was just a slash. (2) In cricket,* what Americans would call the batsman's* swing. A **backstroke** is not a backswing but a swing by the batsman* for which he takes a step backward to position himself before swinging; a **forward stroke** is a swing for which he strides forward.

stroppy. Navy* slang for obstreperous, after WWII entering general use to mean angry, hardheaded, or difficult to control.

struck on. Slang equivalent to the American "stuck on" or "have a crush on."

student union. Not a labor union for students but an organization that provides snack bars, alcoholic bars, and numerous nonacademic activities at colleges* and universities.*

stuff. (1) As a verb, to have sexual relations. To **get stuffed** is roughly equivalent in meaning and vulgarity to the American "go fuck yourself." Most other idioms and colloquial usages have to deal with more standard meanings of stuff, as for example a **stuffed shirt** for a pompous fool. (2) Technically, wool fabric without a nap or pile, sometimes used generically for any wool fabric but falling from all but technical use in the twentieth century, except in legal circles, where barrister's* gowns are made from stuff. *See also* silk.

stumer. Slang for a bad cheque* or a forged check, and figuratively from that for anything phony or worthless.

stumps. In cricket,* the upright posts of the wicket;* to **draw stumps** or to **up stumps** is to end the match by removing the wickets. Also called **sticks**.

sturdy beggar. An able-bodied person, from the Poor Law* of 1536 that refused relief to "sturdy beggars."

sub. (1) An advance on wages or a loan against expected income, a shortening of subsistence money.* (2) In the army,* a subaltern.*

subaltern. In the army,* the lowest ranking officer;* prior to the twentieth century, this term referred to all officers below the rank of captain,* both lieutenants* and ensigns* or sub-lieutenants.* However, after major reorganization in the regiments* just before WWI, which lowered the number and increased the size of companies* and often passed company command to majors,* junior captains were sometimes called subalterns as well. In general, the subaltern commanded a portion of a company, usually a section* in the nineteenth and a platoon* in the twentieth.

sub-fusc. Dull or dusky in color. At some universities,* this indicates student "uniform" worn under or in place of the academic gown,* particularly the female student's dark dress or dark skirt with white blouse and dark stockings; when said of a person, it indicates they are dull or boring.

subject. What Americans call a citizen, as all are subjects of His or Her Majesty. *See* Majesty, His/Her/Your.

sub-lieutenant. (1) In the army,* the officer* Americans call a second lieutenant, used in some regiments* since the eighteenth century but by the twentieth century used throughout the army. *See also* ensign; subaltern. (2) In the navy, the officer below lieutenant,* equivalent to the American ensign.

subscription. What Americans call a donation. One collects subscriptions for a charity, for example, or for gifts around the office. At the same time, many subscriptions may be voluntary only in name, such as an officer's* subscription to the mess* or the subscription to a club,* and Americans would call these dues or fees.

subsidy. Originally, the subsidy was "extra" revenue given by Parliament* to the monarch, and until the eighteenth century the term was often used synonymously with tax,* as a tax had to be passed to provide such subsidy. In more modern times, it has come to mean governmental assistance given to anyone, as it does in contemporary America.

subsistence money. Money advanced to workers to live on while work is being done before the actual pay is given, or, recently, travel expense money.

subvention. A grant or subsidy from a governmental authority.

subway. An underground passage for pedestrians; the train Americans call a subway is called the Underground.*

succession. The inheritance of the monarchy. In Britain, succession passes to the eldest direct heir, excluding Catholics,* males given preference. In practice, this means sons first; if no sons are alive, then a grandson may inherit. If no son or grandson is living, then the eldest daughter (Elizabeth II) succeeds. If no children or grandchildren exist, then a brother succeeds (James II or William IV), and if no brother lives, then a sister may take the throne (Mary I, Elizabeth I, Mary II, or Anne). If no children, brothers, or sisters are still living, then succession passes to cousins (George I or Victoria). This is notable principally because the title* moves this way only among royalty;* in the nobility,* titles* may be inherited only by males; if the male line dies out, the title disappears. As a result of the Glorious Revolution of 1688, a Catholic may not succeed to the crown and, as head of the Church of England,* the monarch may not be divorced, a rather ironic touch considering it was Henry VIII's desire for a divorce that formed the Church of England to begin with. *See also* Appendix II.

sucks to you. A public school* idiom before WWII used as a general expression of contempt. There doesn't seem to have been any sexual innuendo, just a suddenly popular catchphrase for "that'll show you," or "take that!"

suction cleaner. What Americans call a vacuum cleaner.

Suez. The Suez Canal, built by the French to connect the Mediterranean and the Red Sea in Egypt* in 1869 but partially purchased by the British in 1875. Free and open passage through the canal was a major element of British foreign policy, as the canal was the major link between England* and India,* and Suez, despite its nominal French and Egyptian control, was regarded as British territory, guarded by British troops from 1883 to

1956. In 1956, Egypt nationalized the canal, causing the British and French to send paratroops and a fleet in coordination with an Israeli attack on Egypt; world opinion was inflamed by this "imperialist" act, and the United States threatened to cut off all aid, which caused the immediate withdrawal of all forces. For that generation, Suez was a major crisis, marking for conservatives a humiliating demonstration of Britain's decline and powerlessness and for the liberal-intellectual community a clear demonstration of the immoral nature of their government* and society in general, making a scar that ran through British society much like Vietnam later scarred American and that was the immediate trigger for the explosion of the "angry young men" phase of literature. *See also* East of Suez.

Suffolk. A county* or shire* on the eastern coast of England,* originally the southern portion of East Anglia.* This area has some of the richest agricultural land in all of the nation and active fishing ports, and it has long been associated with a self-sufficient, insular village* life. It has also been the inspiration for much of the most famous English landscape painting, home at times to Constable, Turner, and Gainsborough. *See also* Norfolk.

suffragan. *See* bishop.

sugar. British sugar takes several forms: **castor** (sometimes **caster**), which is similar to American granulated sugar but somewhat finer; **icing**, which Americans call confectioner's or powdered sugar; **Demarara**, raw or "natural" brown crystals (from the settlement in British Guiana); **Barbados**, soft brown sugar, also sometimes called **soft sugar** or **sand sugar**. At the table, it is generally kept in a **sugar basin** rather than a sugar bowl. Before the twentieth century, it was commonly purchased in a large solid mass, called **loaf sugar**, from which small lumps* were broken off for use. **Barley sugar** is not a type of sugar but a candy made from boiled sugar formed into a sticklike shape, usually somewhat twisted.

sugar soap. A substance used to remove paint.

sultana. Similar to what Americans call a raisin but more golden in appearance, made from seedless grapes. *See also* currant.

summat. Something, used primarily in dialects from northern England.*

Summer Time. *See* BST.

sums. What Americans call math but often used figuratively to mean any kind of calculation; to **do one's sums** is to figure or consider all the aspects of the problem, similar to the American "add it all up."

Sun. A daily tabloid newspaper,* established in 1964 in hopes of being a "classless" paper with serious reporting, a dismal failure until 1970 when a new owner changed the paper into a gaudy, vulgar scandal sheet, something like the approach of the American *National Enquirer* applied to politics, daily news, and sports as well as to TV stars' sex lives and UFOs, with bingo contests and photos of nude women thrown in; the newspaper quickly achieved and sustained the largest daily circulation for almost two decades and spawned numerous imitators. The *Sun* is now clearly the most popular working class* paper, which led to all sorts of political confusion in the 1980s as it was more fervently supportive of Margaret Thatcher than even the *Telegraph.* Non-*Sun* readers see it as a symbol of practically all the "decline" in modern Britain, and by American journalistic standards that could be seen as something of an understatement. *See also* page three.

sun blind. Not what Americans call a Venetian blind but an awning.

Sunday. The English Sunday has been legendary since the mid–nineteenth century. For all practical purposes, the country is closed on Sunday, even today, even in London.* Theatres are dark, restaurants are closed, pubs* are open for only a few brief moments in the afternoon, few professional sports are played, and of course shops,* department stores, and markets* are shut. The curious point is that the country is otherwise not particularly religious; the churches are empty. The primary impulse seems to be class-oriented: Sunday was, and is, the only day the British working class* has off, and the rest of society seems determined to remove all possible temptations from them during that time. During the 1980s, some relaxation of the Sunday regime began, but it is at present still minimal. In Scotland* or Wales,* it is if anything worse, for the local communities are more religious in a Calvinist manner. Most families have a Sunday dinner* served in midafternoon, usually consisting of a roast joint,* potatoes* and other vegetables, and a major dessert. *See also* Saturday.

Sunday performance. Under the strict "Sunday Closing" laws, all theaters are normally dark on Sundays. Thus, theatre clubs almost always held their performances on Sunday afternoons, because the theatres were empty and private clubs were still allowed to operate on Sundays. This is why almost all avant-garde drama, such as Ibsen, Shaw, and all the 1920s expressionists, first made their English appearance in Sunday performances.

Sunday Schools. When originally organized in the 1790s, these were real schools that met on Sunday to teach reading and writing to illiterate children who worked the other days of the week. The gradual spread of general education during the nineteenth century meant that by the twentieth century the schools concentrated primarily on religious instruction.

Sunday supplement. The magazine included with the Sunday newspaper.*
These supplements are often as extensive and attractive as regular magazines. However, the term is also used as an adjective for anything that is
glossy, attractive, fashionable, but shallow in thought. Also called **colour
supplement**.

Sunday Times. Like all Sunday newspapers,* the *Sunday Times* is a completely independent paper, and it shares no editorial content with its apparent namesake the *Times** (although since 1966 they have both been
owned by the same person). However, like the *Times* during the week,
the *Sunday Times* is seen as the most sober, reliable, and accurate of the
Sunday papers, even though it was the first paper to introduce the Sunday
supplement* in 1962 and is now an immensely heavy, feature-laden publication.

Sunday tripper. A day-tripper* on Sunday, generally used like the American Sunday driver to indicate someone who clogs up the roads and sights
and generally gets in the way.

Sunderland. A city on the northeast coast of England* near Newcastle,*
which, in the nineteenth century, was a prominent coal port, and, in the
twentieth century, a center of modern industrial development.

sun-filter cream. What Americans call sunscreen.

Sunningdale. A village southwest of London,* now a suburb associated
with stockbrokers* and similar City* types, with a nationally famous golf
course.

super. Good, great, attractive, wonderful, and so forth. This was widespread slang among the trendy* and young during the 1960s, usually pronounced as "SOOOOOpah!" but its use has faded among later generations.

superannuated. Old-fashioned; more common today as a term meaning
someone who is old enough to be forced into retirement, which is often
called **superannuation**.

superannuation scheme. What Americans call a pension plan. *See also*
scheme.

superintendent. In the police,* the rank above Chief Inspector;* the rank
above that is a **Chief Superintendent**, which is primarily administrative but
may still have some criminal duties. The ranks exist with equal status in
both uniformed and detective branches.

supermarket. Used now as a generic term for any self-service food store; the larger supermarkets on the American style are often called **superstores** or **hypermarkets** and may be enormous even by American standards.

superstore. *See* supermarket.

supervisions. *See* tutorials.

supper. This usually means a late and light meal. Until late nineteenth century, the basic meals were breakfast,* dinner,* and a snack called supper; the evening meal eventually expanded somewhat, but in the working class* was generally called tea,* although many respectable families continued to call it supper instead. However, in the upper levels of society—who now have breakfast, lunch,* and dinner—supper is a light meal eaten very late, such as after the theatre, when dinner has been unusually light or early. In families in which the adults ate evening dinner, the children's separate meal before bedtime was sometimes also called supper. In recent years, some people from the professional classes have begun to use supper as a basic term for the evening meal, saving dinner for something more formal, while those in lower levels often use the term for a bedtime snack.

supplementary benefits. What Americans call welfare, benefits paid by the government* in addition to the standard benefits paid through national insurance* for persons who demonstrate special need.

supply teacher. What Americans call a substitute teacher.

supporter. What Americans call a sports fan, usually football* or rugby.*

Surbiton. A town* south of London,* seen as the quintessential middle class* suburb with all the common attitudes of suburbia.

surgeon. In Britain, surgeons and physicians were separate professions until very late in the nineteenth century. The surgeon was the handyman of the medical profession, someone who did actual manual labor, so to speak, and was thus a Mr* rather than a Dr* who was able to dispense medicines. The advances made by surgeons through anatomical studies in the nineteenth century upset this relationship, so that by the late century all GPs* were officially "Physicians and Surgeons." When a doctor specifically calls himself a surgeon and retains the Mr, he is indicating he is a specialist, and thus more expensive than a mere Dr but not necessarily more educated or experienced. *See also* consultant; doctor.

surgery. A doctor's office, even if no operations are done there; also used to mean the hours when the doctor is actually in the office. These hours often surprise Americans, as most doctors hold surgery in the evening so patients don't have to miss work, a practice unknown in America.

surgical spirit. What Americans call rubbing alcohol.

surplice. A loose, white gownlike vestment worn by the priest and the choir in a Church of England* service. *See also* cassock.

Surrey. A county* or shire* immediately southwest of London,* one of the Home Counties* and site of much of the traditionally "English" countryside, a mixture of fields, woodland, the rolling hills of the North Downs,* gentle river valleys, and striking country houses.* **Surrey side** is the south side of the Thames in London.*

surrounds. In a room, the trim, such as the baseboards and the windowsills.

surveyor. (1) An appraiser or inspector. For example, when property is for sale, a surveyor might be called in to estimate its true value, or an insurance firm might have its own surveyors examine a property before putting a value on the insurance policy. A **chartered surveyor** is such an appraiser who is also a member of a professional society of surveyors and thus, like a chartered accountant,* an experienced, senior member of the profession. (2) Historically, many government officers are called surveyors from an ancient sense meaning superintendent that no longer is used except in these old titles. (3) In building construction, an architect often splits the duties with a surveyor who does much the same work as the person Americans call a contractor; more specifically known as a **quantity surveyor**, he converts the architect's drawings into practical building plans and estimates materials, costs, and labor, and so forth.

suspenders. *See* braces.

suss. Slang since the 1920s for suspicion, especially of a crime, used by both criminals and police. In the latter half of the century, the term spread into general usage, where it means to investigate, study, or come to understand.

Sussex. An ancient kingdom in the south of modern England,* since 1888 two counties, **East** and **West Sussex**. Including seacoast areas and the South Downs, they are now two of the most varied of English counties. Northern areas are agricultural, although Sussex had been famous for iron before the industrial revolution, and since WWII these areas have felt much pressure from suburban development from London.* Shaw placed both his Heartbreak House and Horseback Hall here as representative of all the wasted talents of the upper classes* of Edwardian England. *See also* Home Counties.

swallowtail. A morning coat* on which the front was cut away sharply and the back slit so that the overall effect resembled a swallow's tail.

swanning about. Traveling with no apparent goal or purpose, like swans in motion, usually meaning a very relaxed holiday.

Swansea. A port town on the south coast of Wales,* long associated with Welsh industry, especially tin and steel, and with coal shipping, but perhaps best known to readers as the site of Dylan Thomas's *A Child's Christmas in Wales*.

swan upping. A trip to find and mark swans on the beak, rather like a brand; the annual upping to find the Queen's swans on the Thames* is the most famous example.

swatch. A channel of water between sandbanks, or between a sandbank and the shore, also called a **swatchway**, both terms used primarily in the eastern areas of England.*

sweat. Usually as **old sweat**, army* slang for an old soldier, especially Regular Army.*

sweater. Although American usage describes the same garment, the British tend to speak of a sweater only in relation to sports, where it is often worn as part of the sports outfit. Heavier sweaters worn in daily use to keep warm and dry are usually called jerseys,* while lighter ones for males are called pullovers* and, for women, jumpers.* In the 1970s and '80s, sweater also was extended to include the garment Americans call a sweatshirt. *See also* cardigan; twin set.

swede. A turnip with yellow flesh, what Americans usually call a rutabaga; these are basically used as feed for livestock—when Hardy's Tess has to harvest them, she has sunk as low as possible in the rural scale of things.

sweet. What Americans call candy. When used in relation to a meal,* however, it means a dessert of any kind, in restaurants often selected from those displayed on a **sweet trolley**.* A **boiled sweet** is a candy made from boiled sugar, like lemon drops or similar hard candy in America. A **sweet kiosk*** is a small booth or stall* that sells candies; a **sweet shop** a more permanent shop,* like the American candy store; and the **sweet trade** is the overall business of producing candies and similar treats. **Sweetmeats** are preserved or candied fruits. However, **sweetbreads** are most definitely not candy, but rather the pancreas or thymus gland of an animal, chopped, cooked, and eaten as a delicacy; Americans know the word, but the British eat them considerably more often. *See also* afters; pudding.

sweet oil. In cooking, olive oil.

swift. A dirty-brownish bird, similar to the swallow in appearance but with much wider wingspan. It migrates to the south of England* during spring and summer, during which time it nests in chimneys, in thatch,* under roofs, or in cracks in walls, and flies almost without break, often at great height.

swill. As a verb, to clean something by rinsing rather than by a complete wash.

swimming bath. *See* bath.

swimming costume. What Americans call a swimsuit or bathing suit.

swine. Although a generic name for pigs, swine is used in that sense almost as rarely as in America. Most often, it is heard as a widely used insult for someone who acts in a disgusting or personally unacceptable manner. Although used on many occasions about many activities, it is perhaps most often used of a man who does not act properly toward a lady,* and there is a strong flavor of class insult about it, as it is most often said by the respectable and the middle class about someone who acts as if from a lower class. Americans occasionally call someone a pig in some of the same situations, but not nearly as often. Unlike the American pig, however, swine is not used as slang for policemen.

swingeing. This word sounds sexually suggestive but actually just means gigantic or strong, as a "swingeing blow."

Swing, Swing Together. The opening words and commonly used title of the *Eton Boating Song.*

swing the lead. In military slang, to loaf or malinger. This was first a navy* saying, "swing the leg," which makes more sense, but soldiers misheard it and the corrupted version spread through the army* and from there into the rest of society.

swing tickets. In a store, the price tags or labels on clothing, attached by a string.

swish. Fancy or elegant, usually not with any imputation of homosexuality.

Swiss bun. *See* bun.

Swiss cheese plant. A type of climbing houseplant with holes in the leaves.

Swiss Cottage. The neighborhood in London* south of Hampstead Heath,* so called for a tavern built there in the Swiss chalet–style in 1840 before residential development began.

Swiss roll. A sponge cake spread with jam* and rolled up, then sliced crossways, what Americans call a jellyroll.

switchback. (1) On a road, the kind of sharp turn that Americans call a hairpin curve. (2) In an amusement park, what Americans call a roller coaster.

sword dance. In England,* this is a form of male morris dancing* (often with wooden swords), most common in the northeastern areas, in which a group of dancers maintain contact with each other through complex maneuvers by holding onto the tip of the next man's sword, interweave swords to make geometrical patterns, and/or use clashing swords to mark rhythms for the dancing. In Scotland,* it is a solo dance like a jig in which the dancer moves his feet between the blades of crossed swords on the floor.

swot. To study quickly but intensely; Americans cram for their tests. However, a swot is a person who studies regularly and does very well in classes, and the term is always used in schools as an insult rather than as a term of admiration.

syllabub. A dessert of whipped cream flavored with sugar, spice, and wine, brandy, or cider;* also made as a drink without whipping the cream. Both forms were known and popular before Shakespeare's time, but are relatively rare in the twentieth century except in "olde Englishe" affairs.

T

TA. Territorial Army. *See* territorials.

ta. (1) Casual thanks, originally only used by Cockneys* but spreading through much of society by the late twentieth century. **Ta ever so** is thanks very much. (2) In Yorkshire* and other northern areas, still heard as a form of thee or thou, as in "Has ta plenty?" for "Have you enough?"

tab. At Cambridge,* an undergraduate student.

table. To put on the table for discussion, the opposite of the American sense of to put out of sight in order to forget it.

tablet. Of soap, what Americans call a bar.

Tadpole and Taper. Political hacks with no views of their own, from two characters in Disraeli's *Coningsby*.

Taffy. A Welshman, a corruption of Daffyd, or David, similar to mick* in offensiveness.

tails. A man's coat that reached to about knee-length in back but with the back slit up to the hips, and with the material of the front cut away below the waist, first popularized in Britain as a riding* coat in the late eighteenth century and then spreading throughout the world as a man's fashion. By about 1840, tails had become the standard formal wear that continues into the present but had been replaced for daily wear by the frock coat.* *See also* cutaway; morning coat; white tie.

take. Regularly used in numerous idioms where Americans would use have or get, as in **take tea/food**/et cetera for "have some tea/food/et cetera; **take a pew** for "have a seat"; **take a fancy to** for "get to like"; **take advice** for "get advice," especially legal advice; **take up a post** for "accept or get a job"; or **take against** for "turn against" or "have a funny feeling about."

takeaway. Cooked food that you can carry away from the restaurant. Fish and chips* might qualify, as many takeaways can be eaten on the run, but most people tend to use the term in relation to curries* or Chinese foods rather than finger foods and often take the food home to reheat it for the table.

taken short. Had a sudden need to use the toilet.

tallboy. The piece of furniture Americans call a highboy.

tally-ho. The traditional cry in fox hunting* when the fox is first spotted, now used to mean any target is in sight.

tallyman. Not a man who counts but a man who sells items door-to-door that are paid for in installments, each of which he must come and personally collect.

Tam O'Shanter. The Scottish version of the beret, often called simply a **Tam**.

Tanders. *See* St. Andrew's Day.

T & G. *See* TGWU.

tandoori. A dish from India, chicken cooked inside a clay pot; sometimes used generically for any Indian food. *See also* curry; vindaloo.

tanner. Slang for a sixpence.* *See also* Appendix I.

Tannoy. A loudspeaker used for speeches or announcements, a brand name used generically for what Americans usually call a PA (public address) system.

tantalus. A cabinet or case used for storing liquor, with a glass front that can be locked.

tap. What Americans usually call a faucet.

taped. Slang for what Americans usually call sized-up, from WWI use of measuring tape for laying out the spacing of men before assaults.

taproom. In a hotel, what Americans call the bar.

ta-ra. Another form of ta-ta.*

tarmac. Tar macadam, what Americans call asphalt, named for the inventor of the substance, and more loosely applied now to any smooth paving, such as highways* or (especially) airport runways. Technically, the macadam is the stone, the tarmac is the stone and tar together, but few except engineers make the distinction.

tarn. In northern England,* a small lake.

tart. (1) What Americans call a pie, usually with a fruit filling. Originally, a tart was the same as a pie, but after about 1800, the term was applied to pies without a top crust, usually to small, individual serving-sized pies. A **jam tart** is an individual serving-sized tart with a jam* filling; in a **Bakewell tart**, the jam is strawberry. *See also* flan. (2) In mid–nineteenth century, the term appeared as rhyming slang*: jam tart = sweetheart; unlike most rhyming slang, it was shortened to the second word rather than to the first, and until the early twentieth century it was used, at least among Cockneys,* as an affectionate term, often calling the wife or regular girl friend the **old tart**. But somehow as it spread to the rest of society, it lost its affection and was quickly applied to a prostitute, as it also does now in America. **Tarted up** means dressed in fancy but gaudy or revealing clothes, or, as used among conservative speakers, simply wearing heavy makeup.

tartan. Cloth made in a plaid pattern. The original use was to make the kilt,* and sometimes a kilt is called a tartan. In Scotland,* particular plaid patterns of the tartan are thought to belong to and identify each of the clans,* although recent research has indicated that this usage was in fact invented as an advertising gimmick by cloth manufacturers during the fashion for Scottish history provoked by Sir Walter Scott's novels; many plaid patterns have existed for centuries, but they were not really tied to particular clans. *See also* plaid; trews.

tar water. A common home remedy made by steeping tar in water, taken for any and all ills.

tass. In Scotland,* a small cup.

tat/tatt. Worthless stuff, junk.

ta-ta. Good-bye. This is used only for casual farewells but has been widely used in almost all classes* for about 150 years.

Tate. The Tate Gallery, a museum in London* on the bank of the Thames* devoted to English art and artists, with some modern art from other nations.

Tattersall's. (1) The primary betting circle at a race course, so called from Tattersall's Committee, the original regulator of on-track betting. *See also* ring. (2) The primary auctioneer of race horses, originally at Hyde Park Corner,* now in Brompton* in London.*

tattoo. A military pageant or drill done primarily for show, usually at night; the most famous is the annual Edinburgh Tattoo.

tatty. Cheap, tawdry, worthless; sometimes, worn or tattered.

Taunton. A town in southwestern England* noted for its dissenter* traditions and its apples grown in the surrounding valley called the **Taunton Deane**.

tawse. In Scotland,* a leather strap, one end of which is split into several strips, generally used for corporal punishment in schools.* *See also* cane.

tax. *See* cess; death duties; income tax; poll tax; rates; VAT; window tax.

taxi. This word was (and is) used only for the motorized cab,* because the first such vehicles in London* in 1907 had a German invention called a taxameter or taximeter that automatically measured distance traveled and computed the fare owed by the rider. The term was almost immediately shortened to taxi, and as such it spread throughout the world. The London taxi in particular has long been a model of convenience for the passenger: Ugly, boxy, high-roofed, and styled like no normal car, it was (and is) immediately recognizable and easy to enter and exit. *See also* hackney; hansom; mini-cab.

tea. Tea appeared in Britain at about the same time as coffee* in the late seventeenth century but made little impact until colonists began to grow it in India and Ceylon in the 1830s, producing a tea that was much cheaper than the previous China teas. By the mid–19th century, tea had become ubiquitous, encouraged in no small measure by the rise of respectable society that needed a tasty, stimulating, but nonalcoholic drink. Tea went everywhere, although the upper classes in general drank tea only for refreshment and snacks, never with or after meals (except perhaps breakfast), continuing to prefer coffee instead. By the end of the nineteenth century, most Britons were drinking tea six or seven different times a day, not counting the cups brewed up for visitors or in emotional crises that made the housewife with a teapot a national stereotype.

Americans often see tea as a woman's drink, but in Britain it was and is drunk by everyone and, if the question ever arose, was seen as a much more macho drink than coffee, which until very recently was thought to be drunk only by effete bohemians,* except after dinner* with brandy and cigars. In provincial and working class* homes, a man's tea mug is usually a pint* in size, about double even American coffee mugs. In the second half of the twentieth century, tea drinking began to decline among the younger and the more prosperous; coffee returned to favor with much of the middle class, but perhaps the biggest inroads were made by American-style soft drinks. Even so, the British still average more than six cups a day per person. Curiously to Americans, tea remains the preferred morning beverage in almost all levels of society and is often drunk at breakfast and/ or elevenses* even by people who do not touch it the rest of the day.

Except perhaps for the first cup of the day, tea is almost always automatically served with milk, with sugar optional, although some sophisticates prefer lemon to milk. However, people at the lower end of the social scale generally put milk in the cup first, while those at the upper end start with the tea. True British tea is always brewed with the tea leaves loose in the pot and then poured through a small strainer into the cup; only in recent years have tea bags made any significant inroads. Tea is always hot; iced tea is never seen, even in midsummer. **Tea caddies** are canisters for holding the tea leaves before brewing.

Of the various types of tea: **Green tea** is technically unfermented tea, meaning it is steamed before drying so that it stays green in color, but in practice it usually means a China tea, as most teas from there are green; **Oolong** is partially fermented, left in the sun for a few hours after the green tea stage, which turns it orange or copper-colored, and comes only from China; **black tea** is fully fermented by drying the leaves before crushing them and then leaving them to ferment for a time before drying them again, which turns them black, but in practice, this usually means Indian tea, as most from there are so processed. **Pekoe** is a standard grade of quality and size, not a type of tea—pekoe, orange pekoe, and flowering pekoe progressively; **Souchong** is a grade below pekoe, and **Lapsang souchong** is a Chinese black tea of this grade with a very strong taste sometimes compared to tar. **Gunpowder tea** was green tea in the form of very small pellets. **Darjeeling** is an Indian tea generally thought the most subtle and is thus comparatively expensive. **Assam** is also an Indian tea, much more robust and bitter than Darjeeling. Most British tea, as in America, is blended, meaning several types of tea are mixed together; the most common blends are: **English Breakfast Tea**, a mix of India and Ceylon teas that has a strong taste and as the name suggests is used like the American morning cup of coffee to help the drinker wake up; **Earl Grey**, a blend of China teas originally made for an Earl* Grey, the most popular choice for afternoon tea.

Tea was so ubiquitous that the name was also applied to various meals in the afternoon. At the lower levels of society, it is the evening meal served usually about 6 to 6:30, as soon as Dad gets home from work. Before WWII, it was often little more than tea and bread and butter, but now it generally involves some meat or fish and chips.* That the meal took its name from the beverage indicates not only the prevalence of the drink but also that the drink had become a major source of calories, from the amounts of sugar added to it, the quantity of which increased the further down the social scale one traveled. (The ubiquitous "One lump or two" question is thus more a sign of the respectable middle class than of concern for the guest's tastes, signifying that the hostess knows no one who would take more.)

The tea Americans think of as quaint and stereotypically British, however, is the afternoon tea, a snack served by the middle and upper classes around 4:00 or 4:30 to tide them over until dinner.* These are often substantial repasts, with sandwiches* and cakes,* perhaps more food than found in the working class meal, but are still usually served with no utensils, except of course a spoon for stirring the tea, and thus clearly a snack. Sometimes an afternoon tea might also include meat or hot dishes; if so it is usually called **high tea** and substituted for the evening meal, often served an hour or so later than afternoon tea. A **cream tea** is an afternoon tea without sandwiches, usually with only tea, scones,* jam,* and whipped or clotted cream.* At work, the **tea break** comes about 3:30, still called a tea break even when people take coffee instead. A **tea boy** is a boy who brings around the tea for office breaks but who also has other duties in the office, but a **tea lady** is usually a mature woman who does nothing but serve tea, coffee, and snacks in the office, often selling them. A **tea cosy** is a thick cloth cover that fits over a teapot to keep the tea from cooling off too fast. A **tea towel** or a **tea cloth** is what Americans usually call a dish towel, used to dry dishes and not solely linked to tea. For **teacake**, *See* cake.

A **tea shop** is a restaurant specializing in afternoon teas and lunch* and having an almost all-female clientele; tea shops appeared first in the late nineteenth century to provide lunches for respectable female office workers and through the first half of the twentieth century remained the unchallenged domain of the middle-class female shopper; most have disappeared now, overwhelmed by the multitude of restaurants and snack bars. The

tea dance was a dance held in the afternoon around time for afternoon tea, usually in hotels, throughout the first half of the twentieth century. It was practically the only place for public dancing except at formal balls,* since there were no night clubs,* and thus where one went to tango or listen to the modern dance bands; since WWII these have faded away. *See also* ABC; caff; char; Corner House; meals; Mother, be; urn.

teacher training college. Special schools that trained teachers for primary school* work. They ended in 1975 when all such training was moved to "colleges of education" which were part of other institutions, in an effort to force all teachers to earn a "real" degree.*

teaching block. A building with school classrooms in it. *See also* block.

tearaway. A young hoodlum. Also sometimes called a **tearabout**.

teat. What Americans call a nipple on a baby bottle; also sometimes any other fixture that looks or operates in the same way.

technical college. An institution of higher education that specialized in technical and vocational subjects; reorganized in 1967 as polytechnics.*

technical school. A state-supported secondary school from 1944 specializing in technical and scientific subjects, intended to counterbalance the grammar schools,* now absorbed into the contemporary comprehensives.*

Teddy boy. In the 1950s and 1960s, a young man usually assumed to be a kind of hoodlum who affected dress that looked somewhat Edwardian, although usually with an Elvis Presley hairdo. The phrase has since been used as a generic term for young punk or hoodlum, no matter what the particular style of dress involved. *See also* Mods; Rockers; skinhead.

Telecom. *See* British Telecom.

telegram. As in America, the telegram was used to send quick messages. However, due to the urban density of London* in particular, it was extremely common from mid-nineteenth century well into the 1920s to use the telegraph the way we now use the telephone. Mail delivery might take as much as a whole day, so for faster communication, people would send a telegram from the local post office, which would be received at the post office nearest the addressee and then delivered immediately by a delivery boy. It need not indicate an emergency, just a quick message, and literature of the period is full of casual invitations to dinner and such, all of which arrive by telegram and carry no more urgency than phone calls now carry.

Telegraph. A daily newspaper,* in appearance probably more like the paper of a midwestern American city than any other British paper, but much more than the *Times** the paper of choice for the rank-and-file Conservative* voter, especially the suburban middle class,* famous for its letters signed in the manner of "Angry in Tunbridge Wells" and its interest in sex scandals, which are reported in the same staid tones as foreign political correspondence. In 1961, a *Sunday Telegraph* with similar views and appearance began publishing.

telephone. Until privatization in the 1980s, telephone service was provided by the post office.* British phones rang with a double ring and now beep with a double beep. In pay phones, called callboxes,* the caller inserts no coins until the call is completely connected, at which point you hear a number of beeps until you put in the coin, then the beeps stop and you can speak.

telly. TV.

Temple. In London,* the home of the legal profession, so called not due to reverence for lawyers but because the site originally belonged to the Knights Templar. The core of the site is the **Temple Church** south of Fleet Street,* dating to the twelfth century, but the legal profession resides in the outlying buildings, which had been used as a law students' hostel when Henry VIII confiscated the property and were then leased in perpetuity by the lawyers' society. Of the original three buildings, two remain, the **Inner Temple** and **Middle Temple**, each with its individual chambers* and large dining halls, and they have been augmented by the additional Inns of Court* north of Fleet and the Strand.* All barristers are still required to maintain membership in one of the remaining four groups in order to practice. The **Temple Bar** is the point at which Fleet Street changes to the Strand and was the point at which the City* ended its jurisdiction, marked by a gate until 1878, now by a strange statue of a dragon on a traffic island; it has nothing to do with the legal bar* but refers instead to its use as a bar to admission for the monarch, who must ask permission of the Lord Mayor* before passing the bar and entering the City.

ten-a-penny. Very cheap and easy to find, about the same as the American dime-a-dozen.

ten-by-eight. The photo print that Americans call eight-by-ten; British practice is to always put the larger number first. *See also* four-by-two.

tenner. A ten-pound* note.*

tennis. The modern form of the game known as lawn tennis was invented in England in 1873 as a variation of badminton and made a sudden surge to popularity among the upper layers of society. The class* factor was especially pronounced, as play required an expanse of flat lawn available only to the wealthy, at private clubs* or at their own estates. But perhaps a greater factor in its popularity was that it and croquet were the only games of the era played by men and women together; its energetic play meant it was left to the young people, thus providing about the only un-chaperoned meeting place for young couples of the respectable, wealthy classes.

ten p. A coin worth ten new pence,* in use since 1971. *See also* Appendix I.

ten-pin. What Americans call bowling, distinct from bowls.*

term. (1) A period during which university,* college,* or other school* is in session. At Oxford* and Cambridge,* terms are eleven weeks long (although students are only required to be present for the central eight of those), and there are only three terms a year: beginning in October (**Michaelmas term**), January (**Hilary term** at Oxford, **Lent term** at Cambridge), and April (**Trinity term** at Oxford, **Easter term** at Cambridge). Public schools* and other universities follow similar patterns but with individual variations in dates. State schools also have three terms, from September through mid-July, with two weeks holiday between terms and another week off at half-term,* midway through each term. (2) In Westminster* law courts before 1873, cases were tried during only four periods each year, each quite brief: **Hilary term**, January 11–31; **Easter term**, April 15–May 8; **Trinity term**, May 22–June 12; and **Michaelmas term**, November 2–25. By 1873 the crush of cases was so great that they could not be confined to such brief periods, so these dates were expanded, but the terminology continued to be used in legal circles. *See also* sitting.

terminological inexactitude. It is a convention of Parliament* that one member* may never call another member a liar; he or she may, however, accuse others of terminological inexactitude.

terrace. A row of houses,* usually a full block long, all sharing walls, as might be called row houses in America. These began in the eighteenth century and are often associated with the Georgian and Regency periods, as exemplified by the famous terraces in Bath,* and were often built around a square or circle. The individual houses were often quite narrow and several floors* high. To Americans this arrangement sounds like cheap housing, but almost from the beginning terrace houses have been among the most expensive forms of housing available. In the late nineteenth century, however, the style was adapted for quick, cheap housing for the working class* and in most modern literature a reference to terrace houses automatically means working-class residents; for the most part these have now been replaced in middle-class favor by the semi-detached* house and in council* planning by blocks* of flats.* Many country houses* have a terrace that is like an American patio, a stone or paved area directly beside the house where people may gather, and some multistoried buildings have terraces in the sense of balconies outside some rooms on upper floors, but terrace houses have neither of these; the name came about through purposeful misuse of the term by real estate developers.

terraces. Stands without seats at a football* field, the standing room. The terraces provide a way for fans to see a match cheaply and thus contain the most vocal and dedicated fans. But the crush of bodies standing together for the whole game means that the terraces are usually packed only with young men, often drunk, and most of the violence associated with British football breaks out here. Recently, some measures have been taken to eliminate or severely modify the terraces after a number of people were crushed to death against a fence on the terraces in **Hillsborough** in 1989.

territorials. The Territorial Army, soldiers not from the colonies* but from reserve units formed according to geographical areas within Britain.* These operated like the American National Guard, to provide support and meet emergencies within Britain, and were not expected to go overseas. *See also* Home Guard; line; regiment; Regular Reserve.

Terylene. A synthetic fabric Americans call Dacron.

Tesco's. A large chain of supermarkets,* often used generically for any supermarket.

Test. A Test Match, a cricket* match involving teams representing two countries. Since 1966, Tests have been played with England on a regular four-year cycle, teams from Australia, South Africa (except during sports bans), Pakistan, India, West Indies, and New Zealand visiting England on regular rotation in a four-year cycle during the summer, while England in turn visits Australia every four years in the winter and alternates visits to the other countries in the remaining years, usually taking one winter in four off. *The* Test is England-Australia. *See also* Ashes.

TGWU. Transport and General Workers' Union, the largest union in the free world, its membership including bus and truck drivers, dockworkers, and so forth.

Thames. Pronounced tems, the principal river of England.* By American standards very short and mild, it runs through London,* where it is broad and deep enough to be navigable by oceangoing vessels, which made London one of the world's principal ports. This is the river along which British history and culture have grown, its banks holding most of the royal homes and castles, such as Richmond,* Hampton Court,* and Windsor,* as well as Oxford,* and the Thames valley is generally known as one of the loveliest river valleys anywhere. The **Thames Barrier** is a set of enormous movable barriers in the river at Woolwich,* begun in 1972, designed to protect London from a tidal surge that would inundate it due to the gradual sinking of the land; it has yet to be used. People coming to London often hope to **set the Thames on fire**, as Americans used to say "set the world on fire."

Thames Water Authority. Since 1974, the authority that supervises both water supply for London* and sewage and pollution control in the Thames* basin; its policies and wide-ranging authority have made major strides in cleaning up what had been one of the world's most intensely polluted rivers.

that. Very or so, as in "I was that upset!"

thatch. A roofing material of bundles of straw or reeds, which are layered in a deep and steep incline over the house, almost always a cottage.* Centuries ago these were common, but they were gradually replaced by cheaper and more permanent roofing materials; in the modern world, thatch roofs are quaint and part of "our heritage," and extremely expensive to maintain, and are thus found almost exclusively on weekend and retirement country cottages for the relatively well-to-do.

that was. Previously called or named; thus, "Miss Smith that was" means a married woman whose original surname was Smith.

thick. (1) Slow-witted or dull, as in "He's a bit thick" or "thick as a plank." (2) Intolerable, as in "that's a bit thick." (3) Closely allied, intimate, friendly, as in the common "thick as thieves" but also used without comparison, as in "the boys were quite* thick."

thing, old. *See* old thing.

thing, the. That which is right, proper, socially acceptable, as in, "that's hardly the thing, old boy." *See also* done; ticket, the.

third. *See* degree.

third man. In cricket,* the position as far away as possible from the batsman,* behind and to the off* side; this is the hardest area to hit the ball to purposely, and thus if there is a player positioned there, he is usually the kind of fielder you might forget, hence another allusion for Graham Greene's *The Third Man*. Ironically, the term surfaced in a related real-life situation in the 1950s, after the defection of Burgess and Maclean, to indicate the suspected third Russian spy in British intelligence, who turned out to be Philby.

Third Programme. The BBC* radio service from 1946 presenting "cultural" programming, sharing a wavelength previously used only for sports broadcasts, both eventually evolving into Radio 3 in 1970.

Third Reading. *See* reading.

Thirty-Nine Articles. The thirty-nine basic statements of faith for the Church of England,* adopted in 1563.

Thistle, Order of the. A Scottish honorary order, limited to sixteen members. Although, as with so many things Scottish, there are claims of ancient organization, the order in its current form began in 1703. *See also* honours.

Thomas, John. *See* John Thomas.

thorpe. In Middle English, a small hamlet or outlying settlement, now found only in ancient place-names.

Threadneedle Street. The site in London* of the Bank of England,* sometimes also a synonym for the Bank, which is also called the **Old Lady of Threadneedle Street** for its conservative practices.

threepence. Originally a small silver coin worth three pence,* in 1937 replaced by a large, twelve-sided nickel-brass coin that stayed in use until decimalization in 1971; the latter often called a **threepenny bit** or **thrup'ny bit** and both were often called **thruppence** in common pronunciation.

threequarter back. In rugby,* one of the backs who line up leading away from the scrum,* to whom the halfback throws the ball, the fastest and most flexible of the backs.

Throgmorton Street. The site in London* of the Stock Exchange.*

thruppence. *See* threepence.

thrush. The most common songbird of Britain, a small brownish bird related to the American robin.

Tichborne Dole. One of the oldest and most romantic of the charitable doles.* In the twelfth century, Lord Tichborne ironically promised his crippled and dying wife to give to the poor the crops in whatever area she could crawl around; she managed twenty-three acres* but also pronounced a curse should the dole ever be stopped. The family annually gave away bread made from wheat grown on the land for 600 years, but an attempt to quit the dole seemed to activate the curse, so in 1835 the dole was renewed, too late for the last son, who died without issue in 1859, fulfilling the curse. The estate was claimed by the **Tichborne Claimant**, an impostor from Australia, resulting in an incredibly complex civil lawsuit, the longest criminal case in English history, and numerous fictional retellings, such as Josephine Tey's *Brat Farrar*.

tichy. In the early twentieth century, short; used to describe a person, after a famous short comedian, Little Tich, named for the Tichborne Claimant.*

tick. (1) What Americans call a checkmark. (2) Credit, usually **on tick**. (3) A very brief moment, as in "I won't be a tick." (4) To **tick-off** someone is to issue a reprimand or blame them in detail, as Americans often say "tell off"; however, while the recipient may be angry after a **ticking-off**, he is not "ticked off" as in America. *See also* ticking over.

ticket, the. Slang for the right thing, as in "That's the ticket."

ticket of leave. In the nineteenth century, a licence* that (a) allowed a transported* felon to return from Australia or (b) allowed a convict to leave prison* before the end of his or her sentence with certain conditions, roughly the same as the modern American parole system.

tickettyboo. Military slang before WWII meaning okay, everything working fine; generally disappearing except in caricature in the late twentieth century.

ticking over. Going along well but only enough to get by, originally said of a car idling.

tiddler. A runt, from a very small minnowlike fish called a tiddler. **Tiddler's ground**, however, is a place where you get rich quick, from a children's game and rhyme in which **Tom Tiddler** has to protect his base from others who try to sneak onto it, like the American games of red light–green light or statues.

tiddly. Drunk, used primarily by women trying to be cutesy. The term seems to be rhyming slang:* tiddly wink = a drink.

tidy. To put in order; Americans tidy up, but Britons generally just tidy.

tie. In England* it was common in the late nineteenth century for public schools* to use the modern–style long tie as part of their uniforms; hence, each school had a tie in a pattern, usually diagonal stripes, that was unique to its students. As long ties spread into daily dress for men, many continued to wear the tie from their old school as a signal to other old boys.* Similarly, clubs* and military regiments* adopted tie colors and patterns of their own. Thus, the man's tie became far more than just a matter of fashion or personal whim each morning; by about 1920 a man's tie signalled his place in society. The practice continues into the present, diluted somewhat by the pressure of fashion and perhaps even more by the large number of other groups who have also adopted ties, but it is nonetheless still a significant factor in dress and in social relationships. *See also* Ascot; old school tie.

tied cottage. *See* cottage.

tied house. A pub* that is either owned by or contracted to a single brewery, operated like American franchises, so you can only buy one brand of beer* there, as opposed to a free house.*

tiffin. What Americans call lunch, a slang term originally from India and used primarily by the military and Australians.

tights. What Americans call pantyhose, although also used for the heavier knit item Americans also call tights. Since pantyhose have become common, some people use tights to mean any women's nylon stockings* as well.

till. What Americans call a cash register. The term was originally used for the money drawer at a bank teller's window or under the shop* counter and was simply transferred to the whole apparatus when the machines came into use.

timber. While Americans use this term usually for the trees, Britons tend to use it to indicate the cut and shaped pieces of wood Americans call lumber.

time. (1) Time for the pub* to close, the time beyond which no more drinks can be legally served, most commonly as "Time, please," or "Time, gentlemen." *See also* licensing laws. (2) When writing a time, the British generally use a period rather than a colon—7:30 is 7.30, for example. Time is generally told in the same way as in America; however, in late twentieth century, many public services, such as trains, busses, and some government operations, have adopted the continental twenty-four-hour clock, so some listings will show 2100 or 21.00 for 9:00 P.M. For differences in the counting of seasonal and yearly time, *See* calendar. *See also* half.

Times. A newspaper in London* since 1788, almost from the beginning regarded as the most authoritative of all newspapers but also perhaps the dullest. It is often seen as the voice of the Conservative* party, but in practice it is more the voice of Oxbridge,* public school* society, which makes it potent among the upper levels of government bureaucracy, the clergy,* and the traditional professions, and thus the voice of the ongoing Establishment as distinct from any particular party or government. Announcements of births, deaths, weddings, and so forth carried in the *Times* define the membership of real Society; it also carries the most famous and difficult crossword.* It ran personal ads on the front page until 1966. It is a daily, a separate paper from the *Sunday Times.* *See also* TLS.

timeserver. Not a person who puts in time without enthusiasm but rather a person who changes his or her opinions to suit the mood of the times or, more often, the mood of the boss.

timetable. Britons use this term not only for trains or planes, as in America, but for other lists of times Americans usually call schedules, such as times for classes at a college.*

tin. (1) What Americans call a can, as in tinned vegetables. *See also* biscuit tin. (2) A container used for baking, such as a cake* tin or a pie* tin. (3) Money, especially coins.

tinker. Originally a traveling craftsman who repaired pots and pans, thus often synonymous with vagrant or gypsy.*

tinkle. A phone call.

Tintagel. Pronounced tinTAY-jel, a village on the northern coast of Cornwall*; the now-ruined castle on **Tintagel Head**, a rocky, picturesque promontory, is the legendary birthplace of King Arthur, and the modern village is extremely popular with tourists.

Tintern Abbey. A thirteenth-century abbey* near Monmouth,* just inside the Welsh border, falling into ruins in the late sixteenth century. Popularized by Wordsworth's poem, it became one of the most popular and romantic ruins in the nation.

tip. What Americans call a garbage dump. Thus, a **tipper** would be what Americans call a garbage truck. *See also* midden.

tips. Cigarettes with filters.

tipstaff. A sheriff's* officer, such as a bailiff* or a courtroom usher, from the staff normally carried by him before the twentieth century.

tipsy cake. *See* cake.

titbit. What Americans call a tidbit.

titchy. Tichy.*

titfer. A hat, from rhyming slang:* tit for tat = hat.

tithe. Not a donation but an actual tax of 10 percent of income paid to the Church of England* and collected at the local parish* level, used to support the local church and priest; this could be paid in cash or in kind. **Great tithes** were those of the land and crops, with collected produce stored in the church's **tithe barns**; **small tithes** were those of local wages and minor produce. If there was a vicar,* he usually received only the small tithes. Tithes were supposed to be paid by everyone, but many people tried to avoid them, so that the local priest often spent much of his time acting as tax-collector. Resentment was widespread, particularly among Catholics* and nonconformists* who were forced to pay the tithe even though attending other churches. In 1836, a rent charge was substituted for payment in kind, and the charge was finally shifted to owners rather than tenants in 1891, but agitation continued until the tithe was completely abolished in 1936, replaced by a form of annuities that will cease in 1996. *See also* living.

titivate. Completely unrelated to titillate, this was a jokey early nineteenth-century term meaning to finish up the details of dressing; since the end of the century, it has almost always applied only to women to describe what Americans often call "touching up" the makeup, hair, and so forth. However, since WWII ignorance has sometimes led to its confusion with titillate even among reputable writers.

titles. Titles of the nobility* are inherited only through male heirs, and all titles held by a man are passed to the heir in a lump. The exception is that, if a nobleman has two or more titles, his eldest son may use the second-highest as his own title until such time as he inherits the principal title; this is, however, a **courtesy title** only and is used only until the father dies. Women may not inherit a title (except in very rare instances), although they may inherit the property associated with a title. If there are no male heirs, the title dies out. *See also* baron; baronet; dame; duke; earl; knight; Lord; marquess; royalty; succession; viscount.

titmouse. Not a mouse but a type of bird, so called because most are mousy in color. They are very small and live throughout the United Kingdom.

TLS. *Times Literary Supplement,* a weekly newspaper/magazine in 1902 published as a supplement to the *Times,** in 1914 becoming a separate entity. Its book reviews and discussions of current affairs have made it one of the most significant and influential of twentieth-century literary reviews.

toad in the hole. A dish made of sausage baked inside a batter.

toast. As in America, toasted bread,* but very often served with a topping that Americans would rarely consider, such as beans* or spaghetti.*

tobacconist. Someone who sells cigarettes and other tobacco products, almost always a tiny shop* that also sells newspapers,* candy, and so forth.

tod, on my. Alone; rhyming slang: Tod Sloan (a jockey) = own.

toff. From mid–nineteenth century, an extremely well-dressed man, generally used by the lower classes* about men of the upper. In the latter parts of the century, this was generally an admiring term, often implying all the gentleman's* traits, such as education and honor, as well as fashion, but it could always be turned into an insult by a change in tone. After WWI it began to be more consistently negative, implying someone who not only looked but acted superior (*See* toffee-nosed). Before WWI, a **toffer** was a high-class prostitute, suitable for trade with toffs. Probably a corruption of tuft.*

toffee, for. Not at all or no matter what the reward, as in "I can't do maths* for toffee."

toffee-nosed. The attitude Americans usually call stuck-up, drawn more from the toff* than from the candy. One of the RAF's* favorite terms during WWII, it was used for anyone who pulled rank, acted in a superior fashion, or tried to enforce minor regulations.

toft. In northern England,* a small isolated farm.

togs. Clothes, in the nineteenth century a lower class* usage that became more widespread in the twentieth century.

toilet. This sometimes confuses readers of works written before the twentieth century. The word entered English from France (toilette) after the Restoration to mean the process of getting dressed, used almost always of women and including the entire process of cleaning, makeup, hair-dressing, and dressing. This usage continued well into the twentieth century, long after it had narrowed in America to mean only the plumbing fixture that played a minor part in the complete toilet. During the eighteenth century, it was fashionable to receive visitors during this process, and that reception was also called the toilet, but it meant visitors were seen while having one's hair done, not while sitting on a toilet. In general, the British still use toilet only in this meaning, if they use it at all, and use lavatory* for the plumbing fixture; hence, **toilet soap** is what Americans call bath soap, while **toilet table** is what Americans now call a makeup table and a **toilet cover** the cloth on such a table.

tolbooth. In Scotland,* not a toll booth but a town hall; this often included the local jail or prison,* so the term is also sometimes used for a jail. The **Old Tolbooth** in Edinburgh* was a prison* familiarly called "the Heart of Midlothian" before Scott made it the setting for his novel.

Tolpuddle martyrs. Six men from the village of Tolpuddle who were transported* in 1834 as punishment for engaging in trade union* activity.

tombola. What Americans call a raffle.

Tommy. (1) A soldier in the army,* from the name Thomas Atkins that was used like the American John Doe on sample military forms after 1815 to indicate a private soldier. It is always used like the American GI to mean the guys in the lower ranks, never officers.* (2) *See* tommy-rot.

tommy-rot. Nonsense, worthless stuff. In no way related to the Tommy* as soldier, this comes from earlier slang **tommy** for the food, tobacco, and so forth, given to navvies* in lieu of cash wages, or possibly from the army* bread called tommy from the late eighteenth century.

tom-noddy. A noddy,* usually a great fool, in the same way that an American tom-fool is more stupid than just a fool.

tompion. A pocket watch, named after the seventeenth century inventor who developed the dead-beat escapement and balance spring that gave watches real accuracy.

ton. (1) Heavier than an American ton, 2240 pounds. (2) In slang, anything large or great, as in "tons of money"; sometimes this is more specifically 100, so that "going a ton" means driving at 100 mph and "cost a ton" could mean either "cost a lot" or "cost 100 pounds." (3) In swank slang, pronounced in the French* manner, style, flair, or tone.

tonne. A metric ton—1,000 kilograms.

toothful. A small amount of liquor.

tooth glass. The glass used for rinsing after brushing your teeth.

top. To kill, most often said of hanging; the slang has been around so long it is now practically standard usage.

top drawer. Among the very best society.

top hat. *See* silk hat.

top hole. Excellent, superb. This is one of those stereotyped phrases, like "I say," "absolutely smashing,*" or "what ho," that Americans see as typically English, but for the most part it seems to have been confined to the 1920s public school twit* character, such as Peter Wimsey or Bertie Wooster, and it disappeared, if it ever in fact existed, after WWII except when a writer wants to trot out that particular literary stereotype.

top liner. What Americans call a headliner, the person in a show with top billing.

top of the pops. Much admired, from a popular television program of that name that featured popular groups and hit songs since the early 1960s.

top up. Refill a glass or other container that is not yet empty, most often said about liquor.

tor. A rocky peak or hilltop, sometimes just a pile of rocks, used primarily in the southwestern peninsula area of England.*

torch. What Americans call a flashlight. When the British say **flashlight**, they mean what Americans call a flash or flashbulb for a camera.

Torpids. At Oxford,* boat races held in February.

Torquay. Pronounced torKEE, a resort town on the south coast of England* east of Plymouth,* popular since the early nineteenth century as the center of what is often called the English Riviera, despite hoteliers like Basil Fawlty.

torte. Sometimes what Americans call a tart or a pie, sometimes what Americans call a cake, especially one of several layers with icing or filling between. *See also* cake; gateau.

Tory. One of the two primary English political parties,* appearing in the late seventeenth century as supporters of James II. The name first appeared as an insult, from a name for Irish highwaymen. The party was primarily the party of the landed gentry* and was a strong supporter of monarchial rights, which left it out of power during the constitutional monarchies of the early eighteenth century, but it eventually became the dominant party and had uninterrupted control of the country for fifty years before 1830, during which it established some kind of standard for reactionary, corrupt, and self-interested politics. The Reform Bill* of 1832 so destroyed its bases of parliamentary power that it collapsed, reappearing in significantly modified guise as the Conservative* party, but members of that party are still called Tories today.

tosh. Nonsense, generally used only among the public school* class.* *See also* pish.

tot. (1) A small drink, especially of rum or other hard liquor. (2) The total of a set of figures; to do the addition is to **tot up.** (3) Junk, particularly items rescued from the trash pile to be re-used or re-sold.

Tottenham. An area of London* north of the City.* In Shakespeare's day, a byword for sturdy Englishness, and in the nineteenth century full of cheap drapers;* it is now predominately Black.*

Tottenham Court Road. In London,* the northward extension of Charing Cross Road,* associated in mid–twentieth century with cheap furniture dealers.

tottie. Since late nineteenth century, a high-class prostitute.

touch down. In rugby,* what would be called a touchback in American football, when the player touches the ball to the ground behind his own goal line. No points are scored or lost, and the ball is brought back out to the twenty-five-yard line where play resumes.

touchline. In football* (soccer) and rugby,* the sideline.

touch wood. This is done for good luck, same as the American "knock on wood."

tout. Essentially, one who supplies information to a bookmaker about the condition of horses, but sometimes used to indicate a bookmaker's assistant.

towelling. The material Americans usually call terrycloth; hence, a **towelling robe** is a bathrobe.

Tower. Almost always the **Tower of London**, a fortress on the Thames* at the eastern end of the wall of the City.* The still extant White Tower dates to William the Conqueror, but the fort expanded quickly to maintain clear control of the city for the Crown* and was also used as a royal palace.* By the sixteenth century, however, the primary function of the Tower was that of a royal prison,* but by the late seventeenth century that function too had for the most part ended, with the exception of special modern prisoners Roger Casement and Rudolf Hess. The Tower also housed the Mint* until 1810. But by the eighteenth century the Tower was primarily a storage facility for valuables, due to its great security, and the Crown Jewels* continue to be stored there, still guarded by the Beefeaters.* Otherwise, its primary function today is as a tourist attraction. The Tower also marks the dividing line between the City and the East End.*

tower block. *See* block.

Tower Bridge. The bridge in London* over the Thames* just east of the Tower,* built in 1896. This is the drawbridge with the Victorian Tudor towers that is so often pictured in tourist brochures and is consequently mistakenly called London Bridge* by many Americans.

Tower Hamlets. The contemporary borough* of London* including the bulk of the East End.*

town. Technically, a community chartered* by the monarch as a town, which means it has an independent council.* In practice, size has little to do with the term, as town is used most often to mean a community with a market* or with more than one church,* or both, and thus often includes boroughs and cities* as well. A **cathedral town** is a town with a cathedral, usually implying that religion is a major industry. In this work I have used town in most entries in the American sense—anything between 1,000 and 100,000 in population; if I mean a specific British usage, I have always used a*. *See also* dormitory; expanded town; hamlet; new town; village.

Town. London.* Almost always, one goes "up" to Town, no matter where one begins the journey. **London Town**, however, does not exist as a separate entity in the way that the City* of London does but is merely a poetic usage. *See also* country; down.

town hall. The site of the local governmental authority, generally used metaphorically for the local government itself, as Americans use city hall.

town house. Modern real estate euphemism for a terrace* house.

Toxteth. A neighborhood of Liverpool,* now primarily Black* in population, coming into national prominence after a number of riots there in 1981.

track. Usually a path, but sometimes used for a larger road* if it is narrow, unpaved, and rarely used.

Tractarian. Alternate name for the Oxford Movement,* from the *Tracts for the Times* issued by the intellectual leaders of the movement.

trade. Perhaps the single oddest aspect of the British class* structure that developed in the nineteenth century is the general detestation and ostracism of persons "in trade," by which is meant anyone involved in retailing. People in trade constitute a separate and distinct class, which, whatever its wealth, is often ranked by the snobbish below even criminals and the homeless, no matter how much money they may be worth. This is confusing to Americans, where the all-but-universal goal is to start one's own business. British wealth and the Empire were both the direct result of trade and tradesmen, such as the East India Company* that conquered India purely as a trade venture, yet no one wants to know a tradesman.

No one really has a good explanation for this view. Some suggest that trade requires no special education, but the British in general distrust all education; others suggest the tradesman must pretend to be a servant to all, but then servants are generally held in greater general esteem than tradesmen. Whatever the reason, to be in trade, or even come from a family that was once in trade, is to be thought unfit for social contact with any other classes. This is not to imply that persons in trade have no power or authority—after all, the City* has been governed by its livery companies* for centuries, and a significant number of life peers* come from the ranks of successful businesspersons. But socially, they are expected by the rest of society to stick to each other. However, if wealthier tradespeople can distance themselves from actual contact with their customers, they may be considered to be in business* rather than in trade; this isn't as good socially as being a minor government bureaucrat or even a butler,* but it will allow them entry into the homes of the middle class.

To state things in this way seems exaggerated, but it is all but impossible to find a tradesman depicted positively in British literature or entertainment, and it is an element from the nineteenth-century class structure that is particularly resistant to change—attacks on Margaret Thatcher, for example, whether from left or right, sooner or later focused on her being a "jumped-up grocer's* daughter," and a considerable amount of the contemporary disdain for Indian immigrants is related not only to race but also to the highly visible proportion of them who open shops.*

Trade Descriptions Act. A 1968 law dealing with truth-in-advertising and labeling of products; often heard as **Trades Descriptions Act**.

tradesman. A shopkeeper.* *See also* trade.

trade union. Not an organization of tradesmen* but what Americans call a labor union. *See also* TUC.

trading estate. What Americans usually call an industrial park.

Trafalgar Square. A large square in London* immediately north of Charing Cross.* The square itself was finished in the 1840s, named in celebration of the great British naval victory, and is decorated with two large fountain pools and a gigantic pedestal topped with a statue of Nelson, with the four famous British lions at the base. Almost from the beginning, it seems to have become the home of all London pigeons.

traffic warden. A uniformed person engaged in enforcement of traffic and parking regulations; although administered and paid by the police,* traffic wardens are not police constables.*

train, in. In process, on schedule.

trainers. Any soft shoes for running.

trannie/tranny. A small transistor radio.

transport. Any trucking operation; sometimes used to mean any vehicle, so that "I'll lay on transport" means "I'll arrange a car for you," but in other idioms almost always indicating trucks and hauling.

transport/transportation. Historically, shipment of undesirables out of England* to somewhere else overseas. In a nation that had limited prisons* and even less sense of how to use them, the only real punishment available was execution; thus, as an alternative, during the Restoration the English began simply sending the criminals away. No established country would have them, of course, but the colonies in America had just opened up and Georgia in particular was thus used for several decades. Gradually, the American colonies grew to such size that they too resented being used as a dumping ground for criminals, and then the American Revolution firmly closed off that option. But new discoveries had led to a settlement at Botany Bay, now called Australia, and from 1788–1868 most convicts were transported there, after which the practice ended. Most persons were transported for a fixed term, but few chose to return after their term was up. Most of the offenses so punished were, by modern standards, quite petty.

Transport, Ministry of. From 1920, the national ministry* responsible for the national roads* and highways,* temporarily merged in the early 1970s into the Department of the Environment* and almost immediately separated again.

transport café. What Americans call a truck stop, a cheap diner with starchy traditional food, frequented by lorry* drivers. *See also* caff.

traps. What Americans call luggage.

traveller. Anyone who travels, but more specifically a person Americans call a traveling salesman, also called a **commercial traveller**. Generally, a salesman **travels in** his product; thus a man who "travels in ladies underwear" sells it rather than wears it. "No travellers" signs in pubs,* however, bar gypsies* rather than salesmen.

Travellers'. A gentlemen's club* in London* in Pall Mall.* Founded in 1819, it required all members to have traveled at least 500 miles (now 1000) away from London before joining.

traybake. A cake baked in a flat sheet.

treacle. Originally, this was a medicine, an eighteenth-century cure-all. By the early nineteenth, it was common to mix treacle with a thick sugar syrup to make it easier to swallow, so that now the name is used for the syrup, similar to what Americans call molasses though perhaps not quite as dark or thick. Paler types are sometimes called **golden syrup. Treacle sponge** is the cake* Americans usually call gingerbread.

tread. Still in widespread use as a verb to mean step; as a noun, what Americans call the steps on a stair. *See also* steps. The **treadmill** was a wheel of steps on which prisoners were forced to walk for hours each day in many prisons* throughout the nineteenth century.

Treasury. The ministry* of the government* responsible for national financial affairs. Originally during the medieval era, these were handled by the Exchequer,* which was the monarch's financial department, but increasing complexity of financial affairs led to formation of a small Treasury in the Tudor era. After the Restoration, this came to be seen as the single most significant ministry of the government, and the "First Lord" of the Treasury soon began to be called the Prime Minister* and take authority for all governmental activity, with financial responsibility passing to the "Second Lord," the Chancellor* of the Exchequer. In 1833, all financial authority formally passed to the Treasury, with Exchequer used to mean only the national accounts in the Bank of England,* though in typically English fashion the ministry head was still called the Chancellor of the Exchequer. Very roughly, in the modern government, Inland Revenue* collects the tax money, the Exchequer takes care of it, and Treasury determines where, when, and if it will be spent; Treasury has much more power than its American counterpart because Treasury, not Parliament,* makes the national Budget. Since 1961, a third member of the Cabinet is also in the Treasury, the **Chief Secretary to the Treasury**, who is in theory in control of the nuts and bolts of daily operation while the Chancellor deals with the Budget and policy.

Treasury Bench. The front bench* in Parliament* of the party* in power, where the most significant members of the Cabinet* sit.

treat. Generally lower class usage indicating something is attractive or positive, as in "looks a treat."

trendy. Fashionable, but applied to ideas, causes, or politics as well as to clothes and music, and almost always derogatory, implying the person takes up a subject or an item only because it is the fashion.

Trent. The principal river of the Midlands* of England,* flowing to the sea at the Humber* on the northeast coast. Connected to other Midlands rivers by a series of canals by the early nineteenth century, it was part of the transportation network for the industrial revolution.

trews. Primarily in Scotland,* trousers,* but more specifically ones made of tartan* cloth and either short and worn by men under the kilt or long and tight and worn now by women.

trick cyclist. A psychiatrist, military slang from WWII used now in educated portions of society.

trifle. A dessert usually made from layers of sponge cake spread with jam* then topped with custard, fruit, and/or cream; variations abound, in recent years usually involving gelatin.

trillion. *See* billion.

Trinity. (1) A college* of Cambridge,* the largest at either Oxbridge* university, although with less than 650 students minuscule by American standards. **Trinity Hall**, however, is a separate and older Cambridge college. (2) A college* of Oxford,* generally seen as a refuge for not particularly academic boys from public schools.*

Trinity Sunday. The Sunday after Whitsunday.*

Trinity term. *See* term.

Tripos. At Cambridge,* the honours* exam. *See also* degree.

tripper. *See* day-tripper.

trolley. Not a streetcar but rather a small cart, such as a tea* trolley or a dessert trolley; the term is used also for a hospital gurney.

troop. In the cavalry,* a unit, usually two per squadron,* roughly equivalent to the company* in the infantry and usually commanded by a captain.*

trooper. Generally, a soldier in a cavalry* unit; specifically, a rank equivalent to the infantry private. As everything in the cavalry was supposed to be more glamorous than in the infantry, one who swears in an exceedingly colorful manner swears like a trooper.

trooping the colour. Before the late nineteenth century, an army* ceremony in which the regimental* flag was paraded in front of all the soldiers to make sure they would be able to recognize it at all times. The ceremony has disappeared except in the Guards* regiments, who annually troop the colour in London* on the monarch's official birthday in June, a ceremony including inspection of the troops by the Queen.*

trotters. Pig's feet.

trousers. The men's outer garment Americans usually call pants. A **trouser suit** is a woman's outfit with trousers and a jacket, what Americans call a pantsuit, although usually women's long pants are called slacks.* *See also* breeches; drawers; knickers; pants; plus-fours; trews.

Truancy Officer. What Americans once called a truant officer. *See also* Educational Welfare Officer.

truckle bed. What Americans call a trundle bed.

truncheon. The long nightstick or billy club carried by the police constable.*

trunk call. What Americans call a long-distance call.

trunk road. A main highway,* usually an A* road with a single digit number.

try. In rugby,* a score in which a player crosses the goal line with the ball in hand and then touches the ball to the ground, worth four points (three in professional games). A **kick after try** is the free kick after scoring a try; it must be kicked by the scorer and is worth two points if successful.

try it on. Not to wear clothing to see if it fits but rather to do something to see if you can "get away with it."

TT. A teetotaler.

tube. (1) What Americans call a straw, as in a soft-drinks tube. (2) A roll, as in a tube of candy.

Tube. The Underground.*

TUC. Trades Union Congress. Founded in 1868 to coordinate campaigns for legalization of union* activity, in the twentieth century the TUC has come to be the symbolic representative of all unionism. The TUC is a coordinating council for most unions, but its greatest influence is through the Labour* Party, which the TUC in effect invented and which it still finances through union contributions. In fact, the TUC has very little power over individual unions, but in practice, as the ostensible voice of unions, the TUC is blamed by the middle class* and gentry* for every labor-related fault and thus is often depicted as a red-flag-waving bunch of communists out to destroy the nation.

tuck. Candies and such, usually meaning things sent from home to children away at school,* often in a **tuck box**. A **tuck shop** is a candy store near to a school. To **tuck in/into** is to eat eagerly; when children are put to bed, the parents usually **tuck up** the child.

tuft. At Oxford* and Cambridge,* a gold tassel worn before the 1890s on the academic cap, signifying the wearer was the son of a peer;* thus in collegiate slang, a nobleman. *See also* toff.

tummy. As in America, a euphemism for stomach or intestines, but while Americans tend to use it only with children, the British tend to use it with adults as well; a **tummy bug**, for example, is an upset stomach, usually accompanied by diarrhea. The word didn't appear until late nineteenth century, as a childish mispronunciation of stomach, which at that time was the preferred euphemism for belly,* which was the old standard term. *See also* gippy tummy.

Tunbridge Wells. A town south of London* with mineral waters, a popular spa and resort since the Restoration, with a somewhat more serious and staid reputation than Bath* but not so serious and respectable as Leamington Spa;* given the appellation Royal* by Edward VII.

tunny. The fish Americans call tuna.

tup'ny. Costing tuppence;* hence used figuratively to mean something worthless. Something called **tup'ny ha'p'ny**, two penny half penny,* is even more worthless or cheap. A **tup'ny one**, however, is a punch in the jaw.

tuppence. A coin worth two pence,* used from the late eighteenth century until 1971; figuratively used to mean something of little or no value, as in **don't care tuppence** for "couldn't care less."

turf. Usually referring specifically to the racetrack, as most horse racing* is done on grass courses. Hence, a **turf accountant** is what Americans call a bookmaker. The **Turf** is a club* in London* in Piccadilly* for the racing-mad members of the gentry.* To **turf out**, however, is to throw someone out of a room unceremoniously.

turk. Someone bad-tempered, cruel, or uncontrollable, after the presumed nature of the Turks in Turkey; also during late nineteenth century applied to what Americans call a juvenile delinquent.

Turkish. A cigarette made from Turkish tobacco, more expensive and theoretically a more sophisticated taste. *See also* gasper; Russian.

turn. (1) In general use, a shock or surprise, as in "gave me a turn." (2) On the stage, what Americans usually call an act, as in a "comic turn."

turning. As a noun, a side street.

turn off. In business, to fire someone.

turn out. To clean in detail, especially of a room by moving the furniture out of the way.

turn over. (1) Of a motor, as in a car, to run. (2) Of a room or building, to search.

turnpike. A toll road, so called from the wooden pole that barred entrance to them. First authorized in 1663, a number of these were built as private enterprises during the eighteenth century and were pioneers in new road-building techniques, particularly the use of macadam* surfaces. The turnpikes were never particularly popular, as they were quite expensive and, to protect the surfaces, often restricted the kinds of vehicles that could use them; turnpikes were most often used only by the stage coach* system. *See also* Mile End.

turn up. As a noun, an unexpected reversal, a surprising conclusion.

turn-ups. What Americans call cuffs on trousers.*

turps. Turpentine.

turtle. When used in relation to voice or sound, this refers not to the shelled animal but to the turtle dove.*

Tussaud's, Madame. A world-famous wax museum in London* in the Baker Street* area since 1832; most allusions are to its "Chamber of Horrors" depicting famous murderers.

tutor. (1) In a college* or university,* a fellow* who is directly responsible for the education of one or more undergraduates, usually through the tutorials.* Originally, the tutor's first job was to make sure the students paid their fees but this responsibility gradually expanded to personal supervision of all studies. As a rank, the Tutor is essentially the same as a Fellow, ranking below a lecturer.* A **private tutor** also prepares students for their final exams at college but is not a member of the faculty, being rather a person hired by the student to help with individual needs. (2) In private homes, a person responsible for teaching the children who remained at home. In practice, however, the term was almost always male; a female who did the same thing was a governess.* Before the nineteenth century, many of the gentry* would receive all their education from tutors, but after the rise of public schools,* tutors generally simply prepared boys for public school entry.

tutorials. At Oxford,* weekly meetings between a faculty member and a student, usually about an hour during which the student reads an essay on an assigned research topic and the tutor* critiques it. Called **supervisions** at Cambridge,* this method rather than one of lectures* and tests is the traditional British method of collegiate education.

TV Times. A national weekly magazine listing program schedules for ITV* and Channel 4;* the *Radio Times** has monopoly rights to the BBC's* schedules.

twa. In Scotland,* two.

twat. A stupid, obnoxious person. This usage is derived from vulgar slang for female genitals, a very old term that during the nineteenth century was so out of fashion that some writers misused it hilariously, the most famous being Browning who thought it was something a nun wore. *See also* twit.

twee. Cute, but often implying cutesiness done on purpose.

Tweed. A river in southeastern Scotland.* Near the North Sea* coast it serves as the border of England* for a few miles and thus is sometimes used figuratively for all the Scottish border. The famous tweed cloth was originally made from wool woven in the area.

tweeny. A maid* of all work in a large house, one who has no fixed place but changes duties constantly as other servants* need help.

Twelfth Night. The feast of the Epiphany, celebrated on the night of January 5 and the day of January 6, marking the last of the twelve days of Christmas.* In Shakespeare's time, this was more important than Christmas itself, as it was something of a winter Mardi Gras, a time of feasts, parties, and officially sanctioned public misbehaviour, often with plays, mummers,* and lots of drinking. The re-invention of Christmas during the Victorian era gradually overwhelmed the Twelfth Night celebrations and by the twentieth century they had all but disappeared.

twenty. A pack of cigarettes containing twenty. This is, of course, the way they are sold in America, but in Britain cigarettes have been sold in smaller packs of ten and even sold individually by the tobacconist.* By the 1980s, the American-style pack had become standard, but many people still ask for twenty rather than for a pack.

twerp. Slang for a silly insignificant person, usually a man.

Twickenham. Pronounced TWICKnum, a suburb on the southwest side of London* near Richmond,* noted primarily as the site of a major rugby* stadium.

twig. As a verb, to suddenly understand, equivalent to the American "catch on" or "get it."

Twining. The foremost English tea* brand, dating to Thomas Twining, the first businessman to serve prepared tea in London* in the early eighteenth century.

twining plant. Any plant that climbs or grows around a stake or post.

twin set. A woman's jumper* and matching cardigan.* Sometimes it seems that a strand or two of pearls are part of this outfit, but they are merely typical accessories, not part of the twin set itself.

twist. (1) A swindle or con game; hence, as a verb, to cheat. However, a **twister** is someone who can't be cheated. (2) A piece of paper with the ends twisted together, used to hold small items. *See also* screw; spill. (3) In the eighteenth century, this was generally brandy and eggs mixed in a drink; in the mid–nineteenth century, brandy and gin;* since then, gin and hot water. (4) **In a twist** or **round the twist** is upset or angry. *See also* knickers.

twit. A foolish person, so often a "little twit" that it also means insignificant. This was 1920s slang that has hung on to become almost standard usage and, while it is insulting, it is not vulgar or sexual in connotation, quite distinct from twat.* In this work, I use the term "public school twit" to indicate a particular character type that surfaced early in the twentieth century, a genial young man with money who gave no outward sign of intelligence; in fiction Bertie Wooster and the other residents of the Drones Club are the archetypes, with Peter Wimsey and Albert Campion hiding their talents behind this facade. The term twit, however, is now used much more broadly and much more insultingly, particularly since Monty Python spread it far outside collegiate slang.

TWOC. Taken without owner's consent, a police* locution for a stolen car.

two-fisted. Unlike the American usage that implies a man is a macho, red-blooded fellow, this usually means someone with two fists, a clumsy person without coordination, what Americans sometimes call ham-fisted.

two-two. Of guns and ammunition, what Americans call a .22 caliber.

two up and two down. The standard arrangement of rooms in a cheap semi-detached* or working-class* terrace,* with a kitchen and a sitting room* downstairs and two bedrooms upstairs.

TW3. *That Was the Week That Was*, a popular satirical BBC* TV program of the 1960s, the model for a brief American version during the same period.

Tyburn. The site of London's* gallows from the fourteenth century, when it was well outside the City,* on the site that now is the northeast corner of Hyde Park* at Marble Arch.* Most executions were done here until 1783, when the execution site was moved to the gates of Newgate.* Surrounded by open space, the hangings here drew enormous crowds noted for their vulgarity and festive attitudes, particularly during the eighteenth century. The **Tyburn Tree** was a permanent gallows erected here from 1571–1759. A **Tyburn ticket** was a reward of £20 or an exemption from parish* taxes in return for the testimony that led to a conviction and hanging. *See also* capital punishment.

Tyne. The river that runs through Northumberland* and emerges into the North Sea* at Newcastle.* The county* of **Tyne and Wear** was formed in 1974 to encompass the industrial areas usually called Tyneside.*

Tyneside. The area along the shores of the Tyne* near its mouth, especially Newcastle,* long synonymous with heavy industry, particularly shipbuilding, and in the late twentieth century just as synonymous with unemployment and labor unrest.

U

U. (1) For a movie, standing for Universal, the equivalent of an American G rating, suitable for audiences of all ages. (2) In terminology first used by Alan S. C. Ross but popularized by Nancy Mitford, English society can be divided into U and non-U. U is the upper class, **non-U** the middle class* that may try to appear like the upper class but that fails (lower middle and working class* don't enter into the terminology at all). Ross and Mitford originally used the terminology in a linguistic sense, pointing out numerous ways in which a person's vocabulary identified his or her class, and many such usages have been noted throughout this work. Since the first formulation, many others have adopted the terminology and applied to it other aspects of society than just vocabulary, often in a reverse snobbish sense about upper-class habits they think ought to be changed.

UDC. Urban District Council. *See* council.

UDR. Ulster Defence Regiment, a reserve army* force only in Northern Ireland.*

Ugandan affairs. When an African princess claimed she was "discussing Ugandan affairs" when caught in a sexual liaison, the magazine *Private Eye** throughout the 1980s used "discussing Ugandan affairs" or "discussing Uganda" whenever its writers wanted to suggest a subject had been having illicit sex without bringing down libel charges on their heads, and the term has percolated into other segments of society.

UK. United Kingdom. *See* Britain.

ulcer. While Americans use this only for sores inside the stomach, Britons use it for external sores as well.

Ulster. (1) An ancient kingdom of northern Ireland,* one of the last areas to be conquered by the English during the seventeenth century. The name was given to the area of six counties where the Protestants soon colonized and developed a majority and is now often used to indicate the United Kingdom* province of Northern Ireland.* (2) A man's overcoat, double-breasted and belted, so called because it was introduced by a tailor in Belfast* located in Ulster in 1867.

Ulster Unionist. *See* Unionist.

Ulster Volunteer Force. A paramilitary protestant force in Northern Ireland* from 1966, formed to counter the Provisional IRA and immediately outlawed. The **Ulster Volunteers** was a similar private army formed in 1912 to oppose home rule* for Ireland.*

umbrella. The umbrella is inextricably associated with the Englishman, but it was not always so; Americans assume that the regularity of the rain makes umbrellas common, but rain seems to have little to do with it. The first ones were used only to keep out the sun; such umbrellas have slipped in and out of women's fashions several times and are more often called parasols. The waterproof versions appeared in the eighteenth century and were often associated with servants* and others who could not afford good hats. By the early nineteenth century, respectable men had begun to carry them, but Emerson observed in midcentury that they could often be seen walking through the rain with umbrellas still tightly furled, a practice still common. There is also an unspoken understanding that umbrellas can be used by men only in urban areas; in the countryside, only women and clergymen may carry umbrellas in the rain, although men may shelter under them if holding them over women. Similarly, even in urban areas, working class* males almost never will carry an umbrella, and no one associates either the Irish or the Welsh, who get even more rain than the English, with regular umbrella use.

uncle. Slang for a pawnbroker.

uncrushable. Of clothing, what Americans call wrinkle-free or permanent press.

under. As a prefix in titles, what Americans usually prefer to call assistant, as in undersecretary* or under manager.

underdone. Of cooked meat, what Americans call rare.

Underground. In London,* the Underground Railway, what Americans usually call the subway. The modern Underground is the primary commuter transportation of the city, growing from a private underground railway connecting Paddington* and King's Cross* in 1863 to seven competing lines joined into a single system in 1912, now with nine different routes criss-crossing beneath central London. The **Circle Line** forms a loop connecting all the railway* stations of the city, and the other lines connect various suburbs with some portion of the central London area: **District Line** runs east-west through the southern part of the City, **Central Line** runs similarly through the central area, and **Metropolitan Line** along the northern edge; **Northern Line** runs north-south and the **Bakerloo Line** southeast-northwest through Charing Cross;* **Piccadilly Line** runs southwest-northeast through Piccadilly;* the **Victoria Line** runs from the south through Victoria* and then crossing to the north-east; and the new **Jubilee Line** runs from Charing Cross to the Hampstead* area. This was the first subway system in the world, and the visitor is often surprised to discover that many of the stations are a century or more old. Liverpool* also now has an Underground.

undersecretary. *See* permanent secretary; secretary.

understrapper. A colloquial term for a subordinate of any kind.

unemployment. The British have provided various national unemployment insurance or benefits since 1911, and since 1946 have administered these as part of national insurance.* These benefits are most often called the dole,* and although conservatives have always complained about layabouts* on the dole, the payments even today are hardly luxurious: In 1991, an unemployed married man received £60·40 per week, plus an additional £6·15 per child at home, and the paradigmatic layabout, the unemployed school-leaver,* received only £19·40.

Union, Act of. *See* Scotland.

Unionist. A political group favoring complete union of Ireland* and Great Britain,* first used in the late eighteenth century. The term was revived during the debate over home rule* in the late nineteenth and then taken as a party name by Liberals* who broke away over the issue and joined the Conservatives.*

Union Jack. The flag of the United Kingdom,* combining the St. George Cross of England* and Wales* and the St. Andrew's Cross of Scotland.*

United. (1) In the names of several famous football* clubs,* an indication that the club was originally formed as a private club by members of unions;* **Manchester United**, for example, was originally a team of railway workers in Manchester,* and **West Ham United** were iron workers in the East End* of London.* (2) The **United Oxford and Cambridge Club**, a club* in London* near Trafalgar Square,* its members often ironically described as united only against everyone else.

United Kingdom. *See* Britain.

unit trust. A financial organization similar to the American mutual fund. Someone with a share in one of these is a **unit holder**.

Univ. Casual name for **University College**, one of the oldest colleges* of Oxford.*

university. The British university is much more like American Ivy League colleges than the large institutions Americans think of as universities. Technically, students study at a college,* but only a university can grant a degree,* so all the associated colleges eventually send their students to sit* an exam for a degree* from the university; thus, the university has only an influence on what is studied and in no way can it be said to administer or supervise individual colleges in the way an American university administration sets requirements and daily regulations. For centuries there were only two universities in England: Oxford* and Cambridge,* both very medieval in their customs and organization, with Trinity (in Dublin) and Edinburgh* similar in age and methods. During the Victorian era a number of new universities opened to expand higher education to include science and engineering in particular, and most admitted nonconformists.* These are often now called redbrick universities* (from their typical architecture), but they were modeled on Oxford and Cambridge and are just as eccentric and individualistic in their organization and methods. An even greater explosion came in the 1960s, with sixteen new universities opened primarily to expand opportunities for students otherwise unable to pay traditional university fees; most of these are more American in their procedures, with more regular classes, lectures, and testing than older tutorial* systems. Even so, there are still only forty-three universities in Great Britain (the United States has about 1200 for something less than five times the population), enrolling about 0.5 percent of its population (compared to the United States current 5 percent of total population or 2 percent in France), so degrees are still extremely rare and their holders far more unusual; even jobs of extremely high status do not necessarily require a degree the way they do in America. However, many career-oriented and technical studies are taught in polytechnics,* which do not grant degrees, rather than in universities as in America. *See also* academy; further education; London University; Open University; term; vice-chancellor.

University College. (1) A college* in the Bloomsbury* area of London,* in 1826 called London University but having changed its name when it affiliated with the new London University* in 1836. Established as the first nonsectarian college, it accepted Catholics* and nonconformists* and offered a variety of subjects for study. Now it also includes the Slade* art school. **University College School** was a public school* founded in 1830 as an affiliated institution, but it moved in 1907 to Hampstead Heath.* (2) *See* Univ.

University Library. The library of Cambridge* as a whole, like the Bodleian* at Oxford.* Publishers are required by law to present a copy of all published works to this library.

Unknown Warrior. The tomb of an unidentified soldier inside Westminster Abbey, symbolic of all the dead of WWI.* Memorial services and ceremonies for the war dead, however, are held at the Cenotaph.*

unmentionables. From the mid–nineteenth century, underwear; the term was used only by the excessively proper or genteel.*

unsound. In civil service* usage, the worst insult that can be spoken about a colleague, meaning that he is not completely a team player but is given to thinking for himself.

up. (1) Torn up or broken up, as in "the road is still up." (2) **Up the** . . . is used in the lower class* to mean not "stick it up the . . . " but rather "up with the . . . "; hence, Up the Irish! and Up the Rangers! and so forth are all cheers, not insults. (3) *See* down.

up and up. In Britain, this phrase means regularly moving up or improving, as opposed to the American meaning of honest or aboveboard.

upper class. This is not a commonly used term in Britain, although it does appear; I have used it in many entries as a form of shorthand to include all those layers at the genuine top of the social scale, which in general means both the nobility* and the gentry* but also includes those portions of the middle class* with sufficient family wealth or status to share similar social customs. Perhaps the best simple definition is that the term covers those families who could send their sons to one of the better public schools* if they so chose. This group, however, is not at all a uniform group defined purely by wealth, but rather still contains numerous serious class and wealth distinctions within it; for these, *See* Appendix III.

upping. *See* swan upping.

upright chair. What Americans call a straight-back chair.

upstanding, be. Stand up, said before formal toasts and in some other formal situations.

up sticks. To move your dwelling, or just to move, usually implying a certain amount of speed, a term borrowed from hockey,* where it means "lift up the stick* and run as hard as you can."

urn. Almost always the tea* urn, a large pot used in offices, churches, clubs, snack bars, and so forth, when tea must be provided for a large crowd.

U. S. Useless, worthless, not from comparisons with Americans but from the RAF* in the 1930s which used **u/s** to abbreviate "unserviceable."

usher. (1) A doorkeeper, especially in a courtroom. (2) In some public schools,* a headmaster's* assistant who also teaches.

using language. Swearing. *See* language.

usquebaugh. The root word in Scotland* from which whisky* eventually evolved, still occasionally used for Scottish homebrew.

usual offices. A real estate euphemism for an indoor toilet.

utter. As an adjective, as in "utter misery," this is standard usage; however, the term has often been used without a noun following, as in "how utter!" and as such is part of a usually quite affected subculture of the upper levels of society claiming particular sensitivity and artistic sensibility. This is one of the usages Gilbert puts into the mouth of Bunthorne's circle in *Patience*, and it surfaces in literature and films on a fairly regular basis, used by the contemporary equivalent of such poseurs.

V

V. The two fingers held up in the shape of a V was a gesture popularized by Churchill in WWII as the "V for Victory" sign. However, if the fingers are held aloft with the hand turned so the back of the hand faces outward, this is the traditional British equivalent of the American "giving the finger," quite crude and vulgar, a fact Churchill was certainly aware of and from which he probably took a lot of mischievous pleasure.

vac. Vacation, especially a vacation between school terms.* *See also* long vac.

vacherin. A dessert of cream, fruit, and meringue.

vacuum flask. What Americans call a thermos.

vade-mecum. A notebook, from Latin meaning "go with me," used by the public school* class.*

vale. A broad valley, flat or with very gently undulating hills. *See also* dale; dell.

Valentine's Day. As in America, February 14, long a day devoted to lovers. Cards appeared in the late eighteenth century, well before Christmas* cards, and were spectacularly fancy during the Victorian era. The cards and interest in the holiday appeared to be dying by WWI but were revived again in the late twentieth century, perhaps under American influence.

Vale of Evesham. *See* Evesham.

Vale of the White Horse. *See* White Horse.

valet. A man's personal male servant,* often called a **gentleman's gentle-man** because, standing in such close proximity, he might act as an advisor as well as a servant. Jeeves is the ideal, although rarely matched in reality, for in most cases the valet had no more status and was treated no better than was a lady's maid.* The word, although French, is pronounced VALit. *See also* butler.

valve. Of radios and televisions before transistors, what Americans call a tube.

van. (1) This term is used for any large truck, including almost anything smaller than what Americans call a semi. (2) On a train, the luggage car. (3) A caravan.* (4) The post office* uses roaming vans with signal detectors to identify homes using TV sets without buying a licence.*

V & A. The Victoria and Albert Museum, a massive collection of antiques and curiosities begun with the items brought together for the Crystal Palace* exhibition of 1851, housed since 1909 in a gigantic building south of Hyde Park* in London.* For the most part eschewing paintings and sculpture (with notable exceptions), the museum displays enormous collections of practically everything else, from silver to furniture to musical instruments to historical fashions, with examples drawn not only from European history but from all parts of the world.

variety. The form of entertainment that Americans usually called vaudeville. It's no longer clear, if it ever was, just exactly how variety differed from the music hall,* except that variety was less vulgar, both in its content and in its typical audience, and that variety struggled through until the rise of television, on which, unlike in America, it is still regularly seen.

VAT. Introduced in 1973, this is essentially a sales tax, although the various British governments* have made special effort to claim that it isn't. The tax is levied on the "value added" each time a product changes hands on its way to the final commercial sale, with complicated paperwork that allows each business to pass along some of the tax to the next purchaser. But to the final purchaser, the person on the street, what it meant in the 1980s was a 15 percent sales tax.

Vauxhall. (1) Pronounced VOXall, originally a village on the south side of the Thames* across from Pimlico.* In the eighteenth century, **Vauxhall Gardens** were a large and extremely fashionable amusement park with fireworks, orchestras, entertainers, restaurants, and lots of leafy bowers for assignations. Becky Sharp's visit in *Vanity Fair* was fairly typical until the gardens finally closed in 1859. Since then the area has been developed and joined to the urban mass of London* on the south side of the river. **Vauxhall Bridge** in 1816 was the first iron bridge across the Thames, although it was replaced in 1896 with the contemporary version. (2) An automaker associated primarily with estate wagons;* owned since 1926 by GM, recent models have been the same as American Chevettes, Novas, and Cavaliers.

VC. Victoria Cross, the highest medal for military bravery. Instituted in 1856, the medal could be awarded to all ranks (and occasionally to civilians), and carries the same kind of status as the Congressional Medal of Honor in America. *See also* Appendix VI.

veg. Any vegetable; rhymes with hedge. The standard full meal* for the middle class* is often described as **chop* and three veg**, the three veg (never "three veges") usually potatoes,* peas,* and sprouts.*

vegetable marrow. *See* marrow.

Venture Scouts. A branch of the Boy Scouts* open to older teenaged boys and girls.

veranda. *See* porch.

verge. The side of the road or highway,* usually grassy; many Britons go for picnics on the verge of highways, which seems an odd place to look for the quiet of the countryside.*

verger. In a church,* the person who acts as caretaker of the interior of the church. In literature, the verger is usually something of a wimpish figure, particularly when compared with the sexton.*

Very. What Americans call a flare, named for its inventor; when shot into the air, it is fired by a **Very pistol**.

vest. What Americans call a man's undershirt; what Americans call a vest is called a waistcoat.* A **string vest** is an undershirt made from a heavy mesh with no sleeves and with narrow straps over the shoulders.

Vesta. What Americans call a wooden match, from a brand name used for one of the earliest types in the 1830s and still used in modern brand names.

vestry. (1) A room or a small building attached to the church,* usually for keeping the priest's vestments and similar items and also used for meetings by the laymen, called **vestrymen**, who deal with the parochial affairs of the church. A person **born in the vestry** is illegitimate, as the parents have not been in the actual church.* (2) A board of laymen who often met in the vestry to deal with any and all parish* business, used to identify many parish councils* until 1894.

vet. As a verb, to test or investigate; people needing a security clearance, for example, must be vetted. What Americans call a vet (or veteran) is usually called an **ex-serviceman**. However, vet is also used as in America for a veterinarian.

veteran. *See* ex-serviceman.

vicar. In the Church of England,* the parish* priests were supported by a tax called the tithe* rather than by salary from the state or donations in the collection plate. In many cases, the person appointed as parish priest, called the parson* or rector,* chose to live off the income without the bother of actually acting as priest in the parish, or even going near it. He was able to do this by hiring a substitute for a fee, usually that portion of the tithe called the small tithe, which consisted only of a tithe of local wages, considerably smaller than the great tithe of local land produce. This substitute was called a vicar, which means a stand-in, from an older Catholic practice of using vicars to stand-in for a monastery that collected the tithes (also indicated in the description of the Pope as the Vicar of Christ). The vicar was a qualified clergyman, lived in the parish, usually in a vicarage,* preached, performed weddings* and funerals,* and otherwise acted as the local priest. But officially, he was just a stand-in, even if he lived there all his life. Consequently, vicars were almost always very poor, and they often resembled the stereotype of Goldsmith's Vicar of Wakefield, gentle, simple, devout men who had no understanding of finance or the real world; otherwise, why would they have taken on the job to begin with? In literature, their parishes are actually held together on a day-to-day basis by their levelheaded wives (for some reason, vicars, no matter how poor, are almost always married). The practice was so widespread that it became common practice to call all parish priests vicars, even if they weren't, and this practice has continued in many places even after the tithes formally ended. Curates* of an absentee priest often also came to be called vicars. *See also* clergy; minister.

vicarage. The house provided for the vicar,* but more than just a house. In most village* life, the vicarage is the center of respectable social life, focussing not on the vicar but his wife, who was often much more authoritative and influential in daily parish* life than the vicar. *See also* parsonage; rectory.

vice-chancellor. In a university,* the actual chief administrative officer; the chancellor* of a university is an honorary post.

Vickers. A manufacturer of weapons, most noted for the Vickers machine gun used during WWI.

Victims Support Scheme. A volunteer organization devoted to aid for victims of crime. *See also* scheme.

Victoria. *See* Victoria Station.

Victoria and Albert Museum. *See* V & A.

Victoria Cross. *See* VC.

Victoria Embankment. *See* Embankment.

Victoria Memorial. The large statue of Queen Victoria in London* at the end of the Mall* in front of Buckingham Palace.*

Victoria Station. The terminus in London* of trains serving southern England.* The station lies between Pimlico* and Belgravia,* and the immediate neighborhood is often called **Victoria**. Originally built in 1860, the modern structure in 1909, it is the station most clearly associated with holiday travel, as both the terminus of the trains to Brighton* and other southern resorts and of the boat train* to Dover.* It is also a major transfer point for Underground* lines, a principal terminus of London busses,* and the origination point for much coach* service to the countryside.

video nasty. A videocassette with either pornographic or very explicitly violent content.

viewpoint. Not an outlook on life or an opinion, but rather a scenic spot with a great view; for the American viewpoint, the British generally use **view**.

villa. The term is borrowed from Italy, where it meant a country estate, but by the time it reached England,* it meant this only in implication. For the English, the country estate is called a country house;* thus, in typical real estate practice, houses that could by no stretch of the imagination be called country houses were called villas instead, to give them some added social status. The term was especially popular during the Victorian era as railroad construction allowed the suburbs to spread into the countryside around London* and other industrial centers, and it gradually came to be an accepted description for any suburban house suitable for the middle class.* In general, the name was even more popular in the suburbs around Birmingham* or Manchester,* where the newly enriched middle class were even more interested in demonstrating their status, than around London, and entire developments might be given the name of Such-and-such Villas. Some individual villas were large enough to be surrounded with landscaping, but the villa need not be a free-standing house; it could be a semi-detached,* as long as it made some pretense to architectural distinction and was suitable for middle-class occupation. To find a literary character in a villa is thus to find a character who insists on his or her status as a member of the middle class (and is a bit insecure about it).

village. Technically, a village is a distinct English community with its own parish* church,* which in practice usually means a community of less than 1,000 people. Until the early nineteenth century, almost all English life was village life. Because of the ancient tradition of commons* and of each parish's domination by a local, large landowner, people congregated in the village and walked from there to their work in the fields, rather than living on isolated farms as Americans did. This changed after the enclosures,* as villagers no longer had access to the common land that had supported them, small farmers were encouraged to live within their now enclosed fields, and urban industry drew away workers. Villages declined into little more than a place for the local squire's* farm hands to sleep, with a shop* and a pub* and perhaps a craftsman or two to sustain them. But the village remained a magic place in the imagination of the urban dweller, and practically everyone, especially in the middle classes,* dreamed of a time when the family could return to the "simple life" of the village, a prospect offered first by trains* and now by cars (a development that has, in turn, led to a flooding of villages near all urban centers with commuters, often then resulting in more damage to the villages than poverty and the enclosures ever managed). But the village has such a mythical power that the American reader can trust almost no literary descriptions of them; along with the country house,* they form a Disneyland version of England whose spell practically no writer or filmmaker can completely escape. Curiously, unlike the American small town, the village is rarely idealized as a "good place for families"; rather, the ideal village is a community where someone can live quietly (usually without children) in a cottage* with a nice garden* among people who all "know their place." *See also* borough; hamlet; market; town.

vindaloo. A meat dish originally from India; technically, it differs from curry* in that the meat is marinated and then cooked in a vinegar sauce rather than a water-based sauce. Except on Indian restaurant menus, the term is loosely used to mean any particularly hot, spicy meat dish with rice, and has in recent years perhaps replaced fish and chips* as the food most closely associated with the working class,* particularly young males; it is a very common takeaway,* the spicier and hotter the better, reversing centuries of British distaste for spicy flavoring. *See also* tandoori.

viper. The only poisonous snake in Britain. Also called an **adder**.

viscose. A type of material Americans call rayon.

viscount. Pronounced vye-count, a noble ranking between a baron* and an earl,* but also sometimes the younger brother of an earl. The title is from the French indicating a vice-count, in England* meaning an assistant to an earl, and was often in the late medieval era used for the sheriff* of a county.* His wife is a **viscountess**; they are formally styled Viscount and Viscountess (Title name) and addressed as My Lord* and My Lady* respectively. Their children, however, are simply the Honourable* (First name Family name).

visitor. (1) A school* inspector. (2) A prison visitor.*

viva. An oral exam, from the Latin *viva voce*, with living voice.

VO. Royal Victorian Order.*

voe. In Scotland,* either a narrow gully in cliff country, or a sharp-sided or narrow inlet.

volatile salts. In the eighteenth and nineteenth centuries, a rising agent for cooking, similar to modern baking soda but made from ammonia. *See also* sal volatile.

vol-au-vent. A small puff pastry usually filled with meat or fish and sauce.

vole. A small animal similar to the mouse or rat found in the countryside, especially in fens* or along streams,* where it is often called a water-rat.

voluntary school. A school* supported neither by tuition fees nor tax money but by public donations. In the twentieth century, this usually means a school run by a religious group, most of which now accept some government grants* and state supervision for secular parts of the curriculum but retain control over religious instruction.

Volunteers. Regiments* of foot soldiers that were not part of the regular army,* a local militia formed among men of a county* or smaller local unit. Originally, these were self-supported units that the men joined for the glory of doing so while retaining their daily work, and they acted as a potential reserve for the army. After the 1881 reorganization of the army, these were standardized as "reserve" units for various regiments of the line,* but before WWI were again reorganized and subsumed into the Territorial Army. *See also* territorials; Yeomanry.

vote of confidence. In Parliament,* a vote taken when an unpopular action has been taken by the government.* In essence, the House of Commons* is asked if it still supports the Prime Minister.* If a significant part of the ruling party members defect, then the Prime Minister can no longer govern and is expected to call a new election.* There is no American equivalent.

voting. The right to vote has grown very gradually. Within chartered boroughs,* local elections* carried their own rules, determined by charter and local practice. But members* of Parliament* were elected only by a very small proportion of the populace. From 1430 until the Reform Bill of 1832, these were men who had a freehold* providing at least 40 shillings* of income* per year, although within boroughs this requirement might vary. After 1832, the franchise was extended to £10 copyholders* and £50 leaseholders, while householders* paying £10 in the boroughs were given the vote. In 1867, the limits were reduced to £5 leaseholders in the counties and any rentpayers of £10 or more in the boroughs; in 1884 extending to householders in the counties. In 1918, the vote was extended to all men over twenty-one and, under pressure from the suffrage movement, to women over thirty (on the assumption that most women wouldn't publicly admit to thirty, even to vote), finally reduced to twenty-one in 1928. In 1969, the voting age was reduced to eighteen.

voting paper. What Americans call a ballot.

voucher. *See* luncheon voucher.

VT. Videotape.

W

WAAC. Women's Auxiliary Army Corps, a WWI force, changed to ATS* in 1938.

WAAF. Women's Auxiliary Air Force, WWII terminology, changed to WRAF* in 1948.

Wadham. A college* of Oxford.*

waffle. To act like a politician; that is, to avoid the question, to change position continually, or to state the obvious as if it were obscure.

wage packet. Pay packet.*

wages clerk. The clerk who handles the payroll.

waistcoat. What Americans call a man's vest. *See also* vest.

waiting woman. A female servant;* very different from a lady-in-waiting.*

waits. Groups of strolling Christmas carolers. Before the early nineteenth century, this was a town band or a group of musicians hired by the town.

wakes. Originally, a night the village* or town* stayed awake. This most often happened on Midsummer's Eve* or the eve of the saint's day of the local church,* when spirits were thought to be at large and a particular danger to sleepers, so that festivals or holidays often followed the vigil. By the turn of the twentieth century, in smaller towns of the north of England* or the industrial Midlands,* the wakes had evolved into a vacation period, sometimes of several days, shared by all the businesses and workers in a single town. But in late twentieth century, the term is rarely used, most preferring holidays.* *See also* bank holiday.

Wales. Wales was once a series of separate domains in the mountainous far west of Britain, in almost constant warfare along the marches* with the English, but by the early thirteenth century, these domains had at last been subdued into a unified kingdom. Uneasy relations with the English continued until in 1282 the English at last conquered the Welsh kings. This did not necessarily bring peace, as Shakespeare's history plays show, but gradually English law and customs were enforced, and in 1543 Henry VIII at last succeeded in bringing about a formal union of England and Wales, with English laws, religion, and language and Welsh representation in Parliament;* formally they became the "united kingdom" of England and Wales, but the union was so complete and long-lasting that Wales was simply accepted as part of England until the twentieth century. Many of the Welsh* retained their own language for family and daily life, but it had almost disappeared from public usage until quite recently, when intellectuals began attempts to preserve and revive it, in hopes of eventual recognition of a separate Welsh nation again. The Welsh rather easily rejected Catholicism, but in the nineteenth century the area, then devoted almost completely to coal mining, was swept by a wave of evangelical fervor that made its people almost uniformly nonconformist.* *See also* Plaid Cymru.

walking. A sport Americans call hiking. Walking holidays are quite common among the middle class,* but the walker usually spends the evening in pubs* or country inns rather than camping out. *See also* rambler.

walking gentleman. Not a gentleman* who takes recreational walks but in the theater what Americans usually call an extra or a super.

walking stick. *See* cane.

walking suit. Not a man's casual suit but a woman's outfit of matching skirt and jacket, with the skirt hem at about ankle length rather than floor length, first appearing around 1901 and in theory disappearing in the 1920s when all skirt lengths rose to the vicinity of the knee. However, many middle- and upper-class* women still wore heavy tweed* suits of matching skirt and jacket in the village* and countryside* until late in the century, and these too were sometimes called walking suits.

walk out. To go courting, to be going out regularly with someone.

Walks. The gardens* of Gray's Inn,* in the late seventeenth century used for public promenading.

Wallace Collection. In London* a museum of paintings mostly drawn from the private collection of a nineteenth-century duke,* especially noted for its eighteenth-century French paintings, famous Dutch paintings, and historical armor.

wallah. Someone in charge of something. Brought from India,* the term is primarily used by military and civil service* types and usually carries a touch of irony or implies that although the wallah may have some authority, such as a **pay wallah**, he isn't really "one of us." A **desk wallah** is a bureaucrat. A **box wallah** was a peddler in India and is thus often a pejorative term for someone in trade.* Thackeray's Boggley Wallah was pure invention, as the term was not used in place-names. *See also* pop-wallah.

wallet. Often not the small thing with money and credit cards but what Americans call a briefcase. *See also* notecase.

wallop. Beer;* the term sounds like a colorful regionalism but was first noted in 1935 and made its mark as WWII military slang.

wall safe. Not a place for jewelry but a cupboard for food in the kitchen.

wally. A spectacular fool. In general, a person "looks a wally" rather than "looks like a wally."

Walthamstow. A suburb of northern London,* in the nineteenth century a center of William Morris's esthetic movement, celebrated in museums there, but the town itself has become synonymous with modern drab, featureless, communities.

Walworth. An area of London* south of Elephant and Castle,* a separate village when Dickens's Wemmick and his Aged P lived there, now indistinguishable from the rest of Southwark.*

Wandsworth. A neighborhood on the south side of the Thames* in London* between Battersea* and Putney;* **Wandsworth Prison** there is the largest British prison, used primarily for recidivists.

wanker. Generally, a useless, incompetent person; more specifically, one who masturbates, as **wank** or **wank off** is to masturbate. Also **whanker**. The RAF* in WWII popularized the term in both meanings.

want. Still sometimes used to mean need, as a person "in want" or a person who "wants for" something. Similarly, Britons often say want to mean "ought to have," as in "That boy wants a good beating."

Wapping. The riverside area of the East End* directly to the east of the Tower,* long the principal dock area of London,* with attendant slums, much bombed in WWII and now part of the large urban renewal project called the Docklands.*

warbler. A small songbird associated with summer, as it returns from migration usually in May. The most common varieties are the **garden warbler**, from its willingness to visit the gardens* of houses as well as the countryside, and the **reed warbler**, which likes the marshes and fens.*

ward. (1) A **ward in Chancery** is a ward whose guardian has been appointed by a court, usually the Chancery.* A ward was almost always an orphan, and the most common guardian was a godparent, but might also be an uncle and aunt until the modern social-service era, when the courts are more likely to appoint foster parents. *See also* christening. (2) A small district within a town or city that elects its own representative on a local council,* usually electing an alderman.*

warden. A supervisor, but only of specific institutions. Primarily, the warden heads an institution where members or patients are residents as well, such as some colleges* at old universities* (e.g., Zuleika Dobson's grandfather), or some charity homes; he is never the head of a prison, who is always called a governor.* A **church warden** is a layman, usually one of a pair, one selected by the parish* priest and the other by the parishioners, who represent the lay public in workaday activities of the church.* Thus, Trollope's Warden Harding, although a member of the clergy,* is not a church warden but a warden who supervises the residential home for the old men maintained by the Church.* *See also* traffic warden.

warder. A prison* guard.

Wardour Street. A street in Soho* in London,* long the site of many major movie company headquarters, so the term is a generic term for the film business. However, before the rise of film it was synonymous with antique dealers who mostly sold fakes; hence, **Wardour Street English** is arch vocabulary of the ye olde Englishe school.

wardrobe. A piece of furniture in which you store clothes, also called an armoire. In modern homes that have what Americans call closets, the closets used for clothes are still often called wardrobes.* *See also* cupboard.

ware. Beware, heard mostly in **ware language**—"watch your language!"

warehouse stores. What Americans call discount houses or discount stores.

warn/warning. *See* caution.

War Office. The ministry* of government* responsible for administering the army* (the navy* was controlled by the Admiralty*), formally organized in 1785, headed by a **Secretary for War**. The Office was officially submerged within the Ministry of Defence* in 1964.

War on Want. A charitable organization aimed at wiping out world poverty. *See also* want.

warrant card. The ID card carried by the police.*

Warwick. Pronounced WORrick, a small town southeast of Birmingham,* known for its medieval castle built and used by the various Earls* of Warwick so prominent in Shakespeare's history plays.

Warwickshire. A county* in western England* surrounding Warwick* and Stratford,* small and agricultural after Birmingham* and Coventry* were separated into a separate metropolitan county in 1974.* Associated with Shakespeare, it is also Isaac Walton's and George Eliot's countryside.*

was at. A very specialized but socially significant usage, meaning attended, though not necessarily graduated from, a public school,* as in "he was at Eton,*" and thus is "one of us." So far as I can find, no one ever "was at" a comprehensive.*

wash. (1) In stock exchange* practice, to unnecessarily buy and sell shares* in order to generate commissions. (2) Among the genteel,* one often asks a guest if he would like a wash or needs to wash his hands as a euphemism for, "Do you need to use the toilet?" (3) Something that **won't wash** is not dirty but rather is unreasonable or unbelievable.

Wash. A large bay in eastern England,* the one that looks on the map like a notch cut out of the coast north of Norfolk.*

wash cloth. Generally used only for a dishcloth; the cloth for washing a person is usually called a flannel.*

washing powder. Laundry soap. *See also* washing up.

washing up. Doing the dishwashing. Hence, **washing-up powder** is often different from washing powder* and is in fact often a **washing-up liquid**.

wassail. Once common at Christmas* celebrations, the wassail was a toast drunk from a large communal bowl; in the twentieth century it has all but disappeared except in ye olde Englishe festivities for tourists.

wastebook. A daily journal or running record used in bookkeeping.

waste ground. What Americans call a vacant lot.

waste-paper basket. Never shortened to the American wastebasket.

watch out for. Not as in America "be careful of," but rather just "look for."

water biscuit. *See* biscuit.

water closet. *See* bathroom.

water hen. *See* moorhen.

water ice. What Americans call a sherbet.

Waterloo. The battle in 1815 in Belgium in which the British army* and allies defeated Napoleon for the last time was a cause of great rejoicing and patriotic fervor at the time and has continued to be one of the most often memorialized events in British history, ranking perhaps just below Trafalgar.* **Waterloo Station** is on the south side of the Thames* in London* just across from the Whitehall* area; the principal terminus of many train routes to the southern parts of England, it also is a major connection for Underground* service. **Waterloo Bridge** crosses the Thames, connecting the Strand* to the south in **Waterloo Road** that runs past the station and leads to the new South Bank* arts centers; the previous bridge (1817) was much admired for its nine arches of considerable architectural flair (although it was also sometimes known as a haunt of prostitutes) but the new version (1945) is purely functional, with extremely heavy auto traffic.

water meadow. A meadow* that is regularly flooded by the stream running by it, sometimes naturally but often intentionally by irrigation.

waterproof. What Americans call a raincoat.

Watford. A large suburban town northwest of London,* in the mid–twentieth century noted for its publishing industries; most magazines of the nation, though edited in London, were actually printed and published in Watford. The **Watford Gap,** however, is quite different, a broad valley just southeast of Rugby* between the hills at the northern extreme of the Cotswolds;* the Roman road called Watling Street* passed through the "gap" and modern canals, railroads, and now motorways* have followed its lead, so that numerous important junctions of all three lie within the vicinity and the gap itself is sometimes seen as the southern boundary of the Midlands.*

Watling Street. A Roman road running almost perfectly straight from London* to near modern Leicester* and then turning west to near modern Shrewsbury,* a route followed by much of the modern A5,* leaving London by way of the modern Maida Vale.* The other portion (although not always called Watling Street) took an equally straight route southeast from London to Dover,* on the route followed closely by the modern A2, making its major turn at Canterbury.* This, rather than the Pilgrim's Way,* was the most common route used by medieval pilgrims to Canterbury; it would have been used by Chaucer's pilgrims leaving from Southwark* and was also the Dover Road* down which David Copperfield walked.

wax jacket. A weatherproof cotton jacket, both lightweight and warm.

way in/out. These terms are generally preferred to the American enter and exit.

WC. The most genteel euphemism for toilet, from the water closets that were the first water-flushed toilets, introduced in the early eighteenth century and suddenly abandoned in favor of the outdoor earth closet. *See* bathroom.

w/e. Weekend.*

Weald. A large predominantly wooded area of Kent,* Surrey,* and East Sussex,* the woods interspersed with farms and estates.

wear. Put up with, as in "I won't wear such nonsense."

weasel words. Statements that are purposely ambiguous, statements Americans would say could be weaseled out of. *See also* stoat.

weatherboard. What Americans call clapboard.

weathercock. What Americans call a weathervane.

Webb. A type of lettuce similar to American iceberg.

wedding. From 1753–1837, weddings had to be held in a Church of England* church* to be legal, but after the formation of the national Registry,* couples could be married in civil ceremonies at the local register office.* The Church of England wedding service is the model for most such services in America. The traditional **wedding cake** is usually multilayered and multitiered with white icing, as in America, but it is also usually a fruitcake rather than a white or sponge cake. *See also* banns; divorce; marriage.

wee. As an adjective, small, tiny, cute; as a noun, a short period of time, as in "bide a wee." The curious thing about this word is that it was originally commonly found in England* during Shakespeare's time. But in the late eighteenth and early nineteenth centuries it became a signature word for Scots,* and now is so much part of the Scottish stereotype that it is almost never used elsewhere except in an imitation of a Scot. A **wee drop** or a **wee dram**, however, is a drink of whisky* that is rarely wee.

week. When used with a day, as in "Monday week," this means either a week in the future (a "week from Monday") or a week in the past (a "week ago Monday"), depending on the tense of the verb.

weekend. Until very recently, this was a term used only by the middle and professional classes.* What with the English Sunday,* for most people the weekend was basically limited to Saturday* night, except for occasional observances of St. Monday.* The OED shows the earliest use of the term in 1870, which corresponds with the rise of the suburban house or country house* for the professional and business classes. For the most part, the men in these houses found it inconvenient to do little more than commute to and from their fancy new homes during the week, so many used the weekend as a time to entertain, during which guests were invited to stay and dinners or parties were held. Guests arrived on Saturday afternoon, had a dinner* or party, spent Sunday in country pleasures, games, or other casual activities around Sunday dinner, and then left after Monday breakfast, as professional people could of course be a few hours late getting to the office. Tradition says the boundaries of the weekend were originally defined by the Foreign Office*: Foreign dispatches arrived from Dover* at 10:30 and were not sorted and distributed until after 11:00, so people who cleared their desks early Saturday afternoon would have no work to do on Monday until at least 11:00. Although widespread use of the automobile and changes in modern office and work hours have encouraged more weekends on the American pattern (late Friday afternoon to Sunday evening), the British still for the most part think of the weekend as starting Saturday afternoon; even a **dirty weekend**, a quick weekend away for illicit sex, is more likely to occupy Saturday and Sunday nights, as in Alan Ayckbourn's *Norman Conquests*, rather than Friday and Saturday.

Weetabix. A brand of breakfast* cereal, whole wheat flakes shaped into something similar to a small American shredded wheat biscuit, that turns almost instantaneously into a soggy pulp when milk is added.

weird. In Scotland,* destiny or fate, although an archaic term no longer heard; to **dree one's weird** was to accept or give in to one's fate, an idiom apparently invented by Walter Scott and then passing into Scottish usage.

Welch. *See* Welsh.

well and truly. Absolutely, completely, as "well and truly finished."

wellies. Wellingtons.*

wellingtons. Several types of knee-high boots. These were worn as a part of normal men's fashion in the early nineteenth century, especially by the Duke of Wellington who gave them their name. However, late in the century a rubber version appeared, and it quickly became adopted as standard wear for all outdoor work in the rain, so that in the twentieth century, wellingtons are synonymous with heavy-duty rain boots.

Wells. A small town near Bath* known for its cathedral* begun in the twelfth century and called by many guidebooks the most beautiful in England.

Welsh. The English long have regarded the Welsh as a primitive, superstitious, and emotional people, like Shakespeare's Glendower, but no one has any plausible explanation of why backing out of a debt is called **welshing**. In the modern world, Wales has meant coal and nonconformist* religion, and the stereotypical Welshman is a short, dark-haired extrovert who is a great singer (from all that hymn singing) with a ready laugh and working class* habits. **Welsh rabbit** is a dish of melted cheese and beer poured over toast, a reference to both the Welsh diet of cheese and the poverty of the region; rabbit is in fact the real name of the dish, but it was made more "respectable" as **Welsh rarebit** during the late nineteenth century, to little point except confusion, as common pronunciation continues to be rabbit. **Welsh nuts** are a high quality coal that comes in very small pieces. For obscure reasons, the Welsh regiments* in the army* officially spell this as **Welch**.

Wembley. The largest stadium in the Greater London* area, located in suburban Wembley northwest of the Paddington* area, used for the annual Cup* Final, roughly equivalent to the American Super Bowl, and other sporting events, outdoor rock concerts, and so forth, that require seating for huge crowds.

wen. A congested city, from an ancient word meaning tumor or wart (Shakespeare called Falstaff a wen); the **Great Wen** is London.*

Wendy house. A child's playhouse, named for the house in *Peter Pan*.

went. A corruption of wend, for travel, used in many parts of the countryside* to indicate a path or road. Hence, the **four wents** is a crossroads.

Wesleyan. A name often used to indicate the Methodists,* due to their founding by the Wesleys.

Wessex. Originally a kingdom of the Saxons centered on the Chilterns* before the Normans invaded, at which point the kingdom disappeared. Hardy's Wessex is purely fictional and unrelated geographically, situated much further west, primarily in modern Dorset.*

West Country. The southwestern area of England.* There are no specific boundaries but it is generally west of Winchester,* roughly the counties* of Cornwall,* Devon,* Somerset,* Gloucestershire,* and Wiltshire.*

West End. Originally the area to the immediate west of the old City* walls, much more fashionable than the East End* as it lay along the route to Westminster.* In general, it is the area along the Strand,* still noted for prestigious hotels and shops.* But this was also the area in which the eighteenth and nineteenth century theaters grew up around Covent Garden* and Drury Lane,* and the term is now more often synonymous with theater, restaurants, and similar entertainment, used much like Broadway in America, although the theater district now extends from the Strand through Soho* to Piccadilly.*

Western Road. The old highway from London* to Bristol,* followed now by the A4;* it left the old City* by way of the Strand.*

Westminster. A palace* in London* on the Thames* now housing the Houses of Parliament.* Begun by William I, parts of the original still remain inside the latest rebuilding after an 1834 fire. Since 1332 it has contained a room used by a national parliamentary body. The current building houses both Commons* and Lords* and is usually identified by the clock tower called Big Ben.* Westminster is often used as a synonym for all the legislative parts of the government.* However, prior to the mid–nineteenth century, Westminster was a synonym for all royal* government, due to the City* of London's legal separation from the area called Westminster, where the monarch and the court resided, first in Westminster Palace and then in Whitehall* Palace. Until 1883, it was also synonymous with the national legal courts,* as all royal courts held sessions there. For the school, *See* Westminster School.

Westminster, City of. The part of London* initially centering on the royal court* at Westminster* Palace, outside the legal jurisdiction of the City* of London and thus over the years developing its own local governmental practices and laws. Before the nineteenth century, London technically consisted of two cities,* London and Westminster, plus the borough* of Southwark,* all of which had begun to grow together but were still governed separately. After organization of the County of London in 1888 and later of Greater London* in 1965, Westminster retained its independence and even expanded its boundaries, and currently it includes not only the areas immediately around Westminster but also most of the West End,* Mayfair,* Soho,* the major parks,* and the Paddington* areas as well.

Westminster Abbey. Originally the church of a Benedictine abbey to the west of the City* of London* along the Thames,* the abbey* has been the primary church of English royalty* since Edward the Confessor built the first portions and was buried there. As such, it has been regularly used for coronations, royal weddings, and other state occasions and also is the site of graves or memorials for many of the nation's most significant persons, both nobles* and commoners.* *See also* cathedral; Poet's Corner; St. Paul's.

Westminster Cathedral. A Roman Catholic cathedral* in London,* home of the ranking Catholic archbishop in Britain;* finished in 1910, it is located near Victoria Station* and is in no way related to Westminster Abbey.*

Westminster School. A public school* founded by Elizabeth I and housed on the grounds of Westminster Abbey,* still one of the most influential of such schools. The schoolboys also provide the choirs for the Abbey.

Westmorland. A county of England* in the northwest, lying between Cumberland* and Lancashire* and containing much of the Lake District,* before tourism devoted primarily to sheep grazing. In 1974 it was subsumed in the new larger county of Cumbria.*

Weston-super-Mare. Usually pronounced mare not mah-ray, a resort town near Bristol* at the mouth of the Severn;* by all accounts a pleasant resort but decidedly on the wrong coast and originally working class,* so now patronized for the most part only by the conservative or the unfashionable.

wet. In the 19th century, drunken or acting as if drunk. In the 1920s the term resurfaced as racy slang for dull, stupid, or what Americans now call wimpy, then faded somewhat only to reappear in the 1980s as political usage for Conservatives* who did not unwaveringly support all Thatcherite policies, in American terms someone who claimed to be a conservative but still had "liberal" sympathies. *See also* dry.

Weymouth. A port on the south coast of England* near the Bill of Portland,* popularized as a seaside resort by George III's regular visits. This is Hardy's Budmouth, and *The Trumpet Major* is a good description of the place at its fashionable height in the early nineteenth century.

whacking. Unusually large or strong, often seen or heard as **whacking great**.

what. The stereotypical exclamation of public school twits,* military types, and comic old lords,* often as "Eh, what?" This is not intended to actually be a question, but is merely an equivalent to the modern American "you know," used to underline or emphasize a statement, as in "not quite the thing, what?" and it's not actually clear if anyone outside comic stereotypes actually says this with any regularity.

what ho. *See* I say; top hole.

what price. Originally "what is this really worth when you consider everything?," as in *What Price Glory?*, probably from racing odds, but by WWII it was also used much more generally to mean "what do you think of?," as in "what price a goose for the dinner?"

What's all this then? The stereotyped first words out of the mouth of a bobby* on reaching a disturbance or crime.

What's the odds? Not a question about betting odds but rather used to mean "what's the difference?"

wheat. *See* corn.

whelk. A shellfish, larger than a winkle* but eaten in much the same way, particularly popular on holidays at the seashore, although declining in popularity in recent years. They were so easy to sell that **couldn't run a whelk stand** is commonly used to indicate an incompetent.

when he/she/it's at home. A very widespread idiom, almost always used as part of a question, such as "What's that when it's at home?" To ask it is to ask, "What does it really mean?" but it also implies that the person or topic under discussion is pretentious, pompous, or unnecessarily euphemistic.

when pigs fly. A widespread idiom used for never, similar to and as widely used as the American "when Hell freezes over."

wherry. A rowboat large enough to carry passengers: sometimes also a light, small barge.

Whig. From the late seventeenth century, one of the two primary English political parties.* Sometimes said to stand for "We Hope in God," the name was originally applied as an insult, from a group of peasant Scots* rebels, to those who opposed putting James II on the throne, and the party in early days came to be associated with a mild form of antimonarchism and what passed for liberalism, meaning support for large landholders and wealthy merchants rather than absolute monarchial rights. By the late eighteenth century, it was primarily the party of those who were "out" or who disliked William Pitt, who controlled the Tory* party. As outsiders, they supported reforms, and in a brief period of power instituted the Great Reform Bill of 1832, shortly afterward coming to be called the Liberal* party.

whiles. Sometimes, primarily in Scotland* and northern England.*

whinge. To whine or complain; also **winge.***

Whip. (1) In Parliament,* a member* whose duty is to see that the back benchers* show up and vote as necessary for party* proposals. The name suggests the difficulty he sometimes faces. The Whip is the most significant party member not actually in the Cabinet,* because he actually persuades or "twists the arms" to get the votes. This is always done in a gentlemanly fashion, of course: When a vote is needed, the Whip sends a note, also called a whip, to the missing member requesting his or her presence, underlined to show the importance and urgency; thus a "three-line whip" is underlined three times and means "Get over here now, Or Else!" (2) In fox hunting,* the person who whips in the hounds,* also called a **whipper-in.**

whippet. A dog similar to the greyhound but usually a bit smaller, used sometimes for hunting, as greyhounds once were, and for dog racing.

whip-round. A collection for donations, as in a whip-round at the office for a funeral wreath, equivalent to American "passing the hat."

Whipsnade. A large zoo in the Chilterns,* run by the London Zoo* and designed so that the animals live in large open enclosures rather than in cages.

whisk. Applied both to the electric appliance Americans call a mixer as well as to the utensil Americans also call a whisk; also called an **egg whisk**.

whiskey. What Americans call Irish whiskey. *See also* whisky.

whisky. What Americans call Scotch. *See also* whiskey.

whist. Until the invention of bridge,* the primary social card game of Britons of all classes. The game is played by two pairs of partners, and the object is to take tricks by playing the highest card; the scoring system is comparatively complex, and it was Edmund Hoyle's attempt to codify this that made his name synonymous with the rules of card games. Unlike bridge, there is no bidding, first play going automatically to the person on dealer's left, and the trump suit is determined by the dealer turning over the last card of the deal. The partnership requires intricate interplay without discussion (one theory of the name is the constant insistance that the players stay silent), but nonetheless it was the primary social card game in clubs,* coffeehouses,* and at country house* weekends.* The game began to lose its social cachet in the 1920s as bridge became a middle class* passion, but whist has not completely died out. A **whist drive** is a form of tournament or party at which whist is played with progressive partners and/or opponents, often organized by the vicar's* wife for charity purposes.

Whitaker. *Whitaker's Almanac*, the foremost almanac since 1868.

Whitbread. A major brewer of beer.*

Whitby. A port on the northeast coast of England* near Scarborough,* in the seventeenth century a major ship-building center, and in the whaling era the center of England's whaling activity.

white. Of coffee* or tea,* with cream or milk. *See also* whitener.

Whitechapel. In London* the part of the East End* close outside the east wall of the City,* inland from Wapping* and east of Aldgate.* Almost from the first, this was the poorest of the poor neighborhoods, famous worldwide for its slums and often used in the nineteenth century as a synonym for all of the East End; Jack the Ripper's crimes were called the Whitechapel Murders, for example, although the first occurred in Spitalfields.* Although there had been Jews* in the area since the seventeenth century, the area was flooded with refugees in the late nineteenth century, making it a center of sweatshops in the clothing trade and encouraging markets such as Petticoat Lane;* by the late twentieth, many of the slums had been cleared and the Jews replaced by a new wave of Asian immigrants, many still in the clothing business.

White Cliffs. *See* Dover.

white ensign. The identifying flag of the Royal Navy.* *See also* ensign.

white feather. A symbol of cowardice, so widely understood since the late nineteenth century that proper young girls during WWI would try to pin them on strangers of military age found in civilian clothes; the term has for the most part fallen from use except in historical fiction.

Whitefriars. An area of slums south of Fleet Street,* demolished during the late nineteenth century, forcing most of the Cockneys* into the East End.*

Whitehall. A street in London* leading from Trafalgar Square* to Westminster,* along which most of the major government offices are located. Hence, it is often used figuratively to mean the government.* The street takes its name from the **Palace of Whitehall** which was originally built by Wolsey, confiscated by Henry VIII, expanded in 1622, and used as the principal residence of the monarch from Elizabeth I until a fire destroyed it in 1698. St. James's Park* was its backyard, so to speak.

Whitehall farce. Not a comment on government activity but a set of successful examples of "British farce" in the 1950s at the Whitehall Theatre, of the type parodied in the recent hit *Noises Off*.

White Horse. There are several of these figures in various parts of England,* each cut into the side of a hill by removing all the turf so that the white chalk underneath is visible in the shape of a horse. The most famous is southeast of Oxford* in the **Vale of the White Horse**, a wide river valley whose horse figure is 350-feet long and is visible all across the valley. The figures are premedieval and no "experts" agree as to their purpose or significance.

whitener. Artificial cream. *See also* white.

white night. A sleepless night.

white paper. A printed statement of government* policy. *See also* Blue Book; green paper.

White's. A gentlemen's club* in London* in St. James's* Street, the first such, founded in 1693 as a club for Tories* and still extremely conservative in membership and practices, its members noted for limited intellectual capacity coupled with a limitless capacity for liquor.

white tie. In the twentieth century, an indication of "formal" dress. Invitations or announcements saying "white tie" meant tails,* stiff shirt, and white tie for men; as opposed to **black tie**, meaning the shorter dinner jacket,* cummerbund, and black tie. Women could judge from this clue the level of formality and jewelry that would be appropriate for their evening gowns.

white wax. The substance Americans call paraffin; British paraffin* has nothing to do with wax or candles.

Whitmonday. The Monday following Whitsunday,* one of the original bank holidays* but now taken on the last Monday in May whether actually Whitmonday or not. *See* Whitsun.

Whitstable. A seaside town on the southern shore of the Thames* Estuary, just north of Canterbury,* noted primarily for its oyster trade until in the twentieth century it became a minor seaside resort and home to a number of lower middle class* retirees.

Whitsun/sunday/tide. Whitsunday, the seventh Sunday after Easter,* is usually called Pentecost in American churches. This and the Monday and Tuesday following were one of the major holidays of the year, reflected in selection of Whitmonday* as a bank holiday.* This was a time of feasts and games, often called **Whitsun Ales**, especially when the food and drink were used to raise charity money for local parishes.* Most village fêtes* occur about this time, even today when most of the old local customs have died out. Whitsunday is a quarter day* in Scotland.*

wholemeal. What Americans call whole wheat, as in wholemeal bread.

whortleberry. Another name for the bilberry.*

WI. Women's Institute.*

wick. Nerves or feelings, as in "That really gets on my wick," generally used in Cockney* or military slang.

wicket. In cricket,* roughly analogous to home plate in baseball. The wicket itself is made of three vertical sticks, or stumps,* lightly stabbed into the ground; balanced on top of these three stumps are two small wooden pegs called **bails**, the whole wicket looking like a tall *m*. There are two wickets sixty-six feet apart. The batsman* stands in front of one, while the bowler* must throw the ball from behind the other one. Points are scored by hitting the ball and running between the wickets. The batsman is put out when the wicket is broken by a thrown ball or by a player holding the ball while the batsman is outside of the crease* after hitting the ball, but he may also be put out if the wicket is broken by a bowled ball or if his own bat hits the wicket while swinging. Unlike baseball, the bowler does not bowl to the batsman; rather, he "attacks" the wicket, in hopes of knocking over the wicket, and the batsman hits the ball to protect the wicket. In addition, the part of the field between the two wickets is sometimes called a wicket rather than a pitch.* *See also* sticky wicket; wide.

wicketkeeper. In cricket,* the fielder roughly analogous to the American baseball catcher. He stands directly behind the wicket* and batsman* and fields any bowled balls that the batsman does not hit or short hits behind the batsman and receives throws from other fielders in an attempt to put the running batsman out by knocking over the wicket while the batsman is out of the crease.*

widdershins. Counterclockwise; hence, used generically for the wrong direction or the wrong way to do things.

wide. (1) Originally, lax or immoral, fading from use in the mid–nineteenth century. Then, in the 1930s the term **wide boy** surfaced, meaning someone who lived by his wits at the boundaries of legality; this meaning, however, may have grown out of the cricket term below. (2) In cricket,* a ball bowled* so far away from the batsman* that it could not possibly strike the wicket.* If so ruled by the umpire, a wide counts as a run for the batting team; however, the batsman may try to score by running if the ball is so wide it rolls away from the wicketkeeper,* and he may also try to hit the ball as well, but if he does so and the ball is caught in the air by a fielder, he is not out.

wideawake. A soft felt hat with a wide brim.

widgeon. A kind of duck primarily found in Scotland.*

widow's benefit. Various payments to widows under the national insurance,* in 1988 replacing a previous payment but still colloquially called a death benefit.* These payments currently include a one-time lump sum of £1,000, an allowance for support of children remaining at home, and/or a pension lasting until the woman is sixty and qualifies for her own pension. *See also* child benefit; single parent benefit.

wife-sale. *See* divorce.

wig. As a verb, to do what Americans call chewing someone out. A **wigging** is thus a stiff lecture or reprimand.

Wigan. A coal and industrial town in northwestern England* near Manchester.* In the 1920s, Wigan was synonymous with the provincial, good for a laugh just by saying the name, rather like Scunthorpe* today.

Wight, Isle of. *See* Isle of Wight.

wilderness. When said of politicians, the time spent out of office. Winston Churchill spent the most famous time in the wilderness during the 1930s.

Willie. *See* John Thomas.

willow. The cricket* bat,* from the wood from which it is made.

Wilts. Abbreviation for Wiltshire.*

Wiltshire. A county* or shire* in southwestern England,* primarily dairy and grazing, the bulk occupied by the barren Salisbury* Plain; the shire has a reputation for strange people and stranger happenings. In 1974, the coastal areas were separated to form the county of Avon.* *See also* moonraker.

Wimbledon. Originally a village on the eastern side of Richmond Park,* it grew into a prosperous town in the eighteenth century. The **Wimbledon Common** was one of the earliest commons* to figure in national battles for preservation of open space, but the principal fame of the town belongs to the Wimbledon All England Lawn Tennis Championship played there in June since 1877, the most prestigious and fashionable tennis championship in the world.

Wimpole Street. A street in London* north of Oxford Street.* Although known primarily as the home of Elizabeth Barrett before she married Browning, it was the London center for doctors' offices (and homes) and thus all but synonymous with the professional upper–middle class,* for example, Shaw's Henry Higgins. In the twentieth century, however, the most fashionable doctors have moved to nearby Harley Street.*

Wimpy bar. Now a generic term for a place to get hamburgers or other fast foods, from the first London* chain of American-style burger restaurants, named after the character in the American Popeye cartoons.

winceyette. The cloth Americans generally call flannelette.

Winchester. (1) A town near modern Southampton,* in Saxon times the capital of England and a major center of the wool trade until the sixteenth century. The cathedral* is one of the oldest in the country, the present building dating to the eleventh century. Until eclipsed by Oxford* and Cambridge,* the cathedral was the primary center of learning for all of England. It is called Wintonchester in Hardy's works and was the model for Trollope's Barchester. (2) Technically **Winchester College**, located in Winchester, one of the oldest public schools,* noted for especially high academic standards and intellectual graduates while still conferring enormous social status. The school motto is "Manners maketh man." *See also* Wykehamist.

windcheater. The jacket Americans call a windbreaker; breaking and wind are only used together in Britain to mean a fart.

winder. On a watch, what Americans call the watch stem.

Windermere. The largest lake in the Lake District.*

Windmill Theatre. A theatre in Soho* in London,* famous in the late 1930s and during the WWII years* for its nude women, who were allowed to perform only as long as they never moved, since movement would legally make them sexual rather than artistic displays. Times change, and the theatre has long since been driven out of business by entertainment that makes its daring seem almost childishly innocent. *See also* Raymond's.

window tax. A tax begun in 1696 not as an attempt to regulate windows but as a primitive form of graduated tax, in which the wealthy ostensibly paid more than the poor. After 1782, when the rate for houses with more than ten windows went up, the tax was widely avoided, many householders bricking up windows or building new houses with fewer windows than necessary, until it was reduced in the early nineteenth century and finally eliminated in 1851.

windrow. A row of cut and raked or piled hay or sheaves (sometimes peat), arranged so as to let the wind dry it before restacking it for permanent storage.

Windscale. The first British nuclear electric power plant, on the seacoast of the Lake District,* now called **Sellafield**.

windscreen. The part of a car Americans call the windshield.

Windsor. A town on the Thames* west of London* and site of the primary home of the English monarchs since William the Conqueror began a fortress there. **Windsor Castle**, begun by Henry II, was extensively remodeled for George IV, and all the various kings* and queens* have lived there regularly during their reigns. Queen Elizabeth II uses it for the most part as a country house,* spending most weeks in London and most weekends at Windsor. In 1917, George V officially changed the family name of the royal family* to that of the **House of Windsor**, primarily to give to what was in fact a German family tree a good English name during the war with Germany, and so it has remained since. In theory, this should change when Prince Charles succeeds to the throne, as his father's family was not Windsor, but Elizabeth II decreed in 1952 that her successor would still be known as a Windsor. The **Duke of Windsor** was a title* given to the former King Edward VIII after his abdication in 1936 and is not a title that has been used for any other person. *See also* Buckingham Palace; Balmoral; Sandringham.

wind up, put the. A widespread idiom meaning to disturb or upset; to **get the wind up** is to be disturbed or frightened.

wine bar. A bar that serves wine, and often food, rather than beer* and liquor like a pub.* Although some have been in business for decades, they became faddishly popular during the 1970s and were closely associated with the British version of yuppies.

wine lake. Used in the 1980s by columnists and politicians about the vast quantities of wine stockpiled by the EEC,* particularly in France,* in order to maintain prices artificially. *See also* butter mountain.

wing. (1) The part of a car Americans call the fender. *See also* fender. (2) In hockey* and football* (soccer), the two players on the outside ends of the forward* line, offensive players and among the best athletes on the team. Also called **winger**. The term is also used for a threequarter back* in rugby* stationed near the edge of the field. (3) In the RAF,* a unit of several squadrons,* commanded by a **Wing Commander**. *See also* Appendix V.

winge. *See* whinge.*

winkle. (1) A tiny sea snail, eaten mostly by the working class,* going out of favor in late twentieth century. **Winkle pickers** are a man's shoe with very sharp toes, from the small sharp instrument used to pick the winkles from their shells. Sometimes called a **periwinkle**. *See also* whelk. (2) To pry out or to discover after much digging around, from prying the winkle out of its shell.

wireless. The radio. After the rise of TV, the radio began to be called the radio, so wireless is fading from use at present, but in the first half of the century it was the primary term in use.

wire mesh. What Americans call window screen.

wire netting. What Americans call chicken wire.

wire screen. What Americans call a screen door, rarely seen on homes.

wire tray. What Americans call a cake rack.

wire wool. What Americans call steel wool.

Wisden. An annual almanac of cricket* since 1864, in standardized volumes with yellow covers, regarded as *the* authority for cricket scores and history.

witness box. What Americans call a witness stand in a courtroom.

wizard. Slang meaning great or wonderful, usually associated with schoolboys prior to WWII and the RAF.*

wobbly, throw a. Have a fit or throw a tantrum.

Woburn Abbey. *See* Bedford.

wodge. A lump or irregular piece.

wog. Originally, an Egyptian. From that, it was expanded to include many other racial groups. British racial epithets are, like many other nations', sometimes used very specifically and sometimes very generally. Wog is one of the most flexible, for there have been many who say "all wogs begin at Calais," on the coast of France. In a broad sense in late nineteenth century, wog was applied to Egyptians and Arabs, and possibly to Greeks and Turks who live in the same vicinity and are dark,* while nigger* was applied to Indians, not Africans. Only gradually, after British expansion into Kenya and South Africa and then later under the influence of American entertainment, did nigger shift in the early twentieth to mean black African, while wog shifted to mean Indian. For the most part, the British refused until very recently to see this and similar terms as offensive or insulting.

Woking. Pronounced WOE-king, a large town west of London,* almost completely devoted to housing for commuters.

wold. High open land, not used for cultivation. The **Wolds** is the upland area of northeastern Lincolnshire.* *See also* Cotswolds; Weald.

Wolverhampton. A town north of Birmingham,* famous for its toy manufacturing but usually seen as Little Nell saw it, a nightmarish industrial wasteland.

woman named. In a divorce* case, the woman with whom the husband is supposed to have committed adultery. *See also* corespondent.

Women's Institute. A social, educational, and charitable organization for women, usually middle class,* national in membership but confined primarily to small town life in their activities; ironically referred to as **jam and Jerusalem** for their most common activities in earlier days of the 1920s, making jam and singing *Jerusalem.**

Women's Land Army. *See* land girls.

women's suffrage. *See* voting.

wonky. (1) Rickety, unstable, unreliable. (2) Crooked, illegal.

wood. Generally used in the singular, while Americans prefer the plural woods, to mean an area of trees, usually also meaning natural growth as opposed to man-made plantations.* *See also* copse; forest; hanger.

woodbine. A plant similar to what Americans call honeysuckle. **Woodbines** are a brand of cigarettes, often used generically for all cigarettes.

Woodstock. A village near Oxford,* before the Civil War* site of a royal residence and later the site of Blenheim.*

wood straw. The packing material in the form of wood shavings Americans call excelsior.

wool. In addition to the cloth, this is also used to mean yarn.

woollies. Any nice warm wool garment. Most of the time this term means a sweater of some type, but it can also refer to underwear, especially that worn by old ladies.

woolsack. The cushion used by the Lord Chancellor* when attending Parliament.*

woolton pie. *See* pie.

Woolwich. Pronounced WOOLidge, a riverside village east of London* transformed by Henry VIII into the major naval dockyards of the nation, in 1716 becoming the **Royal Arsenal**, the major weapons facility of the nation until 1963 and also home to the army* school for artillery and engineering officers until it merged with Sandhurst* in 1940; also now the site of the Thames Barrier.*

Worcester. Pronounced WOOSter. (1) A town in west-central England,* significant especially in eighteenth and early nineteenth century industry for its gloves, porcelain, and the famous sauce that was invented here in 1825 (often in Britain called Worcester sauce rather than Worcestershire sauce). (2) A college* of Oxford,* one of the smallest and traditionally the poorest.

Worcestershire. A county* or shire* of England* on the southeastern border of Wales, primarily hilly country with orchards; in 1974 joined with Hereford* to make a single new county. *See also* Evesham.

words, have. To have not just words but angry words; hence, to quarrel. Different from **have a word with**, which means to discuss or more often to advise so as to prevent a developing problem.

work, in. To have a job.

workday. What Americans call a weekday.

workhouse. *See* Poor Laws.

working class. This term is used for the broad majority of urban workers who do not fit into any of the middle class slots, meaning in practice people who work in factories or with machines or do some form of manual labor.

This is an urban phenomenon, and primarily only since the late nineteenth century, when urban society had finally been accepted as the norm for most people. The significant factor, when compared to American use of the term, is that the large group accepted itself as a separate broad class with its own culture and, unlike American factory workers, made no attempt to adapt that culture to appear to be middle class. It had its own religions—primarily Methodist* or other nonconformist;* its own entertainments—the music halls;* its own social centers—the pubs;* its own slang and dialects; eventually its own political party—Labour;* its own newspapers; and rather than being embarrassed by these things, as a group it became rather aggressively proud of them. Strong divisions existed within the general class, particularly between the respectable, religious, teetotalling portions and the Alfred Doolittle brigades, but even the most respectable person made little or no attempt to cross the line into the middle class. In recent years, the term has come to imply unemployed persons with this cultural background, as most of the nation's contemporary unemployment is in these kinds of jobs. For more detail, *See* Appendix III. *See also* accent; Cockney; gin; North; rhyming slang.

working party. A committee with only temporary duties.

work of national importance. During WWII, a job that could exempt a man from military service.

works. Always used in the plural to mean a singular factory.

works outing. What Americans call a company picnic.

work-to-rule. An industrial action* in which all workers follow all the rules and procedures of their jobs down to the tiniest detail. This procedure is often used in lieu of a strike and is often more effective, since in most cases this can paralyze any business or governmental department so completely that nothing gets done while the employer still has to pay the workers.

work your ticket. To get out of a contract. The derivation comes from the military, where the ticket was the certificate of honorable discharge, and one wanting out of the army* had to "work his ticket" to get out without losing the honorable discharge.

world and his wife. Lots of people, like the American "everybody and his dog."

World Service. *See* BBC.

Wormwood Scrubs. A prison* in London* in the Hammersmith* area since 1874, often used as synonymous with prison itself. The name comes from the open space with scrubby little trees on which the prison was built, not from slang for punishments there.

Worthing. A large resort town on the southern coast of England* west of Brighton,* considered quite dull and sedate due to the large number of retirees who settle there.

Worzel Gummidge. The scarecrow in a popular children's TV show.

wot. Lower class* and provincial pronunciation and spelling of what; especially common is the use of wot or **as wot** to mean which, who, or that, as in "the man as wot left the parcel" or "the man wot came in late."

wotcher. Hello or hi ("what cheer?"), used among the working class.*

WPC. Woman police constable. *See* PC.

WRAC. Women's Royal Army Corp, since 1948. *See also* army.

WRAF. Women's Royal Air Force, since 1948. *See also* air force.

wrangler. Not a cowboy but a graduate with honours* in math at Cambridge.*

wrapover. A skirt Americans call a wraparound.

wren. The smallest of the common birds of Britain,* usually brownish in color, nesting in trees or hedges* and usually found year round.

WREN. Women's Royal Navy. (The *E* means nothing and was added to simplify pronunciation of the acronym.) *See* navy.

writer. In Scotland,* a unique usage indicating a member of the legal profession, such as a solicitor* or a notary.

writing block. Not the agony of staring at a blank page but a tablet of paper to write on.

wrong'un. A bad person, from a cricket* term often applied to a googly.*

WRVS. Women's Royal Voluntary Service, a national charity organization originally formed for WWII air raid duties, now providing aid such as meals-on-wheels or disaster relief.

Wykehamist. A graduate of Winchester,* from the founder's name.

wynd. In Scotland,* a narrow alley.

X

X. For a movie, the code indicating children under eighteen are not allowed.

x factor. In labor relations, any special situation requiring additional pay, such as split shifts.

Y

yard. A space covered with concrete; before the twentieth century, this was merely an enclosed space, such as the yard of an inn. What Americans call a yard around a house, the British call a garden.*

Yard. Scotland Yard.*

Yarmouth. There are two of these: One is a port and popular resort on the eastern coast in Norfolk,* once the source of most bloaters;* in *David Copperfield*, Mr. Peggotty's boat/house rested on the shore there, and Steerforth drowned in the harbor. The other Yarmouth is a much smaller port on the Isle of Wight* that was significant in naval affairs during the sixteenth century.

yarn. What Americans call embroidery thread; what Americans call yarn is usually called wool.*

year dot. Long, long ago; Americans usually say "the year one."

yellow. Yellow lines are painted in the street parallel to the curb to indicate parking restrictions. A **single yellow** means no parking 8 A.M. to 6 P.M. (except Sundays); a **double yellow** means no parking ever; a broken yellow line means parking is okay except at posted times.

yellow card. In football* (soccer), a yellow card is raised by a referee to indicate that a player has committed a major foul.

yeoman. Originally a servant of a noble* who was given some responsibilities, the term was most commonly applied to the followers a noble counted on when he needed soldiers. In return for their military service, yeomen were usually given plots of land and thus, as the copyholder* gradually replaced the yeoman, the term came to mean an independent farmer who tilled his own land, socially not a gentleman* because he actually worked the farm but higher ranking socially than a farmer, who usually was merely a tenant rather than an owner. The term also developed a stereotype—bluff, hearty, dependable, strong, perhaps not bright but with a heart of oak.* More recently, the term has fallen into disuse, the line between yeoman and farmer blurring, but the term is still used for the character type. *See also* squire.

Yeomanry. A volunteer cavalry* force recruited during the Napoleonic wars from among the local yeomen* and used as a reserve. During the Boer* War, many were sent to South Africa in volunteer units recruited from the many different Yeomanry units in England, but otherwise the Yeomanry did not go overseas until WWI. *See also* regiment; territorials; Volunteers.

Yeomen of the Guard. A ceremonial guard at the Tower,* from an earlier body that acted as the personal bodyguard of the monarch from Henry VII's day; nicknamed Beefeaters.*

yett. In Scotland,* a gate.

yew. A dark green evergreen tree, especially associated with churchyards where so many still grow. Tradition says a large number were planted about the time of Agincourt* because the wood was used in longbows.

y-fronts. Men's underwear similar to the kind Americans call jockey shorts, a brand name often used generically.

YHA. Youth Hostels Association, since 1930 provider of numerous hostels for hikers, not always young, across the nation.

yob/yobbo. A hooligan, but usually a northern one, identifiable by heavy work boots* used more for kicking than for working (boy spelled backwards).

yonks. A long time, casual usage in late twentieth century.

York. The principal city of Yorkshire,* one of the island's oldest communities, significant since the Roman era. The cathedral,* called the **York Minster**, is a Norman building on a site in use since the seventh century, when York was one of the principal centers of European Christianity, and it continues as the second most important religious community in England, with its archbishop* the second-ranking clergyman of the Church of England.* The modern city still has most of its medieval walls and many other buildings from that era, when it was the center of the wool trade. The **Duke of York** is a nonhereditary title for the second son of the monarch. *See also* riding.

Yorkshire. A county* or shire* in northeastern England* so large it was divided into three administrative areas called ridings* until 1974, when it was at last divided into five separate counties: **North, South**, and **West Yorkshire** and Cleveland* and Humberside.* In the medieval era, York* challenged London* as a commercial center, and the shire's status was underlined by appointment of its own archbishop.* Much of the industrial revolution developed in the southern areas around Leeds,* Bradford,* Sheffield,* and Hull,* but even so, the dominant images of the area were the moors* of the north and west, epitomized in the Brontë novels of the nineteenth century and the James Herriot stories of the late twentieth century. Thus, despite its industrialization, Yorkshire held a position similar to that of Texas in American lore: a vast, wild, frontierlike place where everything was *more*—the passions more passionate, the repression more repressed, the weather more violent, and so forth—and whose livestock-raising inhabitants often saw themselves as from a separate country, only connected to the rest of England by the accident of geography, with their own ways of doing things and their own views of life, and with their own accent that was a source of English humor as early as Chaucer and is often impenetrable to outsiders; the one major difference is that the stereotypical Yorkshireman's personality is much closer to that of the native New Englander's close-mouthed frugality than to the Texan's braggardly ebullience.

Yorkshire pudding. *See* pudding.

you lot. A lower class* usage meaning all of you.

Young Farmers. In rural areas, an organization for ages ten to twenty-five similar to American 4-H Clubs.

young fogey. A term used in the 1980s for the relatively young and prosperous who espoused so many ideas formerly associated only with old fogeys of the Conservative* party.

Your Grace. The proper form of address for a duke,* duchess,* or archbishop.* *See also* Your Lordship.

Your Ladyship. A form of address for anyone formally called a Lady.* My Lady* is actually preferred, but as late as the early eighteenth century there was a distinction made between the two, with Your Ladyship being used only for wives of barons* and bishops* and My Lady for all married women above that rank. Probably as a form of flattery, most were elevated over the years to My Lady, so that in the twentieth century we find numerous instances of people reversing the practice and using Your Ladyship on the assumption that it increases the respect shown beyond that indicated by a mere My Lady. **Her Ladyship** is used when speaking about, but not to, a Lady; however, this phrase is also widely used sarcastically when speaking about someone who is stuck-up. *See also* Your Grace; Your Worship.

Your Lordship. A form of address for anyone formally called a lord,* for a judge,* or for a female sheriff.* Except for the female sheriff, My Lord* is actually preferred, but as late as the early eighteenth century there was a distinction made between the two, with Your Lordship being used only for barons,* bishops,* and judges and My Lord for all above that rank. Probably as a form of flattery, most were elevated over the years to My Lord, so that in the twentieth century we find numerous instances of people reversing the practice and using Your Lordship on the assumption that it increases the respect shown beyond that indicated by a mere My Lord. **His Lordship** is used when speaking about, but not to, a Lord; however, this is also widely used sarcastically when speaking about someone who is stuck-up. *See also* Your Grace; Your Worship.

Your Worship. A respectful form of address to magistrates* or mayors.*

Youth Custody Centre. *See* Borstal.

yule log. Once common throughout Britain,* the yule log was a large log burned only on Christmas* Eve; it was supposed to burn for a minimum of twelve hours, and failure to do so meant bad luck in the coming year. The practice has all but disappeared, partly due to changes in Christmas activities and partly to the disappearance from homes of large fireplaces.

Z

Z-car. A police patrol car, from the use of Zulu as the call sign for such radio-equipped cars; the name was spread, and possibly invented, by a popular TV series of the 1960s.

zebra crossing. What Americans call a pedestrian crosswalk, indicated by white and black stripes alternating across the street. *See also* Belisha beacon; pelican crossing.

zed. The letter *Z*.

zigger-zagger. A large rattle* that makes its rasping sound by swinging the rattle portion around a handle, most commonly found at football* matches.

zimmer. The aluminum walker used by the elderly or infirm.

zip. What Americans call a zipper.

zizz. A nap.

Appendixes

Appendix I: Money and Values

No one can hope to understand the literature of a society without some understanding of the finances of that society. Money counts, and in a novel, play, or film, you have to know something about the money to know just how much it counts. Unfortunately there is no simple way to explain money and wealth in a different place or time.

The reader of any "foreign" literature faces two separate problems with money: (1) What is the currency itself?—for example, What are the names of the coins, their relative values, and so on? (2) As tourists often ask, "What's this in real money?"—for example, What does the amount mean in relation to something we can understand in our own lives? How much is a lot of money, and how much is next to nothing? These questions are in turn complicated by time factors, since inflation, the growth of wealth, and social changes all affect the "real" value of any amounts mentioned in a particular work.

The following will attempt to deal with these questions.

CURRENCY AND COINS

For Americans, who have always had a decimal coinage, the old English system provided much amusement as well as confusion. In fact, the English system was not just another eccentricity but rather the monetary system that had been in use across western Europe since introduced by the Romans, whose basic value was the libra, translated as the pound but still noted as £. This unit was divided into 240 denarius, in England eventually corrupted into the word pence but still written as *d*. The English also borrowed an intermediate value from the French (Charlemagne, not William), who divided the livre into 20 sols or sous, in England called shillings and written as *s*.

Notation. Prior to 1971, all English accounts were written in 3 columns: £, *s*, *d*. Prices and wages were quoted in whatever might be most convenient: thus, 25 shillings might be written either as 25s or £1,5s, and usually expressed as "one pound five." When people gave prices as *x* and *y*, they meant shillings and pence; thus, "ten and six" meant "ten shillings and six pence." Over the years, the *s* for shillings got flattened out in writing, so that ten and six, for example, was usually written as 10/6 rather than 10s6.

In 1971, all this ended, as Britain officially joined the ranks of decimalized coinage, with one pound made up of 100 new pence, and all notations are now written approximately the same way as Americans write amounts, but with the British decimal: one pound, five pence = £1·05. Amounts less than one pound are written with a *p* following to indicate new pence, as in 59p.

Coinage. Over the centuries, a number of different coins (and notes) were issued, the most prominent of which are outlined below:

Before 1971

coin	value	substance	dates	nicknames
farthing	¼ penny	silver	1279–1672	
		copper	1672–1860	
		bronze	1860–1961	rag
halfpenny	½ penny	silver	13th c.–1672	ha'p'ny, brown
		copper	1672–1860	
		bronze	1860–1971	
penny		silver	8th c.–1797	
(two or more		copper	1797–1860	copper
= pence)		bronze	1860–1971	
two pence	2 pennies	copper	1797–1971	tuppence, cartwheel
threepence	3 pennies	silver	1551–1937	thruppence, joey
		nickel	1937–1971	threepenny bit
groat	4 pennies	silver	13th c.–17th c.	
		silver	1836–1856	fourpenny bit, joey
sixpence	6 pennies	silver	1551–1980	tanner, crookie, fiddler, sprat
shilling	12 pennies	silver	1504–1971	bob, drake, stag
florin	24 pennies	silver	1849–1937	
		copper/ nickel	1937–1971	

coin	value	substance	dates	nicknames
half-crown	2½ shillings	gold	1470–1551	piece
	(30 pennies)	silver	1551–1946	
		copper/ nickel	1949–1971	
crown	5 shillings	gold	1526–1551	
	(60 pennies)	silver	1551–1951	
		copper/ nickel	1951–1971	
noble	80 pennies	gold	1344–1634	angel
10 shilling	10 shillings (120 pennies)	note	1914–71	
mark	160 pennies	*		
sovereign	20 shillings	gold	1489–1660	
		gold	1817–1914	quid, canary
20 shillings	20 shillings	gold	1660–85	broad
pound	20 shillings	note(green)	1914–83	quid, oncer, bradbury
guinea	20 shillings	gold	1663–1813	quid, canary
	21 shillings	*	1817–1971	
five pound	5 pounds	note		fiver

(*Term for this amount was used with no actual coin in circulation; *See* dictionary entry for details.)

Since 1971

value	substance	size and shape
1 pence	bronze	(about size of American nickel)
2 pence	bronze	(about size of American half-dollar)
5 pence	copper/nickel	(about size of American quarter)
10 pence	copper/nickel	(about size of American half-dollar)
20 pence	copper/nickel	(about size of 5p but seven-sided)
50 pence	copper/nickel	(about size of American silver dollar, seven-sided)
1 pound	yellow colored copper/nickel	(a thick coin, about the size of three quarters stacked)

The new notes are much smaller than the old ones, but each note is a different size, with the £5 the smallest, shorter and wider than an American bill, and the others progressively larger. Each note has a white base but the ink is a different color: £5 = blue, £10 = brown, £20 = purple, £50 = yellow-brown.

In order to simplify the changeover, the one shilling coin was given the value of 5 new pence, and the florin (or two shilling) the value of 10 new pence, and both coins stayed in circulation but were not newly minted. The sixpence was used for 2½ new pence until 1980; there was also a new halfpenny, but it was discontinued in 1984.

VALUE

Nothing is more difficult than to try to translate the "value" of a currency over time. One of the most logical methods is to try to look at comparative prices, but even this analysis is not much real help. For example, a pint of beer in a pub in 1910 was usually 2d, and a pub pint now costs 100 to 125 times that amount, so perhaps we should simply multiply any pre-WWI figure by 100 or 125. But a comparison of wages of the same era would suggest an increase of barely half that amount, while today's wages would not only buy more beer but also a lot of other things that didn't even exist in the Edwardian era. Similarly, we know the price of bread over several centuries, but even so, where does that leave us? A "typical" weekly budget for a family's bread a hundred years ago was about 6s—why not compare that amount to the cost of seven loaves of bread now? But for the "typical" laborer of those days, bread was more than half of the food eaten, and in expenses, well over half the family budget; how does that compare to a family that now spends less on bread for a week than on snack foods or on meat for a single meal? In 1850 Mrs. Beeton estimated that a family needed £150/yr to afford a full-time, live-in maid. A modern family would need 250 to 300 times that amount to afford such a servant. But the 1850 family didn't have refrigerators, cars, televisions, washer-dryers, vacuum cleaners, frozen dinners, microwaves, and so on, items that both do parts of the maid's work and also have to be paid for before the family can even consider a maid. Another way of comparison is to look at prices in relation to the value of gold; a decent man's suit in the Restoration cost about an ounce of gold, and a decent man's suit in the 1980s also cost about an ounce of gold, and thus the price of gold could be used as a constant. But a man of the Restoration wore his suit every day for several years, so in essence it was not a suit but his entire wardrobe, while modern man has several suits, clothes for relaxation and play, for vacation, and so on, which somehow must be factored in, even without considering government manipulations of gold prices during the era of the gold standard.

The point of all this discussion is that there is no simple, and ultimately no genuinely accurate, answer to the question "What is that worth?" The best we can do is approximate. And any approximation is *very* approximate. There is so much more to buy now that it is all but impossible to understand the value of money in times when such things were undreamed of, when even the very wealthy depended on their own lands for the bulk of their food and thus had comparatively little food expense, and when everything else was handmade by people who had for the most part no concept of leisure time. Economists and historians have tried, particularly since the computer made it possible to figure in many factors, but no two experts agree. What follows is an approximation based on comparisons of several such estimates. What I have tried to do is provide a formula that will give something more than a hint as to whether an individual transaction is cheap or expensive, whether a tip is miserly or ostentatious, whether a wager is modest or foolhardy, and to give the reader a way to know where we would place such a character on our own social scales if we were to meet him or her today.

One further word of explanation. Somehow, even after we translate historical pounds into modern pounds, we must then retranslate that into modern dollars. For our purposes, this requires a somewhat more complex calculation than simply checking the day's exchange rates. In a purely financial sense, the standard of living in Britain, as in the rest of Europe, is significantly lower than that in America. That is to say, if two persons had identical jobs in the two countries, the American would be paid considerably more in almost all cases. At the same time, prices for most consumer goods in Britain are equal to or higher than those for the same goods in America,—identical cars cost more, food costs as much or more, gasoline is almost three times as expensive, and so on. But in a social sense, the British, like most of the other Europeans, seem to get "more bang for the buck," so to speak; somehow, they seem to live far higher on the social scale than they would live in America on a similar amount of money. A family might have a live-in au pair to care for the children full time, for example, on an income that in America could not afford to send the children to part-time day care. In the course of preparing this book, I have toyed with a number of different formulae that attempt to express this, some of them quite complex, but in the end it seems most helpful to the American reader to take the simplest route and simply convert pounds to dollars at the approximate exchange rates of the early 1990s. In that way, the American reader can gain some insight not only into the financial values but also the social values of the two countries and be surprised or shocked that the British have been willing or able to pay so much more (or less) than Americans will for the same goods and services. But it must be stressed that this is only the roughest of figures, and that it tries to express in a number many factors that are ultimately not quantifiable.

Needless to say, all of these figures will be out of date by the time a reader actually sees them. They are based on 1991 estimates; make your own adjustments as necessary to deal with the inflation that is sure to come after this book goes into print.

Additional caveats: It should be remembered that, particularly when characters who head family estates mention "income," that is a gross, not a net, figure. Thus, in *Pride and Prejudice* Mr. Bingley's £4,000 to £5,000, although well over a million dollars *a year* in contemporary terms, is not really that large, because for a country gentleman that represented what the entire family—of which he was the head—was expected to gross each year from all their land rents and other investments. From that Mr. Bingley would have to operate all the family estates, with wages, machinery, repairs, new investments, and so forth, all deducted from that income, which for many nobles and gentry often left barely half the figure as actual net income for all the family together. There is no doubt that Mr. Bingley was a very rich man indeed, but his actual income as we understand the term today cannot be figured merely by multiplying a few figures. At that same time, "income" for a town man, a younger son, someone with a specific bequest, or an actual businessman or worker, would mean what we think of as income today, the actual take-home pay, and its comparable value can be computed fairly straightforwardly. Similarly, any large amounts before 1900 can and should be mentally increased another 30 to 50 percent because they were, by modern standards, practically tax-free.

At first glance, some of these equivalent values, when applied to historical figures, seem incredibly high, but they are, if anything, extremely conservative. The real Duke of Derby in the late 1870s, for example, had an income of over £75,000 a year, by the table below the equivalent of more than $9,000,000 *a year*. But that sum represented not just his income, but all the family income, hardly an outrageous amount when compared with, for example, the Rockefeller family as a whole. When compared with major entertainers of our day like Oprah Winfrey or Michael Jackson who are reported to make $30 to $60 million a year; with movie stars paid $15 million plus a percentage for a single film; or with the likes of John Gutfreund, Ivan Boesky, and others, such a figure seems positively minuscule for the man considered by most people to be the head of the richest family in England and possibly the world at the time.

Similarly, although we think of inflation as a fact of life, its movement through British history is not a constant. In particular, there was a major deflation in the second half of the nineteenth century, so that the pound of the 1870s was worth considerably more than it had been in the 1850s, and there was another similar if less pronounced deflation in the late 1920s, so that thirties-era money was worth somewhat more than it had been a decade earlier.

Sample Author of Period	£1	1s	1d	1 farthing
Shakespeare	£160–70	£8·20	70–75p	17–20p
	$325–50	$16.50	$1.25–50	35¢
Restoration writers	£140–45	£7	60p	15p
	$275–85	$13.50	$1.15	30¢

Sample Author of Period	£1	1s	1d	1 farthing
Austen	£120	£6	50–55p	12–13p
	$220–40	$11.50	95¢–$1	25¢
Dickens, Brontës,	£50–55	£3	22–24p	5–6p
early Trollope	$105	$6–6.25	45¢	11¢
Trollope (Pallisers)	£55–60	£3·20–3·40	25–30p	6–7p
	$120	$6.50	55¢	13–14¢
Doyle, Shaw	£50–55	£2·75–3·00	20p	5–6p
	$103	$4.85	40¢	10¢
Sayers, early Christie	£27·50	£1·35	13p	3p
	$55	$2.65	22–25¢	5¢
Waugh	£30	£1·50	15p	
	$60	$3.00	30¢	
postwar Christie*	£15	75p	6–7p	
	$30	$1.50	12–13¢	
Osborne, early Pinter*	£6–7	35p	3.5p	
	$13.75	65–70¢	5–6¢	
late 1970s-early 1980s	£2–2·50			
	$4–4.50			

(*From the end of WWII into the late 1970s, Britain went through several sharp devaluations, so figures for this period are only the roughest of estimates.)

Appendix II: Reigns and Historic Dates

William I	1066
William II	1087
Henry I	1100
Stephen	1135
Henry II	1154
Richard I	1189
John	1199
Henry III	1216
Edward I	1272
Edward II	1307
Edward III	1327
Richard II	1377
Henry IV	1399
Henry V	1413
Henry VI	1422
Edward IV	1461
Edward V	1483
Richard III	1483
Henry VII	1485
Henry VIII	1509
Edward VI	1547
Mary I	1553
Elizabeth I	1558
James I	1603

Charles I	1625
(Cromwell)	1649
Charles II	1660
James II	1685
William III/Mary II	1689
Anne	1702
George I	1714
George II	1727
George III	1760
George IV	1820
William IV	1830
Victoria	1837
Edward VII	1901
George V	1910
Edward VIII	1936
George VI	1936
Elizabeth II	1952

For generations, British schoolchildren have learned history in relation to the reigns of the Kings and Queens. Thus there are few specific historical dates that all persons are expected to know. The most common of these include:

1066 William the Conqueror invades England, Battle of Hastings, end of Anglo-Saxon rule and beginning of Norman rule

1415 Agincourt

1534 Founding of the Church of England

1536 Dissolution of the Monasteries

1588 The Armada

1605 Gunpowder Plot, Guy Fawkes's arrest

1649 Charles I beheaded

1660 Restoration of Charles II

1745 Bonnie Prince Charlie's uprising

1805 Battle of Trafalgar, death of Nelson

1815 Battle of Waterloo

1832 First Reform Bill

1857 Indian Mutiny

1914 beginning of WWI

1939 beginning of WWII

1956 Suez crisis

Appendix III: Class Structure

While finding one's proper place in the family is the great theme of American literature, it is a relatively minor aspect of British, where the great theme is one's proper place in society, reflecting British society's general obsession with social class. Arguably the last major British work showing members of different classes mixing together as social equals was Chaucer's *Canterbury Tales*. Because of this national obsession, it would be impossible to try to "define" the changing faces of the class system in the short space available here—almost any British novel or play is an attempt to explicate this relationship in some way. However a few points that often confuse American readers should be explained.

First, class in Britain is incredibly complicated. Americans, particularly those who grew up in small towns, know that America has great social divides of its own between various classes, but they are related directly to a single factor—money. In Britain, money counts, but only in part; even more important is the source of the money.

Since Britain has retained many of the noble titles and ranks, Americans tend to think of the class system as a holdover from the medieval era. But British nobility really dates only from the Restoration and early eighteenth century. The "modern" class system actually dates from the early nineteenth century and is a creation of the urban middle class. Prior to the Napoleonic Wars, Britain really had only two classes, the gentry (which included the nobility) and everybody else. Within the gentry resided not only all the landowners but also almost all the lawyers, doctors, clergymen, and government and military officers, and among themselves they mixed fairly easily, even to choosing marriage partners. Among "everybody else" some distinctions might exist, particularly in the towns, but these were related primarily to factors of wealth, and they play little part in our considerations since there was little or no literature that recognized these people. By the time of Jane Austen, this picture was clearly changing, due to the rise of the new industrialist class with the immense wealth they produced for themselves and the concurrent growth of urban workers. The wild career up and down the social scale of Defoe's Moll Flanders would be incredible in the world of Brontë's Jane Eyre or Dickens's Little Em'ly and inconceivable in the worlds of Agatha Christie's or Rudyard Kipling's characters. The urban industrialized world was an insecure world for all who were in it; only the tiniest margins divided the successful from the unsuccessful, and there was nowhere to go if one failed, except to live in utter poverty. Perhaps because of this insecurity, the urban middle class became obsessive about minute social details; numerous divides, almost as deep as those between the gentry and everyone else, appeared within the middle class itself, and a new divide appeared as well that separated the middle class from what was eventually called the working class.

In the single most curious and confusing aspect of the change, the shop-keeper who had been the very definition of middle class in the past was in effect thrown out of the middle class. Those who were "in trade" were not accepted among the "real" middle class, who were in business or the professions rather than trade. This distinction was accepted in all levels of society; persons in trade were perceived as belonging to something like an untouchable caste in social situations. This attitude has continued into the present, with the almost visceral hatred of many people from all levels of society for Margaret Thatcher sooner or later having revealed itself through insults about her grocer father.

Similarly, there arose a new servant class. Before urbanization, practically everyone spent some time as some form of servant, and then went on to be something else—artisan, farm worker, mother, and so forth. In the nineteenth century urban areas, domestic service became a career; for the most part, once in, one stayed. Married servants of childbearing age were not acceptable, which made those in service part of a dead-end class that could not propagate itself. But it was a distinct class separate from the working class, replenished primarily by village girls coming to town rather than by children of industrial workers, and with its own complex rules and status system.

In rural areas, the independent farmers who had grown up after the enclosures added another layer of complexity; because they were land-owners, they had high status, but because they actually worked their own lands, they were little better than common tradesmen. And thus they tended to also be treated as a separate class, middle class for political purposes but not gentry or real middle class for social purposes.

By the late nineteenth century, we could thus define the following gen-erally recognized classes, in roughly descending order of status:

• Nobility
• Gentry (noninheritable titles, landowners, leisured)

- Professional gentry (civil servants, clergy, lawyers, officers from gentry families)
- Middle-class public servants (from nongentry families)
- Middle-class professionals (doctors, lawyers, officers, dons, from professional families)
- Modern professionals (engineers, architects, headmasters)
- Middle-class businessmen (industrialists, brokers, bankers, foreign traders)
- Middle-class merchants (wholesalers, operators of chains of shops, etc.)
- Servants of gentry
- Office workers (clerks, bank tellers, bookkeepers, schoolteachers)
- Farmers
- Shopkeepers
- Servants of middle class
- Artisans (including actors and musicians)
- Shop assistants
- Skilled industrial workers
- Semiskilled industrial workers
- Manual laborers (urban or rural)

Even this representation is only a broad generalization. Over these were layered a number of other distinctions, the most profound being the separation of respectable and nonrespectable. Thus, in certain social situations a respectable working man's wife outranked a duke's daughter, and each of the classes already noted were themselves subdivided according to the nature of their respectability. Number of servants was a critical distinction. No one without a servant could even pretend to be even in the lower–middle class, and every higher class was understood to have an ever larger minimum essential complement of servants. Since WWII, the number of servants has drastically declined, but they still remain a sort of benchmark of the middle class, so that the most financially-strapped wives of that class still insist on a char lady several days a week or on an au pair. Similarly, those who had attended a public school formed a class that crossed other class lines. Within many classes, further distinctions were marked by attendance at Church or chapel, with of course Catholics generally in a separate class structure of their own. In addition, each of the classes developed their own rituals and customs, so as to distinguish between those who were properly born to the class and those who had merely sneaked into it by getting a job or wealth above their stations; thus, persons could find themselves outcasts for calling luncheon dinner, for having tea at the wrong time of afternoon, for saying or not saying *h* sounds, for opening the umbrella, for wearing a homburg when a derby should be worn, for taking tea in the parlour, for wearing an apron rather than a pinafore, and on and on. The government census might list only five classes, but in real life thirty to fifty might be more accurate.

Further complication was provided by the clear understanding among all groups that a woman must assume the class of her husband. She could drag him down, but she could not raise him up. Thus, marriage became the ground on which class battles were and still are most openly fought; as marriage suitability is a primary subject of the literature from Jane Austen to Fay Weldon, we need not expand on it here. However, the need to ensure that one's children only came into contact with persons who were suitable was perhaps the major factor in the rise of what we now call Victorian morality; the consignment of women of practically all classes to a form of purdah from which they have only recently begun to emerge came first and foremost from an attempt to guarantee that they could not be tempted into any liaisons that might destroy their chance for a "good" marriage. Only women from the working classes or the borderline groups, such as office workers and shop assistants, could hold jobs, and then only until marriage. And every care was taken on the job to underline the limited social status of the women to make sure they didn't "take advantage" and "seduce" a male from a higher class.

Likewise, neighborhoods and streets became socially exclusive with an intensity unknown on the continent, where classes shared the same buildings but on different floors, or in the United States before the advent of modern suburbia. In America, people live in houses, various sizes, various shapes; in Britain, one lives in a country house, a terrace, a semi-detached, a villa, a bungalow, and so forth, each type indicative of a specific station on the class scale.

Americans of course are familiar with a similar scale of social status; what made Britain different was that these groups, once established, lived socially exclusive lives within almost hermetically sealed containers. Although I have listed the major classes in a ranking order, in most daily life this ranking was not much of a factor—one simply did not mix with persons not of one's own class for any reason except unavoidable business transactions. It was not only possible but was thought desirable for children within a class to grow up, go to school, marry, and raise their own families without ever having any personal contact with any persons outside their own class (except of course with servants). Americans tend to see class as a matter of those on the outside and those on the inside, with the outsiders pressuring to be accepted by the insiders; in Britain, everyone (except possibly the monarch) is an outsider to other classes, and everyone is an insider within his or her own class. Thus there has been very little pressure to break the system open—most people saw no reason to "improve" themselves, as there was no central group of "average" people toward which they might want to progress. Thus, while in America ambition means a desire to move up in status, in Britain, ambition was desirable only in the sense of making enough money to secure your family's future; ambition in the sense of rising to a new class was unacceptable. (There are two exceptions only: merchants and professionals could aim for a country house and provisional entry into the gentry; and respectable workers could aim for clerical or shop assistant work, which usually meant a cut in pay.) And under no circumstances would children be allowed to consider careers or spouses that might suggest a decline in class.

This complex, unofficial, but completely understood and accepted Victorian social arrangement continued through most of the twentieth century and, if anything, intensified, primarily because those at the lower end began to see themselves as a working class. Through the trade union movement and the Labour party, its members came to see themselves as a unit that need not try to sneak into the middle class to have social value, and in many ways began to take pride in the things that made them different from other groups. Thus, many "workers" actively resisted the kind of homogenization toward the middle class that took place with American workers, ultimately validated after WWII by the rise of British working-class writers and intellectuals and particularly of rock-n-roll musicians who adopt working-class poses and accents in much the same way American groups adopt Black sounds and styles.

At the same time, the aristocracy and gentry lost their political and financial power, through a combination of political reforms, agricultural depressions, and death duties. The aristocracy and gentry still retained their social cachet, but the actual running of the country shifted to the upper levels of the middle class who made up the civil service, legal professions, and the intellectual community, concentrated among the graduates of the public schools. The third major change has been the wave of dark-skinned immigrants since the end of Empire whose presence has introduced race into the already complex issues of class; if anything, the immigrants have lowered the status of trade even more, as the bulk of small shopkeepers in the major cities now seem to be Indian, Chinese, or Caribbean in origin. Not that race has never been an issue—outside of Ireland, any Irish automatically were ranked at the bottom of the heap, no matter what their profession; Jews were tolerated but not accepted; and Scots or Welshmen were always second-class members of any specific English class (no matter how many generations the family had lived in England), just as the English were equally suspect in Scotland or Wales. Finally, within the last decade, as in America, it has become increasingly common for married women to continue to work outside the home, raising a certain amount of confusion as to the precise boundaries of any particular class group; however, as class strictures about marriage continue to be quite strict, it is relatively rare by American standards to find couples in which the wife would work at a job associated with a class significantly different from that of her husband.

Because Americans tend to see the middle class as made up of the people in the middle—represented by the average person—we are often confused by the use of the term in British literature and life. The middle and the upper classes both were and are, by American standards, *very* small. Henry Fielding, for example, estimated the gentry of his day at less than 1200 people. In the late nineteenth century, Debrett listed fewer than 6,000 families in the land-owning gentry, from a population of about 30 million, and if anything that number has declined as population increased. Similarly, the 1901 census showed only 400,000 persons (just over 1 percent) with an income of £400 (contemporary American equivalent of $40,000 to $45,000), and there seems never to have been more than about two million servants, totals indicating that there could have been no more than a million families, probably much less, from the shopkeeping class upwards who kept servants at any time before WWII. Thus, even including its lowest reaches, the middle class at any time before WWII would consist of no more than 5 percent to 8 percent of the nation, and the gentry barely 1 percent. That number clearly has expanded in the postwar world of office workers and suburban development, and most professionals who would have thought of themselves as gentry now see themselves as middle class, but even so, middle class in any British sense of the term still makes up less than 20 percent of the nation. The minute distinctions within the various broad class groupings meant that most people lived within very tightly constrained worlds, even in a city like London, with so many significant social distinctions to be made that the individual person might know less than 100 "suitable" people in a lifetime, and in the higher social reaches outside the city, minor gentry like Jane Austen's Emma, for example, might live in a daily world of barely a dozen people.

Britain has survived because the class system, though rigid in daily life, has been fluid in the long term. People can change their class. Education, money, talent, even sometimes marriage can move a person into higher places on the social scale; nothing *legal* prevents a person from rising or falling. But unlike America, where you can move overnight if the money is right, the movement is much slower. The person who moves up a class may hold a better job, live in a better neighborhood, and so on, but may still never be accepted socially in the new class, and the children will also have some problems, but the grandchildren will have few if any. The speed of social change suddenly increased during the 1980s, but distaste for the new yuppies and their insistence that money was the only class distinction that mattered was even more pronounced among Britons than among Americans, so it is unclear whether such social mobility will continue in the near future when stock and real estate markets stabilize or decline.

One final factor should be noted. In general, Americans associate class obsession with women more than with men, and American wives are in general far more likely to notice social slights than American husbands. Among the British, men have generally been as sensitive to class distinctions as the women.

Appendix IV: Calendar of Holidays and Festivals

In most cases, dates within the year are referred to in most literature and conversation by name; that is, people are more likely to say Lammas than August 1. However, for the convenience of the reader faced with a specific date, the following calendar lists the major holidays and saints' days common in Britain.

Fixed dates:

January

1	New Year's Day
6	Twelfth Night/Epiphany
20	St. Agnes's Eve
25	Burns Night

February

2	Candlemas
14	Valentine's Day

March

1	St. David's Day
25	Lady Day

April

1	All Fools' Day
23	St. George's Day

May

1	old May Day

June

11	St. Barnabas's Day (Barnaby Bright)

June

23   Midsummer Eve
24   Midsummer

July

12   Boyne
15   St. Swithin's Day

August

1   Lammas
24   St. Bartholomew's Day
31   All Hallow's Eve

September

29   Michaelmas

November

1   All Saints' Day/All Hallows
2   All Souls' Day
5   Guy Fawkes Day
11   Martinmas/Remembrance Day
23   St. Clement's Day
25   St. Catherine's Day
30   St. Andrew's Day

December

25   Christmas
26   Boxing Day
31   Hogmanay

Moveable feasts related to Easter:

41 days before   Shrove Tuesday
40 days before   Ash Wednesday/beginning of Lent
3 weeks before   Mothering Sunday
2 weeks before   Carling Sunday
1 week before   Palm Sunday
Thursday before   Maundy Thursday
Friday before   Good Friday
EASTER: first Sunday after a full moon on or after March 21
Monday after   Easter Monday/Bank Holiday
1 week after   Low Sunday
5 weeks after   Rogation

40 days after	Ascension
7 weeks after	Whitsun
8 weeks after	Trinity

Other variable dates:

March
last Saturday   beginning of BST
May
first Monday   May Bank Holiday
last Monday   Spring Bank Holiday
August
first Monday   old Summer Bank Holiday
last Monday   Late Summer Bank holiday
October
last Saturday   end of BST
November
Sunday nearest Nov 30   Advent

Appendix V: Military Ranks

For convenience of reference, the most typical ranks used in the British military are listed below, arranged so that roughly equivalent ranks are parallel. Units of command are not listed for the navy, as the types of ships commanded by each rank changed fairly regularly, or for the RAF, as RAF units are included in the name of the rank itself.

Army	Typical Command	RAF Equivalent	Navy Equivalent
Field Marshal		Marshal of the RAF	Admiral of the Fleet
General	Army	Air Chief Marshal	Admiral
Lieutenant General		Air Marshal	
Major General	Division	Air Vice-Marshal	Vice-Admiral
Brigadier	Brigade	Air Commodore	Rear Admiral
Colonel	Regiment	Group Captain	Captain
Lieutenant-Colonel	Battalion	Wing-Commander	Commander
Major	Company (or Staff)	Squadron Leader	Lieutenant Commander
Captain	Company/Platoon	Flight Lieutenant	Lieutenant
Lieutenant	Platoon/Section	Flying Officer	Sub-Lieutenant
Sub-Lieutenant	Platoon/Section		
Warrant Officers	non-command duties	Warrant Officers	Warrant Officers (Master, Engineer, etc.)
Sergeant-Major	Regiment/ Company	Sergeant-Major	Bosun
Sergeant	Platoon/Section	Sergeant	Bosun's Mate

Army	Typical Command	RAF Equivalent	Navy Equivalent
Corporal	Squad	Corporal	Coxswain
Lance-Corporal			
Private (trooper/ gunner)		Aircraftsman	Rating

Appendix VI: Honours and Initials

Unlike many continental Europeans, the British are chary of wearing medals and badges in public, but they are meticulous about noting them in print. Thus, British visiting cards, signatures, and biographical data often seem to Americans like Scrabble kits, each name followed by a welter of random letters indicating various honours, orders, societies, and degrees. The most significant or well known of these are listed here in a single chart for convenience, in official order of precedence. This list includes only official honours awarded by the monarch; many other initials, such as BA, RA, and so forth, representing degrees or honorary and professional societies are discussed in the main text but not included here as they are not part of the formal honours system. Nor are all the official honours listed here—there are nearly one hundred of them, including numerous honours related to those below but for persons from various colonies and dominions; police awards; and single event medals that for reasons of space have not been discussed in the main text. The honours listed below are the ones most visible, and all are discussed in the main text.

VC (Victoria Cross)
GC (George Cross)
KG (Order of the Garter)
KT (Order of the Thistle)
GCB, KB, CB (Order of the Bath)
OM (Order of Merit)
GCMG, KCMG, CMG (Order of St. Michael and St. George)
VO (Royal Victorian Order)
GBE, KBE, CBE (Order of the British Empire)
DSO (Distinguished Service Order)

OBE, MBE (Order of the British Empire)
DSC (Distinguished Service Cross)
MC (Military Cross)
DFC (Distinguished Flying Cross)
DCM (Distinguished Conduct Medal)
GM (George Medal)
Police Medal
DSM (Distinguished Service Medal)
DFM (Distinguished Flying Medal)
AFM (Air Force Medal)

Selected Bibliography

DICTIONARIES, GLOSSARIES, AND REFERENCE WORKS

No one could begin to deal with British language and usage without an immeasurable debt to and reliance upon the *Oxford English Dictionary*. This work in particular would not exist without it. In addition, the following reference works generally available to American readers and librarians were consulted in some detail for various topics:

Abbott, P. E., and J.M.A. Tamplin. *British Gallantry Awards*. Garden City, New Jersey: Doubleday, 1972.

BBC Pronouncing Dictionary of British Names. 2d ed. Oxford: Oxford University Press, 1990.

Beeching, Cyril Leslie. *A Dictionary of Eponyms*. 2d ed. Oxford: Oxford University Press, 1988.

Bentley, Nicolas, Michael Slater, and Nina Burgis. *The Dickens Index*. Oxford: Oxford University Press, 1988.

The Book of Common Prayer and The English Hymnal. Oxford: Oxford University Press, 1976.

Bullock, Alan, and Oliver Stallybrass, eds. *The Harper Dictionary of Modern Thought*. New York: Harper & Row, 1977.

Chapman, Robert L. *New Dictionary of American Slang*. New York: Harper, 1986.

Clark, Audrey N. *The New Penguin Dictionary of Geography*. London: Penguin, 1990.

Clark, John O. E. *World Wise: A Dictionary of English Idioms*. New York: Henry Holt, 1990.

The Concise Dictionary of National Biography, 1901–1970. Oxford: Oxford University Press, 1982.

Coyle, L. Patrick. *The World Encyclopedia of Food*. London: Francis Pinter.

De Sola, Ralph. *Abbreviations Dictionary*. 5th ed. New York: Elsevier, 1978.

Drabble, Margaret, ed. *The Oxford Companion to English Literature*. 5th ed. Oxford: Oxford University Press, 1985.

Eagle, Dorothy, and Hilary Carnell. *The Oxford Literary Guide*. Oxford: Oxford University Press, 1977.

Evans, Ivor H., ed. *Brewer's Dictionary of Phrase and Fable*. 14th ed. New York: Harper & Row, 1989.

Foreign & Commonwealth Office. *Britain 1991: An Official Handbook*. London: HMSO, 1991.

Forster, Klaus. *A Pronouncing Dictionary of English Place-Names*. London: Routledge & Kegan Paul, 1981.

Fowler, H. W. *A Dictionary of Modern English Usage*. Oxford: Oxford University Press, 1926.

————. *A Dictionary of Modern English Usage*. 2nd ed. Revised by Sir Ernest Gowers. Oxford: Oxford University Press, 1965.

Frewin, Anthony. *The Book of Days*. London: Collins, 1979.

Green, Jonathan: *The Slang Thesaurus*. London: Penguin, 1986.

Grote, David. *Common Knowledge: A Reader's Guide to Literary Allusions*. Westport, CT: Greenwood Press, 1987.

Gulland, Daphne M., and David G. Hinds-Howell. *The Penguin Dictionary of English Idioms*. London: Penguin, 1986.

Haigh, Christopher, ed. *The Cambridge Historical Encyclopedia of Great Britain and Ireland*. Cambridge: Cambridge University Press, 1990.

Hanks, Patrick, and Flavia Hodges. *A Dictionary of First Names*. Oxford: Oxford University Press, 1990.

Hole, Christina. *A Dictionary of British Folk Customs*. London: Paladin, 1978.

Holder, R. W. *The Faber Dictionary of Euphemisms*. London: Faber, 1989.

Horton, Chris, ed. *Encyclopedia of Cars*. New York: Mallard Press, 1990.

Johnstone, William D. *For Good Measure: A Complete Compendium of International Weights and Measures*. New York: Holt, Rinehart and Winston, 1975.

Kenyon, J. P., ed. *A Dictionary of British History*. New York: Stein & Day, 1983.

Kightly, Charles. *The Customs and Ceremonies of Britain: An Encyclopedia of Living Traditions*. London: Thames & Hudson, 1986.

McDonald, James. *A Dictionary of Obscenity, Taboo and Euphemism*. London: Sphere, 1988.

Mawson, C. O. Sylvester, and Charles Berlitz: *Dictionary of Foreign Terms*. 2d ed. New York: Barnes & Noble, 1979.

Moore, Margaret. *Understanding British English*. New York: Citadel Press, 1989.

Moss, Norman. *The British/American Dictionary*. rev. ed. London: Hutchinson, 1984.

Ousby, Ian, ed. *The Cambridge Guide to Literature in English*. Cambridge: Cambridge University Press, 1988.

Partridge, Eric. *A Dictionary of Catch Phrases: British and American from the Sixteenth Century to the Present*. New York: Stein and Day, 1979.

————. *A Dictionary of Clichés*. 5th ed. London: Routledge & Kegan Paul, 1978.

————. *A Dictionary of Slang and Unconventional English*. 5th ed. New York: Macmillan, 1961.

Paxton, John. *The Statesman's Yearbook*. New York: St. Martin's, annually updated.

Payton, Geoffrey. *Webster's Dictionary of Proper Names*. Springfield, MA: Merriam, 1970.

Rawson, Hugh. *A Dictionary of Euphemisms & Other Doubletalk.* New York: Crown, 1981.

Room, Adrian: *Dictionary of Changes in Meaning.* London: Routledge & Kegan Paul, 1986.

———. *Dictionary of Coin Names.* New York: Routledge & Kegan Paul, 1987.

———. *Dictionary of Confusing Words and Meanings.* New York: Dorset, 1986.

———. *Dictionary of True Etymologies.* London: Routledge, 1988.

Sadie, Stanley, ed. *The Norton/Grove Concise Encyclopedia of Music.* New York: Norton, 1988.

Schur, Norman W. *British Self-Taught: With Comments in American.* New York: Macmillan, 1973.

Thorburn, Archibald: *The Complete Illustrated Thorburn's Birds.* New York: Gallery, 1989.

———. *The Complete Illustrated Thorburn's Mammals.* New York: Gallery, 1989.

Webster's Sports Dictionary. Springfield, MA: G & C Merriam, 1976.

Weinreb, Ben, and Christopher Hibbert, eds. *The London Encyclopedia.* New York: St. Martin's, 1985.

Whitaker's Almanack. London: J. Whitaker & Sons, updated annually.

Wintle, Julian, ed. *Dictionary of Modern Culture.* London: Ark, 1984.

Wood, F. T., and R. J. Hill. *Dictionary of English Colloquial Idioms.* revised ed. London: Macmillan, 1979.

GUIDES, TRAVEL BOOKS

Banks, R. R. *The Penguin Guide to London.* 7th ed. London: Penguin, 1977.

Baxendale, Kenneth William. *Charles Dickens' London.* East Wickham, England: Alteridem, 1986.

Burton, Anthony. *Walking Through History.* London: Queen Anne Press, 1988.

Crowl, Philip A. *The Intelligent Traveller's Guide to Historic Britain.* New York: Congdon & Weed, 1983.

Daiches, David and John Flower. *Literary Landscapes of the British Isles: A Narrative Atlas.* New York: Penguin, 1981.

Dale, Alzina Stone, and Barbara Sloane Hendershott. *Mystery Reader's Walking Guide: London.* Lincolnwood, IL: Passport, 1987.

Defoe, Daniel. *A Tour Through the Whole Island of Britain.* abridged. London: Webb & Bower, 1989.

Hannah, Jean. *Coping With England.* New York: Basil Blackwell, 1987.

Hebbert, Antonia, ed. *Secret Britain.* Basingstoke, England: Automobile Association, 1986.

London. Harrow, England: Michelin, 1988.

Mason, Mercia. *Oxford and Cambridge.* 3d ed. London: A & C Black, 1987.

Morton, H. V. *I Saw Two Englands.* London: Methuen, 1989.

Nicholson, Louise. *Fodor's London Companion.* New York: Fodor's, 1987.

Ousby, Ian. *England.* London: A & C Black, 1989.

———. *Literary Britain and Ireland.* 2d ed. London: A & C Black, 1990.

Piper, David. *The Companion Guide to London.* 6th ed. London: Collins, 1977.

Theroux, Paul. *The Kingdom By the Sea: A Journey Around Great Britain.* Boston: Houghton Miflin, 1983.

Tucker, Alan, ed. *The Penguin Guide to England & Wales*. New York: Penguin, 1989.
Walford, Edward. *Old London: Belgravia, Chelsea & Kensington*. London: Village Press, 1989.
———. *Old London: Haymarket to Mayfair*. London: Village Press, 1989.
———. *Old London: Highgate & Hampstead to the Lea*. London: Village Press, 1989.
———. *Old London: Hyde Park to Bloomsbury*. London: Village Press, 1989.
———. *Old London: Paddington Green to Seven Sisters*. London: Village Press, 1989.
———. *Old London: Westminster to St. James's*. London: Village Press, 1989.
Weisser, Henry G. *Understanding the U.K.: A Short Guide to British Culture, Politics, Geography, Economics and History*. New York: Hippocrene, 1987.

HISTORY, COMMENTARY, SATIRE

Adams, Robert M. *The Land and Literature of England: A Historical Account*. New York: Norton, 1983.
Allen, Charles, ed. *Plain Tales From the Raj*. London: Futura, 1976.
Andrew, Christopher. *Her Majesty's Secret Service: The Making of the British Intelligence Community*. New York: Viking, 1986.
Arnold, Peter, ed. *The Complete Book of Card Games*. London: Octopus, 1989.
Bailey, Adrian. *The Cooking of the British Isles*. New York: Time-Life, 1969.
Barker, Theo, ed. *The Long March of Everyman: 1750–1960*. London: Penguin, 1978.
Berriedale-Johnson, Michelle. *The Victorian Cookbook*. New York: Interlink, 1989.
Bigelow, Marybelle S. *Fashion in History: Western Dress, Prehistoric to Present*. 2d ed. Minneapolis: Burgess, 1979.
Boucher, Francois. *20,000 Years of Fashion: The History of Costume and Personal Adornment*. New York: Abrams, 1966.
Briggs, Asa. *A Social History of England*. London: Penguin, 1985.
Brockett, Oscar G. *History of the Theatre*. Boston: Allyn & Bacon, 1968.
Brooke, Iris. *A History of English Costume*. New York: Theatre Arts, 1979.
Cannadine, David. *The Decline and Fall of the British Aristocracy*. New Haven, CT: Yale University Press, 1990.
Caldwell, Doreen. *And All Was Revealed: Ladies' Underwear 1907–1980*. New York: St. Martin's, 1981.
Castronovo, David. *The English Gentleman: Images and Ideals in Literature and Society*. New York: Ungar, 1987.
Cooper, Jilly. *Class: A View From Middle England*. London: Methuen, 1979.
Coxe, Antony Hippisley. *A Seat at the Circus*. rev. ed. London: Macmillan, 1980.
Critchfield, Richard. *An American Looks at Britain*. New York: Doubleday, 1990.
Cunnington, C. Willett. *English Women's Clothing in the Nineteenth Century*. New York: Dover, 1990.
Dahrendorf, Ralf. *On Britain*. Chicago: University of Chicago, 1983.
Deighton, Len. *The Cookstrip Cookbook*. New York: Bernard Geis, 1965.

De Marly, Diana. *Fashion for Men: An Illustrated History*. London: Batsford, 1985.

Donaldson, Gordon. *Scotland: The Shaping of a Nation*. rev. ed. London: David & Charles, 1980.

Drabble, Margaret. *A Writer's Britain: Landscape in Literature*. New York: Thames & Hudson, 1987.

Farwell, Byron. *Mr. Kipling's Army: All the Queen's Men*. New York: Norton, 1981.

Fraser, Antonia. *Royal Charles: Charles II and the Restoration*. New York: Knopf, 1979.

Frost, David, and Antony Jay. *The English*. New York: Avon, 1969.

Fussell, Paul. *Wartime: Understanding and Behavior in the Second World War*. New York: Oxford University Press, 1989.

Gardner, Brian. *The East India Company*. New York: Dorset, 1990.

Gathorne-Hardy, Jonathan. *The Unnatural History of the Nanny*. New York: Dial, 1973.

George, M. Dorothy. *London Life in the Eighteenth Century*. 2d ed. Chicago: Academy Press, 1984.

Gibbs, Philip. *England Speaks*. New York: Literary Guild, 1935.

Glyn, Anthony. *The British: Portrait of a People*. New York: Putnam, 1970.

Graves, Robert, and Alan Hodge. *The Long Weekend: A Social History of Great Britain 1918–1939*. 2d ed. New York: Norton, 1963.

Hartley, Dorothy. *The Countryman's England*. London: Batsford, 1935.

Hazleton, Lesley. *England, Bloody England: An Expatriate's Return*. New York: Atlantic Monthly Press, 1990.

Hibbert, Christopher. *Daily Life in Victorian England*. New York: American Heritage, 1975.

———. *The English: A Social History 1066–1945*. New York: Norton, 1987.

Hobsbawn, Eric. *The Age of Revolution: 1789–1848*. New York: Mentor, 1964.

Hobsbawn, Eric, and Terence Ranger, eds. *The Invention of Tradition*. Cambridge: Cambridge University Press, 1984.

Hoskins, W. G. *The Making of the English Landscape*. London: Hodder & Stoughton, 1955.

Keegan, John. *The Second World War*. New York: Penguin, 1990.

Kerridge, Roy. *Bizarre Britain: A Calendar of Eccentricity*. Oxford: Basil Blackwell, 1985.

Laslett, Peter. *The World We Have Lost: England Before the Industrial Age*. 3d ed. New York: Scribner's, 1984.

Laver, James. *Manners and Morals in the Age of Optimism: 1848–1914*. New York: Harper & Row, 1966.

———. *Taste and Fashion*. London: Harrap, 1937.

Levenstein, Harvey. *Revolution at the Table*. New York: Oxford University Press, 1988.

Levi, Peter. *The Life and Times of William Shakespeare*. New York: Henry Holt, 1989.

Levin, Bernard. *Run It Down the Flagpole: Britain in the Sixties*. New York: Atheneum, 1971.

Lewis, Lesley. *The Private Life of a Country House (1912–1939)*. London: Futura, 1982.

Lloyd, Christopher. *The Well-Tempered Garden*, new edition. London: Penguin, 1987.

McNeill, William H. *Plagues and Peoples*. New York: Anchor, 1976.

Machin, G.I.T. *Politics and the Churches in Great Britain 1832 to 1868*. Oxford: Clarendon Press, 1977.

Marcus, Steven. *The Other Victorians: A Study of Sexuality and Pornography in Mid-Nineteenth-Century England*. New York: Norton, 1985.

Mayer, Tony. *La Vie Anglaise*. Translated by Christopher Sykes. London: Victor Gollancz, 1960.

Mitford, Nancy, ed. *Noblesse Oblige*. New York: Atheneum, 1986.

Morris, Jan. *Oxford*. rev. and updated. Oxford: Oxford University Press, 1987.

Muir, Richard. *The English Village*. London: Thames & Hudson, 1980.

Neuberg, Victor. *Gone for a Soldier: A History of Life in the British Ranks from 1642*. London: Cassell, 1989.

Newton, Michael. *Armed and Dangerous: A Writer's Guide to Weapons*. Cincinnati: Writer's Digest, 1990.

Opie, Iona and Peter. *The Lore and Language of Schoolchildren*. Oxford: Oxford University Press, 1959.

Orwell, George. *The Road to Wigan Pier*. New York: Harcourt Brace, 1958.

Owen, John B. *The Eighteenth Century: 1714–1815*. New York: Norton, 1976.

Packard, Jerrold M. *The Queen & Her Court*. New York: Scribner's, 1981.

Parkinson, C. Northcote. *Parkinson's Law: And Other Studies in Administration*. New York: Ballantine, 1975.

Parrott, E. O., ed. *The Dogsbody Papers: Or, 1066 and All This*. New York: Viking, 1988.

Pitman, Jack. *England Ebbing*. New York: Stein & Day, 1987.

Priestley, J. B. *The Edwardians*. New York: Harper & Row, 1970.

Pritchett, V. S. *London Perceived*. New York: Harcourt, Brace & World, 1962.

Rackham, Oliver. *The History of the Countryside*. London: Dent, 1987.

Russell, Douglas A. *Costume History and Style*. Englewood Cliffs, NJ: Prentice-Hall, 1983.

St. Auban, Fiona. *Ackermann's Illustrated London*. London: Wordsworth, 1985.

Sampson, Anthony. *Anatomy of Britain*. New York: Harper & Row, 1962.

———. *The Changing Anatomy of Britain*. New York: Vintage, 1984.

Smith, B. Webster, ed. *The English Counties*. rev. ed. New York: Norton, 1959.

Smith, Godfrey. *The English Companion: An Idiosyncratic Guide to England and Englishness from A to Z*. New York: Clarkson N. Potter, 1984.

Smith, Michael. *The Afternoon Tea Book*. New York: Collier, 1986.

Stone, Lawrence. *The Family, Sex, and Marriage: In England 1500–1800*. abridged ed. New York: Harper, 1979.

———. *Road to Divorce: England 1530–1987*. Oxford: Oxford University Press, 1990.

Sutherland, Douglas. *The English Gentleman*. New York: Penguin, 1980.

———. *The English Gentleman's Child*. London: Debrett, 1979.

Swinburne, H. Lawrence. *The Royal Navy*. London: Black, 1907.

Tannahill, Reay. *Food in History*. New York: Stein & Day, 1973.

Thompson, F.M.L. *The Rise of Respectable Society: A Social History of Victorian Britain 1830–1900*. Cambridge, Mass: Harvard, 1988.

Trevelyan, G. M. *English Social History: A Survey of Six Centuries Chaucer to Queen Victoria*. New York: McKay, 1965.

Tuker, M.A.R. *Cambridge*. London: Black, 1902.

Walden, Hilary. *Harrods Book of Traditional English Cookery*. New York: Arbor House, 1986.

Walmsley, Jane. *Brit-Think, Ameri-Think*. New York: Penguin, 1987.

Warner, Philip. *The British Cavalry*. London: Dent, 1984.

Welsby, Paul A. *A History of the Church of England, 1945–1980*. Oxford: Oxford University Press, 1984.

Wilson, C. Anne. *Food and Drink in Britain*. London: Penguin, 1976.

Winn, Dilys, ed. *Murder Ink*. New York: Workman, 1977.

————. *Murderess Ink*. New York: Bell, 1981.

Yarwood, Doreen. *500 Years of Technology in the Home*. London: Batsford, 1983.